The Decolonization Reader

The process of decolonization transformed colonial and European metropolitan societies culturally, politically and economically. Its legacy continues to affect postcolonial politics as well as cultural and intellectual life in Europe and its former colonies and overseas territories.

This authoritative collection of pioneering essays by many of the world's leading scholars addresses the key issues of decolonization and provides an illuminating introduction to and a critical definition of this emerging field. Grouped around the most salient themes, this compilation includes discussions of metropolitan politics, gender, sexuality, race, culture, nationalism and economy, and thereby offers a comparative and interdisciplinary assessment of decolonization.

The Decolonization Reader will provide scholars and students with a thorough understanding of the impact of decolonization on world history and cross-cultural encounters worldwide.

Contributors to this volume are: Jean Marie Allman, Joseph S. Alter, Charles Ambler, Dipesh Chakrabarty, Frederick Cooper, Paul Darby, Christopher Flood, Hugo Frey, David Gilmartin, Dane Kennedy, James D. Le Sueur, John Lonsdale, William Roger Louis, Aletta J. Norval, Cora Ann Presley, Ronald Robinson, Catherine R. Schenk, Andrew Selth, Heather J. Sharkey, Martin Shipway, Pierre van der Eng, Frederic Wakeman, Jr., and Crawford Young.

James D. Le Sueur is associate professor of history at the University of Nebraska-Lincoln and senior associate member of St Antony's College, Oxford. He is the author of *Uncivil War: Intellectuals and Identity Politics During the Decolonization of Algeria* (2001), and has edited various collections on decolonization.

The

Decolonization

Reader

Edited by

James D. Le Sueur

Routledge
Taylor & Francis Group

NEW YORK AND LONDON

First published 2003

Simultaneously published in the UK, USA and Canada
by Routledge
29 West 35th Street, New York, NY 10001
and Routledge
11 New Fetter Lane, London EC4P 4EE

Routledge is an imprint of the Taylor & Francis Group

Typeset in Perpetua and Bell Gothic by
RefineCatch Limited, Bungay, Suffolk
Printed and bound in Great Britain by TJ International Ltd, Padstow, Cornwall

Library of Congress Cataloging in Publication Data
The decolonization reader / [edited by] James D. Le Sueur.
    p.   cm.
  Includes bibliographical references and index.
  ISBN 0–415–23116–7 (alk. paper)—ISBN 0–415–23117–5 (pbk. : alk. paper)
  1. Decolonization.   2. World politics—20th century.   I. Le Sueur, James D.

  JV151.D36 2003
  325′.3—dc21   2002037053

British Library Cataloguing in Publication Data
A catalogue record for this book is available from the British Library

ISBN 0–415–23116–7 (hbk)
ISBN 0–415–23117–5 (pbk)

Contents

Acknowledgements

The authors and publishers wish to thank the following for their permission to reproduce copyright material:

Essays from *The Journal of Imperial and Commonwealth History*: "Imperial History and Post-Colonial Theory" by Dane Kennedy, vol. 24, 3 (1996): 345–363; "The Imperialism of Decolonization" by William Roger Louis and Ronald Robinson, vol. 22, 3 (1994): 462–511; "Madagascar on the Eve of Insurrection, 1944–47: The Impasse of a Liberal Colonial Policy", by Martin Shipway, vol. 24, 1 (January 1996): 72–100; "Decolonization and European Economic Integration: The Free Trade Area Negotiations, 1956–58", by Catherine R. Schenk, vol. 24, 3 (1996): 444–463, by permission of Frank Cass Publishers.

"Conflict and Connection: Rethinking Colonial African History" by Frederick Cooper is taken from *American Historical Review* (December 1994): 1516–1545 by permission of the American Historical Association and the author; " 'Our Strike': Equality, Anticolonial Politics and the 1947–48 Railway Strike in French West Africa" by Frederick Cooper is from *Journal of African History* 37 (1996): 81–118 by permission of Cambridge University Press and the author; "The Youngmen and the Porcupine: Class, Nationalism and Asante's Struggle for Self-Determination, 1954–57" by Jean Marie Allman, *Journal of African History* 31 (1990): 263–279 by permission of Cambridge University Press; "Mau Maus of the Mind: Making Mau Mau and Remaking Kenya" by John Lonsdale, *Journal of African History* 31 (1990): 393–421 by permission of Cambridge University Press; "Alcohol, Racial Segregation and Popular Politics in Northern Rhodesia" by Charles Ambler, *Journal of African History* 31 (1990): 295–313 by permission of Cambridge University Press; "Zaire: The Shattered Illusion of the Integral State" by Crawford Young, *The Journal of Modern African Studies* 32, 2 (1994): 247–263 by permission of Cambridge University Press; "The Mau Mau Rebellion, Kikuyu Women, and Social Change" by Cora Ann Presley, *Canadian Journal of African Studies/Revue canadienne des études africaines* 22/3 (1988), 502–527 by permission; "Decolonising 'French Universalism': Reconsidering the Impact of the Algerian War on French Intellectuals" by James D. Le Sueur, *Journal of North African Studies* 6/1 (Spring 2001), 167–186 by permission of Frank Cass Publishers. "Marshall Aid as a Catalyst in the Decolonization of Indonesia, 1947–49" by Pierre van der Eng is from *Journal of Southeast Asian Studies* XIX, 2 (September 1988): 335–352 by permission of Cambridge University Press; "Democracy, Nationalism and the Public: A Speculation on Colonial Muslim Politics" by David Gilmartin, *South Asia* 14, 1 (1991): 123–140 by permission of The South Asian Studies Association and the author; "Race and Resistance in Burma, 1942–1945" by Andrew Selth, *Modern Asian Studies* 20, 3 (1986): 483–507 by permission of Cambridge University Press; "Celibacy, Sexuality, and the Transformation of Gender into Nationalism in North India" by Joseph S. Alter, *Journal of Asian Studies* 53, 1 (February 1994): 45–66 and "Licensing Leisure: The Chinese Nationalists' Attempt to Regulate Shanghai, 1927–47" by Frederic Wakeman, Jr., *Journal of Asian Studies* 54, 1 (February 1995): 19–42 reprinted with permission of the Association for Asian Studies, Inc. "Colonialism, Character-Building, and the Culture of Nationalism in the Sudan, 1898–1956" by Heather J. Sharkey, *The International Journal of History and Sport* 15, 1 (April 1998): 1–26 by permission of Frank Cass Publishers; "Decolonization, demonization and difference: the difficult constitution of a nation" by Aletta J. Norval, *Philosophy and Social Criticism* 21, 3 (1995): 31–51 by permission Sage Publications Ltd (© Sage Publications Ltd, 1995); "Football, Colonial Doctrine and Indigenous Resistance: Mapping the Political Persona of FIFA's African Constituency" by Paul Darby, *Culture, Sport, Society*, vol. 3, 1 (Spring 2000): 61–87 by permission of Frank Cass Publishers; "Questions of decolonization and post-colonialism in the ideology of the French extreme right" by Christopher Flood and Hugo Frey, *Journal of European Studies*, xxviii (1998): 69–88 by permission of Alpha Academic; "Postcoloniality and the Artifice of History: Who Speaks for 'Indian' Pasts?" by Dipesh Chakrabarty, *Representations* 37 (Winter 1992): 1–26 by permission of the University of California Press.

Every effort has been made to obtain permission to reproduce copyright material. If any proper acknowledgement has not been made, we would invite copyright holders to inform us of the oversight.

Note: The text and/or notes of some contributions have been abridged.

An introduction:
Reading Decolonization

RELATIVELY YOUNG, THE STUDY of European decolonization in Africa and Asia is one of the fastest growing and most dynamic areas of research today. As a political, cultural, social, economic, and intellectual phenomenon, decolonization became such a fierce feature of everyday life in metropolitan Europe, its colonies, and its overseas possessions that it would be inconceivable to write the history of the twentieth century without giving primary importance to it. Yet, despite the prominent place that decolonization occupies in the history of the twentieth century, there has not been a concerted effort to offer a collection of essays covering a variety of approaches to the study of decolonization from within a wide range of metropolitan and colonial contexts.[1] *The Decolonization Reader* is such an attempt, for it offers a comparative overview of the field and highlights some important thematic trends in past and current scholarship.

By the nature of its scope, this *Reader* is multifaceted. It is intended to be an introduction to the history of decolonization in Africa and Asia; it makes available for a general audience an exceptional collection of original and important contributions to the field; it offers a useful means to contrast and compare the process, events, and salient issues of decolonization in different historical contexts, from several points, and from within different academic traditions; and, perhaps most important, it is intended to encourage further research in the field. With this in mind, the articles and central themes covered in this volume are by no means exhaustive; rather, they are, as I see it, representative of the trends and the talents of the field's leading scholars. And, without claiming to be a comprehensive account of all aspects of decolonization, the number and variation of the essays presented in this volume were selected based on the author's ability to illustrate – each in distinctive ways – that decolonization must be thought of as a complex and highly differentiated subject of inquiry.

While researchers have become increasingly comfortable with nuanced studies of decolonization, comfort with the use of the neologism of "decolonization" has been long in coming. For example, as Raymond F. Betts argues in *Decolonization* (1999), this "awkward and inelegant" word only entered into usage in the 1930s, and since then "decolonization" has become "work-a-day, rather like other 'de' prefixed words that denote cleansing changes."[2] Decolonization, as a word, has thus been applied to the act or the concept of (anticolonial) cleansing. It can also be applied, more theoretically, I think, to decisive efforts to reconsider the act of writing about European colonialism and the end of empire. As I have written elsewhere, one of the ways by which today's historians can make history more responsible and responsive to the changes that have taken place as a result of European decolonization, is to begin to think of colonialism and decolonization as dialogical processes.[3] Thinking of colonialism and decolonization as dialogical is crucial, I believe, because in this way metropolitan and indigenous voices carry equal weight. This collection is one such effort to represent this dialogical relationship at work because, as a whole, it affords a plurality of views from a plurality of nations, epochs, and traditions in which no single "voice" is given sway over another. However, I would add further definition to this a neologistic analysis by stating that when the word is used in this volume, its general meaning is that of a process by which colonial powers – in this case European nations and administrators – left, whether voluntarily or by force, from their overseas possessions in various areas of Africa and Asia. As a matter of definition, therefore, I take decolonization to mean (almost without exception) a process during which hard-won battles were waged between nationalists and metropolitan colonial powers.

Furthermore, I view the seeming awkwardness of "decolonization" referred to by Betts not as something to decry but as something to embrace, for when researchers study issues posed by decolonization they inevitably enter into a field of inquiry whose very subject is that of contest and change. It is no surprise that one of the most hotly contested and dynamic fields of study today is precisely this open-ended (or to use Bett's expression, "loose-ended") subject that is perhaps all the more fortunate to be condemned to be in full dispute as long as the legacy of decolonization remains in play. Hence, from my perspective, decolonization's open-ended quality does not diminish the relevance of history and of our contemporary inquiries; in fact, it reinforces the value of research because this open-endedness demonstrates that there is something worth grappling with and arguing about. In other words, the epistemological ruptures ushered in by the demise of European hegemony – otherwise known as the "end of empire" – and the transitions to what I call historical postcolonialism (by which I mean the period following independence) have encouraged and enlivened discussions of decolonization.

As the historical phase that bridged the gap between colonial and postcolonial worlds, decolonization has its own dramatic and rich legacy. Virtually every colonized territory in Africa (from Algeria to post-apartheid South Africa, and in Asia from Myanmar to Shanghai), passed through the doors of decolonization within the span of a few decades. In Africa alone, more than fifty new states were created from the 1950s onward. Because of this, it becomes clear in journeying through this collection that in both scholarship and practice, decolonization remains unfinished business.

That said, it is well known that scholars as well as political and intellectual critics of colonial regimes have been writing about these effects for years.[4] One of the most famous, of course, was the Africa nationalist and intellectual Kwame Nkrumah, who created his own neologism, "conscienscism," in 1964, which he identified as a "philosophy and ideology for decolonization."[5] One of the other important social critics and intellectuals who helped re-define the significance of decolonization for intellectuals in the "developing world" was Ngugi wa Thiong'o. Ngugi urged in *Decolonising the Mind* (1986) that African writers could go a long way in reclaiming their identity by rejecting the language of the colonizer and writing in their native tongue after independence (in his case rejecting British English for Kenya's Kikuyu language).[6]

In addition to Nkrumah and Ngugi, many others remain concerned about the status of the postcolonial condition, neocolonialism, and the future of post-independent states as well as transformative effects of the loss of empire on metropolitan nations themselves. Many scholars (including several in this volume and especially Dane Kennedy) have long since argued that colonial history in general and studies in decolonization in particular have generally been separated into two camps: the metropolitan transfer of power and the nationalist perspectives.[7] During the latter half of the twentieth century, these two modes of writing about decolonization have existed side-by-side, often and unfortunately with very little interaction between the principal practitioners. Nevertheless, in recent years there has been considerable improvement of the relations between what I would term metropolitan-oriented and nationalist-oriented historians, but these changes have been fostered largely by the development of a third line of inquiry: postcolonial studies.

There is no question that postcolonial studies has had little patience for metropolitan-centered scholarship or the historiography of *imperium*, though it has often even remained at odds with the nationalist tradition as well. Impressive terrain has been covered with postcolonial studies, beginning perhaps with the path-breaking questions posed by Edward Said's *Orientalism* and then more recently by the Subaltern Studies group.[8] The result has been decisive and in many cases divisive – with the historiography of empire and decolonization altered significantly. As a result of the many debates stirred by the Subaltern Studies group, we are witnessing renewed interest in nearly every aspect of colonialism, and as central as postcolonialism may have been to rejuvenating interest in such studies, it has also been exposed to considerable criticism from historians (several appearing in this volume), who although willing to embrace much of postcolonialism's methodologies and comparativist framework, have been uncomfortable with the jargon and ahistorical tendencies of postcolonialism's principal advocates.[9]

In this sense, postcolonialism – as a theoretical platform from which to reconsider all dimensions of colonialism – has come to researchers interested in decolonization as a double-edged sword: one side used to sharpen the methodologies of the scholars of the colonial world and the other to cut away at the remains of the historian's enterprise. The overt indictments and not-so-covert contempt lurking in the postcolonial worldview, especially the charge that the Western notion of history has been used as a means to dominate other non-Western cultures, is particular salient to historians of empire, all the more so because postcolonial theorists have not been shy about expressing their suspicion if not derision for Western historians and scholars.

Postcolonial studies has, as a matter of principle, challenged the status and relevance of metropolitan European narratives, forcing many to reconsider so-called Western or Euro-centric teleologies. At the same time, many colonial historians have continued with business as usual, too often put off by the verbose and seemingly unnecessarily steep prose (indeed anti-prose) of postcolonialism's chief spokespeople. However, both Western and non-Western scholars have been obligated in recent years to reevaluate the nationalist narratives of African and Asian states. The disagreement is far from settled. But it has certainly altered how the history of decolonization will be written in the future.

At the very least, concerns raised by cultural theorists have fostered an appreciation for questions that had not been considered by the two dominant traditions. Issues of identity, cultural hybridity, mimicry, and representation have all taken more prominent places in the study of decolonization – even by mainstream historians today. Furthermore, researchers using cultural theory have brought studies of gender, race, social class, immigration, political ideology, and religion to the forefront. Without question, the combination of cultural and postcolonial theory has allowed many scholars across an increasingly large variety of fields to think of decolonization in a global context and outside purely national narratives or the metanarrative of European hegemony. New theories and scholarship in colonial history have in turn fostered a desire to look for evidence of the changing status of European culture during decolonization. As a result, researchers have begun to study decolonization from within the British, French, Dutch, Belgian, and other countries' experiences, and, at the same time, they also assess the impact of decolonization on emerging nations, metropolitan states invested in the empire debates, and on Cold War superpowers such as the United States and the former Soviet Union.

The new and dynamic studies of decolonization provide future evidence that the colonial question remains important for several reasons. Chief among these is what I would term the "echo factor." By this I mean that the trauma and the burdens of colonial relations between the colonizer and the colonized as well as the after-effects of anticolonial violence continue to echo in contemporary debates (academic or otherwise) over language, ethnicity, immigration, gender relations, race, political ideology, and religion in former colonies and in metropolitan Europe. Aware of the echoing of these debates, I have chosen the articles for *The Decolonization Reader* in a concerted effort to bring a combination of approaches (theoretical and historical) to bear on the problem of decolonization from within a variety of national and metropolitan perspectives.

To this end this volume presents readers with articles on European decolonization in Asia (India, Indochina, Indonesia, Burma, and Shanghai) and throughout the continent of Africa (from North to South). This comparative approach (which loosely brackets out decolonization in the Middle East and Latin America) offers a means to assess many shades of European decolonization. In an eclectic spirit of highlighting some of the best original research published first in the leading academic journals, and in an effort to bring to the fore some of the principal themes of decolonization, I have divided the present *Reader* into eight sections. Each section attempts to treat decolonization from several angles and from several national and metropolitan contexts. The eight sections are, one could argue, somewhat fluid; nevertheless, they represent what I would term the salient themes of decolonization. These topical sections include:

1   Defining Decolonization
2   Metropolitan and International Politics
3   Economy and Labor
4   Nationalism and Anticolonialism
5   Race and Ethnicity
6   Gender and Sexuality
7   Culture and Contexts
8   Postcolonialism: After Decolonization

Aside from the issue of geographical range, these thematic sections also present a divergence of disciplinary and methodological trends relevant to each central category. In offering these sections considerable care has been taken to provide readers with an appreciation for the evolution of the field of decolonization studies itself.

There can be little question that over the past few decades decolonization has truly come into its own. The essays presented in this *Reader* are evidence of the maturity and diversity of approaches to the study of what has now become an independent field of inquiry. And the field of decolonization, as represented by many of its most talented practitioners from several disciplines here, has clearly come of age. There is nothing awkward or inelegant about it now.

Notes

1   This is not to suggest, however, that there have not been other important collections on the subject of decolonization. For examples of other collections on European decolonization see: Prosser Gifford and Wm. Roger Louis (eds), *Decolonization and African Independence. The Transfer of Power, 1960–1980* (New Haven: Yale, 1988), A. J. Stockwell and A. N. Porter (eds), *British Imperial Policy and Decolonization, 1938–1964* 2 vols (Basingstoke: Macmillan, 1987–89), W. H. Morris-Jones and Georges Fisher (eds), *Decolonization and After: The British and French Experience* (London: Frank Cass, 1980), and Wolfgang Mommsen and Jürgen Osterhammel, *Imperialism and After: Continuities and Discontinuities* (London: German Historical Institute, 1986).
2   Raymond F. Betts, *Decolonization* (New York: Routledge, 1998), 1.
3   See James D. Le Sueur, "Decolonizing 'French Universalism': Re-considering the Impact of the French-Algerian War on French Intellectuals," Chapter 5 below.
4   There are many writers who come to mind here, beginning with V. I. Lenin's landmark critique of capitalism, *Imperialism, the Highest State of Capitalism* (New York: International Publishers, 1969). See also Kwame Nkrumah, *Neo-Colonialism: The Last State of Imperialism* (New York: International Publishers, 1969), Jean-Paul Sartre, *Colonialism and Neo-Colonialism* (London: Routledge, 2001), and Ngugi Wa Thiong'o,

Decolonizing the Mind: The Politics of Language in African Literature (London: James Curry, 1986).

5   See Kwame Nkrumah, *Consciencism: Philosophy and Ideology for Decolonization* (New York: Monthly Review Press, 1964/revised edition 1970). See also Kwame Nkrumah, *Neo-Colonialism: The Last Stage of Imperialism* (New York: Humanities Press, 1965).

6   See Ngugi wa Thiong'o, *Decolonising the Mind: The Politics of Language in African Literature* (London: James Curry, 1986).

7   For the best discussion of this issue see: Dane Kennedy, "Imperial History and Post-Colonial Theory" and Frederick Cooper, "Conflict and Connection: Rethinking Colonial African History," reproduced below.

8   See Edward W. Said, *Orientalism* (New York: Vintage, 1979). For an overview of the the Subaltern Studies group see Renajit Guha and Gayatri Chakravorty Spivak (eds), *Selected Subaltern Studies (Essays from the 4 Volumes and a Glossary)* (New York: Oxford, 1988).

9   Among others, I am referring to Gayatri Chakravorty Spivak and Homi Bhabah. See Spivak, *A Critique of Postcolonial Reason: Toward a History of the Vanishing Present* (Cambridge: Harvard, 1999), Spivak et al., *The Spivak Reader: Selected Works of Gayatri Chakravorty Spivak* (London: Routledge, 1995), and Bhabha, *The Location of Culture* (London: Routledge, 1994).

PART ONE

Defining Decolonization

DEFINING DECOLONIZATION

THIS SECTION ADDRESSES TWO CENTRAL issues concerning the writing of colonialism and decolonization: perspective and history. Dane Kennedy in "Imperial History and Post-Colonial Theory" and Frederick Cooper in "Conflict and Connection: Rethinking Colonial African History" argue that the historiography of colonialism since decolonization (the postcolonial era) has changed significantly. Both authors endorse the changing methodologies and epistemologies, and each stresses the need to go still further in the direction of finding new means of comparison and in eroding European biases with regard to the era of colonial retreat.

Cooper and Kennedy concur that European categories and teleologies need to be re-examined and even, in some cases, subverted. Cooper argues that researchers have recently come to question critical notions within the study of decolonization such as the distinction between anticolonial politics and nationalism. Even metanarratives such as anticolonialism and nationalism, Cooper contends, obscure the nuances of colonial history and the interactions at the heart of decolonization. This means that researchers can no longer be content with analyses of decolonization that depend on the "nationalist" and "anticolonial politics" as the primary means of interpreting historical events. Similarly, while Kennedy acknowledges that historians cannot turn a deaf ear to the challenges postcolonial theorists present, he cautions against putting aside the question of history. When history is sidelined in favor of ahistorical analyses of literature, for example, researchers of the so-called postcolonial exempt from discussion all forms of causality, "context, and chronology." The result, Cooper and Kennedy insist, is a deceptive historical and conceptual blurring, which ultimately renders comparisons within different historical contexts meaningless. Both Cooper and Kennedy ask for a regeneration and to some degree a de-centering of Western scholarship, and they also call attention to the problems of undifferentiated, ahistorical analyses represented in much of postcolonial studies today.

Chapter 1

Dane Kennedy

IMPERIAL HISTORY AND POST-COLONIAL THEORY

THE HISTORIOGRAPHY OF BRITISH IMPERIALISM has long been coloured by the political and methodological conservatism of its practitioners. Arising as it did from the imperial metropole in the late nineteenth century, it originally served as an ideological adjunct to empire. Its purpose was to contribute historical insights into past exercises in overseas power that could be used to inform and inspire contemporaries to shoulder their obligations as rulers of a world-wide imperial system. Decolonization robbed imperial history of most of its practical incentives. Yet it continued to cling to the methodology and *mentalité* of 'the official mind', as Ronald Robinson and John Gallagher termed it in their enormously influential work.[1] The persistence of this paradigm is evident even in the most recent scholarship. Peruse any issue of *The Journal of Imperial and Commonwealth History*, for example, and you will find a succession of articles that still tread the path pioneered by John Seeley more than a century ago. They remain wedded to the same official documentation, persist in addressing the same political, economic, and military manifestations of power, and continue to employ the same narrative conventions. They seldom stray from an adamant empiricism. On the rare occasions they do flirt with theory, it generally derives from well-worn models. P. J. Cain and A. G. Hopkins' acclaimed new two-volume study of *British Imperialism*, which is widely regarded as the most important and innovative contribution to the field since Robinson and Gallagher, resembles nothing so much in its theoretical stance than that old war-horse of imperial theory, J. A. Hobson, with a pinch of Schumpeter thrown in for flavour.[2] This return to the concerns of Edwardian radicalism is taken within the field for theoretical daring. It is hardly surprising, therefore, that imperial history has acquired a reputation for insularity and inattention to the methodological advances made both by historians in other fields and by scholars in related disciplines.

Perhaps because so many historians of British imperialism have been content to plough the same narrow plot over and over again, their professional domain has been invaded in recent years by a wide array of academic interlopers. Interest in imperialism and colonialism has intensified among specialists in anthropology, area studies, feminist studies, and, above all, literary studies. The latter have proven especially energetic and adept at claiming squatters' rights over imperial history's unclaimed provinces. Armed with the latest post-structuralist theories, the literary invaders have opened up and exploited some surprisingly rich and provocative intellectual terrain. It is their colonization of imperial studies and its implication for the field that this essay proposes to address.

There can be no mistaking the success that literary scholars have had in making the topic of imperialism their own. Teaching positions in colonial and post-colonial literatures appear to be one of the booming fields in English departments these days. New works with titles like *The Rhetoric of Empire* seem to come off the presses every week. Thick anthologies of influential and representative essays have begun to appear for use as textbooks in college courses. Leading theorists such as Edward W. Said, Homi K. Bhabha, and Gayatri Chakravorty Spivak have become superstars of the academic firmament. In America, *The Chronicle of Higher Education* has highlighted the phenomenon with a feature story, the popular academic journal *Linguafranca* has attacked it in a cover story, and *Time* magazine has devoted several pages to a flattering profile of Said, its principal founder. In Britain, interest among the intellectual community has been equally intense. Clearly this is a scholarly industry to be reckoned with.

The problem is that historians of British imperialism have for the most part failed to reckon with it. This is a pity both for the historians, whose methodological horizons could be broadened by serious engagement with this literature, and for the literary scholars, whose theoretical excesses could be checked by the sober scrutiny of the historians. In proposing that historians enter into a dialogue with their literary trespassers, I do not mean to suggest that the two parties can be entirely reconciled with one another. Some of the differences that divide them are unbridgeable. Even so, a good deal can be gained, I believe, from historians conducting a critical reconnaissance of the territory that literary theory has claimed as its own. So let us explore.

I

The new and growing body of scholarship that concerns us here is generally known either as colonial discourse analysis or post-colonial theory. Colonial discourse analysis refers to the examination and interpretation of particular colonial texts. Post-colonial theory refers to the political and ideological position of the critic who undertakes this analysis. In practice, the two terms have become virtually interchangeable, so much so that several recently published 'readers' have put them in harness in their rather ponderous, mirror-imaged titles – *Post-Colonial Theory and Colonial Discourse* and *Colonial Discourse, Post-Colonial Theory*. Although objections have been raised to the teleological implications of the hyphenated tag 'post-colonial', its evocation of an anti-imperialist political stance and a post-structuralist theoretical one has ensured its usage. Indeed, the label 'post-colonial theorist' seems to carry rather more cachet among the practitioners of the trade than 'colonial discourse analyst', even though the latter designation is often the more accurate one. Perhaps the term 'analyst' has unwelcome associations with financial and/or military functionaries; certainly the term 'theorist' has an inflated prestige in lit-crit circles these days. For the sake of convenience and consistency, I will refer to this literature as post-colonial theory, but I caution that much of it is less engaged in developing a body of theory than in making gestures of obeisance to it.

It is generally acknowledged that Edward Said's seminal study, *Orientalism* (1978), is the foundational text for post-colonial theory. Its transfiguration of the term 'oriental-ism' from an arcane field of academic study to a synonym for Western imperialism and racism has been accepted and applied across a wide spectrum of scholarship, as has its central thesis and theoretical concerns. Said starts from the post-structuralist premise that knowledge is a discursive field derived from language and he draws from Foucault the insight that its significance lies embedded within systems of power. His study of Orientalism, by which he means Western representations of those parts of the world the West identifies as the Orient, seeks to show that this body of knowledge tells us little about the so-called Orient, which may or may not exist outside the Western imagination, but much about the West's efforts to impose itself on the peoples and cultures who came under its hegemonic sway. *Orientalism*, then, pushes past the con-ventional conception of imperial power as a material phenomenon, presenting it instead as an epistemological system. Moreover, because the West's power is linked to the cultural representations it constructs and imposes on the minds of colonizer and colonized alike, it is able to survive the political decolonization that occurred after the Second World War. Indeed, it exists even within the purportedly objective scholarship of Western academia. The full implication of this analysis is that the dismantlement of Western modes of domination requires the deconstruction of Western structures of knowledge. Hence the claim that this is a *post*-colonial theory.

These central propositions have been endorsed, elaborated upon, and modified in varying respects by subsequent practitioners of post-colonial theory. Although Said has his critics within the fraternity, his influence has persisted to a remarkable degree over the years since *Orientalism* first appeared. Many of the weaknesses as well as some of the strengths of his enterprise have become magnified in the works that have followed its lead.

Perhaps the most obvious characteristic of post-colonial scholarship is its theoretical promiscuity. Said draws mainly on Foucault for inspiration, but other influences on his work include Antonio Gramsci and Erich Auerbach. This odd menage create certain tensions and contradictions in his argument. Aijaz Ahmad has observed that Said vacillates between a Foucaultian position that places the origin of Orientalism in the Enlightenment project of the eighteenth century and a Auerbachian stance that traces it all the way back to classical Greece. Dennis Porter has pointed out that Said's use of Foucault is at odds with his use of Gramsci – the former presents a totalizing conception of power that absorbs knowledge itself while the latter conceives of hegemony as historically contingent and subject to subversion. Various critics have drawn attention to the ambivalence, if not outright obfuscation, in Said's position regarding the funda-mental question raised by his study: is it possible to attain a true knowledge of the Other? For Said to charge that the West's representations of the Orient are distorted seems to suggest that he regards an undistorted representation as attainable, but this conflicts with his post-structuralist insistence that the Orient is nothing more than a discursive phantasm. 'Orientalist inauthenticity is not answered by any authenticity', notes James Clifford.[3] Such are the conundrums that arise from the effort to appropriate incompatible theoretical perspectives.

Said's progeny have taken the turn to theory in ever more tortuous directions. As Stefan Collini has remarked with regard to cultural studies in general, it suffers from 'a disabling deference to the idea of "theory" '.[4] In addition to the obligatory bows to Foucault and Gramsci, post-colonial theorists have drawn upon Althusser, Bakhtin, Barthes, Benjamin, Derrida, de Man, Fanon, Heidegger, Lacan, and other mainly post-modernist theorists. Conspicuously absent from the post-colonial canon is Marx, whose work is considered irredeemably Eurocentric. This seems rather ironic in light of the fact that, except for Fanon, none of the names cited above ever exhibited the slightest intellectual curiosity in the issue of European colonialism or the concerns of non-European peoples. Yet the fascination with such theorists, especially if they are French, continues to run high among the post-colonial coterie. The latest initiates into the canon appear to be Foucault's contemporaries, Gilles Deleuze and Felix Guattari, whose Wilhelm Reich-inspired work *Anti-Oedipus* is advanced by Robert Young as an important new source of post-Saidian inspiration.[5]

The infiltration of these varied theoretical influences into post-colonial studies makes for a literature that is often dense and sometimes impenetrable. Arguably the most fashionable figure in the field at the present time is Homi Bhabha, whose ruminations on the cultural effects of colonialism draw inspiration from post-structuralist psychoanalysis and semiotics.[6] Traces of Lacan, Derrida, and the like are all too visible in the style and substance of his essays, which pose a formidable challenge for those who seek to decipher them. One of Bhabha's most sympathetic commentators has suggested that his baffling prose is a deliberate strategy to disorient the reader so as to prevent 'closure' and thereby subvert the 'authoritative mode' of Western discourse, a claim also offered in defence of Gayatri Chakravorty Spivak, whose work is often equally difficult to penetrate.[7] One has to admire the over-the-top audacity of this assertion, but the fact remains that the principal reason readers have trouble with Bhabha, Spivak, and certain other post-colonial theorists is because they make such indiscriminate use of words, expressions, concepts, and doctrines from so many different, sometimes incompatible sources. The literary scholar Elaine Showalter rightly complains that the 'difficult languages of high theory . . . have become a new orthodoxy as muffling as scholastic Latin, expressive straitjackets which confine all thought to a prescribed vocabulary'.[8] Post-colonial theorists' vocabulary has become clotted with highly specialized, often obscure terms like heteroglossy, alterity, aporia, synecdoche, aleatory, elide, and metonymy. Even familiar words such as gaze, gesture, site, space, efface, erase, and interrogate have taken on highly specialized, almost metaphysical meanings in their writings. Metaphor has metastasized into metaphoricity, narrative into narrativity, origin into originary, fact into facticity. One critic of this plethora of arcana has put tongue-in-cheek in recommending a *Devil's Dictionary of Cultural Studies* to make its terminology accessible to the uninitiated.[9]

It is easy, of course, to mock almost any academic genre for its jargon, but what makes post-colonial theorists especially vulnerable to criticism are the claims they make for the relationship between language and liberation. Language, as they see it, is the key to emancipation from colonial modes of thought. This is the objective the Kenyan novelist and essayist Ngugi wa Thiong'o has referred to as 'decolonizing the mind'.[10] His strategy for doing so has been to reassert the use of his native tongue (although this does not extend to the programmatic tracts in which he presents his rationale for doing so). The strategy adopted by the post-colonial theorists is to subject the language of the colonizers to critical scrutiny, deconstructing representative texts and exposing the discursive designs that underlie their surface narratives. This is seen as an act of trans-gression, a politicized initiative that undermines the hegemonic influence of Western knowledge and brings about the 'cultural decentering of the [European] centered world system.'[11] Bhabha, for example, presents his work as an effort to turn 'the pathos of cultural confusion into a strategy of political subversion'.[12] Its intent is to escape from the totalizing claims of the West.

For the sake of argument, let us accept the post-colonial theorists' assertion. Let us agree that the non-Western world remains in thrall to the discursive system of the West, to the system that Said identifies as Orientalism. How do the post-colonial theorists propose to liberate these hostages? By writing in a manner that is utterly inaccessible to most of them? By writing as the acolytes of Western theorists? By writing to mainly Western audiences from mainly Western academies about mainly Western literature? By writing? These questions may seem unnecessarily harsh, but they force to the fore the premise that stands at the heart of post-colonial theory's sense of itself – the notion that the sort of recondite textual analysis it practises offers a weapon to break free from the cultural and indeed political oppression of the West. One need not be a Marxian materialist – though this stance has supported a healthy scepticism regarding post-colonial theory – to consider this proposition as dubious, if not delusional.

The issue that concerns us here, however, is not what this literature can or cannot do to decolonize the minds of contemporary non-Western peoples, but what it can or cannot do to deepen our understanding of the history of colonialism. What complicates this issue is that post-colonial theorists hold contending views about the value of historical analysis. For post-modernist purists like Homi Bhabha, history is nothing more than a text, a 'grand narrative' that operates according to the same rules of rhetoric and logic as other genres of Western writing. As such, its significance is limited to the part it plays in the discursive field that the post-colonial critic seeks to dismantle, rather than the contribution it makes to our knowledge about the nature of colonialism. Bhabha keeps out the stuff of history by plucking random works of literature and other texts from their contextual soil and sealing them in the hermetic chambers of a psycho-analytic essentialism. Suspicion of history as an accomplice to the West's discursive drive to dominate the Other is a disturbing motif within a significant element of post-colonial theory. Edward Said's position is an ambiguous one, professing on the one hand the importance of a historicized understanding of Orientalism, while suggesting on the other hand that the discipline of history is itself implicated in the Orientalist enterprise. John MacKenzie complains that Said's efforts to achieve a historicism untainted by Orientalist assumptions are essentially ahistorical, a charge that I think overstates the case, obviating the opportunity for interdisciplinary dialogue.[13] The same accusation can be made, however, against some of Said's confederates. Gayatri Spivak praises the members of the Subaltern Studies group for engaging in what she regards as the deconstruction of a 'hegemonic historiography' and urges them to break from the premises of historical analysis altogether.[14] The influential cultural critic Ashis Nandy denounces historical consciousness as a 'cultural and political liability' for non-Western peoples.[15] In *The Intimate Enemy*, his best-known work, he proclaims that his aim is to present 'an alternative mythography which denies and defies the values of history'.[16] This view of history as a mythography concocted by the West to further its hegemonic ambitions is one that Robert Young argues to be at the core of the post-colonial critique. He traces the intellectual genealogy of this effort to expose, decentre, and deconstruct what are seen as the totalizing claims of 'white mythologies', or history as it has been practised in the West.[17] For historians who have come under the influence of post-colonial purists, this attack on history has occasioned considerable hand-wringing. Some of the younger members of the Subaltern Studies school of Indian historigraphy in particular have begun to agonize about whether it is possible to write history when 'Europe works as a silent referent to historical knowledge itself'.[18] This is a real and serious epistemological problem, and I do not wish to demean the struggle to reconstruct history from a non-Eurocentric perspective. But this is not the agenda of the post-colonial purists, whose efforts instead are directed against an historical mode of understanding altogether.

What happens when history is set aside? Some recent examples of post-colonial scholarship suggest that it leads to a wilful neglect of causation, context, and chronology. The authors of *The Empire Writes Back: Theory and Practice in Post-Colonial Literatures* blithely pour the literatures of Africa, Australia, the Caribbean, the United States, and other regions of the world into the same post-colonial pot, ignoring their profoundly different historical experiences except insofar as their 'complexities and varied cultural provenance' are taken as signs of the decentring pluralism that identify them as post-colonial literatures.[19] Laura E. Donaldson acknowledges the need to address 'concrete historical circumstances' in the introduction to her *Decolonizing Feminisms: Race, Gender, and Empire-Building*, but this appreciation is quickly forgotten as she flits from *Jane Eyre* to *Uncle Tom's Cabin* to *The King and I* (the novel, the play, *and* the film) as well as a bewildering array of other texts in an analysis that conflates colonialism with racism, sexism, and oppression in general.[20] One of the most egregious examples of this aversion to history is David Spurr's *The Rhetoric of Empire*.[21] Subtitled 'colonial discourse in journalism, travel writing, and imperial administration', this astonishing book insists that the same discursive forms recurred over more than a century in the diverse genres of writing that Western travellers, officials, and others produced about the profoundly varied peoples across the globe with whom they came in contact. In this 'global system of representation',[22] it seems to make no difference whether the rhetoric is British, French, or American, whether the author is Lord Lugard, André Gide, or Joan Didion, whether the text is a colonial report, a scholarly treatise, or an article in *National Geographic*, or whether the place is nineteenth-century South Africa, early twentieth-century Mexico, or the contemporary Middle East. All are indiscriminately advanced as evidence of the depth of the West's discursive drive for power and domination. It might be supposed that reductionism could not be carried much further, but Spurr shows otherwise. Following in the footsteps of Derrida, he tracks his quarry all the way back to writing itself: 'The writer is the original and ultimate colonizer, conquering the space of consciousness with the exclusionary and divisive structures of representations'.[23] Rarely does a theory chase its own tail with such single-minded intensity. We will not trouble Spurr with such obvious questions as whether he too is complicit as a writer in this colonization of consciousness or whether the imperial implications of writing are also applicable to the literatures of non-Western societies. We will merely observe that his analysis is entangled in what post-colonial theorists might call a 'double bind': it seeks to convict historically specific parties of historically specific crimes while exonerating itself of any accountability to historical specificity.

II

Fortunately, other literary scholars have shown far more sensitivity to the historical record in their work. While operating under the general rubric of post-colonial theory, these scholars have rejected the anti-historical orientation of the theoretical purists. They recognize the distinction that exists between history as a text and history as a tool, between its presence as a discursive product and its use as an analytical practice. By placing their arguments in an historical context and testing them against the historical evidence, they have enriched our understanding of the imperial experience in ways that historians have been slow to appreciate.

This increased fraternization with history has inspired its practitioners to question some of the cruder premises that post-colonial theory brought to the study of imperialism. One of the most dismaying of these is the tendency to essentialize the West, a discursive practice no less distorting than the West's tendency to essentialize the Orient. In Said's *Orientalism* and much of the scholarship it has inspired, the West is seen as an undifferentiated, omnipotent entity, imposing its totalizing designs on the rest of the world without check or interruption. Ironically, this stress on the power of the West countenances the neglect of that power as it was actually exercised in the colonial context, ignoring 'its plural and particularized expressions'.[24] Further, it fails to appreciate the uncertainties, inconsistencies, modifications, and contradictions that afflicted Western efforts to impose its will on other peoples. Marxist-inspired critics in particular have taken post-colonial theory to task for ignoring what Sumit Sarkar calls 'the microphysics of colonial power'.[25]

If post-colonial theory is to move toward a more nuanced, historicized understanding of the colonial experience, it also has to overcome its tendency to abstract the colonized Other as an undifferentiated, unknowable category. Given their ideological loyalties, this may seem a rather surprising position for the proponents of post-colonial theory to take, but it derives directly from their answer to a crucial question: can the deconstruction of the West's misrepresentations of the Other open the door to a true representation? Most theoretical purists say 'no', arguing that any effort to retrieve the experiences and attitudes of the colonized is doomed to failure because it is inescapably enmeshed in the positivist premises of Western knowledge. Homi Bhabha argues that the best that can be done is to monitor the traces of the colonized inscribed in the margins of the colonizer's discourse, an enterprise enigmatic enough in its interpretation of silences, ambivalences, and contradictions to escape almost any kind of external assessment. Gayatri Spivak insists that the voice of the colonized subject, and especially the colonized female subject, can never be recovered – it has been drowned out by the oppressive collusion of colonial and patriarchal discourses.[26] The implication of this stance is made clear by Gyan Prakash, who declares that the 'shift to the analysis of discourses' means the abandonment of a 'positivist retrieval' of the experience of the colonized and the search instead for the random discursive threads from that experience that have become 'woven into the fabric of dominant structures'. While Prakash is seduced by the prospect that the 'relocation of subalternity in the operation of dominant discourses leads . . . to the critique of the modern West',[27] others are appalled by this abandonment of the effort to recover the 'subaltern' or colonial subject's experiences. Critics complain that the Derridean turn in post-colonial theory denies agency and autonomy to the colonized, whose struggles against colonial rule and strategies to turn it in their favour are too abundant and abundantly recorded to be dismissed as mere echoes in the chambers of Western discourse. Apart from Prakash, few historians are likely to adopt the stifling stance of the theoretical purists, and there are signs that an increasing number of practitioners of post-colonial studies have begun to back away from it as well. Robert Young concedes in his latest book that the discipline has 'reached something of an impasse' growing in part out of a realization that 'the homogenization of colonialism does also need to be set against its historical and geographical particularities'.[28] And Sara Suleri complains in *The Rhetoric of English India* that post-colonial theory 'names the other in order that it need not be further known', and that its practitioners 'wrest the rhetoric of otherness into a postmodern substitute for the very Orientalism that they seek to dismantle'.[29] Even Edward Said has recently warned against viewing the West and the rest as essentialized dichotomies. He has retreated from his earlier position regarding the pervasiveness of Western power by examining the work of Yeats, Fanon, and other voices of cultural resistance to that power.[30]

Whether figures such as Yeats and Fanon are entirely representative of colonized peoples' reactions to colonial rule, however, is open to question. What Said's use of them signifies is post-colonial theory's residual obeisance to its literary studies roots, with its privileging of canonical authors. Hence the almost ritualistic re-examination of Charlotte Brontë, Kipling, Conrad, Forster, and the like in volume after volume of post-colonial scholarship. While recent efforts to extend the post-colonial inquiry to non-Western writers should be regarded as an important step forward, it remains the case that attention tends to focus on those Westernized authors who have obtained at least provisional admission into the Western canon, such as Achebe, Naipaul, and Rushdie (though Naipaul's status, in particular, is questioned by some post-colonial theorists because of his contrarian political views). It would be useful if post-colonial scholarship made more effort to situate these writers within the class structure of their home societies and the cultural context of a transnational intelligentsia so as to avoid simplistic generalizations that their work embodies some nationalist or 'Third World' essence. It would be even more useful if it freed itself from the constraints of a canon altogether. The recent upsurge of studies of travel literature can be seen as one of the ways it has sought to do precisely that, but the abiding limitation of this genre is its Eurocentric character. While some practitioners of post-colonial theory have managed to take up topics and texts that are entirely outside the bounds of any Western-derived canon, the most interesting instances generally have come from scholars trained in disciplines other than literature. Thus, one of the challenges that continues to confront post-colonial theory is to open its inquiries to a wider range of voices, especially those from colonial and ex-colonial territories.

III

What, then, does post-colonial theory offer to British imperial history? With its mind-numbing jargon, its often crude essentializations of the West and the Other as binary opposites, and, above all, its deeply ingrained suspicion of historical thinking, one might well wonder if it has anything to offer. In John MacKenzie's view, it does not.

Such a conclusion, I suggest, profoundly misjudges the potential of post-colonial theory to enrich the inquiries of imperial historians. For all its faults, this body of scholarship has inspired some valuable insights into the colonial experience, and historians would do well to take notice. It has reoriented and reinvigorated imperial studies, taking it in directions that the conventional historiography of the British empire has hardly begun to consider. It has raised provocative, often fundamental questions about the epistemological structures of power and the cultural foundations of resistance, about the porous relationship between metropolitan and colonial societies, about the construction of group identities in the context of state formation, even about the nature and uses of historical evidence itself. These preoccupations are in no way limited to the literary proponents of post-colonial theory: similar inquiries have arisen among anthropologists, area studies specialists, feminist scholars, and others whose methods may seem somewhat less inimical to imperial historians, but whose concerns are often no less challenging to their practices. This essay, however, has focused on the literary scholarship inspired in large measure by Said because it has been the most audacious in its application of post-structuralist theories and the most uncompromising in its relationship to historiographical traditions.

The principal aim of this scholarship has been to reframe and reassess Europe's impact on the rest of the world – and the reciprocal effects on Europe itself – by shifting the focus from the material to the cultural realm. The contribution of post-colonial theory to this effort lies first and foremost in its appreciation of the relationship between knowledge and power. Said's central premise, derived from Foucault and embraced by other post-colonial theorists, holds that the imperial power of the West was bound to and sustained by the epistemological order the West imposed on its subject domains. While imperial historians have attended to the issue of power since the inception of their field of study, and while their inquiries have given rise to a sophisticated body of work that traces the exercise of power from coercion to collaboration, the fact remains that the circumstances that allowed relatively small contingents of Europeans to acquire and maintain authority over vastly larger numbers of Asians, Africans, and others represent one of the most persistent conundrums to arise from the study of Western imperialism. The post-colonial theorists have opened up a new and intriguing avenue of inquiry into this problem by probing the assumptions and intentions that underlay the efforts to give meaning to the colonial encounter. They have argued that these discursive practices were every bit as expressive of power relations as the more conventional manifestations of those relations in politics and other material realms. Heretofore their work has been more successful in suggesting an intent on the part of colonial rulers than in establishing an effect on colonized subjects: this has been a recurrent point of criticism of Said and his student Gauri Viswanathan, for example. However, they have been helped in their endeavours by others, notably historical anthropologists like Bernard Cohn, whose path-breaking work on British India has demonstrated a direct relationship between the acquisition of knowledge about subject peoples and the imposition of authority over them.[31] The marriage of this research to the insights from post-colonial theory has shown that a fuller understanding of the West's success in imposing itself on the rest of the world requires a deeper appreciation of its cultural and ideological dimensions.

Post-colonial theory's insight into the pervasive nature of Western constructions of the Other has made it clear that much of what we thought we knew about societies that had been subjected to colonial rule was distorted by the discursive designs of the colonizers. This realization has compelled scholars to re-examine the circumstances under which particular peoples became identified as members of particular tribes, castes, races, faiths, nations, and other culturally-defined collectivities. Once again, the theoretical positions advanced by the post-colonial contingent have converged with the empirical researches of others, particularly specialists in the anthropology and history of ex-colonial societies. An exceptionally lively and important body of scholarship has arisen that examines the colonial construction of collective identities. What had long been thought to be the primordial affiliations of tribe and caste, for example, are now seen to have assumed much of their modern shape as a result of contestatory processes arising from the efforts of colonial authorities to impose order over subject peoples who sought to resist those demands. Similarly, religious communalism and other markers of group identity such as race and ethnicity appear to have taken new and more virulent forms under colonialism as a result of its determination to classify and categorize. The influence of post-colonial theory has been felt in studies of peasant consciousness, of gender and sexuality, of the body and disease, and of imperial ideology. Our under-standing of the nature and impact of colonialism has been profoundly reconfigured as a result of these and other works, and at the heart of this reconfiguration lies the post-colonial premise that the categories of identity that gave meaning to colonizers and colonized alike cannot be taken for granted: they must be problematized and presented in the context of power.

The final point is that this problematizing of identity has provided an opportunity to overcome what D. K. Fieldhouse described a decade ago as the Humpty-Dumpty syndrome in British imperial history.[32] Since decolonization, the study of the British empire has shattered into a multitude of separate fragments, with the most significant break occurring between the imperial experience as it has been portrayed from the metropole and from the periphery. By presenting a case for understanding the con-struction of cultural difference as a binary process – we define ourselves in the context of how we define others – post-colonial theory has insisted that the metropole has no meaning apart from the periphery, the West apart from the Orient, the colonizer apart from the colonized. The dominant party in these parings has its own character shaped as a consequence of the shape it gives the character of the other. This is almost certainly the most significant contribution that post-colonial theory has made to the study of colonial practice. Sometimes, as in Edward Said's effort to read plantation exploitation in Antigua as the silent referent in Jane Austen's *Mansfield Park*, the case for a connection between imperial periphery and centre seems strained.[33] But just as often it has worked, supplying fresh insights into the imperial experience and its impact on Britain. Javed Majeed has made a persuasive case for viewing the development of Philosophic Radicalism in the context of colonial India in the early nineteenth century.[34] Moira Ferguson has shown that the abolitionist-inspired debate about colonial slavery helped to shape Mary Wollstonecraft's critique of gender relations in British society.[35] Robert Young has exposed the importance of mid-nineteenth-century racial theory on the development of Matthew Arnold's famous notion of culture.[36] More generally, post-colonial theorists have shown that the 'languages of class, gender, and race [were] often used interchangeably',[37] connecting imperial metropole and colonial periphery in surprising and significant ways. Evidence that historians have begun to take heed of the insights advanced by post-colonial scholarship can be found in works such as

Antoinette Burton's provocative analysis of the efforts by British feminists to appropriate the ideology of humanitarian imperialism to their cause and Lynn Zastoupil's careful study of the influence of John Stuart Mill's career in the India Office on the development of his ideas.[38] Post-colonial theory, then, has contributed to the task of restoring the relationship between centre and periphery, of recovering the connection between the history of Britain and the history of its imperial dependencies – in effect, of putting Humpty-Dumpty back together again. It has done so by demonstrating that imperialism was a process of mutual interaction, of point and counterpoint that inscribed itself on the dominant partner as well as the dominated one. And it has made it clear that any assessment of this interaction which ignores the cultural dimension – that is, the realm of mutual representations of the self and the other – is one that misses what may well be the most persistent and profound legacy of the imperial experience.

IV

I began this essay with a rather polemical metaphor that portrayed post-colonial theory as a colonizing discipline, subjecting a province of historical studies to its alien rule. Insofar as this metaphor resonated with readers, it did so because it pandered to the widespread perception that disciplinary boundaries are akin to ethnic or national ones, abstract entities that must be patrolled and protected at all costs against outsiders. I intend now to denounce this metaphor as misleading and even destructive. It connotes a defensive mentality that hinders rather than advances scholarship and knowledge. While I have argued that there is a great deal wrong with post-colonial theory, I have also suggested that it offers interesting and useful avenues of inquiry that imperial historians would do well to examine. What we need at this stage is a full-fledged critical dialogue between the two parties, a dialogue that exposes areas of difference and delineates points of convergence. There are, in fact, some signs that this has begun to occur. John MacKenzie has made a vigorous, albeit defensive, intervention that has already stimulated debate.[39] My intent has been to push this dialogue in a direction that will encourage imperial historians to rethink their practices in response to post-colonial theory. Whatever the outcome of such a rethinking, it promises to take the historiography of imperialism in fruitful, if unfamiliar, directions.

Notes

1 Ronald Robinson and John Gallagher with Alice Denny, *Africa and the Victorians: The Official Mind of Imperialism*, 2nd edn (London, 1981).

2 P. J. Cain and A. G. Hopkins, *British Imperialism: Vol. 1, Innovation and Expansion; Vol. 2, Crisis and Deconstruction* (London, 1993).

3 James Clifford, 'Orientalism', *History and Theory*, 19, no. 2 (1980), 209.

4 Stefan Collini, 'Badly Connected: The Passionate Intensity of Cultural Studies', *Victorian Studies*, 36, no. 4 (Summer 1993), 458.

5 Robert J. C. Young, *Colonial Desire: Hybridity in Theory, Culture and Race* (London, 1995).

6   See Homi K. Bhabha, *The Location of Culture* (London, 1994).

7   Robert Young, *White Mythologies: Writing History and the West* (London, 1990), 156, 158.

8   Elaine Showalter in 'The Rise of Theory – a Symposium', *Times Literary Supplement*, 4763 (15 July 1994), 12.

9   Daniel Cotton, 'Discipline and Punish', *Victorian Studies*, 36, no. 4 (Summer 1993), 463.

10 Ngugi wa Thiong'o, *Decolonizing the Mind: The Politics of Language in African Literature* (Heinemann, 1986).

11 Frederick Buell, *National Culture and the New Global System* (Baltimore, 1994), 221.

12 Bhabha, 'Interrogating Identity', *Location of Culture*, 62.

13 John M. MacKenzie, *Orientalism: History, Theory and the Arts* (Manchester, 1995), xvii, passim.

14 Gayatri Chakravorty Spivak, 'Subaltern Studies: Deconstructing Historiography', in Ranajit Guha (ed.), *Subaltern Studies IV* (Delhi, 1985), 332, passim.

15 Ashis Nandy, 'History's Forgotten Doubles', *History and Theory: Theme Issue 34. World Historians and Their Critics* (1995), 65.

16 Ashis Nandy, *The Intimate Enemy: Loss and Recovery of Self under Colonialism* (Delhi, 1983), xv.

17 Young, *White Mythologies*. For a more subtle reading of these anti-historical tendencies in post-colonial theory, see Buell, *National Culture*, ch. 9.

18 Dipesh Chakrabarty, 'Postcoloniality and the Artifice of History: Who Speaks for "Indian" Pasts?', *Representations*, 37 (Winter 1992), 2.

19 Bill Ashcroft, Gareth Griffiths and Helen Tiffin, *The Empire Writes Back: Theory and Practice in Post-Colonial Literatures* (London, 1989), 11.

20 Laura E. Donaldson, *Decolonizing Feminisms: Race, Gender, and Empire-Building* (Chapel Hill, 1992), 9, passim.

21 David Spurr, *The Rhetoric of Empire: Colonial Discourse in Journalism, Travel Writing, and Imperial Administration* (Durham, 1993).

22 Spurr, *Rhetoric*, 10.

23 Spurr, *Rhetoric*, 93.

24 Nicholas Thomas, *Colonialism's Culture: Anthropology. Travel and Government* (Princeton, 1994), x.

25 Sumit Sarkar, 'Orientalism Revisited: Saidian Frameworks in the Writing of Modern History', *The Oxford Literary Review*, 16, nos. 1–2 (1994), 217.

26 Gayatri Chakravorty Spivak, 'Can the Subaltern Speak?', in Gary Nelson and Lawrence Grossberg (eds), *Marxism and the Interpretation of Culture* (Urbana and Chicago, 1988), 271–313.

27 Gyan Prakash, 'Subaltern Studies as Postcolonial Criticism', *American Historical Review*, 99, no. 5 (Dec. 1994), 1482, 1483.

28 Young, *Colonial Desire*, 164, 165.

29 Sara Suleri, *The Rhetoric of English India* (Chicago, 1992), 12–13.

30 Edward W. Said, *Culture and Imperialism* (New York, 1993), ch. 3.

31 Bernard S. Cohn, *An Anthropologist among the Historians and Other Essays* (Delhi, 1990).

32 David Fieldhouse, 'Can Humpty-Dumpty Be Put Together Again? Imperial History in the 1980s', *Journal of Imperial and Commonwealth History*, 12, no. 2 (Jan. 1984), 9–23.

33 Said, *Culture and Imperialism*, ch. 2.

34 Javed Majeed, *Ungoverned Imaginings: James Mill's 'The History of British India and Orientalism* (Oxford, 1992); Gauri Viswanathan, *Masks of Conquest: Literary Study and British Rule in India* (New York, 1989).

35   Moira Ferguson, *Colonialism and Gender Relations from Mary Wollstonecraft to Jamaica Kincaid: East Caribbean Connections* (New York, 1993), ch. 2.

36   Young, *Colonial Desire*, chs. 2 & 3.

37   Tim Youngs, *Travellers in Africa: British Travelogues, 1850–1900* (Manchester, 1994), 6.

38   Antoinette Burton, *Burdens of History: British Feminists. Indian Women, and Imperial Culture, 1865–1915* (Chapel Hill, 1994); Lynn Zastoupil, *John Stuart Mill and India* (Stanford, 1994).

39   MacKenzie, 'Edward Said and the Historians' and *Orientalism*; Martha L. Hildreth, 'Lamentations on Reality: A Response to John M. MacKenzie's 'Edward Said and the Historians', *Nineteenth-Century Contexts*, 19, no. 1 (1995), 65–73.

Chapter 2

Frederick Cooper

CONFLICT AND CONNECTION
Rethinking colonial African history

THIS ARTICLE IS PART OF AN EFFORT to bring historiographies of
Africa, Latin America, and Asia—with their particular scholarly traditions,
insights, and blind spots—into relationship with each other, avoiding the assumption
that interaction simply means borrowing from apparently more "developed" historiographies. South–South intellectual exchange is not new. The earliest attempts by
African intellectuals to confront the issues of colonialism and racism, beginning in the
nineteenth century, entailed contacts forged with Americans of African descent and
later with anticolonial leaders from Asia and the Caribbean. Later still, the limitations
of anticolonial ideologies and of nationalism were analysed in Africa with the help of
arguments originating with Latin American dependency theorists.

The Subaltern Studies Group has had a particularly empowering effect on the
scholarship of once-colonized regions, for it has put the process of making history into
the picture. While striving to recover the lives of people forgotten in narratives of global
exploitation and national mobilization, this collective of historians has called into
question the very narratives themselves, indeed, the source material, theoretical frameworks, and subject position of historians. The "subalternity of non-Western histories" as
much as the subalternity of social groups within those histories has been uncovered.
Those histories exist in the shadow of Europe not solely because of colonization's
powerful intrusion into other continents but because Europe's self-perceived movement
toward state-building, capitalist development, and modernity marked and still mark a
vision of historical progress against which African, Asian, or Latin American history
appears as "failure": of the "nation to come to its own," of the "bourgeoisie as well as of
the working class to lead."[1]

In these pages, I want to explore the ways—with parallels and differences—in
which historians of Africa have confronted the experience of colonial rule. To the
African historian, the value of Indian historiography is not that our colleagues offer
ready-made solutions to our problems but that all of us are engaged in different ways
with closely related debates. Both historiographies wrestle with—but do not quite
escape—the dichotomous vision characteristic of colonial ideologies, originating in the

opposition of civilized colonizer and primitive colonized. The risk is that in exploring the colonial binarism one reproduces it, either by new variations of the dichotomy (modern versus traditional) or by inversion (the destructive imperialist versus the sustaining community of the victims). The difficulty is to confront the power behind European expansion without assuming it was all-determining and to probe the clash of different forms of social organization without treating them as self-contained and autonomous. The binaries of colonizer/colonized, Western/non-Western, and domination/resistance begin as useful devices for opening up questions of power but end up constraining the search for precise ways in which power is deployed and the ways in which power is engaged, contested, deflected, and appropriated.

With Africa's independence, historians were strongly moved to find a domain that could be defined as both unambiguously African and resistant to imperialism. In the historiography of Subaltern Studies, the clarity of such categories is questioned, but they keep coming back in the very concept of the subaltern and in Ranajit Guha's insistence that one can examine the "autonomous" domain of the subaltern and reveal people acting "on their own."[2] Guha, like many African historians, wants his subalterns to have a rich and complex consciousness, to exercise autonomous agency, and yet to remain in the category of subaltern, and he wants colonialism to remain resolutely colonial, despite the contradictions of its modernizing projects and its insistence on maintaining boundaries, despite its interventionist power being rendered contingent by the actions of subalterns.[3] Colonial discourse, Subaltern Studies rightly points out, has tried to contain its oppositions—whether in the form of its "liberal" ideas of self-determination or the "irrational" actions of "primitive" people—within its own categories. How far colonial discourse could actually contain its challenges and tensions remains in question.

The Subaltern Studies Group has turned what could be yet another exercise in Western self-indulgence—endless critiques of modernity, of the universalizing pretensions of Western discourse—into something more valuable because it insists that the subject positions of colonized people that European teleologies obscure should not simply be allowed to dissolve. While profiting from the insights of Subaltern Studies to reexamine work in African colonial history, I also hope to push back the dualisms that are coming in the rear door in both historiographies. African historians' use of the concept of "resistance" is generally less subtle, less dialectic, less self-questioning than Indian historians' deployment of the idea of subaltern agency, yet both concepts risk flattening the complex lives of people living in colonies and underestimate the possibility that African or Indian action might actually alter the boundaries of subordination within a seemingly powerful colonial regime. The critique of modernity has its own dangers, as Dipesh Chakrabarty recognizes in warning that too simple a rejection could be "politically suicidal."[4] One can agree with Guha and his colleagues that Marxist master narratives of relentless capitalist advance are yet another form of Western teleology—as are nationalist metanarratives of the triumphal takeover of the nation-state— yet historians should not deprive themselves of the analytical tools necessary to study capitalism and its effects around the world—in all their complexity, contingency, and limitations. Nor should the recognition of the violence and oppression within the generalization of the nation-state model around the world blind us to the potential for violence and oppression that lies in other social formations. I am also trying to push capital and the state back in, making them the object of an analysis more nuanced and interactive than attacks on metanarrative and modernity.

There are reasons for different emphases in the historiographies of the two continents. Subaltern Studies emerged in the 1980s, nearly forty years after India's independence, as a critique of an established nationalist interpretation of history, as well as of "progressive" arguments, whether liberal or Marxist. Africa's independence movements are more recent, their histories only beginning to be written. Africans' and Africanists' disillusionment with the fruits of independence in the 1970s took the form of an emphasis on the external determinants of economic and social problems, and hence a look toward Latin American dependency theory. Most important of all have been the obstacles to the density of debate possible in India: the catastrophic economic situation Africa faced, particularly since the 1980s, and the harsh material conditions in which African scholars and educational and cultural institutions function.

Different experiences give rise to different initial assumptions. The category of subaltern is an intuitively attractive point of departure for South Asianists, given the widely shared perception of social distinction in India as long-lasting, coercive, and sharply delineated, even when scholars put the bases of social distinction in question. Recent generations of African scholars have witnessed—and often been part of—a moment, perhaps not to be repeated, of considerable mobility and category jumping, reflecting the sudden expansion of education systems in the 1950s, the post-World War II export boom, the precipitous Africanization of the civil service, and the rapid development by African rulers of clientage networks and distributional politics. Whereas many scholars have been trying to pull apart and examine the idea of an essential "India," others have felt they had to put together "Africa" in the face of general perceptions of everlasting and immutable division. Subaltern Studies' critique of ways in which a nationalist state picks up the controlling project of a colonial state gives rise to sympathetic echoes among Africans and Africanists—disillusioned with post-independence states—but also to a measure of skepticism about conceivable alternatives, given bitter experience, as in contemporary Somalia, with what "communities" can do to one another when a state loses its controlling capabilities in the age of automatic weapons.

What follows is a consideration of African historiography, stressing the connections between the "resistance" model that was crucial to its development and the new scholarship on colonialism. Both concepts, I argue, should be further scrutinized. Politics in a colony should not be reduced to anticolonial politics or to nationalism: the "imagined communities" Africans saw were both smaller and larger than the nation, sometimes in creative tension with each other, sometimes in repressive antagonism.

The burst of colonial liberations that followed Ghana's independence in 1957 led Africanists to project backward the idea of the nation. The new states of Africa needed something around which diverse peoples could build a sense of commonality. Africa scholars, as one acute observer put it, acted like the "Committee of Concerned Scholars for a Free Africa."[5] The first generation of historians of Africa, seeking to differentiate themselves from imperial historians, were eager to find a truly African history.

African resistance to European conquest and colonization both ratified the integrity of pre-colonial polities and structures (themselves a major topic) and provided a link between them and the nationalist challenge to colonial rule. Resistance was the key plot element in a continuous narrative of African history. Terence Ranger argued specifically for a connection between "primary resistance movements" in the early days of colonization and "modern mass nationalism." Early resistance implied mobilization across a wider network of affiliation than kinship units or "tribes" provided, and this enlargement of scale created a basis for subsequent movements. In a detailed study of a revolt in Southern Rhodesia, Ranger pointed to the role of spirit mediums in mobilizing rebels across a large region and providing a coherent framework for the resistance.[6]

While analyses such as these attempted an Africa-centered perspective, they paradoxically centered European colonialism as the issue that really mattered in the twentieth century. An apparently populist rhetoric concealed the privileging of African elites—in the 1960s as much as the 1890s—by virtue of their anticolonialism and downplayed tensions and inequalities within African societies. Sensitive to these historiographical issues, Ranger himself stepped away from the linearity of his earlier argument and advocated a more multivalent and nuanced approach to African political mobilization. Nonetheless, studies within the resistance framework conclusively showed that colonial conquests and heavy-handed interventions into African life were vigorously challenged, that guerrilla warfare within decentralized polities was as important as the fielding of armies by African states, that women as well as men engaged in acts of resistance, and that individual action—moving away from the tax collector or labor recruiter, ignoring orders, speaking insolently, and criticizing the claims of missionaries, doctors, and educators—complemented collective actions.[7]

For the authors of the UNESCO history of Africa (a collective series intended to reflect the first generations of post-independence African and Africanist scholarship), the key issue of the early colonial era was the defense of sovereignty. Adu Boahen, the editor of the relevant volume, saw African societies in the late nineteenth century as dynamic, moving toward a form of modernity that retained sovereignty but selectively engaged with European commerce, religion, and education. The dynamism of African societies before colonization is no longer in question, but Boahen's conception grants Western modernity too much power—particularly in its emphasis on the strength of the state as a marker of political progress and a unit for social advancement—while it fails to address the contradictions stemming from specific social structures within Africa. Boahen has little to say about Africans who conquered other Africans or about the slaveowners in coastal Dahomey or Sahelian Sokoto or island Zanzibar who made other Africans bear the burden of expanding commerce. Sovereignty was not the only issue facing Africans, and the European invasions entered a long and complex process of state-building and oppression, of production and exploitation, as well as a history of small-scale producers and merchants for whom the overseas connection offered opportunities they did not want to give up and oppressions they wanted to contest.[8]

Here, I will break the linearity of the discussion of the historiography itself for a moment and point to another pioneering approach. In 1956, K. Onwuka Dike, generally regarded as the first African to become a professional African historian, authored *Trade and Politics in the Niger Delta*, seeking to make a decisive break with the imperial historians who had been his mentors and to write history from an African perspective. His book is less remarkable for the new sources it used than for the matter-of-fact way in which it analysed interaction. Africans do not appear in this text as either resistors or collaborators in the face of European involvement in the Delta; Europeans, indeed, appear as actors in the universe of different actors within the region, all trying to work with the opportunities and constraints of overseas trade and regional political structure. Dike knew what the Delta traders could not—that the European traders' metropolitan connections would one day break the framework of interaction—but he nonetheless provided an account of African agency intersecting with European in a crucial moment of history.[9]

Resistance had a special power in the two decades after Dike's study appeared. Scholars and journalists wanting to make the world aware of anticolonial movements in Africa—Thomas Hodgkin and Basil Davidson the most knowledgeable among them— sought to show the complex roots of political mobilization, from Africa's own traditions of rule to memories of battles against foreign conquerors, to religious and labor movements that provided an experience of organization culminating in the development of nationalist political parties. Dike's own project took on a nationalist bent as well: the "Ibadan" school emphasized the integrity of pre-colonial African societies, which sometimes appeared as precedents for independent Africa. J. F. Ade Ajayi termed colonialism an "episode in African history," a break in the otherwise continuous exercise of African political agency.[10] What was most neglected was colonial rule itself: to my cohort in graduate school (1969–74), studying pre-colonial history or resistance constituted genuine African history, but bringing a similar specificity of inquiry to that which was being resisted risked having one's project labeled as a throwback to imperial history.

Questionings of the nationalist metanarrative came from two generations of African scholars. B. A. Ogot, the senior historian of Kenya, in an essay of 1972 on the "Loyalist crowd" in Mau Mau, pointed out that the violent conflicts of the 1950s could not be reduced to a simple morality play: both sides had their moral visions, their moral discourses. The "Loyalists" saw themselves as engaged in a defense of a way of life in which Christianity, education, and investment in small farms were the means to progress. Colonial policy could be contested within limits, but to the Loyalists the young rebels were violating Kikuyu traditions of respect for elders and threatening the community.[11] Some twenty years later and across the continent, Mamadou Diouf published a book that debunked Senegal's basic myth of resistance, the battle of Lat Dior and his Wolof kingdom against the French. Lat Dior, Diouf argued, was defending "the privileges of the ruling class and the traditional field in which it exercised its exploitation" as much as sovereignty. His study entailed a complex engagement with how power was mobilized and contested within Africa and the extent to which the long-term French presence first made the emergence of a Lat Dior possible and then rendered the continued existence of this sort of polity impossible.[12]

The metanarrative of nationalist victory—and many of the tales of "resistance"— have most often been told as stories of men, with a rather macho air to the narrating of confrontation. Women's history, to a significant extent, began by arguing that "women could do it, too" or by adding African patriarchy to the colonial object of resistance. As historians increasingly showed that economic and social activity was defined, contested, and redefined in terms of gender, the gendered nature of politics needed to be examined as well. The contestation of gender roles within the Mau Mau movement is being explored by Cora Ann Presley, Luise White, and Tabitha Kanogo, while Timothy Scarnecchia shows the masculinization of African politics in the 1950s in Harare. Housing regulations that effectively disallowed women access to residential space except through a man meant that women on their own were by definition outside the law, and they were driven into certain niches in the unofficial economy. For a time, such women worked with a male-led union-cum-political movement to challenge the way the state defined and constrained urban women. The movement failed; and, when nationalists later began to challenge the colonial state in other ways, their quest to balance respectability against the movement's need to recruit migrant male laborers meant that they, too, treated such women as dangerous and disruptive. Nationalism in the 1950s explicitly constructed itself in masculine—as much as class—terms, leaving aside its own more ambiguous history.[13]

Apartheid in South Africa affected women in particular ways: through male-only labor compounds, the policing of migration, the feminization of rural poverty, and a complex hierarchy of residential rights that divided black workers and families. Protest was thus also shaped by gender. Women led bus boycotts and demonstrations against the application of pass laws to women. A strong and sustained series of women's protest movements in the Herschel district of Cape Province reflected the circumstances of women in the context of increasing male out-migration, but the more formally organized Industrial and Commercial Workers' Union largely shunted women aside.[14]

The heroic narrative fell victim not only to wise elders and young scholars with new questions but also to continuing crises in Africa itself. African novelists were the first intellectuals to bring before a wide public inside and outside the African continent profound questions about the corruption within postcolonial governments and the extent to which external domination persisted. Growing disillusionment made increasingly attractive the theories of "underdevelopment," which located the poverty and weakness of "peripheral" societies not in the colonial situation but in the more long-term process of domination within a capitalist world system. The debate that dependency theory unleashed had the beneficial effect of legitimizing among African intellectuals the notion that theoretical propositions were not mere impositions of Western models on a unique Africa but offered ways of understanding the predicament Africa shared with other parts of what had come to be called the "Third World." The direct link in bringing dependency theory to Africa from Latin America was Walter Rodney, a Guyanese of African descent, instrumental in founding the "Dar es Salaam" school of radical African history. It may be that an engaged expatriate was better positioned than were Tanzanians to open the challenge to nationalist conventions, the tragic counterpart to this being Rodney's assassination after his return to Guyana and the detention, in their own country, of several Kenyan historians who had questioned reigning myths.[15]

The issues opened by dependency theorists prompted an increasing interest in Marxist theory among Africanists and Africans in the 1970s and opened the possibility of a dialogue across the continents. Ironically, dependency theory emphasized common subordination and gave little place to African or Latin American agency. Certain Marxist approaches assumed the dominance of capitalism, although a useful contribution of African history to Marxist theory would be to point to the limits capital encountered in trying to tame Africa's labor power. More recently, poststructuralist theory has turned toward an examination of discourse and modes of representation—including the scholar's own—but often at the cost of surrendering the tools with which to undertake studies of global power and exploitation. For all the critique and counter-critique among these approaches, there has been a certain facility with which historians outside the African continent have slid from one paradigm to another, post-Marxism and poststructuralism embodying this tendency in their very labels. To many American or European scholars, insisting that Africa had a history—irrespective of what one said about it—was evidence of a progressive bent; African history was subaltern studies by default.

The notable exception to this observation comes from the part of Africa that did not fit into the 1960s narrative of liberation from white rule, South Africa. My cohort of graduate students in the United States felt that the history of South Africa was not African enough. South African expatriates contributed the most in the 1970s to the focus on that region, and as they did one of the sharpest theoretical divides opened up: a "liberal" view that stressed African initiative and Afro-European interaction stymied by the rigid racism of Afrikaners versus a "radical" paradigm that saw South African racism as itself a consequence of the way in which capitalism emerged in the late nineteenth and early twentieth century. Within the "radical" approach, one branch tended toward a structuralist conception of an unfolding logic of capital determining South African history, but another looked directly to the inspiration of European and American social historians to uncover the ways in which Africans carried out their struggles and forged community as well as class. South African historians shared some of the "history from the bottom up" concerns with Subaltern Studies but generally not their conception of the subaltern's autonomy. Charles van Onselen has most sharply described the element of shared culture across racial divisions and antagonisms within poor farming communities, and likewise the efforts of diverse and changing groups of blacks and whites to make their way in the rough world of urbanizing Johannesburg. The most interesting autonomist argument—independent of Subaltern Studies—comes from Keletso Atkins' analysis of a distinctly African work culture, although her point is that this work culture influenced and constrained the apparently dominant work culture of developing capitalism.[16] South African history in the 1970s and 1980s was thus distinguished by a focused debate— only occasionally engaging the historiography of the rest of Africa—over race, class, and capital. In the 1990s, poststructuralist questionings of the categories and narratives of Marxist history have been strongly resisted in South Africa by those who insist that here, at least, the lines of power and exploitation are clear. This is a useful debate and also opens opportunities for engagement with the issues being raised by Subaltern Studies.

Over the past several years, a new colonial history has emerged, in dialogue with anthropology and literary studies and ranging over many areas of the world. Anthropologists questioned past and current modes of ethnographic inquiry, suggesting the need for a more contextual and historical examination of the apparatus that collected and classified knowledge of Africa or Asia. Literary critics began to study the politics of representation and the process by which the assertion within European discourse of a sense of national or Continental identity depended on inscribing "otherness" on non-European populations. Both scholarly traditions encouraged an examination of the categories and tropes through which the Africa of explorers, missionaries, settlers, scientists, doctors, and officials was symbolically ordered into the grid of "tribe" and "tradition." Historians explored how censuses defined or reified such categories as caste, how medicine defined susceptibility to disease in racial or cultural terms, how colonial architecture inscribed modernity onto the built environment while appropriating a distilled traditionalism to its own purposes, and how missionaries sought to "colonize minds" by forging an individual capable of thinking about his or her personal salvation, separated from the collective ethos of the community.[17] The Subaltern Studies Group took the further step of asking whether categories of colonial knowledge set the terms in which oppositional movements could function and in which colonialism itself could be critiqued.[18]

This trend has opened up possibilities of seeing how deeply colonies were woven into what it meant to be European and how elusive—and difficult to police—was the boundary between colonizers and colonized. It is nonetheless open to the danger of reading a generalized "coloniality" from particular texts, abstracting what went on in colonies from local contexts and contradictory and conflictual global processes. Even as subtle and interactive an argument as Homi Bhabha's treatment of mimicry, in which the colonized person's acting as if "white but not quite" destabilizes the colonizer's view of boundaries and control, relies on detaching the dyad of colonizer/colonized from anything either subject might be engaged in except their mutual confrontation.[19]

It is far from clear what Africans thought about the symbolic structure of colonial power or the identities being inscribed on them. The cultural edifice of the West could be taken apart brick by brick and parts of it used to shape quite different cultural visions. Piecing together such processes is one of the most promising endeavors being undertaken by innovative scholars. A scholarly trend that began from the opposition of "self" and "other" has thus ended up confronting the artificiality of such dichotomies and the complex *bricolage* with which Africans in colonies put together practices and beliefs.[20]

The problem of recovering such histories while understanding how colonial documents construct their own versions of them has been the focus of thoughtful reflections by Ranajit Guha. At first glance, these contributions may appear to the African historian more as sound practice than a methodological breakthrough. African historians cut their teeth in the 1960s on the assertion that colonial sources distorted history, and they saw the use of oral sources—as well as reading colonial documents against the grain—as putting themselves on the path to people's history. But Africa scholars put more emphasis on showing that Africans had a history than on asking how Africans' history-making was implicated in establishing or contesting power. Guha and his colleagues, facing the rich but problematic corpus of Indian colonial documents, have provoked a useful discussion over the conceptual difficulties in the attempt to recover consciousness and memory outside of a literate elite—and the ultimate impossibility of true knowledge across the barriers of class and colonialism—while African historians have tried to see how far one could push with nondocumentary sources. There is room here for exchange across differing perspectives, although Gayatri Chakravorty Spivak's rhetorical question "Can the Subaltern Speak?" may tempt the historian struggling for his or her modest insights to ask in return, "Can the theorist listen?"[21]

Recognition of the much greater power of the Europeans in the colonial encounter does not negate the importance of African agency in determining the shape the encounter took. While the conquerors could concentrate military force to defeat African armies, "pacify" villages, or slaughter rebels, the routinization of power demanded alliances with local authority figures, be they lineage heads or recently defeated kings. A careful reading of colonial narratives suggests a certain pathos: the civilizing mission did not end up with the conversion of Africa to Christianity or the generalization of market relations throughout the continent, and colonial writing instead celebrated victories against "barbarous practices" and "mad mullahs." Colonial violence, in such a situation, became "acts of trespass," vivid and often brutal demonstrations distinguishable for what they could violate more than what they could transform.[22]

The economic geography of colonization is as uneven as the geography of power. Colonial powers established islands of cash crop production and mining surrounded by vast labor catchment areas in which coercion and, as time went on, lack of alternatives were necessary to extract laborers. To a significant extent, the wage labor force that capital could use—whatever the wishes of employers—was largely male and transitory, in large measure because Africans were seeking to incorporate periods of wage labor into their lives even as capital was trying to subordinate African economies. It took the wealth and power of South Africa—where a racialized version of "primitive accumulation" took place through the relative density of white settlement, the impetus of gold mining after the 1880s, and the agency of the state—for labor power to be detached from its social roots. Even in South Africa, the struggle over how, where, and under what conditions Africans could actually be made to work never quite ended. Elsewhere, some of the greatest success stories of colonial economies came about through African agency: the vast expansion of cocoa production in the Gold Coast at the turn of the century, Nigeria from the 1920s, and the Ivory Coast from the 1940s was the work of smallholders and did not depend on colonial initiatives. Cash cropping was neither a colonial imposition nor an unmediated African response to price incentives; it gave rise, in certain places, to accumulation without producing a bourgeoisie. This is the kind of history that Subaltern Studies scholars want to have told, a history that breaks out of the molds of European modernity and Afro-Asiatic stasis, yet these farmers' experience cannot easily be contained within a notion of subalternity.[23]

The juxtaposition of a disruptive but concentrated colonizing presence and a large and unevenly controlled "bush" had paradoxical consequences: fostering episodic exercises of collective punishment or direct coercion against unwilling workers or cultivators on whom the effects of routinized discipline had not been successfully projected; making the boundaries of African communities more rigid and their "customary law" more categorical than in days before colonial "progress", marginalizing educated and Christian Africans as the colonizing apparatus assumed control and established alliances with "traditional" leaders; fostering commercial linkages that enabled Africans who adapted to them to acquire collective resources that later enabled them to resist pressures to enter wage labor; expanding an ill-controlled urban economy that offered opportunities for casual laborers, itinerant hawkers, criminal entrepreneurs, and providers of service to a migrant, largely male African working class, thus creating alternatives (for women as well as men) to the roles into which colonial regimes wished to cast people; and creating space for missionary-educated Africans to reject mission communities in favor of secular roles in a colonial bureaucracy or to transform Christian teaching into critiques of colonial rule.[24]

This is not just an argument about African "adaptation" or "resistance" to colonial initiatives. Rather, it is an argument that policy and ideology also reflected European adaptation (and resistance) to the initiatives of the colonized. This notion extends to the periodization of colonial history: Imperial conquerors began by thinking they could remake African society and rationalize the exploitation of the continent; by World War I, they were largely frustrated in such endeavors and began to make—through policies of "indirect rule" and "association"—their failures sound like a policy of conserving African society and culture; by the late 1930s, the imagined Africa of "tribes" was proving unable to contain the tensions unleashed by the much more complex patterns of economic change; in the late 1930s and 1940s, Great Britain and France tried to re-seize the initiative through a program of economic and social development; African political parties, trade unions, and rural organizers turned the development initiative into a claim for social and political rights, effective enough for the abdication of power and responsibility to become increasingly attractive in London and Paris; most recently, the tendency of Western powers to write off Africa as a continent of disasters and bad government is a sign that the development framework still has not pushed Africans into the role of a quiet and productive junior partner in the world market.

Ranajit Guha has characterized colonization as dominance without hegemony, a direct contradiction of the trends in metropoles to envelop the exercise of power under universal social practices and norms.[25] The claim of a colonial government to rule a distinct people denied the universality of market relations, revealed the limits to capitalism's progressive thrust, and led colonial regimes to seek legitimacy by hitching themselves to indigenous notions of authority and obedience. Nationalists, seeking to displace colonial rulers without undermining their own authority, continued to practice dominance without hegemony.

The distinction between capitalist universality and colonial particularism is a compelling one, but Guha does not get to the bottom of it. He misses the implications of the limits of coercion, and he underplays the dynamic possibilities stemming from the partial and contradictory hegemonic projects that colonial rulers attempted: the disputes within colonizing populations and metropolitan elites over different visions of colonial rule and the space that efforts to articulate hegemony opened up for contestation among the colonized. He implicitly draws a contrast between colonial dominance and metropolitan hegemony that the exclusions and violences of twentieth-century Europe belie. Guha's insight, however, offers an opportunity to explore the tensions of particularism and universality within colonies themselves and in a dynamic interconnection of colony and metropole. As I will argue below, the inability of colonial regimes to establish and maintain "dominance" amid the uneven effects of capitalism led them to deploy the "universalistic" conceptions of social engineering developed in Europe, only to find that their own hopes for the success of such technologies required giving up the beliefs about Africa on which a sense of "dominance" depended.

The incompleteness of capitalist transformation in a colonial context has been a major theme of Subaltern Studies, but the tensions of colonialism in a capitalist context are equally important to analyze. Just as elusive are the conceptual categories with which scholars try to understand the movements that have challenged colonial and capitalist power in Africa, Asia, and Latin America.

At one level, the concept of resistance is generally accepted and unproblematic. In the clash of African and colonial armies, individual acts of disobedience or flight, and the elaboration of powerful arguments for liberation, colonial rule has been continually and severely challenged. But much of the resistance literature is written as if the "R" were capitalized. What is being resisted is not necessarily clear, and "colonialism" sometimes appears as a force whose nature and implications do not have to be unpacked. The concept of resistance can be expanded so broadly that it denies any other kind of life to the people doing the resisting. Significant as resistance might be, Resistance is a concept that may narrow our understanding of African history rather than expand it.

Scholars have their reasons for taking an expansive view. Little actions can add up to something big: desertion from labor contracts, petty acts of defiance of white officials or their African subalterns, illegal enterprises in colonial cities, alternative religious communities—all these may subvert a regime that proclaimed both its power and its righteousness, raise the confidence of people in the idea that colonial power can be countered, and forge a general spirit conducive to mobilization across a variety of social differences. The problem is to link the potential with the dynamics of a political process, and this problem requires careful analysis rather than teleology. It is facile to make causal generalizations across diverse circumstances, as Donald Crummey does in proclaiming, "Most popular violence is a response to state or ruling-class violence," and it is questionable to link all acts of assertion with a military metaphor, as James Scott does in terming them "weapons of the weak."[26]

Foucault saw resistance as constitutive of power and power of resistance; he denied that there was a "single locus of great Refusal." He found "mobile and transitory points of resistance, producing cleavages in a society that shifts about, fracturing unities and effecting regroupings." Although "strategic codification" of those points can make for revolution, such a process cannot be assumed, and his stress was on the continual reconfiguration of both power and resistance. In the current atmosphere of postcolonial pessimism, such an idea resonates: even the counterhegemonic discourses of the colonial era and the subversions of European notions of modernity become enmeshed in concepts—the nation-state most prominent among them—that redeploy ideas of surveillance, control, and development within post-independence politics, fracturing and producing unities and reconfiguring resistances. In such a light, Subaltern Studies scholars have scrutinized the reconfiguration of power-resistance at the moment of nationalist victory.[27]

The difficulty with the Foucauldian pairing of power and resistance lies in Foucault's treatment of power as "capillary," as diffused throughout society. However much surveillance, control, and the narrowing of the boundaries of political discourse were a part of Europe in its supposedly democratizing era, power in colonial societies was more arterial than capillary—concentrated spatially and socially, not very nourishing beyond such domains, and in need of a pump to push it from moment to moment and place to place. This should be a theoretical rallying point for historians: they have the tools (and often the inclination) to analyse in specific situations how power is constituted, aggregated, contested, and limited, going beyond the poststructuralist tendency to find power diffused in "modernity," "the post-enlightenment era," or "Western discourse."

The resistance concept suffers from the diffuseness with which the object of resistance is analyzed, as well as from what Sherry Ortner calls "thinness." The dyad of resistor/oppressor is isolated from its context; struggle within the colonized population—over class, age, gender, or other inequalities—is "sanitized"; the texture of people's lives is lost; and complex strategies of coping, of seizing niches within changing economies, of multi-sided engagement with forces inside and outside the community, are narrowed into a single framework.[28]

Some of the best work in African history discards the categories of resistors and collaborators and starts with the question of how "rural people saw their circumstances, made their choices, and constructed their ideas about the larger society."[29] One can trace the way in which women in Central Africa became more vulnerable to both predators and protectors during the nineteenth-century slave trade, then made use of the colonial peace and cash crop outlets to gain a measure of economic influence, but subsequently became more dependent on men's remittances from wage labor. Or one can see how some women in Nairobi found a niche in providing cheap services to male wage laborers, subsidizing the economic designs of the colonial state while subverting the cultural designs of producing a well-controlled city and working class. And one can see how African religious movements refashioned Christian doctrines in relation to the local power structure, defining a moral community in which the officially sanctioned structures of chieftaincy became irrelevant.[30]

I am arguing here for the complexity of engagement of Africans with imported institutions and constructs, as opposed to James Scott's emphasis on a "hidden transcript" among colonized people that develops among them only to burst forth into a "public transcript" in moments of confrontation.[31] My approach also differs from Ranajit Guha's quest to explore the "autonomous" domain of the subaltern, although the complex and varied practice of historians in the Subaltern Studies collective, more so than the manifestos, is filled with stories of engagement.

In discussing labor, as Dipesh Chakrabarty points out, the historian can usefully invoke general theories about "abstract labor," a set of relationships characteristic of capitalism, while preserving a notion of "real labor," located in his case in the systems of authority and clientage of Bengali villages and the power structure of colonial India. In my own research on Africa in the era of decolonization, I examine both the tensions between African labor movements whose demands are shared around the capitalist world—wages, family welfare, security, and working conditions—and whose rhetoric invoked the universality of wage labor through a demand for equal pay for equal work, and a political movement focusing on self-determination for all Africans. Ironically, the wave of strikes and general strikes in French and British Africa from the mid-1930s into the 1950s drew on the integration of workers into a wider population—which provided food to sustain strikers and at times brought about generalized urban mobilization—yet the workers' demands distanced them from that population.[32]

Colonial regimes sought to regain the initiative through "stabilization," to form the poorly differentiated, ill-paid population that moved in and out of urban jobs into a compact body of men attached to their employment. They wanted employers to pay workers enough to bring families to the city so that the new generation of workers would be properly socialized to industrial life and separated from the perceived backwardness of village Africa. The dynamic of the situation lay in the fact that trade unions were able to capitalize on this yearning for predictability, order, and productivity—on officials' hope that Western models of the workplace and industrial relations might actually function in Africa—to pose their demands in ways officials found difficult to reject out of hand. Unions seized the developmentalist rhetoric of postwar imperialism and turned it into claims to entitlements, even as officials began to concede that a unionized work force might aid stabilization.

By the mid-1950s, colonial regimes feared that their development initiatives were being undermined by rising labor costs, and they began to pull back from their own universalizing stance. They realized that conceding African politicians a modest measure of power in colonial governments would force them to weigh the cost of labor against the territorial budget. A national reference point now seemed less threatening economically than a universalistic one. This time, colonial officials guessed right, for nationalist leaders, granted limited territorial authority, quickly set about disciplining African labor movements in the name of a single-minded focus on a national unity defined by the political party.

One can read the actions of labor movements in French and British Africa as one example among many of African militance or as an instance of the universal struggle of the working class or as the successful cooptation of an unquiet section of the African population into a set of structures and normalizing practices derived from Europe. All three readings have some truth, but the important point is their dynamic relationship: labor movements both brought material benefits to a specific class of people and opened new possibilities for other sorts of actions, which themselves might have mobilizing or normalizing consequences. In this period, labor had a window of opportunity it lacked before and lost afterward, facing a colonial regime invested in a tenuous development initiative and fearing the mobilization of an unpredictable mass. The tension between the demands of labor and efforts to forge unity against the colonial state was often a creative one—except in the too-common instance in which party elites fearful of organized challenges and insistent on the supremacy of the national struggle moved to deny the tension and suppress such movements.

Rural mobilization, which was sometimes led by "organic intellectuals" emerging from a peasant milieu, also developed in alliance and tension with movements led by Western-educated people from towns and constituted a challenge to the tyranny of colonial agricultural officers with their ideas of scientific agriculture. Rural political discourse sometimes focused on the integrity and health of the local community, and it also deployed the transcendent languages of self-determination, Christianity, or Garveyism. But, as Norma Kriger has shown, the connections of cultivators with the commercial economy and the state were so varied and complex that "polarizing society along racial lines" was difficult for radical movements to accomplish.[33]

Whether nationalist movements by themselves were strong enough to overthrow colonial rule is unclear, but a variety of social movements from labor unions to anticonservation movements disrupted the economic project of postwar colonialism while discrediting its hegemonic project. Unable to get the Africa they wanted, European powers began to think more seriously about the Africa they had. Empire became vulnerable to another of bourgeois Europe's contradictory tendencies: the calculation of economic interest. By the mid-1950s, France and Great Britain were adding up the costs and benefits of colonial rule more carefully than ever before and coming up with negative numbers.

To the extent—never complete—that issue-specific or localized movements came together in the 1940s and 1950s, the threads also came apart, leaving the unsolved problems of the colonial era to new governments and a tenuously constituted political arena. It is to the problem of framing the national question in relation to other political questions that I now turn.

From the cauldron of politics in the 1950s and 1960s, nation-states emerged across the African continent. Benedict Anderson's conception of the nation as an imagined community should be set against two related notions: the nation was not the only unit that people imagined, and the predominance of the nation-state in post-1960 Africa resulted not from the exclusive focus of African imaginations on the nation but from the fact that the nation was imaginable to colonial rulers as well. Pan-Africanism—embracing the diaspora as well as the continent—had once been the focus of imagination more than the units that eventually became states, but pan-Africanist possibilities were written out of the decolonization bargains.[34] Regional federation, though once a basis of French administration and of the mobilization of trade unions and political parties, fell victim to a French program of "territorialization" and to the interests in territorial institutions that the partial devolution of power to individual colonies gave African politicians. At the same time, linguistic and ethnic groups were denied a legitimate place in politics—which did not prevent them from becoming even more salient and more sharply demarcated in postcolonial politics—and the menace of "tribalism" was used by governing elites to try to eliminate many sorts of subnational politics. In the confrontations of the 1950s, colonial states used violence to exclude certain options, for example, the explicit leftism and the premature (in official eyes) claims to independence of the Union des Populations du Camaroun or the antimodern radicalism of Mau Mau rebels in Kenya.[35] Imperial bureaucrats, however, gave up aspects of their own imaginings: the idea that social and economic change could be directly controlled by those who claimed already to have arrived was lost in the struggles over decolonization. Where the imagination of anticolonial intellectuals in Africa and imperial bureaucrats overlapped was in the formal apparatus of the nation-state, the institutions and symbols contained within territorial borders.

Pan-Africanism actually predated nationalism—defined, as it should be, as a movement to claim the nation-state. Leading intellectuals, notably Léopold Senghor, navigated the perspectives of Pan-Africanism, nationalism, and a desire for social and economic reform in complex ways: Senghor's "négritude" embraced essentialist notions of African culture yet inverted the valuation placed on them, erasing difference and eliminating conflict within an idealized Africa. Senghor was just as brilliant at analyzing and working through the specific social structures of his own Senegal: a Christian politician with a political machine based on Muslim brotherhoods, a poet who expressed his ideas of Africa through the French language, a man who defended Africa from a seat in the French legislature, a romantic defender of African village life who after independence sought to use trade and aid to transform an African nation. Living these complexities entailed pain and difficulty, but there is no indication that Senghor—or the many others navigating similar currents—experienced them as personally destabilizing, as intellectually contradictory, or as threatening to his sense of cultural integrity: *in between* is as much a place to be at home as any other. The implications for the historian are crucial: we must analyse the culture of politics and the politics of culture by constantly shifting the scale of analysis from the most spatially specific (the politics of the clan or the village) to the most spatially diffuse (transatlantic racial politics) and examine the originality and power of political thought by what it appropriated and transformed from its entire range of influences and connections.[36]

The triumph of nationalist movements appears less as a linear progression than as a conjuncture, and the success of African political parties less a question of a singular mobilization in the name of the nation than of coalition building, the forging of clientage networks, and machine politics. For a time, nationalist parties made the colonial state appear to be the central obstacle facing diverse sorts of social movements, from labor to anti-conservation to regional movements. Coalition politics may not have been the stuff of revolutionary drama, but it was often conducted with enthusiasm and idealism. The give-and-take of this era forced—and allowed—colonial governments to make a necessary imaginative leap themselves. They came to envision a world that they no longer ruled but that they thought could function along principles they understood: through state institutions, by Western-educated elites, in the interest of progress and modernity, through integration with global markets and international organizations. British archives, notably, disclose that top echelons of government wanted to believe all this but were not quite convinced. A non-hostile postcolonial relationship was the best they thought they could achieve. In the process, they could eliminate some enemies, but in other cases the one-time Apostles of Disorder—Kwame Nkrumah, Jomo Kenyatta, Nnamdi Azikiwe—were remade in the colonial imagination into the Men of Moderation and Modernity.

The nationalist parties paid a price for their conjunctural coalitions: the social struggles they tried to attach to their cause remained unresolved. As Aristide Zolberg first showed in 1966, the public's nationalist sentiment was actually quite thin. Attempts at building national institutions were inevitably read as building up particularistic interests: for the leader's tribe, for his class, for his clientele, for himself. New states, taking on a transformative project at which European powers had failed, were politically fragile and ideologically brittle, their insistence on unity for the nation and development denying legitimacy to the social movements out of which political mobilization had often been achieved.[37]

The idea of the nation, as Benedict Anderson stressed, emerged in a particular historical context, when the circuits along which creole elites (starting in Latin America) moved and built their careers began to exclude the metropole and focus on the colonial capital and when print capitalism provided a medium to establish a bounded identity. Europe learned to imagine the nation from the tensions that emerged within its old empires and passed the imaginative possibility along to its new colonial conquests. Partha Chatterjee reluctantly grants Anderson a point: the kind of politics that eventually took over colonial states was this nation-centered one, focused on the European-defined boundaries and institutions, on notions of progress shaped by capitalism and European social thought. In making claims on colonial powers, nationalists became caught up in the colonial regimes' categories; nationalism was a "derivative discourse." Chatterjee finds possibilities for "a 'modern' national culture that is nevertheless not Western" but locates them in a spiritual domain set outside economy and statecraft. The Indian elite, drawing its power both from notions of caste and communalism rigidified by British rule and from its immersion in colonial commerce, was willing neither to undertake a drastic assault on the Indian past nor to repudiate those elements of the colonial present from which it benefited. At some moments, more radical appeals—notably those of Mohandas Gandhi himself—were necessary to widen the mobilization of the Indian National Congress; but, as victory came into sight, the Congress leadership's immersion in the economic, political, and ideological structures of the Indian state marginalized alternative visions. The institutions of state and the goal of state-directed development were only a part of Indian politics in the twentieth century, but they were the politics that triumphed.[38]

Both Anderson and Chatterjee do more than take the nation and nationalism from the realm of "natural" sentiment to social construct; they do so in a way grounded in material conditions and aspirations of certain social groups, in the life trajectories of those who imagined the nation, in the networks of intellectuals and political leaders, in the ways in which ideas were circulated. The "state" should be examined with the same care as the "nation"—its institutions and rhetorics carefully scrutinized. One can agree up to a point with Anthony D. Smith that particular qualities of the colonial state— "gubernatorial, territorial, bureaucratic, paternalist-educational, caste-like"—were carried over to postcolonial states, yet African rulers gave their own meanings to institutions they took over, adapting them to patrimonial social structures and complex modes of representing power.[39]

To historicize the nation-state is not, however, to postulate that it is Africa's "curse," as Basil Davidson called it. One should not assume the innocence or autonomy of community or "civil society" any more than that of the nation, and the articulation between state and social units within and beyond it is where analysis should focus. The "national order of things" should neither be taken as natural nor dismissed as an artificial imposition on Africa. State and nation need to be examined in relation to diasporic communities, to the migratory circuits around which many people organize their lives, to the structures and rules—from market transactions to factory discipline—that also cross borders, and to the cleavages that exist within borders and at times both destroy and remake the nation-state.[40]

In concluding this discussion, I turn to a view of colonialism and resistance that in the recent past would have been a likely starting point: Frantz Fanon. The West Indian psychiatrist and intellectual who devoted much of his life to Algeria and was read as a voice of the "African Revolution" epitomizes the anti-imperialist who crosses borders. His view of violence negating the psychological power of colonialism captured the imagination of other African intellectuals and, above all, those in the West who did not have to face the consequences of that violence.

Fanon was no nationalist. For him, nationalism was a bourgeois ideology, espoused by those who wanted to step into the colonial structure rather than turn that structure upside down. Nor was Fanon a racialist: he criticized "négritude" and saw no solace in the sharing of a mythic black identity, opposing a universalistic notion of liberation to arguments about authenticity or cultural autonomy. Fanon's future came out of the struggle itself: " 'The last shall be first and the first last.' Decolonisation is the putting into practice of this sentence."[41]

Yet Fanon was also denying colonized people any history but that of oppression, any ambiguity to the ways they might confront and appropriate the intrusions of colonizers. Instead, he provided a sociological determinism: the petty bourgeoisie was absorbed in mimicking the culture of the colonizer and was best understood in terms of psycho-pathology; the working class had become a labor aristocracy intent only on capturing the privileges of white workers; the peasantry and the lumpenproletariat, by contrast, were the true liberationists, the last who would become first. The categories were actually colonial ones, and the irony of Fanon's fervent argument was that it allowed—by its inversionary logic—France to define the present and future of people in colonies.

Fanon's reduction of ideology and political strategy to traits of social groups in effect created purge categories: the organized worker or the petty bourgeois, like the kulak of the Stalinist Soviet Union, was a traitor by definition. And the singularity with which the "anticolonial" eclipsed all other notions of affiliation or common interest implied postcolonial uniformity as much as anticolonial unity.

Some African leaders were saying exactly that. Sékou Touré, one of Africa's most notable radical nationalists, himself once a trade unionist, spoke on the eve of his assuming power in Guinea of the new imperatives of African rule. Trade unions were "a tool" that should be changed when it got dull; striking against the "organisms of colonial-ism" had been a legitimate action, but a strike "directed against an African Government" was now "historically unthinkable," and the labor movement was "obligated to reconvert itself to remain in the same line of emancipation" as the government. Sékou Touré was to practice what he preached by destroying the autonomy of the trade union movement and jailing much of its leadership. Other once-autonomous, once-activist organizations were similarly destroyed, coopted, or marginalized in many African countries.[42] There were, of course, complex questions to be faced about the role of unions, of regionally or ethnically based associations, of representatives of farmers, traders, and other economic interests in postcolonial polities, as well as questions of allocating more resources to groups that had fared well or badly under colonial rule. But Sékou Touré was not issuing an invitation to a debate. Nor were his fellow leaders who made the national ideal compulsory, via such devices as one-party states and such ideological constructs as Mobutu's *authenticité* or Kenyatta's *harambee* (pulling together). The last were now declared to be first. The others deserved to be last.

This is not to deny Fanon's critique of the self-serving nationalists of his day or the appeal of his call for a liberation that overrode national or racial chauvinisms. The issue is one of facing consequences. The casting out of all but the True Anticolonialist from the political arena and the reduction of entire categories of people to class enemies gave an exhilarating legitimacy to state projects, which were often deflected into less liberationist goals than Fanon had in mind. Enthusiasms for projects of state-building, modernization, and development, in the name of the market or of socialism or of good governance, have consequences, too. Those who find in notions of "community" or "new social movements" a welcome antidote to one sort of oppression need to worry about the other forms of oppression that lie within them. For the historian, searching for those historical actors who found the true path is a less fruitful task than studying different paths into engagement with colonization as well as the tensions between different sorts of liberations, between local mobilization and state institutions, between cultural assertion and cultural interaction.

For the historian who seeks to learn what can be learned about the lives that African workers or market women lived day by day, the Manichean world of Frantz Fanon is no more revealing than a colonial bureaucrat's insistence that such people stood at the divide between African backwardness and Western modernity or a nationalist's dichotomy between an authentic community and an imposed westernization. The Guinean port worker was not just seeking European wages or fighting colonialism: he may also have used his job for a colonial firm to seek autonomy from his father, just as his wife may well have been acting within the urban commercial sector to attain a measure of autonomy from him. As a trade unionist, he drew on organizational forms and institutional legitimacy from the French model of industrial relations, but union and political activities also drew on and contributed to webs of affiliation, languages of solidarity, and a range of cultural institutions that colonial officials did not understand and could not adequately monitor. The worker and the market seller were remaking institutions and their meanings even as they used them.

The concept of subalternity also does not categorize the lived experience of such people, but Subaltern Studies historians are not saying that it should. Their emphasis is on the tension between such experiences and the historical process that generates the categories of knowledge themselves. The tension defines a valuable entry point for probing colonial experiences and an essential reminder of the scholar's inability to escape the implications of the material and cultural power that Europe exercised overseas. Yet, as we look ever more deeply into the contested spaces of colonial politics, we would do well to look beyond the notion of subalternity—and conceptions of colonialism that assume its ability to coerce, coopt, and categorize challenges into its own structure of power and ideology—in order to pry apart further the ways in which power was constituted and contested. The violence of colonizers was no less violent for the narrowness of its range and the limits of its transformative efficacy, and the totalizing arrogance of modernizing ideologies is not diminished by the fact that Africans often disassembled them and created something else. But if "subalterns" are to be seen as vital parts of history, the possibility, at least, that the very meanings of domination and subalternity could be undermined should be kept open. And if, at the same time, we are to follow the call of Chatterjee and Chakrabarty to "provincialize" European history—to subject its universalizing claims to historical examination rather than use them as measures of other people's histories—we should move beyond treating modernity, liberalism, citizenship, or bourgeois equality as if they were fixed and self-contained doctrines unaffected by the appropriations and reformulations given to them by processes of political mobilization in Asia, Africa, or Europe itself.[43]

Nationalism, meanwhile, can be explored in tension with a range of social movements, and, as with the colonization process, the ability of nationalist parties to subsume other sorts of mobilizations under its roof should be seen as contingent and partial. The forms of power in Africa after decolonization—the institutions through which it is exercised and the idioms in which it is represented—reflect not so much the all-consuming thrust of the national order of things but the fragilities, the compromises, and the violences of insecure leaders that emerged in the process of ending colonial rule.

In Africa, the encounters of the past are very much part of the present. Africa still faces the problems of building networks and institutions capable of permitting wide dialogue and common action among people with diverse pasts, of struggling against and engaging with the structures of power in the world today. Africa's crisis derives from a complex history that demands a complex analysis: a simultaneous awareness of how colonial regimes exercised power and the limits of that power, an appreciation of the intensity with which that power was confronted and the diversity of futures that people sought for themselves, an understanding of how and why some of those futures were excluded from the realm of the politically feasible, and an openness to possibilities for the future that can be imagined today.

Notes

1   Dipesh Chakrabarty, "Postcoloniality and the Artifice of History: Who Speaks for 'Indian' Pasts?" *Representations*, 37 (1992): 19; Ranajit Guha, "On Some Aspects of the Historiography of Colonial India," in Ranajit Guha and Gayatri Chakravorty Spivak, eds., *Selected Subaltern Studies* (New York, 1988), 43.

2   Guha, "On Some Aspects," 39, 40.

3   Gayatri Chakravorty Spivak, "Subaltern Studies: Deconstructing Historiography," in Guha and Spivak, *Selected Subaltern Studies*, 15.

4   Chakrabarty, "Postcoloniality and the Artifice of History," 23.

5   John Lonsdale, "States and Social Processes in Africa: A Historiographical Survey," *African Studies Review*, 24, no. 2/3 (1981): 143.

6   Terence Ranger, "Connexions between 'Primary Resistance' Movements and Modern Mass Nationalism in East and Central Africa," *Journal of African History*, 9 (1968): 437–53, 631–41; Ranger, *Revolt in Southern Rhodesia, 1896–7* (London, 1967).

7   Terence Ranger, "Religious Movements and Politics in Sub-Saharan Africa," *African Studies Review*, 29 (1986): 1–69. For a comprehensive review of recent literature, see Allen Isaacman, "Peasants and Rural Social Protest in Africa," in Frederick Cooper, Allen Isaacman, Florencia Mallon, William Roseberry, and Steve J. Stern, *Confronting Historical Paradigms: Peasants, Labor, and the Capitalist World System in Africa and Latin America* (Madison, Wis., 1993).

8   A. Adu Boahen, "Africa and the Colonial Challenge," in A, Adu Boahen, ed., *Africa under Colonial Domination, 1880–1935* (Berkeley, Calif., 1985), 1–18.

9   K. Onwuka Dike, *Trade and Politics in the Niger Delta 1830–1885: An Introduction to the Economic and Political History of Nigeria* (Oxford, 1956).

10 Thomas Hodgkin, *Nationalism in Colonial Africa* (London, 1956); Basil Davidson, *The Liberation of Guinea: Aspects of an African Revolution* (Harmondsworth, 1969); Davidson, *In the Eye of the Storm: Angola's People* (Harmondsworth, 1972); J. F. Ade Ajayi, "The Continuity of African Institutions under Colonialism," in Terence O. Ranger, ed., *Emerging Themes in African History* (London, 1968), 189–200.

11 B. A. Ogot, "Revolt of the Elders: An Anatomy of the Loyalist Crowd in the Mau Mau Uprising," in B. A. Ogot, ed., *Hadith 4* (Nairobi, 1972), 134–48. See also Bruce Berman and John Lonsdale, *Unhappy Valley: Conflict in Kenya and Africa*, Book 2: *Violence and Ethnicity* (London, 1992).

12 Mamadou Diouf, *Le Kajoor au XIXᵉ siècle: Pouvoir ceddo et conquête coloniale* (Paris, 1990), 283.

13 Luise White, "Separating the Men from the Boys: Constructions of Gender, Sexuality, and Terrorism in Central Kenya, 1939–1959," *International Journal of African Historical Studies*, 23 (1990): 1–27; Cora Ann Presley, *Kikuyu Women, the Mau Mau Rebellion, and Social Change in Kenya* (Boulder, Colo., 1992); and Tabitha Kanogo, forthcoming study of women in Kenya; Timothy Scarnecchia, "The Politics of Gender and Class in the Creation of African Communities, Salisbury, Rhodesia, 1937–1957" (Ph. D. dissertation, University of Michigan, 1993). Norma J. Kriger writes of gender— as well as age—cleavages in *Zimbabwe's Guerrilla War: Peasant Voices* (Cambridge, 1992).

14 Cherryl Walker, *Women and Resistance in South Africa* (London, 1982); William Beinart, "*Amafelandawonye* (the Die-Hards): Popular Protest and Women's Movements in Herschel District in the 1920s," in William Beinart and Colin Bundy, *Hidden Struggles in Rural South Africa: Politics and Popular Movements in the Transkei and Eastern Cape, 1890–1930* (Berkeley, Calif., 1987), 222–69; Helen Bradford, *A Taste of Freedom: The ICU in Rural South Africa, 1924–1930* (New Haven, Conn., 1987); Belinda Bozzoli, *Women of Phokeng: Consciousness, Life Strategy, and Migrancy in South Africa, 1900–1983* (Portsmouth, N.H., 1991).

15 Ayi Kwei Armah, *The Beautyful Ones Are Not Yet Born: A Novel* (Boston, 1968); Chinua Achebe, *Man of the People* (New York, 1966); Walter Rodney, *How Europe Underdeveloped Africa* (London, 1972).

16 Monica Wilson and Leonard Thompson, eds., *The Oxford History of South Africa*, 2 vols. (New York, 1969–71); Frederick A. Johnstone, *Class, Race and Gold* (London, 1976); Harold Wolpe, "Capitalism and Cheap Labour Power in South Africa: From

Segregation to Apartheid," *Economy and Society*, 1 (1972): 425–56; Charles van Onselen, *Studies in the Social and Economic History of the Witwatersrand, 1886–1914*, 2 vols. (London, 1982); Charles van Onselen, "Race and Class in the South African Countryside: Cultural Osmosis and Social Relations in the Sharecropping Economy of the South-Western Transvaal, 1900–1950," *AHR*, 95 (February 1990): 99–123; Shula Marks, *The Ambiguities of Dependence in South Africa: Class, Nationalism, and the State in Twentieth-Century Natal* (Baltimore, Md., 1986); Keletso E. Atkins, *The Moon Is Dead! Give Us Our Money!: The Cultural Origins of an African Work Ethic, Natal, South Africa, 1843–1900* (Portsmouth, N.H., 1993).

17   See Frederick Cooper and Ann Stoler, "Tensions of Empire: Colonial Control and Visions of Rule," *American Ethnologist*, 16 (1989): 609–21; and Nicholas B. Dirks, ed., *Colonialism and Culture* (Ann Arbor, Mich., 1992); Talal Asad, ed., *Anthropology and the Colonial Encounter* (London, 1973); Edward W. Said, *Orientalism* (New York, 1978); Bernard S. Cohn, *An Anthropologist among the Historians and Other Essays* (Delhi, 1987), 224–54; Megan Vaughan, *Curing Their Ills: Colonial Power and African Illness* (Cambridge, 1991); Jean Comaroff and John Comaroff, *Of Revelation and Revolution*, Volume 1: *Christianity, Colonialism, and Consciousness in South Africa* (Chicago, 1991); T. O. Beidelman, *Colonial Evangelism: A Socio-Historical Study of an East African Mission at the Grassroots* (Bloomington, Ind., 1982); Gwendolyn Wright, *The Politics of Design in French Colonial Urbanism* (Chicago, 1991).

18   Ranajit Guha, "The Prose of Counter-Insurgency," and Dipesh Chakrabarty, "Conditions for Knowledge of Working-Class Conditions: Employers, Government and the Jute Workers of Calcutta, 1890–1940," in Guha and Spivak, *Selected Subaltern Studies*, 45–84, 179–232; Partha Chatterjee, *Nationalist Thought and the Colonial World: A Derivative Discourse?* (London, 1986).

19   Homi Bhabha, "Of Mimicry and Man: The Ambivalence of Colonial Discourse," *October*, 3–4 (1985): 125–33.

20   Achille Mbembe, "Domaines de la nuit et autorité onirique dans les maquis du Sud-Cameroun (1955–1958)," *Journal of African History*, 32 (1991): 89–122; Luise White, "Cars Out of Place: Vampires, Technology, and Labor in East and Central Africa," *Representations*, 43 (1993): 27–50; David William Cohen and E. S. Atieno-Odhiambo, *Burying SM: The Politics of Knowledge and the Sociology of Power in Africa* (Portsmouth, N.H., 1992); Leroy Vail and Landeg White, "Forms of Resistance: Songs and Perceptions of Power in Colonial Mozambique," *AHR*, 88 (October 1983): 883–919; Kwame Anthony Appiah, *In My Father's House: Africa in the Philosophy of Culture* (New York, 1992); V. Y. Mudimbe, *The Invention of Africa: Gnosis, Philosophy, and the Order of Knowledge* (Bloomington, Ind., 1988).

21   Guha, "Prose of Counter-Insurgency"; Jan Vansina, *Oral Tradition: A Study in Historical Methodology*, H. M. Wright, trans. (Chicago, 1965); David William Cohen, *The Combing of History* (Chicago, 1994); Gayatri Chakravorty Spivak, "Can the Subaltern Speak?" in Cary Nelson and Lawrence Grossberg, eds., *Marxism and the Interpretation of Culture* (Urbana, Ill., 1988), 271–313.

22   I am following the insightful argument of David Edwards, "Mad Mullahs and Englishmen: Discourse in the Colonial Encounter," *Comparative Studies in Society and History*, 31 (1989): 649–70. The colonial assault on "barbarous practices" has been most fully explored in the case of slavery. See Richard Roberts and Suzanne Miers, eds., *The End of Slavery in Africa* (Madison, Wis., 1988); Frederick Cooper, *From Slaves to Squatters: Plantation Labor and Agriculture in Zanzibar and Coastal Kenya, 1890–1925* (New Haven, Conn., 1980).

23 Frederick Cooper, "Africa and the World Economy," in Cooper *et al.*, *Confronting Historical Paradigms*.

24 Martin Chanock, *Law, Custom, and Social Order: The Colonial Experience in Malawi and Zambia* (Cambridge, 1985); Kristin Mann and Richard Roberts, eds., *Law in Colonial Africa* (Portsmouth, N.H., 1991); J. F. A. Ajayi, *Christian Missions in Nigeria, 1841–1891: The Making of a New Elite* (Evanston, Ill., 1965); Luise White, *The Comforts of Home: Prostitution in Colonial Nairobi* (Chicago, 1990); Claire Robertson, *Sharing the Same Bowl?: A Socioeconomic History of Women and Class in Accra, Ghana* (Bloomington, Ind. 1984); Beidelman, *Colonial Evangelism*; Comaroff and Comaroff, *Of Revelation and Revolution*.

25 Ranajit Guha, "Dominance without Hegemony and Its Historiography," in Ranajit Guha, ed., *Subaltern Studies VI: Writings on South Asian History and Society* (Delhi, 1989), 210–309.

26 Donald Crummey, "Introduction: 'The Great Beast,'" in Crummey, ed., *Banditry, Rebellion, and Social Protest in Africa* (London, 1986), 1; James C. Scott, *Weapons of the Weak: Everyday Forms of Peasant Resistance* (New Haven, Conn., 1985).

27 Michel Foucault, *The History of Sexuality*, Volume 1: *An Introduction*, Robert Hurley, trans. (New York, 1978), 95–96; Chatterjee, *Nationalist Thought and the Colonial World*.

28 Sherry Ortner, "Resistance and the Problem of Ethnographic Refusal," *Comparative Studies in Society and History*, 37 (1995): 173–93.

29 Beinart and Bundy, *Hidden Struggles in Rural South Africa*, 31.

30 Elias Mandala, *Work and Control in a Peasant Economy* (Madison, Wis., 1990); Karen E. Fields, *Revival and Rebellion in Colonial Central Africa* (Princeton, N.J., 1985).

31 James C. Scott, *Domination and the Arts of Resistance: Hidden Transcripts* (New Haven, Conn., 1990).

32 Dipesh Chakrabarty, "Marx after Marxism: History, Subalternity and Difference," *Meanjin*, 52 (1993): 421–34; Frederick Cooper, *Decolonization and African Society: The Labor Question in French and British Africa* (Cambridge, 1996).

33 Beinart and Bundy, *Hidden Struggles*, esp. 31–37; Steven Feierman, *Peasant Intellectuals: Anthropology and History in Tanzania* (Madison, Wis., 1990); Kriger; *Zimbabwe's Guerrilla War*, 157.

34 Benedict Anderson, *Imagined Communities: Reflections on the Origin and Spread of Nationalism*, rev. edn. (London, 1991); J. Ayodele Langley, *Pan-Africanism and Nationalism in West Africa, 1900–1945. A Study in Ideology and Social Classes* (Oxford, 1973).

35 Richard A. Joseph, *Radical Nationalism in Cameroun: Social Origins of the U.P.C. Rebellion* (Oxford, 1977); Achille Mbembe, *La naissance du maquis dans le Sud-Cameroun: Histoires d'indisciplines (1920–1960)* (Paris, 1993); Berman and Lonsdale, *Unhappy Valley*.

36 Janet G. Vaillant, *Black, French, and African: A Life of Léopold Sédar Senghor* (Cambridge, Mass., 1990); Appiah, *In My Father's House*; Mudimbe, *Invention of Africa*. See also Edward Said's impassioned defense of colonial and ex-colonial intellectuals' engagement with European literature and culture as well as his critique of nationalist thought, in *Culture and Imperialism* (New York, 1993).

37 Aristide Zolberg, *Creating Political Order: The Party-States of West Africa* (Chicago, 1966); Cooper, *Decolonisation and African Society*.

38 Anderson, *Imagined Communities*; Chatterjee, *Nationalist Thought and the Colonial World*; Partha Chatterjee, *The Nation and Its Fragments: Colonial and Postcolonial Histories* (Princeton, N.J., 1993), 6.

39 Anthony D. Smith, *State and Nation in the Third World: The Western State and African*

Nationalism (Brighton, 1983), 56; Jean-François Bayart, *L'état en Afrique: La politique du ventre* (Paris, 1989).

40   Basil Davidson, *The Black Man's Burden: Africa and the Curse of the Nation-State* (New York, 1993).

41   Frantz Fanon, *The Wretched of the Earth*, Constance Farrington, trans. (New York, 1966), 30. See also Frantz Fanon, *Black Skin, White Masks*, Charles Lam Markmann, trans. (New York, 1967), 226–29.

42   Exposé de M. le Vice Président Sékou Touré à l'occasion de la conférence du 2 février 1958 avec les résponsables syndicaux et délégués du personnel RDA, "Le RDA et l'action syndicale dans la nouvelle situation politique des T.O.M.," PDG (9)/dossier 7, Centre de Recherche et de Documentation Africaine, Paris; Cooper, *Decolonization*, chap. 11.

43   Chatterjee, *Nation and Its Fragments*, 237–38; Chakrabarty, "Postcoloniality and the Artifice of History," 20.

PART TWO

Metropolitan and International Politics

METROPOLITAN AND
INTERNATIONAL POLITICS

I T IS A TRUISM THAT European metropolitan governments and societies dealt with the issues of decolonization on their own terms and in accordance with their own internal imperial hierarchies and priorities. The three articles selected here reveal the degree to which two European metropolitan governments (Britain and France) differed in their response to the destabilization of European colonial power in Africa and Asia. William Roger Louis and Ronald Robinson, Martin Shipway, and James D. Le Sueur's chapters illustrate that neither the British nor the French could have been prepared for the monumental changes each metropolitan country faced in the immediate aftermath of World War II. In fact, World War II unleashed a series of events that unbalanced the already wobbly system of power in Africa and Asia, thus paving the way for a combination of unforeseen changes and predictable responses to the changing balance of power.

To begin, in "The Imperialism of Decolonization" William Roger Louis and Ronald Robinson brilliantly tease out the question of whether decolonization, from the historian of the British Empire's point of view, ought to be seen as a point of weakness or strength. Challenging popular belief that the British decolonization following World War II was a sign of weakness, Louis and Robinson suggest that British decolonization can be seen as a dynamic and interactive effort to rebuild the world's geopolitical stage. Moreover, reconsidering the transformation of the British colonial policy after World War II, Louis and Robinson explain how the Cold War undercut the anticolonial movement and encouraged American policy makers to back the British imperial system. With sweeping scale, they also argue however that British decolonization was far from monolithic and as much influenced by American pressures and concerns about the Soviet Union as it was by purely imperial concerns. According to them, this means that subtle variations in British decolonization require researchers to look beyond the surface and see decolonization as an interactive phenomenon in which the British negotiated postcolonial boundaries of control with indigenous leaders from within an ever-growing international financial and political system.

Martin Shipway's "Madagascar on the Eve of Insurrection, 1944–47: The Impasse of a Liberal Colonial Policy" concentrates on French colonial concerns by focusing on the Malagasy insurrection of 1947. For Shipway, Madagascar offers a unique and understudied window into French colonial policy because the crisis illuminates the degree to which instability in French overseas possessions was, to a large degree, a result of the chaotic nature of the French metropolitan government in the aftermath of World War II. Hence, unlike the British case as outlined by Louis and Robinson, Madagascar demonstrates how out of control French colonial policy makers were. The failures of France to frame a coherent and unified policy eventually forced the French state to rely on the age-old doctrines of military repression. In this sense, Shipway argues that Madagascar became but one significant example of the inherent instability of the newly created Fourth Republic and was an important event in a long chain of colonial mismanagement (Indochina and Algeria were others), which brought about the end of the French empire and led, in very direct ways, to the collapse of the metropolitan government (the Fourth Republic) itself.

In "Decolonizing 'French Universalism': Reconsidering the Impact of the Algerian War on French Intellectuals," James Le Sueur continues with the theme of French experience, but turns from the issue of the French government to the role of French intellectuals during the French–Algerian War (1954–1962). In this chapter, Le Sueur argues that the war transcended military and governmental considerations and influenced debates about national identity and intellectual legitimacy in France. This is because the war in Algeria forced a profound re-evaluation of French intellectuals' perceptions of themselves and of their society in broad cultural and political terms, especially concerning the notion of "French universalism." In analysing the influence of the war on intellectuals and on the "universalism" upon which the French republican politics rested, Le Sueur reassesses the effects of the anticolonial struggle within metropolitan France. He does this by placing the debates about the Algerian conflict within larger disputes over comparability of French and Soviet imperialism in 1956 and controversy over the limits of an intellectual engagement toward the end of the conflict. Two key examples of intellectual engagement are considered: the creation of the Comité d'Action des Intellectuels contre la Poursuite de la Guerre en Afrique du Nord and the "Jeanson Network." Both movements demonstrate the paradoxes of post-World War II intellectual life in France. And both reveal fundamental tensions in the metropolitan political and cultural worlds because, in the face of the nationalist revolution in Algeria, the intellectuals discussed in this chapter either came to terms with the diminishing status of French culture by accepting the downscaled version of France's place in the world or reasserted the universal principles of the so-called 'Rights of Man' ideology by embracing the revolution itself and by joining Algerian nationalists in a 'treasonous' revolt against their own government.

Chapter 3

William Roger Louis and Ronald Robinson

THE IMPERIALISM OF DECOLONIZATION

I T O U G H T T O B E A C O M M O N P L A C E that the post-war British Empire was more than British and less than an *imperium*. As it survived, so it was transformed as part of the Anglo-American coalition. Neglecting the American role, imperial historians often single out British enfeeblement as prime cause of an imperial demise. The presumption is that an imperial state caved in at the centre like Gibbon's Rome, with infirmity in the metropole and insurgency in the provinces. For the 'Gibbonians', the Empire therefore ends with political independence. Dependent though they remained in other ways, the new states are said to be decolonized. Historians of the cold war necessarily take more account of invisible empires, but the imperial effects of the trans-Atlantic alliance are not their concern, except for some writers who suspect that the expansion of American capitalist imperialism swallowed up the Empire. Far from being decolonized, in this view, the British system was neo-colonized more intensively under new management. Each of these interpretations may be true in some instances, given a particular definition of empire. The overall picture is none the less confusing. To see the transformation of an imperial coalition as if it were the collapse of an imperial state is like mistaking the melting tip for the iceberg. Without defining the relativities of imperial power, it is hard to tell how much metropolitan infirmity, nationalist insurgency, and American or Soviet expansion contributed to whatever happened to the post-war Empire.

The difficulty of attributing the fall to British decline is that it leads us into paradox. Colonial emancipation is not necessarily a sign of metropolitan weakness. Virtual independence was conceded to Canadian, Australasian, and South African nationalists before 1914, when Britain was at her strongest. Conversely, when she was much weaker during the inter-war years, the Empire reached its greatest extent, with the addition of much of the Middle East and more of Africa. By 1940, when there was scarcely strength to defend the home islands, the British were able to crack down on nationalists in India, Egypt, and Iran and mobilize the Empire for war. When peace came, a bankrupt metropole somehow reconstructed the imperial system in the familiar Victorian style of trade without rule where possible, rule for trade where necessary. The 'Imperialism of free trade', or rather, of the sterling area continued. Weak or strong, the metropole was clearly not the only source of imperial strength. Gibbon will not help us with these difficulties. How is the survival of the Empire to be explained? Was it in fact decolonized by the 1960s, or informalized as part of the older story of free trade imperialism with a new American twist? It is with the answers given by British and American officials at the time that this article is concerned.

A more refined notion of the ingredients of imperial power is required to explain the Empire's capacity for regenerating on alternative sources of strength and for exchanging informal and formal guises. In peace time the United Kingdom government invested relatively few resources in the imperial upkeep. The British state provided military forces in emergency, a string of bases from Gibraltar to Singapore, and not least the necessary prestige. Whitehall monitored what was in effect a self-generating and self-financing system. It could not have been otherwise. Had ministers tried to project so vast an empire with metropolitan resources, they would have been driven from office before they ruined the country. At the centre of an imperial economy, the international financial and commodity markets of London held the system's bread and butter together, whether the branches were politically dependent or not. Most of Britain's chief trading partners belonged to the sterling area. Imperial preferences encouraged their exchanges. Tight state controls over capital and commodity movements persisted from wartime into the mid-1950s. No longer the hub of a global economy, London remained the central banker and market for the world's largest trading area.

Our hypothesis suggests that, more than a project of the British state, imperial sway by 1939 derived mainly from profit-sharing business and power-sharing with indigenous elites overseas. At the country level, the system relied on unequal accommodations with client rulers or protonationalists who multiplied British power locally with their own authority for their own advantage. Contracts could not be too unequal or collaborators would lose their constituents and the system would break down. As local sub-contractors became better organized the terms for co-operation turned progressively in their favour. The final settlement would be with national successors who would secure British economic and strategic assets under informal tutelage. Local bargains could not be struck to imperial advantage if other great powers competed in the bidding. Inter-national alliances – at least 'hands-off' arrangements – were essential if the Empire were to be defended and the imperial balance sheets kept out of the red. The object was not that Britain should sustain the Empire, but that the Empire should sustain Britain. From Canning to Churchill, British geo-strategists looked to 'the continuous creation of new sources of power overseas to redress the balance of the Old World'.[1] They once sought those sources of power in Latin America. They found ample reward in India. In the 1900s they looked to the Japanese alliance and the Anglo-French and Anglo-Russian Ententes. They were to turn to the United States. The various local coalitions depended on international alignments to tilt internal and global balances in their favour.

Finally, the system required the tolerance of the British voter. Terms for the metropolitan contract were those of 'empire on the cheap' – that tax payers should not be asked to meet the cost at the expense of their home comforts; that a benign imperial image assuage the latent forces of anti-imperial opinion; that British industry remain strong enough to drive the imperial economy; and that the economic prizes to be won were worth more than the imperial cost of winning them. The state of imperial power at different places and times may therefore be measured in the contracts required to win collaboration and head off resistance at international, metropolitan, and local levels. Bargains were interdependent. As we have argued in an earlier essay,[2] an alteration of terms at one level implied corresponding changes on the others. The Second World War overthrew the balance of pre-war terms. A different Britain re-formed the post-war Empire in another world.

I

Clement Attlee's government faced devastating problems of economic recovery in 1945–46. When American Lend-Lease ended, he protested that the very living conditions of people in the British Isles depended on the continued flow 'both of food and . . . raw materials' from the United States.[3] There were no dollars to pay for them.[4] The cumulative shortfall on current account stood at £10 billions. Even if the economy could be re-jigged to export 75 per cent above pre-war levels, the estimated balance of payments deficit would still be running at over a billion pounds in 1951. Fifteen billion dollars was owing to Washington. Three billion pounds was due to sterling countries, especially to India and Egypt for defence costs. The British were no longer the creditors, but the debtors of the Empire. John Maynard Keynes, the Treasury's most influential adviser, concluded: 'We cannot police half the world at our own expense when we have already gone into pawn to the other half.'[5]

There was no recourse but to go cap in hand for a dollar grant or loan. With or without the American loan, ministers had to choose between financing their domestic recovery and their imperial commitments. To reduce food rations further was not practical politics. In 1945–46, as in every budget thereafter, the promised welfare state competed with the Empire for scarce resources. The Treasury warned: 'a straight issue would be reached with the Middle East and India. Either they would have to lend us the money for our troops there, or we should have to move our troops out.'[6] Keynes emphasized that, 'the American loan is primarily required to meet the political and military expenditure overseas.' Without it 'a large-scale withdrawal . . . [from our] international responsibilities' was inevitable.[7]

On what terms would Washington with its plans for global free trade agree to underwrite Britain and the Empire? During the eighteen months between the end of the hot war and the beginning of the cold, most Americans regarded empires as obsolete. British claims to world power seemed pathetic. To save their wartime ally from 'starvation corner', Congress wrote off the Lend-Lease debt, but saw no reason to rescue the Empire. In return for a dollar loan of £3.75 billion, which the Canadians topped up to £5 billion, the British were forced to make the pound convertible into the dollar within twelve months. The imperial economy, in effect, was to be dismantled.[8] Meanwhile, nationalist protests against stringent economic controls erupted throughout the dependent Empire. Imperial contracts were falling apart at all levels in 1945–47, as Attlee recognized. 'It may be,' he foresaw in March 1946, 'we shall have to consider the British Isles as an easterly extension of a strategic [arc] the centre of which is the American continent rather than as a Power looking eastwards through the Mediterranean to India and the East.' In Attlee's forthright estimate, 'we cannot afford . . . the great sums of money for the large forces involved.'[9] His acidic foreboding of Britain reduced to a small Empire in Africa seems, in retrospect at least, more realistic than his Foreign Secretary Ernest Bevin's case for holding the Middle East. Much depended on 'what the Americans are prepared to do.'[10]

The Cabinet debate echoed in the Colonial Office where J. S. Bennett argued that 'the United States cannot be expected to underwrite the British Empire either *in toto* or unconditionally. In consequence, the system and objectives of [pre-war] colonial administration . . . no longer correspond to the realities of the situation.' Either the British could 'hang on' until international and related internal pressures became overwhelming, as in India, or they could wind up colonial commitments in the Middle East and South-East Asia in return for 'maximum practical' support from the United States. 'The Colonial Empire . . . would thus be reduced to Africa, the Pacific and the Caribbean.'[11] But British recovery depended largely on the imperial cohesion of the sterling area. From the economic standpoint, Hilton Poynton commented: 'The point surely is that USA must help the British Empire to underwrite the world.'[12] The issue remained in doubt up to the end of 1947. By that time the Americans were doing a great deal to prop up the Empire, especially in the eastern Mediterranean and the Middle East. Meanwhile the Cabinet withdrew the troops fighting the communists in Greece and gave up the Turkish commitment. They were determined to leave India, Burma, and Ceylon, and they were soon to abdicate in Palestine.

Attlee felt morally obliged to concede Indian independence. For all that, the British were being driven out. The National Congress had gained the momentum of a popular movement in the 1930s, but the outbreak of war put an end to provincial power-sharing with Indian ministers. After crushing the 'Quit India' rising of the Congress in 1942, the Raj relied on Muslim collaborators for the war effort, and alienated its remaining indigenous support. By 1945, the Viceroy, Lord Wavell, could no longer rely on Indian loyalty in the army and public services. The pre-war contracts for local co-operation had run out of time. In John Gallagher's irreverent metaphor, nationalists and imperialists were propping each other up like punch-drunk boxers lest they both fall into chaos. One question only remained – how to find a viable and amenable successor. At the Indian elections of 1946 the avowed British intention to leave in 1948 evoked not one possible successor but two. Fearing entrapment in a terrible communal war, Attlee and Lord Mountbatten, the last Viceroy, brought the departure date forward to 1947. The emergency enabled Mountbatten to settle with Congress for a strong central government over most of the subcontinent. In exchange, Congress yielded to Jinnah's claims to Pakistan. Both new states unexpectedly joined the Commonwealth, which now began its uncomfortable mutation from an English-speaking club to a multi-racial association.

There had been no significant superpower intervention in India, as there was to be in Palestine. Since the Indian empire had always drawn its strength from local allies more than from the metropole, the idea that the British 'transferred power' is a half truth. The other half is that the divided communities once articulated by the Raj had become nationalized. It was the emergence of two national fronts of non-cooperation that drove the bitter transition to a relatively stable and scarcely revolutionary succession. A partition that left the Indian Army divided between two hostile states was the solution that the British had tried above all to avoid. Informal affiliations none the less continued to serve imperial objectives in unforeseen ways.

In Palestine, there were no effective power-sharing contracts to expire.[13] Separate administrative arrangements with the Arab and Jewish communities had been incompatible, especially after the Arab revolt in 1936. As Bevin complained, President Truman's intervention on behalf of Jewish refugees and Zionist aspirations exacerbated the conflict. When the plan for partition gained momentum in 1947, Attlee and Bevin were ready to throw in their hand. Even Churchill insisted on withdrawal: 'there is the manpower of at least 100,000 men in Palestine who might be at home strengthening our depleted industry. . . . What good are we getting out of it?'[14] After the attempt at convertible sterling in July 1947 turned into a disastrous run on the pound and exhausted almost all of the American loan, the imperative to leave Palestine became overwhelming. On 15 May 1948, the British withdrew from an imbroglio in another communal war that was disrupting their Arab alliances throughout the Middle East. Against the advice of the Secretary of State, George C. Marshall, Truman immediately recognized the state of Israel. An American-sponsored government had taken over much of the British Mandate. Zionist contracts with the White House had prevailed. Two can make viable imperial contracts. Three is a crowd. Four is an impossibility. Palestine showed how an intrusive superpower allied with a nationalist revolt could upset the collaborative equations of Empire.

The ensuing Arab–Israeli war eventually forced the Americans to resume their partnership with the British. Washington felt morally obliged to defend Israel while the British were treaty-bound to defend Transjordan. Washington and London could easily be drawn into the war by proxy on opposite sides. 'This must not be allowed to happen,' Truman vowed after his election in November 1948.[15] He compelled the Israelis to withdraw from Egyptian territory by ultimatum, though they acquired the territory of the Negev. At Bevin's request Truman appeased the Arabs by agreeing to incorporate Arab Palestine into British-allied Jordan.[16] The Anglo-American schism over Palestine had to be repaired to bring about an armistice and a *de facto* territorial settlement.

II

As the cold war intensified from 1947 to 1951, competition between the two super-powers came to the rescue of the Empire. Faced with the Czech crisis and the Berlin blockade, the United States hastened to strengthen Britain and France in defence of Western Europe. As Senator Henry Cabot Lodge, Jr., told the Senate Hearings on the North Atlantic Treaty, 'we need . . . these countries to be strong, and they cannot be strong without their colonies'.[17] After the fiasco of convertibility, the dollar underwrote the sterling area up to 1951, and at need thereafter. Under the Truman Doctrine, American power reinforced the traditional imperial 'Great Game' of checking Russian advances into the eastern Mediterranean and the Middle East. By the end of 1947, the American Chiefs of Staff had recommended 'all feasible political, economic, and if necessary military support . . . to the United Kingdom and the communications of the British Commonwealth'.[18] With the Maoist triumph in China and the Korean War, Washington relied on the British and French empires to block Sino-Soviet expansion into the lands on the rim of southern and western Asia. Much as some American officials disliked it, the State Department and the Pentagon found their 'most important collaborators' in the British and their Empire-Commonwealth.[19]

After 1947 the Americans subsidized the imperial system generously in one way or another to defend the United States. Robert Hall of the Cabinet Office summed up the tally in 1951: 'We have had . . . an average of over a billion dollars a year . . . since 1946 and of course under Lend/Lease we had a great deal more. In fact our whole economic life has been propped up in this way.'[20] Keynes had earlier underlined the imperial effect: 'America . . . was underwriting British policy in other parts of the world.'[21] Marshall Plan aid and the Mutual Security programme met the otherwise prohibitive charge on the balance of payments of sustaining British power overseas. The British voter could have his imperial cake and eat at the same time. In return, Bevin undertook to assume the lead in saving Europe for social democracy and 'primary responsibility' for defending the Middle East.[22] With joint policies in Europe and mutual support in Asia, the Empire could rely on the American shield against Sino-Soviet intervention. Aligned with Washington's cold war strategy, the keystone of the reconstituted imperial system was thus the Middle East, a region honeycombed with British air bases and military installations. The oil fields there were as vital to European defence as they were to British prosperity. So too were the tin and rubber of Malaya. Whitehall relied largely on the sterling countries between Suez and Singapore for the dollar earnings required to make up the British trade deficit.[23] The potential of Africa's minerals and vegetable oil was also linked more and more to British recovery. With India and Pakistan hived off and Palestine shrugged aside, the Empire reasserted itself in the Middle East and Africa.

Much of the pre-war Empire survived locally to be slotted into the post-war design. Even so, local continuities masked the basic discontinuity. At metropolitan and international levels British imperial power was substantially an Anglo-American revival. Neither side cared to publish the fact, the one to avoid the taint of imperialism, the other to keep the prestige of Empire untarnished. An imperial coalition was as unnatural for the Americans as it was demeaning for the British. Whether or not the Congress needed a Communist devil to assure the American people of the innocence of their global expansion Washington's Cold War approach often departed from London's Great Game of Empire. Endless talks were devoted to straddling the divergence to permit concerted action. A consensual if not a common official mind worked to achieve the 'overlap' of inter-dependence in the cold war. It was not merely a question of 'he who pays the piper'.[24] As Bevin analysed the situation in October 1949:

> Western Europe, including its dependent overseas territories, is now patently dependent on American aid . . . The United States recognises that the United Kingdom and the Commonwealth . . . are essential to her defence and safety. Already it is, apart from the economic field, a case of partial inter-dependence rather than of complete dependence. As time goes by [in the next ten to twenty years] the elements of dependence ought to diminish and those of inter-dependence to increase. The United Kingdom in particular, by virtue of her leading position both in Western Europe and in the Commonwealth, ought to play a larger and larger part in a Western system.[25]

Bevin accepted that, 'In all fields in which the United States makes the major contribution, whether financial, military or otherwise, it is inevitable that proportionate (although not always determining) weight must be given to her views.'[26] Dependence could weaken imperial ties. Interdependence could strengthen them. A study of some regional crises will show how much and how little the Anglo-American alliance disturbed the balance of imperial contracts locally.

So long as the cold war left tropical Africa aside, the Americans had few interests and exerted little influence in the colonial management. In 1948 Attlee's ministers faced a crisis in British West Africa when riots in Ghana and strikes in Nigeria threatened colonial control. Dissatisfied with low prices from colonial marketing boards and inflated charges for British imports, the dollar-earning cocoa farmers and palm oil collectors were turning for economic relief to national leaders. Drs Nkrumah and Azikiwe campaigned for immediate independence. The British took account of American and international anti-colonial opinion. But the balance of payments deficit, together with the Labour Party's expectations of a better deal for African workers, convinced the Cabinet that the iron hand of economic control required the velvet glove of power-sharing.[27] The quasi-democratic reforms of 1951–52 in Ghana and Nigeria aimed at bringing conservative chiefs and their moderate nationalist spokesmen into executive government. The popularity of the traditional allies of colonial adminis-tration would thus be strengthened against their radical critics. By this route, the two dependencies were expected to achieve self-government 'within a generation'.[28] Their connection with the imperial economy eventually would be politically informalized within the Commonwealth.

In British central Africa it was white rather than black nationalists who brought about a crisis from 1949 onwards. Roy Welensky, the European leader in the depend-ency of Northern Rhodesia, could halt the copper mines on which the British economy and large American stock-piling contracts depended. Sir Godfrey Huggins, the premier of self-governing Southern Rhodesia, controlled the railways required for mineral export. To expand the dollar-earning capacity of the region, the agitation of the European miners and tobacco farmers against colonial control had to be appeased. By 1953, under a Tory government, the velvet glove of power-sharing took the shape of a white Rhodesian federation imposed on the black majority.

Under the impact of the Far Eastern crisis in 1949–51, imperial Anglo-Americanism solidified, though with many a crack, from Europe and the Middle East to eastern and southern Asia. Once the People's Republic had driven the Kuomintang regime out of mainland China, Soviet-allied power seemingly dominated the Euro-Asian land mass. As the global balance shifted in July 1949, Dean Acheson, the Secretary of State, accepted Bevin's invitation to make 'a trip around the world . . . in a matey sort of way' to see whether Britain and the United States might pursue a common policy against the spread of communism in the Far East.[29] In a series of private talks they reached a workable consensus in every area but one. To save the Hong Kong trade and to accommodate the Indian championing of the principle of pan-Asian self-determination, the British insisted on recognizing Communist China. The Americans by contrast still recognized and protected Chiang Kai-shek's Nationalist government on Taiwan. With the unexpected outbreak of the Korean War in June 1950, the two policies undercut each other. Taiwan now acquired strategic significance in the American defence of Japan and the Pacific. Acheson told Bevin that if the British wanted their global common front, they had better not keep asking the Americans to abandon Taiwan.[30]

The rift widened in the vicissitudes of late 1950 in the Korean War, despite the common UN cause. A token British force belatedly joined the Americans in repelling the North Korean invasion. But 'it was almost universally felt in England that MacArthur had provoked the [subsequent] Chinese attack in N. Korea' by advancing to the Yalu River and bombing North Korea.[31] Consequently the left wing of virtually all of Attlee's government feared that General MacArthur, if not President Truman (who had admitted the possible use of atomic weapons), was bent on reconquering China for Chiang Kai-shek. Much more important, the allies in NATO bristled at the prospect of the United States becoming absorbed in a major Asian war that could leave Europe undefended.[32]

It was usually the Americans who warned the Europeans of the penalties for aggressive imperialism in the cold war, but when Attlee flew to Washington in December 1950, the imperial boot was on the other foot. The Prime Minister in effect admonished the President against allowing MacArthur any more scope for what most European socialists and Asian nationalists regarded as American imperalist intervention in China.[33] If the American people could not rely on their allies in the East, Truman remarked, they would no longer subscribe to a common front in the West. None the less, the two leaders agreed to put real teeth into NATO. Attlee undertook the trebling of British defence expenditure over the next three years. The Americans promised to 'pick up the tab' on the balance of payments costs.[34] Much of the Anglo-American wartime apparatus for allocating strategic supplies globally was reactivated in the Korean emergency. The reuniting of priorities was symbolized by the recall of MacArthur from Korea four months later and the advent of Eisenhower as Supreme Commander, Europe. The Prime Minister and the President agreed to differ over China for the sake of their 'identity of interests generally throughout the world'. In view of 'Korean aggression', their subordinate officials laid the ground for dealing with other Soviet-inspired Koreas anticipated in Greece, Germany, Iran, and South-East Asia.[35]

The ambivalence of Washington as a centre of Western imperial power emerged sharply in 1949 when Secretary Acheson and Ernest Bevin discussed the domino effect of a Communist China on South-East Asia. In 'a turmoil of revolutionary nationalism' left by the Japanese retreat, the French in Indo-China as well as the Dutch in Indonesia were fighting to regain colonial control. Their intransigence, the State Department believed, was 'doomed to ultimate failure'. They were driving nationalists into the arms of the communists at the cost of draining men and money away from 'the revitalization of Western Europe'. On the other hand, it was feared, 'the only alternative to imperial rule is chaos in Indonesia and communism in Indochina'. European 'self-support' depended on the 'economic attachment' of these areas to their respective metropoles. To ride 'rough-shod' over European pride would strain vital NATO alliances.[36] This was to be the American dilemma wherever colonial empires became involved in the cold war.

Bevin agreed with Acheson on the only way to square the circles of local and international collaboration in this region. They fruitlessly pressed the French and Dutch to follow the American example in the Philippines and to do what the British had done in India and were doing in Malaya. The French and Dutch colonial presence would have to take on the mantle of informal association. Anything that looked like imperialism or Western dictation, Bevin warned, would alienate the newly independent countries of southern Asia. But the Western Allies, with their strategic priorities in Europe and in the Far East, had few resources left for the area. South-East Asia must be persuaded to defend itself, with Indian support. Given political independence, the nationalists would stand on their own feet against the communists. A relatively small amount of economic and military aid from the West would win their alliance and secure Europe's economic assets. Then, as British and American officials agreed, the Western powers could 'keep out of the limelight' and 'pull the strings whenever necessary'.[37]

American anti-colonialism evidently did not extend to informal sway: nor after the outbreak of the Korean War in June 1950 did it run to handing over colonies to communists or to chaos. American subsidies for the defence of Indo-China against the communist Viet-Minh by 1954 fell little short of the French investment. Washington blessed the British colonial campaign against Chinese communists in Malaya. Yet, in January 1949, the Americans had vetoed a Dutch re-conquest of an anti-communist nationalist regime in Indonesia by threatening to end Marshall aid to the Netherlands.[38] Ideally, the United States preferred 'independence' and covert influence to colonialism. In practice the Americans gave priority to anti-communism over anti-colonialism. It was admittedly for the Europeans to decide. Determined not to commit American ground troops to mainland Asia after the Korean truce, Washington necessarily pursued the cold war through imperial proxies. At the local level, the Americans, under protest, acted as sleeping partners in the British and French empires wherever the latter could cope with local communist subversion.

In South Asia the Americans relied chiefly on Britain and the Commonwealth to take the major responsibility. 'We are becoming engaged in a competition with the USSR for the favor and resources of South Asia,' the State Department and the Joint Chiefs of Staff reported in 1949. 'Bearing in mind our commitments elsewhere, it would appear to be in our interest for the British to bear as great a share of this burden as they possibly can.'[39] The demise of the imperial raj served the purpose in unforeseen ways. Despite Jawaharlal Nehru's 'non-alignment', a powerful Indian buffer state stood in the way of Sino-Soviet expansion. A successful Indian democracy would show the rest of Asia that Mao's path was not the only road to modernization. To support Nehru in his involuntary roles, Washington first supplemented and soon surpassed the inadequate supply of British and Commonwealth aid in competition with Moscow. From 1953 to 1961 the foreign exchange costs of Delhi's five-year plans were subsidized by the United States to the extent of two and a half billion dollars. Meanwhile, the British retained a strong market for their exports. India remained an important member of the Commonwealth. From 1949 onward the Pentagon joined the War Office in the traditional imperial great game of securing the Indian sub-continent's frontiers from Kabul and Herat to Rangoon and Singapore. As F. P. Bartlett, Director of South Asian Affairs in the State Department, observed, Curzon's strategy in 1889 for containing Russian expansion in central Asia 'applied very much today'.[40]

Unlike the Indians, the Pakistanis joined the Baghdad and SEATO defence pacts under direct and indirect Anglo-American auspices, and provided strategic air bases. In return they received two billion dollars of military and economic aid in the 1950s.[41] They were soon affiliated more closely with the United States than with the Common-wealth. Under the shadow of cold war, a once British Empire modulated strategically into an Anglo-American field of influence, and thence into a predominantly American commitment. Similarly, in the ANZUS pact of 1951, the American 'off-shore island' chain around Communist China took in the Australasian Commonwealth. Australia and New Zealand, none the less, continued to be bound up with Britain financially and commercially in the sterling area up to 1960.

III

At the centre of the post-war Empire, paramountcy in the Middle East worked through a network of client dynasties that were in the political, military, and financial grip of British diplomatic missions, military bases, and oil companies. Americans in the tradition of the open door objected to these discriminatory satrapies. In 1945 the State Department regarded them as 'outmoded' and 'dangerous to peace'.[42] The Kings and Emirs asked for American help to escape the imperial thrall. By the end of 1947 Marshall had undertaken with Bevin to restrain the oil rivalry, and to abstain from intervening competitively in British relations with Egypt, Iraq, Jordan, and the Gulf states.[43] Communist encroachment threatened the security of the Middle East, especially the oil fields of the two allies. By July 1950, British and American officials agreed that a Soviet attack on Iran would 'raise the question of a general war'. The northern Iranian frontier was the 'stop line' equivalent to the 38th parallel in Korea. No less important, the Middle East had become an area of Anglo-American interdependence in oil. Any conflict between Middle Eastern client governments and the oil companies could open the way to Soviet influence. Early in 1951 Washington as a precaution urged on the British the wisdom of conceding a fifty-fifty share in the Anglo-Iranian Oil Company's profits to the Shah's government. The American oil company in Saudi Arabia (Aramco) had already yielded as much. The British company, however, was slow in following the American example until it was too late. In May 1951 the Iranian premier, Mohammed Musaddiq, put Anglo-American solidarity to the test by nationalizing the Anglo-Iranian concession.

A legacy of the British Great Game in south-western Asia, the Pahlavi dynasty in Teheran had been in every sense a creation of the British. Under the Shah, Mohammad Reza, Iran produced more oil than all the Arab states combined and figured largely in the sterling balance of payments. If Musaddiq were 'allowed to get away with it', Emanuel Shinwell, the Defence Minister, warned Attlee's Cabinet that other clients would nationalize their way to financial freedom. 'The next thing might be an attempt to nationalise the Suez Canal.'[44] But to reoccupy the Abadan oil fields would be costly and militarily precarious.[45] Washington warned that use of force could provoke a communist rising with Soviet backing in northern Iran. With American co-operation, the British resorted to blockading Iran's oil exports. When Musaddiq refused to talk to the British any longer in October 1952, the Americans attempted to broker a settlement.

The Americans now feared that strangling Iran's main revenue would prove a double-edged weapon. If rising economic discontent destroyed Musaddiq's popularity, he could only turn to the pro-communist faction for support. Moscow in that case might bail out his regime. On several occasions American officials, such as Defense Secretary Robert Lovett, argued for going it alone and lifting the oil embargo to save Musaddiq as the only non-communist leader in sight; but, as a British official put it to Acheson, 'the choice before you is whether Iran goes Commie, or Brit[ain] goes bankrupt'.[46] Acheson decided that 'only by correlating our efforts with the British' could the Middle East be stabilized.[47] The Anglo-American blockade continued. In March 1953 President Eisenhower's National Security Council, like Truman's before it, first considered settling with Musaddiq without the British. Charles Wilson, the Defense Secretary, asked 'whether [the United States] were not in fact in partnership with the British in Iran'. John Foster Dulles, now Secretary of State, acknowledged that 'this had been the case until fairly lately, but that the British had now been thrown out'. The President stated that he 'certainly [did not] . . . want a break with the British'.[48] Dulles eventually decided that selling out to Musaddiq might have grave effects on United States oil concessions in other parts of the world. 'We cannot force the British hand,' he concluded.[49]

In August 1953 the critical problem of saving Iran from communism without damaging the British required a desperate gambit. A coup promoted by British and American intelligence services restored the Shah to power on the shoulders of the army of General Fazlollah Zahedi. American military aid consolidated the regime and strengthened the Iranian buffer in the northern tier of Middle Eastern defence. Washington willy nilly had taken over the senior part of partnership in Iran. The consequent oil settlement in 1954 registered the shift in local collaborative terms. The percentages of the consortium were: Anglo-Iranian Oil Company, 40 per cent; Royal Dutch-Shell, 14 per cent; Standard Oil of New Jersey, 7 per cent; Socony Vacuum Oil Company, 7 per cent; Standard Oil of California, 7 per cent; Gulf Oil Corporation, 7 per cent; Texas Company, 7 per cent; Compagnie Française des Pétroles, 6 per cent; and a 5 per cent interest by a group of nine American independents. Much of the British oil stake had been saved, but the Americans now held 33 per cent of the Iranian market. Even though the percentage of the American independents was minor, the reason for their inclusion was significant. If they were left out, warned a former Ambassador to Britain who had oil contacts, Lewis Douglas, there would be an explosion in the United States Senate that would blow the new consortium into 'little bits as effectively as a hydrogen bomb'.[50]

There was complaint in some British circles that the Americans had taken over a British monopoly. But it was not the case that the Americans had ousted the British in Iran. They had taken over when the British could no longer cope. Lord Salisbury, the influential Tory minister, warned against recrimination: 'If we give the impression in Washington that we are only concerned with our oil to the exclusion of . . . keeping Persia in the anti-communist camp, we may lose all control over American actions. That would be disastrous.'[51] The Americans were highly sceptical of the ability of the Anglo-Iranian Oil Company to adjust to twentieth-century conditions, but Eisenhower, like Truman before him, was certain that 'US–UK agreement is necessary for any settlement of Middle Eastern problems'.[52] Vulnerable to Soviet pressure in the Middle East, the British had to keep in line with American cold war strategy, just as American strategy had to align on the strong points of the British Empire. If Washington forced the British to change their unrealistic imperial policies in Iran, Egypt, and elsewhere, Dulles admitted in April 1954, it would 'have the effect of tearing the free world coalition to pieces'. Nevertheless, he continued, the Americans could not 'go on forever' avoiding these great issues. 'The peoples of the colonial states would never agree to fight Communism unless they were assured of their freedom.'[53] For the British, the Iranian crisis had demonstrated another, equally compelling, principle. If Musaddiq's view had prevailed, then nationalists throughout the world might abrogate British concessions. Intervention could be effective. But as a precedent for Suez, the British lesson from the Persian oil crisis was disastrous.

IV

In the Tory governments 1951–57, first Churchill and then Eden fell increasingly out of step with their wartime comrade Eisenhower. In the Far East the allies divided bitterly over Communist China, Taiwan, and Quemoy. To Washington's dismay, London and Paris took advantage of the advent of 'peaceful co-existence' to initiate dealings with Moscow. They went to Geneva in 1954 and partitioned Indo-China with Chairman Mao. Dulles lamented, 'We can no longer run the free world.'[54] For the Americans, the British appeared far too ready to insure their eastern Empire at the expense of 'free world' territory. Tory ministers in Whitehall did indeed resolve to rebuild imperial strength, which they regarded as the main opportunity for national solvency. American financial aid dwindled from 1952 to 1956. Despite recovery, British exports could not balance overseas payments under the overload of debt, social welfare, and massive rearmament. Two solutions were discussed in 1952. One was to expand exports to hard currency markets by £600 million a year at the expense of austerity at home and power abroad.[55] The other was through tighter imperial control to develop dollar-earnings and savings in the sterling system.[56] Washington prodded London towards convertibility and the General Agreement on Tariffs and Trade. As Harold Macmillan put it, 'This is the choice – the slide into a shoddy and slushy Socialism [as a second-rate power], or the march to the third British Empire.'[57] In the continual fear of a run on the pound, the Churchillians marched to the imperial drum up to 1956. International confidence in sterling seemed to depend on Britain acting as a great imperial power. 'Our economic survival in the next year or two will largely depend upon world confidence in sterling.'[58] This might be muddled economics, but it was good Tory politics.

At the same time, the British relied on Washington not to retaliate against their discriminatory imperial economy. They hoped that American capital would share in developing sterling area assets. They needed the backing of economic and military aid from Washington to sterling countries in order to stabilize them against Soviet influence. In the last resort, the Cabinet relied on American strategic cover in Europe and the world at large. Yet the British aspired to a sterner, less dependent imperialism. By their own reckoning, they were caught between their vision of the Brutishness of the Third British Empire and their actual dependence on the Americans.

Friction was most acute in the Middle East. Anxious to keep up international confidence in sterling, especially after losing Abadan, London meant to confront 'nationalists sapping at our position as a world power'.[59] On the other side of the Atlantic, influential officials were bending policy in favour of substituting direct American alliances for British influence in the Arab states. For a time in 1953, Dulles pressed the British to evacuate the Suez base unconditionally in the hope of winning the good will of General Neguib and Colonel Nasser. The Americans expected the British to concede the Buraimi oasis to please the new King of Saudi Arabia, Saud Ibn Abdul Aziz al-Feisal, thereby to protect Aramco and the connection between that country and the United States. To Churchill and Eden, the Americans seemed far too eager to woo Arab nationalists away from Soviet blandishments at imperial expense. Washington certainly looked forward to some such outcome in the long run. But the Pentagon and the Treasury wanted the British to bear the burden in the Middle East. The State Department did not want to weaken NATO. Given the heavy demand on American resources, and in view of Eisenhower's conservative fiscal policies, it seemed wiser for the time being to rely on the existing imperial positions in Libya, Jordan, Iraq, and the Gulf states.

Despite the deviations, the Americans generally returned to supporting British positions in the Arab states. With the French, the British and Americans doled out arms supplies to the region and so regulated the balance of power. Aided by the Americans, the British in 1954 at last achieved a Suez base treaty with a right of re-entry in case of war. Together, the two allies had tried and failed to entice Egypt into the western alliance and peace with Israel. Despite misgivings, Washington backed the military association of Iraq with Iran and Turkey under British auspices in the Baghdad Pact. It was not the Americans but the British who finally tried to go it alone when the rivalry between the American cold war and the imperial Great Game came to a head in 1956. The Suez Crisis thus becomes a touchstone of the inquiry into the nature of post-war imperial power.

Once the evacuation of some 80,000 troops at Suez had been scheduled, the British had few cards to play in Cairo, except remote control of the White Nile in Uganda. Throughout the Arab Middle East, anti-British feeling combined with resentment against American sponsorship of Israel. The Egyptians united behind Gamal Abdel Nasser. Like Musaddiq, Nasser skilfully played the American and Soviet ends against the British middle. Unlike the Iranian leader, he had no oil to embargo, and the Russians agreed to buy his cotton. By November 1955 the Egyptian premier had clinched the Czech arms deal with Moscow and upset the regional power balance. The Soviets were dangling economic aid for his Aswan dam project as well as arming his Syrian allies, and offering munitions to Saudi Arabia and Yemen. As the Americans admitted, the communists had executed 'a brilliant series of economic forward passes', and mounted a 'new and monumental threat' to the Middle East.[60] Eisenhower saw the beginning of a great struggle between communist and free world economies for control over the development of the Third World.[61] Dulles averred that no cleavage between British and American policy could be allowed, if the Middle East and Africa were not to become another Communist China.[62]

It had long been evident, according to Sir Humphrey Trevelyan (the British Ambassador in Cairo) that the British retained their position in the Middle East only because of the relatively low level of Russian intervention. Anthony Eden commented: 'We are [now] compelled to outbid them, or lose the main source of [oil] on which our economy depends.' Only by enlisting the Americans and their money could the British stave off Russian influence in Cairo and over the Canal. 'On our joint success in excluding the Russians from this [Aswan] contract,' Eden wrote to Eisenhower in November 1955, 'may depend the future of Africa.'[63] A joint bid was entered with 330 million American dollars and 80 million British pounds.

London and Washington saw eye to eye on the danger that the Egyptian ruler represented. By June 1956 he was viewed as an involuntary pawn of the Russians. He was inciting the Arab states to rise against Western domination. Eisenhower and Dulles feared not only for 'the jugular vein' of Western Europe's oil; they also believed that Nasser was rallying the Arabs for a final assault on Israel.[64] To Eden, the Egyptian 'Mussolini' with his pan-Arab ambitions threatened to become 'a Caesar from the Atlantic to the Gulf . . . It is either him or us.'[65] From March 1956 the British Cabinet set in train plans to reinvade Egypt. Three months later, the Anglo-American offer for the Aswan dam was cancelled. It was no longer possible to get Congressional aid for so menacing a regime. In riposte on 26 July after the last British troops had left the Suez base, Nasser nationalized the Suez Canal Company. British and French control of the Canal was the final emblem of his country's bondage. The result was explosive. The Canal carried two-thirds of Europe's oil supply.

The Americans also wished for Nasser's downfall, but, as Eden was repeatedly told from April 1956 onwards, they were unalterably opposed to military intervention. Dulles suspected a British attempt to manoeuvre Washington into reasserting British imperial supremacy in the Middle East.[66] If Egypt were invaded, the President predicted, every Arab state would swing towards Moscow. Revenge would be taken on American as well as British oil companies, and the British thus would lose the assets and the prestige they hoped to secure.[67] Washington preferred covert methods of a kind familiar in Latin America. They had succeeded in Teheran, and the CIA was already plotting a coup against the pro-Nasser regime in Damascus. The Americans had every reason to dissociate themselves publicly from British military action.

The Great Game was now being played for the highest stakes in the cold war. Eden's ministers agreed with the Bank of England that Egyptian 'piracy' on the Canal 'imperils the survival of the U.K. and the Commonwealth, and represents a very great danger to sterling'.[68] An expedition was prepared 'to bring about the fall of Nasser and create a government in Egypt which will work satisfactorily with ourselves and other powers'.[69] Harold Macmillan, Chancellor of the Exchequer, pointed out that Nasser, like Arabi Pasha in 1882, would block the Canal in self-defence. In that case, American finance would be needed to meet the dollar cost of alternative oil supplies from Venezuela and the Mexican Gulf. The British presumably took it for granted that their ally would gladly accept and pay for a *fait accompli*. There is only circumstantial evidence that they meant to stage a 'Boston Tea Party' in reverse on the Nile. At Eisenhower's request, the British waited to see if Dulles could persuade Nasser to 'disgorge the canal' to international management. The indefatigable Dulles failed on this occasion. Keeping Washington in the dark, the British decided to go it alone, or rather, with the French and the Israelis. On 5 November 1956 an Anglo-French expedition landed on the Canal in the guise of peace-keepers come to stop a second Israeli–Egyptian war.

In the event, forebodings were realized. The Canal was blocked, pipe lines were sabotaged, and the oil ceased to flow. Far from saving sterling, the intervention set off a disastrous run on the pound. As the reserves ran out, Macmillan presented his colleagues with two alternatives: either to float the pound – a 'catastrophe affecting not merely the [British] cost of living but also . . . all our external economic relations'; or to ask for massive American aid.[70] Only after Eden had agreed to leave Egypt unconditionally did Eisenhower rescue the pound, with a billion dollars from the International Monetary Fund and the Export-Import Bank. As the expedition took to its boats, Nikita Khrushchev rattled the nuclear sabre over London and Paris. Eisenhower shielded his errant allies with a similar threat against Moscow.

It was the Americans, not the Russians, who had vetoed the Anglo-French effort at imperial reassertion in the Middle East and North Africa. At the peak of the crisis, Dulles told the National Security Council, in a now famous comment, that for many years the United States had been 'walking a tight rope' between backing Europe's empires and trying to win the friendship of countries escaping from colonialism. Unless the United States now asserted leadership, all those countries would turn to the Soviet Union.[71] Eisenhower asked: 'How can we possibly support Britain and France if in doing so we lose the whole Arab world?'[72] The Americans insisted that their major European allies give priority to the cold war over their empires. Yet the prize of Arab friendship eluded the righteous. The Arabs gave the credit for defeating imperialism mostly to the Egyptians and the Russians. Nasser and Nasserism were exalted. It was Eden who was toppled. American anti-imperialism in the Middle East provoked anti-Americanism in Europe and threw NATO into disarray. It was difficult not to fall off Dulles's tight rope.

A triumph for the non-aligned nations, the Suez fiasco was a disaster for the Empire. It ended British aspirations to imperial dominance in the Middle East. It showed that international confidence in the sterling empire still rested on the alignment of Anglo-American aims. Once and for all, it was established that Britain had to work in concert with the United States in the 'peripheral regions' no less than in Europe or suffer humiliating consequences. What Dulles called the 'violent family quarrel' over Suez had exposed the American essentials underlying British imperial power for all to see. The colonial periphery of the First Empire had become the centre of the Third.

V

In 1957, at Bermuda and later in Washington, Macmillan, now Prime Minister, and Eisenhower hastily revised and renewed the Anglo-American contract. Once more, as in 1947, the British were cutting their European and imperial commitment to save their payments balance.[73] Once again, the Americans repaired British power as the 'core of the [revitalized] NATO alliance and . . . an important element in SEATO and the Baghdad Pact'.[74] Like Attlee and Truman before them, the two leaders pledged 'joint policies' over the whole range of world affairs.[75] Bevin had looked forward to equality. But this time the Prime Minister spoke of British 'junior partnership' and declared 'inter-dependence'. With the Soviet Sputnik signalling nuclear parity with the United States, 'no country can do the job alone'.[76] The extreme danger of the Allies acting at cross-purposes in Suez fashion had become undeniable.

The understandings reached at Washington in 1957 initiated a concerted Anglo-American strategy in Asia and Africa to match the closer relationship in Europe. Eisenhower equipped the British with ballistic missiles and agreed to covert joint leadership in NATO. In return, Macmillan undertook not to negotiate with Moscow over disarmament or Germany without the Americans. He also agreed to keep his troops on the Rhine. As an American official put it, 'They can't ask for a 50 per cent interest in the political profits and then draw down their share in the firm's assets from 30 to 10 per cent . . . if . . . sterling is really heading to disaster, we will have to bail them out in our own interests.'[77] There would be no more British talk of seating Communist China at the United Nations. It was understood that independence for co-operative nationalists was the best chance of saving Africa from communist subversion. Under the Eisenhower doctrine, which carried with it an allocation of up to 200 million dollars a year for the Middle East, the Americans were taking over the lead there as elsewhere. Nevertheless, the British position in Iraq and the Gulf states was to be respected and supported. The oil there was vital to British prosperity, Washington noted, and the British would fight for it. Along those lines, the President and the Prime Minister subscribed to 'coordinated effort and combined planning in the field of production, defense and economic warfare' towards a global common front.[78] In 1958 they faced the sequel of the Suez Crisis together.

Eisenhower found the root of the trouble in 'Nasser's capture of Arab loyalty and enthusiasm throughout the region'.[79] A Nasserite coup had ejected Soviet influence from Damascus and had merged Syria with Egypt in the United Arab Republic. Pan-Arab disturbances, seemingly directed from Cairo and Damascus, were undermining every ally of the West from Beirut to Kuwait and Aden. In the spring of 1958 the Americans prepared for military action with British participation in support of President Chamoun in Lebanon. To strengthen their clients, the British in turn had supported the proposal of their most loyal collaborator in the Middle East, Nuri al-Said of Iraq, to form a union of Iraq and Jordan. On 14 July, however, another 'pro-Nasser, anti-Western coup' swept away the pro-British regime and the Hashemite dynasty in Baghdad.[80] Would Brigadier Abdul Qasim's revolutionary junta join forces with Nasser's United Arab Republic, or would he oppose Nasserite aggrandizement with communist support? The question had wide ramifications. The British had lost their Iraqi air bases, they might lose their Iraqi oil fields,[81] and worse still, Qasim might invade Kuwait, which was now the chief supplier of oil to the sterling area. The Americans feared that if the King of Jordan fell the Israelis would move into the West Bank and start a general war in the Middle East.

Now it was Eisenhower's turn to fulminate against 'the struggle of Nasser to get control of these [petroleum] supplies – to get the income and power to destroy the Western world'.[82] Like Eden in 1956, he felt that 'the most strategic move would be to attack Cairo[83] and 'turn Israel loose on . . . the head of the snake'.[84] Unlike Eden, the President knew 'of course [that] this can not be done'. Critics in Congress and the world at large, Foster Dulles added, would say 'we are simply doing what we stopped the British and French from doing'.[85] But pro-Western rulers from Turkey and Israel to Saudi Arabia and Pakistan had requested immediate American or Anglo-American military support. Either the United States and Britain would have to respond, according to Eisenhower, or they would have to 'get out of the Middle East entirely'.[86] On the day of the Baghdad coup, brushing aside the Prime Minister's idea of a joint expedition to clear up the whole situation in the Middle East, the President ordered the Marines into the Lebanon.[87] By agreement, the British sent a contingent to Jordan as an insurance for the King and a warning to Qasim.

Most of Asia and much of Africa condemned the military intervention. 'If we stay on,' Eisenhower was advised, '. . . the USSR will beat us to death in public opinion. We must adjust to the tide of Arab nationalism . . . before the hot heads get control in every country. The oil companies should be able to roll with the punches.'[88] Such were the guidelines of American and Anglo-American policy thereafter. In October 1958 Eisenhower's Marines left the Lebanon. Macmillan in turn withdrew the troops from Jordan and Washington provided most of the money needed to support the King with a credible army.

It was recognized after 1958 that friendly regimes, if only to survive, had to temper their pro-Western stance and share power with the more moderate pan-Arabs. As Macmillan put it, the cold war in the Middle East and elsewhere had become a question of winning the battle against 'so-called neutralism'.[89] The British accordingly dismantled their formal controls over Kuwait. They trod warily in Iraq, where Anglo-American co-operation aimed at encouraging Qasim 'to resist pro-communist and pro-Nasserite forces equally'.[90] Qasim denounced his British defence treaty, left the Baghdad Pact, and took military aid from Moscow. But the Iraqis resisted Soviet pressure to nationalize the British and American oil concessions through the 1960s. Qasim's army had to be paid. Forewarned by Musaddiq's fate, even revolutionary nationalists could not afford to lose three-quarters of their revenue. In Iraq and Iran the politics might be nationalized, but the invisible empire of oil remained.

Throughout the 1950s Anglo-American strategy rested on an oil cartel that allegedly fixed prices and divided 'producing and marketing territories' for 85 per cent of the world's supply outside the United States.[91] The five American and two British multinationals involved represented the substance of empire in the Middle East. Their interests were so enmeshed with Western economic and strategic security that American anti-trust proceedings against them hung fire throughout the decade. The American companies with more capital expanded their areas of production in the region more than the British. Through the opening of new oil fields, American influence was eroding British sway in much of the Middle East and North Africa. Most of the 'British' Middle East became an Anglo-American concern after 1958. Only in the Gulf states and the Red Sea could British power cope single-handed. It was not a matter of simple metropolitan enfeeblement. All the combined influence of the United States and Britain proved insufficient to shape the turmoil of pan-Arabism into stable informal sway.

VI

The new Tory government of 1957 under Harold Macmillan set sights on an empire in the post-colonial world. A system of influence was to be won by converting discontented subjects into loyal allies. The strategy was nothing if not Anglo-American. Imperial defence was realigned on joint plans for by-passing the Canal and re-routing Europe's oil supplies around Africa. As the 'air barrier' over the eastern Mediterranean 'thickened', the only sure way for reinforcing the security of the Gulf states and the Indian ocean seemed to be a string of airfields connecting Kano (in Northern Nigeria) to Nairobi and Aden.[92] Control in the Red Sea became the pivot of the scheme. The Middle East Command moved its headquarters to Aden – the only major base left in the Arabian peninsula. The Colony also housed the regional oil refinery of the Anglo-Iranian Oil Company (now British Petroleum). But the local nationalists listened to the 'Voice of the Arabs' broadcasts from Cairo and could no longer be kept at bay with colonial gradualism. In 1958 the Colonial Secretary, Alan Lennox-Boyd, set about saddling the trade-unionized port with the clutter of tribal sheikdoms inland in a federation weighted in favour of collaboration with the British after independence.[93] It was an unlikely scheme. In Aden the British were gambling against the odds for high strategic stakes.

During the scramble into Africa in the 1890s Lord Salisbury had worked at keeping hostile powers away from the upper Nile region and the Horn of Africa. Five decades later the British were pursuing a similar plan in the colonial scramble out of Africa. Only the method and the enemies had changed. In 1957 the members of Macmillan's government were bent on erecting buffer states against 'the southward drive of Nasser and the Russians' towards the projected trans-African life line to Aden and Singapore. For that purpose it was essential for the British and Americans to persuade the peoples of Somalia and Ethiopia 'to live together as good neighbours'. Ethiopian co-operation depended largely on American subsidies to Emperor Haile Selassie. 'Inevitably, American money would have to finance the greater part of this policy.'[94]

At first, the Nile Valley had been sealed off in the Sudan, where the British had advanced the anti-Egyptian party to independence by 1956 in the course of outbidding Cairo and the pro-Egyptian party for Sudanese loyalty. Two years later, General Ibrahim Abboud's coup in Khartoum re-opened the way for Nasserite influence. For 'a counter-poise' the British turned to the Somalis.[95] In the familiar style, Macmillan's government bought nationalist co-operation with imperial strategy at the price of independence. After the United Nations had decreed independence for Italian Somalia in 1960, the Cabinet with American support united the British Somali clans with their neighbours in a greater Somali state. Given their national aspirations, Lennox-Boyd judged, 'the moderate political parties and mass of the people would cooperate fully' with the Western powers.

British officials concentrated on independence for tropical Africa after 1957 – independence in the north-east, independence in the west – above all independence to prolong imperial sway and secure British economic and strategic assets. It was increasingly urgent to exchange colonial control for informal empire. To turn this trick, the last aces in the African colonial hand would have to be played before they were forced. In West Africa the game had already been played out with some success despite errors. The constitution that Attlee's government had introduced into the Gold Coast (Ghana) in 1951 had been designed for the British to share power with conservative chiefs and nationalists.[96] It was a British initiative. However, the psephology proved mistaken, and Kwame Nkrumah's young 'Independence Now' party won an unexpected majority in the Legislative Assembly; he had to be let out of jail and endowed with the executive power intended for his 'elders and betters'.[97] First as 'Leader of government business', and soon as Prime Minister, Nkrumah won prestige as the next ruler of Ghana. His Convention People's Party undermined the chiefs' hold over their local communities and won more elections. The British Governor had 'only one dog in [his] kennel'. As the only effective collaborator with the colonial administration in sight,[98] the Ghanaian leader was able to bargain his country's way to political, if not economic, independence by 1957. Whitehall was consoled that Ghana had been stabilized under British influence.[99] But, as Lord Home, the Commonwealth Secretary, observed, Nkrumah 'sees himself as a Messiah sent to deliver Africa from bondage.'[100] He was becoming the Nasser of black Africa.

According to the French, Nkrumah's progress spawned nationalists and dis-couraged the friends of colonial gradualism throughout West Africa and beyond.[101] Concessions yielded in Accra were immediately demanded in Lagos and Dakar. Colonial governors warned that if the claims to power of 'responsible' national leaders were denied they would lose their followers to revolutionaries. Step by step behind the Ghanaians, the Nigerians, followed by the Sierra Leonians, advanced to political independence in 1960 and 1961 respectively. A Nigerian federation was negotiated to yoke the radical Yoruba and Ibo leaders of the southern provinces with the conservative pro-British emirs in the Muslim north. With 'our very good friend'[102] Abubaker Balewa, the northern leader, as federal prime minister, the British had done their best to construct a reliable and congenial succession. Partly as a result of the domino effect, but chiefly because of the writing on the wall in Algeria, the French followed the British example in West Africa in 1960. The acceleration to independence had made sport of imperial time tables. In the 1930s the Colonial Office expected the tropical African empire to last into the twenty-first century, and in 1945, for another sixty years. By 1950 the end of colonial rule in Nigeria and Ghana was predicted for the 1970s. In fact the span of imperial longevity in West Africa was cut off within a decade.

The pace of events in this region owed little to direct pressure from the super-powers. Until 1960 Soviet intervention remained prospective rather than actual. With little leverage in tropical Africa, Eisenhower and Dulles found that 'we must tailor our policies . . . to . . . our overall relations with the metropolitan powers' in NATO. 'Premature independence would be as harmful to our interests . . . as . . . a continuation of nineteenth century colonialism.'[103] Paris was thus enabled to ignore American advice and continue the Algerian war with American financial support. London proceeded single-handed with its own collaborative arrangements in tropical Africa. From 1956 onwards, none the less, Washington, fearing a build-up to another Suez, pressed the colonial powers to consult and coordinate their African policies with the Americans in the councils of NATO. Anglo-American diplomacy narrowly placated the Graeco-Turkish struggle over Cyprus that imperilled a vital Western base and the integrity of NATO and CENTO. Salvation in 1960 took the form of rule of the once-exiled Archbishop Makarios over an independent Cyprus.[104] To coordinate the African policies of the NATO powers proved even harder.

At Dulles's request in June 1959, Macmillan instructed his officials to survey the African endgame in a comprehensive inter-departmental report under the auspices of the Africa Committee of the Cabinet chaired by Burke Trend of the Cabinet Office and composed of representatives of the Colonial Office, Foreign Office, Commonwealth Relations Office, the Treasury, and the Ministry of Defence.[105] Written as a possible basis for Anglo-American consensus, the document testified to the shared belief that Africa's future would be shaped by the relationship between Britain and America. British officials approached the crisis of African independence with no solid belief in the potentiality of black nationalism among so many divided ethnic communities. They regarded the freedom movements as essentially anti-European, not to say racist. What impressed them was the speed with which handfuls of urban nationalists were stirring up popular black resentment against white rule.[106] 'Africanism', as some preferred to call it was spreading from the Niger to the Zambesi and the Nile. The agitation could be contained at local levels, but the use of force would defeat the object. As the Colonial Office noted, 'It would be difficult for us to create some new authoritarian force artificially, and if we tried to do so . . . to the exclusion of people like Nkrumah or [Obafemi] Awolowo [in Nigeria] or [Julius] Nyerere [in Tanganyika] – it would probably lead to the creation of a revolutionary force against the set-up that we had created.'[107] The good will of amenable national leaders had to be won before independence, if they were to be allied after independence.

Anticipations of Soviet intervention and fears of an alliance between Nkrumah's pan-Africanism and Nasser's pan-Arabism multiplied the significance of local nationalist agitation. In the Cabinet Office's analysis, Moscow was alert to every chance of promoting African freedom movements. The Russians would be competing with the West for the sponsorship of every ex-colonial state. They were already making overtures in Ghana and Guinée as well as Ethiopia. The well-worn phrases of Anglo-American discourse ran through the Cabinet Office report: 'If the Western Governments appear to be reluctant to concede independence . . . they may turn [African opinion] towards the Soviet Union; if . . . they move too fast, they run the risk of leaving large areas . . . ripe for Communist exploitation'.[108] Only nationalists with independence could form a 'strong, indigenous barrier to the penetration of Africa by the Soviet Union and the United Arab Republic'.[109] The American analysis of African prospects followed similar lines. Washington was as sure as London that tropical Africa was far from ready for independence. Every other consideration pointed to the necessity of keeping in step with African national aspirations.

By the late 1950s British hopes for the economic future were veering away from the Empire towards Europe. Sterling was on the verge of full convertibility. The preferences and financial controls of the imperial economy had given way to freer world trade. In 1957 Macmillan had requested a 'profit and loss account' for the colonies that had found, ambiguously, that British trade might be better served if independence came sooner rather than later. Two years later colonial controls were clearly no longer indispensable for metropolitan prosperity. The inevitable political informalization of the Empire in its final stages went hand in hand with the desirable economic informalization of the sterling area.[110]

The economics of dependence after political independence was the key to the Cabinet Office's plan for African informal empire. Since 1957, British and American officials had agreed that the African dependencies must evolve 'towards stable self-government or independence' as rapidly as possible 'in such a way that these [successor] governments are willing and able to preserve their economic and political ties with the West.'[111] Economic and military aid with technical advisers would bind the new states to their former rulers. An ambitious plan for Africa would be underwritten by the Americans.[112] It was all to the good that they had few economic interests and large cold war stakes in the continent. The British would share the profits of American investment. They were relying a great deal on the Americans financially and strategically for the imperial future in Africa. Although some of his officials were talking about an African Marshall plan, Eisenhower and the Treasury wanted the British and French to carry the burden of assistance 'with the Americans picking up the slack'.[113] Whatever the source, the influence to be won from aid would go to the donor. If there were to be an African informal empire, the British Cabinet Office report implied, it would be increasingly Anglo-American rather than British.

Everything now depended on winning and keeping African goodwill. It would all be lost, the Colonial Office feared in 1959, unless the struggle for independence between black majorities and white minorities in Kenya and the Central African Federation could be resolved. 'If we fail to . . . demonstrate that we are not seeking an unqualified white supremacy [there], we may lose West Africa as well.'[114] African good-will rested on the outcome of the racial struggle in East and Central Africa. In Kenya since 1921, a few thousand European settlers, with the racial sympathy of British voters, had vetoed African advancement by threatening revolt. After British troops had put down the Mau Mau rising in the early 1950s, Whitehall had more control over the situation. Even so, Downing Street was reluctant to impose black majority rule on British kith and kin. It might lose the next British election. It would certainly alienate white Southern Rhodesia and the Union of South Africa from the Commonwealth. Yet the Africa Committee report of 1959 argued that unless the British could build 'a viable non-racial state' in Kenya, the entire African position would be jeopardized.[115]

Until late 1959, none the less, Macmillan and Lennox-Boyd were determined that British authority in East Africa would prevail for at least another decade. It seemed vital to secure the air bases at Nairobi and Entebbe and the sea base at Mombasa. Peter Ramsbotham, the Foreign Office liaison with the Chiefs of Staff objected: 'Are we to adopt a political policy in East Africa which is almost certain to poison our future relations with Africa as a whole because of a possible strategic need outside Africa?'[116] By May 1960 it was not practical politics for the Nigerians to give the British base rights in Kano. According to Iain Macleod, who had become Colonial Secretary in October 1959: 'They would be very glad to see their airfields used to help us in a struggle in which we supported Blacks against Whites but might not like them used if we supported Whites against Blacks.'[117] With the collapse of Belgian rule and Soviet intervention in the Congo, the trans-African reinforcement route to the Red Sea and the Gulf proved to be an illusion.[118] Amphibious forces on a scale that Britain could not afford would be needed when the East African bases were lost. The projected informal empire in the Red Sea and the Gulf would eventually then depend largely for defence on the United States Navy.

British Central Africa presented the gravest prospects of racial conflict. Since 1953 the British dependencies of Northern Rhodesia (Zambia) and Nyasaland (Malawi) had been subjected to a federal government dominated by the virtually independent European minority in Southern Rhodesia (Zimbabwe). A quarter of a million whites were consolidating their rule over six million blacks. Reacting to the federal imposition, the Africans organized national parties and worked for black majority rule. In response to the British abdication in West Africa, the Europeans demanded white independence for the whole Federation before they were submerged under an 'uncivilized' African government. By mid-1959 the Colonial Office feared that 'the Federation may simply break up under the mounting pressure of the internal conflict'.[119] At worst, the white Southern Rhodesians would declare independence unilaterally with the support of the South Africans. At best the British hoped that the Federation would become a 'primarily multi-racial community' that could act as a 'shock-absorber' between South African Apartheid and the emerging black states in the north. But, if white domination were maintained by force, 'the whole of the Western position in black Africa, even in those territories (such as Nigeria) which are . . . well-disposed towards us, will be gravely shaken'.[120] Given the possible domino effects of pan-Africanism, questions of local racial collaboration had broadened into great matters of continental balance that involved the interdependent interests of Europe and the United States.

In January 1960 the Prime Minister set out on a tour of African capitals in search of African partners and British influence. Macmillan assured the new rulers in Lagos and Accra that the British were on the side of black Africa. In Cape Town and Salisbury (Harare) he warned the Europeans against resisting the 'Winds of Change' from the North. The intransigent Premier of the Federation, Sir Roy Welensky, suspected that, if need be, Macmillan would break up the Federation to appease pan-Africanism. African appeasement was certainly Macmillan's overriding aim. From this standpoint it seemed to him that 'the Africans are not the problem in Africa, it is the Europeans who are the problem.'[121] As the new Colonial Secretary, Iain Macleod, remarked, 'The pace of events in Somalia, Tanganyika, Uganda, and above all the Congo' was overtaking the time tables of mid-1959.[122] In an effort at saving the Central African Federation, Macleod ended Federal police rule in Nyasaland and Northern Rhodesia. Hastings

Banda and Kenneth Kaunda, the African nationalist leaders, were released from prison. But African hatred of the white Federation was such that, within four years, federal government was to end in African rule in independent Malawi and Zambia. Macmillan wanted to avoid a British Algeria in Central Africa. But in 1965 Premier Ian Smith was to declare independence unilaterally to perpetuate white supremacy in Southern Rhodesia, with disastrous consequences for British relations with the Afro-Asian members of the Commonwealth.

Early in 1960 Macmillan and Macleod promoted a compromise to clear the way for independence in Kenya. If the settlers would accept African majority rule, the Africans would guarantee the Europeans' land and commercial stake in the country. Michael Blundell, the leader of the multi-racial New Kenya Party, was chosen to persuade the settlers. Macmillan told him that 'if the multi-racial approach failed the likelihood was that the whites would be driven out of Africa and this could only be of profound detriment to the black.'[123] In March 'a tacit conspiracy'[124] between Macleod and Julius Nyerere's unrivalled TANU party led to Tanganyikan independence in 1961. Uganda followed a year later after a federal compromise between the dominant Baganda and the rest of the country. After one year more the suspected Mau Mau leader Jomo Kenyatta was to rule in Nairobi. The British were scrambling out of colonialism before anarchy invited Soviet penetration in conjunction with pan-Africanism and pan-Arabism. The collapse of Belgian rule and its consequences in the Congo lent speed to British heels.

By the summer of 1960 the darkest scenario of Anglo-American planning was realized in the Congo (Zaire). Western relations with a score of newly or prospectively independent African governments were at stake in the crisis. If the Congo disintegrated, radical anti-Western Congolese factions would bid for Soviet support, which would have repercussions in western, eastern, and southern Africa. The supreme test of Anglo-American solidarity in Africa would be to hold the Congo together and to keep it aligned with the West. After prohibiting political activity for decades, in 1959 the Belgian administration, faced with riots and revolts, offered self-government within four years. Diverse political parties emerged. The anti-colonial coalition that insisted on independence in June 1960 soon fell to pieces. Premier Patrice Lumumba's radical centralists quarrelled with President Kasavubu's federalists who represented various ethnic and provincial societies. When the *Force Publique* dismissed its Belgian officers and mutinied, civil order broke broke down entirely. Belgian troops returned to protect the lives of the 100,000 Europeans. Shortly thereafter Moise Tshombe declared the secession of Katanga province taking with him the bulk of the country's revenue and mineral wealth.

The rump of the Congolese government in Léopoldville required foreign aid if its authority were to be restored. Yet the divided ministers favoured different helpers. Justin Bomboko (Foreign Minister) welcomed the return of the Belgians and looked to Brussels for assistance.[125] Lumumba excoriated the Belgian return, and the Katanga secession, as a Western capitalist plot for a colonial reoccupation. At first Lumumba fruitlessly solicited aid in Washington. The Americans took the initiative in assembling a UN peace-keeping force, chiefly from African states, and called upon the Belgians to withdraw. Afro-Asian opinion sided with Lumumba. Anti-imperial resentment against the Belgian invasion was sapping the good will of black Africa that the West had cultivated so sedulously. The Belgian forces merely withdrew to their bases and the Belgians remained in Katanga. When the United States and the United Nations failed to respond to Lumumba's plea to throw the Belgians out immediately, he called for Soviet aid and appealed to the non-aligned powers for support. Brussels protested that the 'US was seeking [to] cut Belgium off and out from [the] Congo entirely, and injuring NATO in [the] bargain'.[126] General de Gaulle supported the Belgians. The activities of the UN officials in the Congo represented an Afro-Asian menace to the influence of the French over their neighbouring excolonial territories. King Leopold's Congo Free State had been set up in 1885 to exclude international rivalry from the heart of Africa. In reverse, the disintegration of the state brought about the alliance of indigenous factions with rival powers and involved the whole of tropical Africa in one way or another in the cold war.

Eisenhower and Macmillan agreed that Lumumba must be removed or 'fall into a river full of crocodiles' before he handed over the richest country in the region to Russian managers and technicians.[127] Covert plans to ensure his disappearance were laid.[128] Meanwhile there was another possibility that tested Macmillan's resolve to placate black nationalism at European expense in Central Africa. Katanga formed part of a multinational mineral empire (much of it British and American and controlled by interlocking directorships) that ran by rail to the Zambian copper belt and the Johannesburg gold mines. The company directors were influential in the right wing of the Conservative party. Welensky saw the chance of allying Tshombe's Katanga with his Federation. Why not back the secession and leave the shell of the Congo to Lumumba and the Soviets? Washington also kept the possibility open as a last resort.[129]

For a time, the Americans vetoed the entry of UN forces into Katanga in an attempt to restore unity in NATO. In the end, Eisenhower and Secretary Christian Herter stood for the integrity of the Congo. Not to be tempted, Macmillan stood with them. Like his Foreign Secretary, Lord Home, he feared that the Congo would become another 'Korea'. According to Home:

> The great danger of the Congo situation has always been the danger of outside intervention & the creation of a situation very similar to that which occurred in the Spanish Civil War & Korea . . . the only hope of averting that was intervention by U. N. & our line has been to give complete support to Mr Hammarskjold.[130]

The Under-Secretary at the Foreign Office, Lord Lansdowne, who served as envoy to the Congo, wrote: 'I cannot emphasise too strongly how unrealistic . . . is the theory that an independent Katanga can exist along side a truncated Congo.'[131] The Congolese could not afford to lose Katanga. The Americans would not tolerate such a disastrous move in the cold war. Independent black Africa as a whole would be alienated.[132] The British, after much debate on the dilemma of the wealth of the copper belt versus the larger issue of the Congo and the cold war, did not want to risk their chances of informal empire in black Africa.[133] The Congo crisis showed that the interdependent interests of the Western allies could all be lost if they were to act independently. Post-colonial sway in Africa would have to be concerted as part of the Western coalition under American leadership.

The Congo held together. Zaire became, for better or worse, a vast client state of the United States. The Congolese type of breakdown, however, was soon matched in the

Nigerian civil war and later with Sino-Soviet intervention in Portuguese Africa and Rhodesia. Latter-day Lumumbas abounded. Castro, as Macmillan remarked, became Eisenhower's and Kennedy's Nasser,[134] and Panama their Suez. Cuban forces were to fight in Angola. The cold war fed upon internal instability, whether through colonial or ex-colonial proxies.

VII

In conclusion, we have given an account of what officials believed was happening to the Empire. Their evidence has its limitations. Groping among their illusions for the reality at times of crisis, they did not always find it where they expected. For all that, where the estimates proved unrealistic they were soon corrected. It is the corrections that offer the surest evidence of how the Empire was being made, unmade, and remade.

If the assessments of Attlee and his Treasury advisers in 1945 are credible, the collaborative basis of the pre-war Empire went down in the Second World War. The calculus of Bevin and Marshall suggests that the post-war system regenerated on American wealth and power. Compared with this reinforcement, the loss of India in the imperial Great Game seems almost derisory.[135] With economic recovery and a brief respite from overseas payments deficits, the system under Churchill and Eden regained a tentative dynamism of its own, until in 1956 Eisenhower jolted Eden into realizing that imperial dynamics were still reciprocal. Until the late 1950s British prosperity relied on an imperial economy of which the discriminatory integrity required American toleration, dollar underwriting, and strategic protection. In all these ways, the post-war Empire represented not a continuation, but a more formidable and a more vulnerable innovation. If the system were to succeed in securing and developing the sterling area, it had to operate as a project of the Anglo-American coalition. Such was the common prayer in Whitehall and Downing Street from Attlee to Macmillan.

By comparison the liturgy in Washington dissented in faith and conformed in works. Imperialism was Beelzebub. Ancient antagonism and historic bonds underlay the arguments of exclusive national interest that ostensibly justified the imperial coalition. From ingrained prejudices the Americans were reshaping the Empire in the revolutionary image of the Thirteen Colonies in 1776. The British were welcoming the Americans back into the British family of nations and, informally at least, into the Commonwealth, to which the shared tradition of civil liberties had contributed. Anti-colonialism constrained both sides. For a time, however, American cold war aims ran broadly parallel with British imperial purposes despite the rifts over Communist China and Suez. Committed heavily in the Far East and Europe, and anxious to keep their major allies, Washington depended on imperial proxies in other regions. For all the 'holier than thou' attitudes of the Americans, the British and French Empires were propped up in the democratic cause of saving the global free market from communist annexation. The Americans looked forward in the long run to turning Europe's colonies and client regimes into alliances with national states. So did the British in their own good time. One by one the imperial barriers tottered. Only then did Washington invest its power directly and exert effective influence in local management. Even then the Americans backed the British and French in their efforts at exchanging formal control for informal tutelage. None of the Western powers intended to 'decolonize' their dependencies because they feared 'neo-colonization' by the communists. The relationship between Britain and the United States largely offset British decline in the international system. But at the local level, as Bevin foresaw in 1949, the more American aid was required in competing with the Sino-Soviet bloc for nationalist good will, the more British imperial areas came under American influence.

It follows that the dismantling of the visible Empire is not to be explained in monolithic terms of metropolitan infirmity. With American support or acquiescence, the British had resources enough to deal with local insurgency. Coercion was often threatened. Force was used in Cyprus, Aden, and Malaya with Washington's blessing, and without it in Kenya, Suez, and the Buraimi oasis. The Americans restored much of the British oil fief in Iran, and they refrained from interfering with those in Iraq and the Gulf emirates. In British calculations the necessity for heading off resistance and for winning local collaboration governed the colonial retreat at different speeds in different territories. Just as local imperial authority had multiplied through divided indigenous alliances, so it dwindled in the face of popular national organization. The process had long historical roots. Pre-war power-sharing contracts expired in South Asia without significant superpower intervention, but in Palestine there was American interference. The collaborative arrangements in Egypt had come to an end before the Soviet irruption into the Middle East. Post-war colonial contracts were reaching their term in Ghana and Nigeria before the Russian aid offensive in tropical Africa. Until 1956 the presence of superpowers was by no means the imperative for imperial retreat. Soviet and at times American competition thereafter helped to frustrate the conversion of British pre-war clientships into informal tutelage in most of the Middle East. In tropical Africa after 1958 the danger of Soviet sponsorship multiplied the weight of black nationalism and hastened the dismantling of white supremacy in the eastern and central regions. After Suez, the British concurred with the Americans at last in setting their sights on the post-colonial era. To assert colonial power became counter-productive when it came to bidding against the Soviets for nationalist alliances after independence. According to Anglo-American calculations, the strategic significance of pan-Arabism, of pan-Africanism, and of the non-aligned nations in the cold war motivated the final dismantling of formal empire.

It should be a commonplace, therefore, that the post-war Empire was more than British and less than an *imperium*. As it survived, so it was nationalized and international-ized as part of the Anglo-American coalition. It operated more like a multinational company that, after taking over other peoples' countries, was hiving them off again, one by one, as associated concerns. In this at least, the Empire after 1945 hewed to its original mid-Victorian design. Like the Americans, the Cobdenites in their day had worked for a revolutionary commercial republic of the world, held together by economic attraction rather than by political subordination. Long before Truman and Eisenhower, Palmerston and even Gladstone had discovered that the international economy required imperial protection. Combining the two principles, Victorian imperialism withdrew from countries as reliable economic links and national organiza-tions emerged – while it extended into others in need of development. Such was the genius of British free trade imperialism.

The formal Empire contracted in the post-war years as it had once expanded, as a variable function of integrating countries into the international capitalist economy. Under Anglo-American auspices, the remains of the system were progressively nationalized and in tropical Africa, if not in India and the Middle East, informalized. Only now the American economy would drive the economic development of the system. The ex-colonial powers would share the dividends and the burdens. Most of the new states would have to co-operate with one side or the other in the cold war if they were to fulfil their national aspirations. Though some might choose aid from the Soviet bloc, prospects of development generally depended on the superior economic capacity of the West. After 1956 the British fell in with the American design for Western alliances with freer trade and free institutions. Such was the imperialism of decolonization.

The prescription for British informal sway worked well enough so long as sterling remained central to the economies of many underdeveloped countries. It was ill-suited to the 1950s and 1960s when the rouble and the dollar were contending for the economic and military contracts as well as the doctrinal loyalty of the third world. Competition devalued, if it did not entirely debase, the currencies of informal sway. President Kennedy's 'New Frontier' began where Europe's imperial frontiers had ended. In competition with communist political economics, the 1960s were dedicated to Third World development under the aegis of the United Nations and the World Bank. As things turned out, the new world order needed a good deal of old-fashioned imperial and financial intervention along with the economic attraction. Visible empires may be abolished; the thraldom of international economy remains. There was no conspiracy to take over the Empire. American influence expanded by imperial default and nationalist invitation.

Notes

1   War Cabinet Memorandum by L. S. Amery, 'Notes on Possible Terms of Peace', G.T. -448, Secret, 11 April 1917, CAB 24/10. W. R. Louis, *In the Name of God Go! Leo Amery and the British Empire in the Age of Churchill* (New York, 1992), 68. All references to ADM, CAB, CO, DEFE, DO, FO, PREM, T, and WO classification refer to documents at the Public Record Office, London.

2   W. R. Louis and R. E. Robinson, 'The United States and the Liquidation of the British Empire in Tropical Africa 1941–1951', in Prosser Gifford and W. R. Louis (eds.), *The Transfer of Power in Africa* (New Haven, Conn., 1982), 31–55.

3   Attlee to Truman, 1 Sept. 1945, *Foreign Relations of the United States, 1945* (US Government Printing Office, Washington, DC), VI, 115 (*FRUS* hereafter).

4   Cabinet Memorandum by Lord Keynes, 13 Aug. 1945, CAB 129/1, CP (45) 112, in *British Documents on the End of Empire* (General Editors D. J. Murray and S. R. Ashton), Series A. Vol. 2: *The Labour Government and the End of Empire 1945–1951*, Ronald Hyam (ed.), Part II (HMSO, London, 1992), 1–5 (hereafter *BDEEP – Labour Government*).

5   Quoted in M. W. Kirby, *The Decline of British Economic Power since 1870* (London, 1981), 93.

6   Minute by R. W. B. Clarke to Sir David Waley, 'What happens if we do not get the US Loan?', 15 Feb. 1946, Clarke, *Anglo-American Economic Collaboration*, 147.

7   Minute by Lord Keynes to Sir David Waley, 'If Congress rejects the Loan', 22 Feb. 1946, Clarke, *Anglo-American Economic Collaboration*, 152.

8   On American motives for the loan, see specially *FRUS, 1945*, VI, 54, 110 ff. For British reactions, see Alan Bullock, *Ernest Bevin: Foreign Secretary 1945–1951* (London, 1983), 201–5.

9   Memorandum by Attlee, 'Future of the Italian Colonies', 2 March 1946, DO (46) 27, CAB 131/2.

10 Attlee to Bevin, 1 Dec. 1946, FO 800/475, *BDEEP – Labour Government*, Part III, 222.

11 Memorandum by J. S. Bennett, 'International Aspects of Colonial Policy – 1947', 30 April 1947, CO 537/2057, *BDEEP – Labour Government*, Part II, 418–19.

12 Marginal note by Poynton on Bennett, *idem*, 12 May 1947, ibid., 418.

13 Bernard Wasserstein, *Herbert Samuel: A Political Life* (Oxford, 1992), 262, 266–7.

14 *Parliamentary Debates* (Commons), 31 Jan. 1947, column 1347.

15 Account of conversation with the President, Lewis Douglas to Acting Secretary of State, 12 Nov. 1948, *FRUS, 1948*, V, Part 2, 1572.

16 Acting Secretary of State to Stabler in Amman, 3 Jan. 1949, *FRUS, 1949*, VI, 604. For the British side see especially minute by Sir Orme Sargent (Permanent Under-Secretary), 17 Jan. 1949, FO 371/76336.

17 Hearings in Executive Session on Vandenberg Resolution and the North Atlantic Treaty, 2 June 1949, *Senate Committee on Foreign Relations*, 81st Congress, 1st session, 1949, 256.

18 Agreed State Dept.-Joint Chiefs memorandum, endorsed by Truman; James F. Schnabel, *The History of the Joint Chiefs of Staff*, Vol. 1 (Wilmington, Del., 1979), 93 and Ch. III.

19 See Top Secret Minutes of 7th Meeting of the Policy Planning Staff, 24 Jan. 1950, *FRUS, 1950*, III, 617–22.

20 Alec Cairncross (ed.), *The Robert Hall Diaries 1947–53* (London, 1989), 20 July 1951, 161.

21 Quoted in Susan Strange, *Sterling and British Policy* (London, 1971), 274.

22 Summary of Pentagon Talks, 16 Oct.–7 Nov. 1947, in Bullock, *Bevin*, 468–75; Kennan memorandum, 24 Feb. 1948, *FRUS, 1948*, V, Part 2, 655–57; key British files FO 371/61557–59.

23 Richard Clarke memorandum, 'The World Dollar Crisis', 16 June 1947, Clarke, *Anglo-American Economic Collaboration*, 168–74.

24 Though it was so argued at the time: 'After all,' Sir Roger Makins of the Foreign Office wrote, 'they [the Americans] are paying the piper, and in the last analysis we are dependent on general American support for our security.' (Makins memorandum, 'Some notes on British foreign policy', 11 Aug. 1951, FO 371/124968, *BDEEP – Labour Government*, Part II. 375, note 1). The Foreign Secretary at the time, Herbert Morrison, disliked the emphasis on US dependence. The sentence in the official version of the note was deleted.

25 Cabinet memorandum by Bevin, 'European Policy', CAB 129/37/1, CP (49) 208, 18 Oct. 1949, *BDEEP – Labour Government*, Part II, 344, 347.

26 Ibid., 346.

27 Cabinet memorandum by Creech Jones, 'Gold Coast Constitution', 8 Oct. 1949, CAB 129/36/2, CP (49) 199, ibid., Part III, 46–9.

28 Report of the Committee on the Conference of African Governors, CO 847/36/1, 22 May 1947, Appendix II, *BDEEP – Labour Government*, Part I, 199.

29 Acheson to Douglas, 20 July 1949, *FRUS, 1949*, IX, 50.

30 See Top Secret messages between Acheson and Bevin, 10–15 July 1950, *FRUS, 1950*, VII, 347–90.

31 *Hall Diaries 1947–53*, 8 Dec. 1950, 135.

32   Bruce to Acheson, 5 Dec. 1950, *FRUS, 1950*, VII, 1387–9. See Alan Bullock's analysis of the European context in *Ernest Bevin*, Chs. 21 and 22.

33   US Delegation Minutes of Fifth Meeting of President Truman and Prime Minister Attlee, Top Secret, 7 Dec. 1950, *FRUS, 1950*, VII, 1449–62.

34   *Hall Diaries 1947–53*, 136, 139, 142, 150–3.

35   'Present World Situation', Top Secret, 25 July 1950, *FRUS, 1950*, III, 1658 ff.

36   Quotations from staff paper by George Kennan, PPS/51, 29 March 1949, *The State Department Policy Planning Staff Papers, 1949*, Vol. 3 (New York, 1983), especially 42–4; revised version *FRUS, 1949*, VII, Part 2, 1128 ff.

37   Anglo-American official talks, Washington, 12 Sept. 1949, *FRUS, 1949*, VII, Part 2, 1199.

38   Memorandum of conversation with the Ambassador of Netherlands, 11 Jan. 1949, *FRUS, 1949*, VII, Part I, 139.

39   Report on 'U.S. National Interests in South Asia', Top Secret, 19 April 1949, *FRUS, 1949*, VI, 8–31 (the quotations are on pp. 14 and 28).

40   Memorandum of 19 Jan. 1959, *FRUS, 1958–60*, XV, 154.

41   *U.S. Overseas Loans*, Statistical Annex 1, 26.

42   Memorandum by Loy Henderson, 28 Dec. 1945, *FRUS, 1946*, VII, 2.

43   Anglo-American Pentagon Talks of 1947, Top Secret, Oct.–Nov. 1947, *FRUS, 1947*, V, 575–625. W. R. Louis, *The British Empire in the Middle East, 1945–1951* (Oxford, 1984), 109–12.

44   Confidential Annex to Chiefs of Staff (51) 86, 23 May 1951, DEFE 4/43.

45   Confidential Annex, COS (51) 84, 21 May 1951, DEFE 4/43; Cabinet Conclusions, 12 July 1951, CAB 128/20. See also *BDEEP Labour Government*, I, 87–96; and James Cable, *Intervention at Abadan: Plan Buccaneer* (London, 1991).

46   Acheson to State Department, 10 Nov. 1951, *FRUS, 1952–54*, X, 279.

47   Acheson to Defense Secretary Lovett, 4 Nov. 1952, ibid., 512.

48   Memorandum of discussion, National Security Council, 4 March 1953, ibid., 695.

49   Memorandum of National Security Council discussion, 11 March 1953, *FRUS, 1952–54*, X, 713.

50   Douglas to Sir William Fraser (AIOC), 24 Oct. 1953, FO 371/104642. For the consortium see Daniel Yergin, *The Prize* (New York, 1991), 475–8; David S. Painter, *Oil and the American Century* (Baltimore, 1986), 192–8; and especially for the Iranian side, Mostafa Elm, *Oil, Power and Principle: Iran's Oil Nationalization and Its Aftermath* (Syracuse, NY, 1992).

51   Minute by Salisbury, 22 Aug. 1953, FO 371/104577.

52   At talks in Washington in January 1952, Churchill had stressed that Anglo-American cooperation in the Middle East would 'divide the difficulties by ten'. Truman had declared that 'US-UK agreement was necessary for any settlement of Middle Eastern problems.' *FRUS, 1952–54*, IX, Part 1, 176.

53   Memorandum of National Security Council discussion, Top Secret, 6 April 1954, *FRUS, 1952–54*, XIII, Part 1, 1259.

54   National Security Council memorandum, 24 June, 1954, *FRUS, 1952–54*, II, Part 1, 694–5.

55   Cabinet memorandum by R. A. Butler, 'The Balance of Payments Outlook', C (52) 172, 23 May 1952, CAB 129/52; *BDEEP – Conservative Government 1951–57*, Pt. III, 37–43.

56   Memorandum by Macmillan, 'Economic Policy', 17 June 1952, ibid., 47–50.

57   Ibid., 50.

58   Ibid., 44.

59 Foreign Office memorandum on 'The Problem of Nationalism', Secret Guard [Guard = not for American eyes] 21 Nov. 1952, CO 936/217, with extensive CO minutes.

60 C. D. Jackson to President's Special Assistant, Nelson Rockefeller, 10 Nov. 1955, *FRUS, 1955–57*, IX, 8.

61 President to Secretary of State, 5 Dec. 1955, *FRUS, 1955–57*, IX, 10–12.

62 Dulles, Report to National Security Council, 21 Nov. 1955, *FRUS, 1955–57*, XIV, 797.

63 Eden to Eisenhower, 26 Nov. 1955, FO 371/112739.

64 National Security Council memorandum, 28 June 1956, *FRUS, 1955–57*, XII, 308.

65 Quoted in David Reynolds, *Britannia Overruled* (London, 1991), 203.

66 Dulles's statement at a meeting of the National Security Council, 21 Nov. 1955, *FRUS, 1955–57*, XIV, 797.

67 Memorandum of conference with the President, 31 July 1956, *FRUS, 1955–57*, XVI, 62–8.

68 Quoted in Diane B. Kunz, 'The Importance of Having Money', in W. R. Louis and Roger Owen (eds.), *Suez 1956: The Crisis and its Consequences* (Oxford, 1989), 215.

69 Memorandum by Macmillan, Top Secret, 7 Aug. 1956, E. C. (56) 8, CAB 134/1217.

70 See 'Sterling', 19 Nov. 1956, T 236/4189. See also especially the minutes in T 236/4188 and T 236/4190.

71 Memorandum on National Security Council discussion, 1 Nov. 1956, *FRUS, 1955–57*, XVI, 906.

72 *FRUS, 1955–57*, XVI, 910.

73 Eden had noted on the eve of the Suez crisis: 'we must now cut our coat according to our cloth. There is not much cloth.' P.R. (56) 11, 13 June 1956, CAB 134/1315.

74 Northern European Chiefs of Mission Conference, 19–21 Sept. 1957, *FRUS, 1955–57*, IV, 610.

75 Dulles on agenda for Washington Talks, 17 Oct. 1957, *FRUS, 1955–57*, XXVII, 789–91.

76 Macmillan to Eisenhower, 10 Oct. 1957, *FRUS, 1955–57*, XXVII, 785.

77 Memorandum by Merchant for Dulles, 19 Oct. 1957, *FRUS, 1955–57*, XXVII, 795.

78 As anticipated by Dulles in agenda for Washington Talks, 17 Oct. 1957, *FRUS, 1955–57*, XXVII, 791.

79 President to George Humphrey, 22 July 1958, *FRUS, 1958–60*, XI, 365.

80 As described by William M. Rountree (Assistant Secretary of State), 14 July 1958, *FRUS, 1958–60*, XI, 228.

81 Sir Gerald Templer, Chief of the Imperial General Staff, believed that Arab nationalism in general 'had become a tool of Soviet policy'. 12 Aug. 1948, COS (58) 71, ADM 205/116; see also Templer's minutes in WO 216/917.

82 Memorandum of Conversation between President and Vice-President, 15 July 1958, *FRUS, 1958–60*, XI, 244.

83 Conference with President, 14 July 1958, ibid., 214.

84 Conference with President, 16 July 1958, ibid., 310.

85 Conference with President, 14 July 1958, ibid., 214–15.

86 Conference with President, 14 July 1958, ibid., 213.

87 Telephone conversations and messages between Eisenhower and Macmillan, 14–15 July 1958, ibid., 231–42. The British records of these conversations are in PREM 11/2387.

88 Memorandum of National Security Council discussion, 24 July 1958, *FRUS, 1958–60*, XI, 384.

89   Memorandum of conversation with President, 21 March 1957, *FRUS, 1955–57*, XXVII, 710.

90   Record of conversation between Lloyd and Dulles, 4 Feb. 1959, FO 371/141841; memorandum of conversation between Eisenhower and Macmillan, 22 March 1959, *FRUS, 1958–60*, 216.

91   Memorandum by Legal Adviser (Hager) to State Department, 11 April 1960, *FRUS, 1958–60*, IV, 630–3.

92   Cabinet memorandum by Burke Trend, 1 March 1957, PREM 11/2582.

93   Memorandum by Lennox-Boyd, 'Aden Colony and Protectorate', Secret, 14 Aug. 1959, C.P.C. (59) 12, CAB 134/1558.

94   Minutes by Burke Trend, 1 March 1957, and 20 Nov. 1958, PREM 11/2582.

95   Record of conference between East African Governors and Secretary of State, Entebbe, 7–8 Oct. 1957, Secret, CO 822/1807.

96   Cabinet memorandum by Arthur Creech Jones, 'Gold Coast Constitution', 8 Oct. 1949, CAB 129/36/2 (*BDEEP – Labour Government*, Part III, 46–9).

97   Arden-Clarke to Cohen, Personal, 5 March 1951, CO 537/7181.

98   We have only one dog in our kennel, all we can do is to build it up and feed it vitamins and cod liver oil'; it could only be replaced with one 'of even more extremist nationalist tendencies.' Arden-Clarke to Cohen, 12 May 1951, quoted in Hyam's note on Cohen minute, 11 June 1951, *BDEEP – Labour Government*, Part II, 73–4.

99   'Africa: The Next Ten Years', Interdepartmental Report, June 1959, FO 371/137972.

100   Home hoped that 'the emergence of Nigeria . . . will cut him down to size.' Memorandum by Home, 1 June 1959, PREM 11/2588.

101   C. de Brabant, 'Anglo-French Colonial Cooperation, Principally in West African Affairs' (unpublished M. Litt. thesis, Oxford University, 1989).

102   The phrase of Iain Maclcod in a minute to Macmillan, 9 May 1960, PREM 11/3047.

103   'Statement of U.S. Policy Toward Africa South of the Sahara', 23 Aug. 1957, *FRUS, 1955–57*, XVIII, 79–80; see also assurances to Macmillan at Bermuda Conference, 23 March 1957, ibid., 55–7.

104   See *FRUS, 1958–60*, X, 564–835. For the key British files on Cyprus in relation to other dependent territories, CAB 134/1558 and CAB 134/1559 (Colonial Policy Committee, 1959 and 1960).

105   'Africa: the Next Ten Years', June 1959, FO 371/137972.

106   Ibid.

107   Colonial Office officials went on to draw the lesson they had learned from the Iraqi revolution: 'we would gain nothing by trying to back authoritarians against public opinion.' Minutes of a meeting at the Colonial Office, Secret, 20 May 1959, CO 936/572.

108   'Africa: the Next Ten Years', June 1959, FO 371/137972, 6.

109   Ibid., 29.

110   Cf. P. J. Cain and A. G. Hopkins, *British Imperialism* (London, 1993), II, 281 ff.

111   Agreed U.S.-U.K paper, 'Means of Combatting Communist Influence in Tropical Africa, 13 March 1957', *FRUS, 1955–57*, XXVII, 759.

112   'Africa: the Next Ten Years', June 1959, FO 371/137972, 25–6.

113   For the stalemate in American policy over aid to Africa, March–Dec. 1960, see *FRUS, 1958–60*, XIV, 93–171 *et passim*.

114   'Africa: the Next Ten Years', 23.

115   Ibid.

116   Minute by Ramsbotham, 27 Feb. 1959, FO 371/137951.

117   Macleod to Macmillan, 9 May 1960, PREM 11/3047.

118   Minutes by War Office and Air Ministry, 11 May 1960, PREM 11/3047.

119   'Africa: the Next Ten Years', FO 371/137972, 17.

120   Ibid., 18.

121   Minute by Macmillan, 28 Dec. 1959, PREM 11/3075.

122   Macleod to Macmillan, Secret, 8 Feb. 1960, PREM 11/3030.

123   Note of Meeting, 17 Feb. 1960, PREM 11/3031.

124   John Darwin's phrase: see his account in *Britain and Decolonisation* (London, 1988), Ch. 6.

125   Herter to US Congo Embassy, 12 July 1960, *FRUS, 1958–60*, XIV, 299.

126   US Mission at United Nations to State Department, 14 July 1960, *FRUS, 1958–60*, XIV, 305.

127   Memorandum of conversation between the President and Lord Home, 19 Sept. 1960, *FRUS, 1958–60*, XIV, 495; memorandum from Board of National Estimates to Director CIA, 22 Aug. 1960, ibid., 435–42. The evidence on the British side is fragmentary, but see minute by H. F. T. Smith in the Foreign Office on 'ensuring Lumumba's removal from the scene by killing him'. Minute of 28 Sept. 1960, FO 371/146650.

128   Director CIA to Station Officer, 26 Aug. 1960, *FRUS, 1958–60*, XIV, 443; cf. memorandum on National Security Council discussion, 18 Aug. 1960, ibid., 421 footnote 1.

129   Memorandum on National Security Council meeting, 18 Aug. 1960, *FRUS, 1958–60*, XIV, 424.

130   Minute by Home, *c.* 14 Sept. 1960, FO 371/146644.

131   Memorandum by Lansdowne, 26 Sept. 1961, PREM 11/3/91.

132   National Estimates memorandum, 22 Aug. 1960, *FRUS, 1958–60*, XI, 435–42.

133   See Cabinet Conclusions 74(62), 11 Dec. 1962, CAB 128/36/2.

134   Macmillan to Eisenhower, 22 July 1960, *FRUS, 1958–60*, VI, 1005, note 6.

135   Cf. D. A. Low, 'The Asian Mirror to Tropical Africa's Independence', in Gifford and Louis, *Transfer of Power in Africa*, 3.

Chapter 4

Martin Shipway

MADAGASCAR ON THE EVE OF INSURRECTION, 1944–47

The impasse of a liberal colonial policy

LESS WELL KNOWN THAN France's long, bloody wars of decolonization in Indochina and Algeria, and indeed in many ways the forgotten tragedy of France's withdrawal from colonial empire, is the case of Madagascar, where a peaceful transfer of power in 1960 was achieved in the wake of a bloody insurrection and its brutal repression more than a decade earlier, which decapitated Malagasy nationalism and left upwards of eighty-nine thousand Malagasy dead.[1]

This article focuses on the period leading up to the Malagasy insurrection of 1947, and in particular on the thrust of French colonial policy on the island before the outbreak of violence ushered in harsher methods. As in Indochina, disorder and repression in Madagascar put an end to what had seemed to many a quite promising attempt to set French colonial policy on a new footing in the wake of the 1944 Brazzaville Conference. Indeed, as will be argued, the colony was viewed as a potentially fruitful proving ground for the new *politique de Brazzaville* which emerged from the Conference. Notwithstanding the rather misleading Gaullist propaganda which surrounded the so-called *esprit de Brazzaville*, this policy represented a genuine attempt by a new generation of colonial administrators to ensure a liberal future for France's colonial empire, grandly renamed the French Union (*Union Française*) in March 1945. It will be shown how the insurrection pre-empted an impending reversal in French policy in Madagascar, which had run into an impasse by the end of 1946 at the latest. Thus, when insurrection broke out during the night of 29–30 March 1947, the French were already preparing for a clampdown intended to put them back in charge of an increasingly uncomfortable situation and to provide, in Frank Furedi's description of the classic British emergency, 'a breathing space for the colonial administration to evolve an appropriate response to the challenge it faced'.[2]

How may we explain the impasse in which the French administration found itself in Madagascar? One crucial explanatory factor lies in the instability of metropolitan French politics following the Liberation. The period covered by this article also saw the establishment of a Provisional Government of the French Republic (GPRF) in liberated Paris and de Gaulle's presidency of that government until his disgruntled resignation in

January 1946; the drafting of a new Constitution, its rejection by referendum (in May 1946), redrafting and grudging acceptance by referendum (in November 1946); the increasingly disruptive rivalry and disagreement between the parties of the 'tripartite' coalition which succeeded de Gaulle; and, in particular, the growing hostility of two of those parties, the Socialist *Section Française de l'Internationale Ouvrière* (SFIO) and the Christian Democratic *Mouvement Républicain Populaire* (MRP), towards the third, the *Parti Communiste Français* (PCF), hostility which was to erupt in France's own domestic version of the Cold War by May 1947 at the latest, when Communist ministers were forced to resign from the Socialist-led government of Paul Ramadier. The present author has examined elsewhere how the uncertainties created by domestic political crisis impacted on colonial policy-making, particularly in the case of Indochina; and how domestic crisis served to encourage autonomy and indeed insubordination on the part of senior officials. The metropolitan backdrop is also crucial to what follows.

In this article, however, emphasis is placed rather on two aspects of French policy which derived from the perspective and understanding of French officials, whether in Paris or in the seat of the Government-General at Tananarive. First, it examines the ideological and doctrinal sources of French policy and identifies two apparently complementary but increasingly divergent models for French action in Madagascar. Thus new ideas derived from the Brazzaville model were grafted onto older methods and perspectives going back to the conquest of 1896. Secondly, the article charts the administration's progressive loss of control on the island, starting from the inception of the wartime Gaullist administration in 1943. It is argued that these two aspects of policy worked, or failed to work, together. Thus, as policy-making became a matter of maintaining order, rather than of planning for the future, officials fell back almost instinctively on the traditional assumptions and repressive reflexes of French rule in Madagascar.

I

French colonial officials were well used to viewing Madagascar as a case apart, representing a unique set of problems which made the island as fascinating and elusive for French administrators as it was for the ethnologists, linguists, agronomists, zoologists, missionaries and others, who came in their train. Unsurprisingly, therefore, the new policy which emerged from the 1944 Brazzaville Conference soon developed a Malagasy dimension, as Madagascar became a candidate for autonomy within the proposed overarching framework of the French Union. But this new, self-consciously modernizing and reformist model for policy-making was imposed on an older model of policy in Madagascar, originating in the still influential teaching of Madagascar's first French Governor-General, Gallieni. As with roses so with official doctrine, it was the root stock which exerted an influence on the new graft rather than the reverse.

Madagascar's place in the *politique de Brazzaville* must be understood against the background of the ambiguities surrounding that policy as a whole, following the Liberation and the Gaullists' return to Paris in September 1944. On the one hand, the organizers of the Brazzaville Conference had sought to define a new spirit of reformism, the so-called *esprit de Brazzaville*, and affirmed the will to maintain a new, liberal purpose for the French Empire. According to the Gaullist propaganda surrounding Brazzaville, 'colonialism' and all that that term implied were to be abolished in favour of a new federal structure based loosely on the old Republican ideal of Greater France ('la plus grande France'). In part, this 'generosity' was a response to supposed French gratitude for the Empire's role in the Gaullist wartime campaign, which in Madagascar's case involved glossing over the controversies surrounding the British invasion in 1942 and subsequent Gaullist take-over (see below). But quite apart from its key role as a piece of triumphalist Gaullist propaganda, the Brazzaville Conference was seen by its organizers as at least a partial failure. According to Governor Henri Laurentie, who had largely been responsible for proposing and organizing the conference, Brazzaville's welcome recommendations for humanitarian and social reforms were of less sig-nificance than the more pragmatic, but at the same time more ambitious, proposals for constitutional and political reform which the conference delegates had distorted and rejected. This rejection was marked by the oft-quoted declaration which headed the conference recommendations, against Laurentie's objections, ruling out any possibility even in a remote future of autonomy or 'self-government' (a term left in English to show its inapplicability to the French empire). In this way the 'apolitical' corps of African colonial proconsuls had succeeded in creating a lasting source of friction and uncertainty which was to dog colonial policy-makers throughout the period of decolonization.

In the face of this ambivalence, Laurentie, as Director of Political Affairs in the Ministry of Colonies in liberated Paris, saw his primary task as being to campaign, behind the closed doors of central government and the colonial administration, for acceptance of the logic of imperial reform as he saw it. This logic implied first and foremost an accommodation with the forces of colonial nationalism, and the offer where appropriate of whatever revised status was necessary, including autonomy or self-government, to maintain a given French dependency within the French Union. Each country's constitutional status was to be negotiated as a function of its perceived political culture and development. Thus, as Laurentie explained to a committee drawn up to study (and improve upon) the Brazzaville recommendations:

> Tous les Pays Français ont la vocation à la majorité politique. Certains y sont parvenus: le Maroc, la Tunisie, l'Indochine, la Nouvelle-Calédonie. D'autres n'y sont pas parvenus: ils resteront en tutelle sous l'Exécutif, qui restera pour eux, dans une certaine mesure, le législateur. Mais la tutelle de l'Exécutif sera temporaire: les Territoires unis, suivant leurs affinités, évolueront, soit vers l'assimilation, pour devenir des départements d'outre-mer, soit vers l'association pour devenir des Pays-Unis.[3]

This explanation presents two important elements of Laurentie's vision (a term used advisedly but not derogatorily in this context). First is the crucial but undefined time-table for reform: some territories were deemed to be not yet ready for the accordance of a definitive status within the French Union. Secondly, an element of choice is involved: 'association', a term glossed elsewhere as approximating to autonomy, was thought to be a status which some territories would eschew in favour of the closer political union implied by 'assimilation'. The use of the latter term is an interesting concession by Laurentie, since it formed one of the main planks of his criticism of

Brazzaville that the conference delegates had shown a frustrating attachment to the ultimately meaningless shibboleth, as Laurentie saw it, of traditional assimilation doctrine.[4]

Madagascar was usefully identified as belonging in the category of territories which might accede, in time, to the status of Associated States as opposed to assimilated Overseas Departments (the four *départements d'Outre-mer* created in 1946). Thus, in a confidential briefing to newspaper editors in which Laurentie was at his most expansive, in September 1945, a strong contrast was made with the colonies of Black Africa:

> Il est certain qu'il y en a une [colonie] qui peut tendre vers l'autonomie. C'est Madagascar. L'Afrique Occidentale en revanche, au contraire, devrait plutôt chercher sa voie du côté, je ne dis pas de l'assimilation, parce que c'est un mot qui n'a aucun sens, mais plut't vers une certaine forme de la liberté individuelle plutôt que de la liberté politique du pays pris dans son ensemble; je crois que l'Afrique devrait être un pays où nous serions tout naturellement chez nous tandis qu'au contraire Madagascar peut tendre à devenir une espèce de pays autonome.[5]

The reasons for Madagascar's special status in this ambitious scheme were not difficult to identify: Madagascar was perceived as having a continuous indigenous tradition of political activity, and indeed dissent, and a strong national identity based on its pre-colonial statehood, which, it was believed, could nonetheless be accommodated within a French-oriented framework. Laurentie's theoretical, broad-brush approach was more nuanced than a brief summary can allow. One *caveat* expressed elsewhere is of relevance in the present context. This concerned the envisaged status within the future Associated States of settler communities, the presence of which was likely, if anything, to impede progress towards autonomy. As Laurentie wrote in the *programme général* for the Brazzaville Conference:

> Le mot de self government n'a été que trop souvent prononcé. Nous ne l'écarterons pas à priori, mais nous désirons d'abord nous placer en face de la réalité. Or, lorsqu' on parle de self government, on oublie toujours de demander: je self government de qui? et sur qui?[6]

Clearly this was a matter of prime importance within the North African territories, Morocco and Tunisia as well as Algeria, which were all seen more or less explicitly as *colonies de peuplement*, as opposed to the *colonies d'exploitation* South of the Sahara. But Madagascar's settler community of planters and traders, many of them with roots in the far older colony of Réunion, were more numerous and vocal than in any of France's continental African colonies, their presence part of the rationale of colonial annexation in 1896.

Conversely, from a constitutional perspective, Madagascar represented a far less problematic case for imperial planning than the more 'advanced' dependencies of the Maghreb and Indochina. Indeed, Laurentie and his colleagues at Brazzaville and subsequently were studious in their avoidance of any discussion of Algeria, whose constitutional status was officially that of an extension of metropolitan France. The position of Morocco and Tunisia within a new imperial community was also problematic because of their status as protectorates. The administrative dimension to these constitutional and diplomatic niceties was perhaps decisive as far as Laurentie's interest was concerned. Whereas Madagascar came within the remit of the Ministry of Colonies (renamed Ministry of Overseas France [*Ministère de la France d'Outre-Mer*] in January 1946), the North African protectorates, like the Levant Mandate, were jealously overseen by the *Direction de l'Afrique-Levant* at the Ministry of Foreign Affairs, while Algeria was the responsibility of a powerful Division of the Ministry of the Interior. Both departments maintained an aloof detachment from the planning at the 'junior' Ministry of Colonies. Indochina was a special case again, in part because of its complex structure of colonies and protectorates, but also, not least, because it was still at this period under Japanese control. The Far Eastern colonies stole the limelight largely as a result of the precipitous events which followed the Japanese overthrow on 9 March 1945 of Admiral Decoux's *Vichyste* administration. The March 1945 Declaration on Indochina, which had in fact been drawn up over months as a comprehensive public statement of post-Brazzaville colonial policy, set out the framework for a new Indochinese Federation of five *pays* (Laos, Cambodia and the three separate *ky*, or regions, of what was resolutely *not* called Vietnam). But the Declaration made first use in public of the term 'French Union', and it set down an idea of what was meant by 'Associated State' status.[7] Thus, quite apart from outlining France's proposed negotiating position in Indochina, however vaguely and ambiguously, it also placed a marker for policy in other dependencies, not least Madagascar. This article will return to the possible application of these terms to Madagascar. First, consideration must be given to the second model to which policy-makers were drawn.

In keeping with France's Napoleonic tradition of rational, scientific and centralizing administrative rule, the *politique de Brazzaville* was intended to apply comprehensively to France's imperial system. This rather grandiose imperial planning contrasted sharply, however, with the appeal of an older model for policy derived from the specific traditions and justifications of French rule in Madagascar. As with Marshal Lyautey's Moroccan legacy, and the traditions of the Indochinese Civil Service derived from Doumer and others, colonial rule in Madagascar was indelibly associated with one of the great proconsuls of French colonization: the 'pacifier' and first Governor-General of the island, General Gallieni, whose writings were required reading for any cadet at the *Ecole Nationale de la France d'Outre-Mer*, the prestigious training college (*grande école*) from which all senior officials were recruited. Gallieni's literary and administrative life's work provided the *locus classicus* for many of the traditions and reflexes of the twentieth-century French colonial administration. Alongside the more general intellectual baggage of technical competence and Republican loyalty, therefore, officials learnt from Gallieni the importance of ethnology, philology (officials posted to Madagascar were encouraged to learn the Malagasy language) and pre-colonial history.

Aside from the general importance of these disciplines, every colonial administrator was well drilled in Gallieni's own account and justification of the French conquest and subsequent colonization of Madagascar.[8] According to Gallieni, the French brought down the imperialist Merina monarchy and humiliated the Merina ruling caste (generally, but somewhat misleadingly, referred to in French discourse as the *hova*), abolished slavery and were welcomed as liberators by the oppressed or hostile non-Merina peoples (the so-called *côtiers* or 'coastal peoples').[9] The more socially advanced

Merina, of Malayo-Polynesian origin, were initially forced by the French to withdraw from positions of administrative and military responsibility outside Imerina.

This was the thrust of Gallieni's so-called *politique des races*. Although this proved impracticable, when the Merina proved indispensable to the French colonial administration, it remained part of the French colonial mission to promote the interests of, and more generally to 'protect', the *côtiers*, of Bantu origin. Merina resistance to French authority, including the Menalamba insurrection of 1895–97, the VVS[10] movement of 1913–15 and the unrest of the 1930s, was thus readily interpreted by the French as inspired by reactionary ambitions to restore Merina hegemony and the hated *status quo ante*. The final plank of this 'official version' concerned the role of the Protestant mission churches. The congregationalism of the London Missionary Society had been adopted as state religion of the Merina monarchy in the last decades before 1896. This provided a natural focus for French anglophobia and the basis for the lasting myth of an Anglo-Merina-Protestant alliance, though Welsh LMS missionaries were never entirely plausible as agents of British imperialism. (The Malagasy counterpart of this myth was the belief that outside intervention was just around the corner at moments of crisis, including the 1947 Insurrection.) Moreover, the irony of official French support for the French Jesuit missions as an instrument of anti-Merina policy seems to have been lost on the staunchly Republican and anti-clerical Gallieni.

No doubt social and historical reality was reflected to an extent in Gallieni's version of events, although his part in falsifying the record has been amply documented and argued; in particular, in what amounted to a show trial, two Merina courtiers, Rainandrianampandry and Prince Ratsimamanga, were falsely accused and executed for their alleged involvement in the Menalamba risings.[11] More generally, Gallieni's only partially aborted *politique des races* and its accompanying racial and political doctrine had incalculable effects on Madagascar's social and political organization. What is of chief interest here is the extent to which official French perceptions, barely more than a single generation after Gallieni's departure from the island in 1905, were still guided by the official history of the French conquest; as Tronchon points out, the *hova/côtier* distinction 'correspond plus à un clivage idéologique qu'à une réalité ethnographique ou géographique'.[12] In some isolated cases there was also continuity of personnel, as was the case for Marcel de Coppet, Governor-General at the time of the insurrection, who was called from the brink of retirement to return to Tananarive where he had started his career under Governor-General Augagneur in 1905. This continuity of personnel was even more marked on the Malagasy side: the nationalist leaders Ravoahangy, Raseta and Ravelojaona had been involved in the VVS movement, and Ravoahangy was directly descended from the Merina monarchy.

Reference to this 'official version' of the French mission in Madagascar remained all-pervasive in French official discourse at this period. At a general level, it was ritually reiterated in reports, as if to rally the faithful and initiate outsiders (such as government ministers). Thus in his report to a conference of High Commissioners in February 1947, de Coppet started by reproducing in detail the account given above.[13] Far from seeing Gallieni's doctrine and the *politique de Brazzaville* as mutually exclusive, officials made every attempt to couch the new policy in terms of the older orthodoxy; and Gallieni's authority was explicitly invoked to support both sides in the debate surrounding the application of the *politique de Brazzaville* to Madagascar. Two ways are examined here in which the two policy-making models converged. The first concerns proposals for administrative restructuring of Madagascar along federal lines. In this case, convergence was explicit and potentially fruitful. The second way takes us to the heart of France's policy-making dilemma in Madagascar, and concerns the series of electoral campaigns which marked the period, and which were to become the main battle-ground for the *politique des races* as it was increasingly understood by the French.

Proposals for a federal administrative structure were first made by General Legentilhomme, appointed High Commissioner for the Indian Ocean following the Gaullist take-over in 1943. As a means of coordinating the war effort more efficiently, Madagascar would be divided into five administrative districts staffed and, if necessary, headed by Malagasy administrators. Governor-General Pierre de Saint-Mart, Legentilhomme's successor put the proposals on ice, on the grounds that it would place too great a strain on the colony's wartime budgetary and personnel resources.[14] By the time of the March 1945 Declaration on Indochina, the idea of a federal structure for Madagascar had been taken up by the *Direction des Affaires Politiques* (DAP), by analogy with proposals for Indochina. However, when colonial proconsuls were invited to comment on the applicability of the Declaration to their own territories, Saint-Mart at Tananarive suggested that the terms of the Declaration had awakened old Merina claims to power on the island, and that granting Madagascar a similar statute of autonomy within the French Union would mean reversing Gallieni's policy of holding back the Merina until the *côtiers* caught up socially and politically with their erstwhile overlords.[15] Laurentie, while repeating the argument that Madagascar was not yet ready to choose, nonetheless did not see eye to eye with Saint-Mart on the *problème hova*:

> . . . je vois entre Madagascar et Indochine plus de similitudes que de différences. Je crois que fatalement Madagascar tendra dans l'avenir à une forme d'autonomie comparable à celle à laquelle l'Indochine accède dès maintenant. Dans ce cas et si Madagascar reste une colonie unitaire les Hovas utiliseront leur avance sur le plan culturel et social pour augmenter et consolider cette avance, prendre les postes de direction et rétablir leur domination sur la grande île.[16]

By contrast, Laurentie favoured establishing two separate regimes, 'association' for the High Plateaux (that is, the Merina heartlands of Imerina), and 'direct administration' for the non-Merina in order to contain Merina influence. As he argued:

> C'est bien ce qu'avait voulu Gallieni et c'est reprendre sa politique que de faire de Madagascar une colonie fédérale où comme l'Indochine et grâce à la France les pays composants, distincts par la civilisation, la race et la tradition, pourront garder leur personnalité propre à l'intérieur de la fédération malgache.

In other words, not only was Gallieni appealed to, *pace* Saint-Mart, to justify the new policy in Madagascar, but also an analogy was drawn with the proposed five-way division of Indochina. This was far from the last word concerning the federalization of Madagascar, which Laurentie continued to advocate throughout the period under consideration. But, in the sense that federalization presupposed a long period of reflection and careful planning, it was overtaken by events and never implemented in the form intended by Laurentie.

The second example of convergence between the Brazzaville and Gallieni models is closely related, but by its very nature had more immediate impact. The recommendation by the Brazzaville Conference that Overseas France should be represented in an eventual Constituent Assembly in Paris led to one of the most distinctive features of French decolonization, which was the parliamentary and ministerial experience it offered independent francophone Africa's first generation of political leaders. Colonial representation in the metropolitan parliament represented the extension of existing pre-war practice, since France's older colonies (Algeria, the pre-1789 colonies which were to become *départements d'outre-mer*, the French Indian *établissements* and the Four Communes of coastal Senegal) had enjoyed this privilege going back to the nineteenth century. It also constituted the practical application of France's largely theoretical colonial doctrine of assimilation, itself an offshoot of French Republicanism, with its emphasis both on universalism and on parliamentary legitimacy. Ironically, this most successful and enduring of the Brazzaville recommendations was opposed by Laurentie, partly because he saw assimilationism as a meaningless doctrine, which went against the federal principle he espoused; and partly because it was out of the question that the colonies would ever be granted adequate or equitable representation in the French National Assembly. Indeed, Laurentie's reluctance to embrace the principle might be seen as the administrative counterpart of Edouard Herriot's more famously expressed fear that France might become 'the colony of her former colonies'.[17] None the less, given African enthusiasm for the idea and perhaps the opportunities it offered for French-sponsored political training, the DAP took up the cause in Paris, and threw its weight behind the work of the Commission, chaired by Gaston Monnerville, which met in Paris over the Spring 1945 to debate on an imperial electoral system. Reporting in July 1945, the Monnerville Commission recommended a generous number of colonial seats to be elected by universal suffrage and proportional representation within a single electoral college, thus effectively abolishing the distinction between citizens and non-citizens.[18] One by one these recommendations were diluted or overruled by the Minister of Colonies, Paul Giacobbi who, despite the wide publicity accorded the Monnerville recommendations, steered a more cautious path on the advice of the Governors-General of French West Africa, Cameroun and Madagascar. At a key meeting of the proconsuls in Paris in late July, Laurentie was outvoted, and a more cautious system installed.[19] This was based on a double college, limited suffrage for the non-citizens' college, and huge constituencies embracing two colonies each in the African Federations, and splitting the island of Madagascar arbitrarily into its Western and Eastern halves. According to the Ordonnance of 22 August 1945, Madagascar was to be represented by four *députés*, two citizens and two non-citizens (and a further single *député* for the Comoros which also fell within Tananarive's ambit).

Two general points serve to illustrate the way in which the issue of political representation proved to be inseparable from the *hova/côtier* question. First, Saint-Mart's influence was instrumental in maintaining a double-college system. This was partly in order to preserve the settlers' political influence on Madagascar (and elsewhere); the *Réunionnais* settlers' experience of colonial politics made them a powerful lobbying force in Paris at this time, when settler concerns were finding new vociferous expression in a new organization, the *Etats-Généraux de la Colonisation* (which met for the first time, in Paris, in August 1945).[20] But a further reason for Saint-Mart's campaign was that, as one official in Tananarive explained, voting in a single college would ensure the election of exclusively native *députés*, and Merina at that.[21] However, this was at best a circular argument, since Malagasy social and intellectual elites were dominated by the Merina. Moreover, the double-college system had the effect of concentrating the pro-French and the anti-French votes in the citizens' and non-citizens' colleges respectively, thus ensuring Merina victory in the latter college's seats. As will be seen, by early 1947, the administration was to resort to a single college in Provincial Assembly elections in order to outvote the MDRM party. Secondly, by dividing the island into only two (later three) constituencies, the administration inevitably cut across the enormously complex (and anyway largely invisible) ethnic boundaries, thus ensuring that candidates were almost inevitably, if somewhat simplistically, assumed to belong in one or other of the Merina or *côtier* camps. Thus for the October 1945 and the May 1946 elections, Tananarive and the High Plateaux (that is, broadly speaking, Imerina) fell in the Eastern constituency, ensuring Merina victory (as the French saw it). With the introduction of a third constituency, in November 1946, Imerina was now separated off from the Western and Eastern coastal regions. But this merely served to reinforce the French interpretation of *hova/côtier* rivalry in the coastal constituencies (which were won, respectively, by an established Merina and a Betsimisaraka fighting with Merina backing). In other words, by their own doing, the French now had to rely even more than usual on the distorting prism of their own divisive doctrine.

Thus, convergence of the Brazzaville and Gallieni models tended to work against the liberal thrust of the former. The administrative mechanisms, procedures and vocabulary derived clearly enough from the Brazzaville model prescribed by the new Gaullist hierarchy installed in the Ministry of Colonies in Paris. But the underlying reality was much more readily interpreted in terms of the time-honoured racial doctrine derived from Gallieni. The electoral issue also provided the immediate cause for much of the political instability which marked the period in Madagascar. This was, not least, because of the frequency of elections necessitated by the drawn-out Constitution-writing process in Paris and the rejection in the May 1946 referendum of the first Constitutional draft. As such, it forms the essential background for the gradual loss of administrative control in Madagascar, to which we now turn.

II

High-level debates on doctrine and underlying ideological formation are crucial to an understanding of the official approach to policy-making, but in the end policy is made or broken on the ground. Why and how did the French administration lose its grip on policy in Madagascar? Clearly, the short answer would be to the effect that it never really regained control following the depredations of the Gaullist war effort. Thus, the nationalist *députés* elected to the Constituent Assembly in 1945 were able to play on local unrest and discontent and to take credit for any alleviating measures taken, such as the abolition of forced labour in April 1946. Nationalist momentum increased with the re-election of Raseta and Ravoahangy in the elections to the second Constituent Assembly and the formation of an organized mass party, the *Mouvement Démocratique pour la Rénovation Malgache* (MDRM), and was accompanied from late 1946 by increasing disorder and violence, until the administration set in train the process of dissolving the MDRM. This process was interrupted by the outbreak of the insurrection at the end of March 1947. What needs to be teased out here is how the administration interpreted the political situation in Madagascar, and how the decision was reached to undertake such a drastic reversal of policy as the dissolution of a highly successful political party previously identified, albeit somewhat uneasily, as an *interlocuteur valable* with whom the French could 'do business'.

Although far removed from any theatre of combat, Madagascar's traumatic experience of the Second World War embraced foreign invasion, overthrow of the colonial regime and famine. In common with every other part of the French Empire, the administration changed its allegiance twice. First, in 1940, following Marcel de Coppet's abortive attempt (in his first tour of duty as Governor-General at Tananarive) to rally to the side of the British and de Gaulle, *colons* and administrators forced his resignation and declared for Vichy. Then, in December 1942, following the British occupation of the naval base at Diego-Suarez in June, and other parts of the island in November, de Gaulle negotiated with Churchill the take-over by his own men of the Government-General in Tananarive. General Legentilhomme's mission, as High Commissioner for the Indian Ocean, was to take the island in hand and, in particular, to gear its economy to the Gaullist war effort. His thoroughness brought the island to the brink of crisis. Responding too readily to the arguments of his advisers at Tananarive, Legentilhomme increased the penalties inflicted under the native penal code, the *indigénat* (and applied it to women), and doubled the requirements of the *prestations* system, according to which able-bodied Malagasy worked for a given number of days per year as directed by the local administration. As a Paris official later concluded, Legentilhomme 'y est allé fort, trop fort'.[22] In response to the threat of famine following drought in late 1943 (a threat no doubt compounded by the socio-economic effects of the war effort), Legentilhomme introduced a Rice Bureau (*Office du Riz*) responsible for rationing supplies of the Malagasy staple.

From the start, therefore, the new Gaullist colonial administration found itself reacting to events in Madagascar. In December 1943, René Pleven, Commissioner for the Colonies in de Gaulle's French Committee for National Liberation (CFLN), made a special trip to Tananarive to announce a special package of reforms pre-empting and in some cases exceeding the recommendations to be made at the Brazzaville Conference a few weeks later, including the promise of increased political representation. And yet, both at Brazzaville and in subsequent months, Governor-General Saint-Mart was instrumental in delaying some of the more radical reforms recommended, including the abolition of forced labour and the *indigénat*, until the end of hostilities, in spite of pressure from Pleven's officials. As Laurentie wrote in April 1944:

> J'ai peine à admettre qu'un régime entièrement supprimé au Cameroun et en AEF [Afrique Equatoriale Française] et pour ainsi dire entièrement supprimé en AOF [Afrique Occidentale Française] où il disparaîtra complètement dans neuf mois doive être maintenu même partiellement à Madagascar. En dehors des arguments d'ordre moral et politique qui commandent cette suppression, je n'ai pas besoin de vous rappeler que l'emploi de la main d'oeuvre prestataire est le système le plus anti-économique

qui existe. Le rendement de cette main d'oeuvre est plus faible que celui de toute autre.[23]

Meanwhile in Madagascar, a Committee of Public Safety was formed to protest against the pressures imposed by Legentilhomme's harsh regime, in particular the Rice Bureau. Its members, including such nationalist figureheads – and future political rivals – as Joseph Ravoahangy and Joseph Ravelojaona, also took the opportunity to campaign discreetly for the cause of Malagasy independence.[24] They may have been emboldened in their longer-term political aims by the Government-General's insensitivity. In response to one appeal by the Committee in January 1945, Saint-Mart's Secretary-General in Tananarive argued that it was nonsense to talk of the Malagasy starving when only rice was rationed, ignoring the political significance of this one crop.[25] Significantly, it was during this period that the JINA was formed, and that the *Parti National Socialiste Malgache* (PANAMA), formed in 1941, first mobilized successfully at a national level: these two clandestine organizations were to spearhead the insurrection.[26]

In the end, Saint-Mart's arguments concerning the war effort were unanswerable, and it was only with the end of hostilities, and the preparations which followed for elections to the Constituent Assembly in Paris, that a sense of progress was achieved. These first elections of the post-war period were also the first democratic elections to a metropolitan institution for all but the pre-1789 colonies of India, the Caribbean and Senegal. Notwithstanding the momentous nature of the event, the elections were a triumph of compromise and improvization in Madagascar as elsewhere across the Empire, given that the administration had to organize an election in six weeks, following the Ordonnance of 22 August 1945 which set down the modalities of the election. In the circumstances, the two rounds of the election in October November 1945 passed off without serious incident, notwithstanding Tananarive's reports of tensions in the capital and campaigning in favour of total independence.[27]

More remarkable than the administration's successful management of the election was its failure to foresee – or prevent – the victory in the non-citizens' college of Joseph Ravoahangy in the Eastern constituency, and Joseph Raseta in the Western constituency. Although neither result was overwhelmingly decisive, it may be significant that victory was predicted in both cases for candidates who were both more moderate nationalists and better known amongst the Merina intellectual elite, Ravelojaona and Razafintsalama respectively. The campaigns fought in the two constituencies differed significantly. Thus, in the capital the contenders' main platform was one of independence, ostensibly inspired by Brazzaville, developments in Indochina, the San Francisco Conference and especially the Atlantic Charter; while the campaigns fought by Raseta and Razafintsalama in the West stressed Malagasy unity and were, according to the official report, expurgated for consumption by those wary of anything coming from Imerina. Even in the West it was noted that the election was dominated by a bloc of Merina civil servants working for the Nationalist cause.[28] Thus, not only was the election interpreted in terms of the *hova/côtier* distinction, which was to be expected, but this was presented in a way which subtly discounted nationalist successes. Moreover, the fact was duly noted that both Ravoahangy and Raseta had been involved in the VVS rebellion thirty years previously. Indeed, preliminary moves were made with a view to having Ravoahangy's victory disallowed given his conviction in the VVS affair. But the proceedings were abandoned on the grounds that Ravoahangy's nearest rival was also a nationalist, that invalidation would be seen as a metropolitan backlash and that further nationalist victory in a subsequent electoral campaign would constitute a serious political defeat for France; the *beau geste* was thus to leave Ravoahangy in post.[29]

Any official complacency in the face of Ravoahangy's and Raseta's election was rapidly dissipated over the course of the following few months. Thus, in a report on Malagasy nationalism produced by the DAP in March 1946, a few weeks after the formation in Paris of the MDRM, a new urgency may be detected, notwithstanding considerable continuities in theme and content. VVS was again invoked, as the author noted that, with France weakened and preoccupied by her position in Europe, as in 1915, the same men were still agitating. Foreign involvement was suggested, since Gallieni's old theme of supposed British interest and involvement in the island had been revived by the very recent memories of the British invasion in 1942. (Moreover this was a theme with resonance for Gaullists, given the flare-up of Anglo-Gaullist antagonism which the invasion provoked.) Ominous importance was ascribed to the presence of British, American and South African Consulates-General on the island. Even PANAMA rated a rare mention in the report, although it was suggested that both it and the Committee of Public Safety had lost political importance since Malagasy nationalists had attained respectability through electoral success. In contrast with Laurentie's optimistic assessments the year before, analogies with Indochina were now to be discouraged. The latest version of the *hova/côtier* question was also more alarmist: the report saw as over-optimistic Tananarive's view that Merina nationalism had not yet 'contaminated' the *côtiers*. As it was argued:

> D'ores et déjà, il faut ramener à ses limites réelles ethniques et géographiques, qui sont la race hova et l'Emyrne, le nationalisme malgache. Il faut chercher à le calmer en donnant satisfaction à celles de ses aspirations qui sont légitimes, en flattant aussi certaines ambitions. Il faudra enfirn dissocier les populations côtières et celles des hauts-plateaux, leur donnant une administration particulière . . . L'insurrection ouverte est peu probable, mais le maintien de l'ordre est à envisager avec plus de vigilance que par le passé.[30]

It will be noted how the report's author combined elements of the two policy-making models: federation and political concessions were now explicitly conceived as ways of containing the Merina. In this way the tone was set for policy over the coming twelve months.

This hardening of the official line may be attributed to several factors. At a general level, the decisive shifts in political circumstances which occurred in Paris in early 1946 brought about a change of heart in the Ministry. Thus, de Gaulle's resignation in January 1946 as President of the GPRF removed at a stroke the principal ideological and institutional pillar supporting the *politique de Brazzaville*. As if to confirm this loss of ideological control, officials at the Ministry of Overseas France saw the constitution-making process for the French Union being taken over by the coalition of Socialists and Communists (the former more or less in thrall to the latter for the moment), which was instrumental in establishing a highly liberal – and, as the DAP saw it, unworkable and incoherent – structure for the French Union. The Malagasy *députés* played a key role in this process, alongside their African and other colonial counterparts in the Constituent

Assembly. Specifically, they took the unusual step of drafting their own law repealing the 1896 law and declaring Malagasy independence within the French Union. Laurentie's subsequent analysis of the abortive work of the first Constituent Assembly, which led him to contemplate resignation, attributed blame squarely to the PCF, which he saw as seeking to wreck the emerging Constitution to its own treacherous ends.[31] It was well known that Ravoahangy and Raseta, apart from their key role in VVS, had also been prominent in the short-lived *Parti Communiste de la Région de Madagascar* (PCRM) during the period of the Popular Front; Communist sympathies were increasingly sufficient to condemn the two men, though the PCRM's relations with the metropolitan party had never been close or orthodox.

The political and constitutional upheavals of early 1946 also brought opportunities for a new start. The new Minister, freshly styled Minister of Overseas France, was the veteran Socialist Marius Moutet, Minister of Colonies in Léon Blum's Popular Front government of 1936; initially at least, he was seen by officials as an improvement on his conservative and undynamic predecessor, Paul Giacobbi. (Jacques Soustelle, Gaullist liberal and future Algerian *ultra*, had briefly succeeded Giacobbi as Minister until de Gaulle's departure.) Moreover, his appointment was a chance for Paris to galvanize the colonial administration by replacing its top officials, including Laurentie's two foremost antagonists: Pierre Cournarie, Governor-General at Dakar, and Saint-Mart, who returned to Paris in February. As Laurentie wrote to Moutet in April, following the rejection of the constitutional draft in the referendum of that month:

> Il faut battre aux prochaines élections RAVOAHANGY et RASETA. Je vous épargne tous les indices qui me portent à croire que non seulement Monsieur de SAINT-MART n'y parviendra pas, mais que la prolongation de son règne risque encore d'aggraver un mal déjà si manifeste. La France a le besoin le plus impérieux et le plus urgent aujourd'hui à Madagascar de provoquer un choc moral qui rende aux indigènes une certaine somme de confiance et d'élan.[32]

The man charged with bringing about this moral shock was Marcel de Coppet, whose credentials were impeccable as both a colonial liberal and an old Madagascar hand. Apart from his familiarity with Gallieni's Madagascar, de Coppet also enjoyed immense prestige as an intellectual boasting André Gide for a friend and Roger Martin due Gard as father-in-law. As an SFIO activist of long standing he had been appointed Governor-General at Dakar by the Popular Front (that is, by Moutet), and then at Tananarive in 1939–40.[33]

Appointed in mid-May 1946, de Coppet's mission was to reinforce the liberal basis of French policy and at the same time to tighten the administration's grip. Following the heavy hints of the DAP, one of de Coppet's early reports back to Paris, in the wake of the elections, attributed the rapid evolution of events in Madagascar to Saint-Mart's administrative insufficiencies: alongside various relics of colonialism, such as Saint-Mart's refusal to grant audiences to individual Malagasy, de Coppet noted the lack of organization at the Government-General, undermanning of the police and *gendarmes*, disorganization in the *Direction des Affaires Malgaches* (DAM, Tananarive's equivalent of the DAP) such that they had again been unable to predict the outcome of the elections, and gross underspending of political funds, indicating that the elections had been unprepared (although political expenditure increased in the three months of Secretary-General Boudry's acting Governor-Generalship). In conclusion, de Coppet foresaw a long haul ahead if France's position in the colony was to be restored.[34]

But de Coppet was not to be allowed the breathing-space necessary for the long-term strategy which he envisaged. Raseta's and Ravoahangy's triumphant re-election in May 1946 represented a kind of Rubicon for the *députés'* Malagasy nationalist following, now represented by the newly formed MDRM. With the administration barely emerging from the doldrums of Saint-Mart's regime, the cause of *rénovation malgache* was increasingly borne along by its own momentum. Officials analysing the elections were probably right to play down the political coherence of the movement, which had hardly had a chance to organize more than a very loose network of electoral committees, but insufficiencies at the level of elite coordination only pointed up the party's largely unearned success in mobilizing an electorate. Ravoahangy's success in increasing his majority from sixteen to thirty thousand was attributed to Ravoahangy's supposed mystique, founded on his status as Madagascar's first representative in Paris, who had rubbed shoulders with metropolitan politicians. He was also widely given credit for the largely symbolic reformist measures of this period including the formal abolition of forced labour and the granting of citizen status to French imperial subjects.[35] As de Coppet commented: 'Le succès aussi bien de RAVOAHANGY que de RASETA n'est pas celui d'une idée politique mais le fait d'un engouement populaire dû en grande partie aux réformes présentées comme leur oeuvre propre.'[36]

It was noted also that the MDRM's overall aim had been modified from that of total independence to a more acceptable position of independence within the French Union. In this way, the MDRM was deemed to have stolen the programme of its rival, the equally new *Parti Démocratique Malgache* (PDM) and beaten its candidate, Ravelojaona, on his own platform. The point for the administration was the primacy of political effect over doctrinal substance: the MDRM was still understood to be a separatist party, and Ravoahangy in particular was believed capable of winning, whatever he proclaimed.

The conclusion drawn from this epitomization of charisma and popular support – the Malagasy press inevitably drew parallels with Gandhi – was that Raseta and Ravoahangy were to be stopped. But how? Aside from administrative action, the obvious means was by exploiting a viable opposition. And yet neither the PDM nor a third party, the *Mouvement Social et Politique Malgache* (MSM), controlled by the Catholic missions, was capable of rivalling the MDRM, despite, or perhaps because of, the fact that these two parties gathered together the majority of the (pro-French) Malagasy intellectual elite.[37] In the wake of the May 1946 elections, a newly formed fourth political party offered potential as the desired counterweight to the MDRM. The *Parti des Déshérités Malgaches* (PADESM), formed in June 1946 by a group of non-Merina intellectuals, aimed to provide a counterweight to Merina power by rallying together the *côtiers* and the *hova mainty*, that is the 'black' (*mainty*) descendants of the Merina kingdom's slave caste. The success of the MDRM had certainly reawakened fears of Merina revival, especially given Ravoahangy's royal forebears, and this was to be a significant factor for social unrest in the months to come. At the same time, PADESM's programme was calculated to appeal to French administrators remembering their gallieni. In July 1946, the *Direction des Affaires Malgaches* noted only the other parties' unease with regard to the newcomer.[38] In a subsequent, much fuller report to Moutet (undated but pre-dating the October 1946 elections), the DAP outlined the role to be allotted the PADESM in the French scheme of things. The importance of the *hova mainty* in the Malagasy ethnic equation was, the report stated, that they constituted two-thirds of the population of the High Plateaux and represented Madagascar's democratic element; that they had clear ethnic affinities with the *côtiers*, and the same aspirations: and that they could develop into a powerful socio-political movement. Although not spelt out explicitly, the administration's role was seen as instrumental in promoting the PADESM:

> Le 'Parti des Déshérités' peut devenir un atout unique pour maintien de la cause française; il convient done de ne pas laisser échapper une occasion qui ne se représenterait pas. Il semble que le Gouvernement local ait *le devoir d'appuyer en toutes circonstances* un parti qui désire une évolution de Madagascar certes, mais dans le cadre de la souveraineté française et ce qui compte aussi dans le cadre de sentiments affectueux envers la mère-patrie.[39]

It was further noted that the party received no directives from any metropolitan party (although the PCF, which was the only metropolitan party really at issue, had initially encouraged the new party), and that while it would need to be closely watched, there seemed little reason to doubt its pro-French tendencies. It should therefore be trusted, not that the French had an overwhelming choice in the matter. While the files contain no evidence to support allegations that the PADESM was a French creature, therefore, the report sets out the rationale for the official heavy-handed support which the party was to receive in the forthcoming elections.[40]

In the few months that followed the elections, as a new constitutional draft was debated in Paris and fresh elections were prepared, the administration's efforts in Madagascar were taken up with parrying the MDRM and seeking to stem a tide of violence sweeping the island. De Coppet was punctilious in maintaining cordial relations with Raseta and Ravoahangy, before their departure for Paris. Raseta's attitude was resolutely placatory: in a speech in Tananarive, he exhorted his public to achieve true independence by staying calm and working hard.[41] Once in the capital, the two *députés* continued their campaign for acceptance of their proposals for Madagascar and for the French Union as a whole. Drafts of a blueprint for the French Union based on the model of the United Nations were thus presented, not only to Laurentie, but also to Ho Chi Minh and Pham Van Dong, in France for the Franco-Vietnamese conference at Fontainebleau. While Ho's response is not recorded, Laurentie engaged in critical but friendly correspondence with the document's authors, Jacques and Raymond Rabemananjara, whom he also entertained to dinner. In ironic counterpoint to this display of good manners on all sides, the administration was increasingly preoccupied with the growing numbers of violent incidents including rowdy demonstrations, friction between Senegalese and Malagasy *tirailleurs*, strikes, attacks on isolated French and Malagasy officials, murders, raids on arms supplies, and so on. De Coppet's response to many such incidents was to report to Paris that they had no bearing on the political situation. On Laurentie's instructions, however, the DAP kept a file of these incidents, and in August 1946 advised de Coppet that, though individual incidents might not form part of a campaign of violence, they were nonetheless inspired by political agitation, and in turn had an impact on the political stability of the colony. At this stage Paris only issued a standard exhortation for stern measures and great vigilance on the part of the administration.[42] One milestone passed without serious incident, however: demonstrations and calls for independence by the MDRM on 6 August 1946, the fiftieth anniversary of French colonization, did not lead to the disturbances feared by the administration.[43]

The decisive switch in official attitudes towards the MDRM was triggered by the November 1946 elections which brought a third electoral 'defeat' for the administration in barely more than a year, with the re-election of Raseta and Ravoahangy and the election of a third MDRM *député*, Jacques Rabemananjara, in the newly created Eastern constituency. (As noted above, the new electoral boundaries meant that Ravoahangy's constituency was now that of the High Plateaux.) The results were not quite the foregone conclusion that might have been expected, except in the case of Ravoahangy's re-election at the hands of the Merina. Thus Raseta's re-election was at the second round only, with a majority of only 2,731; Rabemananjara, a Betsimisaraka fighting on his home territory with Merina support from the MDRM machine, also brought off a comfortable but not overwhelming victory.

Quite apart from the results, however, the campaign alone generated sufficient acrimony to determine the battle-lines for the political struggles which underpinned the insurrection four months later. This acrimony was all the more marked for being determined primarily by the party structure which for the first time opposed MDRM candidates and those of the newly mobilized PADESM. The administration could now point to formal, institutionalized evidence of the *hova/côtier* divide. On the one hand, the election of Raseta in particular brought appeals from intellectuals and dignitaries of the majority non-Merina populations on the West coast. They described intimidation by MDRM electoral officers and hired thugs and the threats of reprisals when a Malagasy government took over in a promised near future, and they protested at the plain fact of a Merina elected primarily by Merina 'immigrants'. The defeated PADESM candidate, Totolehibe, even called for Raseta's disqualification.[44] On the other hand, Raseta countercharged with allegations of official support for the Sakalava Totolehibe; Ravoahangy and Rabemananjara similarly raised objections to their treatment by officials and the privileges accorded supposed 'official' candidates.[45] Indeed, Laurentie discouraged Moutet from pursuing the calls for Raseta's disqualification on precisely these grounds, arguing that Totolehibe could all too easily be presented as an official candidate or one at least enjoying official favour; as he suggested, the evidence for such charges could readily be found in reports from Tananarive.[46]

Official policy in the four-month interlude between the November elections and the outbreak of the insurrection was increasingly a matter of crisis management rather than active policy-making, as the administration sought to interpret – in an increasingly critical light – the actions of the MDRM while simultaneously dealing with the mounting violence in Madagascar. It must also be viewed against the wider backdrop of metropolitan and imperial crisis. What, for example, was the impact of the political vacuum which followed the elections in France? As the parties of France's 'tripartite' coalition (SFIO, MRP, PCF) struggled over more than a month to form an acceptable government, two substantial briefings were prepared for the Government by the DAP over the signature of a caretaker Minister and addressed to two politically neutralized Presidents of the GPRF. The first of these was to the outgoing Prime Minister, Georges Bidault (MRP), whose under-developed interest in Madagascar had been stirred by a veritable oath of fealty received from a group of (non-Merina) dignitaries in Tuléar, and was dated 25 November, four days before the resignation of his Government. The second was addressed to Léon Blum on 12 December, the day of his nomination as

Prime Minister and four days before he formed an all-Socialist interim cabinet. To Bidault at least, Moutet's officials took the comparatively easy option of restating a bland official position:

> C'est au moment où nous adoptons à Madagascar la politique la plus libérale que certains en abusent dans un intérêt de parti. Je pense que nous irons assez loin dans l'octroi de libertés politiques, mais toujours dans le respect des intérêts de la France et de tous les groupements ethniques de la Grande-Ile.[47]

Blum's briefing was more complete but even more formulaic, as its authors set out the steps already taken to stem the progress of Merina nationalism.[48] Quite possibly this restatement of classic doctrine was an attempt to present the veteran Socialist Blum with a *fait accompli*, rather than risk an embarrassing and time-consuming re-examination of the assumptions underlying policy in Madagascar. This might be compared with the rather more concrete and irrevocable *fait accompli* which was being prepared on the ground in Indochina.

Insofar as a coherent policy could be delineated to Blum, it now reflected a fairly comprehensive fusion of the Brazzaville and Gallieni models. If intentions are counted as well as actual accomplishments, this policy included the creation of territorial assemblies organized on ethnic lines, the establishment of provincial training centres for non-Merina recruits to the administration (the first of which was due to open in Tuléar on 1 January), the encouragement of Merina 'repatriation' to Imerina, the counter-propaganda measures by which the Malagasy press had been tamed (which included the arrest of militant journalists in May 1946). In practice, the administration was most obviously committed to a continuation and intensification of its contest with the MDRM, now cast as the villain of the piece. Alongside a rather optimistic forecast of falling MDRM support based on the November 1946 results, the letter to Blum provided a revealingly frank, indeed even exaggerated, assessment of the causes of the party's success: sound organization, even sounder finances, and authority and political astuteness on the part of its leaders. Although Communist Party support was not ruled out, it was recognized that Merina supporters were prosperous enough to keep the party afloat, and that the *députés*' authority was self-generating. Frankness was marred by the usual ethnic blind-spot, however: while accepting the astute move by which a Betsimisiraka had been chosen to contest the Eastern constituency, and despite the dismal results obtained by PADESM candidates, such as Totolehibe, the DAP still stressed the value to France of 'ethnicity'. Totolehibe, it was believed, could have beaten Raseta if only he had shown more personality and commitment in his campaign, and thus gained more support than the 'spontaneous' support of his fellow Sakalava.[49] Although no explicit parallels were drawn with Indochina's precipitate descent into war over these same few weeks, the letter to Blum repeated one of the fallacies – or at best over-simplifications – of post-Brazzaville policy-making in the Far East, according to which it was believed official liberalism could be reinforced by a show of military force. As Moutet's official argued:

> Il ne saurait, certes, être question d'envisager l'utilisation de la force, mais à mon sens la présence à Madagascar d'unités métropolitaines douées

d'un armement moderne et réparties dans les principaux centres de
l'Ile, d'avions de type récent, d'une unité navale importante en permanence
dans les eaux malgaches, épaulerait efficacement la politique de ralliement
autour de notre Drapeau.[50]

This, it was suggested, would reassure the settlers and, more importantly, allow the
administration to maintain a liberal stance without its generous actions being interpreted as signs of weakness. Even without a display of military might, however,
officials would be expected not to remain passive in the forthcoming battles for
influence.

These careful formulae pointed to an increasingly vigorous and practical use of
force and administrative *fiat*. This took two forms. First, officials continued to take an
interventionist line in the remaining elections, this time by the drastic expedient of re-
writing the rules. Elections to the five provincial assemblies in January 1947 returned
MDRM majorities in all but the Northern province of Majunga and the exclusion of all
other parties in the Tamatave and Tananarive assemblies. The official response was to
rule that members of the more important Representative Assembly would be elected by
a single college, thus ensuring an anti-MDRM majority alliance of Europeans and the
PADESM. A repeat of this result in elections to the Council of the Republic (the Fourth
Republic's Upper House), was only prevented by the direct intervention of Blum's
successor as Prime Minister, Paul Ramadier.

As if this step was not itself a clear enough indication of official antipathy towards
the MDRM, secondly, official electoral tactics were accompanied by moves to remove
the party from the political scene altogether. The justification for this lay in the administration's attribution of blame to the MDRM for the continuing disintegration of law and
order on the island. There is no doubt as to the seriousness of the various explosions of
violence reported back to Paris, nor for that matter of the involvement of individual
MDRM party members and officials. The pattern of violence reported at various points
on the island over a period stretching back to June 1946 was also compellingly consistent: typically, local administrators reported the influx of MDRM propagandists
leading to attacks on local officials, on detachments of the native auxiliary militia and on
PADESM supporters, and to more general lawlessness, such as cattle-rustling. As noted
above, these incidents had been played down in the period preceding the November
1946 elections. Thereafter, a new note of urgency may be detected. Thus, in his analysis
of events at Ifanadiana, de Coppet presented two overlapping interpretations, both
indicting the MDRM: the events were either the doing of overzealous local agents,
or they were overseen by national party leaders. In favour of the first diagnosis it was
noted that the MDRM's campaign was more effective in more backward regions (that is,
notwithstanding the party's supposed identification with the Merina cause), thus feeding
on and intensifying local unrest. The alternative hypothesis addressed the longer-term
aims of the MDRM:

> . . . la pensée et les tractations qui ont présidé à sa création ont largement
> dépassé le champ d'une simple préparation aux luttes électorales à venir.
> De là à penser qu'il s'est agi de dresser un véritable complot contre la
> souveraineté française en créant une situation qui la mette en péril, il n'y a
> qu'un pas.[51]

These two hypotheses overlapped in the suggestion that local leaders were forcing the pace, leaving the national leadership with the choice between coming out into the open or losing face by disavowal. But the conclusion was clear in either case: de Coppet now called for the evidence to be drawn together which would allow him to set about disbanding the MDRM. Laurentie's hand-written instruction on this report gave the go-ahead for this process on 5 January 1947.

III

Given the outbreak of insurrection at the end of March 1947, which effectively pre-empted any French moves towards disbanding the MDRM, it is impossible to assess the impact on policy of official attitudes in early 1947. We can only guess whether or not the administration, faced also with full-scale war against the Viet Minh in Indochina, would have taken the political and military risks involved in banning the MDRM, without the spur of insurrection. In the light of the foregoing, however, two conclusions may be drawn.

The first is that the rationale for official liberalism on the Brazzaville model had been discarded for Madagascar by January 1947 at the very latest. The outward form remained, at least: in a further letter to Blum, Gaston Defferre, standing in for Moutet while the latter inspected the battlelines in Indochina, could still define emancipation as the goal of French policy. However, this goal was not to be achieved at the pace demanded by the MDRM, nor at the expense of French authority or of French prestige in the eyes of the masses, especially the *côtiers* who had placed their trust in their French protectors.[52] This 'official version' now worked to discredit the MDRM at every turn, even on their strongest ground: the party's extensive charges of official electoral malpractice were shown to be groundless; worse, they were described as a deliberate ploy to wear down the administration with the sheer weight of protests. It was also clear that the Brazzaville-inspired fiction of political and legal equality for France's new category of Overseas Citizens was wearing very thin. Great emphasis was placed by de Coppet on ensuring legal impartiality in proceedings against trouble-makers. Regrettably, this led to unacceptable delays as suspects released on bail awaited trial. A letter from the DAP in February 1947 assured de Coppet that, the separation of powers notwithstanding, his own powers to issue orders to the Procurator-General in Tananarive were considerable. As the letter explained, the rapidity of the legal process was paramount when dealing with less highly evolved groups for whom punishment effectively makes an example of malefactors only when it immediately follows the crime.[53] One final factor may be mentioned here: events in Indochina were portrayed as a step in the right direction. As de Coppet argued in a cable forwarded to Moutet in Saigon, the reaffirmation of French sovereignty in Indochina could not fail to have a positive effect on the Malagasy masses.[54]

The second conclusion that may be drawn concerns the readiness with which the French administration thus felt able to interpret the insurrection itself. Indeed, rather than coming as a 'bolt from the blue', the actions undertaken against French military and administrative posts in the night of 29–30 March 1947 were seen as the culmination of almost a year of unrest and violence. In a sense, therefore, *mutatis mutandis*, the French were merely being consistent in applying the same interpretation. With the dubious benefit of hindsight, therefore, officials now took the next logical step in their interpretation of the insurrection. Thus, an early report, dated 2 April, suggested that the events of 29–30 March had been preceded, perhaps even prepared, by an apparently coherent series of events. Looking back, the author was able to detect a pattern of escalating violence, in which, for instance, the incidents recorded in the first three months of the year had already shown symptoms of incipient insurrection. The degree of tendentious speculation that passed as analysis in the administration's haste to understand what was happening in Madagascar may be gauged from the report's conclusion, here quoted in full:

> C'est en effet sur le MDRM qu'en toute objectivité l'attention est appelée.
>
> Cette technique des incidents préparatoires et des foyers multiples d'agitation qui a été mise en oeuvre à Madagascar écarte l'idée de mouvements sporadiques et conduit à penser que seul un parti organisé a pu créer la situation à laquelle nous devons faire face.
>
> Une autre question se pose: dans quelle measure les Nationalistes malgaches ne suivent-ils pas les événements d'Indochine et ne sont-ils pas en liaison avec les Viet-Namiens?[55]

It is not the purpose of this article to consider in detail the French response to the insurrection in the months and years that followed. None the less, the line of argument presented in this report must be appreciated in the light of what happened next, in particular the raising of the three Malagasy *députés'* parliamentary immunity, their arrest, trial and imprisonment. Could the administration think of no other interpretation either of the period preceding the insurrection or of the insurrection itself? In particular, little mention is made of the PANAMA or JINA, and this author has found no official discussion of the possibility that the MDRM's organization and leadership at national or provincial levels might have been guided by distinct organizations, including even the old networks of the PCRM which, recruited in rather unorthodox manner on the basis of existing social groups rather than individual membership, had then provided the embryonic structure of JINA. At the very least, officials might have drawn an analogy with the real domestic issue of Communist entryism and infiltration (*noyautage*) of French institutions.

What seems certain is that the dossier built up against the MDRM by the French served their purposes very well in the immediate aftermath of the insurrection's outbreak. The official depiction of a monolithic MDRM dedicated to Merina restoration, and hence the self-fulfilling prophecy of MDRM disloyalty, allowed the French not only to find a justification for crushing rebellion, but also to defeat their most troublesome political opponent. Some inkling of the longer-term consequences of this action was evinced by de Coppet in a dispatch to Paris in August, in which he presented the arguments for and against banning the PDM, the MDRM's defeated electoral rival, which was now showing every sign of taking up the MDRM's banner of independence. As he argued, breaking with the PDM, in the absence of the MDRM, would mean breaking with an important part of the Merina elite. This would leave the French with no other resource than a racial policy, but without the counterbalance of a consensal political and administrative structure based on Brazzaville-style federalism. As he argued, racial policy should never simply pit one race against another; but the circumstances developing in Madagascar pointed increasingly to precisely such an outcome.[56] In the present context, this argument may be glossed with the observation that the French colonial administration had thus unwittingly succeeded in creating the very circumstances which its policy had been designed to prevent. Far from decapitating the forces of supposed Merina imperialism, the ill-conceived hybrid of the Brazzaville and Gallieni models of policy had served merely to disrupt the political life of the island and to impede the development of a mature and coherent Malagasy national movement.

Amongst the innumerable crises, emergencies, police actions, counter-insurgency campaigns and plain wars which marked the decolonization process after 1945, Madagascar serves as an instructive example of colonial initiative pre-empted by a direct, violent challenge to colonial rule. The breakdown of French policy studied here, over the brief period which led from the 1944 Brazzaville Conference to the outbreak of insurrection in March 1947, demonstrates many of the contradictions faced by various colonial administrations after 1945. Can one reconcile a modern analysis of colonial realities with the received wisdom of colonial tradition? Can one recognize nationalist aspirations without accepting nationalist calls for independence? And, more generally, can one square the obvious need for wholesale imperial and colonial reform with the desire for imperial continuity? In the French case, these questions were all the more pressing for the fact that officials were working against the background of profound domestic crisis, which meant that France had a pressing nationalist agenda of her own. Thus, allowance had always to be made for the steady leaching away of political authority from the brand new but fatally flawed regime of the Fourth Republic. The outbreak of insurrection in March 1947 was a significant contributory factor in the crisis culminating two months later in the expulsion of Communists from the Ramadier cabinet, which marked the onset of France's domestic Cold War. Madagascar thus took its place in the canon of French colonial disasters which were to lead to the downfall of a Republic and the end of an Empire.

Notes

1   The debate surrounding this controversial estimation of Malagasy casualties is discussed in what remains the standard work on the insurrection, J. Tronchon, *L'insurrection malgache de 1947* (Paris and Fianarantsoa, 1974, repr. 1986), 70–4.

2   F. Furedi, 'Creating a Breathing Space: The Political Management of Colonial Emergencies', in R. Holland (ed.), *Emergencies and Disorder in the European Empires After 1945* (London, 1994), 94.

3   Bureau d'Etudes, 3e séance, 20 March 1945, Archives d'Outre-Mer (AOM), AP/214bis (Affaires politiques file, box 214bis; a further number in references indicates a dossier).

4   M. J. Shipway, 'The Brazzaville Conference, 1944: Origins of a Policy . . . and a Myth', in *Quinquereme*, 13 (1990–91), 53–70.

5   Conférence de presse (Directeurs de Journaux), 14 Sept. 1945, Archives Nationales (AN), 72AJ539 (Laurentie papers, box 539); see also the reporting of an earlier, less confidential briefing, in *Le Monde*, 15 Sept. 1945.

6   Programme général de la Conférence [de Brazzaville], AOM, AP/2288.

7   M. J. Shipway, 'France's "crise coloniale" and the breakdown of policy making in Indochina, 1944–1947', unpubl. D.Phil. thesis (University of Oxford, 1992), 44–47, 102ff.

8   H. Deschamps, *Histoire de Madagascar* (Paris, 1st edn. 1960); H. Deschamps and P. Chauvet (eds.), *Gallieni pacificateur, écrits et discours du général Gallieni* (Paris, 1949).

9   Except in direct quotations, and in reference to the so-called *hova/côtier* question, this article employs the conventional term Merina to refer to the people as a whole. Their land is Imerina (sometimes rendered in French as *l'Emyrne*, though the more usual term was the *Hauts-Plateaux*, covering Imerina and parts of Betsileo-land to the South). The capital of Imerina, Antananarivo, was universally referred to as Tananarive in the colonial period. The term *hova* more properly designates those Merina free persons not of the *andriana* (or nobility). The term *côtiers* embraces the other peoples of Madagascar, officially seventeen in number (e.g. Betsileo, Betsimisaraka, Sakalava, qqv., though Betsileo were sometimes counted as *hova*) and united only perhaps by not being Merina.

10 *Vy, vato, sakelika*, meaning iron, stone, branching.

11 Stephen Ellis, *The Rising of the Red Shawls: A Rising in Madagascar 1895–1899* (Cambridge, 1986), and *Un complot colonial à Madagascar: L'affaire Rainandrianampandry* (Paris, 1990).

12 Tronchon, *L'insurrection malgache*, 13.

13 'Situation politique à Madagascar, Exposé fait par M. le Haut-Commissaire à la conférence des Hauts-Commissaires en février 1947', in ibid., 242–8. Governors-General were renamed High Commissioners in Jan. 1946, at the same time as the Ministry of Colonies was renamed Ministry of Overseas France.

14 Legentilhomme's original proposal is absent from the files, but cf Tel. no 212, Saint-Mart to Colonies (Algiers), 10 July 1943; No. 2515/CAB, Legentilhomme to Colonies (Algiers); and 'Note sur le projet portant réorganisation administrative de la colonie de Madagascar et dépendances', 10 July 1943: AOM, AP/2409.

15 Tel. no. 154/CIR/AP. Colonies à Dakar, Douala, Brazzaville, Tananarive, ref HL/og, 24 March 1945, AOM, Tels/888; and see Saint-Mart's reply. Tel.no. 584, Tananarive to Colonies, 6 April 1945, AOM, Tels/895.

16 Tel., Colonies to Tananarive, 10 April 1945, AP/3575.

17 Programme général de la Conférence [de Brazzaville], AOM, AP/2288; Herriot's warning in the National Constituent Assembly in Aug. 1946, quoted in A. Grosser, *La politique extérieure de la IVe République* (Paris, 1961), 250.

18 Rapport de la Commission chargé de l'étude de la représentation des territories d'Outre-Mer à la future Assemblée Constituante, AOM, AP/214/III.

19 See Laurentie's NOTE au MINISTRE au sujet des élections coloniales, ref. HL.CM, 4 Aug. 1945, AOM, Cab (Dossier du Cabinet du Ministre), 10; and his correspondence with his liberal ally, Aimé Bayardelle, Governor-General at Brazzaville, in AN, 72AJ539.

20 G. Wright, *The Reshaping of French Democracy* (London, 1950), 204–5.

21 Rapport politique mensuel, 15 juillet-15 août 1945, AOM, AP/3257/10.

22 Note pour M. le Directeur des Affaires Politiques, DAP 1er bureau, 17 July 1947, AOM, AP/3271/2.

23 Tel. no. 574, Colalg/AP1. 1 April 1944, AOM, Tels/850; Saint-Mart's reply, Tel. no. 447, 12 April 1944, Tels/868.

24 Tronchon, *L'insurrection malgache*, 24–25. For their more public role, see for example Tel. no. 125 Tananarive to Colonies 20 Jan. 1945, AOM, Tels/895.

25 Tel. no. 125, Tananarive to Colonies, 20 Jan. 1945, AOM, Tels/895.

26 Tronchon, *L'insurrection malgache*. 23–4.

27 Rapport politique mensuel, 15 juillet-15 août 1945, loc. cit.

28   Note au Ministre, a/s/ Elections législatives, no. 15.374, 17 Dec. 1945, AOM, AP/936.

29   Ministre des Colonies to Président de l'Assemblée Nationale Constituante, no. 19.719, 21 Dec. 1945; and covering note signed Chimier; AOM, AP/935.

30   Note pour M le Directeur du Cabinet, no. 3269, 18 March 1946, AOM, AP/3271/2.

31   Note personnelle pour Monsieur le Ministre. 'Situation politique des colonies au début de juin 1946', 4 June 1946, AOM, AP/214bis/V.

32   Note pour M. le Ministre, à l'attention spéciale de M. le Directeur du Cabinet, AN, 72AJ540.

33   Biography in Tronchon, *L'insurrection malgache*, 217.

34   De Coppet to Min. de la France d'Outre-Mer (FOM), no. 251-CFC, 8 June 1946.

35   Haut-Commissaire, Tananarive (DAM 1er bureau) to FOM, no. 174-DAM, 5 June 1946, AOM, AP/3257/5. See Grosser, *La politique extérieure*, 247–51.

36   De Coppet to FOM, no. 230-CF, 3 July 1946, AOM, AP/3257/5.

37   De Coppet to FOM, no. 258-CF/DAM, 10 July 1946.

38   De Coppet to FOM, no. 258-CF/DAM, 10 July 1946, loc. cit.

39   Note pour Monsieur le Ministre, Objet: Parti des Déshérités Malgaches, Secret, AOM, AP/3272/2.

40   Cf. Moutet's marginal comment, that the report reflects the 'Conclusion personnelle du rédacteur de la note', loc. cit.

41   De Coppet to FOM, no. 250-C, 8 June 1946, and no. 230-CF, 3 July 1946, AOM, AP/2357/5.

42   DAP, 1er bureau, to Tananarive, 23 Aug. 1946, AOM, AP/3257/6.

43   Tel. no. 1906, de Coppet to FOM, 8 Aug. 1946, AOM, AP/3257/9.

44   De Coppet to Moutet, no. 563-CFAP, 16 Dec. 1946, AOM, AP/1076.

45   Qqv., various tels, in AOM, AP/3257/5.

46   Note au Ministre, Invalidation de M. Raseta, no. 91, 4 Jan. 1947, AOM, AP/1076.

47   Moutet to President G. P. R. F., no. 143, Secret, AOM, AP/3257/13.

48   Minister FOM to President G. P. R. F., no. 247 Secret, 12 Dec. 1946, AOM, AP/3257/13.

49   S. Tønnesson, *1946: Le declenchement de la guerre d'Indochine* (Harmattan, 1987).

50   Ibid.

51   De Coppet to FOM, no. 564-CFAP, 16 Dec. 1946, loc. cit.

52   Defferre to Président G.P.R.F., no. 3, 3 Jan. 1947, AOM, AP/3257/4.

53   Minister FOM (DAP) to HC Tananarive, no. 104, 2 Feb. 1947.

54   Tel. no. 3741, 28 Dec. 1946, quoting de Coppet's no. 2802, AN, 72AJ540.

55   Note, 'Aggravation de la situation politique à Madagascar', 2 April 1947, AOM, AP/3257/1.

56   HC, Tananarive (DAM) to FOM (DAP), no. 453 CF/AP, 8 Aug. 1947, AOM, AP/3257/8.

Chapter 5

James D. Le Sueur

DECOLONIZING 'FRENCH UNIVERSALISM'

Reconsidering the impact of the Algerian War on French intellectuals

Introduction

MORE THAN ANY OTHER colonial confrontation, the French-Algerian War (1954–62) forcibly demonstrated North Africa's impact on a major European power. The war in Algeria triggered a series of events that toppled the Fourth Republic, affected intellectual life and destroyed long-standing myths about the universality of French culture. On a grand scale, therefore, the decolonization of Algeria forced a fundamental reconsideration of politics, the status of intellectuals and the role of French culture in the world. This reconsideration had, in fact, become so extreme that by the conclusion of the war in March 1962, the French nation was suffering from an unprecedented identity crisis. In short, the French-Algerian War and the process of decolonization disrupted France and French perceptions of France on a level not seen since the German Occupation and, one can argue, even since the French Revolution. Unquestionably, France and Algeria continue to feel the repercussions of this 'uncivil war', and historians have only just begun to delve seriously into this troubled past. Recent brazen admissions of torture by French generals such as Paul Aussaresses and Jacques Massu have renewed national and international debates over how historians of modern France and the French government ought to proceed.[1]

Due to the severity and the importance of the Algerian crisis, there is a sense of urgency to research on the French-Algerian War because it continues to affect France and Algeria, and by extension Europe and North Africa. Furthermore, because the legacy of decolonization is seldom effortlessly forgotten, memory of the war will continue to pass from national history into national mythology. This is most certainly the case with regard to Algeria because the legacy of the war and decolonization reverberate in contemporary debates over historiography, language, ethnicity, immigration, gender relations, political ideology, morality, torture, violence and religion. The Moroccan-born novelist and writer Tahar Ben Jelloun best characterizes the extent of this legacy in his recent book *French Hospitality: Racism and North African Immigration*:

Between France and Algeria, a memory still survives. But it is not a healthy one. It is a wounded part of a shared history that has not managed to accept reality. Neither the war of liberation nor the independence that followed have really been recorded in the great book of French history. A kind of amnesia affects that part of the story of decolonisation, which has been stated but not assimilated into France's social and political awareness.[2]

For political historians of France, the French-Algerian War is thus one of the most important moments of the twentieth century. French intellectuals' responses to the war and to the changes it brought became such a strident feature of everyday life in the *métropole* that it would be impossible to present an accurate portrait of the post-World War II era without weaving the colours of the Algerian debates into France's social fabric. However, despite the seminal place the war and decolonization occupy in the tapestry of modern France, a proper assessment of its impact on the life-world of intellectuals has suffered much neglect. In part, this is attributable to a noticeable tendency among many historians of twentieth-century France (until recently) to marginalize colonial history, or to write the history of French decolonization following a core–periphery model. This core–periphery model tends to view decolonization through the lens of convenient notions of colonial hegemony – Eurocentric by nature and superficial by deed. This lens projects France's image onto the passive colonies, as receptacles of French ideas, politics and problems. Some efforts have been made to correct this imbalance, such as Robert Malley's *The Call from Algeria* (1996). This chapter is meant to complement and extend this and other praiseworthy efforts to reverse the optics in the writing of history about Algeria and France.

In many ways, however, this chapter is unconventional. In it I will illustrate how the French-Algerian War transcended military and political concerns but its goal is not to illuminate France's impact on Algeria and the Maghreb but rather the war's impact on French intellectuals. Ultimately, this means that we must be prepared to see colonialism and decolonization as a dialogical process, where historians chart the pathways of communication between two or more interlocutors (or communities), rather than as a monologue where subservient and mute colonies listen to the humdrum voice of European colonial powers. Having said that, I must issue a caveat here: this article does not focus on the relationship between Algerian intellectuals and French intellectuals. Rather, it investigates the relationship between the international dimensions of the war in Algeria and French intellectuals' domestic politics. Specifically, it will demonstrate how the war determined, undermined and, in many cases, set the parameters of debates in France over national identity and intellectual legitimacy for French intellectuals.

In short, I believe that an understanding of the period of decolonization – especially the decolonization of French Algeria, which after all was the only French overseas possession actually administered (from 1848) as if it were three regular French provinces – should provide historians with a useful vantage point from which to view one of the most important questions – if not the most important question of the modern period – the question of identity. It is no accident that the decolonization of French Algeria triggered a fundamental re-evaluation of French (especially French intellectual) identity.

By 1954, when the war of liberation began, after 124 years of colonization, the French population in Algeria numbered almost 1 million, the Muslim population about

8 million. The transition away from European colonial hegemony was especially poignant for France. More than other European states, decolonization threw metropolitan France into severe political and economic crises. The reasons for this are clear: its colonial 'superpower' status had become part and parcel with French national identity; France had a large settler population in Algeria; the military was still reeling from its recent, stinging defeat in Indo-China; and many French politicians and intellectuals continued to insist on France's civilizing mission and the universalism of French culture. For over a hundred years French colonial theorists had applied enormous pressure on the national community to affirm that civilizing mission and to ensure that colonialism and universalism would be the measure of French national eminence. This, of course, would have grave consequences during the era of decolonization.

The importance of decolonization is no doubt attributed to the fact that the process of decolonization overlapped with (and perhaps even triggered) the issues posed by postmodernism. Decolonization – as a political cultural and intellectual phenomenon – highlighted the ambiguities and strains in the traditional boundaries between the observer and the observed. In other words, decolonization upset the colonial imbalance and threw the European world-view into chaos. As Martin Evans explains:

> Decolonisation revealed the world as fluid, decomposing, recomposing and changing and destroyed the historical certainties that underpinned the imperialist preconceptions of the world. The emergence of liberation movements in Indochina and North Africa turned the colonial world upside down, and revealed its myths as historical and cultural, rather than natural and eternal. Suddenly, colonised peoples, whom imperialism had confined to the margins of history as inert objects, showed themselves to be dynamic subjects capable of overthrowing French colonialism.[3]

In other words, the effects of decolonization on the French intellectuals' conceptions of selfhood very closely resembled the transformative effects that modernity once had on pre-modern conceptions of the identity.

In order to underscore why decolonization was so important for France, I would like to consider a claim Charles Taylor (1992) has made in his recent book, *Multiculturalism and the 'Politics of Recognition'*.[4] According to Taylor, modern conceptions of personal identity emerged following the collapse of the Old Regime's rigid and fixed social categories. In other words, Taylor locates the emergence of the modern self at the crisis point when the static categories of social ranking gave way to the pressures of modernity. It is possible to apply the mechanics of this same theory to the decomposition of the colonial world. Because colonialism implied relatively static categories of identity (with some important exceptions), there was a stable sense of the French national identity *vis-à-vis* Algeria during the colonial era. There were also pragmatic aspects of this identity. For example, in Algeria, all but a handful of elite Muslims were literally considered second-class citizens. Europeans, in the same French 'provinces', were legally and socially 'superior'. It follows, using Taylor's remarks about identity, that decolonization – like modernity in Europe – would force a fundamental reconsideration of the idea of self, both in France and in Algeria.

It also follows that French intellectuals reflecting on this changing identity ushered in by decolonization would pay a heavy price for theorizing about French and Algerian identity during the war. For example, in an interview I conducted with the French philosopher, Paul Ricoeur, he stated that the French-Algerian War was enormously important for French intellectuals because it unleashed a crisis of French identity. But why did it do so? Because the war and the whole process of decolonization challenged the seminal assumption about French culture. In Ricoeur's words, the war forced an 'honest coming to terms' with the fact that French culture was not 'universal'.[5] In a very profound sense, decolonization in North Africa set the terms by which the entire French nation (and especially intellectuals) could adjust to a scaled-down post-colonial world devoid of France's civilizing mission.

It must also be noted that, on the political level, the French – especially the intellectuals – seldom agreed with one another anyway, and the French Fourth Republic was exceptionally fragile when the war broke out on 1 November 1954. Struggles among communists, non-communists, Marxists, non-Marxists, liberals and non-liberals were commonplace within the patchwork of French national politics. The Vichy purges of the Nazi collaborators and the beginnings of the Cold War only served to accentuate these debates. However, struggle or no struggle, one idea in which many French intellectuals continued to believe explicitly or implicitly was *French* universalism. The notion of French universalism also formed the bedrock of French colonial policy, especially in Algeria. It was this universalism (a product of the French Revolution and the Enlightenment), ironically, that, according to historians, allowed many intellectuals to waver uncomfortably on the Algerian question because French colonialism in Algeria simultaneously contradicted and affirmed universalist intentions and ideals.

While French and Algerian intellectuals rethought the question of national and personal identity, tried to comprehend the loss of *French* universalism, and attempted to understand the national significance of the demise of French power overseas, the French-Algerian War also presented them with a unique opportunity to re-assert intellectual legitimacy. At the very least the war opened doors to new paradigms of identity politics. After all, crisis can be a time of enormous productivity, and this was certainly the case for French intellectuals. The desire to reassert intellectual legitimacy was no doubt due to the fact that the war erupted at the precise moment when French intellectuals, especially the French left, realized that it was entering a period of crisis. Violence, identity and the question of intellectual legitimacy, therefore, forced intellectuals during the war to make a choice: either situate their privileged status as intellectuals within the new France, the post-colonial France, or attach their status as intellectuals to an empire in peril. Very few intellectuals (Jacques Soustelle is among the important exceptions) opted for the latter.[6]

To best demonstrate how the war in Algerian impacted French intellectuals, I have chosen to focus on two episodes of heightened intellectual and political activity during the war: the formation of the anti-colonial movement in 1955 called the Comité d'Action des Intellectuels contre la Poursuite de la Guerre en Afrique du Nord (hereafter referred to as the Comité) and the actions of a group of avant-garde intellectuals, the so-called 'Jeanson Network', accused of treason in 1960 for aiding the Front de Libération Nationale (FLN). I am aware that the Comité and the Jeanson Network do not speak for the totality and complexity of the war, and that Algerian voices are generally not present here, but I have selected these issues as important examples of how the decolonization of French Algeria conditioned debates among intellectuals over legitimacy and identity in

France. I have addressed the issue of the war's impact on Algerian intellectuals elsewhere.[7]

Anticolonialism and intellectual identity

On 5 November 1955, in the Salle Wagram (an important auditorium and meeting hall in Paris), the Comité was founded by Dionys Mascolo and Louis-René Des Forêts, Robert Antelme and Edgar Morin with this telling statement: 'In addressing ourselves against this war [in Algeria], we defend our own proper principles and liberties. The war in North Africa puts, in fact, the Republic in danger'.[8] Understanding that events in Algeria directly impacted political life in France, the Comité's four initiators wanted to assemble something similar to a federation of intellectuals which would fight against the colonial regime and underscore the group's independence from political parties.[9] Their success was astonishing. In a very short time, they succeeded in collecting the signatures of hundreds of writers, . . . artists (including André Breton) professors and journalists on their first manifesto.[10] The signers of the manifesto called for all other like-minded intellectuals and writers to join them in their 'just cause' and their struggle against repression, racism, blocked negotiations, and for the liberation of the continent of Africa.[11]

It was a force to be reckoned with, but soon after it was formed, the Comité's anticolonial agenda provoked a heated and thoughtful debate with Jacques Soustelle, the last governor general of Algeria (from 1955–56) about intellectual legitimacy. It was certainly no accident that Soustelle, the man who led the charge against this anticolonial Comité, was also one of France's preeminent anthropologists. Yet, as an anthropologist, Soustelle was incredibly Eurocentric and believed himself to incarnate the virtues of modern France. As an intellectual, Soustelle unquestionably privileged the French nation as a bearer of progress and civilization and made no apologies for it. Additionally, he believed that French technology, progress, science and rationality was superior to the Algerians' indigenous culture and religion, Islam, which he distrusted. Hence, in his press release issued on 7 November 1955, Soustelle challenged the anti-colonial Comité's right to speak for the Algerian nationalists' cause and to address the public as intellectuals. He followed this bold claim with a piece published in *Combat* on 26 November, which he poignantly called 'A Letter of an Intellectual to a Few Others'. This was not a response to the Comité per se but rather to a few intellectuals, whom Soustelle considered his intellectual peers.[12] Soustelle stated that as an academic he maintained his firm belief in the value of thought, research, and intellectual engagement. On the other hand, he argued, the Comité had substituted the politically 'vague passion-ate images' (of anticolonialism) for the rigors worthy of the intellectual's profession.[13] In addition, Soustelle continued, this (or any) anticolonial movement was bound to be careless and dishonest. Intellectuals, he wrote, were 'only justified if there behave in this instance and more than ever as intellectuals, that is to say with concern for honesty and clarity which are in some respects our mark'.

The following week on 3 December 1955, the Comité published its 'Response to the Governor General of Algeria'. In self-defence, the Comité characterized intellectuals as those who can use 'scientific rigor' in order to analyse a political situation as complicated as that of Algeria.[14] The Comité confronted Soustelle with his failure as a professional intellectual to see the French role in the conflict, for misrepresenting the historical dimensions of colonialism, and for escalating violence through his policy of repression. Furthermore, it claimed that Soustelle had forfeited his intellectual legitimacy by insisting that the conflict's violence originated with the Algerians.[15] Soustelle's silence on the reasons for Algerian nationalists' violence deformed the French intellectuals' identity. This was especially true since French intellectuals needed to be honest about colonialism: 'Who rapes, pillages, kills, massacres and tortures, in effect, in Algeria? The French authorities, isn't it?'[16]

The Comité therefore defended Algerians by distancing itself from the practices of French colonialism (especially those of Soustelle), and in an effort to drive the legitimacy wedge between colonialists and anticolonialists intellectuals, it opened the topic of torture. Evoking the wounds of the Nazi era, the Comité asserted that France had become a '*régime concentrationnaire*' in Algeria and this pervaded all levels of the French bureaucracy, police, and administration.[17] France needed to stop this fascist, colonial behaviour immediately. The Comité called on Soustelle (as a politician, but not as an intellectual) to commission an inquiry into the reported human rights' violations in Algeria. If this were not done, and since violence was systematic, the French military and civilians would be guilty of collective assassinations.[18] Only if Soustelle had the courage to face the horrors of colonialism, could the truth come out and could France and Algeria remain on good terms. The Comité stated, '[t]he path that we want to see our country take is neither abandonment nor war: it is that of co-operation in friendship and confidence between two peoples equal in responsibilities and dignity'.[19]

Naturally enough, Soustelle continued with business as usual. As governor general, Soustelle tried to implement his key policy, that of integration. Without question there was a deep-seated paternalism in Soustelle's policy and a very stable sense of French authority. Consider for a moment a 'declaration' he delivered on Radio-Algérie in January 1956, which illuminates his Panglossian view of French colonialism:

> For Algeria's own good, she must stay French. Algeria without France would mean poverty in countless ways. Who else in the world would replace what France gives to Algeria? Who else would replace the millions of francs that Algerian workers send from metropolitan France? Foreigners who encourage the rebellion or who give advice to France are interested in Algeria only because they want to drill oil wells and dig mines there, but they are not interested in building roads or constructing schools. I say that the separation of Algeria and France would be for Algeria, and especially for its Muslim people, the worst of all catastrophes. Secession is ruin.

And he continued:

> Neither directly nor indirectly, through whatever form it may be, will I allow secession. As long as I am responsible here, as long as I am in charge of Algeria, everyone, friends and adversaries alike, should know that I will not consent to anything which will distance Algeria from France.[20]

In other words, to Soustelle's understanding, France and Algeria could never be separated; colonialism was the best of all possible worlds; there was no political solution for

Algeria outside of France; the Algerian Muslims were, in a sense, capable of being true citizens because they were slowly being Westernized by French civilization.

As Soustelle asserted his role as a political leader to the Muslim and European population in Algeria, the epistolary polemic continued between him and the Comité. On 10 January 1956, the Comité re-issued its call for authentic intellectual activity by stating that when it came to colonialism, intellectuals and governmental authority were incompatible. It was therefore 'sadly comical' to engage in a polemic with a governor general masked in an intellectual's uniform.[21] And it was 'comical' because Soustelle had tried to preserve the respect due to him as an intellectual while simultaneously upholding the intellectually and morally dubious policies of the French government in North Africa – especially the practice of so-called concentration camps in Algeria; furthermore, it was 'sad' because this cost lives and paralleled attempts by the German Gestapo to cover its systematic tortures with propaganda. Soustelle and men like him simply corrupted France from within, which was as dangerous to the French nation as collaboration had been. Soustelle had become a propagandist, a vicious politician. That was all. Hence, by becoming a vehicle of an oppressive state, Soustelle forfeited his privileged status as a French intellectual. '[Soustelle had] not known how to remain an intellectual, according to the intellectuals', the Comité argued, because he had transgressed the border separating intellectuals from the state. In other words, Governor General Soustelle's role as a propagator of colonial warfare and a de facto defender of torture removed him categorically from the roster of legitimate French intellectuals even before he was replaced as governor general by the new resident minister Robert Lacoste in 1956.

In effect, the Comité had won the battle with Soustelle for the right of anti-colonialists to call themselves intellectuals. The Comité–Soustelle debate was one of the first important signs of how the war would affect the composition of intellectuals within the *métropole*. However, a simple question still remained. Could the Comité sustain its cohesion and its monopoly of intellectual legitimacy given its diversity of intellectual and political commitments? In other words, could the Comité sustain its cohesion and its monopoly of intellectual legitimacy given the political diversity of its constituency?

The limits of a unified anticolonialist movement were soon tested as the Comité's intellectuals dealt with divisions within Algerian nationalism itself. Choosing which Algerian nationalist group to support – the FLN or Messali Hadj's MNA (the Movement National Algérien) – undermined unity by raising the issue of whether the Comité as a group could determine orthodox anticolonialism.[22] Put differently, could the Comité legitimately endorse one form of Algerian nationalism over another? Inevitably, the question of Algerian nationalism directly impacted the unity of the anticolonialist movement in France.

Discord within the Comité: is there orthodox anticolonialism?

Aside from the general agreement that France was inevitably intertwined with the events in Algeria, the question of choosing sides created deep fissures which ran the length of the French intellectual community. Yes, the Comité had proved itself to be firmly on the ground of intellectual legitimacy because it had so far shown that it would stand up for universal justice and equality, but where would this newly created federation of intellectuals go from here? How could it move from theory to practice? In this next phase, this struggle to create a praxis of anticolonialism, the Comité was not coherent and proved incapable of finding a comprehensive position. This paralysis was not entirely its fault; there were several important phenomena simply beyond its control: the problem of violence in Algeria, Cold War politics and other domestic affairs. However, the issue of choosing sides in the conflict between rival Algerian nationalist groups nearly destroyed the Comité.

Importantly, the Comité tended to side with the FLN for various reasons, and the preference of the Comité's leaders for FLN over the MNA created the first crack in the wall of a united anticolonial front. There are many examples of this, but one striking one occurred when two Comité members, Francis and Colette Jeanson, published their *L'Algérie hors la loi*, a book favouring the FLN. Immediately, another prominent Comité member, the *pied noir* journalist, Jean Daniel, attacked their endorsement in an article called 'Between Sorrow and Shrugged Shoulders'. Daniel criticized the Jeansons for making it appear that the FLN was the only Algerian nationalist movement French intellectuals could support. And, Daniel correctly predicted that choosing sides in the Algerian nationalist question would destabilize the anticolonial movement. But this was demonstrative of another, more dangerous concern. Daniel insisted that in choosing sides, Francis Jeanson was guilty of the same sin as Soustelle because 'Jeanson believed himself to incarnate Algeria'.[23] In other words, the Jeansons' self-arrogation of the position of a legitimate anticolonialist intellectual illustrated a larger problem that would henceforth colour all leftist intellectuals' discussions of Algeria. As Daniel put it: 'There is now an orthodox anti-colonialism just as there is an orthodox communism. The dogma of this orthodoxy is not the well-being of the colonised but the mortification of the colonisers'. In this sense, Daniel claimed, Jeanson's solidarity with the FLN evidenced bad faith because the Jeansons were acting as if they were uniquely 'qualified to give out certificates of Algerian patriotism to the Algerians of [their] choice'.

On 26 January, the well-known anarchist writer, Daniel Guérin, published a similar critique of the Jeansons' work in the interest of 'public opinion'.[24] Beginning with praise for what he considered a courageous and over-due book on Algeria, Guérin attacked its treatment, 'without any attempt at impartiality', of the diverse tendencies of the Algerian revolutionaries. According to Guérin, the Jeansons' wilful omission of Messali Hadj, claimed by many to be the father of Algerian nationalism, was unjustified and unfounded.

Francis Jeanson responded to Jean Daniel, but not to Guérin, in an unpublished but semi-open letter. Knowing that *L'Express* would not publish it, he had copies printed and sent to approximately 100 'well chosen' Parisian intellectuals.[25] Jeanson argued that membership in the Comité should produce reciprocal respect for individual political differences.[26] However, Jeanson chastised Daniel for pretending that a real political force existed inside Algeria other than the FLN. As a result, Jeanson defended himself against Daniel's charge that he was dividing the French left with radical, orthodox, anti-colonial politics. The time had come, Jeanson contended, to choose between Algerian resistance organizations because there were only two real political forces left in Algeria: the army and the resistance (*maquizards*). Fence-sitting at this point only played into the hands of neo-colonialism disguised as current anticolonialism.

Ironically, however, the death blow to the Comité came not with disagreements within the Comité over which nationalist position to take *vis-à-vis* war in Algeria, or even over which nationalist group to endorse, but with the Soviet army's suppression of the Hungarian nationalists in November 1956. On 23 October 1956, students at Budapest University set off a national uprising by demonstrating for national independence. Within five days, the country was almost completely liberated from the Soviets. But, by 4 November, the Soviet tanks had entered the capital, and Igmar Nagy, the leader of the independence movement, first sought refuge in the Yugoslav Embassy but was soon captured and deported to Romania. The Soviet suppression of Nagy's movement created a problem for French intellectuals: as they sought to adjust to the shifting sands of universalism, the anticolonialist intellectuals, during their debates with Soustelle, had made a convincing argument about the need to condemn colonialism around the globe based on universal political principles. In fact, the Comité had made the universalism of the French republican 'Rights of Man' ideology the hallmark of its crusade against colonialism in North Africa and the foundation stone of intellectual legitimacy. However, Nagy's arrest and deportation – and the arrest of hundreds of opposition intellectuals by the Soviet regime – forced the Comité once again to rethink its own legitimacy because the universalism of its message would again be called into question if its members did not unilaterally condemn this new Soviet imperialism. To understand the full import of this catch-22 position, it is helpful to recall the intent of the founders of the Comité. Embittered by the ineffectual partisan politics of the post-WWII era, the initiators wanted to keep the Comité apolitical. However, after the Soviets smashed Hungary's democratic uprising as the world looked on, it was clear that politics could not be kept out of the Comité. Communist or non-communist sympathizing intellectuals faced an incredible dilemma: would they criticise or break away from the French Communist Party in order to save the Comité from disgrace?

The first move by important members of the Comité came on 8 November 1956, when the directors of the left-oriented *France Observateur* published its text 'Against Soviet Intervention'.[27] Those who signed the text agreed that 'socialism' could not be 'introduced with bayonets'. On 9 November 1956, in an article for *L'Express*, Jean-Paul Sartre denounced the crimes of Budapest: 'I entirely and without any reservations condemn the Soviet aggression. Without making the Soviet people responsible, I repeat that its current government has committed a crime . . . which today goes beyond the Stalinism that has already been denounced'.[28]

If the political effects of taking sides with different Algerian nationalist movements already put the intellectual unity of members of the Comité on shaky ground, Budapest was the ultimate and most destructive test of whether the universal foundations of anticolonialism, as embodied in the Comité, could withstand both domestic and international scrutiny. The executive head of the Comité discussed its position *vis-à-vis* Hungary, and on 21 November the Comité asked its members to choose from among three possible responses to Budapest: 1) to concentrate on fighting against the war in Algeria, despite the similarities between the Soviet suppression of Hungary and French pacification of Algeria; 2) to condemn, with equal force, the war in Algeria and the repression of Budapest; 3) not only to condemn, without reserve, the force used in Hungary, but to demand that all members of the Comité announce publicly their condemnation of the Soviet Union.[29]

Reactions were diverse but resulted in the dissolution of the Comité. For example, Jean-Marie Domenach, the editor of the moderate left Christian journal *Esprit*, admitted that the events of Budapest posed questions 'of logic, of coherence, and of morality'.[30] Knowing that the success of his journal depended on public opinion, Domenach continued, it was not possible for him to continue collaborating with a committee, which did not publicly condemn the Soviet intervention in Hungary. Then, in a general meeting of the Comité on 26 November, Daniel Guérin spoke out against denouncing the Soviet suppression because, unlike Domenach, he argued that it was a 'bad idea' to risk destroying a committee whose, 'unique mission was to continue to struggle against the war in Algeria'.[31] Sartre also started his own petition to voice opposition to the Soviet suppression of Budapest.[32]

Ironically, Budapest helped destroy the Comité by separating the Comité from its original apolitical objective, which was to fight against the war in Algeria.[33] Understandably, the Comité's founders were dismayed at its sudden downfall. Edgar Morin recounted its paralysing effect: 'It was not possible to denounce French imperialism in Algeria, without denouncing something analogous to what the Soviet Union was doing in Hungary'.[34] In his private notes just after Budapest and in reference to the attempt to call for a meeting of the Comité to denounce Budapest, Dionys Mascolo asked himself ironically: would a vocal communist member of the Comité participate today in a 'meeting for the right of people to dispose of themselves' against a communist regime with the same level of commitment as he displayed in attacking French policy in Algeria. 'Sinister joke . . . Now the Comité is paralyzed by the smallest possibility of talking tomorrow of the people's right to dispose of themselves'.[35] Mascolo then asked the communists to leave the Comité in order for it to continue its war against colonialism.[36] Seeing the damage that the communists' refusal to leave had caused to the Comité, he resigned on 11 November 1956, and he wrote the following:

> It is not only odious, it is ridiculous to protest against the arrest of a few militant anticolonists in the company of men who elect to treat the workers, soldiers, and intellectuals in the Hungarian insurrection as fascists just as Soustelle and the traitors of the socialist government of the official France call the Algerian militants terrorists and bandits. I am not sectarian, but anticolonialism should be total: It is a principle.[37]

Budapest, however, was not an isolated incident of discord among the members. It merely pushed the left-oriented Comité over the precipice. The Comité's assumed universalism and unity ensured by the open political battles with Soustelle suddenly dissipated as it confronted a new species of imperialists: the Soviets. By late 1956, the French-Algerian War and other world events momentarily rendered it impossible to unify intellectual identity and orient public opinion through such a large organ as the Comité, and many French intellectuals asked themselves if they would have a chance to restore universalism.

The Jeanson network, or the treason of the French 'self'?

For some of the important members of the Comité the answer was, yes, there would be another chance, but this chance would come with the aid of the FLN, and it would radicalize the idea of intellectual engagement and challenge the very idea of universalism.

Francis Jeanson, for example, took the initiative to mobilize the French left, or 'avant-garde' intellectuals, as he called them. After the Comité dissolved, Jeanson went underground and created a sophisticated network which provided weapons, money, and supplies to the FLN. Eventually, he attracted a large group of committed intellectuals who followed him into clandestineness. It was his affiliation with the FLN that eventually drove him underground in 1957.[38]

Jeanson's decision to enter into a political alliance with the FLN was therefore taken with two primary objectives in mind: (1) ending the war in Algeria by supporting the only effective Algerian revolutionary movement, and (2) unifying the French left in order to save French democracy. This unity was particularly important because the principal issue for the French left was no longer merely cultural and political reconciliation with the Algerians. Rather, many leftist intellectuals wanted to use the idea of universal revolutionary activity – embodied in the Algerian FLN – as a means to re-unite the fragmented left in order to secure individual and collective political freedoms in France.

In making this co-operation between the revolutionary French and Algerian public, Jeanson believed that he could foster intellectual engagement based not only on 'theoretical' concerns but also on those 'inscribed within an everyday context'. In other words, French intellectuals' calls to end the French-Algerian War would make it possible to bridge the gap between 'action' and 'practical reflection' by illustrating to the French public that there really was 'something to do' for the Algerians.[39] Aware that the consequence of taking the FLN's side would lead to the charge of treason, Jeanson claimed that the charge was false because, according to France's official rhetoric, the rebellion was merely a civil war in which the Algerians were considered 'French citizens'.[40] But the crime of collaborating with these 'French citizens' (the FLN) was worth the penalty, he claimed, if the alternative was to admit that he belonged to the same community of men as General Massu and Prime Minister Debré. Moreover, since it appeared indisputable in 1960 that the Algerians would achieve political independence and that France was heading toward fascism by prolonging the war, he argued that it was in France's political interest to guarantee future relations with the Algerian government. The dual purpose, saving France and ensuring that the French would not be condemned 'en bloc' as fascists by the Algerians after independence, would forge a future Franco-Algerian solidarity.[41]

In the May 1960 issue of *Esprit*, Jean Daniel disagreed with the French avant-garde's position on the FLN, which endorsed violence. 'Violence', he claimed, 'had posed the problem; it did not suffice to solve it.'[42] As for the commitment of the French left, Daniel wrote that it wanted to profit from the revolutionary spirit of Algerian nationalism and this 'intellectual slippage was very perceptible'.[43] As a result, Daniel continued, the French avant-garde left had overlooked fundamental and disturbing facts about Algerian nationalists in order to blindly 'sacralise' the FLN as a revolutionary movement. This activity of the French left was no better than 'Stalinist intellectuals [who] sacralised the Communist Party'.[44]

Les Temps modernes replied to Daniel.[45] Admitting that it desired the unification of the left with the FLN, Sartre's journal stated that it was important not to accept de Gaulle's version of peace with Algeria because: 'if de Gaulle makes peace, it will be good for the Algerians, but bad for the left'. The real political problem was simple: 'Peace . . . did not justify the Gaullist order'.[46]

The so-called 'Jeanson Network' was discovered in early 1960. In total, 23 members of the network, 17 French and six Muslims were arrested, while five – including
Jeanson – managed to avoid arrest.[47] The network's trial, which began on 5 September
1960 and lasted for months, provoked an unprecedented national debate on the political
limits of intellectual engagement and the impact of the war on France and the intellectual community.[48] It forced avant-garde leftist intellectuals to face the legal charge of
treason, which the anticolonial Comité never confronted. Eventually, nine members of
the Jeanson network were acquitted; 15 (including Jeanson and four others still at large)
were sentenced to the maximum sentence which was ten years and 70,000 NF in fines,
and three others received less severe penalties. Perhaps, it was just this charge of treason
that created the greatest fissures within the French intellectual community. Yet, for
Jeanson's supporters there was a common cause: motivating French public opinion
against the war in Algeria and using the possibility of a civil war in France to rejuvenate
the French left.

Out of this changing relationship among the members of the French left and
between the French and Algerians, a central question emerged: whose war was the
French-Algerian War? Jeanson himself tried to answer this question with his *Notre guerre*,
published at the end of 1960 because he realized that the war had called French identity
into question. It was, Jeanson wrote, in order 'to really be French' that intellectuals like
him were 'now working to reconstitute a national community' by fighting alongside the
FLN.[49] Hence, the question was not whether or not the war was a French or Algerian
one, but rather how the French could engage in the war which was not their own on the
side of the Algerians in order to reconstruct their own national community without
becoming any less French? Jeanson did not deny the implicit risk of losing one's French
identity during the struggle. In Jeanson's words, those working with the Algerians
'faced two inverse risks: that of being so accepted that we become submerged, absorbed
lost, Algerianized; and that of being rejected for having kept our distance'. The network
members tried to account for this, he said, by attempting 'to be totally *with*, and in
consequence, totally *ourselves* . . . For three years, we have worked *for* the FLN . . .
without being "under its orders", or without being "for sale"'.[50] Hence, the problem for the
French was to show political solidarity with the Algerians and yet maintain their autonomy from the Algerians.

As for the charge that the French involved in the Jeanson network were betraying
their national community, Jeanson claimed that '*the real TREASON* was the renunciation
– active or passive – of the profound resources of the country, the only chance to realise
an effective community, of everything that can, in the end, constitute a real showing of
France at work'.[51] It was only by working for the conclusion of a warranted peace, a
concrete peace, which could assure a continued co-operation and friendship between
the French and Algerians, that the 'Gaullist magic' could be dispelled. That was the true
meaning of the war for France. It was, in fact, according to Jeanson, the only way to
restore France's real significance in the world. In other words, if France did not live up
to its political and moral heritage, which was founded on the universal principles of
equality and fraternity, it would never be in a position to recover its status as a world
leader, nor would its intellectuals be able to hold their heads high. And, for the avant-
garde French left, trapped by de Gaulle's illegitimate rise to power in 1958, trapped by
the illegalities of the French army and the unstoppable use of torture and mass killing,
trapped also by their own desire to take an active role in a nationalist revolution that was

not their own, the paradox was obvious: how could the French avant-grade left not be, as Jeanson said, 'Algerianized' through its involvement in the Algerian Revolution?

In this sense, following Charles Taylor's argument cited above, the French-Algerian War was the ultimate political litmus test for French intellectuals who were placed in the awkward position of defending the universal values of their personal, collective, and national identities on the one hand, and, on the other hand, siding with a people who largely denied this universalism. It was unquestionably a cruel paradox: to affirm and subvert at the same time. This is certainly what Paul Ricoeur had in mind when he stated that the decolonization of French Algeria provoked a national crisis the likes of which had not been seen since the Enlightenment and the demise of the Old Regime. To affirm by subversion, this was for intellectuals such as Jeanson, the only truly orthodox anti-colonial position. Finally, what is particularly significant about this period and these series of political transformations is that they unleashed intellectual and ideological processes and positions that eventually heralded the advent and the crisis of the post-modern intellectual.

Notes

1   See 'Je me suis resolu à la torture . . . J'ai moi-même procédé à des executions sommaires', *Le Monde*, 24 Nov. 2000; 'Si la France reconnaissait et condamnait ces pratiques, je prendrais cela pour une avancée'. Entretien avec le général Jacques Massu, vainqueur de la bataille d'Alger, *Le Monde*, 22 Nov. 2000; and General Aussaresses, *Service Spéciaux Algérie*, 1955, 1957 (Saint-Amand-Montrond: Perrin, 2001).

2   Tahar Ben Jelloun, *French Hospitality: Racism and North African Immigrants*, trans. Barbara Bray (New York: Columbia University Press 1999) p. 11.

3   Martin Evans, 'The French Army and the Algerian War: Crisis of Identity' in Michael Scriven and Peter Wagstaff (eds.), *War and Society in Twentieth Century France* (New York: Berg 1991) pp. 152–3.

4   Charles Taylor, *Multiculturalism and the 'Politics of Recognition'* (Princeton: Princeton University Press 1992).

5   Interview with Paul Ricoeur, Paris, 20 Oct. 1993.

6   James D. Le Sueur, 'Before the Jackal: The International Uproar over *Assassination!*', an historical essay accompanying *Assassination! July 14*, by Ben Abro (Lincoln: University of Nebraska Press 2001).

7   Mouloud Feraoun, *Journal, 1955–1962: Reflections on the French-Algerian War*, ed. and intro. James D. Le Sueur, trans. Mary Ellen Wolf and Claude Fouillade (Lincoln: Nebraska, University of Nebraska Press 2000) and James D. Le Sueur, *Uncivil War: Intellectuals and Identity Politics During the Declonization of Algeria*, with a foreword by Pierre Bourdieu (Philadelphia: University of Pennsylvania Press, 2001).

8   Comité d'Action des Intellectuels contre la Poursuite de la Guerre en Afrique du Nord (N. p. n.d.) p. 2.

9   Edgar Morin, *Autocritique* (Paris: Seuil 1970) pp. 191–3.

10 Among the names on the original manifesto in November 1955 were: Claude Lévi-Strauss, Paul Ricoeur, François Mauriac, Georges Gurvitch, Roger Martin du Gard, Louis Massignon, Gaston Wiet, André Breton, Jean Wahl, Jean-Paul Sartre, Régis Blachère, Jean Daniel, Marguerite Duras, Henri Lefebvre, Jean Cocteau, Jean-Jacques Mayoux, Jean-Marie Domenach, Jean Genet, and Charles-André Julien.

11   Comité d'Action des Intellectuels p. 2.

12   About the Comité, Soustelle says that 'a certain number of honorable signatures mixed with unknown ones, who, without doubt, were desirous to leave their obscurity, and with a few *demoiselles* quite unqualified to treat the problems of which they knew nothing. As much as I worried little about the specialists, the unknowns and the *demoiselles*, I attached greater importance to the opinions of writers and professors [*universitaires*] that I respected and among whom I counted friends. That is why I decided to respond'. Jacques Soustelle, *Aimée et souffrante Algérie* (Paris: Plon 1956) p. 170. Among the '*demoiselles*' to whom he was referring were Marguerite Duras, Simone de Beauvoir and Françoise Sagan.

13   Jacques Soustelle, 'Lettre d'un intellectuel', *Combat* (26 Nov. 1955), p. 1.

14   'Réponse au Gouverneur Général de l'Algérie', Comité d'Action des Intellectuels contre la Poursuite de la Guerre en Afrique du Nord (Paris, 3 déc. 1955) p. 2.

15   Ibid. p. 3.

16   Ibid. p. 2.

17   Claude Bourdet, 'Votre Gestapo d'Algérie', *France Observateur* (13 Jan. 1955) pp. 6–7.

18   Comité d'Action des Intellectuels, 'Réponse au Governeur Général de l'Algérie' (Paris, n.d.) p. 2.

19   Ibid. p. 4.

20   Déclaration de Monsieur Jacques Soustelle Gouverneur, Général de l'Algérie, Radio-Algerie, 12 January 1956.

21   'Réponse du Comité, 10 January 1956, in 'Réponse au Gouverneur Général de l'Algérie', p. 6.

22   Messali Hadj (1898–1974) was one of Algeria's most important nationalist leaders. During the French-Algerian War, he directed the Movement National Algerien (MNA), which was the rival of the FLN.

23   Jean Daniel, 'Entre le chagrin et le haussement d'épaules', *L'Express* (13 Jan. 1956) p. 11.

24   Daniel Guérin, 'L'Algérie hors la loi', *France Observateur* (26 Jan. 1956) p. 12.

25   Jeanson wanted to offer a response to Daniel, one which would be private enough to keep the already skeptical public opinion from turning against intellectuals and the higher causes of Algerian nationalism and anticolonialism. Interview with Francis Jeanson, 11 Dec. 1993.

26   Francis Jeanson to Jean Daniel (16 Jan. 1956) p. 1. Archives Guérin, 721/91/4, Bibliothèque de Documentation Internationale Contemporaine (BDIC), Nanterre.

27   'Contre l'intervention', *France Observateur*, 8 Nov. 1956. Also reprinted in full in: Jean-François Sirinelli, *Intellectuels et Passions Françaises: Manifestes et pétitions au XXe siècle* (Paris: Fayard 1990) pp. 177–78.

28   Jean-Paul Sartre, 'Après Budapest', *L'Express* (9 Nov. 1956) p. 15.

29   Comité d'Action des Intellectuels to its members, Paris (21 Nov. 1956) Fonds *Esprit*, ESP2. El-02.02, Institut Mémoire de l'Edition Contemporaine (IMEC), Paris.

30   Jean-Marie Domenach to the Comité d'Action des Intellectuals, Fonds *Esprit*, ESP2, El-02.02, IMEC.

31   Daniel Guérin, *Ci-gît le colonialisme: Algérie, Inde, Indochine, Madagascar, Maroc, Palestine, Polynésie, Tunisie – Témoignage militant* (Paris: Mouton 1973) p. 95.

32   Interview with Francis Jeanson, 11 Dec. 1993.

33   Interview with Edgar Morin, 4 Dec. 1993.

34   Morin, *Autocritique* (note 13) p. 197.

35   Notes of Dionys Mascolo. Private papers of Dionys Mascolo.

36   Interview with Dionys Mascolo, 16 February 1994.

37   Dionys Mascolo to the Comité, 19 Nov. 1956, Mascolo papers.

38   Jeanson claimed that it was important for him to go into hiding and was actually asked to do so by the leader of the FLN in France because he had 'in his hands' all the information concerning the FLN's activities in France. Interview with Francis Jeanson, 11 December 1993.

39   'Francis Jeanson, Lettre à Jean-Paul Sartre', *Les Temps modernes*, 169–70 (April–May 1960) p. 1541.

40   Ibid. p. 1544.

41   Ibid. pp. 1546–7.

42   Jean Daniel, 'Socialisme et anti-colonialisme,' *Esprit* 284 (May 1960) p. 810.

43   Ibid. p. 811.

44   Ibid. pp. 813–14.

45   'Réponse à Jean Daniel', *Les Temps modernes*, 169–70 (April–May 1960) pp. 1530–4.

46   Ibid. p. 1534.

47   Jeanson was in Switzerland throughout the trial.

48   4 September 1960 when *Le Monde* announced that 121 intellectuals (writers and artists) had signed the Manifesto for the 'right of insubordination' against the French-Algerian war. The Manifesto of the 121 was made public on the day before the trial of the 'Jeanson network' began in Paris. Dionys Mascolo, one of the original founders of the Comité was again one of the principal motivators for the Manifesto of the 121. They included France's most prominent leftist intellectuals including Robert Barrat, Simone de Beauvoir, André Breton, Marguerite Duras, Michel Leiris, Jérôme Lindon, Dionys Mascolo, Jean-Jacques Mayoux, Jean-Paul Sartre, and Pierre Vidal-Naquet. However, a group of moderate French intellectuals quickly countered the Manifesto of the 121. This group, led by Maurice Merleau-Ponty, signed a less provocative manifesto which underscored the moral choices the government was forcing upon the youth, but did not advocate the right of desertion. The signatures on the manifesto totalled over a thousand. Among the names were Raymond Aron, Jean-Marie Domenach, Roland Barthes, Georges Canguilhem, Jean Cassou, Jean Dresch, Claude Lefort, Jacques Le Goff, Edgar Morin, Paul Ricoeur, and Daniel Meyer.

49   Francis Jeanson, *Notre guerre* (Paris: Minuit 1960) pp. 14–15.

50   Ibid. p. 48.

51   Ibid. p. 117.

PART THREE

Economy and Labor

ECONOMY AND LABOR

HISTORIANS AND POLITICAL OBSERVERS have often said that the issue of international economy and labor were central dimensions of post-World War II decolonization in Africa and Asia. Decolonization, as a historical process, was so tied to economic considerations that it would indeed be impossible to study the waning of European political power overseas without giving primary consideration to these issues. The three essays selected here underscore the importance of economic considerations and highlight the differences in the way in which economic issues factored into the political equations of decolonization in Indonesia, French West Africa, and for British policy makers.

Pierre van der Eng's "Marshall Aid as a Catalyst in the Decolonization of Indonesia, 1947–49" affords unique insight into the complex relationship between economic aid from the United States and the political policies of the Dutch government in Indonesia. Van der Eng goes against dominant perceptions of the use of Marshall Aid by the United States as an instrument of US political policy and argues that Dutch decisions to abandon politico-military operations and cede the eventual independence of Indonesia under Sukarno's presidency were based not only on ideological considerations and domestic pressures but also on fiscal ones. These considerations eventually salvaged the Dutch economy and led to an economic boom for the Netherlands. Consistent with this argument, van der Eng suggests that it was the Dutch realization that financial assets in Indonesia might be in jeopardy that ultimately triggered the full-scale military assault on the newly declared Republic of Indonesia (established in the wake of the Japanese withdrawal in August 1945). The military/police actions, which commenced in July 1947, evoked immediate criticism by the United Nations Security Council. However, despite the controversy in the UN and the fear that aid to the Dutch would become a political liability for the US State Department, the US never really threatened to block Marshall Aid to the Netherlands; instead, it was the threat of international alienation as evidenced by UN's suspension of aid that brought increased pressure on the Dutch government. Ultimately, in agreeing to the transfer of power on 27 December 1949, the Dutch government secured huge financial rewards and relieved the Netherlands of its financial obligations toward Indonesia. In short, from an economic standpoint, while the Dutch bemoaned the loss of Indonesia, they, perhaps unfortunately, profited greatly from it in the form of international aid, whereas Indonesians and the Indonesian state did not.

Also interested in the relationship between colonial policy and international financial pressures, Catherine R. Schenk examines British changes in the economic system in "Decolonization and European Economic Integration: The Free Trade Area Negotiations, 1956–58." Schenk argues that historians must now look at the complexities of British colonial policy, and to demonstrate this she focuses on the relationship between decolonization and the European Economic Community (EEC). As the British tried to achieve integration with the European economy, they found it more difficult to pursue their own unique colonial policy and therefore became increasingly reluctant to give themselves over to the terms of European integration. Furthermore, unable to find a final agreement on the terms of integration, the attempt to arrive at European integration served to highlight the tension among European powers on the colonial question and between Britain and its new Commonwealth trade members. Schenk concludes that Britain instigated few economic initiatives and proved far more reflexive than proactive. In the end, Britain found itself torn in two directions and able to appease neither metropolitan nor ex-colonial powers.

Frederick Cooper in " 'Our Strike': Equality, Anticolonial Politics and the 1947–48 Railway Strike in French West Africa" tackles another aspect of economic concern. By focusing on the 1947–48 railway strike in West Africa, Cooper moves from macro to micro to macroeconomics. Cooper is able to do this by distilling the central questions to ones such as what was the relationship of strikes to trade union activity and what were the the connections between anticolonial movements in the colonies and French metropolitan planning. In addition to the well excavated archival sources, which include police files and spy reports, Cooper turns to oral history to give the study added human dimension and depth. Cooper's analysis of the railway strike thus helps researchers to understand how African workers were able to mobilize the rhetoric of French imperialism against the colonial structures and bosses in French West Africa.

Chapter 6

Pierre van der Eng

MARSHALL AID AS A CATALYST IN THE DECOLONIZATION OF INDONESIA, 1947–49

T HE UNITED STATES DID NOT give Marshall aid to Western Europe for purely humanitarian reasons. Aid was also, perhaps even mainly, provided to serve the economic and political purposes of the United States. In studies dealing with the Marshall aid programme, the suspension of aid to the Dutch colony of Indonesia, and the seeming threat to halt the stream of dollars to the Netherlands, has been used as an example to prove that the programme was an American instrument of political power. In studies dealing with the decolonization of Indonesia, it is also alleged that the menace of adjournment of Marshall aid forced the Dutch to retreat from their colony in December 1949. However, primary sources show that neither the offer of Marshall aid in June 1947, nor the seeming threat to halt aid to the Netherlands in December 1948, prevented the Dutch government from pursuing its own way in the process leading to the independence of Indonesia. The Dutch cabinet was not sufficiently impressed by both the offer and the threat to keep it from engaging in military "police actions" in July 1947 and December 1948 against the nationalist Republic of Indonesia.

Although the occurrences in 1949 seem to indicate otherwise, I will argue in this chapter that Marshall aid was not the blunt instrument of United States power as some allege. At most it was a catalyst, which induced the Dutch government to assume that with decolonization Dutch interests would be better served than by stubbornly sticking to its own conviction on how to guide Indonesia to prosperity, democracy and independence. Concluding, I will argue that giving in to decolonization was an economically rather rewarding choice for the Netherlands, which provides part of the explanation why the post-war economic recovery of the country was so remarkably successful.

Dutch dollar shortage and colonial politics

Until the Second World War the Netherlands East Indies (henceforth Indonesia) was of great economic importance to the Netherlands. Dutch industry obtained part of its raw materials from Indonesia. In 1938, 8 per cent of Dutch imports originated from and 10 per cent of Dutch exports went to Indonesia. The foreign trade of Indonesia was formally controlled by the Netherlands, which disposed of the foreign currency earned by Indonesian companies. Most importantly, the Netherlands could count on the transfer from Indonesia of profits made by Dutch companies, pensions for former civil servants and managers, and interest and redemptions of Dutch loans. In 1945, it was estimated that in 1938 almost 14 per cent of Dutch national income originated directly and indirectly from Indonesia.[1]

Immediately after the Second World War the Netherlands badly needed the foreign exchange, which was earned previously in Indonesia, to defray the huge deficit on its balance of payments. Many goods were in short supply in Europe and had to be imported from the United States, but there were insufficient dollar earning exports to pay for these imports. In 1946 and 1947, 12 and 14 per cent respectively of Dutch national income originated from foreign credits and from the sale of foreign assets, gold and foreign exchange in Dutch hands.[2] Dutch financial reserves were considered to be insufficient to maintain the deficit on the balance of payments for several years at a row. A swift recovery of the financial-economic relations with Indonesia was therefore regarded to be an absolute necessity for Dutch economic recovery. A number of Dutch statesmen expressed their anxiety in public at several occasions. The Dutch Prime Minister for the Catholic Party, Louis J. M. Beel, was very succinct in a meeting of Dutch cabinet in April 1947: "If we leave Indonesia, the Netherlands will go bankrupt."[3] This was a major reason for the Dutch government to support the recovery of Indonesia as far as the financial resources allowed.

In August 1945 the colonial administration in Indonesia had taken up again the task which Dutch colonial politics had imposed upon itself before the war. Indonesia was to be guided again to prosperity, democracy and to an undermined independence in a union with the Netherlands. The country had suffered a lot from devastation during the war in 1941–42 and the Japanese occupation. Production of rice per head on Java had declined by almost 40 per cent between 1940 and 1945.[4] Previous foreign exchange-earning plantations and estates had been neglected or occupied by Indonesians for food cropping. Sugar factories and public buildings had been ruined or ransacked. The necessary economic aid to the population consisted of distributing imported rice and textiles. In providing this relief the colonial administration was primarily dependent on the loans the Netherlands issued and on the monopoly of purchase and sale of export products like rubber, copra and tin.

Next to material problems, the colonial administration had to come to terms with the existence of the Republic of Indonesia, which had been established in August 1945 by the nationalist movement. The Republic was guided by Sukarno and controlled most of rural Java and a large part of Sumatra. The principle of Indonesian independence was negotiated between the Republic and the Netherlands. Both parties agreed in the Treaty of Linggajati in November 1946 to the establishment of an Indonesian federation, in which the Republic was to become one of the member states. However, differences of opinion about the interpretation of the treaty prevented agreement being reached in the first half of 1947 on concrete steps toward Indonesian independence.

Financial aid to Indonesia had been considered by the Netherlands government as an advance, to be repaid later. But in March and April 1947 the Dutch cabinet started to realize that the Netherlands lacked foreign exchange to continue financing both its own and Indonesian economic recovery. The Minister of Finance for the Labour Party, Pieter Lieftinck, drew the attention of his colleagues to this problem in several cabinet meetings. He scorned the option of abandoning Indonesia, because he wanted to preserve the extensive Dutch assets in Indonesia.[5]

For that reason the Dutch government agreed to launch an all-out military action against the Republic. This action was to serve three goals. First of all it was to undermine the strategic and political position of the Republic. Second, rural stocks of foodstuffs and export products were to be taken for distribution to other parts of the country and to earn foreign exchange. Lastly, it had to prove to the United States that the Dutch had mastered the situation in Indonesia and that there were no obstacles to the releasing of a 100 million dollar loan by the Exim Bank for special projects to improve the Indonesian infrastructure. The loan agreement had already been reached in 1946, but disbursement had been held back, because of American opinion that there was no guarantee that the projects could be carried out as agreed.

The first "police action" started on 20 July 1947 under the code name "Operation Product". Under pressure from the Security Council of the United Nations the Netherlands had to adjourn the action on 4 August. Through the mediation of a committee of the United Nations, negotiations with the Republic on Indonesian independence had to be resumed. The captured stocks were smaller than expected; therefore extra rice imports continued to be necessary. Above all, the Indonesian Republic gained international political sympathy now that it was the underdog. Under pressure of public opinion the United States kept refusing to disburse the Exim Bank loan.

Marshall aid and Dutch colonial politics

In the meantime representatives of sixteen Western European countries had gathered in Paris in July 1947 to negotiate a concrete reply to the offer of financial aid by the American Secretary of State, George C. Marshall, on 5 June 1947. This Conference for European Economic Co-operation (CEEC, which was to be the base for the OEEC, later OECD) aimed at designing a joint European Recovery Program (ERP). State Department representatives had notified the participants that the amount of Marshall aid in the period 1948–53 would be established according to the expected deficit with the United States on the combined European balance of payments in ERP.

At the State Department the importance of the overseas colonial territories of Belgium, France, the Netherlands and the United Kingdom for the bridging over of the European dollar deficit had been recognized. These areas were therefore included in the estimate of the total deficit. Because Indonesia had suffered most during the Second World War, its deficit was estimated to be 400 million dollars, whereas the deficit of all European "dependent territories" was taken to be 460 million dollars.

The fact that Indonesia would be drawn into the Marshall aid programme was considered to be a delicate matter in the Netherlands. Although Lieftinck wanted to ask for a loan to bridge over the period until Marshall aid would be released, the best he achieved was an instruction by the Dutch government to its Commissioner for General Affairs, the high ranking civil servant Hans M. Hirschfeld. After having participated on behalf of the Netherlands in the negotiations in Paris, the commissioner had gone to Washington for subsequent talks on ERP in October 1947. Hirschfeld was instructed to draw the attention of State Department representatives to the dilemma the Dutch government was facing in Indonesia. However, the commissioner defied the instruction, replying that it would be "inopportune" to do so. He argued: "For such action the political sky should be cleared first."[6] This no doubt shows what latitude Hirschfeld could permit himself and in what esteem he was held in the Dutch cabinet.

In December 1947 the Director of Economic Affairs in Indonesia, Jacob E. van Hoogstraten, went to the United States in order to acquire loans for Indonesia. He was dissuaded in advance by Hirschfeld from issuing public statements about the participation of Indonesia in the Marshall aid programme and from asking in talks at the State Department how much aid Indonesia could expect to receive. Hirschfeld anticipated that inquiries about the amount of aid would draw attention in the American press to Indonesian participation in the programme. This could result in negative reactions in American Congress and endanger aid to Indonesia.[7]

Van Hoogstraten was allowed to explain at the State Department that at most the foreign exchange reserve would allow Indonesia to make both ends meet until mid-1948, and that in the situation of distress which would occur the Netherlands would not be able to render assistance. The Americans explained to him that financial aid would not be given, unless clear political improvements were realized. "Not because the State Department attaches much value to this, but because it needs a change in the public opinion to justify supporting us in Congress", wrote Van Hoogstraten to his superior, the Lt. Governor General of Indonesia, Hubertus J. van Mook.[8]

In spite of the continuing postponement of the Exim Bank loan to Indonesia, American policy was favourable to the Dutch political stand. The State Department expected that the political instability with which the Republic had to cope made her susceptible to communist influence. Furthermore, the Netherlands had in 1946 promised in principle to guide Indonesia to independence. The Dutch were also granted the benefit of the doubt, because after the first "police action" their military power seemed to exceed the strength of the Republic. The State Department did not want to risk alienating the Netherlands and therewith perhaps other colonial powers in Western Europe. On the other hand the State Department did not want to force colonized peoples into the communist camp, by estranging them with a pronounced policy towards Indonesia. Such a policy could also not be too outspoken, because the United Nations had declared itself in favour of the right of self-determination for all colonized countries. The United Nations was held in great esteem by the American public, which opposed colonial relations in general.[9]

At the State Department policy was weighed carefully, but its officials shared the Dutch conviction that economic recovery of Indonesia would be essential to Dutch economic recovery and therefore to the decline of the Western European dollar deficit.[10] This conviction was also incorporated in the proposal for the amount of Marshall aid and the distribution of the total sum, which Marshall sent to Congress. It should be added that in its contemplations the State Department considered recovery and opening up of the Indonesian economy important to the American economy. Indonesia was praised for its supply of all kinds of "strategic" raw materials, like rubber, palm oil, tin and natural oil. Above all it was considered that a substantial amount of American capital was invested in Indonesia, which would be secured with a roseate Indonesian economic future.[11]

But at the State Department the officials were not convinced in advance of the positive attitude of Congress. A conspicuous Dutch step as a token of goodwill toward decolonization was assumed to have a positive impact on public opinion and on those of members of Congress. That was why the American member of the mediating United Nations committee asked Marshall to inform the Dutch ambassador in Washington, Eelco N. van Kleffens, that accepting the agreement as proposed by the committee would not be unwelcome.[12] The American ambassador in The Hague also notified the Dutch cabinet informally that a Dutch refusal "would endanger Dutch participation in the European Recovery Program".[13]

In the next meeting of cabinet only Lieftinck suspected "intolerable blackmail". But in his opinion the threat had become quite harmless, because cabinet had already agreed to give its consent to the proposal. Only the Minister of Justice was prepared to do without Marshall aid if necessary. Lieftinck pointed out, however, that a delay of financial aid would mean a disaster for the Netherlands: "Theoretically it is possible to turn down the aid according to the Marshall Plan; practically this is impossible." Cabinet agreed on the assumption that the Americans had wanted to point out "that it would be politically very favourable for the Netherlands, when an agreement would be reached with the Republic of Indonesia, before aid to the Netherlands and Indonesia based on the Marshall Plan would be discussed in Congress".[14] On 17 January 1948 an agreement was signed by Dutch and Indonesian Republican representatives on the American navy ship *Renville*. In the agreement the principle of a future independent Indonesian federation was reconfirmed.

Marshall aid to the Netherlands was not really endangered in this case. At the Dutch embassy in Washington it was even noted: "As far as the Dutch embassy has been able to check it was *never* intended to put the knife on the Dutch throat; the support to the Kingdom in Europe under the Marshall Plan has never been at stake."[15] At the State Department, officials did not want to push matters to the extreme, because they considered Dutch co-operation in ERP to be essential to the success of the programme. This was given priority over a quick solution of the Indonesian problem. The American government could not have afforded to offend the Netherlands by openly condemning its colonial policy, while stressing to Congress that the economies of the Netherlands and Indonesia could not be considered apart. After the signing of the *Renville* agreement Congress agreed to the proposed amount and distribution of Marshall aid. This gesture no doubt strengthened Dutch attitude in the process of decolonization.

Dutch officials expected that an agreement for a dollar loan to Indonesia to bridge over the period until the Marshall dollars would start to flow would soon be reached. They also expected that the Americans would show understanding for Dutch financial-economic demands in discussions about decolonization. These demands concerned above all the take-over of Indonesian debts by the new Indonesian government, the guarantee of the rights of possession of Dutch companies in Indonesia and a guarantee of financial transfers to the Netherlands. But an American loan stayed out, because at the State Department it was argued that the United States had to be neutral in the Dutch-Indonesian conflict and could not give one party an economic advantage over the other. As long as the guarantee of Dutch interests in Indonesia was not sealed, the Dutch government was reluctant about increasing the Indonesian deficit with the Netherlands very much. Only by very strict cuts in the import programme was Indonesia able to maintain its deficit on the balance of payments. Inevitably its gold and foreign currency resources declined to 624 million guilders and its long-term debt to the Netherlands increased to 871 million guilders by 1 July 1948.[16]

The fact that at the State Department the Netherlands and its overseas territories were considered to be an economic unity, appeared to be a problem when the outcome of the provisional allotment of Marshall aid to the Netherlands became known. In the American scheme the dollars earned by Dutch oil companies on the Dutch Antilles in the Caribbean were cancelled against the dollar deficit of Indonesia. It therefore looked as if the Dutch kingdom as a whole would not be allotted enough.[17] In June 1948 the Dutch tried to convince the Americans that Indonesia had its own foreign currency régime which could not be linked to the Dutch dollar revenues in the Caribbean. Thereupon the OEEC partners called the Dutch representative to account and wondered whether Indonesia should be included in the aid programme, now that it appeared to have its own foreign currency régime in contrast to the British and French overseas territories. After a hasty Dutch appeal in Washington with the Economic Co-operation Agency (ECA, the American body which organized the Marshall aid), ECA adopted the Dutch view. It allotted Marshall aid separately to Indonesia, although the Netherlands was considered to be the receiving country.[18] This forced the OEEC partners to withdraw their objections and give up hope of claiming the Indonesian share.

That the Netherlands was considered to be the receiving country was no disadvantage. In July 1948 it appeared that Indonesian export production was quickly recovering and with it the Indonesian monetary reserves. The Indonesian dollar deficit was not considered to be the major problem, but the Dutch dollar deficit became looked upon as "very precarious".[19] Indeed, the Indonesian deficit on the balance of payments for 1948 of 438 million guilders would turn out to be lower than that for 1947. In the end Indonesia was allotted for the fiscal year 1948/49 64 million dollars as a gift, 15 million as a loan and 20.5 million to be spent in OEEC countries.

After the *Renville* agreement the negotiations about Indonesian independence stagnated. The Netherlands felt itself strengthened by the superior military and economic position of its colonial administration in Indonesia and the implicit support of the United States. Pending the negotiations between Dutch and Indonesian Republican representatives the colonial administration established several Indonesian states outside Republican territory. It also installed a provisional federal government in which non-Republican Indonesians participated. Republican officials resisted the establishment of more states than originally agreed to in the Treaty of Linggajati, and the premature installation of a federal government. The Dutch negotiators tried to persuade them to accept participation in the federal government and to agree to a union between the Netherlands and the forthcoming federal Indonesian republic. The federation was meant to curtail the political influence of the Republic of Indonesia in the new state. The union was intended to safeguard a Dutch say in the politics of the future United States of Indonesia, and to guarantee the economic co-operation between both states. The Republican negotiators tried to drag out the negotiations, because the Republic of Indonesia had to cope with internal political controversies. A new stalemate was developing, and already in June 1948 a new military action was alluded to in the Netherlands.[20]

Before the deadlock was actually reached, officials at the State Department realized that Marshall aid to Indonesia could be endangered as long as unambiguous steps toward decolonization were not agreed to.[21] American economic aid to Indonesia could result in the impression that the State Department provided the Netherlands with an economic and therefore with a political-military advantage to the Indonesian Republic. As such the State Department would *de facto* abandon its neutral stand in the matter. Officials of the Indonesian Republic accused the Netherlands in the American press of misusing Marshall aid for financing its military force in Indonesia. State Department spokesmen denied such accusations and also received a Dutch guarantee that no such thing happened.[22] Formally considered, these accusations were indeed untrue, but practically seen Marshall dollars enabled the Netherlands to spend free dollars on imports for the military force in Indonesia.

The State Department officials still had to weigh American policy carefully in the second half of 1948. The American member of the mediating United Nations committee, H. Merle Cochran, thought that advocates in the Netherlands of a new military action could be curbed by informally notifying the Dutch about the American problem. He produced a proposal on 10 September 1948 for concrete steps toward independence, which was backed by the State Department. With the increasing tension of the Cold War, it became more important for the Americans to prevent communist influence from gaining a decisive foothold in the Indonesian Republic. Therefore the American opinion won ground that the Republic of Indonesia had to regain its economic strength and that its government had to be assisted in establishing political control in its area. To the Americans the Dutch had to make concessions to their conception of the road to independence of the future Indonesian republic. Such concessions would reinforce the position of the moderate government of the Republic relative to communist opposition.

The apparent threat to Marshall aid

In an attempt to break the impasse, a memorandum to the Dutch government was prepared at the State Department to elucidate the American point of view. On 3 December the Deputy Minister of Foreign Affairs, Robert A. Lovett, cabled a draft to Cochran. He argued that the Netherlands would be able to win a military action easily, but that it would have to deal with a guerrilla warfare with disastrous effects afterwards: "Such outcome would seriously deplete resources of Netherlands and tend nullify effect appropriations made to Netherlands and Indonesia under ECA, or jeopardize continuance thereof.[23] A day later Lovett notified Cochran that the last few words would be omitted, both because it would be inappropriate to threaten a future NATO ally, and as it was possible that the threat did not have to be carried out.[24] The State Department was non-committal, however, in the final version which was handed to Stikker at his return in the Netherlands on 7 December. In the memorandum it was stated that the State Department would feel free after a military action to take measures "as the changed circumstances might require".[25]

The memorandum caused quite some commotion in Holland and was withdrawn the next day, after informal insistence by both Cochran and Van Kleffens in Washington. Although the Dutch government realized the implicit significance of the memorandum, this did not have a decisive impact on the decision to start a second military "police action". The members of cabinet did not expect that Marshall aid to the Netherlands would be endangered. They were aware that international pressure would be brought on the American government to cease aid to the Netherlands, but speculated that a successful action and an immediate installment of a loyal Indonesian Federal Interim Government would present the outside world with accomplished facts. This was supposed to halt all American doubts about the whole procedure. With the continual violations of the truce by Republican armed forces as an excuse, the Dutch cabinet already agreed on 13 December to the preparations for a new military action.

The American embassy in The Hague enquired informally after the possible economic and social consequences of a military action for the Netherlands. According to Hirschfeld, the economic effects could not be estimated. The social consequences — by which for instance strikes were meant — from the side of the "reliable" (non-communist) Dutch trade unions would be negligible, according to the commissioner. He expected more danger from boycotts organized by British and American trade unions.[26]

A day after the Dutch had started the second "police action", ECA announced on 20 December the suspension of Marshall aid to Indonesia and amplified in a press statement:

> ECA-funds can only be spent if there is reasonable assurance that their expenditure will actually contribute to economic recovery. In view of developments in Indonesia in recent days ECA considers that conditions favourable to continuation of an effective economic assistance program do not now exist. The further commitment of ECA-funds would therefore be unjustified.[27]

State Department officials stressed that the United States did not intend to support sanctions against the Netherlands, nor to bring about a break with the Netherlands on the Indonesian question.[28] Suspending aid to Indonesia would be least harmful to the Netherlands and would prevent actions by American trade unions. Officially it was stated that Indonesia would be able to spend the remaining amount as soon as negotiations between the Netherlands and the Republic would be resumed. In press statements it was emphasized that the aid was interrupted for economic reasons, not because the aid would have been misused for military purposes by the Dutch. Every possibility of denouncement of the Marshall aid programme was to be prevented.

The suspension of aid to Indonesia can indeed be regarded as a symbolic act. It was meant to be a gesture to the discontent in American public opinion and Congress. The actual delivery of goods was not suspended, but rather the procurement authorizations for Marshall aid goods. From the allotted 64 million dollars were 61 million had already been granted in authorizations. The loan and the conditional aid were not affected at all. That was why Hirschfeld could report to his superiors: "In a material sense this is no severe blow, especially not because the already granted matters can proceed".[29] The outside world was ignorant about the amount of money which was actually involved. Estimates appearing in the papers were higher.[30]

Not the suspension of aid to Indonesia, but a new resolution of the Security Council of the United Nations was the reason for realizing a ceasefire on Java on 31 December and on Sumatra on 5 January. At that moment the Dutch army had conquered large parts of the Republican territory and captured the principal Republican leaders. Various countries urged in the United Nations for a suspension of aid to the Netherlands. Representatives of the Republic of Indonesia did not neglect to point out that Marshall aid had enabled the Dutch to finance the second military action. Public opinion got worse for the Netherlands, when the *New York Times* revealed on 13 January 1949 that Holland had received 400 million dollars as Marshall aid, whereas it had cost the Netherlands 436 million dollars to maintain the army and air-force in Indonesia.

Although pressure on the American government increased, it kept refusing in public statements even to consider suspending aid to the Netherlands. The argument it used was that economic aid should not be used for political purposes. In public statements the State Department stressed that blocking aid to the Netherlands would also mean that aid to other countries should be stopped for political reasons, for example, to Great Britain for its policy concerning Palestine. It also emphasized that it would not be very efficient to weaken economically a future NATO partner.[31] Although they did not intend to give in to outside pressure, State Department officials did not omit to pass on the pressure to the Dutch. Lovett revealed to Van Kleffens on 11 January "that public and Congressional opinion might force us in a direction which would be extremely adverse to the interests, both of the Netherlands and the United States, including jeopardizing ECA-aid to Holland and the North Atlantic Security Pact".[32]

Until half way through January the Dutch cabinet had been rather stoical under mounting pressure. It had regretted in public that the American government gave way to political arguments, but did not directly fear the possibility of endangering economic aid to the Netherlands. It had to be realized, however, that in the long term Holland would not be able to defy the wrath of the rest of the world, with only Belgium as a loyal partner. Also now that Dutch participation in the North Atlantic Treaty Organization (NATO) and even the genesis of the organization were challenged, cabinet willingness to accept any realistic solution grew.

A federal interim government could not be installed, because the non-Republican Indonesians refused to cooperate, before having consulted the captured Republican leaders Sukarno and Hatta. On 28 January 1949 the Security Council of the United Nations, explicitly sponsored by the United States representative, accepted a new resolution. This resolution urged the Dutch government to install a federal government before 15 March 1949, and to commence serious negotiations about the transfer of sovereignty before 1 July 1950. In an attempt to keep the initiative in Dutch hands, and to refute the mediation by the United Nations, Beel proposed a plan to transfer sovereignty to a federal government of the United States of Indonesia on 1 April 1949. In this government a third of the seats would be reserved for Republican representatives. It was to be installed without an interim period. By treaty the Netherlands would keep certain rights concerning Dutch-Indonesian economic, financial and military co-operation, on the condition that before 1 July 1950 the Dutch-Indonesian union would be established and an Indonesian constitution would be accepted by an elected government. By accelerating the establishment of the United States of Indonesia, Beel hoped to exclude the Republic from further negotiations and to secure the federalization of Indonesia, even though this could mean a diminution of Dutch influence on the establishment of the Dutch-Indonesian union.

A breakthrough in Dutch colonial politics

Initially the Dutch cabinet resisted the proposal of the High Commissioner, but within two weeks it changed its mind. Only Sassen did not agree and resigned. An argument for the majority for the Dutch ministers to concede to this new stand was the fact that the non-Republican Indonesian representatives were positive about the proposal. But there was another reason for the change of opinion. It explains why the other ministers for the Catholic Party did not follow their political compatriot Sassen, and why a split in the coalition cabinet did not emerge. This argument was provided by a lengthy note Hirschfeld sent on 1 February 1949 to his superiors in the Council for Economic Affairs, a sub-committee of Dutch cabinet.

The commissioner stressed that in the end a stubborn Dutch attitude could endanger Marshall aid to the Netherlands. At least it was likely that the allotment of aid to Indonesia for 1949/50 would be much lower than expected. He argued that it would become very difficult to realize decolonization of Indonesia against world opinion. This would be so for three reasons. First, because the Dutch had always stressed that the economic recovery of Indonesia would be essential for Dutch economic recuperation; second, because of the international obligations the Netherlands had entered into; and lastly, because of the great dependence on foreign aid. According to Hirschfeld, Holland would not be able to finance the economic rehabilitation of Indonesia, and without this recovery a large amount of invested capital in Indonesia would be scrapped. The centre of gravity of Dutch policy had to be the financial-economic issues instead of the political-military points. Because the main object of the United States was to see to it that a new Indonesian state would be primarily anti-communist, Hirschfeld concluded:

> If the government will be anti-communist, the political structure will be rather indifferent to us in the long run, at least as law and order are realised in Indonesia in such a way, that economic life can develop and Europe and America will not be discriminated. The strength of our policy in Indonesia before the war was the open-door policy. Maintaining such a expediency is an essential point. [. . .] Our real interest in Indonesia from the economic point of view now is the maintenance and in the near future the recovery of our investments in Indonesia.[33]

Until the commissioner's note, the Dutch argument had been that the economic importance of Indonesia for the Netherlands had to be conserved through political regulations. Hirschfeld was the first to provide the insight that the economic importance of Indonesia could be preserved by giving in to Indonesian political demands. This was very important, because in the meantime the Indonesian debt to the Netherlands had increased to about 1.2 billion guilders.[34] As in previous notes written by Hirschfeld for his superiors, his clear way of ascertaining the problems and providing a solution was hardly a matter of debate in the Council for Economic Affairs. On 7 February its two prominent members, the Labour Minister of Finance, Lieftinck, and the Catholic Minister of Economic Affairs, Johan R. M. van den Brink, both pressed the point in cabinet that as soon as possible a Dutch-Indonesian financial-economic agreement had to be signed. According to Van den Brink this was urgent, because "on these points matters of prestige are far less important to the Indonesian".[35] This Dutch business-like approach of the decolonization of Indonesia was strengthened by further events in February and March 1949.

A few days after Hirschfeld had written his note, Senator Owen Brewster introduced

an amendment in the American Senate to the bill which would facilitate the commitment of Marshall aid for 1949/50. The motion put forward that all American aid to the
Netherlands should be suspended, until the Dutch had finally ended the military action,
had withdrawn their troops, had released the Republican leaders and had started reliable
negotiations with the Republic.[36] The senator's motives were less noble than they
seemed to be. In an amplification to his vote Brewster stated: "Dutch business has shut
American business out of the lucrative Indonesian market, yet American money is
directly financing the Dutch colonial adventure."[37] Brewster was counted among the
notorious opponents of economic aid to Western Europe, and his vote was an attempt to
discredit the Marshall aid programme in general.

Brewster's initiative was not applauded by the State Department, because of the
risk of delay to the further allotment of Marshall aid. The American representative of
the ECA in the Netherlands was urgently asked to come to Washington to testify at a
Congressional hearing. He stated that without Marshall aid the Netherlands would
become an unwanted economically unstable factor in Western Europe.[38] On top of that
Secretary of State Marshall himself dissuaded the vote in an address to the Senate. He
considered unilateral steps by the United States to be "untimely and inappropriate".[39]
Pending the motion, State Department used it to put pressure on the Netherlands.
Cochran notified the Dutch representatives that the State Department would have to
give in to the vote if a tentative agreement with the Republic about its recovery in
Yogyakarta was not reached.[40]

Apparently American support for the Dutch position was withering. The most
important issue to the Americans was the anti-communist inclination of the new Indonesian government. Such proneness would be both a guarantee for American-Indonesian
political cooperation as for the American economic interest in the country. However,
the tension was mounting between two elements of American foreign policy: Atlantic
cooperation with colonizing nations and sympathy for decolonization. In the United
Nations many countries expected a clear stand of the United States, but the country did
not consider itself in a position to make a choice. On the one hand it did not want to
neglect the security aspect, on the other it could not afford to let the United Nations
down. To keep on carrying its own point, State Department officials agreed to forcing
the Dutch to make a move.

When it appeared that the Dutch had not carried out the last resolution of the
Security Council of the United Nations, the new Secretary of State, Dean Acheson,
instructed the special ambassador for the Marshall aid programme in Europe, Averell
Harriman, to increase pressure on the Dutch cabinet. Harriman hinted to the Dutch
representative in Paris on 5 March that the military aid, which the Netherlands expected
to receive in accordance with the still to be signed North Atlantic Treaty, would also be
endangered, as long as the Netherlands had not accepted the pending mediating United
Nations resolution to the full.[41]

In a first reaction, the Dutch Minister of Foreign Affairs, Stikker, stated that he
wanted to make a reservation to Dutch commitment to NATO.[42] He received the
consent of his colleagues in cabinet to do so, but cabinet also agreed to agree
"reluctantly" to a "symbolic return" of the Republican government to Yogyakarta.
Stikker indeed made the reservation in conversations with Acheson just prior to the
signing of the North Atlantic Treaty on 31 March. Stikker stated that it would not
do to mix up two unsimilar matters as military assistance and decolonization. He

told Acheson that he would not sign the treaty, as long as the American reservation was not withdrawn. Acheson, however, put forward that the American government had to take notice of an increasingly unfavourable attitude of the American public and Congress, and he repeated that the Netherlands could forget about military aid as long as decolonization would not be settled.[43] Stikker did sign the treaty on 4 April 1949.

The prompt swing-over of Stikker suggests that his threat was nothing more than a theatre scene which cannot be taken seriously. The actual decision to agree on how to proceed with the Indonesian question had already been reached on 23 March, after a "ruling" of the United Nations to recover the Republican government and to accept a preliminary conference between Dutch and Republican officials before a concluding Round Table Conference (RTC). The Dutch cabinet agreed to leaving the Beel Plan and accepting this breakthrough for two major reasons. We have already acknowledged that the financial-economic point had been first put to the Dutch cabinet in the beginning of February. In the beginning of March a second point had become urgent too, namely the security policy of the Netherlands. As a matter of fact, at this stage both issues were being viewed as one. With the mounting tension of the Cold War, economic recovery of the Netherlands was no longer conceived to be a goal in itself, but as a means to serve another purpose: the defence against communism. This purpose was to be achieved both by building up a welfare state as well as by an actual military build-up. The two were only possible with economic recovery, for which it had become important to consent to an accelerated political independence and economic recovery of Indonesia. Although it seemed to be otherwise, the State Department never threatened to block Marshall aid to the Netherlands, nor was such a seeming threat the decisive argument for the Dutch government to give in to Indonesian independence.

Towards Indonesian independence

In the month of April serious talks were resumed on Indonesian independence, which resulted on 7 May 1949 in an agreement to recover the Republic in Yogyakarta and to hold the concluding RTC in August 1949. This cleared the way for military aid to the Netherlands. Brewster's motion did not reach the finishing line. Its sting was pulled out by an amendment, which stated that the United States could withhold assistance to aid-receiving countries against whom the United Nations Security Council "is taking preventative or enforcement action".[44] This definitely ended the threat that Marshall aid to the Netherlands had seemed to be under.

Dutch officials urged for resumption of Marshall aid to Indonesia and for granting the 100 million dollars Exim Bank loan. In Paris talks had been taken up about the distribution of Marshall aid for 1949/50. The Netherlands had claimed 89 million dollars for Indonesia. However, the OEEC partners did not seem to be willing to adopt Indonesia in the proposal for the distribution of aid, because Harriman had urged for cuts in the original claims of the participating countries. A Dutch appeal to ECA resulted in an informal instruction to the OEEC to earmark 50 million dollars for Indonesia, although the European representatives proposed a symbolic 10 million dollars. This indicates to what extent the American government stood behind the Dutch again.

During the RTC the representatives of the Republic agreed that the new Indonesian state was to accept all the debts of the colonial administration. In total Indonesia took over domestic and foreign debts to the amount of 4.9 billion guilders. Above all, it guaranteed all future transfers of Dutch companies in Indonesia to the Netherlands and recognized the rights of possession of Dutch enterprises. When the final financial-economic agreement with the Indonesians was discussed in Dutch cabinet, the ministers approved with unceremonious satisfaction.[45]

A remunerative choice

The Dutch ministers could indeed lean back with contentment in their chairs. After the outbreak of the Korean war in 1950 prices of raw materials on the world market went up very quickly. Private enterprise in Indonesia was one of the leading suppliers of raw materials like rubber, palm oil, tin and natural oil. Nearly half of the invested foreign capital in Indonesia was in Dutch hands. Although foreign companies in Indonesia did not produce up to pre-war standards and according to their capacity, because of labour disputes and the many discouraging changes in export regulations, their profits were substantial. Van Hoogstraten reported in January 1956 in his capacity of general representative of Dutch trade and industry in the Far East, Australia and New Zealand:

> We have needed to exercise patience with Indonesia in our Western way of pushing matters and in the last six years since the transfer of sovereignty this patience has brought grist to the mill of Western interests — although this is sometimes forgotten. Many Western enterprises in Indonesia have even made in these last few years more profits, and have been able to transfer these profits to outside Indonesia in foreign currency, than on average in many past year.[46]

A peak in this stream of foreign currency was reached in the second half of 1952, when 495 million guilders worth of foreign currency and gold reached the Netherlands in half a year.[47] The stream kept on flowing until December 1957, when in reaction to the conflict between the Netherlands and Indonesia about Dutch New Guinea all Dutch enterprises in Indonesia were seized and somewhat later nationalized.

The Dutch ministers could also throw a satisfied retrospective glance at what they had achieved, because by agreeing to the decolonization of Indonesia they had secured to their own conviction the Marshall aid for the period 1949–52 and the military aid for the period 1949–60. Above all, the independence of Indonesia discharged the Netherlands from the obligation to take care of economic recovery of Indonesia. In the period 1949–60 the most important share of aid to Indonesia was supplied in the form of loans, gifts and supplies of agricultural surplus production by the United States (586 million dollars), the rest of the Western world (809 million dollars) and Eastern Europe (516 million dollars).

If the Dutch cabinet had chosen in 1949 to follow its own way in the process of decolonization, this would have meant international political isolation for the Netherlands and most probably the international economic solitude of Indonesia. In that case the Netherlands would have been forced to finance the economic recovery of Indonesia out of its own means and it would have missed out on other amounts, which can be summarised as follows:

— Marshall aid (1949–52)	f 3.35 billion
— Military aid (1949–60)	f 4.50 billion
— Take-over of Indonesian debts (1949)	f 4.90 billion
— Financial transfers to the Netherlands (1950–57)	f 3.20 billion
— "Saved" economic aid to Indonesia (1949–60)	f 7.25 billion
Total	f23.20 billion

Note: The exchange rate of the US dollar was 3.80 guilders in the 1950s.

An amount of about 23.2 billion guilders is a minimal estimate. Not included are for instance the costs of a possible guerrilla war or an economic boycott. On the other hand, the nationalization of Dutch enterprises in 1957 and 1958 meant a loss of Dutch capital. In 1966 this loss was claimed by the Dutch cabinet from the new Indonesian government. It was estimated to be 4.5 billion guilders.[48] Agreement was reached, however, on a repayment of 600 million guilders.

This leaves us 22.6 billion guilders, which almost equals 8 per cent of Dutch Net National Product (NNP) in the period 1949–60. In those years about 16 per cent of NNP was spent on average in the Netherlands on net investments in the private and public sector.[49] These expenditures enabled the Dutch government to pursue its policy of industrializing the Netherlands economy in the 1950s successfully. The self-evident supposition is therefore that the Dutch economic recovery in the 1950s was for a substantial part facilitated by the consent of the Dutch cabinet in 1949 to Indonesian independence.

Notes

1   J. Tinbergen and J. B. D. Derksen, "Berekeningen over de Economische Betekenis van Nederlandsch-Indië, voor Nederland", *Maandschrift van het Centraal Bureau voor de Statistiek* XL. (1945): 210–16.

2   P. van der Eng, *De Marshall-Hulp. Een Perspectief voor Nederland, 1947–1953* (Houten, 1987), pp. 167–68.

3   Minutes of Cabinet (13 April 1947) in *Officiële Bescheiden Betreffende de Nederlands-Indonesische Betrekkingen (OB)*, ed. S. L. van der Wal (The Hague, 1971–85) VIII: 302.

4   Production figures from J. E. Metcalf, *The Agricultural Economy of Indonesia* (Washington, 1952), p. 38; population figures from N. Keyfitz, "The Population of Indonesia", *Ekonomi dan Keuangan Indonesia* VI (1953): 633.

5   Minutes of Cabinet (7 March 1947) *OB* VII: 690.

6   H. M. Hirschfeld to C. G. W. H. van Boetzelaer (31 October 1947) *DGEM*, no. 485.

7   H. M. Hirschfeld to C. G. W. H. van Boetzelaer (21 November 1947) *DGEM*, no. 455; C. G. W. H. van Boetzelaer to E. N. van Kleffens (21 November 1947) *OB* XII: 25.

8   J. E. van Hoogstraten to H. van Mook (7 December 1947) *OB* XII: 113; J. E. van Hoogstraten to H. van Mook (8 December 1947), *H. van Mook Papers* at the National Archive (Algemeen Rijksarchief, ARA) in The Hague, no. 250.

9   This paragraph draws on: E. Colbert, "The Road Not Taken: Decolonization and Independence in Indonesia and Indochina", *Foreign Affairs*, LI (1973): 624; and P. J. Drooglever, "The United States and the Dutch Applecart During the Indonesian Revolution", in *Image and Impact: American Influences in the Netherlands Since 1945*, ed. R. Kroes (Amsterdam, 1981), pp. 36–37.

10 E. N. van Kleffens to C. G. W. H. van Boetzelaer (3 December 1947) *OB* XII: 97.

11 R. J. McMahon, *Colonialism and Cold War: The United States and the Struggle for Indonesian Independence, 1945–1949* (Ithaca/London, 1981), pp. 144–48.

12 E. N. van Kleffens to C. G. W. H. van Boetzelaer (9 January 1948) *OB* XII: 483.

13 P. W. Bonsal to G. C. Marshall (11 January 1948), *Foreign Relations of the United States (FRUS)* (1948–VI), p. 75.

14 Minutes of Cabinet (11 January 1948) *OB* XII: 503–504.

15 Note by Embassy Councillor H. A. Helb (16 January 1948) *OB* XII: 555. Compare: McMahon, *Colonialism and Cold War*, p. 177.

16 "De Economische Toestand van Indonesië Medio 1948" (26 August 1948) *DGEM*, no. 455.

17 "Bespreking [. . .] over de Verhouding van Nederland en de Overzeese Gebiedsdelen in het European Recovery Program", E. H. van der Beugel to H. M. Hirschfeld (26 April 1948) *DGEM*, no. 455.

18 "Vergadering van de Committee of Four over de Nederlandsch Overzeesche Gebiedsdeelen", H. M. J. Hart to L. Götzen (31 July 1948) Archive of the Council of Enterprises in Indonesia (Onder-nemingsraad voor Nederlands-Indië, *ORNI*) at ARA, box 162.

19 H. M. Hirschfeld to A. H. Philipse (30 July 1948) *DGEM*, no. 455.

20 R. Gase, *Beel in Batavia. Van Contact tot Conflict. Verwikkelingen Rond de Indonesische Kwestie in 1948* (Baarn, 1986), p. 70.

21 R. A. Lovett to H. M. Cochran (5 November 1948) *FRUS* (1948–VI), p. 465.

22 *Keesings Historisch Archief (KHA)* (1–7 August 1948), p. 7698; *KHA* (12–18 December 1948), p. 7870.

23 R. A. Lovett to H. M. Cochran (3 December 1948) *FRUS* (1948–VI), p. 514.

24 R. A. Lovett to H. M. Cochran (4 December 1948) *FRUS* (1948–VI), p. 516.

25 "Aide-Mémoire from Department to Netherlands Embassy" (7 December 1948) *FRUS* (1948–VI), p. 531.

26 H. M. Hirschfeld to H. N. Boon (17 December 1948) Archive of Secret Documents of the Department of Foreign Affairs, Ministry of Foreign Affairs in The Hague, no. 610.33 (Indonesië – ECA-hulp).

27 R. A. Lovett to H. M. Cochran (20 December 1948) *FRUS* (1948–VI), p. 593.

28 D. Rusk to P. C. Jessup (23 December 1948) *FRUS* (1948–VI), p. 597.

29 H. M. Hirschfeld to L. Götzen (22 December 1948) *DGEM*, no. 457.

30 G. McTurnan Kahin, *Nationalism and Revolution in Indonesia* (Ithaca/New York, 1952), p. 403.

31 McMahon, *Colonialism and Cold War*, p. 261.

32 "Memorandum of Conversation" by R. A. Lovett (11 January 1949) *FRUS* (1949–VII), p. 140.

33 "De Economische Positie van Nederland en de Indonesische Quaestie", H. M. Hirschfeld to the Council for Economic Affairs (1 February 1949) *DGEM*, no. 458.

34 "Nota Inzake de Deviezenpositie", *Bijlagen bij de Handelingen van de Tweede Kamer der Staten Generaal* (1948/49), no. 1202–2, p. 19.

35   Minutes of Cabinet (7 February 1949) Archive of the Council of Minutes (Raad van Ministers, *RvM*) at ARA, box 392.

36   *KHA* (6–12 February 1949), p. 7954.

37   O. Brewster in the Senate (25 February 1949) as cited in McMahon, *Colonialism and Cold War*, p. 276.

38   E. N. van Kleffens to H. M. Hirschfeld (11 February 1949) *DGEM*, no. 457.

39   G. C. Marshall in the Senate (25 February 1949) *FRUS* (1949–VII), p. 223.

40   L. G. M. Jaquet, *Minister Stikker en de Souvereiniteitsoverdracht: Nederland op de Tweesprong tussen Azie en het Westen* (The Hague, 1982), pp. 218–19.

41   "Memorandum of Conversation" by F. E. Nolting (6 March 1949) *FRUS* (1949–VII), p. 303.

42   Minutes of Cabinet (8 March 1949) *RvM*, box 392.

43   D. Acheson to H. M. Cochran (31 March 1949) *FRUS* (1949–VII), pp. 356–57.

44   E. N. van Kleffens to D. U. Stikker (7 April 1949) *DGEM*, no. 458.

45   Minutes of Cabinet (31 October 1949) *RvM*, box 393.

46   "Notities Betreffende de Politieke Situatie in Indonesië bij de Aanvang van 1956" (p. 18), J. E. van Hoogstraten to the Stichting Vertegenwoordiging in Indonesië van de Nederlandse Industrie (16 January 1956) *ORNI*, box 171.

47   *New York Times* (2 January 1953).

48   C. van Esterik, *Nederlands Laatste Bastion in de Oost. Economie en Politiek in de Nieuw-Guinea-Kwestie* (Baaru, 1982), p. 145.

49   *Tachtig Jaren Statistiek in Tijdreeksen 1899–1979* (The Hague, 1979), pp. 144–45.

Chapter 7

Catherine R. Schenk

DECOLONIZATION AND EUROPEAN ECONOMIC INTEGRATION

The Free Trade Area Negotiations, 1956–58

THE 1950s WAS A PERIOD of fundamental change in Britain's economic relations. As the crises and stop-gaps of the late 1940s receded and recovery from the war became more established, the international economic system began to change shape and the role of Britain within it altered. In response to the failure of the institutions devised at the Bretton Woods Conference in 1944 to produce multilateral trade and payments, attention turned to regional solutions to the imbalance left after the Second World War. The result was the formalization of the Sterling Area and the political and economic integration of Western Europe. At the same time as these regional economic systems were being established, Britain's relationship with its overseas territories was undergoing fundamental political change. India and Pakistan led the road to post-war independence in the late 1940s and this process was accelerated through the 1950s as colonies strove to end their constitutional dependence on Britain. The recent economic history of the end of Empire and of British involvement in European integration have, with some recent exceptions, tended to be pursued in parallel. This paper aims to integrate these two strands in the history of Britain's external economic relations by looking at the British attempt to create an industrial Free Trade Area between the OEEC and EEC in 1956–58.

The coincidence of the severing of constitutional ties with many colonies and Britain's increasing interest in becoming part of an integrated Europe has generated three views of this relationship. It was assumed by many at the time and many commentators since, that these two allegiances offered some sort of a choice for British policy-makers. Becoming closer to Europe, it was argued, would necessitate looser economic ties with the Commonwealth and Empire. Thus Camps has described Britain's Free Trade Area initiative of 1956 as a turning-point in British policy when 'Europe began slowly but perceptibly up the scale, and the Commonwealth to move down'.[1] Britain's application to join the EEC in 1961 is therefore viewed as a major policy shift away from its traditional global role and toward a regional one. On the other hand, as colonies distanced themselves from British influence, the process of end of Empire may have accelerated the changing emphasis in British policy toward Europe.[2]

Alternatively, it was asserted at the time that the Empire and Europe were mutually reinforcing. In 1957 Maudling addressed the Council of the European Assembly making clear his belief that

> what strengthens the economy of the British Commonwealth must in the long run help to strengthen the economy of Europe, what strengthens the economy of Europe must help to strengthen the economies of the British Commonwealth. In these matters we are interdependent, there is no conflict but a true interdependence that I believe it is our responsibility to explain.[3]

This interpretation has been adopted by recent writers. Darwin describes the Commonwealth, the United States, and Europe as components of a 'Churchillian Tripod' and argues that British policy was aimed at carefully balancing these three relationships.[4] How this balance evolved and the dynamics of the underlying economic trends still need to be explored.

A closer examination shows that Britain's external economic relationships after 1950 were more complex than they have been described. In particular, it is necessary to examine the impact of policy in Europe and in the Empire on the development of British priorities. The initiative at this time was arguably coming from outside Britain in the form of changes in the international trading system. The present study describes these changes by analysing the interaction between the process of decolonization and Britain's first initiative toward the EEC. The question of the conflict between wider Commonwealth interests and European integration is not the main subject of this article. Although it will be shown that the interests of the independent members of the Commonwealth did overlap with those of the colonies, they were not identical. The episode of the Free Trade Area negotiations is chosen because it raised specifically colonial (as opposed to Commonwealth) issues which have not hitherto been explored. After a preliminary section on changes in trade policy and merchandise flows, the article analyses the attempt to form an industrial free trade area with the EEC, and then Section III examines British endeavours to arrange mitigation for the effect of the Treaty of Rome on the colonies. A further section assesses colonial, Commonwealth, and European opinion on these various issues.

I

The obvious beginning of an investigation of the nature of Britain's external economic policy is to examine the pattern of international trade in the 1950s. Trade relations among Empire countries began to disintegrate from 1953 after the Korean War, well before British initiatives toward Europe. The case which will be argued here is that the Empire and the old Commonwealth were becoming an increasingly hard place for British exports to penetrate.

By the mid-1950s the quantitative importance of Imperial Preference for both Britain and its colonial trading partners had largely been eroded. Inflation after 1932 erased much of the benefit that overseas exporters enjoyed in the British market since most preference offered by Britain was through specific duties rather than on an *ad valorem* basis. This effect was reinforced by liberalization of trade generally and changes in the composition of trade away from imports on which preference was given and towards goods such as raw materials which carried no tariffs. By 1953 the average preference margin on trade between Britain and the Commonwealth was only 5–6 per cent, or half the rate which had prevailed in 1937,[5] although the levels of preference varied widely. In 1958 the preference on particular colonial products ranged from 1 per cent on cocoa and 7–8 per cent on oranges to 10 per cent on bananas and 12 per cent on coffee.[6]

The preference offered to British products in colonial markets is shown in Table 1. This indicates that Imperial Preference was essentially a Commonwealth issue and not a colonial/empire system. In 1955 Britain exported £382m worth of goods to the colonies, of which £146m went to those offering some preference. As seen in Table 1, however, most of these exports were not subject to preferential tariffs. The Federation of Malaya was the only important market for British exports where preference was significant and even here only one third of goods were offered a preference margin which averaged 13 per cent. The larger African and Asian markets did not offer any preference to British goods. The Board of Trade acknowledged in 1956 that the close commercial ties of overseas territories to Britain were not due to tariff preferences but rather to the influence of long-standing technical and commercial connections.[7] By the mid-1950s, as Europe recovered, these informal ties were waning.

Imperial Preference retained political importance as a symbol of British imperial power that outlived its economic rationale. The Empire remained dear to the hearts of sections of the British electorate and, partly for this reason, the British argued strongly that there was no inconsistency between Imperial Preference and European integration. The former comprised negotiated trade agreements on primary products which were bound by reciprocal obligations from the British, while the latter was meant to enhance the industrial trade of Britain. Ministers argued that the contractual agreements with the Empire could operate alongside any agreements Britain proposed to make with Europe.[8]

Table 1 Tariff preferences on British goods (%)

	(1) % of dutiable items on which preference is accorded to Britain	(2) Average level of preference on trade in (1)
Fed Malaya	33	13
Br W. Indies	90	12.5
Cyprus	98	8–10
Malta	56	8–10
Nigeria	nil	nil
East Africa	nil	nil
Aden	nil	nil
Ghana	nil	nil
Hong Kong	neg	neg
Singapore	neg	neg
Small Colonies	substantial	10

Notes: Source, Note on Commonwealth Preference, March 1958, PRO, T 234/219. East Africa includes Kenya, Uganda, and Tanganyika.

Moreover, the preference offered to British products in Commonwealth markets was not considered an obstacle to closer economic association with Europe.[9] The increased opportunities for British trade in Europe were expected to outweigh the negative impact of a decline in preference in the Commonwealth, although officials noted that 'we could not take advantage of these opportunities if we were not competitive with Europe but if we cannot be competitive we shall in the long run be as badly off with protection as without it'.[10] Evidently, Imperial Preference did not offer a viable alternative to European integration. There was no scope for turning back the clock and reinforcing Empire trade as an alternative to or a bulwark against Europe. As early as 1952 the Commonwealth had sincerely committed itself to freer trade and payments on a global scale and was unwilling even to consider reinforcing old Imperial economic ties.[11] In August 1958 Maudling advised the Prime Minister that '[it is] obvious . . . that no expansion of Commonwealth trade on a new preferential basis can be regarded as a possibility'.[12]

These shifts in trade policy accompanied changes in the pattern of merchandise trade itself. The British share of colonial exports overall fell from 31 to 23 per cent between 1953 and 1958. The corresponding share of British exports in colonial markets fell from 29 per cent to 23 per cent in the same period. Table 2 shows the changing nature of trade in manufactures in major colonial and ex-colonial markets between 1953 and 1959.

The decline in Britain's share was mostly offset by increased imports from West Germany into Africa and from Japan into Malaya. By 1959 Malaya was importing half of its iron and steel from Japan and also an increasing proportion of electrical and metal-working machinery, and also textiles. The remnants of Imperial Preference were not sufficient to maintain the British share of this market. The growing proportion of imports from West Germany into the colonies generally reflected the loss of competitiveness of British automobiles and capital goods.

Figures 1 and 2 show the changes in total trade[13] of selected African colonies with Britain. The British share of the African exports remained fairly high but stagnant through the period. Nigerian exports were very concentrated in the British market at the beginning of the decade but declined steadily thereafter. The fall in Britain as a market for colonial imports is much more dramatic. After the Korean War boom and bust of 1951–53, Britain's share of the African markets fell sharply.

Figures 3 and 4 show the trade of these territories with the non-sterling OEEC.

Table 2 Changes in manufactured import market share

Market Per Cent	UK		W. Germany		France		Japan	
	1953	1959	1953	1959	1953	1959	1953	1959
East Africa	81.6	58.9	4.4	10.2	0.6	–	0.9	6.4
Ghana	74.4	60.0	4.6	14.1	–	1.5	8.4	13.0
Malaya	60.3	40.3	5.9	9.3	1.1	2.3	13.8	27.4

Notes: Source, S. J. Wells, *British Export Performance: a comparative study* (Cambridge, 1964), 17. East Africa includes Kenya, Uganda, Tanganyika.

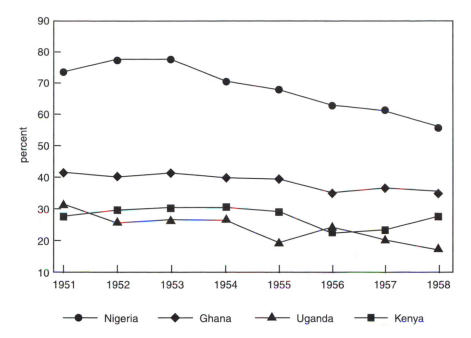

Figure 1 UK share of colonial exports

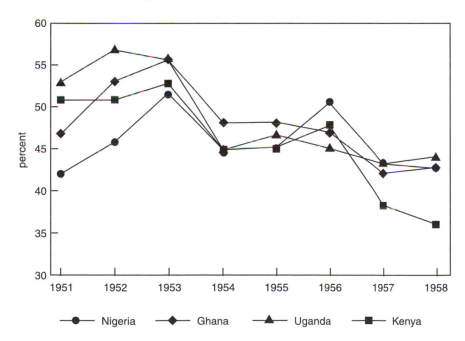

Figure 2 UK share of colonial imports

Europe's share of African exports rose dramatically for Nigeria and Ghana after 1953. After the end of the raw materials boom in 1953, European imports into these markets recovered quickly and held their position through the period.

This changing geographical distribution of trade was not the result of changes in discrimination since most colonies had removed preference in favour of British goods

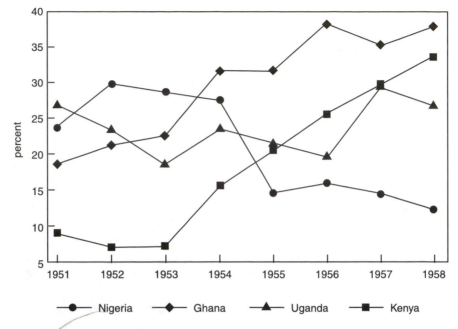

Figure 3 OEEC share of colonial exports

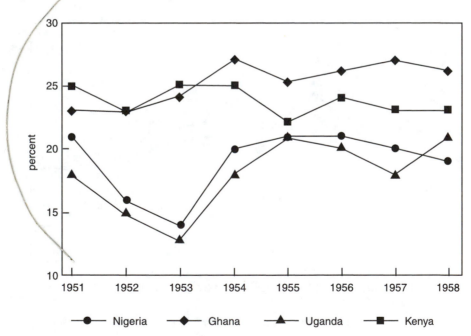

Figure 4 OEEC share of colonial imports

by 1952. Instead, British competitiveness in terms of price and quality declined as European producers recovered from the war and British exporters faced mounting resistance to their goods in colonial markets. It has been argued elsewhere that the sterling area as a whole was an increasingly difficult market for British producers and this conclusion is also valid for the colonial and newly independent part of the sterling area.

II

A key point of interaction between decolonization and Britain's European initiative was the industrial Free Trade Area which Britain tried to negotiate with the EEC nations in the late 1950s. In November 1956 the Chancellor of the Exchequer announced an intention to pursue an industrial free trade area (FTA) in Europe to allow Britain access to the benefits of freer trade in Continental Europe that would result from the introduction of the European Common Market. At this time there were several colonies approaching independence which complicated the arrangements for colonial participation in the FTA. This episode also draws out the distinction between French imperial policy and that of the British, and shows the growing awareness in Europe of Britain's rather delicate position at the head of an empire that was undergoing a political transformation.

The important distinction for colonial interests was to separate industrial from agricultural trade and this was British policy until they were forced into retreat in early 1957. All colonial products entered Britain free from duty, and they generally did not compete with temperate European producers so they were not initially affected by the Common Market on the Continent. As long as the FTA was restricted to industrial manufactures the colonies were also unaffected by British association with the EEC, since the terms would not require Britain either to impose tariffs on colonial imports or to include them in the FTA.

The decision to exclude agriculture from the FTA was not, of course, a disinterested act on the part of a conscientious imperial leader. British farmers themselves were threatened by freer trade with Europe, which would undermine their subsidized position in the protected British market. They did not oppose tropical imports from the Empire that entered duty-free but European producers presented direct competition. In August 1957, for example, Rab Butler wrote to the Prime Minister from his country home regarding the FTA and agriculture: 'this subject is dynamite for and to the County Constituencies', and he warned Macmillan to tread carefully on this issue.[14] The British government, therefore, had its own domestic reasons for trying to insist on an industrial FTA. This was not exclusively or even predominantly an imperial issue.

In 1956 the colonies were surveyed about their attitude to a possible industrial FTA through which Britain could be associated with the European Common Market. Their response broadly fulfilled British expectations by not raising any objections. Only Singapore suggested that it would prefer to be included as this would increase the colony's entrepot trade.[15] In the event, the Empire was brought to the centre of the negotiations in response to a French challenge rather than a British initiative. Late in 1956 the French decided that dependent overseas territories of The Six European nations[16] should be included in the proposed European Common Market. This policy was adopted by the French essentially for domestic political purposes: to reassure the French public that European integration was not going to undermine the country's position as an imperial power. Between November 1956 and February 1957, the British made frequent attempts to persuade the Europeans 'how important it was to have similar arrangements for Colonies in both the Customs Union and the Free Trade Area and urging that before the Six made up their minds what to do there should be discussions between them and us to avoid future difficulties'.[17] The Six avoided consultation with Britain, however, as the issue became a breaking-point for the French in their negotiations with The Six who were forced to concede. In December 1956 the German economic minister complained to the British that the French and Belgians had not sufficiently thought through their plans for the overseas territories. The British representative in Bonn reported that 'It was clear to him [German economic minister] that their main object had been to try to obtain as much money as possible for colonial development from the other Powers concerned, especially Germany, and implied that the Federal Government was not at all enthusiastic.'[18] Nevertheless, the Germans agreed to the terms in order to complete the Messina negotiations.

In mid-February 1957 it was agreed that French, Belgian, and Dutch overseas territories would be full beneficiaries of free trade in their exports to continental Europe. They would also be allowed to impose infant industry protection on their imports from Europe, so long as these restrictions were non-discriminatory. In addition, the French pressured The Six to compile a fund of $581.25 m for investment in these territories over five years. The EEC was thus widened geographically beyond Europe and a development role was added to its responsibilities. This change in emphasis came to be characterized as EURAFRICA to describe the association of non-Imperial European countries with the economic and social development of Africa. Table 3 shows how the EURAFRICA development fund was to be raised. Germany bore most of the development burden since it had no overseas territories to benefit.

The British authorities were sceptical about the political wisdom of such an axis and recognized that in many territories this attempt to link Africa more closely with Europe would be viewed with suspicion. British territories such as Ghana and Nigeria were approaching (or had just achieved) constitutional independence, and were likely to view the EURAFRICA initiative as a way to perpetuate a dependent colonial bond. Ghana, especially, was more interested in creating pan-African ties which would strengthen the continent in a confrontation with developed European powers. British representatives in the African colonies shared these concerns. The Tanganyikan and Kenyan governors complained that if European overseas territories were included in the EEC and Free Trade Area, membership would be on the basis of politics, not economics or geography. This would interfere with regional African development efforts such as infant industry protection.[19]

Table 3 Contribution to development fund ($USm)

	Gross	Net
Germany	200	200
France	200	—
Belgium	70	40
Italy	40	35
Holland	70	35
Luxembourg	1.25	1.25
Total	581.25	

Notes: Source, Telegram from Bonn to Foreign Office, 26 Feb. 1957, PRO, T 234/223. 'Net' is the gross contribution less the allocation for that country's overseas territories.

The European dependent overseas territories were less politically advanced than those of Britain and were more economically integrated with their metropolitan rulers. The African British colonies did not offer preference to imports from Britain and their trade was much more diversified geographically (and in most cases by commodity) than was the case for European colonies. The EURAFRICA concept was therefore considered inappropriate for British dependent overseas territories and contradictory to general African interests.

By bringing their dependent overseas territories into the proposed EEC, The Six raised complex obstacles to any British association with the group. In March 1957 Macmillan noted that 'I understand that as the result of the decision of the six to include colonies in the Common Market a somewhat critical position has arisen.'[20] The proposed FTA was meant to ally *all* EEC participants with other OEEC countries, but Britain was eager to exclude all dependent territories from any FTA in order to hold the line on excluding agriculture. The Treasury and Colonial Office recognized that most, if not all, of the British colonies would be unwilling to join an industrial FTA as they had little to gain and would be unwilling to offer reciprocal liberalization on industrial imports in order to become full members. The European colonies, on the other hand, would have nothing to gain from a FTA unless tropical agriculture was included.

A further complication was posed by the seemingly inexorable progress toward constitutional independence in the Empire. These negotiations over the FTA coincided with independence in two major British colonies – the Gold Coast and Malaya. Differentiating between newly independent countries, those in which independence was imminent, and those beginning the process towards independence was problematic. If only dependent territories were included in the FTA, the benefits of membership would finish with the end of colonial status. This would put an unacceptable obstacle in the way of the process of decolonization to which Britain was committed. On the other hand, if newly independent territories were included, membership would also need to be offered to other independent Commonwealth countries. This geographical expansion would move such a trade agreement well beyond the original concept of a European group and would necessitate even more concessions within the GATT which threatened the viability of GATT altogether. The consequent disruption to the organization of global trade would be compounded by the damage to British interests in any FTA, since it was inconceivable that the large Commonwealth countries such as Australia and New Zealand would join unless they could negotiate the inclusion of their temperate agricultural exports. This would open the floodgates for European penetration of the British agricultural market.

Finally, the need for all members of the Commonwealth to be treated equally in trade with Britain was of paramount concern in order to preserve its unity. Allowing some to be included and others to remain outside would impose an insupportable wedge between members of the 'new-style' Commonwealth which would undermine its viability. Ministers did not want to accelerate the decline of economic cohesion in the Commonwealth at a time when its political ties were loosening.

Just before The Six announced its decision on overseas territories, an OEEC Council meeting was held in Paris to discuss the possibility for a FTA on the lines suggested by the British, and The Six finally met with Britain to discuss the position of overseas territories. The British representatives put their case, outlining their objections to the inclusion of overseas territories as described above, but the European response was not encouraging. The Six kept virtually silent, merely noting that this was an outstanding problem but refusing to elaborate on their position.[21] The British had hoped that any provisions for overseas territories would be kept as vague as possible in the Treaty of Rome establishing the Common Market but they were destined for disappointment. Harkort of the German Foreign Ministry reported that until The Six met in Paris they too had expected that the provisions for the overseas territories would be kept general and that a convention would be negotiated after the Treaty was signed, but the French insisted on detail in the Treaty itself and this was finally accepted by Adenauer.[22]

On 9 March, the Prime Minister met with French Foreign Minister Pineau and voiced Britain's disappointment at the inclusion of the overseas territories in the Treaty of Rome. Macmillan warned that the issue would have to be raised in the GATT and it was agreed that there should be urgent discussion between French and British officials on the issue.[23] At the end of March, Figures of the Treasury met with French civil servant Marjolin to try to persuade the French to agree to exclude overseas territories from any FTA. In particular he emphasized the necessity to invite the Commonwealth in if the colonies were included 'owing to the constant constitutional evolution of colonies'.[24] Marjolin responded that the French did not want to include the large Commonwealth countries since they competed with French farmers, and that perhaps the French overseas territories were not that similar to those of Britain. Nevertheless, if the overseas territories were excluded from the FTA, this would be inconsistent with the Common Market and might do injury to some of the territories included in the Rome Treaty. Despite the failure to agree, Figures emerged from this discussion with the impression that the French were now much more aware of British difficulties.

Meanwhile, also in February 1957, the British position on the FTA was further undermined when Denmark insisted that some provision for agricultural products should be included in the FTA. The British were forced to agree to consider the inclusion of agriculture but still hoped to exclude foodstuffs.[25] In May Faure, French Minister of State, announced that his government would also insist on agriculture being included in the FTA in order to ensure the support of French farmers.[26]

The economic rationale for excluding the colonies was, therefore, eroded on two fronts: by the prospect of including some agricultural products in the FTA, and by the provisions for overseas territories in the EEC. The political obstacles, however, remained. It would still be necessary to make the offer to colonies approaching independence and also, therefore, to the independent Commonwealth. This geographic expansion would make the FTA impossible to negotiate. There was also the prospect of dividing the new Commonwealth between members and non-members. In March 1957, and again in October, Ministers were advised to continue to insist that all overseas territories be excluded from any FTA, although this position might be reviewed when the agricultural policy became clearer.[27]

III

The inclusion of overseas territories in the Common Market opened up a new legal objection to the Treaty of Rome. A customs union among European states was consistent with the GATT since it did not introduce new preferential trading arrangements but merely reduced barriers to trade among members. The provisions for colonies, however, extended the existing preference which they received from their traditional metropole to non-Imperial European countries such as West Germany. The British were reluctant to criticize the Rome Treaty directly because this was an important initiative supported by the Americans which would unite continental Europe, and because a campaign against the Treaty would be inconsistent with their efforts to secure the advantages of being part of an industrial FTA with Europe. The provision for overseas territories, however, would require a waiver in the GATT, and Britain and the Commonwealth planned to insist on mitigation from The Six to redress any harm done to the economic interests of the British colonies in return for granting the waiver.

The economic problems for the British empire lay in the fact that the French and Belgian overseas territories were producers of primary products – especially coffee and cocoa – which competed directly with production in Ghana and the British colonies in East and West Africa. The Common Market was likely to introduce a preferential margin of 16 per cent on coffee and 6 per cent on cocoa produced within their associated territories.[28] Ghana and the African colonies were much larger producers of these commodities than the French overseas territories and enjoyed a large market share in Continental Europe (other than in France) which would only be eroded in the long run by increased production encouraged by the preference margins. Although the immediate economic effects might be limited, the political fallout was expected to be more serious.[29]

In May 1957, British ministers began informal negotiations, first with the Germans bilaterally and then with the Six together, to arrange mitigation for colonial interests. Their strategy was to stress 'the damage – political and economic – which would be done to European interests, particularly in Africa, if our Colonies found that their interests had been sacrificed by the Messina Powers'.[30] It was pointed out to the Europeans that the shifting constitutional position complicated the political consequences of antagonizing the colonies:

> in this regard it is relevant that some important territories, eg. Nigeria, may be emerging as independent countries just at the time in the transitional period when the common tariff on the Customs Union will be beginning to be effective against them. This in itself will provide an opening for countries hostile to the West to win them over by specious trade deals etc.[31]

Nigeria and Uganda were regarded as particularly sensitive as both were affected by forces of nationalism and were geographically strategic. Ghana also needed to be considered, although it was already an independent state, since

> it could not but be of serious consequence to the future relations between West Africa and Europe if both Ghana and Nigeria – whose total populations approximate to nearly 40 million (a larger population than that of the Belgian and French overseas territories taken together) – were to feel their interests to be seriously prejudiced by action taken by the major Western European countries.[32]

The British met with The Six in June 1957 to put their case but were unable to extract any commitments from the Europeans, who preferred to leave mitigation to the institutions established under the Treaty of Rome. The British delegation summed up that 'in brief we got no more out of The Six than we had expected but we have at least made it clear to them that we have a pretty major political problem here. What (if anything) they are prepared to do about it still remains obscure.'[33] Privately, the Prime Minister's advisers had misgivings about the possibility of securing mitigation for the colonies and, in the event, the negotiations were delayed for over a year.[34]

IV

Throughout the OEEC deliberations, the colonies were consulted and kept abreast of developments. On 2 April 1957 a formal meeting took place at the Colonial Office with colonial representatives at which only Hong Kong, Singapore, and Malta expressed a desire to join an industrial FTA. The Colonial Secretary acknowledged these dissensions but noted later 'I have regretfully come to the view that it would be impracticable to negotiate their admission to the FTA.'[35]

Hong Kong emerged as the major colonial critic of an industrial FTA excluding all colonies. After the UN blockade on trade with China in 1951, Hong Kong had rapidly developed flourishing, competitive textiles and footwear sectors, and by the mid-1950s these exports were presenting a serious challenge to British and European producers. In the rare position of being a colony in which manufactures were an important export, Hong Kong naturally petitioned to be included in any industrial FTA. The Governor, Alexander Grantham, made several impassioned pleas that the special interests of Hong Kong should be recognized with membership Failing that, the colony should at least be compensated for being excluded.[36] The British responded that all colonies needed to be treated the same, and as the majority had opted to be excluded, this principle must also be extended to Hong Kong. More convincingly, perhaps, officials noted that European countries were unlikely to open their markets to increased competition from Hong Kong. Many had already imposed a variety of quantitative restrictions on Hong Kong products to protect their domestic producers. Grantham continued to express his disappointment during the next four months, and his case raised considerable sympathy, but the British authorities were not won over. The principle of consistency of treatment of all colonies (including European colonies) was to be maintained.

The Kenyans also raised objections at this point. After the April meeting they suggested that Britain should reconsider the option that the colonies enter the FTA so that their tropical food could be imported into Europe on the same basis as the products of the dependent territories of The Six. This would be useful if the British colonies could maintain their protection against European industrial exports.[37] The rather blunt advice to Ministers from the Treasury was that, although Kenya and Hong Kong disagreed with British policy 'they will have to be disappointed in the interests of the majority'.[38] In October, the Kenyans tried again. The Governor reasserted that Kenya might benefit from association with the FTA since it would allow access to European agricultural markets which were important for the colony's development. He also worried that an industrial FTA would restrict the ability of Britain and Europe to use raw materials from the colonies since the resulting manufacturers might not qualify as 'European'.[39] The Colonial Office replied that Kenya could not join the FTA under GATT if it kept protection on infant industry which was Kenya's policy priority. Britain would press for mitigation of the effects of the Treaty of Rome on behalf of East Africa and, in any case, Britain's market would remain open to Kenyan products. Officials advised, therefore, 'that colonial territories generally, including Kenya, will gain more from adequate mitigation than from association with the FTA and agricultural arrangements, and at the same time the many disadvantages of the latter course, including the weakening of the case for mitigation, will be avoided'.[40] Mitigation of the effects of the inclusion of colonies in the EEC was thus bound up with the exclusion of all colonies from the FTA. Yet, as we have seen, doubts persisted about the prospects for negotiating adequate provisions for the colonies.

Other Europeans appeared to remain optimistic about the prospects for associating all African colonies with a European Free Trade Area despite British objections. Indeed the FTA seemed to offer an opportunity to extend the EURAFRICA initiative. In September 1957 the Council of Europe's 'Study Group for the Development of Africa' asserted that

> one of the objectives of the participating countries' joint effort to develop Africa should be that of liberalising trade between the two continents and in the interior of each . . . Negotiations now in progress at the OEEC on the creation of a European Free Trade Area provide an opportunity for action in this direction, so as to offset any distortion of trade patterns consequent upon the association of only part of Africa with the Common Market of The Six countries of the EEC.[41]

Evidently British officials still had not convinced the Europeans of the seriousness of their obstacles to such association. In October they met with representatives of the Council of Europe[42] and warned of the difficulty of coordinating development plans for different territories (this had not been very successful under the Colombo Plan). The Europeans were also cautioned that since there was no expressed desire for co-ordinated policy from the Africans, 'they may feel that this might mean a continuation of "colonialism" in another guise'.[43] Finally, officials noted that Britain could not afford any extra capital for African development.

Representatives of the independent Commonwealth had an opportunity to express their views on the colonial issue at their Trade and Economic Conference in July 1957.[44] They were mainly interested in the possible benefits their exporters might reap from the settlements on mitigation, since the British expected any concessions to apply to all affected countries and not just the colonies. In the end the Commonwealth expressed general agreement with the British policy, which was to exclude all overseas territories from the Free Trade Area, to accept reluctantly the inclusion of overseas territories in the Treaty of Rome, and to aim for mitigation for the interests of affected exporters through the GATT.

In October 1957 the OEEC formalized its efforts to achieve a European Free Trade area which would unite members of the EEC with other members of the OEEC by establishing an Inter-Governmental Committee chaired by Reginald Maudling. The question of the inclusion of overseas territories was deferred at the request of The Six, although all other forty-five points on the agenda were addressed during the first two meetings of the Maudling Committee.[45] At this time, Britain was forced to declare its willingness to negotiate ways to liberalize agricultural trade progressively within the FTA, although not to remove all protection. It continued to press for the exclusion of food, drink, and tobacco, which were colonial products.[46]

Just as the negotiations became formalized within the OEEC, the prospects for the FTA began to fade. In January 1958 Roger Makins noted in a conversation with Belgian civil servant Baron Snoy et d'Oppuers that

> it seemed to me that the main difficulty still lay with the French attitude. The French appeared to be very sour, particularly with us. Baron Snoy admitted that this was so. He said that in retrospect it was a pity that the phrase 'Free Trade Area' had ever been coined in the GATT. The idea of free trade was anathema to a Frenchman.[47]

In the next few months the likelihood of a FTA receded as the French came up with various counter-proposals which reflected their lack of enthusiasm for the project. For example, they introduced the possibility of negotiating on a product-by-product and country-by-country basis which would no doubt prove very cumbersome and not necessarily result in a FTA. They also proposed that all European countries should enjoy British preference levels on a quota of exports to the Commonwealth, though without offering any concessions to the Commonwealth in return.[48] In mid-November 1958 the French press were told that a FTA was incompatible with the Common Market if it did not apply the common external tariff and aim to harmonize social and economic policy. On 12 December 1958 the OEEC was forced to announce its failure to achieve an alliance with the EEC.

The Six were primarily concerned with shoring up and implementing the terms of the Rome Treaty and were reluctant to dilute these provisions in order to achieve a wider (though more shallow) association with other members of the OEEC. The terms of the Rome Treaty extended well beyond the reduction of tariffs to include co-ordination of economic and social policies, while most of the negotiants of the FTA were unwilling to go much further than agreeing to the reduction of tariffs and quantitative restrictions. More fundamentally, it proved impossible to devise a formula to integrate the common external tariff of the EEC with individual external tariffs of other countries. In short, the inconsistencies between a possible FTA and the already established EEC were too great for The Six to bridge at the delicate time when the provisions of the Rome Treaty were to be implemented for the first time. Finally, for the French, any agreement which did not provide their farmers access to the British market for agricultural products was not worth negotiating.

In November 1959 the European Free Trade Association was formed which reduced trade barriers among Austria, Denmark, Norway, Portugal, Sweden, Switzerland, and Britain only. The EFTA was primarily an industrial free trade area with special, though limited, provisions for agriculture. Although it professed its commitment to achieve an association with the EEC, this was not possible at the time.

V

Despite the fact that this first foray into associating Britain with the EEC was not successful, it served to clarify the issues for the country's changing relationship with the Empire. First, the economic implications for the Empire of Britain engaging more closely with European markets were not great, though they fell disproportionately (New Zealand and the British West Indies were to bear much of the burden). Second, the inclusion of overseas territories in the Rome Treaty drew a sharp distinction between continental Europe's 'old style' imperialism and the new Commonwealth ideas taking hold in the British overseas territories. The frailty and anachronism of French colonial policy were brought into stark exposure when crisis in Algeria brought down the Fourth Republic. When order was finally restored with De Gaulle's Fifth Republic in June 1958, the French empire was hurriedly dismantled.

These negotiations show that the process of decolonization influenced Britain's relations with the rest of the world and that, in turn, its European aspirations forced Britain to confront the changing relationship with the colonies. In practice, it proved impossible to distinguish between dependent colonies and the independent Dominions of the Commonwealth. The over-riding priority was to maintain a semblance of Commonwealth unity by treating all territories the same, even at the apparent sacrifice of individual interests such as those of Kenya and Hong Kong. By 1961 this principle had been abandoned and Britain arranged for members of the Commonwealth to have a variety of associate relationships with the EEC corresponding to their different stages of development.

In the late 1950s, Britain seemed to be reacting to events rather than initiating them. By this time, the country was losing its predominance in colonial markets as the colonies looked to regional trading partners and to recovering European producers. The integration initiative among The Six also posed a challenge for the British that they were initially unable to meet. These two eternal phenomena came together in the episode of the FTA negotiations and exposed the frailty of British policy. British initiatives toward a closer economic association with the European Economic Community continually faced obstacles and a general lack of enthusiasm among Europeans. British efforts to influence the terms of the Treaty of Rome fell on deaf ears and eventually their FTA initiative was rejected. An industrial FTA, or even one with some provisions for agricultural trade, was of little interest to European countries whose farmers wanted access to the British market. Closer integration with the Empire was also a closed door by the mid-1950s as the colonies realigned themselves to cheaper markets and strove for development. In the 1960s Britain found itself forced to make more compromises in its international economic relations with both parties.

Notes

1 M. Camps, 'Missing the Boat at Messina and Other Times?' in Brivati and Jones (eds.), *From Reconstruction to Integration*, 134–43, 141.

2 See, for example, L. J. Butler, 'Winds of Change: Britain, Europe and the Commonwealth 1959–61', in B. Brivati and H. Jones (eds.), *From Reconstruction to Integration: Britain and Europe since 1945* (Leicester, 1993).

3   Text of Maudling's speech to Council of Europe Assembly on 23 Oct. 1957, Public Record Office (hereafter PRO) PREM 11/2531.

4   J. Darwin, *Britain and Decolonisation: the retreat from empire in the post-war world* (London, 1988), 234–5.

5   D. MacDougall and M. Hutt, 'Imperial Preference: a quantitative analysis', *Economic Journal*, LXIV, 254 (1954), 233–57, 256–7.

6   Draft paper by Colonial Office for Secretary of State, 6 March 1958, PRO, T 234/227.

7   Board of Trade paper, 30 Nov. 1956, T 234/223.

8   Extract from Economic Steering Committee minutes, 5 Nov. 1958, T 234/221.

9   Maudling to Macmillan, advice for Macmillan's discussion with de Gaulle, 27 June 1958, PREM 11/2531.

10   Telegram to Commonwealth High Commissioners, 11 Sept. 1956, T 234/213.

11   P. J. Cain and A. G. Hopkins, *British Imperialism: Crisis and Deconstruction 1914–1990* (London, 1993), 287.

12   Maudling to Prime Minister, 5 Aug. 1958, PREM 11/2531.

13   The data for the figures differ from those in Table 2, which includes only manufactures. Data for all figures taken from OEEC, *Direction of International Trade*.

14   R. A. Butler to Harold Macmillan, 24 Aug. 1957, PREM 11/2531.

15   Telegram from Singapore, 8 Oct. 1956, T 234/223.

16   The Six refers to the founding members of the EEC: Belgium, Luxembourg, Netherlands, France, Italy, West Germany.

17   Brief for Prime Minister's visit to Paris, undated (early March 1957), PREM 11/2133.

18   Telegram from Bonn to Foreign Office, 18 Dec. 1956, T 234/223.

19   Telegram from Tanganyika, 1 Oct. 1956, T 234/223. Telegram from Kenya, 13 Oct. 1956, T 234/223.

20   Macmillan to Chancellor of the Exchequer, 5 March 1957, PREM 11/2133.

21   Telegram from Paris to Foreign Office, 18 Feb. 1957, T 234/223.

22   Telegram from Bonn to Foreign Office, 24 Feb. 1957, T 234/223.

23   Record of Prime Minister's meeting with M. Pineau, 9 March 1957, PREM 11/2133.

24   Telegram from Paris to Foreign Office, 23 March 1957, T 234/224.

25   Record of Meeting of OEEC Ministerial Council, Telegram to Commonwealth High Commissioners, 19 Feb. 1957, T 234/214.

26   Telegram to Colonies re: Anglo-French talks on 6 May 1957, 16 May 1957, T 234/225.

27   Report by Economic Steering Committee of Cabinet, 22 March 1957, T 234/224.

28   Memorandum by the Colonial Office, 20 Sept. 1957, T 234/226.

29   Report by the Economic Steering Committee for the Chancellor of the Exchequer, 22 March 1957, T 234/224.

30   Board of Trade report to Colonial Office, 30 May 1957, PRO, CO 852/1730.

31   Brief for Meetings with The Six in Brussels, 19 June 1957, CO 852/1730.

32   Ibid.

33   Telegram from Brussels to Foreign Office, 20 June 1957, CO 852/1730.

34   B. Trend to Macmillan, 1 May 1957, PREM 11/2133.

35   Telegram to the Colonial Governors, 7 April 1957, T 234/225.

36   Telegram from Grantham in Hong Kong, 13 April 1957, T 234/225.

37   Telegram from Kenya to Colonial Office, 23 April 1957, T 234/225.

38   'The FTA, the EEC and OT', report for Ministers, 25 April 1957, T 234/225.

39   Telegram from Kenya, 7 Oct. 1957, T 234/226.

40   Telegram to Kenya, 18 Oct. 1957, T 234/226.

41 Extract from Report to the Consultative Assembly by the Study Group for the Development of Africa, Council of Europe, 12 Sept. 1957, T 234/226.
42 Minutes of a Meeting of Foreign Office and Colonial Office with representatives of the Council of Europe, 14 Oct. 1957, T 234/226.
43 Ibid.
44 Minutes of the Third Meeting of Commonwealth Officials, 9 July 1957, CAB133/192.
45 Maudling to Macmillan, 6 Dec. 1957, PREM 11/2531.
46 Telegram from Secretary of State for the Colonies to Colonial Governors, 18 Oct. 1957, T 234/226.
47 Note by Roger Makins of a talk with Baron Snoy, 20 Jan. 1958. T 234/219.
48 Telegram to British High Commissioners in the Commonwealth, 19 March 1958, T 234/219.

Chapter 8

Frederick Cooper

'OUR STRIKE'

Equality, anticolonial politics and the 1947–48 railway strike in French West Africa

THE STRIKE OF AFRICAN RAILWAY WORKERS which began in October 1947 was an event of epic dimensions: it involved 20,000 workers and their families, shut down most rail traffic throughout all of French West Africa, and lasted, in most regions, for five and a half months. As if the historical event were not large enough, it has been engraved in the consciousness of West Africans and others by the novel of Ousmane Sembene, *God's Bits of Wood*. Sembene dramatizes a powerful strike effort weakened by the impersonal approach of trade unionists, by the seductions of French education, and by the greed of local élites. The strike is redeemed by its transformation into a truly popular movement dynamized by women, climaxing in a women's march on Dakar led by someone from the margins of society and leading to a coming together of African community against the forces of colonialism.

Sembene's novel both complicates the task of the historian and lends it importance: the written epic may influence oral testimony, yet the fictional account enhances the sense of participants that their actions shaped history. When a group of Senegalese graduate students and I went to the railway junction of Thiès to begin a project of collecting testimonies, some informants expressed resentment of Sembene for turning 'our strike' into his novel.[1] What needs most to be unpacked is the connection of the labor movement to the independence struggle: the two were both complementary and in tension with one another. My goal in this article is both to re-examine the question of how to locate the railway strike in the history of post-World War II West Africa and to point to questions that need further research, for the very extensive nature of this social movement – embracing the colonies of Senegal, the Soudan, Guinea, the Ivory Coast and Dahomey and intersecting a wide range of local contexts, communities, and political struggles – means that it contains many histories and requires the attention of many historians. The research begun in Senegal gets at only some of these histories, and time is running out on the lives and memories of the people involved.

The all-too-neat assimilation of social and political struggles is a matter of hind-sight: once independence was achieved, all forms of contestation against French rulers and bosses appear to be part of a seamless pattern of ever-broadening, ever-growing struggle. Some sort of connection is not in doubt; the problem is to pry apart its complexities and ambiguities. The strikers were able to hold out for over five months because they were so well integrated into the African communities in which they lived, but their demands, if realized, would have had the effect of pulling them out of close communities into a professionally defined, non-racial body of railwaymen. The union's goal from 1946 onward was the creation of the *cadre unique*, a single scale of wages and benefits for Africans and white Frenchmen alike. Such a system would widen the gap between the life experiences of railwaymen and those of the peasants, pastoralists and merchants among whom they lived. In political terms one can argue the opposite: to the extent that the strike movement drew from anticolonial sentiments that went beyond the workplace and to the extent that the strike gave Africans a sense of empowerment in their confrontations with the French government, anti-colonial politics risked diluting the work-centered goals of the strike movement. The idea of independence would sever the French connection which was the ideological basis for the railwaymen's claims to equality of wages and benefits with French workers, while opening the union's considerable organizational achievements to co-optation by political parties whose primary concerns lay elsewhere.

In fact, the union and the major political movements of the day remained in uneasy relationship. The men who were the ultimate beneficiaries of decolonization – the Senghors and the Houphouët-Boignys – did not make the cause of the strikers their own. Senghor, more so than other party leaders, maintained contact with the union and when the strike was over moved decisively to bring its leaders into his political fold and under his eyes – a process which increased the union's influence and decreased its autonomy. For many strikers, the behavior of politicians was disillusioning, and for the union structure, the very success of the strike left potentially conflicting alternatives between becoming, as one veteran put it, the 'auxiliaries' of a political party or else focusing as a union on the kinds of claims they could make that stood a good chance of success within the framework of industrial relations emerging out of the strike. If the strike, as a popular movement, gave thousands of people a sense of collective strength the strike – as a process carried out through certain kinds of institutions – defined the terrain of contestation in a narrower way.

This article points to the kind of questions that further oral research across the strike zone will illuminate. Among documentary sources it gives particular emphasis to reports by police spies present at numerous strike meetings. They must of course be used with care, since spies have a tendency to see what their superiors want them to see. But it is clear that the strikers earned the grudging admiration of their opponents, who had clear reasons to try to learn something of what was going on among them. Taken together, available sources offer multiple points of access to an extraordinarily complex social movement.[2]

The context: strike movements and the modernization of imperialism

The strike must be understood in the context of a French government anxious to find a new basis of legitimacy and control in an era when social and political movements in the colonies were asserting themselves with new vigor. These two processes shaped one another: as African movements sought to turn the government's need for order and economic growth into claims to entitlements and representation, officials had to rethink their policies in the face of new African challenges. The truly agenda-setting movement of the immediate post-war years was the Senegalese general strike of 1946. Up to that point, the French sociology of Africa admitted to only two categories, *paysans* and *évolués*. Officials hoped to achieve economic growth by eliminating forced labor, reducing the tax burden on peasants, and improving infrastructure devoted to agri-culture, and to attain political stability by granting *évolués* a modest degree of partici-pation in the governing institutions of France itself. The strike movement – beginning in the port in December 1945, extending to commercial establishments in January, and turning at mid-month into a general strike – involved everyone from African civil servants to dockworkers to market sellers (with the conspicuous exception of railway-men). Confessing his inability to control events, the Governor General welcomed a labor expert from Paris who proceeded to make workers a focus of policy. The general strike ended as officials negotiated with individual categories of workers, granting collective bargaining agreements to each one in turn. By February the strike movement was over, and ordinary laborers had won significant wage increases; government workers were getting family allowances based on a percentage of the indemnities granted to the top ranks; unions were recognized; and wage hierarchies were expanded and bonuses granted for seniority.

Out of the strike came a newly empowered Inspection du Travail that sought to use French models of industrial relations to gain a measure of control over an increasingly differentiated labor force and to promote 'stabilization' as an antidote to the kind of mass, boundary-crossing movement they had just faced. There emerged as well a labor movement able to turn officials' hopes for stability and the assimilationist rhetoric of post-war French imperialism into African workers' claims to French wage and benefit scales. Over the next several years, the labor question focused on the details of what stabilization and 'equal pay for equal work' would mean and on efforts of both workers and labor inspectors to devise an empire-wide *Code du Travail* that would guarantee basic rights and bound conflict within a set of legally defined procedures. Family allowances, minimum wages, wage hierarchies, and trade union rights were all the objects of negotiations, mobilization, and strikes.[3]

Politics was meanwhile being changed from above and from below. Seeking to demonstrate that what were once called colonies were now an integral part of Greater France, citizenship was extended from the few acculturated urban centers to all French territory and – with a limited but gradually expanding franchise – elections were held throughout French Africa from late 1945 onward for positions in the French legislature. As old-line politicians like Senegal's Lamine Gueye tried to maintain control of their parties, 'youth' organizations challenged them in cities and rural constituencies were organized, most strikingly by the Société Agricole Africaine in the Ivory Coast, leading to the formation of a cross-territorial political party, the Rassemblement Démocratique Africain (RDA).

In the middle of the ferment within Senegal over both trade unions and politics was François Gning, Secretary General of the Syndicat des Travailleurs Indigènes du Dakar-Niger, headquartered in Thiès. He had led this union of skilled and long-term African railwaymen since the mid-1930s, and he was an active member of Lamine Gueye's socialist party, the Section Française de l'Internationale Ouvrière (SFIO). His union was the most important group of workers to refuse to participate in the 1946 general strike. His socialist affiliations – the socialists were then in the government in France – were a major factor inhibiting his room to maneuver. It was not a popular stance.[4] As early as December 1945, railwaymen at a meeting in Thiès were talking about a strike, in opposition to Gning. This did not come off, but after the Dakar general strike, Gning and his Comité Directeur decided to start a strike fund, part as sensible preparation, part as delaying tactic. He hoped that 'the example furnished by the groups that recently went on strike will allow railwaymen to reflect on the gravity of an act which constitutes a two-edged sword'.[5]

Politics and trade unionism came together in the opposition to Gning's maneuverings in the principal railway junction and repair center at Thiès. In April 1946, officials reported agitation among the railway workers, who felt they had not received what they deserved from their restraint during the general strike. In May, security officials learned that a movement to oust Gning was being organized by a group from the Union des Jeunes de Thiès, who were also active members of the railway union. Here developed an extraordinary conjuncture of the political ideals of a group of young, educated men and a workforce that was largely non-literate. From mid-1945, the Union des Jeunes was led by a clerk (Abdoul Karim Sow) and a school teacher (Mory Tall), and included several people with clerical jobs on the railway. Its goals were simultaneously political, cultural and intellectual – to promote our 'general development', one leader recalled.[6] Its meetings brought out a youthful vigor against the perceived lethargy of older Senegalese politicians and a new combativeness toward the French, even though neither it – nor any other significant political group – was at this time calling for independence. Its attacks were highly personal – the Commandant de Cercle at Thiès was a target – and the administration replied in kind by transferring Tall to a remote northern town, where he promptly organized another Union des Jeunes. The organization published a newsletter, *Jeunesse et Démocratie*, and entered a complicated dialogue with the local section of the SFIO, also led by Gning. It alternated between criticism of the doyen of Senegalese socialist politicians, Lamine Gueye, and attempts to make up with him.[7] The aggressive moves of the 'Jeunes' to remake politics within the SFIO at Thiès led Gning to resign in frustration as its Secretary General.

Gning was a Catholic and his mentor, Lamine Gueye, while Muslim like most peasants and workers, was from the old élite of the Quatre Communes, which had long enjoyed French citizenship and were seen to be distant by most rural Senegalese. The leaders of the Union des Jeunes were Muslim, and one of them, Ibrahima Sarr, came from a family with connections to marabouts, the leaders of the Muslim brotherhoods which held great influence in rural Senegal. Sarr was also well educated: a graduate of a leading trade school, *écrivain* in the *cadre local supérieure* since 1938.[8]

Gning, an *évolué* conscious of having earned his privileges, was unable to assimilate one of the basic lessons of the January 1946 strike: that workers of all levels were laying claim to basic entitlements. He would not attack the privilege of the top cadres, thinking it inconceivable that an ordinary worker 'receive the same indemnities as a Governor'.[9]

Following their attacks on Gning in the Thiès section of the SFIO, the militants of the Union des Jeunes spearheaded a 'revolution' within the railway union, attacking Gning's non-combative approach, his failure to join the successful 1946 strike, and his alienation of non-élite workers.[10] After meetings of the Comité Directeur, demonstrations calling for Gning's resignation, and a public meeting of 1,000 railway-men at Thiès on 23 May 1946 at which he was repeatedly denounced, Gning resigned. Ibrahima Sarr took over, installing a Comité Directeur largely led by other clerks but including representation of all divisions.[11]

Sarr's inaugural speech to the committee, in May 1946, printed and circulated to the men, was at the same time an attack on colonialism and a perceptive use and extension of the new French colonial rhetoric against the old. He called for

> the liberation of the worker, giving him sufficient means so that he can live honorably and relieving him, above all, of the singular and painful nightmare of uncertainty about the next day, in other words, the abolition of anti-quated colonial methods condemned even by THE NEW AND TRUE FRANCE which wishes that all its children, at whatever latitude they may live, be equal in duties and rights and *that the recompense of labor be a function solely of merit and capacity*.[12]

The new union regime had a base to start: Gning's union was the oldest in French West Africa, and his connections to the Socialist Party and the Government General in 1936–8 and 1944–6 had brought some concessions without strikes. But Sarr was promising to remedy the union's greatest limitation since the 1930s. In fact, the most important railway strike in recent memory, at Thiès in 1938, had been conducted over the opposition of the union, and Gning's élitism had put the largest category of railway workers – the auxiliaries – outside of the union's embrace. Auxiliaries often worked for years if not a lifetime and many were highly skilled; but the railway limited the number of its permanent employees, the *cadres*, to increase its control and decrease its costs. In 1938, a dissident union of auxiliaries had challenged Gning as much as the railway. Their aggressive attempts to shut down the railway had ended in military violence and the fatal shooting of six strikers. The tragic incident was quickly exploited by rightists in Dakar and Paris to eliminate officials who had encouraged bargaining with African trade unions, and the labor movement remained all but dormant until the end of World War II.[13] Reviving his old union after the war, Gning soon learned that the world of labor had changed for good.

Sarr promised to bring auxiliaries and cadres into a single organization and a single struggle. The union's demands consistently had two dimensions: to equalize benefits for all railwaymen in the cadres with no distinctions of origin or race, and secondly to integrate all auxiliaries into the cadres. The demands were both about equity in compensation and about dignity, especially the dignity of lower-ranking workers. The ultimate demand was for a *cadre unique*, a single hierarchy defined by skill and seniority that would set aside the old distinctions of colonial/metropolitan and cadres/auxiliary.

Sarr's other major achievement was to forge a French West Africa-wide movement. The *coup de main* that overthrew Gning had been very much a Thiès-centered event; a mass meeting was its climax. Thiès was a very special kind of place: residence and workplace were thoroughly integrated, and railwaymen from diverse parts of Senegal and the Soudan shared common conditions in this double sense; the bonds formed at Thiès in turn travelled up and down the rail line that ran from Dakar to Bamako. It was not clear at first that the new leaders had support along the line, let alone in the other systems of French West Africa. But within a month of his takeover, Sarr embarked on a series of visits, beginning with the Soudan in June 1946 and culminating in a tour of the other railway lines on the eve of the 1947 strike. He told everyone of his desire to end the distinction between cadres and auxiliaries, pleaded the common cause of the workers against the Federation-wide railway administration, and encouraged the payment of dues and contributions to the strike fund. The union organizations on the different lines brought themselves together as the Fédération des Syndicats des Cheminots Africains, and ceded central direction to the Comité Directeur of the Dakar-Niger branch, headquartered in Thiès. In February 1947, the Dakar-Niger branch claimed to have added over 700,000 francs to the fund of 92,000 left by the old leadership – it was ready for a test.[14]

All this took place against the background of what police reports often called 'effervescence' at various points in the West African railway system and in other professions as well. Dakar now seemed a center of calm, and the Governor General attributed this to the success workers had already achieved in that city. Short, localized strikes and strike threats were reported in Dahomey, Guinea and the Ivory Coast.[15] In 1947, in French West Africa as a whole, 164 collective conflicts were reported to the Inspection du Travail, although the vast majority was settled without incident and strikes focused on wage disputes. By then, 133 unions in the public sector and 51 in the private had been officially organized. In Dakar, 40 per cent of workers belonged to unions; by the next year, officials believed that 20 per cent of all wage workers in French West Africa had joined a union. The large majority of the unions affiliated to the Confédération Générale du Travail (CGT), with the African confederation retaining considerable autonomy despite its affiliation with the communist-led, metropolitan organization. But the Fédération Syndicale des Cheminots remained autonomous of any of the central union organizations.[16]

The other side in the rail dispute was also changing, opening up uncertainty about the status of railwaymen as government employees just as civil servants achieved success in the strike of 1946. The railways had been under the Direction des Travaux Publics. Effective 17 July 1946, they were reorganized as the Régie des Chemins de Fer de l'Afrique Occidentale Française (AOF), which would today be called a parastatal organization and which was described at the time as an 'organization of public utility attached to the private sector and constrained to rules of industrial and commercial operations'. It was administered by a director, M. Cunéo, who reported to a Conseil d'Administration chaired by the Secretary General of the Government General and consisting of 16 members appointed by the administration, eight representatives of the Grand Conseil (the elected legislative body of French West Africa), five representatives of the workers (of whom three were named by the unions), and three representatives of the users of railway services. The board was autonomous in its position, but not in its majority membership, while the status of the Régie implied that its own financial condition – and not the resources of the Government General, or by extension, France – constrained its expenditures. The reorganization meant that railway workers would no longer benefit from a *statut*, as did civil servants, but would come under a *convention collective*, like the metal workers, the bakery workers or commercial workers. Railway workers could not automatically claim the gains acquired by the civil service, and railway officials had an excuse for not responding to political pressure. The Régie became a distinct battleground, consistent with the government's overall strategy of regaining initiative after the unified mobilization it had faced in the general strike of 1946.[17]

The Régie's personnel was organized hierarchically, in a manner parallel to the bureaucracy: the *cadre supérieur* was entirely European, the *cadre commun supérieur* mostly so. The *cadre secondaire* was mixed and the *cadre local* was, essentially, African. All the cadres were either housed or received equivalent indemnities; the indemnities of zone and for family charges were highly skewed toward the superior, largely European, cadres. But most important, the auxiliaries did not receive housing or indemnities; they could be fired for minor offences; they were in many respects treated like temporary workers even though most served for years. And they were the large majority of railway personnel. In 1946, the railway employed 478 Europeans and 1,729 Africans in the various cadres, plus 15,726 auxiliaries.[18] This structure was very difficult to defend in principle – but useful in practice, especially given the precedent set by government cadres in 1946. Government officials, however, did see that a more coherent structure might offer possibilities of reducing the staffing level of the railway. The direction of the railway agreed: they wanted a smaller and more efficient staff – realizing that the days of the derisorily paid multitude were ending – and they wanted the unions to co-operate. There was room for bargaining.

In August 1946 the Fédération des Travailleurs Africans submitted its demands for a *cadre unique* and for the integration, over time, of the permanently employed auxiliaries into the cadre. The Governor General, under current labor law, appointed a Commission Paritaire, in which representatives of the two sides discussed the issues dividing them. Between December and April, twenty rounds of bargaining were held, most of them 'confused, tedious, broken up by stormy discussions'. Unions representing European workers made the procedures more divisive by their overt defense of racial privilege and rejection of the *cadre unique*. In April 1947, the African union, its demands unmet, staged a theatrical coup: it withdrew from the Commission Paritaire and staged a strike at the moment when the President of France and the Colonial Minister – Marius Moutet – were visiting Senegal.[19]

The three-day strike – throughout French West Africa – was a brilliant maneuver, and it appeared to have worked. Under the pressure of Moutet's presence – as well as that of Governor General Barthes, Lamine Gueye, Léopold Senghor, and other luminaries – the parties agreed on the necessity to create a *cadre unique*, but also to reduce the staffing level of the railway, with the layoffs to be worked out by another Commission Paritaire which would consider seniority and skill. The creation of the *cadre unique* would require working out a table of equivalencies, so that people would be slotted into the correct positions.[20]

The acceptance of this protocol suggests that the highest levels of the government were unwilling to contest the principle of the *cadre unique* and the integration of auxiliaries. They did not want to defend overtly the discriminatory structure of a colonial labor force against the universalistic claim to equality among all workers. In April, the most far-reaching issue seemed theoretically solved. The issues over which the October strike was to be fought were less than earthshaking; the Director of the Régie later referred to them as 'points of detail'.[21] The real issue was power: who was to control the process by which new modalities of labor organization would be worked out?

In the months after April, two developments took place. The worsening economic situation in metropolitan and overseas France led to a renewed attempt by officials to hold down prices and wages throughout the French domains, the first attempt in Africa having failed during the 1946 strike. In late April and May, Governors General were told to avoid a 'general readjustment of wages of a profession'. Despite fears of renewed general strikes, officials on the scene had to push for restraint.[22] The wages of railway-men were a major factor in the cost of goods exported and imported. In August, the railway claimed that its 1947 budget was in the red and that the integration of around 2,000 auxiliaries into the cadre would more than triple the deficit and require a 130 per cent increase in railway rates in order to bring it back to equilibrium, in lieu of which a subsidy from the government would have to be forthcoming.[23]

Secondly, in May 1947, the coalition governing France changed. The Communist Party was formally expelled, and a Center-Left coalition took power, although Moutet remained Colonial Minister until November. This meant that certain kinds of debates and certain kinds of compromises did not have to take place within the French govern-ment. The new Cabinet did not overtly reverse past labor or imperial policy – it remained committed to rationalizing the workplace and working for a Code du Travail – but it was more open to other sorts of imperatives. In metropolitan France, a bitter railway strike promptly ensued.[24]

Although the Conseil d'Administration of the Régie des Chemins de Fer overlapped in membership and personnel with the Commission Paritaire that had negotiated the agreement of April, it voted in August to reject the accord. This kind of contradiction was in fact part of what the creation of the Régie was all about: government-appointed members put on their parastatal hats, pleaded autonomy and fiscal accountability, and sent the agreement into limbo.[25]

For the union, this was nothing less than a betrayal. By summer's end, Sarr was mobilizing forces for a strike, and angry workers were even criticizing him for not doing so forcefully enough.[26] They had to cross muddied waters to define issues: the call for a *cadre unique* was a dramatic demand for equal conditions of work – linking the feelings of workers who experienced racial discrimination on a daily basis with the assimilationist rhetoric of the French state – but the other side responded by both accepting and rejecting the *cadre unique*. The union's demand that railwaymen of all ranks be paid the indemnity of zone (the supplement to wages intended to offset geographical differences in cost of living) at the same rate rather than at rates favoring the top ranks was met not with denial but with claims that perhaps the indemnity of zone was a bad idea and should be eliminated for all workers.[27] The issue of integrating auxiliaries into the cadres was not contested either, but issues of effective dates and the standards for integration (general versus selective) were pressed by the Régie.[28] Officially, the disputed issues boiled down to: the effective date for integrating auxiliaries into the cadres; how workers were to be reclassified in forming the *cadre unique*; where examination barriers were to be set for promotions; conditions for leaves; which employees would receive housing; and whether the indemnity of zone would be uniform or would depend on rank.

At the beginning of September, Sarr told an assembly at Thiès that 'The colonialist spirit of the Europeans has once again revealed to us its force'. He explained the detailed issues in dispute. With unanimous agreement, a strike date was set for 10 October. He persuaded proponents of an immediate strike that it was first necessary to make the rounds of the railway depots – including the Ivory Coast, Guinea and Dahomey – and he soon set off on his journey. The Ivoirien union leader, Gaston Fiankan, declared that the

Abidjan-Niger region would join the Dakar-Niger in the strike, and he was soon holding meetings in various locations in the Ivory Coast to consolidate support. As Sarr went off to prosyletize the Soudan, French security reported 'Up to now, he is getting confidence and unanimity for the strike along the entire line'. Returning from the Soudan, Sarr appeared before another assembly at Thiès attended by, according to police, 7,000 people. Awaiting him, the crowd beat drums, engaged in 'wild dances' and waved three big French flags. He was escorted to the meeting by cyclists and arrived amidst cries of 'Vive Sarr'.[29]

Just before the strike deadline – on October 7 by one account – Léopold Senghor came to Thiès to meet in private with the Comité Directeur. He told them he was with them in their struggle. Lamine Gueye, meanwhile, already had a strained relationship with the current union leadership and had had an ugly confrontation in Thiès with the 'Jeunes' when he tried to reconcile them with Gning after Sarr's coup in the railway union. Gueye, according to informants, was willing to talk to the union leaders, but he warned them of the dangers of a strike rather than giving his support. The strikers would remember the difference, even though Senghor failed to back the strikers publicly as he had in private.

The Governor General talked to the union leaders on the eve of the strike and tried to intimidate them. The Inspection du Travail made a last ditch attempt at conciliation. The union felt it had fulfilled all the preconditions for a legal strike by virtue of the fact that it had been jumping through hoops for over a year; officials claimed that these were not the hoops prescribed by law and that the dispute should go to arbitration over the listed items in dispute. An arbitrator and the arbitration appeal panel eventually did hear the case and made their rulings later in the month. This action was too little, too late, and without waiting for the hearing, the union began its strike as planned on 10 October throughout all branches of the railway in French West Africa and on the wharfs in Dahomey and the Ivory Coast under the Régie's jurisdiction. The walkout was virtually complete among the 17,000 railwaymen and 2,000 workers at the wharfs, and it remained that way: on 1 November, 38 Africans were on the job.[30]

Solidarity and survival

Reading police reports – several per day during the five and a half months of the strike – reveals some of its remarkable features: the union's largely successful attempt to preserve unity until January, when the Abidjan-Niger region defected, but the other regions held solid; the fear of the administration that the hiring of strikebreakers or other repressive measures would provoke reactions which it could not control, and its delay for a month before it tried – with only marginal success – to reconstitute a work force and increase traffic; the slowness of African politicians and political parties – and the new institutions of the Union Française – to take cognizance of this act of enormous political and economic importance until the strike was three months old; and the way in which the struggle, as it wore on, became more and more about the strike itself, and its ending reflected the fact that each side had proved its toughness and was ready for the next round – and the next form – of contestation.

The most fascinating question about the conduct of the strike – how such a large and diverse body of workers maintained themselves physically and as a coherent force –

requires further investigation. Asked this question, informants stress solidarity within the railway community, connections to farmers, merchants and others in a position to help, and good preparation by the union itself (see below). The question obviously puzzled officials – who were predicting the strike's imminent collapse from its first days to its final months – and the most perspicacious official accounts reached a surprising and frightening conclusion.

The security services gradually learned that railwaymen had a complex web of affiliation within the communities in which they lived. A police spy overheard reports to a meeting at Thiès of a strike official's tour of Senegalese depot towns: at Kaolack a 'humble cultivator gives us 400F'; at Tambacounda, the merchant El Hadj Abou Sy gave sheep to the railwaymen, and local notables, marabouts and merchants offered 20,000 francs and ten tons of millet; at Guinguinéo investigation of a rumor that the marabouts were hostile to the strike proved false, and the strikers' emissary found that the entire population 'is with us with no reserve'. In fact, the leading marabouts of the Islamic confraternities of Senegal – who were close to the administration – used their influence against the strike but closer to ground level the religious organization seems to have been more supportive. Informants claim that marabouts would not support the strike in public but that many were either supportive or neutral in private.[31]

Other reports suggested that merchants in Senegal played a particularly important role in providing assistance, in the form of money, food and trucks to transport food. This was particularly so in Thiès where the health of almost the entire business community depended on the custom of railwaymen.[32] The newspaper *L'AOF*, read by many *évolués*, publicized a collection drive to benefit railwaymen: it reached 134,615 francs in late November and 454,555 by mid-December.[33] The union, according to an informant, channelled its strike funds to men with families, figuring that single men could improvise more easily. Railwaymen did a great deal themselves to obtain food provisions, drawing on their family members in rural areas, personal connections to merchants, fishermen and farmers, and the organizational efforts of the union.[34]

Women clearly played a major role in the strike, although one female informant distinguished between their participation in the violent strike of 1938 – where she and other women passed stones to male strikers who threw them at police and strike-breakers – and their role in the non-violent, carefully controlled strike of 1947. Testimonies so far collected stress the role of women within family units – their efforts to find food, their work in market-selling or other non-wage activities to sustain family income.[35] They composed songs supporting the strike and its leaders and taunted strike breakers: their position in railway communities created an atmosphere where *défaillants* (strike breakers) would not want to live. This is a subject which requires further investigation, but it appears less likely that women acted as a distinct entity – let alone that such an entity was led by someone from the margins of Muslim society like Sembene's character Penda – than that they acted as parts of families and communities. Sembene's women's march is absent from oral testimonies and the police record. It remains to be seen how much their actions in turn affected the way these structures operated and altered the meanings of gender within laboring communities, as well as the extent to which the increasing value and security of male wage packets changed power relations within households.

In January, three months into the strike, Pierre Pélisson, the head of the Inspection du Travail in French West Africa, reached a startling conclusion about the ability of

Africans to conduct a long strike: 'Here the means of defense are very different – and singularly more effective – than in the case of metropolitan strikes because the roots of the labor force are deeper and its needs less imperious in Africa than in Europe'.[36] Pélisson had been taught an important lesson: the degree of proletarianization was not an accurate measure of the power of strikers, and the success of the strike lay in the integration of the strikers into the strikers' own communities.

Proletarians, politicians and mobilization beyond the railway

It was in regard to other proletarians that the solidarity of the strike movement was the most ambiguous. Pélisson noticed this too, writing that most wage workers outside the railway distanced themselves from railwaymen, and the latter 'have not benefited from their effective support but only from habitual demonstrations of sympathy'. In Dakar, wage workers were in the midst of peaceful negotiations over another round of wage revisions; no general strike movement emerged in support of the railwaymen.

At times, it looked as if the solidarity of the railwaymen would take on an even wider dimension. In early November the Commission Administrative of the Union des Syndicates de Dakar discussed what to do to support the strikers. The leading veterans of the 1946 strike, Abbas Gueye and Lamine Diallo, tried to convince a 'reticent assembly' of the need for a general strike. They pointed out to civil servants in particular that they shared a fundamental interest in a unified indemnity of zone. But other speakers pushed for 'more moderate' approaches, such as protest meetings, collections of funds and delegations to the Governor General, and it was the latter position which prevailed.[37] In Guinea, the Union Régionale Syndicale de Guinée passed a motion of support for the railwaymen, 'whose demands were theirs as well'. But there was no common action for the common demands.[38] In the Ivory Coast in November, the Union Locale des Syndicats, affiliated to the CGT, decided 'that it could not support the action of the railway union because [it was] not affiliated to the CGT'.[39] Around that time, some civil service unions were thinking about a general strike, but they would not act until they heard from the Rassemblement Démocratique Africaine and its leader Houphouët-Boigny. They were to get no encouragement from him.[40]

The trade union movement, in West Africa and in France, did better by the railwaymen in a financial sense. CGT unions in the region contributed, according to a French CGT source, about two million francs. The National Solidarity Committee of the CGT in France gave 500,000, while other contributions came from French railway unions and another CGT bureau. The RDA in the Ivory Coast gave 350,000 – although its support became increasingly suspect.[41]

What other unions and political parties did not do was organize sympathy strikes, stage large demonstrations or otherwise try to turn the strike into a wider social and political movement. The lack of common action is all the more notable because there was considerable trade union anger at the time of the strike over the withdrawal by a new Minister of Overseas France of a Code du Travail which Moutet had tried to implement by decree just before he left office in November 1947. But the causes never were linked, the Code protests fizzled, and the Code debate disappeared into French political institutions for another five years.

Some trade unionists in Senegal were reluctant to lend their support to railway workers in 1947 because railwaymen had not helped them during the general strike of 1946. Moreover, the civil service, metal trades, commerce and industry unions were now engaged in regular negotiations through institutions set up as a result of that strike. The fact that most of the concessions made to civil servants in Dakar were extended to other parts of French West Africa, and the spread of Dakar-type agreements to other key businesses in West Africa changed the politics of labor on a wide scale. Focusing the labor question on union-management relations within each branch of industry, commerce or government and making workers less inclined toward another venture in solidarity had been the Inspection's strategy since January 1946, and Pélisson recognized even in the midst of the railway strike that the strategy was working.[42]

The relationship of the railwaymen to organized politics was equally ambiguous. The RDA, which like the railway crossed territorial borders, maintained its distance. In the run up to the strike, Sûreté thought that the RDA was fighting against the strike call, hoping that its failure would lead to Sarr's ouster and open up the autonomous union to takeover by pro-RDA leaders.[43] In February 1948, the *Voix de la RDA*, published in Dakar, saw fit to rebut a charge that the strike had been called by the RDA by writing, 'Sarr, the federal secretary of the railway union, whose courage and combativity we admire, is not RDA'. The newspaper insisted that it respected 'trade union independence', and that while it agreed with the demands of the union, 'We had the courage to declare to the railwaymen: on the local level we could do nothing. It was the business of the railwaymen and only the railwaymen to take up their responsibilities'. It claimed that the RDA had tried in the metropole to bring pressure on the government to settle the strike and blamed its opponents for the failure of that initiative.[44]

This article probably represented the view of the RDA leadership in Dakar. The leading light of the party, Houphouët-Boigny, was playing a more complicated game. Security officials kept hearing reports of Houphouët-Boigny's covert opposition to the strike. In early November, they reported he had told the strike committee 'that the deputies from French West Africa had not been consulted before the breaking out of this strike, inopportune at this time of year, and that as a result he was not going to be mixed up in their affair'. Two weeks later, security reported, 'In his house, last Sunday, the deputy Houphouët had said to his friends that the strikers have not acted skillfully, that they should have accepted the advantages conceded in the course of this strike, gone back to work in order to renew their demands later and obtain the "full rate" (the full indemnity of zone) by successive steps'. At that point, he said he would go to Dakar to see what he could do.[45]

In Dakar he sang a different tune. Houphouët-Boigny told a meeting called by the Union des Syndicats Confédérés de l'AOF on 7 December that he and his RDA colleague Gabriel d'Arboussier pledged support to the railwaymen 'in their struggle against colonialism' and assured them of the 'presence of the RDA beside you to defend their demands which are legitimate'. The pro-RDA newspaper *Réveil* noted the absence at this meeting of the parliamentarians from Senegal (who were not RDA).[46]

But by this time most of the West African parliamentarians, Houphouët-Boigny included, were pursuing a goal which, however worthy, was not quite the same as the anti-colonialist rhetoric implied. At the time of the union meeting, Houphouët-Boigny and other deputies were in Dakar for the December–January meeting of the Grand Conseil de l'AOF, French West Africa's major deliberative body. They took advantage of their collective presence in Dakar to talk to leading officials and to try to persuade the

Governor General to intervene. Houphouët-Boigny and his rival counselor, Lamine Gueye, both told Pélisson of 'their concern not to mix politics with an affair that must remain strictly professional and simply to bring their purely obliging support to settling a conflict whose importance to the country is considerable'.[47] The parliamentarians told both the Inspecteur Général du Travail and the Governor General that their concern was to end the strike 'so prejudicial to the economy of the country as well as to the interests of the Régie and of the railwaymen themselves'. They were rebuffed by Governor General Barthes, who refused to call into question the October ruling of the arbitrators.[48] But in any case, these interventions show the tone of the politicians two months into the strike: a sentiment of regret over the hardships caused by the strike and hope for a quick settlement, but an evasiveness about the substantive issues and an unwillingness to support the strikers unambiguously and publicly.

Houphouët-Boigny reported the meetings to the Grand Conseil, but the effort of some members to debate the strike failed, as its president, Lamine Gueye, claimed the Conseil had no say on such a matter. Gueye went on to distance himself from the strikers, noting that while the interests of the railwaymen were affected by the strike, 'those of the entire country are as well'. At a subsequent session in January, a counselor from Dahomey, Apithy, introduced a resolution asking for a delegation of the Conseil to try to get the government to intervene and attacked Lamine Gueye for failing to act. But this merely led to a brief and bitter exchange of accusations between RDA and Socialist deputies. Several delegates opposed intervention on the grounds that the Conseil did not have jurisdiction. Senghor said contacts had been made with the incoming Governor General, whose presence would raise the possibility of compromise in this 'painful conflict'. He added, 'The role of Grand Counselors is not to have a partisan debate here or to tear each other up and thus to tear up Africa, but to study the technical means to bring a solution to the conflict'. Apithy withdrew his resolution. French West Africa's most powerful political actors had failed even to express a collective opinion on the most salient issue of the day.[49]

Meanwhile, Houphouët-Boigny was doing his bit to end the strike in his home territory. The railwaymen of the Ivory Coast broke ranks in early January and gave up the strike. Pélisson wrote, 'According to our information, this result is due to M. the Deputy Houphouët who succeeded in persuading the African railwaymen to return to work despite the counter-propaganda of M. Sarr'.[50] The police reports from the Ivory Coast (see below) reveal a pattern of intrigue in January which resulted in the union's defection; Houphouët-Boigny's influence on some members of the union leadership – although not its leader, Gaston Fiankan – may well have been crucial. None of this should be surprising: the Ivoirien branch of the RDA had emerged from a group of cocoa planters and was rapidly expanding its power in agriculture as much as in politics. The harvest-time strike obviously affected their prospects with particular acuity.

Senghor was among the deputies who joined the settlement initiative in December and January. He was the only major political figure at the time to have given some indication of support – if only in private – to the strikers and he remained in contact. Senghor sent a letter to the minister, enclosing a list of demands of the union as well as a 'History of the Situation' written by Sarr. His own interpretation was truly Senghorian: 'In any case, the claims relative to the suppression of racial discrimination seem to me to be well founded, even if one can dispute the wage rates. In effect, one cannot speak of a *cadre unique* if there is discrimination within the interior of the cadre, discrimination which is moreover condemned by the Constitution of the IVth Republic'. He appealed for a settlement not on the basis of the April accords, but on the 'spirit of the Constitution of the IVth Republic which proclaims that the Union Française is a union founded on the equality of rights and duties, without discrimination based on race or religion'. Avoiding the mundane complexities of a labor dispute Senghor defined the issue as one of constitutional principles and racial equality.[51]

By then, the Comité Directeur of the union had already criticized both Senghor and Lamine Gueye 'for having placed themselves on the side of the Administration and for their support of Cunéo'.[52] When the December discussions among parliamentarians assembled for the Grand Conseil meeting and the meetings with the Governor General got nowhere, Fily Dabo Sissoko, deputy from the Soudan, began to intervene as well.[53] Since the Soudanais railwaymen were crucial to the Dakar-Niger branch, officials hoped that he would have sufficient influence to get one group of workers to give up the strike in exchange only for promises that Sissoko would use his good offices on the union's behalf after railwaymen returned to work. Sissoko and his allies told officials that the Soudanais railwaymen had 'total confidence' in the Deputy of the Soudan, and that his intervention would insure that 'the Soudanais will detach themselves from the Senegalese and it is certain that overall movements similar to the strike of 11 October will not recur'.[54] Sissoko suggested token concessions, such as changing the date on which auxiliaries would acquire permanent status, but the real message was 'about the influence that the Deputy Fily Dabo Sissoko could have on the end of the strike'.[55] The Régie agreed to the date change, insisting that this promise 'is made to you and you alone to help you in your good offices to bring about an effective return to work and would only apply if the return occurred on the date indicated'.[56]

Sissoko talked directly with Sarr, who was frightened of the potential split in the strike movement within the Dakar-Niger. But the Comité Directeur would have none of this: they interpreted the offer as a 'word game' and as 'sabotage'. Sarr was instructed on 29 January 1948 to reject Sissoko's initiatives: 'A scalded cat fears cold water . . . and we cannot base our return to work on a promise, above all when that promise is stripped of any guarantee'. Sarr showed the telegram to Sissoko, who was angered and gave indications that he would actively intervene to get the Soudanais railwaymen to go back to work.[57]

The Inspection du Travail in Bamako reported that Sissoko indeed asked workers to go back, effective 2 February. The union appealed to them to hold fast. And this they did: at Bamako only seven workers returned to work on the day indicated.[58] Sissoko's intervention did little more than discredit him, although it may have made the union leadership nervous enough to look more favorably on the next settlement initiative in early March.

It had taken the leading elected politicians of French West Africa two months to intervene, and their efforts over the next two months accomplished little more than splitting the railwaymen of the Ivory Coast from their comrades elsewhere. Although Senghor, in a private letter to the minister, had assimilated the cause of the strikers to his anti-racist cause, he had done nothing to tap the popular mobilization that was part of the strike. Houphouët-Boigny had invoked the spectre of colonialism in a Dakar speech, but at virtually the same time he was working behind the scenes to end the strike in the Ivory Coast.

In Senegal, Senghor is said to have helped to settle the strike. This perception is more a consequence of what happened after the strike than what he did during it. Senghor realized that the union was one of the most important organized blocks of voters in the territory, and he set about straightening things out. He made Sarr a candidate on his ticket for the Assembly of the Union Française, and he was duly elected in 1953. He is remembered in Thiès for having incorporated the railway workers union into his political movement, but with more than a hint that the workers did more for him than he for them.[59]

The story does not end here. As part of the leadership of Senghor's Bloc Démocratique Sénégalais, Sarr – who did not forget his origins – allied himself with the left wing of the party, and in particular with Mamadou Dia, who became Senghor's Prime Minister after independence. But when Dia and Senghor broke, and Dia and his allies were accused of crimes against the state, Sarr, along with Dia, was imprisoned, a fate he had not suffered at the hands of the French government.

None of this negates the argument – which is the main point of Sembene's fictionalized account – that the struggle itself galvanized a *popular* sentiment hostile to the hypocrisies of the colonial regime and led to a sense of empowerment among the strikers whose implications undoubtedly went beyond the sphere of labor. But organizationally, things were not so clear. Neither the major parties nor the major trade union confederations made the railwaymen's cause their own. Neither gave the railwaymen much reason to have confidence in their ability to represent the cause of labor. The strike of 1947–8 was a railway strike of extraordinary proportions, but it began and ended as a railway strike.

The ambivalences of colonial repression

The government side of the issue leaves its puzzles too: why officials allowed a disruptive strike to drag on so long without being either more repressive or more conciliatory. The government at first had no idea that it would face a long strike: 'The strike will no doubt last a few weeks. It is unpopular in all milieux – merchants, politicians, and workers'. This expectation may be why virtually nothing was done until November to try to maintain railway traffic.[60] And the arrogance of the assumption that the Régie would soon prevail no doubt communicated itself to the well-placed network of spies, who kept telling their bosses that the strike was about to collapse. Self-deception was thus an important element in prolonging the strike.

Although the Régie had conceded the *cadre unique* and the integration of auxiliaries in April, it was struggling for the power to give content to those ideas. Increasingly, the strike itself became the principal issue. On the very eve of the strike, Governor General Barthes, in his last-ditch meeting with union leaders, lectured them on 'the terms of the law and my intention of insuring that it is respected'.[61] He immediately (and in accordance with those terms) sent the dispute to an arbitrator and then to an arbitra-tional committee – which on 31 October in effect affirmed the agreement of April 1947 and on the whole agreed with the Régie's interpretation of it. From the first, the Governor General and the Régie insisted that the arbitration proceedings alone had legal standing and that negotiation over them was out of the question. The stance led to a virtual loss of contact between Régie and union, and the Inspection du Travail, whose interventions had been critical to settling previous strikes, was largely frozen out of the action.[62] Only in December were some minor concessions being talked about: making the integration of auxiliaries retroactive to 1 July instead of 15 July, allowing 'individual' reclassifications of some railwaymen in categories where the union had demanded systematic reclassification, and allowing fifteen instead of ten days leave in case of marriages, births and deaths. But it was still on the grounds of the sacrosanct nature of the arbitration decision that the Governor General refused the December initiative of the West African parliamentarians.[63] As late as 3 February, the administration in Dakar claimed that even sending an Inspecteur du Travail to talk to the union would be interpreted as a sign of loss of will, and that it was still necessary that the affair 'end by the total execution of the arbitration ruling'.[64]

Yet at the same time, the administration pulled its punches. At first it did nothing to enforce the arbitrator's judgment: it did not arrest the strike leaders, replace the illegally striking workers with new recruits, or requisition the workers, which would have put them under military discipline. All these options were discussed within the Government General and in Paris, but all were at first considered provocative. Only in the first week of November did the Régie make known its intention to hire replacements for the strikers, and even then the Governor General saw it necessary to explain that 'now, traffic must be assured as far as possible, despite the prolonged absence of African railwaymen'. The minister agreed, but wanted such hiring kept to a 'strict minimum'.[65] Such drastic measures as conscripting strikers into military service were viewed with considerable skepticism at the highest levels of the Ministry. Officials were no doubt reluctant to escalate for fear of going against their own initiatives of the post-war era: to constitute a new approach to labor based on ending forced labor, developing a system of industrial relations, and incorporating trade unions into that system. Measures intended to crush the union and coerce unwilling workers into the workplace would not help the cause. As Robert Delavignette, then head of Political Affairs in the Ministry in Paris, put it 'the strong style directed at the strikers will not itself resolve the problem (one has seen this in the recent past, even in AOF), if the government gives the impression of going back, after a detour, on trade union freedom and on the abolition of forced labor'.[66]

It was only in mid-November that Sarr was brought to court 'for having ordered the strike in violation of the decree of 20 March 1937 on compulsory arbitration'. Fiankan, the Ivory Coast leader, had been prosecuted earlier and sentenced to three months in prison for interference with the liberty to work, although he was not in fact jailed and his conviction was overturned on appeal. Sarr was sentenced on 11 December 1947 to twenty days in jail and a fine of 1,200 francs for leading an illegal strike, but he never served his sentence: in April, after the strike, the appeals court commuted his sentence to a fine of 100 francs, suspended. Significantly, the prosecutors went after Fiankan again immediately after the Ivory Coast strike was broken and they were anxious to remove him from the scene lest he start it up again. He was convicted of threatening people who returned to work and sentenced to six months in prison on 22 January, but his sentence was later reduced on appeal to two months and a fine, and in the end he was pardoned. There were also some prosecutions in Dahomey and Guinea, most of which ended in acquittals.[67]

Nor did the Régie play another card it had: many of the strikers lived in railway housing, concentrated in various *cités* in key depots. One of the demands of the union was to open such housing to auxiliaries: lodging was quite valuable given the poor infrastructure of colonial towns, and the linkage of housing to job was part of the stabilization strategy of post-war governments. The Régie kept threatening to expel strikers from their homes unless they returned to work, but it did not do so.[68] Perhaps its caution came from the notion – repeated often in reports in the immediate post-war years – that African labor was inherently unstable, all too likely to jump from job to job or return to village life. It was the most experienced and skilled workers who were housed, and it would have been consistent with thinking on the 'stabilization' issue for the Régie to fear that once such workers left the *cités*, they might never be heard from again.

The weapons that the Régie was left with, then, were to manipulate the divisions within the work force and try to get enough manpower in place to run the railway system well enough to avoid economic paralysis. By November, the Régie had started to hire new workers and it kept issuing appeals to strikers – with a mixture of promises and threats – to go back individually. The appeal stressed that the Régie had already agreed (and the arbitration award made this explicit) to the reorganization of the cadres, in some form at least, and to the integration of at least a significant number of auxiliaries. The poster distributed to the Ivory Coast, for example, pointed out that these measures would mean a 'large raise' for the cadres and 'a very large raise for qualified auxiliaries'. The threat was that, as of November, strikers had been officially 'detached' from their posts, but that the regime would take them back with seniority intact if they returned immediately and not at all if they held out.[69]

None of this was very effective until the Ivory Coast gave way in early January. As of 1 November, three weeks into the strike, 487 Europeans and 38 Africans were trying to run a railway. By 2 January, 836 strikers had gone back to work and 2,416 new workers had been hired. Even if one accepts the Régie's claim that it really needed only 13,500 men, not the 17,000 it had had before the strike (and after the strike the Régie came up with a new figure of 15,000), the Régie had recovered only little over a quarter of its African workforce. In the crucial 'material and traction' section of the Dakar-Niger line, which included locomotive drivers and other running personnel, less than a sixth of the posts were filled on 2 January. Indeed, the entire Dakar-Niger branch remained solid: 1,125 workers of both races were all there was to do the job of 6,765. The Conakry-Niger line – 1,196 at work out of 2,014 – and the Abidjan-Niger line – 1,424 out of 3,111 – were shakier.[70]

After the return to work in the Ivory Coast, the administration hoped that the other lines would give way, but their most serious attempt, via Fily Dabo Sissoko, to hive off a large section of workers from the union failed. As of 1 February 1948, the active workers as a percentage of theoretical staffing stood at 32 per cent on the Dakar-Niger, 54 per cent on the Conakry-Niger, and 16 per cent on the Benin-Niger. Overall, this meant that 34 per cent of staffing needs were being met.[71]

Officials thought that the union was able to prevent hiring through its influence in the railway centers.[72] Even where new workers were signed on, they did not necessarily work well. For example, attempts to use a mixture of European and African strike breakers on the wharfs in the Ivory Coast 'have not lived up to our hopes' because the men in question did not know how to use the equipment.[73]

Traffic had plunged after the strike and had only partially been restored. In mid-February, passenger traffic on the Dakar-Niger was at 12 per cent of its recent average, goods traffic at 43 per cent. Or the Conakry-Niger, passenger traffic was at 20 per cent, goods at 48 per cent. On the Benin-Niger, passenger traffic stood at 10 per cent, goods traffic at 30 per cent.[74] Its effects were felt not only in the damage it was doing to the French campaign to resupply the metropole, but also in the scarcities of goods that were occurring throughout French West Africa and which threatened the painful effort that was being made to provide incentives to peasants to grow marketable crops and workers to work.[75] In fact, the timing of the strike was crucial in this sense: France had with fanfare launched a 'development' initiative in 1946, and the railway strike served both to undermine its economic goals and take the luster off its ideological intervention.

At the end of January, about 300 men from the French railways were sent to Dakar to provide skilled labor, particularly in the troublesome Traction division. Some white CGT leaders and the anti-colonial press urged them not to act as strike breakers, and apparently some asked to be taken back to France or else subtly undermined their own presence by pretending that their equipment was not properly functioning. The fact that the French locomotive drivers were not familiar with the steam locomotives still in use in Africa – and which African drivers knew intimately – may have contributed to the subsequent decision to accelerate dieselization of the system.[76]

However much the administration's actions fell short of all-out combat, the union's achievement in holding together for so long stands out. There is no question that leadership played a big part in it: the strike had been extensively discussed within railway communities in advance and scrupulously planned. Sarr had made the rounds of the depots and cemented a personal identification of the cause with himself and with the strike committee. He ordered his followers to 'stay home and not to indulge themselves in any outside demonstration or any sabotage' – an order which was by all indications followed.[77] In Thiès, the strikers held daily open meetings, where doubts and concerns were aired, but peer pressure was maintained. Whenever there were signs of wavering along the Dakar-Niger line, Sarr went on tour and reaffirmed the personal ties and the group loyalties. Security officials were convinced that this direct approach was effective: 'Before the passage of Sarr, many of them were getting ready to return to work; afterwards, they have again decided, more so than ever, to continue the strike'.[78] Fily Dabo Sissoko – in the midst of his effort to get the Soudanais back to work – told French officials that 'The Soudanais considered themselves bound to the union Leader by a pact which it would be dishonorable to break'.[79]

However impressive the leadership, collective and personal, it was clearly rooted in railway communities – in towns like Thiès and Kayes, where railway workers and their families lived together as well as worked together, and where they were part of broad networks linking them to merchants and farmers in the area. In any case, Pélisson, the Inspecteur Général du Travail noted a crucial aspect of solidarity on the railway: it crossed all ranks.

> It is important to observe that the [strike] order was followed not only by the agents of the permanent cadre and the auxiliaries eligible to be inte-grated into it, the only people with an interest in the agreement under discussion, but also by the mass of ordinary auxiliaries – manual laborers for the most part – and by the personnel of the wharfs whose situation was not at all in question. Led into this behavior by a limitless confidence in their

leaders and their directions, undoubtedly as well by fear and at times by concern to keep their word, the African railwaymen have until now kept up, calmly and with respect for public order which is much to their credit, a strike whose prolongation seemed, however, more and more like a dead end.[80]

Defection, defiance and an ambiguous resolution

The strike broke first in the Ivory Coast. Pélisson attributed this to the behind-the-scenes machinations of Houphouët-Boigny, but it is also clear that a second tier of union officials staged a kind of coup while Fiankan, the Secretary General of the Abidjan-Niger railway union, was out of the country. The Ivory Coast union was clearly divided, and the officers whom Fiankan had replaced when he became Secretary General had, as early as November, intrigued against him. Fiankan for a time wavered in his support of the strike. Houphouët-Boigny had reportedly told the union leaders of his disapproval of the timing of the strike and their failure to consult him. When the news of the failure of the intervention of the deputies in December reached Abidjan in a telegram from Sarr on 30 December, it led to a tense meeting of a hundred railwaymen, presided over by Djoman, the Adjunct Secretary. Sarr's telegram was pessimistic, but argued that the only way for railwaymen to keep their jobs was to carry the strike to a successful conclusion. Maitre Diop, a lawyer and member of the Grand Conseil just returned from Dakar, confirmed the failure of the Dakar initiative. The Regional Director had shrewdly timed an offer (quoted above) to rehire all workers on the Abidjan-Niger who returned to work at that time, promising wage increases that would flow from the reclassifications approved in the arbitration ruling. The meeting divided between those who favored a return to work and those who wanted to await the return of Fiankan.[81]

The next day, Fiankan was being blamed for his absence (he was in Dakar), and the supporters of the strike were rapidly becoming discouraged. Over the next few days, the failure of the parliamentarians to settle the strike weighed heavily on a divided and depressed group of trade unionists. Sarr was blamed for starting the strike, 'traitors' for trying to end it. Diop and Djoman came out for a return to work. This was decided on 4 January, effective the next day. When Fiankan returned on 5 January, the men had gone back.[82] Meeting with a group of railwaymen at Treichville, Fiankan called them 'traitors to your comrades in Dahomey, Guinea and the Soudan' and demanded why they had gone back. 'It was the Committee in accord with Maitre Diop who gave the order to go back', he was told. Fiankan urged them to strike again. They replied, 'We have suffered enough'.[83]

Leadership was clearly of the utmost importance in maintaining such a strike. The Ivory Coast workers went back essentially under the terms of the arbitration decision, which provided that auxiliaries would be integrated into the cadres in accordance with their qualifications. The members of the cadres were, as promised, taken back to their old posts, but auxiliaries found that the conditions of their return were indeed problematic. The Régie had promised that the strikebreakers hired in the interim – and there were 755 of them out of a theoretical staffing of 3,111 – would keep their jobs, and it was the less senior auxiliaries who would bear the brunt. The Government

General in Dakar – despite fear of trouble from the Governor in Abidjan – was content for the laid off auxiliaries to learn that a 'strike always carries risks above all when it takes place outside legal procedures'.[84]

All this served notice that the government was going to play as tough when workers went back as they had when they were out on strike. Perhaps this experience contributed to the determination of the other regions to hold out and to the union's toughness in the post-strike period.

It was only when a new High Commissioner came to French West Africa that further movement took place. Paul Béchard, taking advantage of his arrival, undertook to talk to the principals beginning 26 February. Béchard as he himself later told it, decided that taking the legalistic line to its logical conclusion – by firing the railwaymen for violation of the arbitration ruling – was 'a brutal solution of rupture with unpredictable political consequences'. He sought a 'last try at conciliation', and he issued a series of proposals based on, but slightly modifying, the arbitration ruling:

(1) In regard to the union's claim to make the integration of auxiliaries retroactive to 1 January 1947, he proposed 1 May 1947 in regard to pay and 1 January 1947 in regard to seniority. The Régie had wanted 1 October and the arbitrator 15 July.

(2) In regard to the reclassification of certain agents in the *cadres secondaires*, Béchard maintained the Régie's equivalence tables, but granted extra seniority to the agents in question.

(3) In regard to where examinations would be required to pass between scales, he placed examination barriers where the Régie wanted them, and also where the union wanted them.

(4) In regard to the union's demand for 15 days annual leave, in addition to a month's vacation, which the Régie had rejected and the arbitrator reduced to ten days, the High Commissioner agreed to 15, but only for family events and only if necessities of service permitted.

(5) In regard to the union's demand for the provision of lodging or a compensatory indemnity to all agents, he agreed with the Régie's position supported by the arbitrator, that this could not be guaranteed for all.

(6) In regard to the union's demand for a uniform indemnity of zone, at the rate then accorded the highest rank – as opposed to the Régie's and the arbitrator's proposal for incorporating the old, hierarchical indemnities into a hierarchical wage scale and adding an indemnity of residence for places with a high cost of living – Béchard held firm to the Régie's position.

The High Commissioner decided in addition that there would be no punishment for striking, that the Régie would take back all its personnel in the cadres, that all auxiliaries currently at work would be kept on, and that striking auxiliaries would be taken back in order of seniority until the staffing levels had been filled.[85] The High Commissioner was trying to avoid the appearance of racial distinction while preserving the hierarchy of rank and the right of the Régie to deal flexibly with the potentially expensive demands for extending the rights to housing downward through the ranks. Union members insisted on a measure of job protection for auxiliaries who had gone on strike, and management agreed to a wage increase of 20 per cent. The Régie and the union accepted these proposals, and the return to work was fixed for that Friday, 19 March. Béchard concluded his report on the strike, 'It left no victors, no vanquished. Reasons for excessive bitterness for one side or the other have been avoided. Work could be resumed on solid bases, ignoring former divisions, in good order and with confidence'.[86]

Sarr, returning to Thiès after signing the agreement, claimed that the High Commissioner had 'given us concessions which the Régie did not want to give us . . . Thus, comrades, our honor is safe and we will return to work having shown that we were men who know what we want'. He did not want strikers to get into disputes with nonstrikers: 'We will resume work calmly, and with discipline'. The end of the strike was celebrated with a long march at Thiès, followed by meetings and dancing. It was an occasion of joy, an expression of confidence in organization and unity. In the years that followed, many children of railwaymen were named after Ibrahima Sarr.[87] The end of the strike is remembered today as a 'magnificent' victory bringing equality and the end of racial discrimination within the labor force, as a 'clear improvement' in the lives of workers, as an achievement won on behalf of the auxiliaries integrated into the cadres.[88]

Aftermath

Almost immediately, the two sides plunged into a struggle over the staffing table, over deciding which auxiliaries would be kept and over how integration would take place. The intensity of the disputes must have reminded everyone concerned of why the strike had been fought so determinedly. Management asserted its prerogative to fire people for incompetence or other reasons; the union had the implicit threat of another strike behind its demands.

The discussions over the labor force reduction lasted over two years. The Régie had intended to reduce its 17,000-man force even before the strike began; such a reduction was its quid pro quo during the April negotiations for agreeing to restructuring the cadres and integrating auxiliaries. In the midst of the strike, and probably for political purposes, it claimed it only needed 13,500. But when it came to listing necessary workers, the Régie found it needed to ponder the question – amidst challenges from the union – and then came up with a figure of 14,748 in June 1948. Given the fact that over 2,000 strike-breakers had been hired (not counting the Abidjan-Niger branch) and had to be kept on under the terms of the Protocol, this meant that as many as 5,000 workers could have lost their jobs. But as further delays ensued – including protracted and heated negotiations throughout the summer – many workers left voluntarily; while new works projects and the need to take care of neglected maintenance increased needs, so that by September the number of workers in jeopardy was around 2,500.[89]

Some of the voluntary resignations apparently resulted from union members making life difficult for the *défaillants* or *jaunes*, as strike-breakers were called.[90] From the very start, the union challenged management on so many points that the director complained that his regional directors find themselves in an annoying situation *vis-à-vis* the unions because of the fact that they are constantly accused of violating the end of strike protocol with threats of informing the Governor General or the Inspecteur Général du Travail. The authority necessary for the execution of a public service is dangerously disturbed.[91]

What was happening was good, hard negotiating, carried out within the new Commission at the federal level (as well as the Conseil d'Administration of the Régie) and within each of the branch lines. The Régie recognized the need to balance its desire to minimize costs with a desire for an 'appeasement policy', and in bargaining sessions the union insisted on 'the social side of the problem'. This meant avoiding brutal layoffs while using the labor force to assure neglected maintenance and the 'modernization of its equipment and its installations', which the Régie had proclaimed its goal. One top official admitted that in the course of 115 hours of meetings, the two sides had come closer together and concessions had been 'pulled out of the Régie', which admitted that its first tables were too theoretical and that more staffing was needed.[92] Then, from June through September, the details of where the axe would fall were negotiated. By this time, attrition had eased the problem somewhat, some of the workers hired during the strike were fired for incompetence and others for faults committed before the strike, and the union negotiated that layoffs take place in three batches, in August, September and October. Lists were generated by trade and seniority, and they were given to the union. Regional commissions heard disputes. Most, according to the Inspection, were settled unanimously. The axe did fall: the August firings consisted of 671 on the Dakar-Niger, 92 on the Conakry-Niger, 112 on the Abidjan-Niger, and 258 on the Benin-Niger, a total of 1,133. In September, 380 workers were fired. At Thiès, where the problem was regarded as 'the thorniest', the Inspecteurs got 348 rehired as temporaries, and encouraged others to seek work as dockers in Dakar or laborers on a development scheme on the Senegal River. In Dahomey and in the Ivory Coast, the union succeeded in getting significant numbers of workers slated for lay off to be reinstated.[93]

The Inspecteur Général du Travail admitted that 'the social malaise remains considerable', particularly the tension between white and black railwaymen. He hoped that the departure of some European railwaymen would ease the way both to hiring more Africans and improving the atmosphere. In any case, Pélisson acknowledged, a bit grudgingly, that the union 'had done its duty in defense of the railwaymen'.[94]

The union had to accept its share of responsibility for the process, but also credit for protecting its own men and inducing strike-breakers to quit. It concluded,

> having rid ourselves of the nightmare of staff compression, the situation of all the comrades who remain will be correspondingly improved. All qualified auxiliaries will soon be integrated into the cadre. The agents of the cadre will in several days receive their recalls, fruits of a struggle that will be forever remembered. Thus all will be paid their true value and the frightening number of auxiliaries will diminish considerably by their integration into the *cadre unique* which does not distinguish white or yellow or black, but only workers, period.[95]

But people did get hurt in this process, and in November a group of auxiliaries massed in front of Sarr's home to protest that the union was not looking after their interests and had not accomplished the promised integration of auxiliaries. They accused him of fostering his own political ambitions.[96] Indeed, the process of integrating auxiliaries was slow and partial, and some railwaymen continued to press (unsuccessfully) to regain the status of civil servants while civil servants pressed (successfully) for their own version of the *cadre unique*, with equal benefits regardless of origin.

The concrete gains were significant. The post-strike plan was for 2,500 auxiliaries to be integrated into the cadres. By 1950, the cadres had gone from around 12 per cent of the work force before the strike to over 31 per cent.[97] A financial evaluation of the Régie in 1952 concluded that the cost of integrating auxiliaries was one of the major factors leading to the high freight charges and precarious financial situation of the Régie, as were the substantial raises – estimated at 77 per cent – given auxiliaries since 1948. Officials pointed out in reply that the costs of the 1947 strike were still being paid and that social relations in French West Africa's largest enterprise were important not only in themselves but were 'necessary, as the strike of 1947 proved, for the sound functioning of the Régie itself. I believe that technical progress and social progress cannot be separated'.[98] This was a lesson that officials could not forget and unions would remind them if they did, while rank and file might remind their union leaders if they neglected the human interests that were at stake.

In the aftermath of the strike, its political implications remained to be worked out. The administration had fought the strike as a labor dispute, not as a contest over colonial authority, restraining its authoritarian hand but stubbornly insisting on following its industrial relations procedures. The union had also fought the strike as a labor dispute, restraining itself from public demonstrations more extensive than the regular mass meetings of railwaymen at Thiès. If the rhetoric of Sarr from his first speech in May 1946 onward was filled with attacks on colonialists, it also contained numerous references to the role Africans had played as in the French military, defending French freedom, and this – along with working side by side with French railwaymen – was seen as legitimating the claim to equality of pay and benefits. Similar strategies were used by others to turn the rhetoric of unity and assimilation in the Union Française into claims to entitlements: the veterans' slogan, for example, was 'equal sacrifices, equal rights'.[99] The French reference point was in fact vital to the union's entire argument: the plea for an end to racial discrimination in regard to indemnities, housing and other issues assumed the existence of a unit within which equality could be pursued.

Forty-seven years later, a former railwayman denied that the 'spirit of inde-pendence' was behind the strike; the central issue was 'respect of professional value'.[100] Yet the political meanings of the strike are more complicated than that. Equality with French railway workers was a formal demand, yet the spirit of defiance and the anger against French colonial practices could not be so neatly bounded. Nor could the self-confidence gained by the disciplined conduct of a social movement over five and a half months and a vast space be limited to the issues formally at stake. In regard to questions of popular consciousness, the vision of Sembene's novel remains germane to histories of the post-1948 era.

But popular consciousness does not make movements in a vacuum. Organization is a key concern, and here one finds a double ambiguity, in relation to trade union organization and to political parties. The community mobilization on which the strike depended was channelled – in the strike and its aftermath – through the railway union and its Comité Directeur. The very success of its negotiations drew it into a framework of industrial relations, modelled on French labor law and French practices. The union, over time, became more of a union.

And whatever the potential implications of the strike to anti-colonial politics, they were in fact channelled through the structures of political parties. The networks created by the union and by the strike as well as the memories and sentiments to which it gave rise were both enlisted in a wider cause and tamed. Senghor was the West African politician who accomplished this with particular acuity. Spending much time as a deputy in Paris and more tending to organizational work in Dakar, Senghor needed a mechanism to get beyond the limitations of the Dakar-centered politics of his mentor, Lamine Gueye. Senghor had not stood publicly by the side of the railway workers. His breakthrough occurred in reaching out to them – as he did to other constituencies via leaders, networks and pre-existing institutions. The Mouride brotherhoods were key constituents in rural areas, labor in the towns. Two of the candidates he kept on his slate after his break with Lamine Gueye in 1949 and his founding of the Bloc Démocratique Sénégalais were Sarr (for the Assemblée de l'Union Française) and Abbas Gueye, one of the heroes of the 1946 Dakar general strike (Assemblée Nationale).[101]

In the memories of participants, there is both pride and bitterness at this process: assertions that the railwaymen's actions set the stage for wider population mobilization, identification with Senghor as a political 'phenomenon'. But one hears from workers as well a disappointment that their own union leaders had become estranged in putting on the *boubou politique* (the robes of politics) and that their interests were being set aside in the scramble for office and the enjoyment of its perquisites. They feared that they would lose the power that derived from their professional focus and become only the 'auxiliaries' of the political parties. By the mid-1950s, the political activities of union leaders would become a source of controversy within the railway union and indeed within the labor movement of French West Africa in general.[102]

Conclusion

There remained, in 1948, a great deal for African union leaders to accomplish, on the railroad as well as outside. But in following up the strike, as much as in the strike itself, they had shown that the representatives of African workers would be present where their interests were being discussed. The 1947–8 railway strike was above all a contest over power within a system of industrial relations that had only just been brought to French Africa. No longer willing to defend explicitly and overtly a system of job classifications by race or origins, colonial officials were nonetheless willing to fight for power within the structure of bureaucratized industrial relations machinery they had created, over the details of what the wage hierarchy would be and the precise terms of access to different points within it. Hierarchy and differential access to resources were to remain fundamental to the modernized colonialism of the post-war era, and the strike of 1947–8 revealed the impossibility of separating neatly the impersonal structure of a modern institution from the racialized history of colonial rule. In so far as the struggle forced colonial officials to assert ever more vehemently that they did not mean for the new hierarchy merely to reproduce the old, in so far as control of that hierarchy had to be shared with a militant union, officials were made to confront the fact that colonial authority was no longer as colonial as it once was. Such a realization was an important part of the reconsideration by French political leaders and civil servants in the mid-1950s of the strategies and institutions on which French rule depended.

The determination and unity of the African railway workers made clear, for then and thereafter, that their voices would be heard. But the government of French West Africa made its point too; African unions could fight and they could win, but within certain legal and institutional structures. The very battle brought both sides ever deeper into those structures, and neither tried to take the battle outside. The railway workers drew on the strength of their communities – ties of family, commerce and religion within Thiès most notably – whereas proletarian solidarity across occupational lines or a wider African mobilization against colonialism could not be organized. At the end of 1948, a government report, reflecting on a year which had witnessed one titanic labor conflict – and a host of routine disputes and negotiations easily contained within the recently created structures of the Inspection du Travail – applauded the form in which the two sides had joined their conflict: 'Social peace can only profit from such a crystalization of forces around two poles, certainly opposed but knowing each other better and accepting to keep contact to discuss collective bargaining agreements and conditions of work'.[103]

Perhaps. The clearest sign that the terrain of struggle became more closely framed, defined and narrowed was that nothing quite like the general strike of 1946 or the railway strike of 1947–8 occurred again under French rule. For the railway and the government, the strike had a high cost in wages and benefits and a higher one in the lesson learned that the new social engineering strategies of the post-war era would give rise to new forms of struggle and new claims to entitlements. The question this would eventually leave in official minds had profound implications: was it politically wise to use France as a model for Africa and assert that the French empire represented a single entity when that legitimated African claims for a French standard of living? For African railway workers integrated into the cadres, the material gains of the strike were considerable, but this achievement left open the question of whether African communities would be strengthened or segmented by the higher incomes of a distinctly defined body of men. The strike of 1947 had drawn its strength simultaneously from the communities of the railwaymen and the union's seizure of the institutions and rhetoric of post-war French imperialism as the bases for its demands. The railwaymen now faced the question of whether their strength could serve a broader population or whether in attaching themselves to the cause of national politics the strength would be drawn out of the labor movement and into political institutions where their interests, their sense of community and their visions would be lost.

Notes

1   The quoted phrase comes from an interview with Amadou Bouta Gueye, 9 Aug. 1994, Thiès. Oumar NDiaye, interviewed the same day, made much the same point. These interviews were part of a workshop and field studies program conducted in August 1994, by Dr Babacar Fall of the Ecole Normale Supérieure, Université Cheikh

Anta Diop, Dakar, and the present author. A series of training sessions for graduate students was led by Dr Robert Korstad of the Center for Documentary Studies of Duke University, and I accompanied groups of students who interviewed eyewitnesses in Dakar and Thiès. The students participating in these interviews included Aminata Diena, Makhali NDaiye, Oumar Gueye, Alioune Ba, Biram NDour, and Ouseynou NDaiye. I was first introduced to strike veterans in Thiès by Mor Sene, son of a railwayman and author of 'La grève des cheminots du Dakar-Niger, 1947–1948' (Mémoire de maîtrise, Ecole Normale Supérieure, Université Cheikh Anta Diop, 1986–7).

2   The spies' reports appear in the archives as 'Renseignements', often with a notation such as 'African source – good'. Most came from the Sûreté at Thiès, where the almost daily mass meetings were held, but reports from other regions are also used. Archival sources from the Archives Nationales du Sénégal include (from the Government General of Afrique Occidentale Française) series K (labor), 17 G (politics), 2 G (annual reports), and (from the government of Senegal) series D (political and administrative files). The series IGT (Inspection Générale du Travail) and AP (Affaires Politiques) are from France, Archives Nationales, Section Outre-Mer, Aix-en-Provence. The abbreviation 'AOF,' for Afrique Occidentale Française, occurs frequently in the notes.

3   Frederick Cooper, 'The Senegalese General Strike of 1946 and the labor question in post-war French Africa', *Can. J. Afr. Studies*, XXIV (1990), 165–215.

4   Renseignements, 9, 27 Apr. 1943, 7 Sept. 1944, 27 Feb. 1945, 11 D 1/1392; Governor General to Minister, 19 Jan. 1946, 17 G 132.

5   Syndicat des Travailleurs Indigènes du Dakar-Niger, Circulaire no. 10, 1 Feb. 1946, signed by Gning, in K 325 (26).

6   Mory Tall, interview, Thiès, 9 Aug. 1994, by Aminata Diena, Biram NDour, Alioune Ba and Frederick Cooper.

7   Commissaire de Police, Thiès, to Commandant de Cercle, Thiès, 22 Aug., 27, 28 Sept. 1945; Renseignements, Thiès, 3 Dec. 1945, 11 Sept. 1946; Commissaire de Police to Chef de la Sûreté du Sénégal, 22 Nov. 1945; Commandant de Cercle, note for Governor of Senegal, 26 Apr. 1946; Chef du 2e Secteur de la Sûreté to Chef de la Sûreté du Sénégal, 20 July, 13 Nov. 1945; Note by Chef de la Police Spéciale du Réseau Dakar-Niger, 7 Aug. 1945, in 11 D 1/1396.

8   On Sarr's background, see Sene, 'Grève des cheminots'.

9   Renseignements, 6 Apr. 1946, K 328 (26); Renseignements, 14 May 1946, enclosing transcript of meeting of 4 May 1946 of Comité Directeur, K 352 (26).

10   'Revolution' was the word used by a strike veteran Adoulaye Souleye Sarr, interview, Thiès, 22 July 1990, by Mor Sene, Babacar Fall and Frederick Cooper. He pointed to the milieu of Thiès as the incubus of the revolution.

11   Renseignements, 22, 23, 24, 25 May 1946, 11 D 1/1392.

12   Renseignements, 28 May 1946, K 352 (26); Sene, 'Grève des cheminots', 46.

13   Iba der Thiam, 'La grève des cheminots du Sénégal de Septembre 1938' (Mémoire de maîtrise, Université de Dakar, 1972).

14   Syndicat des Travailleurs Africains de la Région Dakar-Niger, Transcript of Assemblée Générale of 9 Feb. 1947, K 459 (179); Sene, 'Grève des cheminots', 47–50; Renseignements, 20 June, 2 July 1946, 11 D 1/1392.

15   Governor General to Minister 20 Apr. and 19 June 1946, 17 G 132; Renseignements, Dahomey, June, July, Aug. 1946, and Report of the Gendarmerie Nationale, Porto Novo, 13 Aug. and 18 Sept. 1946, K 352 (26); Renseignements, Guinea, 1 July

1947, Aug. 1947, and Gendarmarie Nationale, Conakry, report, 1, 5 Aug. 1947, K 352(26); Renseignements, Soudan, 8 June 1946, 7 July, 3 Aug. 1947, K 352(26); Chef de la Région Abidjan-Niger to Directeur, Chemins de Fer de l'AOF, 20 Sept. 1946, 17 G 591; Ivory Coast, Police et Sûreté, Rapport Politique Mensuel, 3 Oct. 1946, and Renseignements, 6 May 1947, 17 G 139; Report of Commandant du Peloton de Marché d'Abidjan on strike movement at Tafiré (Korhogo), 16–17 Aug. 1946, 17 G 138.

16   AOF, Inspection Générale du Travail (IGT), Annual Report, 1947, 56–9; *ibid.*, 1948, 83.

17   AOF, IGT, Annual Report, 1947, 60–1; Sene, 'Grève des cheminots', 16. The importance to strikers of the *statut* issue was emphasized by Mansour Niang (interview 4 Aug. 1994).

18   AOF, Direction Générale des Travaux Publics, Direction des Chemins de Fer et Transports, Annual Report, 1946, quoted in Jean Suret-Canale, 'The French West African railway workers' strike, 1947–48', in Robin Cohen, Jean Copans and Peter C. W. Gutkind (eds.), *African Labor History* (Beverly Hills, CA, 1978), 152, n. 5.

19   Inspecteur Général du Travail, 'La Grève des Cheminots de l'AOF (1/10/47–16/3/48)', IGT 13/2; AOF, IGT, Annual Report, 1947, 60; Renseignements, 19 Aug. 1946, 11 D 1/1392; Suret-Canale, 'Railway workers' strike', 134–5.

20   Renseignements, 11, 13 Apr. 1947, and Gendarmerie Nationale Thiès, Rapport, 14 Apr. 1947, K 377 (26); Protocole de fin de grève, 19 Apr. 1947, K 377 (26).

21   Note sur la proposition de loi présentée par M Mamadou Konaté tendant à la création d'un cadre unique des chemins de fer de l'AOF, incl. Cunéo to Governor General 30 Mar. 1950, K 43(1).

22   Circular signed by Secretary General Marat (for Minister) to Hauts Commissaires, 29 Apr. 1947.

23   Note sur l'équilibre financier de la Régie, 12 Aug. 1947, K 459 (179).

24   Marie-Renée Valentin, 'Les grèves des cheminots français au cours de l'année 1947', *Le Mouvement Social*, cxxx (1985), 55–80.

25   Sene, 'Grève des cheminots', 55–7.

26   Renseignements, 25 Aug. 1947, K 377 (26).

27   Governor General to Minister, 28 June, 16 Sept. 1947, K 459 (179).

28   Mémoire of Régie for the Comité Arbitral, 27 Oct. 1947, K 459 (179).

29   Renseignements, Thiès, 1, 11 Sept. 1947, and Renseignements, Ivory Coast, 16, 18 Sept., 1947, K 377 (26); Sûreté, Synthèse mensuelle, Oct. 1947, 17 G 527.

30   Interviews, Amadou Bouta Gueye and Oumar NDiaye, 9 Aug. 1994; Renseignements, 27 May 1946, IID 1/1392; Governor General to Minister, 11 Oct. 1947, IGT 13/2, AOF, IGT, Annual Report, 1947, 62; Sene, 'Grève des cheminots'.

31   Renseignements, 19 Nov. 1947, K 378 (26); renseignements, 29 Oct. 1947, K 457 (179); interviews, Oumar NDiaye and Amadou Bouta Gueye, 9 Aug. 1994, and Mansour Niang, 4 Aug. 1994.

32   Renseignements, 14 Nov. 1947, K 457 (179).

33   *L'AOF*, 25 Nov., 12 Dec. 1947.

34   Interviews, Oumar NDiaye and Amadou Bouta Gueye, 9 Aug. 1994, Mansour Niang, 4 Aug. 1944, and Abdoulaye Souleye Sarr, 22 July 1990.

35   Khady Dia, interview, Thiès, 9 Aug. 1994, by Aminata Diena, Alioune Ba, Oumar Gueye and Frederick Cooper. Abdoulaye Souleye Sarr (interview, 22 July 1990), Oumar NDiaye and Amadou Bouta Gueye (interviews, 9 Aug. 1994) also suggested that Sembene may have elided the role of women in the two strikes.

36   IGT, Report, 24 Jan. 1948, IGT 13/2.

37   Report of meeting, 4 Nov. 1947, K 379 (26); Renseignements, 7 Nov. 1947, K 457 (179).

38   Resolution of Union Régionale de Guinée, 18 Nov. 1947, K 379 (26).

39   Governor, Ivory Coast, to Governor General, 21 Nov. 1947, K 237 (26).

40   Renseignements, Ivory Coast, 9 Nov. 1947, K 379 (26).

41   Suret-Canale, 'Railway workers' strike', 147.

42   IGT, Report, 24 Jan. 1948, IGT 13/2. On the changing struggles in AOF and the debates over the Code du Travail See Frederick Cooper, *Decolonization and African Society; The Labor Question in French and British Africa* (Cambridge: Cambridge University Press, 1996).

43   Renseignements, 1 Sept. 1947, K 377.

44   *La Voix de la RDA* was published regularly as a special section of the *communisant* Dakar newspaper, *Réveil*. This article appeared in no. 283, 5 Feb. 1948.

45   Renseignements, Ivory Coast, 5, 18 Nov. 1947, K 379 (26).

46   *Réveil*, no. 268 (15 Dec. 1947) and no. 269 (18 Dec. 1947).

47   IGT to Governor General, 12 Dec. 1947, K 457 (179).

48   *Ibid.* IGT 13/2.

49   AOF, Bulletin du Grand Conseil, Procès-Verbal, 23 Dec. 1947, 80–1, 31 Jan. 1948, 320–1.

50   Pélisson to M le Deputé Dumas, 6 Jan. 1948, IGT 13/2.

51   Senghor to Minister, 26 Nov. 1947, K 457 (179).

52   Renseignements, 17 Dec. 1947, K 457 (179).

53   Sissoko to Ministry, telegram, 3 Dec. 1947, IGT 13/2.

54   Note signed by Pillot, for the Dakar-Niger Réseau, for M le Directeur Fédéral de la Régie des Chemins de Fer de l'AOF, and sent by Cunéo to the President of the Conseil d'Administration, 19 Jan. 1948, K 457 (179); renseignements, Thiès, 27 Dec. 1947, K 457 (179).

55   Note by Pillot, K 457 (179).

56   Secretary General of Government General, to Sissoko, 29 Jan. 1948, copy enclosed Inspection du Travail, Bamako, to IGT, 7 Feb. 1948, K 457 (179).

57   Inspection du Travail, Bamako, to IGT, 7 Feb. 1948, Moussa Diarra, on behalf of Comité Directeur, telegram to Sarr, 29 Jan. 1948, and Renseignements, 4 Feb. 1948, K 457 (179).

58   Inspection du Travail, Bamako, to IGT, 7 Feb. 1948, K 457 (179).

59   Mory Tall, Oumar NDiaye and Amadou Bouta Gueye (interviews, 9 Aug. 1994). Mansour Niang (interview, 4 Aug. 1994).

60   Directeur Fédéral de la Régie to Directeur de l'Office Central des Chemins de Fer de la France Outre-Mer, 10 Oct. 1947, IGT 13/2.

61   Governor General to Minister, 11 Oct. 1947, IGT 13/2.

62   AOF, IGT, Annual Report, 1947, 62.

63   *Paris-Dakar*, 26 Dec. 1947, and Minutes of Grand Conseil, 24 Dec. 1947, cited in Suret-Canale, 'Railway workers' strike,' 145, 153, n. 25.

64   Affaires Courantes, Dakar, telegram to the new Governor General, Béchard, 3 Feb. 1948, IGT 13/2.

65   Governor General to Minister, telegram, 5 Nov. 1947, and Minister to Governor General, telegram, 7 Nov. 1947, IGT 13/2.

66   Delavignette, 'Grève des chemins de fer et des wharfs en AOF', 13 Dec. 1947, IGT, 13/2.

67   Governor General to Minister, 20 Nov. 1947, IGT 13/2; Directeur, Sûreté, to IGT, 15 Sept. 1948, K 458 (179).

68   Cunéo (Director of Régie) draft letter to all regional directors, 9 Jan. 1948, reminding them that strikers, as of 28 November 1947, had been 'detached' from the Régie and warning them that if they did not return by 15 January they would be dislodged: K 457 (179). For earlier threats, see Renseignements, 19 Nov. 1947, K 378 (26), and Inspection du Travail, Guinea, to IGT, 19 Nov. 1947, K 457 (179).

69   Annex to Renseignements, Ivory Coast, 30 Dec. 1947, K 379 (26).

70   IGT, AOF, to IGT, Paris, 8 Jan. 1948, IGT 13/2; AOF, Inspection du Travail, Annual Report, 1947, 62.

71   On these three lines, 839 workers had returned to their posts (including a few who had never left them) and 2,155 had been hired. Situation de la Régie au 1er Fevrier 1948, K 457 (179).

72   Governor General to Minister, 21 Nov. 1947, IGT 13/2.

73   Directeur Général de l'Office Central des Chemins de Fer de la France Outre-Mer, Note, 15 Dec. 1947, IGT 13/2.

74   Affaires Courantes, Dakar, to Minister, 14 Feb. 1948, IGT 13/2.

75   Inspection du Travail, Guinea, to IGT, 19 Nov. 1947, K 457 (179); Delavignette, 'Grève des chemins de fer . . .', 13 Dec. 1947, IGT 13/2.

76   Gendarmerie Mobile, Rapport, 15 Nov. 1947, K 43 (1); Suret-Canale, 'Railway workers' strike', 140; Abdoulaye Soulaye Sarr (interview, 22 July 1990); Sene, 'Grève des cheminots', 117.

77   Renseignements, 25 Oct. 1947, K 43 (1). His warning was later published in *Réveil*, 20 Nov. 1947. The orders against demonstrations were passed out in the Soudan as well. Renseignements, Bamako, 11 Oct. 1947, K 43 (I).

78   Renseignements; 13 Nov. 1947, K 457 (179), in regard to Sarr's trip to the Soudan.

79   Sissoko therefore saw convincing Sarr as the key. He miscalculated the nature of the union leadership, however, since the strike committee ordered a wavering Sarr not to give in. Governor, Soudan, to Governor General, 12 Jan. 1948, K 378 (26).

80   IGT, Report, 24 Jan. 1948, IGT 13/2.

81   Renseignements, Ivory Coast, 14, 15 Nov., 30 Dec. 1947, K 379 (26). On Houphouët-Boigny's role, see Renseignements, 5 Nov. 1947, *ibid.* and IGT to Deputy Dumas, 6 Jan. 1948, IGT 13/2.

82   Renseignements, Ivory Coast, 31 Dec. 1947, 3, 4, 7, 8 Jan. 1948, K 379 (26).

83   Renseignements, 7 Jan. 1948, K 379 (26). At Port-Bouet the next day, Fiankan was greeted with such hostility that he had to leave. *Ibid.*, 8 Jan. 1948.

84   Governor, Ivory Coast, to High Commissioner, telegram, 12 Jan. 1948, and Affaires Politiques, Administratives et Sociales to Governor, Ivory Coast, telegram, 20 Jan. 1948, K 378 (26).

85   High Commissioner's narrative of strike, 1 Apr. 1948, K 458 (179).

86   High Commissioner's narrative, 1 Apr. 1948, K 458 (179); Protocole de Reprise du Travail, 15 Mar. 1948, IGT 13/2.

87   Renseignements, 16 Mar. 1948, K 458 (179); Sene, 'Grève des cheminots', 104, 112.

88   Abdoulaye Souleye Sarr (interview, 22 July 1990), Oumar NDiaye and Amadou Bouta Gueye (interview, 9 Aug. 1994) and Mansour Niang (interview, 4 Aug. 1994).

89   These ups and downs are traced in IGT to Inspecteur Général des Colonies, 6 Sept. 1948, K 458 (179), and can be followed in Renseignements, June–September 1948, 11 D 1/1392.

90 Inspecteur Territorial du Travail, Dahomey, to IGT, 1 Apr. 1948, IGT 13/2; IGT, Réglement de la grève des chemins de fer africain de l'AOF, 24 Sept. 1948, *ibid.*

91 Directeur Fédéral de la Régie des Chemins de Fer to Inspecteur Général du Travail, 9 Apr. 1948, K 458 (179).

92 Statements of Pillot and Mahé for the Régie and Ousmane N'Gom for the union, Transcript of Meeting of Conseil d'Administration des Chemins de Fer de l'AOF, 25 June 1948, IGT 13/2.

93 IGT, 'Réglement de la grève des chemins . . .' 24 Sept. 1948, IGT 13/2. See K 458 (179) for reports on layoff issues in the different branches of the railway system.

94 IGT, 'Réglement de la grève des chemins . . .', 24 Sept. 1948, IGT 13/2.

95 Circular signed Abdoulaye Ba from the union to union subdivisions, apparently intercepted by Sûreté and filed as Renseignements, 8 Sept. 1948, K 458 (179).

96 'La vie syndicale en AOF', 31 January 1949, AP 3406/1.

97 IGT to Inspecteur Général des Colonies, 6 Sept. 1948, K 458 (179); Directeur Fédéral de la Régie to IGT, 30 June 1950, K 43 (1).

98 Mission Monguillot, 'Situation Financière de la Régie Générale des Chemins de Fer de l'AOF', Rapport 93/D, 10 Apr. 1952; Directeur Général des Finances to Monguillot, 5 May 1952, and High Commissioner to Monguillot, 17 July 1952, AP 2306/7.

99 Myron Echenberg, *Colonial Conscripts: The Tirailleurs Sénégalais in French West Africa, 1857–1960* (Portsmouth, NH: Heinemann, 1991), 152.

100 Mansour Niang (interview, 4 Aug. 1994).

101 'La vie syndicale en AOF au cours de l'année 1948', 31 Jan. 1949, including High Commissioner to Minister, 2 Feb. 1949, AP 3406/1.

102 Interviews, Moussa Konaté, 8 Aug. 1994, and Mory Tall, 9 Aug. 1994. For more on politics and trade unionism in the years after the strike, see Cooper, *Decolonization and African Society*, ch. 11.

103 'La vie syndicale en AOF', 31 Jan. 1949, AP 3406/1.

PART FOUR

Nationalism and Anticolonialism

NATIONALISM AND
ANTICOLONIALISM

DECOLONIZATION COULD NOT have taken place in Africa and Asia without the rise of nationalism and nationalist movements in the decades preceding independence. Nationalism, however, did not come in the same form and varied from context to context. Furthermore, many nationalist movements were allied to ethnic and religious ties, while others remained closely aligned with other ideological and political goals. The essays presented in this section reflect a host of different concerns and offer crucial insights into the rise of anticolonial nationalist movements in India, the Gold Coast, and the Sudan.

David Gilmartin's "Democracy, Nationalism and the Public: A Speculation on Colonial Muslim Politics" investigates the emergence of Muslim politics in colonial India. Using the notion of "the public" developed by critical theorists, Gilmartin argues that Muslim opposition was constructed as a tool to contest European power in the Punjab. Nationalism and the idea of the nation — as a unified and coherent whole — remained a central doctrine of Muslim nationalists such as Muhammad Ali Jinnah, who used the discourses of the public and the nation to solidify a new sense of community among his followers. According to Gilmartin, Jinnah insisted that Hinduism and Islam were religiously and socially divisible. This allowed Jinnah to articulate the idea of two nations, or two public spheres, in colonial India (one Hindu, one Islamic) with differing traditions, social customs, and nationalist traditions. Jinnah's need to view the communities as necessarily different was useful as a means to mobilize Muslim nationalism and ensured the division of Pakistan and India in 1947. This separation has also served to support the rationalization and bureaucratization of state control since independence.

Jean Marie Allman, in a wonderfully argued text, "The Youngmen and the Porcupine: Class, Nationalism and Asante's Struggle for Self-Determination, 1954–57," addresses the issue of divergent forms of nationalism in the Gold Coast (Ghana). Allman argues that, contrary to historiographical trends, Asante nationalism was an important movement that posed an important challenge to Kwame Nkrumah's

British-supported plans for post-independent Ghana. By reinserting the Asante back into the historiography of decolonization, Allman offers an important and nuanced account of Ghana's transition to independence. This account demonstrates that the Asante could be considered an avant-garde resistance movement because it refused to be coopted by Nkrumah's vision of nationalism that, according to the Asante, relied too heavily on British support. Furthermore, and perhaps most interestingly, the text indicates how Nkrumah's vision of nationalism and pan-Africanism failed to embrace a significant nationalist movement within his own country.

Heather J. Sharkey's "Colonialism, Character-Building and the Culture of Nationalism in the Sudan, 1898–1956" analyses how a European educational institution helped form a pro-nationalist culture in the Sudan. By focusing on the Gordon Memorial College, Sharkley demonstrates how the College's formal and extracurricular education of Africans altered African self-perceptions and sense of place within the colonial world. As a result, rather than remaining an educational institution that indoctrinated Africans with British culture, the College created a unique sense of nationalist culture and eventually subverted the intentions of its European creators by fostering a desire of independence.

Chapter 9

David Gilmartin

DEMOCRACY, NATIONALISM AND THE PUBLIC

A speculation on colonial Muslim politics

THE IMPORTANCE OF an emerging 'public' for the history of modern India and Pakistan has recently begun to attract scholarly attention. Historians of Indian nationalism for decades have pointed to the emergence of 'public opinion' and an emerging 'public voice' among the English-educated middle class in India as a critical element in the emergence of Indian nationalism. Drawing on the work of Habermas and others, some have recently sought to define more rigorously the elements that shaped a distinctive 'public sphere' in India, and how these elements differed from those that defined the eighteenth and nineteenth century European experience. Central to these efforts has been a concern to define the ways that the distinctive structure of the colonial state in India shaped distinctive forms of 'public' opinion and activity — including 'democratic' and 'nationalist' activity — in ways that distinguish Indian experience from any model shaped by the experience in Europe.

This chapter will take these concerns as the starting point for a general (and thus somewhat schematic) consideration of the development of a distinctly Muslim public in India (with particular reference to the Punjab) in the late nineteenth and early twentieth centuries. It is the argument here that without some consideration of an emerging 'public', it is impossible to analyse the impact of electoral 'democracy', or the emergence of Muslim 'nationalism', on Muslim politics. It is also the argument that the meaning of 'public' has to be understood in Indian colonial politics not primarily in contrast to the sphere of the 'private', but in contrast to the sphere of the 'particular', a distinction given special meaning by the unique structure of the colonial state in India. Indeed, the significance of this will be evident if we turn immediately to the nature of electoral 'democracy' as introduced into India by the British.

The meanings of 'democracy' in India have been strongly conditioned by the historical origins of India's representative electoral institutions within the political structure of British colonial India. The introduction of 'democratic' electoral institutions was influenced, at least in part, by the spread of nineteenth century liberal ideas from Europe. But of far more immediate practical importance in the introduction of electoral institutions into India was the influence of a 'colonial sociology' that shaped the ways that the British colonial state sought to sink its roots into Indian society. As Bernard Cohn and others have argued, the British justified their authority in India (particularly in the second half of the nineteenth century) by ordering and systematizing a society composed of innumerable, parochial 'cultures' and 'communities'. While colonial power remained rooted in bureaucratic and military power, the state's hold over society rested both on its recognition and protection of these communities, *and* on its claim to the superior, 'scientific' knowledge, which allowed the state alone to order these communities into a rationalized political whole. Such communities might include both those based on genealogical reckoning (caste, tribe, etc.) and those based on religion; but all tended to be defined, in essence, as particularistic groups — that is, groups whose principles of internal organization and definition offered no potential challenge — no alternative, universal principle of ordering to the rationalized, scientific authority of the colonial state.

The establishment of this sphere of the particular played a vital role also in shaping the introduction of electoral institutions in the late nineteenth and early twentieth centuries. Whatever other principles may have been at work, the British introduction of electoral representation into India represented one means by which the British sought to manipulate the political definition of particularistic 'communities' and draw them more fully into the structures of the state in the late nineteenth and twentieth centuries. The introduction of local and provincial elections grew in part, as Anil Seal has argued, from the practical requirements of maintaining support as the Raj penetrated more deeply into Indian society in the later nineteenth century in order to increase its revenues. As the state adopted an increasingly intrusive presence in local society, it sought to legitimate its position by using nominations and elections to committees, councils boards and legislatures to draw local elites more fully into its orbit.[1] Though this represented in part a response to pressure from educated Indians, the central concern of the British was the maintenance of the underlying structure of the Raj. The growth of electoral representation, whatever its potential implications for the future, thus did not emerge in the context of a developing bourgeois public sphere — as it did in late eighteenth and nineteenth century Europe — but rather as a mechanism by which the state sought more effectively to encompass a society composed of innumerable particularistic communities. In defining the state's relationship to local society, the vision of India as a conglomeration of local 'communities' — held in place by a scientific state structure — continued to be central.

The implications of this for the meaning of representation are critical if we are to discuss the relationship of Islam and democracy. The history of Islam as a universal religion bequeathed to the Muslim community a somewhat ambivalent place in British ordering of India's particularistic communities, but the structure of colonial representation nevertheless tended to define a vision of Muslim community that fitted the particularistic structure of colonial India. The importance of Muslim identity as a central element in this fabric was underscored by the early introduction into India of separate Muslim electorates. Separate electorates recognized the distinctiveness and historical importance of a Muslim 'community', and acknowledged as well the desire for separate representation among some prominent Muslim leaders. But to be a Muslim for purposes of separate electorates required no particular statement of principle or belief. Instead, 'objective' census considerations, by far the most important of which was descent, determined who would count as a Muslim. As embodied in separate electorates, the

Muslim community thus became, like 'castes' and 'tribes', a fixed, particularistic community that could be easily encompassed within the structure of the colonial order.

Nothing marked this more clearly than the prohibition in colonial election law against the use of threats of 'divine displeasure' in public electioneering. To 'induce a candidate or voter to believe that he . . . will be rendered an object of divine displeasure or spiritual censure' was officially defined in British election law as a corrupt electoral practice. This law had its origins in the United Kingdom, where the concern was to prevent the exercise of religious 'undue influence' on the free choice of the individual voter within the 'public sphere'. But within the context of the emerging electoral system in India, it took on a very different significance, for here the importance of religious affiliation already had been officially recognized through separate electorates as a key, constituent element in the structure of the representative system. To bar any appeal to 'divine displeasure' or 'spiritual censure' was thus to define, in this context, a particular kind of religious community. Obedience to God's will (or to the *shariat*) had no legitimate place in defining Muslim identity as it was encompassed in separate electorates. Indeed, such laws carried clear implications for the political meaning of 'Muslim community' within the context of India's 'democratic' political institutions. Within the structure of the colonial political system, religion thus was defined essentially as a form of particularistic identity — an identity unconnected with the assertion of any universal principles for individual behaviour or for the definition of the larger political system.

Critically, this had implications also for the colonial structure of Muslim political leadership. Separate electorates implied, as Farzana Shaikh has put it, a form of 'descriptive' rather than 'substantive' representation, a system in which representatives gained legitimacy not for their substantive ability to represent a constituency, but rather for the formal correspondence between their own identification and that of the state-defined 'community' to be represented.[2] For many Muslim leaders, this structure of representation provided a means by which a variety of forms of local wealth, status and power could be translated into legitimate leadership within the structure of state power. Muslims as various as merchants in Bombay, landlords in U.P., 'tribal' leaders in the Punjab, and *pirs* in Sind all claimed the same political status as 'Muslim' leaders. Indeed, privileged descent, wealth, and landed status, were all transformed, through separate electorates, into foundations for 'natural' leadership of the state-defined Muslim community. Though the practical roots of local power might be divorced from personal Islamic behaviour and rooted in diverse forms of local influence, the state's formal definition of the community through separate electorates enabled these leaders, as politically influential Muslims, to claim a legitimate place within the state structure as leaders of an 'objectively'-defined Muslim 'community'.

This is not in any way to suggest, of course, that these Muslim leaders took this formal, 'objective' definition of community (as expressed in the structure of separate electorates) to be a full expression of the nature of Muslim consciousness. To the contrary, as the work of many historians has shown, the period of British rule was one of widespread educational, religious and intellectual reform among Muslims in India, marked by powerful new emphases on education and personal reform as key markers of Muslim identity. Nevertheless, the very prominence of such movements among influential Muslims (including those who profited from separate electorates) suggests another critical feature of the colonial structure: a tendency toward the definition of separate 'political' and 'cultural' realms in the definition of Muslim community and identity. As colonial rulers, the British had self-consciously sought to separate religious ideology from political power. With roots in this context, the most powerful movements of reform (particularly among the ulama and the old *ashraf* elites) focused on the definition of the Muslim community — as a cultural entity — outside the state-supported political realm.

Such reforms were various and were not of course shaped wholly by Muslim responses to the structure of colonial rule; they drew on far older traditions of Islamic discourse. Perhaps nowhere is this more evident than in the dramatic nineteenth century reforms among the ulama, who, at Deoband and elsewhere, drew heavily on the reformist tradition of Shah Waliullah. But such reforms were strongly adapted also to British colonial rule in that they focused on definitions of community linked to the spreading reform of personal religious practice and to the assertion of personal cultural identity independent of the structure of state power. Perhaps most noteworthy in this connection was the transformation of the meaning of the *shariat*, or Islamic law, during this period, as described by historians such as Gregory Kozlowski.[3] For many, and not just among the ulama, personal adherence to *shariat* took on increasing importance as a mark of community identity. But the *shariat* during the colonial period (as developed both in the British courts and among the ulama) itself took on the increasingly pronounced character of a system of 'personal law' — a system of law dealing with a realm of behaviour almost entirely separated from, and opposed to, the realm of political life. Such a tendency in the development of *shariat* had roots extending back into Islamic history well before the colonial era. But the meaning of *shariat* as a system of 'personal' law (in which issues regarding family, inheritance and women assumed particular importance) was increasingly marked as a touchstone of community that operated outside the realm of state-oriented politics.

Indeed, much the same sort of argument could be made for the educational reform movement centred on Aligarh. Though the reforms of Sir Sayyid, and most other so-called 'modernists', were intended to facilitate cooperation with the British colonial state, they also aimed toward the 'cultural' definition of Islamic community in an arena largely independent of state authority. These reforms in fact were intended to preserve the local prestige and power of the *ashraf*, which was rooted in privileged descent, even as they sought increasingly to fuse this local power with a broader 'cultural' definition of Muslim community — instilled at institutions such as Aligarh — that would justify *ashraf* leadership in extra-local affairs. The tendency, whether at Deoband or at Aligarh, was thus for Muslim leaders to seek new 'cultural' definitions of community identity forged in the realms of 'community' life independent of the political structures supporting state authority. Drawing on a long history of Islamic discourse, such developments offered at the same time a mechanism for shaping a coherent cultural redefinition of the community in the face of colonial domination.

Perhaps equally important, these cultural re-definitions of Muslim identity in colonial India also located Muslim communal identity squarely within a discourse of rationalized and internalized self-control over the individual. Though Aligarh and Deoband differed in their approach to community in significant ways, they shared a concern to tie the assertion of Muslim 'community' to the spread of education and reformist rationality. Indeed, both educational movements held at their centre a concern to define boundaries of 'control' around a Muslim community that was shaped not only in a cultural realm independent of the state, but that was defined by the internalization by individual Muslims of a distinctive 'cultural' identity. With the colonial state providing no symbolic definition of Muslim community in India, the assertion of 'community' solidarity required that the individual Muslim himself bring his (or her) inner life and sense of identity under self-conscious personal and rational control. For many *sharif* Muslims, this required the self-conscious acceptance of a concept of 'culture', rooted in descent and history, and spread by education, that gave substance and legitimacy to a culturally independent Muslim community. To many of the reformist ulama, the internalized control of behaviour that increasingly defined the community was even more fundamentally modelled on the triumph of individual rationality (*aql*) over emotion, a process that went hand in hand with the triumph of *shariat* over local custom, and localized kin and caste based identities.[4] Individual rationality and self-control were, in fact, central to the whole educational process that sought to define a new sense of Muslim community in colonial India shaped not symbolically by the state, but by self-controlled individuals.

The language of individual rationality was thus central for the establishment of cultural autonomy among colonial Muslims. Clearly some aspects of these movements, with their definition of a 'private' world open to rational control, and their corresponding definition of new forms of 'public' discussion and debate, call to mind the emerging 'public sphere' outlined by Habermas. But the implications of these movements for the definition of a new, public form of political 'community' in colonial India were limited. Though both the Deoband and Aligarh movements made extensive use of printing and the press to disseminate their ideas among increasingly wide circles of Muslims, these movements did not, in themselves, imply a challenge to the structure of colonial political authority, which encapsulated the Muslim community within the larger 'scientific' structure of colonial rule. Indeed, the potential of both the Aligarh and Deoband movements to transcend this encapsulation was sharply limited in the nineteenth century by the continuing importance in both movements of concepts of authority rooted in the continuing cultural domination of privileged elites. Though holding up a model of rationalized, individual identity as the touchstone of Muslim community, both groups stressed the subordination of the individual to externally provided (if rationalized and internalized) boundaries of control. Whether authority was tied to *sharif* descent and culture or to the interpretation of *shariat*, the movements centred on Aligarh and Deoband both clung to structures of 'community' and authority located not wholly within individual Muslims, but in conceptions of status and knowledge mediated to society by privileged elites. In spite of their emphases on the internalization of identity, neither group could imagine a Muslim community that could exist without their own special claims to authority. Without the ulama, *shariat* would mean nothing; without privileged descent and cultural hierarchy based on *sharafat*, Indian Muslim history and Muslim culture would be unthinkable.

In spite of their emphasis on cultural autonomy, Muslim leaders within both these reform movements thus stressed fixed forms of leadership and authority that fit generally into the structure of ordered particularism and 'descriptive' representation that shaped the overarching political structure of the colonial state. Though they stressed increasing rational control over the 'private' world of Indian Muslims (including women, the domestic realm, the emotions, etc.), they did not politically transcend the 'particular'.

Nevertheless, the rhetoric of both movements — and, in particular, their reliance on printing — carried implications for the emergence of Muslim movements with more radical implications. As Benedict Anderson and other writers on 'nationalism' have argued, the new sense of public community associated with the emergence of nationalism frequently was linked with the changes in popular thinking accompanying new technologies of communication, particularly those associated with what he calls 'print-capitalism'.[5] The spread of printing technology created, he argues, new notions among individuals of their interrelationships, not within a grid of relations and of particularistic communities shaped by the state, but within a 'society' composed of autonomous, and constantly interacting, individuals. The notion of autonomous individuals comprising a 'society' gave rise, in Anderson's words, to an 'imagined community', residing in the creative imaginations of each individual. The result was thus the emergence of a conception of community defined not only independently of the state, but also composed of autonomous individuals. Though the early reformers of Aligarh and Deoband remained largely wedded to a structure of particularist leadership adapted to the colonial structure, their stress on both the dissemination of the printed word and on the internal transformation of the individual pointed the way toward more radical transformations in Muslim thinking.

Critical, in fact, to an understanding of an emerging Muslim 'public' that transcended the particularistic structure of the colonial state was the emergence of a commercial Urdu press in north India rooted primarily in the marketplace rather than in the discourse of reform and the school — a press that ultimately produced idioms of community that differed sharply from those of the reformers of either Aligarh or Deoband. In fact, the connections between the press and reformers are so numerous as to be difficult to disentangle, but the critical point for the analysis here is that for the newspaper editors, publicists and political poets who wrote for commercial publications, it was not primarily the control (or internalized self-control) of the inner life of readers that was the aim. In a commercial world, the individual consumer remained autonomous. The rhetoric of 'community' was increasingly deployed in the press not primarily in the interest of education or rational self-control of the individual, but in the interest of drawing as many readers as possible into the public discourse on which their publications, and the dissemination of their own ideas, depended. Even though the impact of 'consumerism' was extremely limited in Muslim India, therefore, the growing importance of a commercial press signalled the beginnings of critical shifts in communal rhetoric, with the rhetoric of individual autonomy, of inner desires and emotions, assuming critical significance. Central to the 'imagined community' of the new press was not a community bounded by a discourse of rational control over individuals, but a new realm of public community rooted in a discourse of individual autonomy.

Such an argument raises critical questions, of course, about the meaning of the 'public'. It is the argument here, that for all their concern with 'public' discussion and with the creation of a cultural realm independent of the state, the reformers of Deoband and Aligarh did not create a 'public' realm (in contradistinction to the realm of the 'particular'), because they sought essentially to give new vitality and meaning to Muslim identity *within* the particularistic and scientific political ordering of communities that comprised the colonial state structure. Indeed, with direct cultural control of the state closed to them, their emphasis on internalized individual rationality, that controlled not only 'public' Muslim life, but also the internal life of the heart and of the home, defined the cultural means by which they tried to do this. But the emergence of a 'public' defined by the commercial press suggested the emergence also of a new kind of 'public sphere', whose contours, in a sense, stood Habermas' model on its head. The element in this new realm that differentiated it most clearly from the realm of the reformists was the potential it created for transcendence of the discourse of reform, rationality and particularism. Central to the emergence of a Muslim discursive realm that could escape the bounds of particularism was a language that rooted community identity not simply in rational self-control but in the autonomous realm of the individual heart and emotions. Ironically, it was only the insertion of the inner (unreformed and autonomous) heart into the 'public' and political realm that allowed the rhetoric of Muslim community to begin to break out of the encapsulated particularism that defined community identity within the 'scientific' structure of the colonial political system.

In the Punjab, the emergence of this discourse of inner emotion and community was rooted both in the Urdu press's growth in the early twentieth century and in the increasingly important political role played by journalists and poets such as Maulana Zafar Ali Khan and Muhammad Iqbal. Indeed, the importance of these men grew not only with the expanding role of the press, but also with their ability to translate long-established literary idioms of inner emotion and desires — particularly associated with Urdu poetry — into the realm of public debate. Zafar Ali Khan and Iqbal were certainly not the first to make political use of Urdu poetry, but the translation of poetry into essentially a public and political form of expression, disseminated not through private or state patronage but through the press, was a central facet of their careers, and it underscored the new conception of 'community' and of the autonomous political individual that the new discourse of 'print-capitalism' embodied. Urdu poetry represented in the nineteenth century a powerful reservoir of imagery of many kinds, but prominent among these was the imagery of inner desire and emotion, potentially dangerous to the social fabric. Though a vital part of the human make-up, this long had been uneasily confined in the rhetoric of poetry to a private realm, sometimes portrayed as irrational, sometimes as a realm of intuitive, even sufi, knowledge. Indeed, this was a realm that reformers had sought to bring under increasing rationalist control. But with the transformation of political poetry in the press, one can trace the movement of the inner world directly onto the political stage. The private world of emotion — of unrequited desire and longing — in fact came to be central in constituting the Muslim community in a new way, as a product not of cultivated *sharif* culture (however much poetry had been a part of that structure), or personal adherence to the *shariat*, but as a community composed of autonomous individuals, each defined by individual desires. And with this, the autonomous heart rather than the rational mind, became the locus of community identity. As Iqbal put it: 'When several hearts put on a single hue, that is community'.[6]

Given this construction, the key to the public demonstration of community came not through public adherence to proper Islamic norms, but through symbolic action, in which the heart was made public. In the 1920s and 1930s the Punjab witnessed a series of symbolic agitations, focusing on the defense of the Khilafat, the Prophet, or mosques — all symbols of Islamic identity — in which the discourse of personal and emotional identification with Islamic symbols was translated from the press into public action. Such agitations drew on the language of sufi devotionalism, and also on the sensibilities attached to urban public arena performances, including Muharram and the Prophet's birthday, which also stressed (and perhaps increasingly so in the nineteenth century) a public display of personal devotion and inner emotion focused on Islamic symbols. But what distinguished these agitations from such public arena performances was that they were freed from any overtly ceremonial context, and thus from the structures of local authority and obligation that largely shaped them. Tied to the emotive language of the commercial press (and popular oratory), they drew on a discourse of personal autonomy that distinguished them not only from the reformist discourse of individual self-control, but also from the continuing particularism associated with public arena ritual.

Two Punjabi examples of such symbolic agitations — the defense of the Prophet focusing on the Hindu-published pamphlet, *Rangila Rasul* in the late 1920s and the defense of the Shahidganj Mosque at Lahore in the 1930s — illustrate these trends. The agitation over the *Rangila Rasul* ('The Merry Prophet') was rooted in a history of communal polemics in Punjab that had waxed and waned since the emergence of the Arya Samaj in the late nineteenth century. *Rangila Rasul* was an Arya Samaj inspired pamphlet, first published at Lahore in 1924, that satirized the sexual practices of the Prophet Muhammad. This pamphlet was prosecuted under British press laws and was initially proscribed, but after repeated appeals the conviction was overturned on a judgment by Justice Dalip Singh of the Lahore High Court in 1927. Though the British government, putting public order far above any question of free speech, rushed to develop new legislation to control the situation, many leading Muslim writers and orators attempted to turn the case into a symbolic test of 'love' of the Prophet, which came to be portrayed by some as a public touchstone of community. But the differing reactions of Muslim leaders to the situation suggested the critical symbolic importance of the issue among Muslims themselves in defining the public and political meaning of Muslim 'community'.

Virtually all Muslims agreed on the importance of protecting the honour of the Prophet. But the terms in which they called for such protection nevertheless diverged. A Lahore meeting of reformist ulama, for example, asserted that love of the Prophet was of central importance for all Muslims. But they nevertheless made clear their view of the community as one defined in its essence by the *shariat* and by controlled personal behaviour. 'The Musalmans consider insult to the Prophet a most serious offence, which under the Muslim Law is punishable by death', they declared. But for most ulama, this did not involve uncontrolled action. If Muslims acted on the basis of 'feelings' that had been 'involuntarily' excited by the failure of the Government effectively to prosecute the pamphlet, then for that, in spite of the appeal to *shariat*, the ulama could not be held responsible. Indeed, with rational self-control at the centre of their discourse of Muslim identity, the ulama could hardly identify themselves wholly with such an emotional appeal, however sympathetic they might be to the aims of the appeal and however resonant for them the symbols involved. If Muslims lost self-control, they declared, then 'the entire responsibility of exciting religious feelings and making law subservient to feelings', would have to devolve not on the ulama, but 'on the Government'.[7]

But for many Muslim publicists and newspapers, the importance of the issue lay precisely in that it dramatized the subservience of law to feelings. Indeed, this was central to their definition of community. For Sayyid Ataullah Shah Bokhari, for example, a poet, an active Khilafatist and later a leader of the Ahrar Party, it was the *public* display of the heart in the active protection of the honour of the Prophet that defined the real existence of a Muslim community during the *Rangila Rasul* crisis. 'If the Hindus abuse the Prophet in a meeting held in a private building', he said, 'Muslims should not attend it. But if any Hindu in any open meeting or procession uses obscene language about the Prophet he should be killed there and then. Any Muslim who would not be prepared to do this is not a true Muslim'.[8] To control one's emotions in such a circumstance was in Bokhari's eyes almost a crime. His appeal was based not on the letter of the *shariat*, but on *action* in the name of the heart, as the most telling validator of Muslim identity. Nor was Bokhari alone in making such appeals. And the effect was illustrated by the actions of a young Muslim who responded to these appeals in deadly fashion — by assassinating the *Rangila Rasul's* publisher.

This agitation over *Rangila Rasul* had little long-lasting political significance, but in the more broad-based agitation for the protection of the Shahidganj Mosque at Lahore that followed in the mid-1930s, the call for the public display of 'feelings' was again at the heart of public action. The Shahidganj Mosque was a religious site that long had been disputed between Muslims and Sikhs, but was awarded to the Sikhs by a special government tribunal in the early 1930s. Though Muslim groups had made various judicial efforts to regain the site, a sensation was caused in 1935 when the Sikhs in possession of the site demolished the mosque even as negotiations with Muslims were going on. As in the *Rangila Rasul* case, the public display of emotional commitment and sacrifice now played a central role in an agitation for what was portrayed as a 'martyred' mosque, a display that took on even more meaning when a dozen Muslims were killed during subsequent demonstrations. Noteworthy now was the popular rhetoric of the press, which not only played on images of martyrdom and sacrifice, but also employed the powerful imagery of unrequited desire drawn from Urdu poetry. As Maulana Zafar Ali Khan wrote in the *Zamindar*, the youth of Lahore had 'sacrificed themselves like moths on the lamp of Islam' to defend the mosque, even as the ulama remained silent.[9] And another Lahore daily, the *Siyasat*, drew on similar language in attacking those Muslims who had contented themselves with working through institutional political channels while Lahore's youths 'in a state of excitement tore their collars and received bullets in their chests'.[10]

This metaphor of public exposure of the heart thus came to be central to the definition of community itself, a counterpoint to the rationalistic discourse of the ulama and the political machinations of responsible and *sharif* Muslim politicians. Perhaps most important, it suggested a community not only 'imagined' in the language of the press, but one symbolically acted out in the disinterested and purely emotional actions of 'restless' and 'excited' male youths — public actions that embodied, in a sense, the inner world of all Muslims, no matter how outwardly controlled and respectable. Whatever the political and religious organizational structures underlying Muslim community life, it was thus only in public *actions*, that the true heart of the community itself — and thus its true unity — could be publicly exposed.

Indeed, the agitations pointed the way toward the popularization in urban Punjabi politics in the 1920s and 1930s of a conception of community that carried critical implications for the entire structure of politics and for newly-developing institutions of electoral 'democracy'. Increasingly, leading urban politicians and newspaper editors (drawing strength from popular agitations, but sometimes organized also into new quasi-political parties such as the Ahrar Party or the Ittihad-i-Millat) sought to inject into the structure of state politics (and particularly into elections) a new conception of

Muslim leadership based not on a 'descriptive' correspondence between leaders and a state-defined community, but on the same commitment to symbols that was embodied in these agitations. However carefully the British had sought to define through separate electorates a fixed and controlled space for the Muslim community within the state structure, these urban leaders now sought to transform urban elections into a realm for the creation of a new kind of 'public', defined at the intersection of an emerging commercial press, with its appeals to symbols as a focus for Muslim community identity, and an appeal to popular action (including voting) as an expression simultaneously of community and individual autonomy. This was only possible in a realm, such as the cities, where the Urdu press and printing were relatively influential. But critically, and in spite of the central importance in this of an Urdu literary tradition, it was a public created not in a cultural realm separated from politics, but one created within the structure of politics itself, and yet, created in self-conscious opposition to the particularism of the 'scientific' colonial structure.

The importance of this for the subsequent evolution of Muslim politics — and particularly for 'Muslim nationalism' — should not be underestimated, for it pointed toward the emergence of a 'public', in Habermas's sense, that was not encapsulated by the state, but could claim ultimately to exert surveillance over it. But in immediate terms, this had relatively little impact, not only because the urban political realm remained a relatively small and circumscribed one within the structure of British rule, but also because, as the immediate results of both urban agitations and elections suggested, such a construction of community was not readily translated into distinctive forms of lasting political organization in British India. Neither in the *Rangila Rasul* case nor in the Shahidganj agitation were symbolic actions followed by political organization expressing effectively the interests of the Muslim 'community' in its relations with the government — indeed, one might argue that the very nature of the construction of community embodied in these agitations largely precluded such an outcome. The efforts by leading editors such as Maulana Zafar Ali Khan and by popular orators such as Sayyid Ataullah Shah Bokhari to form political groups to contest urban elections also did not — in spite of some electoral success — produce any lasting, 'rational' structures of effective political organization. Indeed, the denouement of such contests usually was bitter infighting, and often a politics of conflicting personal interest that seemed to deny the very foundation of unity on which symbolic community was constructed.

But the critical long-term implications of these developments became evident with the emergence of the demand for Pakistan, for it was only with the emergence of Pakistan that the emotional construction of community in these agitations began to take on a new form. At the heart of this lay the relationship of the construction of community to a discourse of nationalism. In fact, one might argue that the emergence of the Pakistan demand as the centrepiece of Muslim community discourse grew out of this history of popular urban action and agitation — this creation of a new 'public' — in two ways.

On the one hand, the agitational politics of the cities proved critical to the emergence of the idea of a 'nation' — because it helped to define a new transcendent form of community. This new form of community 'imagined' both in the world and in the individual heart, was, like the idea of a 'nation', distinctive precisely because it transcended the world of rationality and 'scientific' classification (even if it gained political meaning in interaction with that world). It transcended the arenas of interests and controls (both internal and external) that shaped all the class, kin-based, and sectarian divisions among Muslims that were products of a fixed and visible outer reality. In the discourse of nationalism, all these divisions dissolved in the face of a larger (or transcendent) communal identity rooted in a place that the rational world could not penetrate — in the heart and emotions of the autonomous individual. Whatever its origins in urban politics, this conception thus exerted a powerful force on the emerging concept of a 'national' identity.

But this was only one side of the coin. The origins of the Pakistan movement can be seen, at the same time, as part of an effort by the political leaders among Indian Muslims to control this nationalist discourse by channeling it toward a new, rational structure capable of containing it, the nation-state. The movement for Pakistan was led by a wide range of Muslims rooted in the rationalistic and reformist discourse of the late nineteenth and twentieth centuries, and the rhetoric of emotional nationalism therefore merged with the rhetoric of control and discipline. Not all the inheritors of Aligarh and Deoband of course supported Pakistan; in the eyes of many of them, particularly those associated with Deoband, its meaning was highly ambiguous.

But the centrality of rationality and self-control in the movement was embodied by Jinnah himself; its meaning for the new state was captured clearly in Jinnah's theory of 'two nations'. Hinduism and Islam were not two different religions, Jinnah declared, but two 'distinct social orders', which produced different 'religious philosophies, social customs and literature'. They were two distinct civilizations, with different histories, epics, heroes, etc.[11] They were therefore two 'objectively' knowable communities, defined by outward, rationally perceived characteristics and histories. The importance of individual self-discipline for the realization of this Muslim 'nation' was suggested by Jinnah's motto for the new Pakistan — 'unity, faith, discipline'. By tying the discourse of nationalism to a new vision of the state, many of the Pakistan movement's leaders thus sought to ground it in a structure rooted in discipline and authority. And given this, the relationship of the state to an emerging 'democratic' public sphere was, from the beginning, a highly ambivalent one.

The role of the 'public' in Pakistan itself is a subject beyond the scope of this paper, but it is worth nothing that the ambiguities in the definition of a national 'public', and in its relation to the state, have continued to shape politics since Pakistan's creation. The history of electoral 'democracy', with its cyclic moves from military dictatorships to parliamentary government, has suggested this, as have the repeated efforts of Pakistani states to devise new means of institutional control and manipulation over a still problematic Pakistani 'public' sphere. General Ayub's 'basic democracies', and General Zia's 'partyless' elections both were means by which the state sought to maintain a legitimizing structure of representative 'democracy' even as the electoral arena was, through attempts to control and fix 'representative' leadership, largely sealed off from effective 'public' debate and action. Nevertheless, the history of the inner realm of active identification with symbols has continued to play an important role in the definition of nationalism and national identity.

As in most nation-states, the emotional rhetoric of national identity was in part displaced at Pakistan's creation from symbols of Islamic community to symbols of the state — the flag, the anthem, the army, etc. But although the history of nationalism in Pakistan is a complex one, with many cross-cutting political, religious and linguistic elements, the tension between the assertion of emotional loyalty to Islamic symbols as an expression of both popular community and individual autonomy, and the assertion of loyalty to the symbols of the state has at times found expression in Pakistan in open political conflict. One prominent expression of this has arisen, for example, in the Tahrik-i Khatm-i Nabuwwat (The Movement for the Finality of the Prophethood), a movement that, in its strongly anti-Ahmadiyya rhetoric and its roots in the popular agitations and pamphlets of the 1930s, stressed the public expression of love of the Prophet as the touchstone of Muslim identity. Drawing as well on the support of many ulama, this movement repeatedly has brought a public Islamic movement into direct conflict with the Pakistani government, and has elicited widespread public agitations in many cities of Pakistan — drawing heavily on an appeal to personal love of the Prophet. That this has represented a potential threat to the rationality of Pakistan's state adminis-tration has been demonstrated by the state's sharp reactions, its declaration of martial law in the Punjab in the 1950s, its imprisonment of key leaders of the movement and adoption of press controls, and ultimately its officially declaring the Ahmadiyya a non-Muslim minority in order to co-opt and control the movement. One can perhaps see similar outpourings in the more recent public agitations centred on the banning of Salman Rushdie's *The Satanic Verses*.

But the limitations of these movements — and the different context created by the existence of the Pakistan state — suggest the degree to which the fusing of nationalism with the identity of the state has in fact succeeded in largely coopting this discourse within a structure of rationalized, bureaucratized administration and state control. The meaning of such symbolic agitations has thus been different in independent Pakistan from what it was in colonial India. But the history of this discourse of the individual heart provides important clues for the understanding the meaning of Muslim national-ism in Pakistan. Further, it suggests the ways that an examination of popular, symbolic action and agitation — and its critical intersection with the discourse of commercial press and publications on the one hand and with the devotionalism of public arena perform-ances on the other — helps us to decipher the meanings of emerging new forms of Muslim community, and the Muslim 'public', that emerged in India under colonial rule.

Notes

1   Anil Seal, 'Imperialism and Nationalism in India', in John Gallagher, Gordon Johnson & Anil Seal (eds.), *Locality, Province and Nation: Essays on Indian Politics, 1870–1940* (Cambridge, Cambridge University Press, 1973) pp. 9–10.

2   Farzana Shaikh, *Community and Consensus in Islam: Muslim Representation in Colonial India, 1860–1947* (Cambridge, Cambridge University Press, 1989) p. 90.

3   Gregory Kozlowski, 'Shah Banu's Case, Britain's Legal Legacy and Muslim Politics in Modern India', in K. Lele (ed.), *Boeings and Bullock Carts: Continuity and Change in Indian Civilization* (New Delhi, Chanakya, 1989).

4   Barbara Metcalf, 'Islam and Custom in Nineteenth-Century India', *Contributions to Asian Studies*, Vol. 17 (1982).

5   Benedict Anderson, *Imagined Communities: Reflections on the Origin and Spread of Nationalism* (London, Verso, 1983).

6   Muhammad Iqbal, *The Mysteries of Selflessness*, trans. by A.J. Arberry (London, John Murray, 1953) p. 12.

7   Account of a meeting of the Jamiat-ul-ulema held on 3 July 1927 at Lahore. H. D. Craik to Government of India, 5 July 1927. National Archives of India, Home Political, file 132/III/1927.

8   Translation of speech of Sayyid Ataullah Shah Bokhari at the Badshahi Masjid, Lahore, 5 July 1927. Quoted in H. D. Craik to Government of India, 7 July 1927. National Archives of India, Home Political, file 132/III/1927.

9   *Zamindar* (Lahore), 24 Aug. 1935. Punjab Archives, Press Branch, file 8331, vol. IV-A.

10 *Siyasat* (Lahore), 13 Aug. 1935. Punjab Archives, Press Branch, file 8331, vol. III-A.

11 Presidential Address of M. A. Jinnah to the 27th session of the All-India Muslim League, Lahore, 22–24 Mar. 1940. S. S. Pirzada (ed.), *Foundations of Pakistan*, vol. II (Karachi, National Publishing House, 1970) p. 338.

Chapter 10

Jean Marie Allman

THE YOUNGMEN AND THE PORCUPINE

Class, nationalism and Asante's struggle for self-determination, 1954–57

At one period Ashanti national sentiment undoubtedly looked forward to the evolution of the country into a separate political unit, in which the Confederacy Council would be the recognized organ of the legislative and administrative authority. But the political integration of Ashanti with the Gold Coast Colony effected by the constitution of 1946 has for the time being diminished the general interest in this aspiration, nor does there in fact appear to be any substantial grounds for its revival.

(W. M. Hailey, 1951)

When on a day in September this year a group of Ashanti youth gathered at the heart of Kumasi up the Subin River and swore by the Golden Stool and reinforced their Oath with the pouring of libation to the Great Gods of the Ashanti nation and the slaughtering of a lamb, an act of faith, of great national significance was undertaken . . . And so Ashantis, backed by their chiefs and Elders, their sons and daughters, and taking guidance by the shadow of the Golden Stool, are now determined to live and die a Nation.

(*Pioneer*, 27 November 1954)

O**N 19 SEPTEMBER 1954**, the National Liberation Movement was inaugurated in Kumase, the historic capital of Asante, before a crowd of over 40,000. Many who gathered at the sacred Subin River that day were dressed in funeral cloth and chanted the Asante war cry, '*Asante Kotoko, woyaa, woyaa yie*'! At precisely midday, the leaders of the new movement unfurled its flag. The flag's green symbolized Asante's rich forests, its gold the rich mineral deposits which lay beneath the earth, and its black the stools of Asante's cherished ancestors. In the centre of the flag stood a large cocoa tree; beneath the tree were a cocoa pod and a porcupine. The graphic was powerful and its symbolism misinterpreted by none. The cocoa pod represented the major source of wealth in Asante and the porcupine (*kotoko*) stood as the age-old symbol of the Asante war machine. Like the quills of the porcupine, '*wokum apem a, apem be ba*' — 'if you kill a thousand, a thousand more will come'.

Over the next two and a half years, the National Liberation Movement (NLM) asserted Asante's right to self-determination in the face of Kwame Nkrumah's blueprint for a unitary government in an independent Ghana: a blueprint co-authored and supported by the British colonial government. NLM leaders alternated demands for Asante autonomy within a federated Gold Coast with calls for Asante's complete secession. Violence plagued the major cities of the region as colonial officials watched their model colony teeter on the brink of civil war. For nearly three years most Asante supporters of Nkrumah's Convention People's Party (CPP) lived in exile in Accra. Indeed, Nkrumah, out of fear for his safety, did not cross the Pra River, the boundary between Asante and the Colony, until well after independence in 1957. In short, the NLM not only posed a serious threat to the stability of Nkrumah's pre-independence government, but it destroyed the illusion, present since 1951 and reflected in Hailey's comment at the beginning of this article, that the Gold Coast's transition to full self-rule would proceed with rapidity and order.

Most scholars who have examined these turbulent years in Ghana's history, drawn by the dynamism and historic destiny of Nkrumah's CPP, have focused their attention on the party which was to lead Ghana to independence. As a result, the NLM has been cast into the murky shadows of historical inquiry and branded as a tribalist, regionalist, parochialist ghost of the past — a fleeting aberration in the Gold Coast-wide struggle against colonial rule. Meanwhile, those who have devoted their careers to understanding the specific dynamics of Asante history have seldom ventured beyond the beginning of the twentieth century. This article is aimed at narrowing that historiographical gap. Its purpose is to extend the oft-debated history of the Asante kingdom into the twentieth century through an examination of the National Liberation Movement. It seeks to understand the NLM on its own terms, as part and parcel of Asante history, not as a brief aberration in the national history of Ghana. Though it is a story of continuity and of Asante tenacity, it is by no means the story of a nation united on an historic march to reclaim its right to self-determination. Indeed, to grapple with the twentieth-century tenacity of Asante nationalism — as manifested in the NLM — is to grapple with the historically-rooted contradictions of that nationalism and to confront many of the social and economic conflicts which pervaded Asante history for at least a century before the NLM's inauguration.

Although many in Accra — CPP members and colonial officials alike — reacted with surprise, if not disbelief, at the news of the NLM's founding, there had been indications as early as November, 1953 that some Asantes were beginning to question the government's blueprint for independence. The first murmurs of discontent arose during the debate over the distribution of seats for the new Legislative Assembly — the body envisioned as leading the Gold Coast to independence. A government report provided for the allocation of seats based on the population of the regions, allotting Kumase two seats and the Region nineteen.[1] In a legislative body which was to contain 104 seats, roughly 20 per cent would represent Asante. This allocation reflected a decline from Asante's 25 per cent share of seats in the 1951 Council. As far as the Asante representatives were concerned, the report reflected a total insensitivity to the historic, economic and political importance of Asante to the Gold Coast. Asante, they argued, should be entitled to no fewer than thirty seats. B. F. Kusi, who had resigned from the CPP a year earlier and who would become a staunch supporter of the NLM a year later, told the Council:

> All Ashantis express the sentiment that Ashanti is a nation and that fact has been accepted. We are not a region at all; we should be considered as a nation . . . Population alone does not make a country.[2]

But despite the burning nationalist pleas of many Asante representatives, the government's report was adopted. Many in Asante decried what they considered to be the government's total insensitivity to Asante's special position in the Gold Coast. Their bitterness was not to subside quickly.

A few months later, Asante discontent with the CPP surfaced within the offices of the CPP itself. As the June 1954 election approached – the election heralded as the last before independence – CPP candidates had to be chosen to stand for the 21 seats in Asante. In many cases, local constituencies disapproved of the candidates selected by Nkrumah and the CPP's Central Committee and submitted their own candidates for registration, defying the party's central authority.[3] As the election drew near some members agreed to accept party directives and removed their names from the ballot, but 32 in Asante chose to stand as independent candidates. Nine days before the election these Asante candidates were among the 81 'rebels', as Nkrumah termed them, publicly expelled from the CPP at a mass rally held in the Subin River valley in Kumase.[4] But the Subin valley had not seen the last of the Asante rebels.

On 13 August, the government passed an amendment to the Cocoa Duty and Development Funds Bill which fixed the price of cocoa at 72 shillings per 60 lb. load – a price which represented only one-third of the average prevailing world market price.[5] The Asante rebels were among those who galvanized opposition in Asante to this government ruling; in the process they transformed the campaign for a higher cocoa price into a political struggle. A leaflet circulating in early September, authored by one of the rebels, made the political connections explicit:

> Ashantis produce more cocoa than the colony. IS THERE ANY COCOA IN THE NORTHERN TERITORRIES [sic]? NO! Why should Government tax cocoa farmers to develop the country in which Ashantis suffer most? . . . Ashantis! Save Your Nation and let others know that we are no FOOLS BUT WISE, kind and also we have the Worrier [sic] Spirit of Our Great Ancestors Within Us.[6]

It was abundantly clear that cocoa and *Kotoko* would stand at the heart of the struggle. Within a few weeks, Asante opposition to the cocoa price mushroomed into a broad-based Asante struggle against the CPP, its economic policies and its blueprint for self-government. The *Ashanti Pioneer*, a local paper whose owner, John Tsiboe, had opposed the CPP from its inception, published an editorial which proclaimed:

> Great events . . . from little causes spring. Like an innocent match flame,
> the strange attitude of the all African CPP Government to the simple
> demand of farmers for a higher local price of cocoa has gone a long way to
> threaten to set ablaze the petrol dump of Ashanti nationalism.[7]

On 19 September, in the Subin River valley, that 'petrol dump' was officially ignited as tens of thousands participated in the inauguration of the Asante National Liberation Movement.

Who was behind this massive resurgence of Asante nationalism? Who in Asante was capable of mobilizing a broad-based popular front of resistance against the government? Who welded the issue of cocoa to the spirit and grievances of *Asante Kotoko*? Scholars primarily concerned with the early years of Ghana national history have offered a variety of answers to these questions. Some, influenced by Clifford Geertz and the notion of 'national integration', saw the NLM as an almost inevitable response to the all-encompassing sovereign civil state – an expression of the primordial attachments of Asantes on the eve of independence.[8] Others, writing after the overthrow of Nkrumah in 1966, assumed the same Ghana-wide historical perspective as did the 'integrationists'. However, they argued in more materialist terms that the NLM was the product of large-scale cocoa farmers, powerful chiefs and businessmen, who exploited tribal attachments to gain the support of Asante workers and peasants in a class struggle against Nkrumah and his party.[9]

Only Richard Rathbone's work, based on extensive research in Asante, has revealed the theoretical limitations of attempts to understand the dynamics of the NLM solely within the context of Ghana national history. Rathbone recognized that the driving force behind the formation of the NLM was not the 'big men' of Asante and that the NLM could not be dismissed as simply the enigmatic expression of primordial attachments. Those responsible for the resurgence of Asante nationalism, for the forging of an Asante popular front of resistance against the CPP were, as Rathbone correctly argued, Asante's youngmen – those very same men who had spearheaded the CPP drive into Asante in 1949–51.[10]

Rathbone made a significant analytical leap in singling out the CPP rebels and their comrades in the Asante Youth Association (AYA) as the catalyst to the political upheaval of the mid-1950s. However, by focusing his concern on the wider contemporary struggle between the youngmen and the CPP during the transfer of power, he did not explore the historical dimension of his ground-breaking analysis. He saw the youngmen as a post-World War II phenomenon: Asante's version of the post-secondary school-leavers, the first mass-politicized generation. While this analysis goes a long way toward explaining the immediate thrust behind the resurgence of Asante nationalism, it cannot account for the conflicts and contradictions inherent in that nationalism; for the events of 1954–7 did not simply represent the struggle of Asante's youngmen against the government of the CPP. Those events also reflected the historically rooted struggle within Asante (and within the NLM) between the aspiring youngmen and the established powers of Asante. It was the outcome of this long struggle, not the lone and immediate aspirations of the youngmen, which would determine the course of Asante's quest for autonomy.

The youngmen of Asante had been a potent and active political force since at least the mid-nineteenth century when they were known as the *nkwankwaa*, a term which has been consistently rendered in English as 'youngmen'. The sense of the term was not that the *nkwankwaa* were literally 'young', but that they existed in often uneasy subordination to elder or chiefly authority. As Wilks writes of the nineteenth-century *nkwankwaa*, they were men who 'belonged to old and well-established families but whose personal expectations of succeeding to office or even of acquiring wealth were low'.[11] Channels for political advancement were obstructed by the traditional requirements of office; channels for economic advancement were obstructed by both the state and its monopoly on trade and what could be termed the rising bourgeoisie or *asikafo* (literally, 'men of gold' or 'rich men').[12] Perhaps best described as an emerging petite bourgeoisie, with an economic base in trading and rubber production and economic interests directed at the establishment of free and unencumbered trade with the coast, the *nkwankwaa*, according to Wilks, probably acquired 'their first experience of political action in the anti-war and anti-conscription movements' of the late 1860s and early 1870s.[13] It was in the 1880s, however, that the *nkwankwaa* made their first serious bid for political power in Asante. It was the Kumase *nkwankwaa* who, angered when *Asantehene* Mensa Bonsu raised taxes and imposed heavy fines for petty offenses, took a leading role in the movement which eventually overthrew the *Asantehene* in 1883.[14] Capable of mobilizing the support of the *ahiafo* (the 'poor' or 'under-privileged'), and in alliance with the *asikafo*, whose economic standing was also threatened by Mensa Bonsu's austerity measures and his state trading system, the *nkwankwaa* were able to carry out a successful coup against the *Asantehene*; and since they were 'unconvinced of the virtues of a monarchical system', they were able to bring Kumase under a 'republican form of government' or a 'Council of commoners and chiefs', albeit for only a brief period.[15]

Though the *nkwankwaa* had made a serious bid for political power in the 1880s, their long-term goals differed markedly from those of the *asikafo* and *ahiafo*. In the last years of Asante sovereignty, the *nkwankwaa* were unable to forge a lasting political alliance capable of effecting a dramatic change in Asante politics.[16] By 1901, Asante was under the complete control of the British and the *nkwankwaa* faced an entirely new political and economic landscape. In the first three-and-a-half decades of the century, before the consolidation of indirect rule in Asante, the *nkwankwaa*, according to a 1924 colonial report, enjoyed a 'feeling of independence and safety which gives vent to criticism of their elders, and a desire when dissatisfied to take the law into their own hands'.[17] Their relationship with Asante's traditional authorities remained uneasy at best. Throughout the 1920s, the *nkwankwaa's* involvement in destoolment cases against numerous *amanhene* ('paramount chiefs') alarmed government officials and traditional authorities alike.[18] With their social and economic position bolstered by the growth in trade and the spread of education, the *nkwankwaa* became more resentful of the powers exercised by the chiefs, namely their ability to levy taxes and impose communal labor requirements. In 1930, the *nkwankwaa* were particularly outraged by news that the *Kumasihene*, Nana Prempe I, and his chiefs were considering a law which would require that a percentage of a deceased person's property be given to the *Kumasihene* and his chiefs. In a letter to the Chief Commissioner, they warned that it was a similar measure which led to the overthrow of Mensa Bonsu in 1883. After discussions with the Chief Commissioner, Nana Prempe I dropped the issue.[19]

That the *nkwankwaa* have origins dating back nearly a century before the founding of the NLM clearly has implications for our understanding of the events of 1954–7. Specifically, these pre-colonial origins allow for an historical (though admittedly tentative) class analysis of the youngmen – an analysis which repeatedly points to the *nkwankwaa's* reliance upon strategic alliances or popular fronts which they have forged with other groups in Asante society to further their own aims, be it an end to conscription, the abolition of communal labour, a lessening in taxes, or the opening up of free trade with the Coast. The *nkwankwaa* have been artful initiators of these alliances, capable of winning the support of the *asikafo* and *ahiafo*. Historically, they have also turned to the chiefs (or certain elements within the ruling elite) to gain the support and legitimacy necessary to further their causes.

That the *nkwankwaa* have had to turn to others, particularly to the chiefs, points to their weakness as a class. It also goes some distance toward explaining their pivotal and dynamic role in the turbulence of Asante politics over the past century. The *nkwankwaa* have displayed an historical ability to take advantage of the fluid nature of Asante politics since the 1880s – galvanizing support in frequently opposing camps around common, though perhaps fleeting, issues, playing power against power. They accomplished this in 1883; and in 1934, in alliance with most of the Asante chiefs, they staged an important, though unsuccessful, hold-up of cocoa in response to the low price being paid for the crop by European merchants. In the following year, partly in response to the growing challenge the *nkwankwaa* posed to traditional authority, the British government decided to centralize that authority by restoring the Asante Confederacy Council, with the *Asantehene* at its helm. Some of the youngmen of Kumase, perhaps in an effort to tear apart the recently restored Confederacy, then collaborated with the *Dadeasoabahene, Bantamahene, Akyempemhene* and *Adumhene* in a plot to remove the *Asantehene*, Prempe II, from the Golden Stool.[20] The conspiracy was quickly uncovered, but the fact that 'irresponsible agitators' could win the support of such prominent chiefs required drastic action. Less than a year later, during 1936, the Council took matters into its own hands: in response to the *nkwankwaa's* vocal opposition to the colonial government's reconstitution of the Confederacy, their reluctance to perform various communal services and their role in the destoolments of so many paramount chiefs, including the attempt to destool the *Asantehene*, the Asante Confederacy Council abolished the office of *Nkwankwaahene* ('leader of the youngmen') and all *nkwankwaa* organizations.[21] The traditional position of *Nkwankwaahene* was not hereditary, nor did it confer membership in any council (whether local or divisional), but it did provide a recognized channel through which the youngmen could collectively criticize the government.[22] It was that channel the Confederacy Council sought to destroy. But the *nkwankwaa's* dissatisfaction could not be eradicated so easily. The Confederacy Council could not simply legislate away the historically entrenched *nkwankwaa* who were intent on attaining political power commensurate with their newly acquired Western education, their growing economic power via the expanding cocoa economy and their widening roles as the clerks, teachers and accountants of the new colonial bureaucracy.

In many ways, the Asante Youth Association, founded in 1947, came to assume the role and functions of the abolished *nkwankwaa* organizations, as its members shared common characteristics, as well as common grievances with their counterparts of the late nineteenth and early twentieth centuries. Most AYA members came from well-established families, but had no prospects of succeeding to traditional office. Their economic and social base remained petit bourgeois, but there had been many important changes over the last fifty years. No longer rooted primarily in petty trade and small-scale rubber production, the youngmen of the post-World War II period were an economically diverse lot. Most had attained some degree of education which led them into such burgeoning occupations as journalism, teaching, accounting and clerking. Some were shopkeepers and small-scale traders and some, were involved in cocoa production (if only in a small way). They were not chiefs (though many were related to chiefs) and they had no realizable aspirations to chiefly office. They can also be distinguished from the old guard intelligentsia – the relatively sparse, though politically significant, group of Asante professionals like K. A. Busia and I. B. Asafu-Adjaye – who had been trained to inherit the government upon the departure of the British, but who had been left out after the dynamic rise of the CPP. They were not the indigent or *ahiafo*, nor were they the *asikafo* whose wealth was based in a powerful combination of land ownership, large-scale cocoa and timber production, trading, transport and construction. They were, quite simply, the youngmen, the *nkwankwaa*, or, for lack of a less cumbersome class definition, the petite bourgeoisie.

Perhaps what most distinguished the youngmen of the post-World War II era from the *nkwankwaa* of the previous decades was that they participated in (and, in some cases, helped to initiate) the mass nationalist movement. Many, including Kusi Ampofu, Osei Assibey-Mensah and Sam Boateng, played key roles in the founding of the CPP in 1949. For them, Nkrumah's party was the organization of the 'common man', the vanguard in a struggle against colonial rule and against the power and privilege of chiefly authority. Thus, the youngmen spearheaded the CPP drive into Asante and, in the process, they mastered the arts of mass mobilization, organization and propaganda. Only a few years later, these skills would be put to the test when the youngmen broke with the CPP and prepared to 'fight fire with fire'.

In 1954, though the political and economic landscape of Asante had changed dramatically since the 1880s, the goals of the Asante *nkwankwaa* were not so different from those of their predecessors. The youngmen continued to seek political power, and through it, economic power. However, instead of confronting the Asante state, the *nkwankwaa* were now confronting the CPP – a party which they had helped to found and build, a party through which they had sought to reach the political kingdom and all else that would follow.[23] Their break with the CPP, though precipitated by the freezing of the cocoa price, was based primarily on a growing perception that the CPP was no longer providing a means toward political and economic advancement; it was no longer offering the political kingdom to the majority of Asante's youngmen. The government's allocation of seats in the Legislative Assembly and the CPP's selection of candidates for the 1954 election were cited as *prima facie* evidence that the CPP did not and could not represent the youngmen of Asante. The freezing of the cocoa price and a development policy that was based on the expropriation of wealth from Asante cocoa farmers only served to reinforce the youngmen's growing alarm that the CPP was seeking to build its kingdom on the backs of Asantes *without* giving the youngmen of Asante a voice in that kingdom or allowing them to reap its rewards.

And just as the *nkwankwaa* of the 1880s had turned to *Akyempemhene* Owusu Koko in their bid to depose Mensa Bonsu, the youngmen of the 1950s turned to the paramount chiefs of Asante in an effort to legitimize their movement, culturally and politically, against Nkrumah. They believed that the support of the chiefs was an ideological necessity: the chiefs would bring with them the support of the spirits and ancestors of the entire nation and the struggle against Nkrumah would become the struggle of the Asante nation against political slavery, economic slavery and 'black imperialism'.

It was recognized in September, 1954 that winning the support of the chiefs would take time and would require tactical manoeuvering, because the chiefs, not without cause, viewed the youngmen of the AYA as traitors. Only months before the NLM's inauguration, the *nkwankwaa* had been adamant supporters of the CPP and were directly associated with the CPP's oft-quoted policy of 'making the chiefs run away and leave their sandals behind'. At the same time, however, the chiefs could ill afford to turn away from any movement which held out the promise of effectively challenging Nkrumah and his attempts to curtail chiefly power. Thus, in an effort at reconciliation with the chiefs, the youngmen coupled their demands for a higher cocoa price and Asante autonomy within a federated Gold Coast with a call for the preservation of chieftancy and posited themselves as the defenders of that 'sacred institution'. As one editorial remarked,

> . . . the youth of Ashanti have made it supremely clear that they would NEVER see the sandals removed from the Ahemfie [palace] to the Arena, the Subin Valley, or even the National museum. They would rather them still [be] kept in the Ahemfie so that the Chiefs could come out of their hide-outs and wear them again.[24]

In another strategic move to enlist the chiefs' support, the youngmen persuaded Bafuor Osei Akoto, one of the *Asantehene*'s senior linguists or *akyeame*, to serve as the new Movement's chairman. Akoto was, as *West Africa* reported, '*persona grata* to Otumfuo himself as well as to most Ashanti Paramount and Divisional Chiefs'.[25] He could provide the youngmen with a direct mouthpiece to the most important traditional rulers in Asante. Moreover, as a former apprentice engineer and fitter and as a major cocoa producer in his own right, Akoto virtually personified the popular front the youngmen were attempting to build. He was a man capable of bridging the gap between chiefs and commoners, cocoa farmers and urban wage earners. Bolstered by Akoto's presence, it was not long before the youngmen made headway with Asante's chiefs. On 11 October, the Kumase State Council voted openly to support the NLM and sealed their vow of support with the swearing of the Great Oath of Asante and with the decision to withdraw 20,000 pounds from the *Asantehene's* New Palace Building Fund for the support of the Movement.[26] Ten days later, the Asanteman Council gave the NLM its full endorsement.[27] Thus, step by step in the days surrounding the inauguration, the youngmen began to forge a popular front of resistance against Nkrumah and the CPP. The links of that front, which bound cocoa farmer to chief to youngman, were forged with the fire of Asante nationalism.

This nationalism was, from the very onset, the justifying ideology of the Movement. It was not, however, its *raison d'être*. The youngmen did not spearhead the formation of the NLM because, as one of their leaflets proclaimed, 'Asante has history'. Their reaction was far from being a primordial, tribal or traditional response thrown up in the face of a new all-encompassing sovereign civil state. Rather, the youngmen's invocation of Asante nationalism represented the very modern use and construction of an ideology to justify opposition to the CPP, to rationalize and legitimize that opposition and, most importantly, to mobilize support and forge the links of a popular front of resistance under their control and direction. That Asante had existed as an independent historic kingdom, though useful, was of secondary importance to the creation of the NLM's unifying ideology, its myth of tradition. Of primary importance were the social, political and class dynamics which shaped the construction of that ideology.

Asante in the 1950s provided fertile ground for the nationalist message of the youngmen. It was a message which appealed to the large class of peasant producers of cocoa who had been unable to mobilize effectively against the price freeze. It appealed to the chiefs who had feared that any vocal opposition to Nkrumah on their part would lead to a further erosion in power. It appealed to the old guard intelligentsia who had lost the political moment to Nkrumah and had shown themselves incapable of mobilizing mass support. Only the *nkwankwaa*, with their long history of forging alliances and their recent experience, via the CPP, of mass mobilization techniques and propaganda, were in the position and had the tools necessary to fertilize and cultivate the grounds of opposition in Asante. They were the political catalyst, just as they had been in the 1880s. They were the only class capable of articulating their *specific* aspirations for political and economic advancement – aspirations which had been historically thwarted by the pre-colonial Asante state, by the structure of indirect rule and now by the bureaucratization and centralization of the CPP – as general Asante aspirations. In short, the youngmen were able to hold together an all-embracing ideology which could articulate the varied and often conflicting aspirations of Asantes. Standing on the platform at the Subin River they presented themselves as 'the people' – the new ideologues of Asante nationalism. They fanned the fires of discontent by pointing to the failures, limitations and corruption of the reigning nationalist movement. They raised the issue of cocoa and resurrected *Asante Kotoko*.

For several months after the inauguration of the NLM, Asante's youngmen appeared to rule the day. Their burning nationalist rhetoric, their threats of secession and their ability to mobilize broad masses of the population in Asante engendered fear in the hearts of many a colonial official who watched as Britain's model colony disintegrated before their eyes. One official in London described his apprehension

> that there might be organized in Ashanti a strong-arm group using firearms who would be prepared, if the need arose, to take to the forest. The country is such that it would not be difficult for 200/300 young men suitably armed to stage a Mau Mau of their own.[28]

Meanwhile, Governor Arden-Clark lamented in a letter home to his wife that the Asantes 'are nearly as difficult and unruly as the Scots once were [and] have suddenly decided that they don't like the present Government, want Home Rule for Ashanti, and are vociferously demanding a Federal Constitution'.[29] By the end of 1954, the colonial government had begun to draw up security schemes and emergency evacuation measures in the event of an all-out civil war.

Perhaps these emergency plans were not entirely unwarranted. For a period of several months, Asante appeared to have seceded in fact, if not in name. When the Governor visited Kumase in March, 1955, he was forced to lie flat on the seat of his car to escape the barrage of stones hurled at him.[30] The irreverence shown by the people in Kumase that day for the highest ranking British official in the Gold Coast was unlike any seen since 1948. It was topped off during the minutes that Arden-Clarke spent greeting the *Asantehene*. During that time, 'one of the NLM boys,' recalled K. A. M. Gyimah, '. . . went and sat in his [Arden-Clarke's] car, and he said that the car belonged to us!'[31]

The symbolism of the youngman's actions was clear to all: the colonial Governor, by siding with Nkrumah on the nature of the post-independence state, had thrown in his lot with the CPP. Thus, neither he nor his vehicle were sacrosanct. The youngman's occupation of the car stood as a popular declaration of Asante's right to confiscate or reclaim that very symbol of colonial officialdom, the Governor's limousine.

Among the NLM's rank-and-file, a popular culture of resistance emerged which was a strange tapestry of old and new, unmistakably Asante, undeniably contemporary. It combined the palanquin and the propaganda van, the gong-gong and the megaphone, the war dance and the rally. Women wore cloth bearing faces of Asante nationalist heros. There were NLM drumming and dance troupes. And there were, finally, the NLM Action Groupers – that self-styled vigilante group aimed at ridding the region of CPP supporters.[32] A *New Republic* journalist, after attending an NLM rally, was both amused and confused by the Movement's Groupers:

> . . . they dressed in the movie version of American cowboy costumes, black satin with white fringe, and they wore high-heeled black, Texas boots brilliantly studded with the letters NLM and the words 'King Force'. They were called to the platform . . . and sang a song. I was told that their throwing arms were not impeded by their tight clothing, and that most of the bomb damage in Kumase, rightly or wrongly, was attributed to them.[33]

One can only hypothesize on the symbolism of the Groupers' attire. To a Western journalist it may have appeared incongruous, gaudy, perhaps even ridiculous. But the brilliant outfits of the Action Groupers were part and parcel of the new popular resistance in Asante, a marriage of old and new. The attire befitted the modern-day Asante warrior.

For several months, the youngmen seemed to preside over this popular culture of resistance, this resurrection of *Asante Kotoko*. Their potency as catalysts, nationalist ideologues and, at times, rabble-rousers, appeared unchallenged and unchallengeable as every Asante's political and economic grievance seemed to be brought under the nationalist rubric. Yet the historical conflicts and contradictions in Asante society could not be negated by or even subsumed within the NLM. In resurrecting *Asante Kotoko*, in enlisting the support of the chiefs, the *asikafo* and the old guard intelligentsia, the youngmen had turned to those very powers who had historically thwarted their bid for political power within Asante. The youngmen thus found themselves pitted against Asante's ruling class in a modern-day struggle over the very definition of Asante self-determination. It was a struggle the youngmen were bound to lose.

By the Movement's first anniversary, it was clear that the youngmen's power within the NLM was rapidly eroding, that control of the Movement was slipping irretrievably from their grasp. Though the youngmen continued to play very visible roles at Movement rallies and as writers for the NLM paper, the *Liberator*, their positions as leaders and decision-makers were gradually usurped by the long-established powers in Asante: the chiefs, the intelligentsia and the *Asantehene*. As one youngman recently recalled, '. . . those who were paying the money for the organization were the people who were actually dictating'.[34] When push came to shove, the energy and zeal of the youngmen were no match for the power and money of the chiefs backed by the political savvy and experience of the intelligentsia. The NLM's Finance Committee, which, according to one youngman, kept its affairs a closely guarded secret, was chaired by the *Kronkohene*, Nana Kwabena Amoo.[35] As early as February, 1954, at the insistence of the *Asantehene*, Kusi Ampofu – a leader of the AYA – was replaced by R. R. Amponsah as the Movement's General Secretary. Amponsah, a member of the royal family of Mampon, left the CPP only days before he assumed this top position in the NLM.[36] Shortly thereafter, Victor Owusu (a member of the Agona royal family who abandoned the CPP the same week as did Amponsah and Joe Appiah) became an ex-officio member of the Asanteman Council. Slowly, and perhaps imperceptibly at first, the NLM's seat of power was moved from the organization headquarters to the *Asantehene's* Palace at Manhyia.

While ex-CPP stalwarts like Amponsah and Owusu and old guard intellectuals from the United Gold Coast Convention (UGCC) like K. A. Busia and I. B. Asafu-Adjaye, not to mention Asante's chiefs, had been at political odds for years, their differences quickly faded in the context of the NLM. A process of consolidation occurred within Asante's ruling ranks, in which the *Asantehene* was instrumental. Nana Osei Agyeman Prempe II was the caretaker of the Golden Stool, the symbol of traditional political authority and the symbolic link between Asante's pre-colonial and colonial past and its present. He was the inspiration for and focus of Asante nationalism. Whoever received his recognition as the legitimate leadership of the NLM would become the Movement's indisputable leadership. In bestowing that recognition the *Asantehene* turned to those who shared his ideological and material interests, those who sought to preserve their own economic and social privilege. He turned to Asante's chiefs, its political intelligentsia, and its *asikafo* because he feared the youngmen and the rabble they could so easily rouse. Perhaps he perceived a threat that if the youngmen retained control of the Movement, they would define Asante self-determination on their own terms or, worse yet, on the terms of those rank-and-file supporters who had stoned the Governor's limousine. In short, the *Asantehene* turned to Asante's fragmented ruling class, including ex-CPP and ex-UGCC political intellectuals, *asikafo* and chiefs, united them and empowered them.

What could the *nkwankwaa* do in response to the consolidation of Asante's ruling class and its usurpation of the NLM? Nothing: the youngmen's potency as catalysts, ideologues and rabble-rousers was inextricably bound up with their impotence as a class. The very ideology they had constructed – Asante nationalism – denied their existence as a class and undermined the legitimacy of their own particular economic and political aspirations. The only way the *nkwankwaa* could have challenged Asante's ruling class and its usurpation of the Movement would have been to win the support of the dispossessed in a direct assault on the hegemony of the *Asantehene*. To do so would have meant challenging the very basis of their own nationalist ideology, and here lay the nub of their predicament. They were incapable of acting as a class; their fate was sealed. Never an officer corps, they were destined to remain the true and loyal foot soldiers of *Asante Kotoko*.

By 1956 Asante's political intelligentsia, backed by the *Asantehene* and the chiefs of the Asanteman Council and the Kumase State Council, had successfully transformed the NLM from an extra-parliamentary movement – a popular front of resistance which embodied the diverse and often conflicting grievances of Asantes – into a proper parliamentary party. This party negotiated at length with the Colonial Office in London and competed in the 1956 general election, winning a majority of seats in Asante.

However, it failed in its national electoral battle with the CPP, Nkrumah's party taking 71 of the 104 contested seats.

In August, 1956, not one *nkwankwaa* from among the group which launched the NLM took a seat in the parliament which led Ghana to independence. In that parliament, with the *Asantehene's* trustworthy supporters present, a compromise solution was worked out between the NLM and the CPP which entrenched the position of the chiefs in the constitution and gave some regional autonomy to Asante. The compromise may not have appeared as much of a victory for Asante in the battle with the CPP, but within Asante it marked a decisive victory for Asante's ruling class. Led by the *Asantehene*, they had succeeded, through constitutional means, in retaining their position – a position rooted in pre-colonial Asante and maintained through British colonial rule. It was a victory of continuity, tenacity and enduring hegemony.

The noted American historian, C. Vann Woodward, has remarked that counterfactual history 'liberates us from the tyranny of what actually did happen'.[37] It is useful here to explore one critical counterfactual question. What if Nkrumah had agreed to the earliest demands of Asante's youngmen for virtual autonomy for Asante? Clearly the terrain of struggle within Asante would have been much different. The fundamental social and economic contradictions between Asante's youngmen, the chiefs and the intelligentsia would have been brought into sharp relief as each group vied for control of an autonomous Asante. Indeed, by agreeing to the youngmen's demands, Nkrumah could have forced into the open the contest in Asante over the definition and control of that nation's self-determination – a contest heretofore distorted and overshadowed by the broader struggle against the CPP. In such a contest, the victory of Asante's ruling class was not inevitable. The formal demand for self-determination having been addressed, it could no longer shape the terrain of political struggle in Asante. Nkrumah would have unleashed upon Asante's ruling class those very youngmen and that very rabble who had transformed the Gold Coast's political struggle in 1948. Indeed, if Nkrumah had conceived of national liberation in terms broad enough to accommodate the demands of the NLM, perhaps the CPP would have found an effective 'ideological insert' into Asante, as Roger Murray describes it, and could have linked itself 'explicitly and concretely with poor farmers, floating agricultural proletariat and zongo dwellers *against* old and new privilege'.[38] In such a scenario, perhaps Asante's *nkwankwaa* would have escaped their fate as loyal foot soldiers of the Golden Stool.

But Nkrumah's conception of national liberation, though broad enough to encompass the entire African continent, was not broad enough to encompass the demand, within his own country, for self-determination in Asante. Thus, the social conflict within Asante has continued to take a back seat to Asante's broader struggle with the central government. The definition of Asante self-determination remains the definition offered by Asante's ruling class on the eve of independence and Asante nationalism remains the province of a ruling class which has consistently used it to foster its own privilege. Asante's youngmen, those who were the catalyst behind the 1954 resurrection of *Asante Kotoko*, remain locked in an historical limbo, prisoners of a nationalism so defined as to render them incapable of effectively challenging Asante's ruling class. Social and economic hegemony continues to be the preserve of those chiefs and political intellectuals who, since gaining control of the NLM, have held securely the reins of power in Asante. Those nameless, faceless men and women – the small-scale cocoa farmers, the *abusa* labourers and the urban workers whose militance and mass support made the NLM an imposing force – stand in foreboding stillness. They have not, as some predicted, been integrated into the modern civil state. They have been, quite simply, disarmed and silenced.

Notes

1   Gold Coast, *Report of the Commission of Enquiry into Representational and Electoral Reform* [Chairman: Van Lare] (Accra, 1953).

2   See Gold Coast, Legislative Assembly, *Debates*, 4–17 November 1953, *passim*.

3   D. Austin, *Politics in Ghana, 1946–1960* (London, 1964), 201. See also, *Pioneer*, 8 May 1954 for an account of local CPP officers' discontent over Nkrumah's appointing of candidates.

4   As Nkrumah wrote, 'I called these people "rebels". Firm action had to be taken. It was vital that the Party should not be allowed to become disorganised or to be weakened by the split that this would ultimately bring about': K. Nkrumah, *Ghana: The Autobiography of Kwame Nkrumah* (London, 1957), 208.

5   For the debates surrounding the passage of the Cocoa Duty and Development Funds (Amendment) Bill, see Gold Coast, Legislative Assembly, *Debates*, 12–13 August 1954.

6   E. Y. Baffoe, 'Cocoa price agitation' (Kumase, 1954).

7   *Pioneer*, 4 September 1954.

8   For a summary of national integration theory, see C. Geertz, 'The integrative revolution: primordial sentiments and civil politics in the new states', in Geertz (ed.), *Old Societies and New States* (New York, 1963), 109–30.

9   See, especially, B. Fitch and M. Oppenheimer, *Ghana: End of an Illusion* (New York, 1966), 59–60.

10   See R. Rathbone, 'Businessmen and politics: party struggle in Ghana, 1949–1957', *J. Development Studies*, ix, iii (1973), 390–401.

11   I. Wilks, *Asante in the Nineteenth Century: The Structure and Evolution of a Political Order* (Cambridge, 1975), 535

12   *Ibid.* 535–9 and 710–11.

13   *Ibid.* 535.

14   *Ibid.* 530.

15   For a brief description of the Council or *kwasafohyiamu*, see Wilks, *Asante*, 540.

16   *Ibid.* 710.

17   Great Britain, *Colonial Reports*, Ashanti, 1923–4, cited in W. Tordoff, *Ashanti under the Prempehs, 1888–1935* (London, 1965), 204.

18   Tordoff, *Ashanti*, 375–82.

19   *Ibid.* 268.

20   *Ibid.* 365–9.

21   Asante Confederacy Council, *Minutes of the Second Session*, 23 January 1936.

22   For discussions of the role of the *Nkwankwaahene*, see K. A. Busia, *The Position of the Chief in the Modern Political System of Ashanti* (London, 1951), 10 and Tordoff, *Ashanti*, 373–4 and 383.

23   This is a paraphrasing of Nkrumah's famous statement, 'Seek ye first the political kingdom, and all things will be added unto you'. *Pioneer*, 5 March 1949.

24   *Pioneer*, 6 September 1954.

25   *West Africa*, 11 December 1954, 1161.

26   Kumase State Council, *Minutes*, 11 October 1954.

27   See *Daily Graphic*, 30 October 1954 and 6 November 1954. See also Public Record Office, Colonial Office [hereafter, PRO, CO.] 554/804: 'A Resolution by the Asanteman Council Praying for a Federal Constitution for the Gold Coast', dd. Kumase, 21 October 1954.

28   PRO, CO. 554/1276: File Minute, dd. 17 May 1955.

29   Cited in D. Rooney, *Sir Charles Arden-Clarke* (London, 1982), 159.

30   *Pioneer*, 23 March 1955; *West Africa*, 26 March 1955, 279.

31   J. Allman, Field Notes: interview with K. A. M. Gyimah (FN/9/1), dd. Manhyia, Kumase, 20 July 1984, 73.

32   The Action Groupers were formed in October, 1954, shortly after the murder of the Movement's Propaganda Secretary, E. Y. Baffoe, by a member of the CPP. Allman, Field Notes: interview with Sam Boateng (FN/6/1), dd. Adum, Kumase, 3 July 1984, 39–40 and interview with Alex Osei (FN/3/1), dd. Asante New Town, Kumase, 26 June 1984, 11–14.

33   A. Kendrick, 'Growing up to be a Nation', *New Republic*, 23 April 1956, 15–16. Cited in Yaw Manu, 'Conflict and consensus in Ghanaian politics: the case of the 1950's', *Conch*, vi, i–ii (1975), 103.

34   Allman, Field Notes: interview with N. B. Abubekr (FN/16/1), dd. Akowuasaw, Kumase, 28 July 1984, 127.

35   N. B. Abubekr recently remarked that if anyone needed money, 'they simply went to Bafuor Akoto and he gave them money . . . Our knowledge of our accounts was limited only to that . . . We didn't know how much we had and we were not told what expenditures there were and all that'. See Allman, Field Notes: interview with N. B. Abubekr (FN/16/2), dd. Akowuasaw, Kumase, 10 October 1984, 189.

36   Allman, Field Notes: interview with Kusi Ampofu (FN/24/1), dd. Asante New Town, Kumase, 15 October 1984, 198. For the reactions of other youngmen, see Allman, interview with N. B. Abubekr (FN/16/1), dd. Akowuasaw, Kumase, 28 July 1984, 127.

37   C. V. Woodward, 'Comments on the panel, *The Strange Career of Jim Crow* Revisited', American Historical Association Annual Meeting, Chicago, IL (December 1986).

38   R. Murray, 'The Ghanaian road', *New Left Review*, xxxii (July/August 1963), 70.

Chapter 11

Heather J. Sharkey

COLONIALISM, CHARACTER-BUILDING AND THE CULTURE OF NATIONALISM IN THE SUDAN, 1898–1956

Building characters and nationalism at the Gordon Memorial College

THE GORDON MEMORIAL COLLEGE was a crucible for the development of nationalism in the Sudan, a *de facto* colony of Great Britain (in nominal alliance with Egypt) from 1898 to 1956. More than any other colonial-era institution, the college shaped a generation of thinkers from the Muslim, Arabic-speaking, riverain North. These individuals, in turn, led the way in developing nationalist ideologies. Although there were other routes to education in the North (for example, along the traditional Islamic path of individual study with learned *shaykhs*, or via a government provincial school), the Gordon Memorial College nevertheless had two clear advantages. First, it provided direct access to jobs in colonial government, often at the highest level open to Northern Sudanese. Second, the college gave its students a strong literary education in both Arabic and English, and provided access to new communications technologies, such as typing and printing, in classrooms and extracurricular contexts. At the same time, the college fostered an ethos of self-sufficiency and group spirit among its students, on the playing field and in the lecture room alike. The result was a set of graduates who possessed both the know-how and the confidence to articulate and disseminate nationalist ideologies.

Many elements contributed to the culture of school at the Gordon Memorial College. This culture was the product of the classroom experience; the official emphasis on the training of clerks, engineers and other government employees; the dress code; athletics; extracurricular activities, such as theatricals, debates and social service clubs; alumni events; and social relationships among students and teachers. A study of this school culture, in its various dimensions, is important for understanding and evaluating the college's impact on the Northern Sudanese men who later became self-avowed nationalists.

In the Northern Sudan as a whole, graduates of the Gordon Memorial College represented a small proportion of the literate population. In 1934, Sir Harold MacMichael, Governor of Tanganyika and the Sudan's former Civil Secretary, wrote:

> By the 'educated classes' is meant, roughly speaking, the townsmen of Khartoum, Omdurman and a few similar centres, who have passed through the governmental schools or, exceptionally, acquired an intelligent interest in the outside world by other means. They number in all, perhaps, some 12,000 including, say, 1,300 graduates of the Gordon College, 2,500 from the primary schools, 400–500 officers and ex-officers and 7,000–8,000 merchants.[1]

In 1939, a memorandum by a committee made up of Gordon Memorial College and intermediate-school graduates estimated that the literacy rate in the country was no more than one per cent.[2] Gordon Memorial College graduates would have constituted a dwindling fraction of this one-percent total, since their proportion *vis-à-vis* other school-goers decreased over time with the expansion of elementary education. For example, whereas Gordon Memorial College students accounted for 13.6 per cent of government school-goers in 1907, they represented only 1.6 per cent of the whole in 1926.[3]

The college had separate curricula for its different programmes. Most programmes ran for four years, although some ran for two. Students in the primary-school section, which existed at the college until 1924, studied Arabic and English (including grammar, dictation, composition, penmanship and translation), the Islamic sciences (including study of the Qur'an, traditions of the Prophet Muhammad, or *hadith*, and so on), arithmetic and geometry, surveying, geography, and drawing. Students in the teachers' and *qadis*' (Islamic court judges') programme followed a similar course but with a much stronger emphasis on Arabic and Islamic studies. In the other programmes, meanwhile, the academic emphasis was on practical education. The Education Department's report for 1907 showed, for example, that students in the four-year civil engineering programme learned how to draw and construct such things as bridges and brick kilns using cheap local materials, and how to plan hydraulic systems using pipes and channels.[4]

Over the years the college's pre-professional programmes became more specialized and more diverse. Courses for teachers, *qadis*, surveyors, and engineers were among the college's earliest priorities; soon afterwards programmes developed for specialized clerks (such as typists), translators, and accountants; later, after the opening of the Kitchener School of Medicine in 1924, the college started teaching biology, chemistry and physics to potential medical school entrants or laboratory technicians.

The size of the college fluctuated over the course of its existence. At its peak in 1930, it held 555 students. Otherwise, it hovered in the 300 to 400 range, so that the school was in fact about the same size in 1938 as it was in 1909. Students entered the college at different ages, depending on their level of preparation. By the 1930s they averaged about 16 years old upon their entry into a secondary programme, and 20 at graduation.[5] In the earliest years of the school, some students entered when they were already past the age of 20. For example, if one biographer is correct in asserting a birth year of 1878 for the *qadi* and Graduates Club activist, al-Sayyid Ahmad al-Fil (d. 1950), then this *shaykh* was 24 years old when he entered the newly-opened Gordon Memorial

College in 1902, and 28 when he graduated in 1906.[6] Colonial personnel records confirm that his classmate, Shaykh Abu Shama Abd al-Mahmud, who became *mufti* (chief Islamic legal expert) of the Sudan in 1938, was born in 1883 and was about 23 when he graduated.[7] College authorities called their students 'boys', but in fact most were poised on adulthood even when they entered.

Notwithstanding its educational and preparatory functions, the Gordon Memorial College also had an important socializing agenda. In the words of Wingate, Governor-General from 1899 to 1916, its goal was 'to regenerate the Sudan' through character-training, thereby 'engendering the English public school code of honour amongst the youth of the country'.[8] British authorities structured the school with the perceived mistakes of India in mind. In 1925 a Foreign Office official, anxious to obtain a full report on the Gordon Memorial College, remarked, 'It is the tragedy of British rule in India that, with the best intentions in the world, we have ruined many a young man by our education, i.e., by unsuitable instruction which did not build up character.'[9]

Britons who worked at the Gordon Memorial College variously called it 'The Eton of the Soudan' or 'Winchester by the Nile'.[10] Students at the school became acquainted with the world of prefects and dormitories, football matches and 'prep' time (designated study hours). But Anglicization had its limits. By the 1920s, as a political mood of Indirect Rule infused British administrators, college authorities began to make a conscious effort to preserve the Sudanese cultural authenticity of their students, to avoid creating individuals like the Bengali Babus or African 'Europeanized natives' who recur as negative stereotypes in imperial discourses.[11] College rules now required students to wear 'traditional' Sudanese clothes, so as to be true to their origins in their appearance. This internal contradiction in the college's agenda – the desire both to change and to preserve the culture of its students – epitomized the paradox within the British colonial enterprise at large.

The Gordon Memorial College was more than a school, it was a culture. Its athletic and extracurricular programmes were as important to student training as its academic core. Indeed, it provided an important market for what one historian has called Britain's 'chief spiritual export': sport.[12] Like a good English public school, the Gordon Memorial College also kept up an 'Old Boys' network, and hosted an annual 'Old Boys' tea party and sports day. Its alumni association was in many ways a precursor to the Graduates' Congress (founded 1938), a forum for nationalist politics. Through its 'Old Boys' activities, the college continued to play a role in the political socialization of its students, years after they had graduated.

The Gordon Memorial College: a showcase of government

Kitchener, commander of the Anglo-Egyptian army of colonial conquest, was the first to suggest founding a school in memory of General Gordon. Kitchener made the proposal in 1898, shortly after the Battle of Karari (Omdurman). In light of some press reports at home that criticized the carnage and plunder of his conquering army, he may have hoped to restore his good image in the British public eye. His proposal elicited an enthusiastic response in Britain, so that within two months a public appeal had raised £100,000 for the venture.[13] Amid much fanfare, Kitchener presided over the opening of the Gordon Memorial College in Khartoum in 1902.[14]

The new college found a *raison d'être* in training young men for administrative jobs. Nevertheless, from the beginning these students shared space in the college with the Education Department, and with the educational and research institutions that this department oversaw. For instance, the college housed two other educational programmes: the Instructional Workshops, opened in 1904 to train carpenters, pipe-fitters, cotton-ginners and other manual labourers; and the Khartoum Military Academy, opened in 1905 to train Northern Sudanese officers for the Egyptian Army in the Sudan. (The workshops operated on the site until 1932 when they merged with the Omdurman Technical School. The military academy closed in 1924 after uprisings that led to the evacuation of the Egyptian Army and the creation of the Sudan Defence Force.) The premier research organization at the college was the Wellcome Tropical Research Laboratories, located on the site until 1934. Donated by the pharmaceutical entrepreneur Sir Henry Wellcome, these laboratories sponsored research in tropical medicine, sanitation and public hygiene, entomology and veterinary science. Also falling within the Gordon Memorial College organization (and under Education Department purview) were the Antiquities Service, the Natural History Museum, the Geological Survey, government-sponsored anthropological work, and eventually, the Ethnological Museum.

Located on the banks of the Blue Nile, a few blocks from the other government departments and from the Governor-General's palace, the Gordon Memorial College had a prime location in the layout of the colonial capital. It occupied a grand, double-winged, Gothic-arched building, newly constructed for its purposes out of red brick. Although early photographs of the building show it set against a bare, dusty plot, its grounds were elaborated over the years – especially after 1916, when the technical-school students built a pump to extend the college's water supply, enabling grass to be sown 'on what was formerly a dazzling waste'.[15] Ambitious British officials of the Education Department lavished their spare time on gardening and landscaping the grounds. They planted lawns, shrubs, and shade trees, such as mahoganies, and laid out beds of roses and cannas. To indulge a passion, they even tended vegetables on the side, making one area of the school look like 'a market garden with its plot after plot of luxuriant vegetables'.[16] The site eventually included tennis courts and playing fields, as well as residence halls and staff houses.

The impressively landscaped grounds of the college, together with the prestige of its educational and research programmes, made the place a showcase for the government. Indeed, it became a standard part of any tourist expedition to the Sudan, and earned mention in travel accounts from the period. For years the college featured in the Khartoum section of Baedeker's *Egypt and the Sudan: Handbook for Travellers*. The college also awed the students who came to it. In his memoirs, Amin al-Tum (b. 1914), who in later years became an important Umma Party politician and a Minister of Defence, recalled his first visit to the college, when he went to sit for the four-day round of competitive entrance examinations. He wrote:

> In spite of our fear of the examinations we enjoyed [our stay], since every-
> thing at the college was new to us. We very much liked the spacious, pretty
> rooms, entirely furnished, that had been prepared for us . . . the dining
> hall for seating hundreds of students at one time . . . the clean elegant
> bathrooms for everyone . . . the fields of greenery and verdant trees, and

the flowers, and the piped water ([through] faucets). For us, all of that was one thrill after another.

Fellow applicants coming from the provinces, where there were fewer amenities, were even more impressed.[17]

Amid these surroundings, the students of the college knew that they were special – not only because so many of them had come to the school hand-picked from the most eminent Muslim families in the land, but also because their studies put them at the centre of the new regime. As one writer has noted, 'The students could, almost every day, see the Director of Education, the Sudan Government, come and go. To them the Gordon College was more than just a college, it was the Government in person. No wonder . . . [they] expected to find government employment after finishing their studies.'[18]

The character-building mission of the Gordon Memorial College

The British officials who formed the new Gordon Memorial College were themselves the products of British public school education. They drew upon their own experience in making the college a public-school-style institution, with prefects and houses, strict schedules, and an emphasis on sportsmanship.[19] In the opinion of Wingate, Governor-General from 1899 to 1916, sport offered a kind of moral uplift to students at the school. He wrote,

> From the first, games have played a prominent part in school life. It was clear that they were destined to form an even more valuable means of moral and physical training in the Sudan than in English schools, where home influences and traditions count for so much more. The slovenliness engendered partly by living on insufficient incomes in ill-arranged houses with meagre accommodation, and partly by a natural tendency to slack habits, can only be remedied slowly and through several missions.

Discipline and the playing of 'games', together with economic development, would help to achieve this civilizing mission.[20] Although academic, job-preparatory training was a priority of the school, the school's character-building activities took up almost as much of the daily schedule as did classes. The college's annual reports have as much to say about these athletic and extracurricular activities as about the content of its academic programmes. This shared extracurricular culture meant that students experienced a similar culture of school in their years at the college, regardless of what they studied.

Athletics were serious business. Of the drill exercises required, the 1929 report noted, 'The system followed is that formerly used by the Egyptian Army and is based on the Swedish system of physical exercises. The instructors are Sudanese ex-sergeants of the Egyptian Army or Sudan Defence Force.'[21] These exercises took place in the college quadrangle, as students flexed legs and arms in unison.[22] Sport, namely football in winter and rounders in summer, was a regular part of the afternoon schedule. Both football and rounders were new to the Sudan, but football especially caught on. A tradition of competitive football matches started after 1917, when a British province governor donated a trophy – the Owen Cup – for which the students of the Gordon Memorial College and the cadets of the Military Academy vied.[23] By 1929 there was also an annual sports day that included track and field events. 'The records in running and jumping,' said the annual report, 'compare favourably with those of a good English Public school.'[24] Many students at the college absorbed the sport ethos, and continued to play football, tennis, and other games in their adult lives.

The Boy Scout movement, founded in Britain by Lieutenant-General Robert Baden-Powell in 1908 to instil the virtues of manliness and obedience in young men, spread throughout the British empire and arrived in the Sudan by 1917. A circa-1919 group photograph evokes its success at the Gordon Memorial College: the picture shows a series of solemn-faced Sudanese youths posed in their turbans and khaki scouting outfits.[25] Scouting became an important activity not only at the college, but at all government primary and technical schools.[26] Scouts learned first aid, tying knots, setting up bivouacs, and other tasks suited to the good citizen and outdoorsman.[27] British teachers and other officials enthusiastically assumed roles as scoutmasters. The Director of Education acted as the commissioner of Boy Scouts for the Sudan, while the Governor-General signed on as the country's Chief Scout.[28] Even Northern Sudanese officials, graduates of the Gordon Memorial College, served on the executive committee for scouting. By 1929 there were 31 Boy Scout troops in the country containing 1,082 scouts and 41 scoutmasters. Six of these troops, containing 252 boys, were at the college.[29] Theoretically membership in the Boy Scouts was voluntary, but in practice it appears to have been obligatory for the school's younger set.[30]

Broadening minds: intellectual activities at the college

When graduates of the college reflected on their school days in later years, they often remembered their literary and social activities most fondly. Debates, theatricals, spare-time reading – these were pursuits that fired their imaginations, helped them to hone their cultural values, and stimulated discussion among them for years to come. No wonder, considering that so many of them went on, in their adult lives, to participate in the world of print culture, to argue for social reforms, and to engage in debates of a concrete political nature with regard to the national future.

Students and teachers found space for extracurricular activities in their busy schedules. By 1915 these activities included regular film showings, which drew male audiences from local townspeople. 'Magic lantern shows', namely slide shows projecting black-and-white or hand-tinted images from thick glass plates, were also a regular feature. Sometimes these shows were accompanied by lectures, as on one occasion in 1915 when a government official (the linguist and Arabist Sigmar Hillelson) spoke on the origin and causes of the First World War. The goal of both films and magic lantern shows was avowedly educational, so that they were screened for content.

The college also developed an active dramatic society, which staged student performances as early as 1915, if not before.[31] Drama, as a prose genre intended for staged performance, was new to the Sudan, and developed most rapidly in the context of the colonial government boys' schools, like the Gordon Memorial College.[32] There, students performed formal pieces in classical Arabic, comics and pantomimes, and sometimes plays of the teachers' or students' own creation. Invariably these plays had a didactic and moralising frame.[33] Early inspiration for the development of drama in these schools appears to have come from two sources: first, the immigrant communities of Khartoum, and especially the Italians, who staged plays at coffee houses in the 1910s;[34] and second, from the British and Egyptian dramatic societies that operated within officials' clubs located in the major towns (specially Khartoum, Atbara, and Port Sudan.)[35]

By 1918 the Gordon Memorial College Dramatic Society was an active body, giving monthly performances of Arabic plays that had been written by the students themselves.[36] In 1921 these plays were attracting audiences of about one thousand people.[37] In a few cases, graduates of the school who had participated in these productions sometimes returned, years later, as teachers, and then infused their interest back into college dramatics. One alumnus, Ubayd Abd al-Nur (1896–1963), a writer and producer of plays for the Omdurman Graduates' Club (founded in 1918), became a history teacher at the college (circa 1930).[38] He instituted classes in acting and diction, the first of their kind for students at the college. Another graduate who returned to the college to teach, Abd al-Rahman Ali Taha (1899–1969) (future Minister of Education) had been an actor in his own schooldays. He helped the students to stage an Arabic production of *Julius Caesar* in 1930.[39]

Beginning in 1933 the annual reports of the college register a change in tone. Now more relaxed, the reports convey enthusiasm for an expansion in extracurricular activities. The report for 1933 noted:

> The life of the boarder has become more interesting and less monotonous than it used to be in the past. Physical Training, extra games such as lawn tennis, ping-pong, hockey, net ball and volley ball, a prize-giving, many new societies and activities, a school magazine, a better stocked library and more efficient methods of teaching have all helped to supplement deficiencies and to infuse new spirit into the old rather monotonous routine of football, drill, class work and a number of taboors [parades].[40]

Three factors may explain this lightening of tone: the appointment of a new Director of Education (R.K. Winter) in the middle of 1932; a need to release the gloom caused by the post-1929 job uncertainties for new graduates; and an easing of political constraints on the educated Sudanese, just beginning to lift after the debacle of the 1924 uprisings, which were the most serious anti-colonial uprisings to challenge the British presence in the Sudan.

The activities inaugurated in 1933 were varied. They included a literary and debating society; a school magazine; a social service committee; a natural history society; an art and music society; and a gardening club. The natural history society raised poultry, visited local sites (such as the dairy, the veterinary hospital, and the zoo), sponsored lectures (such as a talk on locusts delivered by a government entomologist), and so on.[41] The gardening club started a vegetable garden on school grounds. The club's director reported, 'During the term we were able to supply the whole school regularly for nearly two months with salads for lunch and on several occasions we supplied the kitchen with cooking vegetables.'[42]

In terms of their intellectual and ideological impact, however, the debating society and the social service committee were most influential. The debating society sponsored lectures and debates in English and Arabic, often inviting former graduates and present teachers (by this time, Britons and Northern Sudanese exclusively – no Egyptians or Syrians) to participate. These debates maintained a link between past and present students, and presented a rare opportunity for sparring legitimately with Britons. Jamal Muhammad Ahmad (b. 1915), who served as president of the literary and debating society from 1934 to 1935, and as a Sudanese ambassador in later life, praised the 'absolutely free atmosphere' of these discussions.[43] They helped students to develop debating skills that were useful after 1938, when as graduates they entered the arena of organized nationalist politics.

As Sirr al-Khatm al-Khalifa, a Gordon Memorial College graduate, educator and later Prime Minister recalled, debate topics had some relevance to the Sudanese situation. Typical subjects were: 'Is it better to spend more money on elementary education or higher education?,' 'Should women be allowed to work outside their homes?,' 'Should the Sudan emphasize agriculture or industry?', and so on.[44] A quintessentially colonial topic (reflecting British concerns) appeared in the form of: 'A little learning is a dangerous thing.' That particular debate drew in a large audience of graduates, and included British teachers on both sides.[45] One young British official, seconded to the Education Department from his normal duties as an Assistant District Commissioner, wrote to his mother in 1936:

> This evening I have got to deliver a speech in the Literary and Debating Society. I am opposing the motion 'That this house views with satisfaction the replacement of the camel by the motor car throughout the Sudan.' I have really not had time to prepare my speech but I mean it to be a virulent attack on modern inventions and a plea to keep the Sudan as it is.

Much to the delight of E. A. Balfour, he and his side swayed the House and defeated the motion, rising to the defence of the camel.[46]

Another popular Debating Society event was Hat Night. Members wrote topics on scraps of paper and put them into a hat. Each person had to pull out a paper and deliver a spur-of-the-moment speech on the topic there written. Amin al-Tum wrote,

> I remember that I was participating once in one of these evenings and took out my paper, and what should be written on it but 'What would you do if you found yourself with four legs and no hands?' It shook me . . . It was impossible for anyone to think about such a topic . . . but after a few moments I gathered my strength and said, 'I would ask God the Almighty to return me to what I was, with two hands and two legs . . .' My response was a very long and fiery discourse and at the end of the applause the appointed time for speech had ended.[47]

Other typical Hat Night subjects were 'Our Place in the Arab World' and 'Our Civic Duties towards Our Town'.[48] These were the very topics that interested the budding nationalists of the period, who emphasized Arabism and modernity, in addition to Islam, as platforms in the national identity. Modernity was a rubric that included social progress and self-help, and belief in the 'civic duties' that Hat Nights occasionally addressed.

The literary salonist and newspaper publisher Isma'il al-Atabani (b. 1910), another Gordon Memorial College graduate, recalled that Hat Night was so popular that he introduced it to the literary circle of the Graduates' Club in Wad Medani, where he was posted as a government accountant in the early 1930s. The transfer of Hat Night from the college to other milieux suggests the influence of the school in the political and cultural socialization of its students.[49] The transfer of Hat Night to the Wad Medani literary circle, in particular, was significant because it was that group, led by Ahmad Khayr, which claimed to have suggested the idea of the Graduates' Congress (founded in 1938), the body that gave rise to political parties.

The social service committee was important, meanwhile, because it gave students an opportunity to put into practice their ideals of social progress. Within the context of the new Sudanese literary magazines and graduates' clubs, social progress had become a major theme of debate. These debates called for an expansion in education for all social classes and for both girls and boys; for the amelioration of poverty; for the development of health services; and so on. Idealistic graduates of the college rose to meet this vision by initiating projects for social improvement. Most notable were the Ahliyya and Ahfad Schools, a system of primary (and later intermediate and secondary) schools (originally for boys, later for girls as well) offering places beyond those in the government schools; and the Malja al-Qirsh ('Piaster House'), an orphanage that prepared boys for life by teaching trades such as tailoring, carpentry, and so on.[50] These projects relied on donations, both large and small, from the Sudanese population at large, and stressed community self-sufficiency. The idea behind 'Piaster House', in particular, was to collect a piaster from even the pettiest of workers, down to the women who sold *kisra* (sorghum bread) on the streets.[51]

The Gordon Memorial College left its mark in one other spare-time activity, and that was in Arabic and English reading. In 1904, its school library included 'rows and rows of the stirring tales of Defoe, Scott, Dickens, Henty, Ballantine, and Rider Haggard'.[52] Later, Kipling figured prominently (the *Just So Stories* were taught in class), and students read Arthur Conan Doyle, for fun.[53] Admittedly, an important part of the reading that students did on their own in the late 1920s and early 1930s was clandestine, consisting of proscribed Egyptian journals – rich in anti-British rhetoric – that students smuggled into the school. Favourite Egyptian journals for Khidir Hamad and his friends included *al-Siyasa, al-Balagh, al-Risala,* and *al-Thaqafa.*[54] Da'ud Abd al-Latif (b. 1914), a one-time province governor and later an entrepreneur in construction equipment, read leftist anti-colonial literature, which he obtained from a Greek bookseller who first introduced him to Marx.[55]

Through reading, students embarked on other explorations of the mind as well. Amin al-Tum attended the college from 1931 to 1934 and read widely in its library. Aside from reading books of Sudanese history (such as *Osman Digna* [1926], a study of the famous Mahdist general by a British official, H. C. Jackson), he dipped into classical Arabic literature as well. He recalled that the most significant book he read during his schooldays was *al- Bayan wa'l-tabyin*, by the ninth-century Arabic comic writer, al-Jahiz (d. 868 AD).[56] Sirr al-Khatm al-Khalifa recalled that he and his friends at the college read not only classical Arabic literature from the school library, but also works by modern Egyptian writers, such as Taha Husayn. In English literature, students with a solid grasp of the language read avidly from the Everyman Series; simplified versions of Charles Dickens were popular for easier reading.[57]

Many graduates of the Gordon Memorial College were forerunners in the development of modern Sudanese Arabic literature. For them, readings in Arabic and English offered inspiration for literary experiments that proved critical to the development of their nationalist ideals.

The changing and preserving of student identity

British educators were torn within themselves about how to proceed with colonial development, and how to balance the merits of modernity and 'civilization' against the values of local tradition. At the Gordon Memorial College, they therefore pushed and pulled on student identities, on the one hand trying to shape them in their own image, on the other trying to preserve what they saw as the pristine nature of local character.

One way that British officials tried to preserve the identities of their students was by placing them in houses and on sport teams according to their place of origin. Early indications of this practice appear in two photographs of student football teams dating from 1906 to 1915. Captions beneath the pictures suggest that the boys, dressed in football outfits of striped shirts and dark shorts, were organized according to home towns – in this case, Rufa'a and Tokar.[58] The Gordon Memorial College report of 1933 confirms this practice, with regard to the division of boys in the boarding houses that were named after Governors-General.

> As far as possible the boarders are divided up by towns and provinces, i.e., all boys from Rufaa are in Wingate B, from the White Nile in Maffey A, from Kordofan in Maffey A, from Berber in Maffey B and Kitchener, from Halfa in Wingate A, from the Red Sea in Stack, and so on.[59]

Similarly, day students were affiliated with Archer House and grouped in sections depending on their origins in Khartoum, Khartoum North, or Omdurman. A *Handbook of Khartoum Province*, compiled around 1936, indicated that the goal of this housing policy was to promote '*esprit de corps* and healthy local rivalry' among students.[60] Boarding houses contributed to 'team' spirit like the one that developed on the sport field, and at the same time helped to maintain locally-based identities.

The Gordon Memorial College always had a dress code, although it changed over time, and became more 'tradition'-conscious after about 1915. Al-Dardiri Muhammad Uthman arrived as a student at the Gordon Memorial College in 1906, and later recalled, 'The students in those days tended to wear Western clothes topped by the *tarbush* (fez).'[61] The exceptions were the student *qadis*, who wore the dignified *jibbas* (outer cloaks), caftans, and silk belts that were a mark of their profession.[62] Indeed, a set of photographs taken at the college between 1906 and 1915 shows many boys dressed in suits and bowties with *tarbushes*, and others, probably the *qadis* (students), in robes and turbans.[63] Among the pages of al-Dardiri Muhammad Uthman's memoirs, meanwhile, is a class photograph from 1912. Of about sixty students pictured, all but eight were wearing suit and tie.[64]

The dress code had changed dramatically by the 1920s, as a political mood favouring the preservation or invention of 'tradition' developed among British authorities. In 1925

Geoffrey Archer, Governor-General from 1924 to 1926, expressed a hope that 'under moral suasion [from British officials], these Sudanese youths [would] cast off their shoddy European clothes and tarbush and revert to national dress'.[65] By 1930 a huge group photograph of the Gordon Memorial College student body shows a sea of white cotton *jallabiyya*s (robes) and *imma*s (turbans), with not a suit or *tarbush* in sight.[66] Egyptians were for the most part no longer welcome at the college by this time, while the *muwalladin*, Sudan-born males of full or partial Egyptian descent, were finding it wiser to play up the Sudanese side of their identity by dressing for the role.

Trousers and shirts, though proscribed for students at the college after about 1920, definitely had cachet. They appealed to those who saw them as a symbol of escape from manual labour or from low social status. They evoked modernity, education and an office job – what British officials would have sniffed at as 'Effendyism'.[67] (The latter term came from the Ottoman-Arabic term *effendi*, roughly meaning a non-European gentleman wearing Western clothes and the tarboosh, or fez.)[68] Hence the observation in a 1907 Education Department report, which commented on the parents of *kuttab* (elementary vernacular school) students:

> At one end of the scale is the father, generally a black [ex-slave] private soldier, whose highest ambition is centred on his son's wearing a tarbush and trousers, and sitting on an office-stool; at the other extreme is the ultra-conservative Sheikh or his wife, who stipulates that his child shall under no circumstances dress like an Egyptian clerk, and looks with suspicion on the teaching of English or geography.[69]

The cachet of Western clothes may explain why they were a common article for theft in the colonial period. For example, the Monthly Diary for the Eastern and Central Districts of Darfur Province, for May 1934, lists two cases of clothing theft for that month alone, the victims being a Wireless Engineer and a Greek merchant.[70] In the same year, one British official explained to his mother that his house in Singa had been burgled, and that clothes had been stolen, including the trousers of his green pajamas and the coat of his blue pajamas. 'It would not have mattered much if he had taken a pair,' he wrote, '[but] as it stands he has ruined two pairs.' Police detectives later caught the culprit near Karkoj. He was wearing Balfour's 'best shirt and trousers and giving himself out to be a veterinary officer'.[71]

British officials in the Sudan took to heart the English proverb 'Clothes make the man'. They believed that by forcing Northern Sudanese students to appear in traditional clothes, they were preserving something important. In fact, however, British officials effected radical change on students, not by changing the way they looked, but by changing the way they thought.

Officials at the Gordon Memorial College tried to restructure students' thought by stressing imagination rather than rote memorization in learning, even in examination contexts, where they wanted to see some free thinking. To theorists of literacy and cognition today, the change of emphasis would have represented a shift from a predominantly oral culture of education, where rote memorization was important, to a predominantly text-based culture of education, where easy access to cheap printed books released the need for memorization and encouraged straying from the text in independent thought.[72] British teachers at the college would not have seen in this way.

In their view rote memorization led to intellectual stagnation. M. W. Blake, the Head of English teaching at the college in 1929, noted that although the 'Oral English' reached a high standard, students had difficulty composing extemporaneous essays on a given subject. Furthermore,

> Most of the boys still prefer to learn their History notes by heart and, if possible, reproduce them word for word. This was shown clearly in the History examination, when no less than 30 boys failed in the Third Year. The boys are keenly interested in this subject, but they need to learn to think for themselves.

Similarly, in Chemistry and Physics classes, students foundered when it came time to apply their mathematical knowledge to chemical and physical problems (as opposed to recounting formulas).[73]

The radical changes that British education wrought on Sudanese students were often inadvertent. With attention fixed on superficial factors such as food and dress, officials thought little of the implications of new curricula (including such novel subjects as English language and mechanical engineering), new ways of organizing time (as in the regimented school schedule), new approaches to taking and judging examinations, and so on. If the British made an impact, then it was not so much in Anglicizing the students, but in reconfiguring their intellectual and social worlds.

An effect of British schooling that upset parents was the tendency of students and graduates to question their fathers' authority. Parents had feared this possibility when the school opened in 1902.[74] Judging from a comment made by Wingate, the Governor-General, in a letter to Kitchener, parents saw their fears realized by 1915. Wingate wrote that 'some of our most loyal old sheikhs stand aghast at the unfilial attitude of their offspring who have imbibed the poison [of Egyptian nationalist propaganda] and freely kick over parental discipline in their homes'.[75] Other elders disliked pretensions to Englishness among youth. An article in the Khartoum literary journal al-Fajr noted in 1934 that, 'It's very nice that our youths excel at the English language and this is something calling for admiration and pride. But there is something calling for astonishment and confusion and that is the use among these Anglicized youth of English, even with their grandfather in the house.'[76]

Sometime between 1937 and 1943, when G. C. Scott was Warden of the Gordon Memorial College, an article appeared in the Khartoum newspaper al-Nil attacking the lack of discipline at the college and the unruliness or disrespect for elders that it bred among students. Scott felt obliged to draft a letter in response. He wrote:

> The writer of the article truly says that there is matter for complaint in the manners, conduct, and discipline of Gordon College pupils, but what is surprising is that he appears to think that such shortcomings are actually approved of and fostered by the Director of Education and by the Warden and Staff of the College; whereas the real truth is the opposite of this. The writer appears to think that there is some policy of 'freedom', in accordance with which the pupils are not merely allowed to do what they like in manners and conduct, but are deliberately encouraged by the staff to behave in ways which may be suitable in English schools, but which are quite

unsuited in the Sudan; and he warns us against the danger of attempting too sudden a change. Your readers may be assured that there is no such policy of freedom of conduct, that the Director of Education and the Warden and staff of the college entirely agree with him, and have always agreed with him, as to the undesirability of too sudden changes, that they have always considered it of the greatest importance that the pupils should learn nothing of which their parents would disapprove, and that while the pupils are actually in the college and under the care of their teachers they are continually not only encouraged to follow the right path, but also forced to do so by rules the breaking of which means punishment, both corporal and otherwise.[77]

Unintentional though it was, the Gordon Memorial College did change its students, by encouraging them to think in ways that defied not only the colonizers, but their parents to boot.

Conclusion: 'Old Boys' and the socialization of the graduates

As the 'Eton of the Soudan', the Gordon Memorial College developed a custom of hosting annual 'Old Boys' reunions. The college initiated the first of these two-day affairs on 17 January 1913, to coincide with King's Day. Also an annual festival, King's Day was an imperial invention observed throughout the Sudan to honour the visit of King George and Queen Mary on 17 January 1912. In province centres, King's Day included contests such as 'climbing the greasy pole', camel wrestling, water pot races, and, for children, 'bobbing for [coins] in flour'.[78] At the Gordon Memorial College, Old Boys' Day festivities included football matches between graduates and students (sometimes attended by the Governor-General himself), theatrical performances and film showings, and a formal garden tea party.[79]

King's Day and Old Boys' Day were part of the imperial hoopla that helped to keep the British empire in place throughout Africa. Rituals, celebrations and fancy outfits (such as the plumed helmet that Geoffrey Archer, Governor-General from 1924 to 1926, was known to wear on special occasions), were all part of the invented traditions that gave weight and grandeur to the British presence. King's Day, commemorating an otherwise unmemorable event, had analogues elsewhere in Africa, such as in Northern Rhodesia (Zambia), where an annual 'Empire Day' honoured the visit of the Prince of Wales in 1925.[80] The Gordon Memorial College, with its invented tradition of Old Boys' Day, had parallels with other English schools in Africa, such as King's College, Budo and Makerere College in Uganda, the latter having its tradition of 'Old Makerereans'.[81]

At the first Gordon Memorial College Old Boys celebration in 1913, the Governor-General delivered an opening address to an audience of approximately 200 graduates (out of 550 alumni in all).[82] In this first year, graduates travelled from their jobs all over the country in order to attend. As the number of graduates increased each year, however, and as the appeal of the event grew, the size of the Old Boys' Day crowd swelled. By 1919 the government restricted attendance to graduates who worked within 24-hours' travelling distance of Khartoum – and still 300 attended. In subsequent years, only graduates based in the Three Towns (Khartoum, Khartoum North and Omdur-man) were invited. Even then, in 1928, 600 Old Boys came, up from 420 the year before. By 1930, the Education Department reported an increase in attendance from the Three Towns of about 100 guests per year. Indeed, 850 Old Boys attended in 1931.[83]

A 1930 photograph of Old Boys' Day captures the mood of this annual event. Printed textiles decorate the school's courtyard walls; potted plants sit here and there; a string of lights hangs around the square, suggesting a party past nightfall. Long tables covered with white cloths, and rows of mismatched chairs, fill the space. Against this setting, the graduates pose for the camera, dressed in suits and neckties, bareheaded; in suits and bowties, with fezzes; or in immaculate *jallabiyyas*, with *immas*.[84] British officials no longer had the control over clothing that they did during their schooldays at the college. Like an alumni day at any school or university, Old Boys' Day brought graduates together, reminded them of their ties to the college, and fostered a sense of corporate identity among them. This sense of identity later contributed to nationalism.

Old Boys' Day was not the only way in which the college strengthened ties with alumni. School publications, aiming for alumni subscriptions and contributions, also bound students of past and present together. The first school publication of this sort was a *School of Engineering Magazine* that appeared in March 1912.[85] It solicited articles from both students and graduates of the engineering course. Intended primarily to maintain the interest of engineering graduates in technical matters, it also aimed to preserve the bond that graduates felt for the college.[86] The Gordon Memorial College engineering course did produce many eminent graduates, who became literati, nationalists, and politicians, including Muhammad Ahmad Mahjub (1905–76), one-time Public Works Department engineer, poet, literary critic, barrister, and later Prime Minister; Ibrahim Ahmad (1898–1989), an instructor of engineering at the Gordon Memorial College, Minister of Finance and director of the Sudanese National Bank; and Mirghani Hamza (1895–1973), a Public Works Department engineer, literary salonist, and three-time Minister – for Education, Public Works and Irrigation, and Agriculture.[87]

A second school magazine, *Majallat kulliyat Ghurdun* (The Gordon College Magazine), started in 1933 and included articles by students, staff, and later graduates.[88] The first issue of 800 copies sold out immediately. Students purchased 150 copies of that first run, while Old Boys posted in government jobs all over the Sudan – from Wadi Halfa in the North to Malakal in the South, from Port Sudan in the east to El Fasher in the west – bought the remaining 650. Subsequent issues also sold out.[89] This point of contact between students past and present – like the football tournaments of Old Boys' Days – provided another link between alumni and students of the school.

The Gordon Memorial College had an enormous impact in acculturating and social-ising its graduates for colonial service. The character-building aspects of its programme were intended to raise men of strength and integrity who could assume positions of responsibility within the regime. When the dismantling of the colonial system began during decolonization, these graduates assumed leadership as the country made its transition to independence. In playing this role, the Gordon Memorial College was not alone. Other colonial schools on the continent played a similar role in shaping a gener-ation of nationalists under European tutelage. One of the most obvious is Sadiki College of Tunis, the graduates of which led many of the major political movements of Tunisia in the twentieth century, from the Young Tunisians (1909), to the Destour (1920), the

Neo-Destour (1934), and finally, the Socialist Destourian Party (1964).[90] Another is Makerere College of Uganda, which trained a generation of East African nationalists and politicians, such as Julius Nyerere of Tanzania, Milton Obote of Uganda, and Oginda Odinga of Kenya.[91]

In all of these schools, it was not the curriculum which drew students together, but the culture of belonging and of bonding. At the Gordon Memorial College in particular, there was a student culture of sporting events, literary activities, and 'character-building' responsibilities (for example, the chore of weeding the football grounds), and an alumni culture of Old Boys' Days, maintained further afield by the Graduates Clubs in the capital and provincial centres. The two cultures overlapped. Students encountered alumni on the football field during Old Boys' Days, in the classroom on Debate Society nights, and on the printed page, through school magazines. In later years, however positive or negative graduates' recollections of their schooldays came to be, the mere sharing of experiences fostered *esprit de corps* among the men who came to lead the country. Without the intention of British officials, and in many ways contrary to aims, the Gordon Memorial College forged a new culture of nationalism among those it educated.

Notes

1   Harold MacMichael, *The Anglo-Egyptian Sudan* (London, 1934), see pp. 267–70.
2   Sudan Archive Durham (hereafter SAD) 662/15/16–45: Acting Secretary, Graduates' General Congress, to the Civil Secretary, dated 5 July 1939.
3   Annual Report of the Education Department in Sudan Government. *Reports on the Finance, Administration and Condition of the Sudan, 1907* (hereafter *Sudan Gov. Reports*) and The Gordon Memorial College at Khartoum, *Reports and Accounts to 31st December, 1926* (hereafter *Gordon College Rep.*)
4   Annual Report of the Education Department, in *Sudan Gov. Reports*, 1908.
5   *Gordon College Rep.*
6   Mirghani Hasan Ali, *Shakhsiyyat amma min al-Mawrada* (Omdurman, n.d.), p. 15.
7   National Records Office, Khartoum (hereafter NRO) Personnel 4A/2/3: Personnel file of Abu Shama Abd al-Mahmud.
8   Sir Francis Reginald Wingate, 'The Story of the Gordon College and Its Work', in Leo Weinthal (ed.), *The Story of the Cape to Cairo Railway and River Route from 1887 to 1922*, Vol. 1 (London, 1923), p. 589.
9   Public Record Office, London (hereafter PRO) FO 371/10080: Selby, Foreign Office, to Archer, Governor-General of the Sudan, dated [London,] 27 April 1925.
10 SAD 724/14/3: Sir Andrew Balfour Papers. Magazine article, 'The Eton of the Soudan: Gordon College at Khartoum', *Sphere*, 12 November 1904; James A. Mangan, 'Ethics and Ethnocentricity: Imperial Education in British Tropical Africa', in William J. Baker and James A. Mangan (eds.) *Sport in Africa: Essays in Social History* (New York, 1987), pp. 138–71, esp. p. 144.
11 F. D. Lugard, *The Dual Mandate in British Tropical Africa* (Edinburgh, 1922); Mrinalini Sinha, *Colonial Masculinity: The 'Manly Englishman' and the 'Effeminate Bengali' in the Late Nineteenth Century* (Manchester, 1995).
12 J. A. Mangan, 'Britain's Chief Spiritual Export: Imperial Sport as Moral Metaphor, Political Symbol and Cultural Bond', in J. A. Mangan (ed.), *The Cultural Bond: Sport, Empire, Society* (London, 1992), pp. 1–10.

13   Mohamed Omer Beshir, *Educational Development in the Sudan, 1898–1956* (Oxford, 1969), pp. 38–9.

14   Sudan Government, *The Sudan Gazette*, Special Issue, 8 November 1902.

15   *Gordon College Rep.*, 1916, p. 13.

16   *Gordon College Rep.*, 1934 and 1935.

17   Amin al-Tum, *Dhikrayat wa-mawaqif fi tariq al-haraka al-wataniyya al-sudaniyya, 1914–1969* (Khartoum, 1987), p. 9.

18   Bjarne Osvald Holmedal, 'The Gordon Memorial College at Khartoum: Agent of British Imperialism or Cradle of Independence?' (Cand. Philol. thesis, University of Bergen, Norway, 1988), 67.

19   J. A. Mangan, 'The Education of an Elite Imperial Administration: the Sudan Political Service and the British Public School System', *International Journal of African Historical Studies*, XV (1982), 671–99; Anthony Kirk-Greene, 'Imperial Administration and the Athletic Imperative: The Case of the District Officer in Africa', in Baker and Mangan (eds.), *Sport in Africa*, pp. 81–113; and Anthony Kirk-Greene, 'Badge of Office: Sport and His Excellency in the British Empire', in Mangan (ed.), *The Cultural Bond*, pp. 178–200.

20   Wingate in Weinthal (ed.), op.cit. p. 601.

21   Sudan Government, *Annual Report of the Education Department: 1929*, p. 18. (Hereafter *Education Rep. 1929*) p. 18.

22   SAD 778/8/1–41: N. R. Udal Papers. Album of postcards and photographs, chiefly of Khartoum and of the Gordon Memorial College [c. 1906–20].

23   SAD 479/8/4–8: R. C. Garrett Papers. 'History of Football in the Sudan', by R. C. Garrett, dated 1949.

24   Sudan Government, *Annual Report of the Education Department: 1929*, p. 18. The same athletic routine was followed in 1925, as annual report of the college for that year shows. *Gordon College Rep.*, 1925, p. 19.

25   SAD 778/8/38: N. R. Udal Papers. Group photograph of Gordon Memorial College Boy Scouts, seated with Withers, Crowfoot, and Udal [c. 1919].

26   By 1919, there were seventy scouts in the Blue Nile town of Wad Medani, for example. PRO WO 33/997: Sudan Intelligence Report No. 296, March, 1919.

27   SAD 304/5/19: E. C. K. Flavell Papers. Programme, Omdurman Technical School, Scout Display, 4 January 1939.

28   SAD 780/5/15: N. R. Udal Papers. 'The Boy Scout Association Warrant for N. R. Udal of Gordon College Khartoum, to act as Chief Commissioner for the Sudan', dated Imperial Headquarters London, 2 March 1927; and *Education Rep. 1929*, p. 39.

29   *Education Rep. 1929*, p. 39.

30   In 1929 there were 510 students at the college. *Education Rep. 1929*, p. 12.

31   *Gordon College Rep.*, 1915, p. 16.

32   Abd al-Majid Abidin, *Tarikh al-thaqafa al-arabiyya fi al-Sudan, mundhu nash'atiha ila al-asr al-hadith: al-din, al-ijtima', al-adab*, 2nd edition (Beirut, 1967), pp. 302, 345.

33   SAD 769/11/54: T. R. H. Owen Papers. 'Sudan Days', a memoir of T. R. H. Owen's life in the Sudan (1926–53), dated 1960–61.

34   al-Sirr Ahmad Quaddur, *Awraq sudaniyya* (Cairo, 1992), pp. 59–61.

35   SAD G//S 1018: Uncatalogued papers relating to the Dramatic Benevolent Society [1923], donated by Khalid al-Mubarak; SAD 294/7/39–42: A. C. Parker Papers. Playbill, The Atbara Players Society, 15, 17, and 18 December 1930; SAD 203/108: B. Kennedy-Cooke Papers. Theatre programme, along with Kennedy-Cooke's production notes, for a play presented by the Khartoum Musical and Dramatic Society,

7–9 March 1940; SAD 57/1/1–469: G. R. Storrar Papers. Album for 24 June 1926 to 1 August 1927, including programmes for plays staged by the Atbara Players.

36   The Gordon Memorial College at Khartoum, *Report and Accounts to 31st December, 1918*, p. 16; and Amin al-Tum. op. cit. p. 11.

37   *Gordon College Rep.*, 1921, p. 16.

38   Mahjub Umar Bashiri, *Ruwwad al-fikr al-sudani* (Beirut, 1991), pp. 242–4.

39   Ibid., pp. 210–12; *Gordon College Rep.*, 1930, p. 25.

40   *Gordon College Rep.*, 1933, p. 29.

41   Ibid., pp. 32–8.

42   *Gordon College Rep.*, 1934, p. 31.

43   Deng and Daly, op. cit., pp. 122–3; Uthman Muhammad al-Hasan (Ed.), *Jamal Muhammad Ahmad: Rasa'il wa-awraq khassa*, Intro. al-Tayyib Salih (Beirut, 1992), p. 25.

44   Interview with Sirr al-Khatm al-Khalifa, Khartoum, 19 October 1995.

45   Amin al-Tum, op. cit., p. 10.

46   SAD 606/5/43–44, 45–46: E. A. Balfour Papers. Balfour to his mother, dated Khartoum, 3 October 1936; and Balfour to his mother, dated Gordon College 9 October 1936.

47   Amin al-Tum, op. cit., pp. 10–11.

48   Interview with Isma'il al-Atabani, Omdurman, Sudan, 30 October 1995.

49   Ibid.

50   Interview with Abd al-Rahman Abu Zayd. Vice-Chancellor, Omdurman Ahlia University, Omdurman, Sudan, 23 October 1995; and interview with Qasim Badri, President, Ahfad University for Women, Omdurman, Sudan, 25 October 1995.

51   Interview with Isma'il al-Atabani, Omdurman, Sudan, 30 October 1995.

52   SAD 724/14/3: Sir Andrew Balfour Papers. Magazine Article. 'The Eton of the Soudan: Gordon College at Khartoum', *Sphere*, 12 November 1904.

53   SAD 606/5/45–46: E. A. Balfour Papers. Balfour to his mother, dated Gordon College, 9 October 1936; Mahjub Umar Bashiri, op. cit., p. 268.

54   Khidir Hamad, op. cit., pp. 25–6.

55   Deng and Daly, op. cit., p. 104.

56   Interview with Amin al-Tum Satti, Omdurman, 27 October 1995.

57   Interview with Sirr al-Khatm al-Khalifa, Khartoum, 19 October 1995.

58   SAD 778/10/206, 209: N. R. Udal Papers. Football team photos, labelled 'Gordon College. Rufa's boys', and 'Tokar Boys' [c. 1906–15].

59   *Gordon College Rep.*, 1932, p. 28.

60   SAD 678/8/218–19: E. G. Sarsfield-Hall Papers. *Handbook of Khartoum Province*, compiled by E. G. Sarsfield-Hall and E. J. N. Wallis, bound typescript copy [c. 1936].

61   al-Dardiri Muhammad Uthman, *Mudhakkirati, 1914–1958* (Khartoum, n.d.), p. 5.

62   *al-Fajr* (Khartoum), I, 1 April 1935, 830–3.

63   SAD 778/10/1–215: N. R. Udal Papers. Album of photographs covering N. R. Udal's early career at Gordon Memorial College, 1906–15.

64   al-Dardiri Muhammad Uthman, op. cit., p. 6, and photograph facing p. 7.

65   PRO FO 371/10080: Enclosure 1, Archer to Allenby, dated Khartoum, April 27, 1925, in Allenby to Chamberlain, Memorandum on the general situation of the Sudan, dated Cairo, 9 May 1925.

66   SAD 778/13/24: N. R. Udal Papers. Group photograph, Gordon Memorial College boys, dated 1930.

67 This exact term 'Effendyism', appears, for example, in the papers of Mabel and Gertrude Wolff at Durham. See SAD 582/3/4: M. E. Wolff, Inspectress of Midwives, to Director, Sudan Medical Service, dated Omdurman, 16 June 1932.

68 Hans Wehr, *A Dictionary of Modern Written Arabic*, Ed. J. M. Cowan, 3rd edition (Ithaca. NY, 1976), p. 20.

69 Annual Report of the Education Department, in *Sudan Gov. Reports*, 1907, p. 570.

70 SAD 659/4/1–7: K. D. D. Henderson Papers. Monthly Diary, Central and Eastern Districts, Darfur, dated May, 1934.

71 SAD 606/4/87–89, 90–91: E. A. Balfour Papers. Balfour to his mother, two letters dated Singa, 18 January 1934, and Singa, 25 January 1934.

72 Walter J. Ong, *Orality and Literacy: The Technologizing of the Word* (London, 1991).

73 *Education Rep. 1929*, p. 60.

74 SAD 682/14/92–93: E. G. Sarsfield-Hall Papers. Autobiography of Angelo Capato (c. 1860–1937), written c. 1930.

75 SAD 196/2/10–11: F. R. Wingate Papers. Wingate to Kitchener, dated Khartoum, 3 August 1915.

76 *al-Fajr* (Khartoum), 1, 1 August 1934, 215–16.

77 SAD 800/6/1–2: G. C. Scott Papers. Draft letter from G. C. Scott to the editor of *al-Nil* concerning education at the Gordon Memorial College, n.d. [c. 1937–43].

78 SAD 474/26/2–3: I. M. Bruce-Gardyne Papers. Photographs of King's Day events, Gedaref, 17 January 1928; SAD 606/4/90–91: E. A. Balfour Papers. Balfour to his mother, dated Singa, 25 January 1934; and SAD 304/5/3: E. C. L. Flavell Papers. King's Day Sports Programme, Port Sudan, 17 January 1922.

79 *al-Fajr* (Khartoum), I, 1 April 1935, 830–33.

80 Terence Ranger, 'Making Northern Rhodesia Imperial: Variations on a Royal Theme, 1924–1938', *African Affairs*, LXXIX (1980), 349–73.

81 Terence Ranger, 'The Invention of Tradition in Colonial Africa', in Eric Hobsbawm and Terence Ranger (eds.), *The Invention of Tradition* (Cambridge, 1983), pp. 211–62. The 'Old Makerereans' are described in Margaret MacPherson, *They Built for the Future: A Chronicle of Makerere University College, 1922–1962* (Cambridge, 1964).

82 SAD 185/1/132–39: F. R. Wingate Papers. Text of speech delivered by Wingate at the Gordon College Old Boys' Celebration, King George's Day dated 17 January 1913.

83 *Gordon College Rep.*, 1919, pp. 16–17; 1927, p. 30; 1928, p. 37; 1930, p. 31; and 1931, p. 28.

84 SAD 778/13/3: N. R. Udal Papers. Photograph, Sudan Schools Club tea party, 1930. The 'Sudan Schools Club' in the caption implies attendance only of alumni belonging to the Omdurman and Khartoum Graduates Clubs.

85 Mahjub Umar Bashiri, op. cit., pp. 8–9.

86 *Gordon College Rep.*, 1912, p. 12.

87 Mahjub Umar Bashiri, op. cit., pp. 8–11, 291–3, 384–6.

88 *al-Fair* (Khartoum), 1, 16 October 1934, 455. This article advertised the magazine and made an appeal for graduate contributions.

89 *Gordon College Rep.*, 1933, pp. 34–6.

90 Noureddine Sraieb. *Le Collège Sadiki de Tunis. 1875–1956: Enseignement et nationalisme* (Paris, 1995).

91 J. E. Goldthorpe, *An African Elite: Makerere College Students, 1922–1960*, Foreword by Julius Nyerere (Nairobi, 1965); Oginga Odinga, *Not Yet Uhuru* (New York, 1967).

PART FIVE

Race and Ethnicity

RACE AND ETHNICITY

RACE AND ETHNICITY HAVE long been important aspects of the European colonial world. Decolonization is no exception. The complex relationship of race and ethnicity to decolonization is indeed critical to our understanding of how both the events and the process of decolonization unfolded. The essays selected in this section illuminate variations of the questions of race and ethnicity in three colonial contexts: Burma, South Africa, and Kenya. These three areas present researchers with an excellent opportunity to triangulate discussions and inquiries into ethnicity.

Andrew Selth's analysis in "Race and Resistance in Burma, 1942–1945" explains how racial and ethnic distinctions came to play an increasingly important role in the decolonization of British Burma. During World War II, racial divisions crystallized into political ones as the British encouraged various Burmese populations (Muslim Arakanese, Karens, Kachin and Mons) to strengthen ethnic and racial divisions. Selth points out how the encouragement of these divisions during the war had long-standing repercussions, which can still be witnessed throughout the region today. Offering a fascinating account of how the racial questions developed during the Japanese occupation and after the nationalist government was established under Ba Maw, Selth demonstrates that British, Japanese, and local leaders all played roles in the creation of Myanmar's postcolonial ethnic divisions.

Aletta J. Norval's "Decolonization, Demonization and Difference: The Difficult Constitution of a Nation" addresses the issue of race in the context of apartheid and post-apartheid South Africa. Through an analysis of the discourse of apartheid in South Africa, Norval examines how decolonization provided the historical space in which Afrikaner nationalism flourished and in which the social imagination of the engineers of apartheid developed and articulated concepts of race and racial superiority during the 1950s and 1960s. Norval locates much of apartheid ideology, especially the notion of spatial separation, within historical traditions of the Calvinist colonial church in South Africa. Furthermore, by situating apartheid within the rise of other discourses such as African nationalism and even Pan-Africanism, Norval illuminates how Afrikaners attempted to fashion their nationalist and racist program in reaction to other African discourses.

John Lonsdale, in his landmark article, "Mau Maus of the Mind: Making Mau Mau and Remaking Kenya," offers another view of racial prejudice within the European mind during decolonization. As Lonsdale demonstrates, racial stereotypes of the Mau Mau dominated European discussions of African nationalism and worked to strengthen whites' resolve to suppress the Mau Mau revolts with the overwhelming power of the military. By examining how whites reacted to African nationalists such as Jomo Kenyatta and by illustrating that Kenyatta himself framed discussions of Mau Mau along the lines of European stereotypes, Lonsale asks readers to look at the social construction of the Mau Mau in both European and African nationalist political discourses. Hence, coming at the question of Kikuyu society from several directions, Lonsdale demonstrates the power of European racial discourses to frame debates about nationalist movements and even myths about African savagery within African nationalist movements during decolonization.

Chapter 12

Andrew Selth

RACE AND RESISTANCE IN BURMA, 1942–1945

WITHIN SIX MONTHS of receiving its independence from Britain in January 1948, the Union of Burma was wracked by a number of insurgencies. While one of the most serious was by communists denied a place in the new government, at least four others were inspired by racial antagonisms, with Muslim Arakanese, Karens, Kachins and Mons all attempting to assert separatist claims against the Burman-dominated central government in Rangoon. To different degrees, these insurgencies are still continuing and have been joined by the secessionist rebellions of other minority groups such as the Shans and Chins. Indeed, members of almost every major ethnic group in Burma have taken up arms against the central government since 1948 and by a recent count more than a dozen separatist insurgencies are currently being waged against the Ne Win regime.[1] Ultimately, these racial antagonisms have their origins in the country's pre-colonial and colonial past, but the differences which arose after the defeat of the Japanese in 1945 were greatly exacerbated by the events of the war period. Even more than was seen before 1942, racial divisions became political divisions, with the majority Burmans and minority hill peoples tending to choose opposite sides and different visions of the country's future. In this they were encouraged by their imperial sponsors, with effects which can still be seen today.

There have been few careful, objective studies of the various internal and external factors affecting Burmese political developments during the war period. Robert Taylor's 'Burma in the Anti-Fascist War'[2] is a notable exception to this rule, but while effectively dispelling many of the myths that have come to surround the nationalist movement at that time, he tends to concentrate on the complex interrelationships between the different factions in the centre and gives little attention to the racial minorities on the periphery. Given that the most important political actors in the struggle for Burmese independence both during the war and after it were almost without exception ethnic Burmans, this is hardly surprising, but to discount the role of the national minorities in the country's 'frontier fringe' is to overlook factors that were to have a significant impact on the country's political future. Josef Silverstein gives greater weight to racial factors in his study, *Burmese Politics: The Dilemma of National Unity*, but claims that the second world war 'created new conditions that made it possible for the socially and politically divided peoples to come together and lay the foundations for a new, united society.'[3] On the contrary, the war period probably saw a greater hardening of divisions between the majority Burmans and minority hill peoples, as well as the development of new rifts that were to lead directly to the many attacks on the Burmese Union after 1948. In this regard, the policies of the Allies towards the anti-fascist resistance groups among the Burmese between 1942 and 1945 played no small part in the breakdown of the new state.

The political entity traditionally known as Burma has been described as an 'ethnic archipelago',[4] with a central lowland area populated mainly by ethnic Burmans, Mons (also known as Talaings) and pockets of Karens, surrounded by a fringe of largely autonomous hill peoples, possessing distinctive languages, cultures and political traditions. With the exception of the Arakanese in the west (who absorbed many aspects of Indian civilization and once enjoyed an empire of their own) and the Shans on the northeastern plateau (who like their Thai cousins enjoyed a highly sophisticated Buddhist culture) the hill peoples of Burma were much less developed than those living on the central plains. In 1942 these highland communities were largely untouched by the political struggles that were taking place between the British and the emerging Burmese nationalist movements. The one exception was the Karens, large pockets of whom had moved from the eastern hills and settled in the Irrawaddy delta, where they established communities among the Burmans. Estimates vary widely, but in 1941 there appear to have been some 13 million Burmans and 500,000 Karens in the central plains, coexisting uncomfortably with one million Indians and around 150,000 Chinese. In the surrounding highlands there were about 50,000 Chins, 150,000 Kachins, one million Shans and another 500,000 Karens.[5]

When the British deposed the Burmese king Thibaw in 1885, and so completed their three-stage conquest of the country, they 'pacified' the hill people and extended formal control over the frontier fringe, but like the Burmese kings before them the British were satisfied with indirect control over these areas through the traditional chiefs and tribal councils. The remainder of Burma was ruled directly by the colonial administration until 1923, when the Montagu-Chelmsford Reforms of 1919 were extended to Burma. Under the 1923 constitution, however, the frontier fringe, which constituted almost half the area of Burma and held around sixteen per cent of its population, was specifically excluded from the jurisdiction of the new Legislative Council. These 'scheduled areas' remained under the direct control of the Lieutenant Governor and were administered through a separate Frontier Service. This arrangement continued under the Act of 1935, which formally separated Burma from India and gave the Burmese a greater role in their own government. Under a separate Instrument of Instruction the Governor was charged with special responsibilities to protect the interests of the minorities and the Karens, Chinese and Anglo-Indians, like the Europeans, were guaranteed representation through reserved seats in Parliament. While ostensibly to protect the legitimate interests of the minorities and certain economic groups, this system in practice ensured that the elected Burmese seated in the House of Representatives could never command an absolute majority.[6] Thus, as Silverstein has written:

> the evolution of self government in Burma helped to foster and intensify
> ethnic pluralities and national disunity by emphasising differences and by

reducing the national power of the majority, through artificial institutional devices.[7]

This was to have profound effects on the nationalist movement which was then gathering strength.

The modern nationalist movement in Burma was essentially Burman in character. Heavily influenced in its early stages by the Buddhist *sangha* (or monks) it laid stress on Buddhism and particular cultural values such as the Burmese language and Burmese literature. By the 1930s, however, these elements were fading and the movement fell under the influence of laymen, in particular a group of young radicals led by Aung San and other former students from the University of Rangoon. As members of the *Dobama Asiayone* (or 'We Burmans Society') and calling themselves *Thakin* (or 'Master') they opened their ranks to all Burmese, regardless of their ethnic background. In addition to independence for the whole of Burma the Thakins demanded 'internal freedom', defined as 'the welfare of one and all, irrespective of race, religion or class or sex.'[8] The movement attracted some Indians and a number of Mons and Arakanese, but remained overwhelmingly Burman.[9] Calls for a united Burma free from British rule found few sympathizers among the minority peoples, who stood to be swamped by the inevitable Burman majority that would follow independence. Those Karens who were prepared to countenance an end to British colonial rule sought instead a state of their own, in which their rights would be protected. This fundamental difference in perception was manifested in the Burma Parliament where the representatives of the minorities constantly blocked reforms which would have exposed them to greater Burman rule.

Before 1930, the Burmese nationalists had not challenged the British argument that historically the 'scheduled areas' were separated from Burma proper and always had been. The Simon Commission in 1930 and the Round Table Conference of 1931–32, however, acted as foci for local grievances against the colonial regime. Of these, the place of the Indians in the country's administration and commerce was perhaps the most important, but also raised at this time was the abolition of communalism in politics and the physical reunification of Burma—the abolition of the scheduled areas. In addition, a persistent claim by the nationalists was that the British conquest and continued hold over the country stemmed in large measure from its success in dividing the peoples of Burma and using them against each other.[10] The basis for this complaint lay not only in the administrative arrangements instituted by the British since 1885 but also in the practice of excluding the Burmans from the country's armed forces and recruiting only the members of the hill tribes.

Although U Nu has stated that the trouble between the Burmans and Karens began in 1942,[11] there was a long history of communal feeling between the hill peoples and the Burmans. The Burmese monarchy had reviled the minorities as illiterate pagans and treated them harshly whenever their paths crossed. The Karens suffered most, being at the mercy of the Burman communities in the delta. Of all the ethnic minorities it was the Karens in particular who welcomed the advent of the British, seeing in colonial rule the means of gaining protection from the majority race and of getting opportunities previously denied them. As animists they were also more susceptible to Christian influences than the Buddhist Burmans, Mons, Arakanese and Shans, and European missionaries were soon promoting the Karens to the British administration as loyal subjects willing if necessary to protect the interests of the Raj against those of the

Burmans.[12] Karens were recruited to help overthrow the Burmese king in 1885 and, like the Chins and Kachins later, came to be viewed by the British as one of the 'martial races' with which they had become familiar in India. By the beginning of the twentieth century these hill peoples had established themselves as the source of the colony's military manpower.

Before the separation of Burma from India there were no Burmans in the regular Burma Army and, until shortly before separation, none in the military police. There had been some effort to recruit Burmans before and during the first world war, but in 1925 a decision was taken by India Army Headquarters to recruit only Chins, Kachins and Karens. All Burmans then in the army were discharged on the grounds that it was not only unnecessary and uneconomical to retain them, but also unwise. The Burmans in general had not made good soldiers, it was felt, and their loyalty had become increasingly suspect as nationalist agitation mounted. The decision was a blow to Burmese pride and was bitterly denounced in the Burma Parliament, but as defence was an area reserved for the Governor's control there was little the Burman MPs could do. After 1935 the British recognized the need to open the ranks to Burmans, but little effort was made to meet it. In addition, the 'best kind' of Burman youth was not attracted to a career in the armed forces, which tended to be viewed as an instrument of state power in which the minorities helped repress the legitimate aspirations of the Burman majority. As J. S. Furnivall noted: 'the army remained non-Burmese, entirely distinct from the people and an instrument for the maintenance of internal security rather than for defence against aggression.'[13] At the outbreak of the second world war in 1939 only 472 Burmans (including here Mons and Shans) were members of the regular armed forces, although together they constituted 75.11% of the country's population. The figures for the hill tribes were rather different—there were 1448 Karens (9.3% of the population), 868 Chins (2.3%), 881 Kachins (1.05%) and 168 members of other ethnic groups.[14] Of the officers, only four were Burman while 75 came from the minority races.[15] The hurried recruitment of Burmans after Japan declared war in 1941 failed markedly to change this situation and when the Japanese invaded Burma in January 1942 many Burmans deserted, some to join the rebel Burma Independence Army (BIA).[16]

When the more radical young Burmese nationalists failed to make any headway against the British by the late 1930s, they decided that armed action was the only avenue left open to them if they were to achieve independence. After unsuccessful attempts to enlist support from China, they managed to secure the assistance of the Japanese, already preparing for a thrust into Southeast Asia. A small group of Burmese was smuggled out of Burma to Japan and China, where they underwent military training. Except for two Shans, the 'Thirty Comrades' as they became known, were all ethnic Burmans. In January 1942 the group returned to Burma at the head of the invading Japanese. Apart from those Japanese marching with them, their newly formed Burma Independence Army consisted of a mixed group of some 200 Shans and expatriate Burmans recruited in Bangkok the month before. A number were Thai nationals. Hailed as the first truly Burmese army since that of Mahabandoola, however, the BIA quickly attracted a large following. By the time it had reached the capital two months later its number had swollen to over 10,000,[17] most of whom appear to have been Burmans. There was little enthusiasm for the BIA on the part of the national minorities. In more ways than one, the war had become a racial conflict.

As the colonial administration retreated north before the Japanese advance, the communal tensions which underlay Burmese politics since the British conquests the previous century quickly became apparent. The Indians were the first to suffer, as they had in a number of riots before the war, but so, too, did the Chinese and the national minorities. Of the latter, the worst treatment was meted out to the Karens who fell into the hands of the BIA. There were serious outbreaks of racial violence in the Salween district in the east and to a greater extent in the Irrawaddy delta where what amounted to a race war raged among the Burman and Karen communities for some three months or more.[18] These outbreaks were in part a reflection of deep-seated Burman resentment against the Karens, but they were also fired by Burman accusations that the Karens remained loyal to the British and were hiding arms badly needed by the rapidly growing BIA. Whole communities were put under arrest simply because they were Karen and there were a number of public executions, either for 'disloyalty' to the new Burmese regime, or to make an example of those unwilling to cooperate with the BIA. There were also acts of retribution for Karen guerrilla attacks. Ironically, many communities (both Burman and Karen) turned to the Japanese for protection against the rampaging soldiers of the BIA, and Karen counter-attacks.[19] Tensions continued throughout 1943 and although a reconciliation of sorts was achieved between the Burmese nationalists under Aung San and the Karen leaders in 1944, the events of 1942 were never forgotten.

The hill peoples in the northern and western fringes of the country fared rather better. The Shans did not escape one BIA 'spree'[20] but were able quickly to persuade the Japanese to withdraw all their forces from the Shan States and leave them to manage their own affairs, in return for an oath of loyalty to the new regime.[21] Even after Burma received nominal 'independence' from the Japanese and the new government was given jurisdiction over the Shan States, Burmese military units were not permitted to operate there. Nor did the BIA, first reformed and named the Burma Defence Army, then after independence the Burma National Army (BNA), ever operate in the Chin Hills or Kachin areas. Because of the monsoons and transport difficulties, even the Japanese pulled up short of the Burma frontier in 1942 and although they later penetrated as far as Imphal and Kohima in their 1944 U–GO offensive, these border regions remained largely free of foreign troops. The Japanese put some effort into propaganda in an attempt to win over the northern hill peoples, but in general did not attempt to occupy their lands.[22] The main racial conflict in the northeast was the age-old rivalry between the local people and the Chinese, some formations of whom were initially sent by Chungking to help stem the Japanese advance, but who quickly retreated from it. Again, it was ironically the Japanese who were able to protect the local villagers from the depredations of these 'allies'.[23] There were also savage outbreaks of racial violence in the Arakan region, as the local people turned on the Indian refugees fleeing west to British territory. In this area, however, it was the BIA and Japanese together who managed to restore a measure of control and communal order.[24]

When the Japanese invaded Burma, almost the entire British administration managed to escape to India, including its Indian component which had formerly dominated the civil service and private bureaucracy. The country was thus left in the hands of the Burmese, who under Japanese control were permitted to form a subordinate administration in August 1942. A year later Burma was declared an independent country and a national government established under a former Prime

Minister, Dr Ba Maw. The new state promptly declared war on the Allies. Many Thakins were appointed to Cabinet positions or given senior ranks in the renamed Burma National Army. In different ways, Ba Maw and the younger nationalists around him attempted to create a united Burma free of the racial divisions which had marked the colonial regime. In his attempts to forge a unified country under his own totalitarian rule, the President took as an official slogan 'one blood, one voice, one leader'.[25] Ba Maw sent missions to the areas of Karen settlement in an attempt to defuse the resentments left smouldering by the 1942 racial troubles. A Karen was appointed to the new Privy Council. Yet despite these gestures it was clear to the national minorities that the 'one voice' would speak in Burmese and the 'one leader', Ba Maw, would be a Burman. The President's official slogan only served to strengthen fears among the Karens in particular that the Burmans had still not abandoned their 'big race' ways.[26]

The Thakins took a radically different approach, but one which they had espoused during the 1930s. They accepted the diversity of the many races in Burma and sought to reassure the national minorities that under an independent Burmese government their particular cultures and traditions would be respected. The Thakins were at pains to disassociate themselves from the excesses of the BIA and made considerable efforts to heal the scars of 1942. The leaders of some offending BIA detachments were executed. Numerous high-level missions were sent to Karen settlements in the delta, led by Aung San, U Nu and other Ministers in the new government.[27] Mainly through the command-ing personality of Aung San, two Karens, one a Sandhurst-trained former officer in the regular Burma Army, were persuaded to join the BNA. They were placed in charge of a newly-formed battalion of young Karens. A number of Shans also joined the BNA. While these efforts to overcome the racial divisions within the country were partially successful, the Thakins in fact added to them by splitting the national minorities, notably the Karens, into those factions which were prepared secretly to work with the Thakins for the overthrow of the Japanese and ultimate independence, and those who preferred to work with the British and against the inclusion of the minorities in an independent Burma after the war.

The Japanese, too, played a significant role in exacerbating racial tensions during this period. The initial impetus behind the training of the Thirty Comrades and forma-tion of the Burma Independence Army was ostensibly part of a Japanese policy to conduct a *Seisen* or holy war 'to liberate the 130 millions of tropical peoples [from] the colonial policy of the white peoples'.[28] Before and during the invasion of Burma Japanese propaganda broadcasts repeated the slogan 'Asia for the Asians', a theme faithfully taken up by the puppet Burmese government. U Nu, Foreign Minister after 1943, published a document in 1944 which stated that 'it is the duty of all Asiatics . . . to participate in the destruction of the Anglo-Saxon influence in the East'.[29] Teams were sent out to the districts to help cultivate an 'Asian mood'. The Japanese included an Indian on the Rangoon Municipal Corporation in an apparent attempt to win the support of Indians who had remained in Burma, but persistent Japanese propaganda stressing the 'glorious past' of the Burmese and hailing them as 'fellow Buddhists' served only to emphasize that the Japanese saw the Burmans as potential allies but viewed the various minorities with suspicion.[30] Such campaigns only added to the fears of the Christian, Muslim and animist peoples already feeling at the mercy of the Burman majority. This was despite the fact that the Japanese themselves in fact treated all

Burmese harshly, many of them making it obvious that they viewed all members of the local population as racially inferior.

The invasion of the Japanese in January 1942 and the advent of a Burman-dominated government, however nominal was its role, served to polarize racial attitudes in the country. As Ba Maw put it:

> The numerous races that either lived in Burma or met there for the first time under the stark conditions of a total world conflict appeared to be seized by a sudden fear and distrust of one another: the Japanese, the Chinese, the Indians, the Burmese together with the other indigenous peoples, all were turning against one another under the stress of the old, atavistic fear and suspicions, all finding the enemy in the nearest stranger as they did in their tribal days.[31]

Ancient antagonisms, fears and identifications had been revived and intensified. There was little feeling of unity either among the people themselves or between the government and the majority of its subjects.[32] The behaviour of the Burmans as soon as they had achieved a measure of power had served only to convince the hill peoples that their future lay with the return of the British. Not only had the BIA committed atrocities against the Karens, but as time progressed the puppet Burmese government came to be identified with the privations and brutalities endured under the Japanese.[33] In some cases inadvertently, but more often deliberately, these feelings of racial antagonism—both towards the Burmans and the Japanese—were encouraged by the Allies, who saw considerable advantages to be gained in using the minorities, as well as disaffected Burmans, against those holding power in Rangoon.

The anti-fascist resistance in Burma was of two kinds. To most Burmese now, references to 'the resistance' will either evoke memories of the March 1945 rebellion against the Japanese by the Burma National Army and its civilian allies, or else the wider nationalist struggle for independence against the British which culminated in 1948. By the end of 1942 Aung San and his fellow nationalists realized that their 'independence' under the Japanese was a sham and started to plan for an eventual rebellion against their new oppressors. In this they were joined by a loose coalition of communists, trade unions, youth groups, women's and religious organizations, including in 1944 the leading Karen organization. This united nationalist front was known first as the Anti-Fascist Organization (AFO), then as the Anti-Fascist Peoples Freedom League (AFPFL). Some of these groups, notably the communists and the loyal Karens, had managed to make contact with the British in 1942, and while some segments of the BNA were anxious to attack the Japanese without outside help, it was agreed that no move would be made until the ground could be prepared for a coordinated rising. Throughout 1944 the AFO maintained secret contact with the Allies, primarily through the communists, until in early 1945 it realized that there was little time left to rise before the advancing British robbed them of their chance to claim a share of the victor's spoils. In March the BNA marched out of Rangoon, ostensibly to join their Japanese allies at the front but in fact to join the communists and hill peoples in fighting a guerrilla war against them.

After 1942, there appear to have been few direct clashes between Burman troops and the hill peoples, yet the active participation of the latter in the British and American forces further separated them from the majority race in their own country. As Joyce

Lebra has pointed out, the British and Japanese recruited from basically different ethnic groups in Burma.[34] Through their pre-war recruiting policies and force of circumstances after 1942, the British ranks were filled with hill peoples. On the other hand, it was Japanese policy to avoid those ethnic groups recruited by the colonial regimes. While never entirely confident of the loyalty of the Burmese government they had created, the Japanese nevertheless preferred to recruit Burmans and were prepared to train and arm a Burmese army to fight alongside them. Thus the age-old racial antagonisms felt between the peoples of the hills and the peoples of the plain were strengthened and even institutionalized by the wider geo-political struggle between the British and Japanese empires.

To the British, gathering strength again in India, the young nationalists who had marched into Burma with the Japanese were collaborators, guilty of treason against the Crown. Aung San was considered a 'traitor rebel leader' of a 'Quisling army', 'whose hands were dyed with British blood and loyal Burmese blood'.[35] The BIA, and its later manifestations the BDA and BNA, was referred to as the BTA, or 'Burma Traitor Army'. While blame for the British defeat was freely apportioned elsewhere as well, there was a strong feeling among the armed forces that their disastrous campaign against the Japanese had been caused in part by the Burmese. Only some 5000 BIA soldiers had actually fought against the retreating British,[36] but they had added significantly to the fear of fifth columnists among the local population and so caused the Allies considerable concern and confusion. Such was the strength of feeling running against the Burmese (of the plains) in 1942 that the exiled Government of Burma felt obliged to try and counter the hostile and even vindictive attitudes then current. In December the Secretary of State for Burma issued a proclamation reminding the British troops that they would not be returning to Burma 'in a spirit of vengeance'. Yet even he drew a distinction between those Burmese who had not harmed the British and those who had 'deliberately assisted the enemy's war effort'.[37] Later events were to prompt the Supreme Allied Commander, Southeast Asia Command, to issue an order in December 1944 telling the Allied forces that 'we come to the people of Burma as rescuers from a tyrannical foe',[38] and not in order to exact retribution for past acts.

After the retreat from Burma in 1942 the Government of Burma was re-established in Simla, where it continued to exercise de jure control over those remote parts of Burma which had not been conquered by the Japanese. De facto control of these border regions rested, however, with the armed forces. This led to a number of difficulties, resolved completely only when the Allies, at the first Quebec conference in August 1943, created Southeast Asia Command with Lord Louis Mountbatten as Supreme Commander. Under his authority the administration of the liberated areas of Burma was carried out by the Civil Affairs Service (Burma)—CAS(B), largely recruited from officers of the Burma Civil Service. The Governor, Sir Reginald Dorman-Smith, formally retained full executive and legislative powers but acted largely in concert with GAS(B). The Governor's overriding preoccupation was to restore British administration to Burma and to bring the country to such a stage of political and economic development that it could be handed over to a responsible Burmese government as a Dominion within the Commonwealth. He drew a distinction, however, between the dominant Burmans and the hill tribes like the Chins, Kachins and Karens who 'though no other Burmese party had bestirred itself in this way . . . had raised levies and were valiantly fighting the Japanese.'[39] Dorman-Smith felt that it would be wrong to include these 'staunch allies' in a future Dominion of Burma unless they were agreeable. He proposed to London that after the war the frontier areas of Burma still be administered separately.[40] These views were supported by CAS(B) and were subsequently incorporated into a British government White Paper. It was a policy designed both to encourage the expectations of the hill peoples and further to alienate those nationalists seeking immediate independence for the whole of the country.[41]

Communications between the civil authorities and the armed forces tended to be poor and even after the organization of the CAS(B) into one headquarters by Mountbatten there was considerable confusion and even conflict over the policies to be adopted towards the hill peoples in Burma. The demand for 'partisans' led at times to grotesque situations, with the regular British, American and Chinese armies, as well as the various paramilitary and clandestine services, all competing for local recruits. Before January 1944, when Mountbatten assumed overall command of both civil and military affairs in the Southeast Asian theatre, some levies were under the responsibility of the exiled Burma Government and CAS(B), others the Chiefs of Staff in London and others the British Minister of Economic Warfare. Those levies recruited by the Chinese and Americans were in a different position again. The wider political implications of recruiting members of the local population seem not to have been given very careful consideration by those responsible, who were intent on fighting the war and thus grateful for any help they could get. From this confused situation, however, sprang further misunderstandings among the hill tribes which, like those British government policies already mentioned, were to have considerable long-term consequences.

It was here that the activities of the clandestine services and paramilitary organizations operating in Burma at the time assumed particular importance. At one period there were at least a dozen such organizations, each with their own administration, chains of command and personnel. Some were branches of world-wide organizations controlled from London and Washington, while others were of local origin. Their concern for secrecy and their professional jealousies resulted in considerable confusion and overlapping of functions, prompting complaints from both Slim and the American General Joseph Stilwell, who was attempting to work with Generalissimo Chiang Kai-shek in opening the road from India to China.[42] This confusion was reduced to a large degree in late 1944 when Mountbatten decreed that SOE should assume overall command of all clandestine services in the theatre.[43] The nature of their operations still meant, however, that the civilian authorities and to a lesser extent the military command rarely knew details of clandestine activities, nor were they consulted by SOE. While secrecy was often necessary for reasons of security, it seems clear that its need was often invoked to prevent interference in operations which ran counter in some way to the political policies of the civil authorities. According to Maurice Collis, who was given access to Dorman-Smith's papers after the war: 'SOE was concerned only with easing the path for the army by organising sabotage and rebellion behind the Japanese lines: it left political complications to take care of themselves.'[44] These 'political complications' included relations with the hill people recruited as levies, and in organizing resistance groups in Burma it is clear that SOE was prepared to give undertakings and encourage expectations far beyond the level to which it was justified in doing so.

In his official history of the *SOE in the Far East*, Charles Cruickshank states plainly that: 'the embryo guerrilla movement among the hill tribes in Burma which SOE developed successfully was based as much on hostility to the Burmese of the plains as on loyalty to the British regime'.[45] It appears that the hill people were encouraged in their traditional racial enmity towards the Burmans and in their belief that, on the defeat of the Japanese and return of the British, they would be rewarded for their services in a particular way. According to one of the British officers working with the levies in the north, the Kachins were convinced that: 'When the time was ripe the Kachins would move back to Myitkyina and invite the good old, kind hearted *asuya*, the British Government of Burma, to come back and pick up things where it had left off.'[46] Other Kachins were equally convinced that they would be given 'an independent state of their own, separate from the Burmese'.[47] It would not be too far-fetched, perhaps, to assume that the strong anti-colonial sentiments of the Americans at the time, Stilwell in particular, helped heighten the expectations of those hill people under U.S. control. Similarly, the Karens who fought so well against the Japanese in the eastern hills believed that they would be rewarded with their own state. The British officers who worked with them traded on the racial antagonisms fuelled by the troubles in 1942 and apparently encouraged the Karens that their dream of a Karen state might be realized after the war.[48] Like their policy towards the Arabs a war before, it seems that the British government, or at least some of its representatives, were prepared to use the indigenous people to support their own war effort, even to the point of deliberately misleading them as to their rewards after the fighting was over.

The differences with the civil authorities, the extent to which the clandestine services were prepared to act beyond established policies and the degree to which immediate military considerations were given precedence over longer term political consequences can all be seen in the controversy over the arming of the Anti-Fascist Organization in 1944. The Governor of Burma and CAS(B) were aware of the initial contacts between the Burmese communists and SOE in 1942 but considered them merely a 'flirtation' with an 'unrepresentative and revolutionary group'.[49] Further contacts were made, however, continuing after the communists formally joined with the BNA and others in forming the AFO in the first week of August 1944. A request for large-scale arms shipments was then sent to SOE, to help prepare for the planned rising against the Japanese. On its own initiative, SOE afforded the AFO 'formal recognition as the Anti-Axis Association of Burma'[50] and undertook to provide enough arms, ammunition and funds to make such a rising a success. All this was done without any formal consideration of the political implications of arming Britain's former enemies in the BNA.[51] As Donnison suggests:

> It is indeed remarkable that official assurances which contained such far reaching implications for the future should have been made without consulting the Chief Civil Affairs Officer, and apparently without the approval of the Supreme Allied Commander.[52]

The Head of SOE in the Southeast Asian theatre was aware of the step he was taking, however, and advised his superiors in London of his decision. In order to forestall objections from CAS(B) he also sought the support of the Governor of Burma and the military command.

To SOE's mind, the issue was 'fundamentally very simple.'[53] It was recognized that the support of men politically undesirable in the eyes of the civil affairs officers might cause some embarrassment, even difficulties, after the war when the government of

Burma came to be restored. It was also recognized that such a step might even bring closer the independence of Burma and possibly that of India as well. SOE realized, too, the potential problems involved in arming a section of the population which elsewhere it had encouraged the hill peoples to fight. Yet despite these factors, it was felt that to arm the AFO was less of an evil than the prospect of another 5000 soldiers of the BNA adding their support to the Japanese facing Slim in central Burma and crippling his 'fantastic race for Rangoon against the monsoon'.[54] Not only was time running out before the rains were due, but there were at the time severe shortages of Allied manpower and transport aircraft, on which the Fourteenth Army so much depended.[55] Should Slim be unable to reach the Burmese capital before the wet season began the British would have to face the prospect of falling back to their nearest reliable supply point, which was on the Indian border. Besides, SOE felt that there were precedents for their proposal in the assistance given by the Allies to guerrillas in Europe. In the words of a senior SOE staff officer at the time:

> as with Greece and Jugoslavia, it was decided to give priority to winning the war in the shortest possible time rather than to feel constrained by the political complications which would have to be faced on the outbreak of peace.[56]

By late 1944 the Chief Civil Affairs Officer (Burma) was aware that something important was being kept from him. As Allied forces advanced into the Arakan region and northern Burma they encountered AFO guerrillas claiming SOE protection. In February 1945 the matter came to a head, with CAS(B) bitterly protesting the arming of 'criminals' and 'communist terrorists', and claiming that the price of their cooperation would be the right to share in the government of Burma after the war.[57] CAS(B) felt that it was wrong to put the AFO on a par with the French *Maquis* or partisans in other occupied countries in Europe. The Commander-in-Chief of Allied Land Forces, Lieutenant General Sir Oliver Leese, was persuaded by CAS(B)'s arguments and prohibited the further issue of arms to the AFO (and thus also to members of the BNA). SOE was able to carry the day only by appealing directly to Mountbatten. SOE claimed in addition to its earlier arguments that not to arm the AFO would jeopardize similar operations in Malaya and put SOE operatives in central Burma at risk. SOE also stated that 'if arms were denied to the Burmans of the plains when they had been freely issued to the hill tribes, it would sow the seeds of post-war grievance'.[58] Such seeds had in fact already been sown by SOE's earlier contacts with the AFO, but disingenuous though this particular argument might have been, Mountbatten was inclined to accept it.[59] The Supreme Commander permitted the arming of the AFO for a mixture of very hard-headed military and political reasons, justifying his intervention in the controversy by saying that it was a political matter which he felt he must reserve for himself. He gave orders that formal recognition was not to be accorded the AFO as an organization and that no undertakings were to be given to AFO members regarding their status after the war. Guerrillas were to be armed on an individual basis only under the supervision of SOE officers in the field.[60]

In practice, this plan was clearly unworkable. The AFO had been recognized by SOE the previous year and arms were being freely issued by its officers working with the guerrillas. It was apparent in any case that the BNA would turn against the Japanese regardless of Allied policy towards it and there was little chance that SOE would be able to keep it under its direction. By his decision, however, later approved by the War Cabinet in London, Mountbatten in effect recognized the AFO (later renamed the AFPFL) as the most powerful and most representative group in the country, and thus helped establish it as the most potent political force in post-war Burma. The loyal hill peoples who had fought for so long against the Japanese had done so within the ambit of Allied control and had no independent political power base or military force comparable to the AFPFL or BNA.

On the defeat of the Japanese in May 1945 there was, as Silverstein has suggested, a certain feeling of common endeavour and achievement among the Burmese resistance groups, a feeling which the AFPFL quickly sought to draw on and utilize in its negotiations with the British over the future of the BNA and of the country.[61] In a speech given in August 1945, for example, Aung San proclaimed that 'Our brothers in the hills, the Kachins, and the Chins also joined in the resistance. The Karens also fought side by side with us.'[62] Considerable efforts have been made since the war to perpetuate this myth, that the hill peoples 'joined' the Burmese nationalists of the BNA in expelling the Japanese, but the situation was in fact quite different. Both the majority of the hill peoples and most of the British forces in Burma drew a clear distinction between those who had collaborated with the Japanese in 1942–44 and those who had held out against them. As F. S. V. Donnison, a senior civil affairs officer at the time, wrote later:

> To welcome with open arms an army which had fought against the British on the side of the Japanese for just so long as it had suited them, all of whose members were technically guilty of treason, was a poor way in which to reward and put heart into those (Burmese) who had remained loyal to the British connection or who, without necessarily wanting the continuance of this connection, nevertheless were opposed to the communistic ideas and dictatorial attitudes of the Thakins, and at least were prepared to achieve their emancipation along the gradualist lines to which the British were committed.[63]

Many felt the Karens in particular had been betrayed. There are numerous reports of British officers (both civil and military) privately counselling them to insist on a separate state of their own and the attitude of many of the returning Burma Government officials to BNA members provoked a bitterness that remains today.[64]

In the negotiations with the British after the war the predominantly Burman AFPFL was quickly accorded the primary role and the national minorities found it increasingly difficult to receive a hearing. The delegation led by Aung San which visited London in January 1947 to discuss independence terms with the Attlee Government did not include any representatives of the hill peoples. Aung San's commanding personality won a degree of cooperation from some of them at Panglong the next month but a Committee of Enquiry established later that year to determine the best method of associating the frontier peoples with the search for a new constitution served only to reveal the many divisions among them and the difficulties that would be encountered in securing their full support.[65] It soon became clear that, notwithstanding their agreement in London 'to achieve the early unification of the Frontier Areas and Ministerial Burma with the free consent of the inhabitants of those areas',[66] neither the Burmans in the AFPFL nor the British government were prepared to contemplate an independent Burma without them. Nor were they prepared to wait until the concerns of the hill peoples had been met.

It is not easy to isolate the purely racial factors from others which played a role in determining how any Burmese ethnic group responded to the crisis of the second world war. Immediate concerns were inextricably intertwined with the fears and resentments of generations, feelings that existed both outside the sphere of the British colonial administration and within it. It could be argued that in one sense the war was concurrently being fought on three levels. At the international level, it was a war between the Japanese and the British and between their Burmese allies. At another level, the national level perhaps, it could be described as a power struggle between different Burmese factions, each with their own vision of the country's future. At a third level the war could be seen as a racial conflict with both the majority Burmans and minority hill peoples being used by the two (Asian and Occidental) imperial powers to gain control of Burma for themselves. The Japanese sought to use the nationalist aspirations of one racial group while the British sought to take advantage of the hopes and fears of the other. In this struggle both Burmese groups seem to have been betrayed.

Notes

1   P. Janke, *Guerrilla and Terrorist Organisations: A World Directory and Bibliography* (Harvester Press, Brighton, 1983), pp. 135 *et seq.* See also the *Annual of Power and Conflict 1978–79: A Survey of Political Violence and International Influence* (Institute for the Study of Conflict, London, 1979), pp. 416–19.

2   R. H. Taylor, 'Burma in the Anti-Fascist War', in A. W. McCoy (ed.), *Southeast Asia Under Japanese Occupation* (Yale University Press, New Haven, 1980).

3   J. Silverstein, *Burmese Politics: The Dilemma of National Unity* (Rutger's University Press, New Brunswick, 1980), p. 50.

4   B. Crozier, *The Rebels: A Study of Post War Insurrections* (Chatto and Windus, London, 1960), p. 84.

5   These figures are based on the wartime estimates used by C. Cruickshank, *SOE in the Far East* (Oxford University Press, Oxford, 1983), p. 163.

6   J. S. Furnivall, *Colonial Policy and Practice: A Comparative Study of Burma and Netherlands India* (New York University Press, New York, 1956), p. 168.

7   Silverstein, *Burmese Politics*, p. 29.

8   Aung San, *The Political Legacy of Aung San*, compiled by J. Silverstein, Data Paper no. 86, Southeast Asia Program (Cornell University Press, Ithaca, 1972), p. 6.

9   Maung Maung, *From Sangha to Laity: Nationalist Movements in Burma 1920–1940*, ANU Monographs on South Asia no. 4 (Manohar, Delhi, 1980), pp. 197, 230 *et seq.*

10 Silverstein, *Burmese Politics*, pp. 43–4.

11 U Nu, *Saturday's Son* (Yale University Press, New Haven, 1975), p. 164.

12 Furnivall, *Colonial Policy and Practice*, p. 180. See also Furnivall's shorter *The Governance of Modern Burma* (Institute of Pacific Relations, New York, 1958), p. 10 and G. E. Harvey, *British Rule in Burma 1824–1942* (Faber, London, 1946), p. 40 *et seq.*

13 Furnivall, *Colonial Policy and Practice*, p. 183. See also U Ba Than, *The Roots of the Revolution* (Director of Information, Rangoon, 1962), p. 23.

14 Furnivall, *Colonial Policy and Practice*, p. 184.

15 Maung Maung, *Burma in the Family of Nations* (Djambatan, Amsterdam, 1956), p. 90.

16 U Ba Than, *Roots of Revolution*, p. 24.

17 Estimates of the size of the BIA vary greatly depending on the political sympathies of the source. The figure of 10,000 is from Yoon Won-zoon, 'Japan's Occupation of Burma 1941–1945' (unpublished doctoral dissertation, New York University, 1971), p. 173.

18 Ba Maw, *Breakthrough in Burma: Memoirs of a Revolution 1939–1946* (Yale University Press, New Haven, 1968), pp. 187–96 and I. Morrison, *Grandfather Longlegs. The Life and Gallant Death of Major H. P. Seagrim* (Faber, London, 1947), pp. 70 *et seq.* and 183 *et seq.*

19 Ba Maw, *Breakthrough*, p. 155.

20 The term is Maung Maung's, in his hagiographical *Burma and General Ne Win* (Asia, Bombay, 1969), p. 122.

21 Ba Maw, *Breakthrough*, p. 200. Also, Silverstein, *Burmese Politics*, p. 54.

22 F. S. V. Donnison, *British Military Administration in the Far East 1943–1946* (HMSO, London, 1956), pp. 10–11.

23 Ba Maw, *Breakthrough*, p. 202.

24 *Ibid.*, pp. 203–4.

25 *Ibid.*, p. 321.

26 *Ibid.*, p. 195, Morrison, *Grandfather Longlegs*, p. 92. Burmese, for example, was made the official language of instruction in all the country's schools, instead of English.

27 U Nu, *Burma Under the Japanese: Pictures and Portraits* (Macmillan, London, 1954), p. 98, and Maung Maung (ed.) *Aung San of Burma*, Yale University Southeast Asia Studies (Nijhoff, The Hague, 1962), pp. 49 *et seq.* and 72 *et seq.*

28 Quoted in F. N. Trager (ed.), *Burma: Japanese Military Administration: Selected Documents 1941–1945* (University of Pennsylvania Press, Philadelphia, 1971), p. 15.

29 Quoted in Ba Maw, *Breakthrough*, pp. 282–3.

30 Htin Aung, *The Stricken Peacock: Anglo-Burmese Relations 1752–1948* (Martinus Nijhoff, The Hague, 1965), pp. 111–12 and Yoon Won-zoon, 'Japan's Occupation of Burma', p. 189.

31 Ba Maw, *Breakthrough*, p. 205.

32 Silverstein, *Burmese Politics*, p. 49.

33 Taylor, 'Burma in the Anti-Fascist War', p. 167.

34 J. Lebra, *Japanese Trained Armies in Southeast Asia: Independence and Volunteer Forces in World War II* (Heinemann, Hong Kong, 1977), p. 64.

35 The description is Churchill's, given in the House of Commons in 1947 when speaking against the move to grant Burma independence. He is quoted in Donnison, *British Military Administration*, pp. 369–70.

36 *Ibid.*, p. 71 and M. Collis, *Last and First in Burma (1941–1948)* (Faber, London, 1956), p. 187.

37 Quoted in Donnison, *British Military Administration*, p. 72.

38 *Ibid.*, p. 73.

39 Collis, *Last and First*, p. 207.

40 *Ibid.*, p. 199.

41 *Burma: Statement of Policy by His Majesty's Government*, Cand. 6635 May 1945 (HMSO, London, 1945).

42 B. Tuchman, *Stilwell and the American Experience in China 1911–1945* (Bantam, New York, 1972).

43 B. Sweet-Escott, *Baker Street Irregular* (Methuen, London, 1965), p. 234.

44   Collis, *Last and First*, p. 231.

45   Cruickshank, *SOE*, p. 5.

46   I. Fellowes-Gordon, *The Battle for Naw Song's Kingdom: General Stilwell's North Burma Campaign and its Aftermath* (Cooper, London, 1971), p. 18.

47   *Ibid.*, p. 58.

48   Morrison, *Grandfather Longlegs*, p. 17 and H. Tinker, *The Union of Burma: A Study of the First Years of Independence* (Oxford University Press, Oxford, 1957), p. 25.

49   Donnison, *British Military Administration*, p. 348.

50   *Ibid.*

51   Cruickshank, *SOE*, pp. 175–7.

52   Donnison, *British Military Administration*, p. 348 and Cruickshank, *SOE*, p. 170.

53   Sweet-Escott, *Baker Street Irregular*, p. 245.

54   W. Slim, *Defeat into Victory* (Cassell and Co, London, 1956), p. 479 *et seq.* and Cruickshank, *SOE* pp. 170–7. See also Donnison, *British Military Administration* p. 349 and Sweet-Escott, *Baker Street Irregular* pp. 244–5.

55   R. Callahan, *Burma 1942–1945* (Davis-Poynter, London, 1978), pp. 147 and 152–3.

56   J. G. Beevor, *SOE: Recollections and Reflections 1940–45* (Bodley Head, London, 1981), p. 221. See also Sweet-Escott, *Baker Street Irregular*, p. 245.

57   Donnison, *op. cit.* p. 349.

58   Cruickshank, *SOE*, p. 177.

59   Mountbatten, *Report*, p. 143.

60   *Ibid.*, pp. 143–5.

61   Silverstein, *Burmese Politics*, p. 61. See also Maung Maung, *Burma and Ne Win*, p. 137 and U Ba U *My Burma: The Autobiography of a President* (Taplinger, New York, 1959), p. 189.

62   Quoted in Maung Maung, *Aung San of Burma*, p. 98.

63   F. S. V. Donnison, *Burma* (Benn, London, 1970), p. 127. See also Sweet-Escott, *Baker Street Irregular*, p. 248.

64   U Ba U, *My Burma*, pp. 177–85, Maung Maung, *Aung San of Burma*, p. 150 and D. G. E. Hall, *Burma* (Hutchinson, London, 1950), p. 15.

65   *Burma: Frontier Areas Committee of Enquiry: Report submitted to His Majesty's Government in the United Kingdom and to the Government of Burma*, Cmd. 7138 (June 1947) (HMSO, London, 1947).

66   Quoted in *ibid.*, p. 1.

Chapter 13

Aletta J. Norval

DECOLONIZATION, DEMONIZATION AND DIFFERENCE

The difficult constitution of a nation

IN THE IMMEDIATE AFTERMATH of the elections which formally marked the 'end' of apartheid, it is more urgent than ever before to reflect on the discourses informing the constitution of apartheid discourse. Since our present is marked by an explosion of violence in the name of ethnicity and nationalism, often leading commentators to argue that under these circumstances democracy can only die a premature death, such an investigation could bring us closer to an understanding of the role and productivity of the constitution of identities in narrow, exclusivist and identitary terms. The discourse of apartheid, in this sense, points to something beyond the historical context in which it emerged. It marks the space of a danger inherent in all forms of identification. The precise conditions of emergence of this discourse thus signify not a historical aberration, a perversion of discourses on nationhood and identity, but show, in the Wittgensteinian sense, something which could not be said or recognized as an inherent possibility in discourses which purport to be 'western' in their origin.

The contemporary horror of the emerging fundamentalisms, be they of ethnic or religious origin, is indicative of a realization which is only slowly dawning, namely that these phenomena are not external to the project of modernity but have always already been contained in it. It is not the case, as some would argue, that these movements represent a return to the pre-modern; that they are efficacious because they represent deep historical memories and traditional communities, re-emerging in our modern present. Rather, as Anderson holds, they are distinctly modern imaginings. It is precisely their modernity which gives nationalism and ethnicity such contemporary power.[1] They are reassertions of difference against the modern intention of making difference into an offence.[2] These reassertions, however, are presented precisely in the language of modernity, in the name of purity and homogeneity as the basis of the national state. It is this that forces one to ask, without belabouring the point, what role the voyeuristic attention historically given to the apparently 'irrational' violence, not only in South Africa, but also much closer to home, in Europe itself, has to play in the constitution of an imaginary which tries to keep the West pure and intact, a signifier of 'civilization'.

These issues may be investigated indirectly, through an in-depth historical analysis of the constitution of forms of social division characteristic of apartheid itself. In this chapter, therefore, I explore the terms in which apartheid's ethnicist character received its articulation in the formative years of the 1950s and 1960s. In addition, I argue that the dissolution of apartheid, and the possibility of thinking a post-apartheid society, call forth a reflection on the precise strategies utilized in its constitution of identity. That is to say, any thought of a post-apartheid South Africa has, of necessity, to come to terms with the past, not as past, but as ever-present possibility.

Apartheid came into being, on the one hand, as a continuation of the existing project of segregation which drew its boundaries of inclusion and exclusion in terms of a stark division between the 'European' and its other – the 'Native'. On the other hand, it sought to delineate a sense of difference which dissolved the apparent homogeneity of both those categories. As part of an anti-imperialist project, it saw itself as an attempt to carve out a space of existence for a particular ethnic group, the Afrikaners. The category of the European, rather than functioning simply as a barrier between white and Black, came to be articulated as embodying the denial of the difference between Afrikaans and English-speaking South Africans. As important for our discussion as this relation, is the disarticulation of the second category, that of the 'Native', whose singularity was also put into question. Both these dis- and rearticulations were informed by quite specific debates on the character of nationhood within the community of Afrikaner intellectuals, by challenges to apartheid thinking by white liberals and African nationalists in South Africa, as well as by events on the wider African continent. All of these debates contributed to, and shaped the precise constitution of the horizon of apartheid discourse.

My exploration of the various articulating contexts of Afrikaner nationalism takes the form of an analysis of the discourses informing and structuring it. More specifically, I look at how the creation of new knowledges brought into being new subjects and a novel form of social division. In the first place, I give attention to the principle of difference underlying the initial articulation of Afrikaner nationalist ideology, asserting its specificity over and against, not 'Blackness', but the discourses of imperialism, and 'South Africanism'. In this sense, apartheid has to be understood as a response to the dislocations experienced in the nascent Afrikaner community during a period of rapid urbanization in which attempts were made to incorporate them into a social structure which was premissed upon a presumed 'equality' between the different language-groups of the white community. In the second place, I show how these par- ticularistic articulations provided the basis for its expansion into wider and wider domains of the social. Here the focus shifted from the specificity of the Afrikaner's position, to a universalizing discourse on ethnicity as the basis of social division. In the third place, it will be shown how this expansion of apartheid discourse into a social imaginary drew upon and was influenced by the wider context of decolonization. This will involve an analysis of the articulation of African nationalism, both on the African continent and within South Africa itself. Finally, I attempt to draw a set of theoretical conclusions on the nature of identity formation from the discussion. From here it will be possible to point to the contemporary relevance of the articulation and disarticula- tion of the apartheid imaginary.

The principle of difference structuring apartheid discourse drew upon a variety of available debates about the nature and character of nationhood which were articulated in

the precise context of a rejection of a liberal emphasis on individualism and majoritarianism. One such intellectual well-spring was located at the Potchefstroom University of
Christian Higher Education, where Calvinist theology inspired attempts to provide a
systematic account of the distinctions to be drawn between peoples, nations and ethnic
groups. There the scriptural theory of 'diversity in unity' enabled church leaders to
bring about an inversion of the Christian ethos of the uniqueness and importance of
the individual, for the sake of some ultimate good to the group. The position put
forward by these theologians did much to provide apartheid *cum* separate development
with its 'moral' basis. Together with conceptions of cultural difference, articulated by
anthropologists of the day, the notion of divinely ordained peoples bolstered National
Party (NP) doctrine. On the occasion of the second reading of the Promotion of Bantu
Self-government Bill, providing for 'separate homelands' for the African population,
a government minister argued that the 'colour policy' of South Africa was based on
three cornerstones: namely, the fact that God had given a divine task and calling to
every nation; that every nation had an inherent right of self-preservation; and that
the personal and national ideals of every individual and every 'population group' could
best be developed within a national community or sphere.[3] In particular, the notion
of sovereignty of spheres proved to be invaluable to the justification of territorial
separation along ethnic lines. First articulated by Stoker in the 1950s, it was closely
connected to the Calvinist emphasis on the respect for the principle of diversity.[4]
Calvinists held that different societal spheres ought not to be divorced from one
another. Unlike in liberal thought, there was no attempt to separate church and nation
(*volk*), and church and state. Rather, a coherence and coordination between the different
terrains and spheres were sought. Yet, this did not imply a movement towards a nullify-
ing of differences and an eradication of the boundaries between church and state.
National Socialism was not acceptable. Each sphere had its own character, its own
destiny and its own sovereignty. Thus, the Calvinist principle of diversity supported
the separate identity of the Afrikaner people: the Afrikaner could not accept either
'dictatorial absolutism' or 'licentious liberalism'. The institution of the *volk* had to be
regarded as an institution of God.[5]

This principle of difference was considered to be universal, while manifesting itself
variedly in different historical circumstances. What is crucially important about this
theological vision, is that it was easily linked to debates on the nature of apartheid,
especially insofar as its identity was predicated on its opposition to liberalism and
communism. In the wider context of a discussion of terminological distinctions between
volk, nation and race it was, for example, argued that the God-willed diversity and
separateness of nations had to be set in contrast to the liberal ideal of 'deadly uniformity' which left no place for differentiation.[6] Contrary to what liberals thought, the unity
found in Christ was universal and cut across national boundaries, but it did *not* eliminate
these boundaries. While unity in Christ, as a matter of fact, transcended temporal
diversities, it did not abolish them.[7] The abolition of diversity, the elimination of
national and racial frontiers, proposed by liberals and the advocates of 'multi-racialism'
alike, could end only in disaster. Integration would 'wipe out Afrikanerdom' and would
'immerse the developing non-European nations in tribal chaos'.[8] A similar argumentative
strategy was followed in discussions around the notion of freedom. Human beings, it
was argued, were free as such or before God. This conception of the universal equality
of freedom, was supplemented with a conception of the distinct freedoms of human

beings – be they artistic, academic, or religious in character – as well as with a principle of 'developmental differentiation'. Apartheid, it was argued, accepted all these principles. It did not deny freedom, but facilitated its development in different spheres. Notions of freedom and equality were therefore inextricably bound up with division between (racial) groups. Equality existed only 'in the eyes of God' and was consistently held to be in opposition to the freedom inherent in difference. Freedom, in opposition to the liberal understanding, did not consist in an individual capacity for choice. It had to be grounded in the specificity of the community.

These onto-theological debates were easily articulated with contemporaneous discussions of the nature of ethnic difference, and were utilized by the National Party to establish the discursive conditions for the introduction of 'grand apartheid', the division of society into 'homelands', based upon linguistic and cultural (i.e. 'ethnic') differences. A specific theory of social contact underpinned the re-categorization of the 'Native' as 'homogeneous' subject, as previously understood, into separate 'ethnic' groups. It was expressed most clearly in the work of the Tomlinson Commission, appointed in 1950 to conduct an inquiry into 'the rehabilitation of the Native areas with a view to developing within them a social structure in keeping with the culture of the native and based on effective socio-economic planning'.[9] On Tomlinson's view, and it was a view held more generally, 'culture contact' could be understood to lead to different outcomes, depending on the broader context of articulation.[10] He argued that 'two poles of thought have arisen in consequence of contact'. These coincided with the choice between the 'preservation of a characteristic type of existence' (apartheid) on the one hand, and 'fusion of all existence' (liberalism) on the other.[11] The choice was one between 'total separation' and 'total integration'. *Non tertium quid.*

This theory of 'culture contact' was developed within the new context of a fascination with ethnicity as a basis for social division. This was what gave it its novel impact: it was no longer simply a matter of discussing the effects of cultural contact between 'white' and 'Black'. Attention was now focused on the impact of different cultures upon one another. The task of anthropology (*volkekunde*) was held to be the study of cultures, processes of cultural contact and the outcomes of such contact. Culture contact was considered to contain inherent limits. At worst, when its limits were reached, conflict and racial tension would result in the destruction of different peoples. At best, it would lead to what was called 'secondary accretion', or the taking-over of cultural elements from a superior culture. Such accretion would produce 'confused beings', 'Euro-Africans', which, finally, could lead only to a degeneration of morals, instability and a loss of principles.[12] These arguments culminated in an emphasis on the retention of traditional values, such that ethnicity came to be the bearer of all national and cultural values.[13] This, in turn, produced a shift from homogeneous to heterogeneous 'population categories'. It was from there that the redivision of the 'Native' into 'Bantu tribes' was to take place. Drawing on Schapera's *The Bantu-speaking Tribes of South Africa*, the homogeneous category of the 'Native' was turned into a number of 'Bantu' ethnic units. As the secretary of the Department of Bantu Administration and Development, and former professor in Social Anthropology, argued, replacing by 'Bantu' of the 'colourless appellation 'Native' indicated the importance of ethnic and language groups in the ordering of the social.[14] The introduction of the policy of 'positive apartheid', referring to the new 'freedom' allowed each ethnic group, had immediate effects. Africans were no longer to be represented in Parliament by white Native Representatives; they had to find political expression in the so-called homelands. Moreover, the possibility of eventual 'independence' for the 'homelands' was now firmly established. South Africa, it seemed, had been irrevocably divided. Social division along ethnic lines was legally entrenched; territorial expression was given to those divisions. Apartheid now had a 'tidiness, substance and a moral justification' that it lacked before, and it drew on the notion of the sovereignty of spheres, the divinely ordained nature of nations, and the centrality of ethnicity in its development of that 'morality'. A symbolic horizon was thus constituted, a horizon rejecting the possibility of establishing a community in which different cultures could merge peacefully or exist in a single territory. In contrast, it aimed at the entrenchment of communities of unity, of groups based on an identity contained and given in ethnicity.

In moving from the particularity of its inception to a universal set of predicates on the nature of ethnicity and nationhood, apartheid changed from being a mythical principle of articulation, suturing the dislocations experienced by a particular community, to an imaginary which came to structure the whole of South African society. For its ideologues, this imaginary offered two distinct advantages: 'every group would be able to exercise control over its own people . . . and it offered the opportunity of developing equalities among groups.'[15] These 'advantages', however, were clearly dependent on being exercised in separate spheres. In contrast to a 'multi-racial state', which would ostensibly be 'unfair' to minorities, positive apartheid or separate development provided the conditions of possibility for the realization of the legitimate aspirations, not only of the Afrikaner community, but also of the indigenous African population. The principle of difference and the theory of culture contact served, inter-alia, as means to delineate 'positive' or merely differential identities. The structuring of the space of difference, however, could only be accomplished by the drawing of a set of frontiers, distinguishing between those who could occupy that space of differential relations and those who had to be excluded as radically other. In the latter case, two discursive contexts were of specific importance: the rise of African nationalism within South Africa and its precise articulation in a discourse of non-racialism, and the process of decolonization taking place on the wider African continent. For Nationalist ideologues, they were deeply interrelated. The 'right to self-determination', as demanded by 'non-white' peoples, was recognized as one of the characteristic features of the decade. It was maintained that a number of peoples had gained their freedom in Africa, and some others were on their way to it. This movement towards freedom was regarded as an 'irresistible force', one that could not be ignored. The process of decolonization thus came to be articulated, in the South African domestic context, as in accordance with apartheid. However, this displacement was premissed on the firmly held belief that nationalism had to be grounded on a people. Africàn nationalism, on this reading, could not exist. It was not a real nationalism. For nationalism to exist, it had to be grounded in the reality of organic communities. Wider African nationalism thus came to be portrayed as a 'monstrous form' which resulted from the fact that 'national units' were ignored.[16]

Decolonization and the rise of Pan-Africanism played a crucial role in the forging of exclusions in the Afrikaner nationalist imaginary. The symbolization of 'Africa' in the discourse of Afrikaner nationalism in the 1950s drew upon two clearly delimited symbolic funds. The first, I shall call a 'colonial' imaginary, while the second consisted of a more narrowly defined identification with the conception of nationalism as previously discussed. The colonial imaginary provided a setting in which a particular conception of nationalism could be paraded as an answer to the 'fears' raised by the spectre of decolonization. The signifier 'Africa' allowed for the articulation of a vague sense of impending doom and threat, while simultaneously foreshadowing the 'correct' solution to the problem. 'Africa', in the writings of Afrikaner nationalists, did not refer simply to the geographical unity of the content. Rather, it acted as a complex signifier, binding together a series of discursive articulations, providing them with a unity which did not pre-exist those articulations. The symbolic value with which 'Africa' was weighed down thus testifies to its importance in the development of the particular form of difference characteristic of apartheid discourse, as well as to the constitution of the other in this discourse. Throughout the 1950s numerous articles appeared in journals and newspapers attempting both to provide information on 'Africa' and to situate South Africa in relation to the wider African continent. It was held that 'South Africans' (whites) needed to have knowledge of the continent of which, paradoxically, they were a part. While the white indigenous population claimed the name 'Afrikaner', they remained essentially 'South-*Afrikaners*', largely isolated from the continent on which they found a fatherland, and with which their fate would be intimately bound up. The rise of independent African states, the opening of markets and the presence of 'heathen peoples', were amongst the main factors listed as reasons for needing knowledge of Africa.[17] More specifically, concern was expressed with the 'task and Christian calling of the Afrikaner in Africa', as well as with the countering of 'communism' in Africa. The 'spying eye' of communist Russia was at work in Africa: with its 'red fingers' it 'meddled' in the affairs of the 'dark peoples' of Africa. Rising nationalism was argued to be a perfect façade behind which 'Moscow' could do its work. These and other similar discussions contained clear traces of the colonial imagination. So, for example, were the 'races of Africa' depicted as living in a condition of barbarism, as ignorant and superstitious.[18] In contrast to African nationalists within South Africa for whom 'Africa' acted as a symbol of resistance and liberation, Afrikaans poets described the African continent as the resting place of evil spirits; as an unknown land visited by doom and death, as a swamp-like place absorbing and drowning civilizations, giving back nothing in return. Populated by 'primitives', who no longer showed any 'respect' for whites, Africa was indeed the dark continent of colonial imagery. Accounts of the rise of African nationalism, and especially of Pan-Africanism, provided by Afrikaner nationalists reflected, moreover, the emerging consensus within the Afrikaner community on nationhood.[19]

A series of important issues were condensed in the treatment of African nationalism in these writings. While some writers argued that the colour question took the form of a national question in Africa, insofar as the 'desire of yellow and black peoples' for national freedom was a desire for political self-determination, others held that something more was at stake.[20] It was claimed, for example, that Africa posed 'human' rather than simply racial problems. The condition of all those who lived in Africa – traditional indigenous Blacks, white settlers and extremist Pan-Africanists – was posed in existential terms. Living in Africa became a symbol of a condition of uprootedness and confusion: 'The human in Africa is uncertain of himself.'[21] This uncertainty could only be understood in terms of the onto-theological vision which inaugurated the apartheid project: the understanding and characterization of nations, and their role and function in history. Africa acted as a symbol of ontological uprootedness, for its peoples had been doubly alienated from their original conditions of existence. Initially, colonial-ist expansion introduced the indigenous populations of Africa to an essentially foreign, Western culture. While a certain ambiguity towards the aims and effects of colonialism was displayed – it was both a curse and a cure, unsettling a natural order and bringing salvation and (western) civilization – no such ambiguity was present in the portrayal of those Africans who came into close contact with white settlers. Echoing the widely held 'culture contact' theories, they were seen as the enemies of the 'real African', that is, of the traditional African who held on to tribal practices and shunned the emerging Pan-African consciousness. These 'evolués', who claimed to have relinquished their 'Bantu loyalties' by claiming the whole African continent as their heritage, and who adopted the name 'African', were said to be fraudulent figures, for they were not rooted in any real community.[22] The 'thin top layer of developed Africans, under European influence' represented a corruption, not only of real African identity, but also of the very nature of nationalism. Indeed, they were inseparable. Pan-Africanism lacked a 'national context.'

The link between nationalism, in its 'truest form', and ethnic belonging was thus crucial to the rejection of Pan-Africanism, which was portrayed as something coming from outside of Africa, whether from 'foreign' black intellectuals such as Garvey and Du Bois, or from a certain complicity with colonial settlers. It was not of Africa. Indeed, for Afrikaner intellectuals, it was questionable whether Pan-Africanism could be described in terms of the category of nationalism at all. Pan-Africanism, on this reading, was organized on the principle of 'colour consciousness'; it was not a patriotism based on the state or the group. Rather, it designated the awakening of an African conscious-ness, based on racial and social characteristics.[23] This rejection of Pan-Africanism on the grounds of its basis in 'colour consciousness' calls for further explanation. Why would the ideologues of apartheid reject such identification as a basis for national conscious-ness? Two different answers to this problem come to mind. The first is clearly connected to their understanding of nationalism, as based on ethnic groups, or clearly defined communities, bound together by a set of elements, of which race may be one. The second concerns the 'fears' raised by the process of decolonization in the white imagination. Pan-Africanism was not simply a form of unity based on colour conscious-ness. The analysts of Pan-Africanism were, above all, acutely aware of its relational character, of the fact that it was a *response* to colonial exploitation and discrimination. In this, their analysis was acute. For African Nationalists inside South Africa, looking northwards towards the rest of Africa for support and inspiration was indeed the result of a realization that they could no longer hope to achieve fundamental reforms through consultation with South African authorities.[24] In 1946, a Congress Youth League (CYL) policy statement, for example, argued that a prerequisite for the restructuring of society in terms of the dictates of an African nationalism was the recognition of African sovereignty in Africa.[25] The 'Programme of Action' carried forward themes already expressed in 'African Claims', the document drafted by the Atlantic Charter Commit-tee in 1943 which, by drawing on the Ethiopian example, held that foreign domination in Africa had to end.[26] Similarly, the CYL Manifesto of March 1944 also rejected 'foreign leadership' in Africa and claimed a belief in 'the unity of all Africans from the Mediterranean Sea in the North to the Indian and Atlantic Oceans in the South' upon which a new vision of Africa could be built. This was to take place by drawing on the cardinal principles of African nationalism, namely the fact that Africa is a 'black man's country', that Africans, irrespective of 'tribal connection' were one, homogeneous nation; and that an African had to lead Africans.[27] For Nationalist ideologues, the cohesive factor of Pan-Africanism, in the absence of a 'real community', was held to be a common hatred of whites.[28] No real unity could exist across the African continent. Africa was far too divided; indeed, it was held that 'cultural, racial, political and civil heterogeneity' was characteristic of Africa.[29] Pan-Africanism, thus, had to be understood as a process in which links and alliances were forged in the face of a common enemy. These alliances were not 'natural', and they were bound to break down. Yet, they were dangerous, and had to be countered. This was so especially in that Pan-Africanism tended to become associated with the 'threats' of majoritarianism and communism in Africa, especially that of violence and conflict. The images conjured up by the Mau Mau in Kenya, 'Ghana' and the 1958 Accra Conference, were of great importance in the symbolization of decolonization. For example, the portrayal of the pre-independence events in Kenya were covered by some 804 reports in one Afrikaans newspaper alone during the period between 1952 and 1955,[30] and consisted mostly of inaccurate pictures of extreme bloodshed. These images are echoed today, not only within and with reference to South Africa, but also within Europe. Explosions of anger and violence are portrayed as irrational and pre-modern, as essentially other. And today, as then, they are utilized in order to entrench, at best, the existing order; at worst, to argue for 'internal' decolonization. In the Nationalist imaginary of the 1950s and 1960s, these images were conjured up to justify and strengthen the process of territorial division consistent with the view that 'culture contact' had internal limits which, when breached, could lead only to destruction, not only of national communities, but of 'western civilization' as such. Non-racialism, the demand for a unified South Africa, associated with the internal resistance movements, particularly the ANC, as well as liberal and communist visions of an egalitarian society, were thus delegitimated and suppressed.

In the context of the contemporary situation it is important to investigate more fully the articulation of at least certain aspects of the resistance discourses which sprung from the same period, for they contain precisely the vision of social division denied by apartheid ideologues, as well as the imaginaries which have succeeded in hegemonizing the terrain of struggle. The movement from myth to imaginary in apartheid discourse failed to complete itself, precisely as a result of the politicization of its underlying conception of nationhood. This process, which has a long and venerable history, increasingly showed the particularistic nature of what pretended to be neutral and natural. Put differently, it uncovered the very form and principle of ideology. Resistance discourses utilized the language of universalism, in order to put into question the presumed universalism of apartheid. This contestation involved different conceptions of the character of nationhood, all of which, as a matter of principle, had to draw on categories which go beyond the particular. The most poignant expression of this politicization can be found in the document which has come to symbolize the very form of resistance: the Freedom Charter. 'We the people of South Africa': the inaugural words of the Charter drawn up at a Congress of the People in Kliptown in 1955, signify its own universalist passion. In this vision the people is constituted, against apartheid, as a *whole*, as a *community* which overrides national and ethnic differences. Here, South Africa became a unified homeland for all its inhabitants. This unification was, however, articulated not only against apartheid, but also against the particularism of the Pan-Africanists who eventually split off from the ANC. It contained, therefore, a double signification, rejecting both ethnicist and Africanist conceptions of nationhood, and so constituting itself in the field of that multiple rejection, not as a closed space of representation, but as an unfinished project, and as open to criticism. This was evident also in its conditions of production, in its origin of multiple authorship. It did not speak in a single universal language, but in a plurality of voices whose 'non-exclusive summation adds up to a never homogeneous whole'.[31] As Berman in his analysis of the Freedom Charter remarks, the universalist modernity of the Charter turned out to be already 'post-modern' in the sense of presuming plurality and heterogeneity. It is precisely this heterogeneity which is also present in the wider discourse of non-racialism informing the Charter and the hegemonic discourse of the African National Congress (ANC). The doctrine of 'non-racialism', however, became dominant within the ANC only after a period of intense discussion and division within this organization. The politics contained in the Africanist slogan, 'Africa for the Africans', did not succeed in becoming Congress doctrine, and with hindsight it could be argued that this constituted the very condition of possibility for the hegemonic success of the non-racialist ideology. Resistance to the territorial division of South Africa on an ethnic basis, the appeals to universal rights of all citizens, and the general anti-imperialist character of the Freedom Charter, all contributed to the forging of a national-popular will in the Gramscian sense, which could serve as the basis for a challenge to the domination and oppression inherent in the social division characteristic of apartheid.

The remaining question posed by our contemporary condition concerns the extent to which non-racialism can succeed, in principle, in constituting a form of South African identity which would not fall foul of its own universalism. In this respect, it might be enlightening to return to our analysis of the *form* of identity constitution of which apartheid is exemplary. I have argued above that apartheid can be understood, not only as a particular historical form, but as indicative of something inherent in all forms of identity construction. Apartheid, in this sense, acts as a signifier of closure. In it is enacted what Connolly termed the second problem of evil, structured by an ideal of purity of identity.[32] That is, it shows the fact that all identity, in order to constitute itself as such, has of necessity to externalize an other as other, as evil. As I have shown, in the case of the early articulation of apartheid ideology, this process took place in the form of a drawing of frontiers between different conceptions of nationhood; by legitimizing and demonizing those discourses which did not take as their starting-point a rootedness in ethnicity. African nationalism and Pan-Africanism thus came to be thought and external-ized within that framework. If, however, it is a general function of the logic of identity construction that the self can be constituted only by the externalization of an other, could the problems resulting from an identitary conception such as that informing apartheid be avoided at all? In this manner, apartheid can be turned on its head. It no longer shows something only about the logics of racial domination. Far from simply being illustrative, it forces us to rethink the possibilities inherent in a certain western discourse on identity. More specifically relevant to our current questioning, it raises general issues concerning the form that the constitution of political and social identities ought to take in a democratic society. How does one constitute, or enact, what Critchley has called 'a politics of ethical difference', where ethics would consist in the disruption of totalizing politics.[33] If identity requires the articulation of otherness, of frontiers in order to constitute itself as such, the issue here is the manner in which such an articulation takes place and the grounds on which political frontiers are to be drawn.

The constitution of those frontiers, as well as the grounds on which they are being drawn, is *political* in the strict sense of the term. It is a matter of institution of a form of social division, of shaping and framing societal divisions. The shaping of such divisions within a democratic project requires thinking of the relation between identities in terms which allow for contestation and for a recognition of the limitedness or particularity of any and every project. Yet, it has also to aspire to a universal moment in order to constitute an imaginary horizon for the expansion of differentially constituted identities.

Over the past 10 years we witnessed the dissolution of the historical logic of apartheid, that is, of its specificity as a discourse ordering the institution of the social on a precise onto-theological basis. The disarticulation of this logic, however, does not of necessity spell the end of apartheid in a broader sense. Apartheid, as I have argued, is not only the name of a specific historical logic, it is also a mode of identity formation which is exemplary of a certain metaphysical logic. Any new imaginary attempting to fashion a truly post-apartheid society would have to think its own formation in terms of the tension inherent in the term 'post-apartheid'. The latter signifies a mode of being which goes beyond, yet remembers, the logic of apartheid. This beyond cannot be a pure beyond. Apartheid cannot simply be left behind. The 'beyond' has to be constituted with reference to the horizon of which apartheid formed the articulating principle. Such an imaginary would retain it as its other, as a signifier of closure which has to be resisted. Insofar as this is taken as the core of organization of a post-apartheid society, it would have the further effect of recognizing itself as a *particular order*. The principle shaping the form of society would then be articulated around the acknowledgement of its own historical situatedness in the very moment in which it attempts to go beyond that. Such a recognition is a prerequisite for thinking a radical democratic order, for such an order is essentially characterized by the knowledge of its own finitude. Awareness of the constantly present possibility of failure could animate a political project which is based upon the premiss of a restless expansion of democracy to further domains of the social. A post-apartheid order would, therefore, only be properly post-apartheid if it succeeds in ordering itself around the principle of openness and the need for continuous self-creation, resisting forms of closure characteristic of the onto-theological principles of apartheid discourse.

How, then, can this form of identification, this logic which recognizes its own finitude, be thought in the South African context? It is here that a response to those critics of deconstruction who question its relevance to anything outside of a 'European' context, as well as those who argue that its undermining of universalism prevents us from thinking about questions of emancipation, is called for. Homi Bhabha, for example, has argued that theoretical texts committed to the articulation of *différance* cannot but marginalize questions of racial, cultural and historical otherness.[34] A more brutal denial of the possible 'liberatory' effects of a deconstructive reading is stated in explicit reference to the South African context by invoking Habermas: 'Nothing remains from a desublimated meaning or a destructured form: an emancipatory effect does not follow.'[35] For Coetzee, this inaugurates a call for a return to 'reality' as opposed to the text. This reading is echoed in a less crude fashion in Berman's reading of the processes of constitution of the Freedom Charter. For him the critique of the metaphysics of presence sovereignly ignored what was the key issue for the anti-apartheid movement: representation – one person, one vote – the first article of the Freedom Charter.[36] This, however, is to miss the point altogether. For the moment of deconstruction shows its efficacy precisely in the subversion of the search for purity, for fully fledged identities. Its intervention, thus, is not a denial or an affirmation of the right to representation, but a critique of a mode of identity constitution, of which I have argued that apartheid is exemplary. And its emancipatory logic is present precisely in the suspension of emancipation as a universal promise, the promise of a Marxian dream of a transparent society. 'Freedom' in this sense, lies 'beyond' emancipation, beyond eschatological history.[37] It is in this beyond that the forms of identification other than those of apartheid, have to be sought. As I have signalled earlier, the final question in this regard concerns whether the discourse of non-racialism can take us into the beyond of apartheid?

It was pointed out earlier that the Freedom Charter was constituted in a process in which a multiplicity of voices was heard and recorded. This non-unitary origin of the Charter could perhaps lead us to a reading of non-racialism which does not stay at the level of a mere recognition of the plurality of the South African population. For at least on one reading, non-racialism reproduces identitary logics. Its articulation as a bringing together of the Black, white, Indian and 'coloured' groups' presumed the existence of differential communities. While this may have been strategically necessary in the struggle against apartheid, the context of a post-apartheid society raises new questions for us, questions which have to be addressed in the absence of a present enemy. To put it differently, the second question of evil remains. It remains *necessarily* in the sense indicated above, that is, in the sense that any post-apartheid form of social division has to mark the space of antagonism constitutive of any identity. Non-racialism, thought around the givenness of a 'common humanity' is not sufficient for marking this space, for it still dreams of a sutured social space, one in which humanity as such can realize itself, thereby forgetting the inaugural split of all forms of identification. Non-racialism could, however, be thought in another sense by taking, not only its universalist passion, but also the non-presence of identity indicated in the non-racialism as a starting-point. Once again, apartheid can be turned against itself. It is conceivable that the precise condition characterized by its ideologues as one of 'ontological uproot-edness', the *absence* of a *natural* community of identity, can be developed not as a principle of uncertainty, a curse and a lack, but as a positive celebration of the denial of purity as the basis for identity. This would amount to a recognition, no doubt, of the instability and undecidability which, for theorists of 'innocent' modernity, can be nothing other than a 'horror', the psychotic terrain of non-identity. This conclusion, however, does not follow, for non-racialism in the latter sense does constitute the condition of possibility of thinking, from within the South African context, a conception of identity which *articulates* itself in the very moment of the denial of its other, apartheid. It mimics the discourse of identity, and so subverts it in the moment of its constitution. If taken in this manner, 'the people' as a signifier could never be considered as the embodiment of the universal. It would have to retain its character as a *political* project, emphasizing not the attaining of a fully fledged identity, but the keeping open of the space of *identification*, that is, the impossibility and undesirability of closing and overcoming the difference between the universal and the particular. This, I would argue, is the precondition for thinking a radical, democratic, post-apartheid society.

Notes

1   B. Anderson, 'The New World Disorder', *New Left Review* 193 (1992), 7.

2   Z. Bauman, *Postmodernity: Chance or Menace?* (Lancaster: Centre for the Study of Cultural Values, 1991), 5.

3   *Hansard* (Debates of the South African Parliament), 18 May 1959, col. 6289.

4   H. G. Stoker, 'Calvinisme as wortel van ons volksbestaan', *Koers* XIX: 4 (1952), 162–74; and H. G. Stoker, 'Antropologiese wetenskappe en die beeld van God', *Koers* XXVI: 1 (1958), 15–20. (All translations from Afrikaans are mine.) Stoker was influenced in this respect by the Dutch neo-Calvinist theologian Abraham Kuyper (1837–1920), whose work contributed to the emergence of the idea of pillarization (*verzuiling*) in the Dutch context.

5   P. J. Meyer, 'Prof. J. C. van Rooy: Volksman en kultuurleier', *Koers* XXVII: 2 (1954), 93–100, at 95.

6   S. J. Du Toit, 'Opensbaringlig op die apartheidsvraagstuk', *Kores* XVII: 1 (1949), 13–23, at 17.

7   W. J. Snyman, 'Rasseverhoudinge in die Skrif', *Kores* XXV: 3 (1957), 161–74, at 167.

8   L. J. Du Plessis, 'Separate University Education', *Journal for Racial Affairs* 9: 3 (1958), 3–11.

9   Union of South Africa, 'Tomlinson Report' (1955), xviii.

10 J. H. Coetzee, 'Die Volkekunde in U lig', *Kores* XXIII: 6 (1956), 319–37; T. S. Van Rooyen, ''n Nuwe benaderingmetode in verband met die studie van die kontak tussen Blank en die Bantoe', *Kores* XXII: 4 (1955), 226–33; E. F. Potgieter, 'Kontak in Suidelike Afrika. Enkele gevolge en kenmerke van die proses', *Journal for Racial Affairs* 7 (1956), 52–65; N. J. Olivier, 'Ons stedelike naturellebevolking', *Journal for Racial Affairs* 10: 2 (1959).

11 Union of South Africa, 'Tomlinson Report' (1955), 29.

12 Olivier, 'Ons stedelike naturellebevolking', 42.

13 Potgieter, 'Kontak', 52–65.

14 W. W. M. Eiselen, 'Harmonious Multi-community Development', *Optima* (1959), 1–15, at 11. The term 'Bantu' officially replaced 'Native' in National Party discourse in 1952.

15 H. F. Verwoerd, 'Speech in the House of Assembly, 23 January 1962', in A. N. Pelzer, ed., *Verwoerd Speaks* (Johannesburg: Afrikaanse Pres, 1972), 664.

16 J. Strauss, 'Die mens en menslike verhoudinge in Afrika', *Journal for Racial Affairs* 13: 4 (1962), 228–36.

17 J. H. Coetzee, 'Die onbekende Afrika', *Kores* XXIII: 6 (1957), 174–87, at 183.

18 S. J. Du Toit, 'Die Christelike roeping van die Afrikaner in Afrika', *Kores* XIX: 3 (1951), 81–91, at 85.

19 J. H. Coetzee, 'Die indeling en verspreiding van die volke van Afrika', *Kores* XXV: 2 (1958), 275–88; and J. H. Coetzee, 'Nasionalisme in Afrika', *Kores* XXVI: 10 (1959), 351–61; W. Louw, 'Pan-Afrikanisme', *Journal for Racial Affairs* 13: 4 (1962), 211–27; P. O. Sauer, 'Openingsrede', *Journal for Racial Affairs* 9: 4 (1958), 129–36; Strauss, 'Die mens in Afrika'; and T. S. Van Rooyen, 'Die stryd om die siel van die Bantoe', *Journal for Racial Affairs* 14: 3 (1963), 163–72.

20 Coetzee, 'Nasionalisme', 325.

21 Strauss, 'Die mens in Afrika', 236.

22 Eiselen, 'Harmonious Development', 2.

23 Strauss, 'Die mens in Afrika', 235.

24   P. Walshe, *The Rise of African Nationalism in South Africa* (Berkeley, CA: University of California Press, 1970), 332.

25   'Policy of the Congress Youth League', in T. Karis and G. M. Carter, eds, *From Protest to Challenge. A Documentary History of African Politics in South Africa, 1882–1964*, vol. 2 (Stanford, CA: Hoover University Press, 1973), 317.

26   'The Atlantic Charter', in Karis and Carter, *Protest to Challenge*, 213.

27   'Policy of the Congress Youth League', in Karis and Carter, *Protest to Challenge*, 317.

28   Louw, 'Pan-Afrikanisme', 219; Strauss, 'Die mens in Afrika', 235.

29   Coetzee, 'Nasionalisme', 352.

30   P. Hugo, 'Towards Darkness and Death: Racial Demonology in South Africa', *Journal of Modern African Studies* 26: 4 (1988), 567–90, at 571.

31   Cronin, cited in R. A. Berman, 'Rights and Writing in South Africa', *Telos* 75 (1988), 161–72, at 171.

32   W. E. Connolly, *Identity/Difference* (Ithaca, NY: Cornell University Press, 1991), 2.

33   S. Critchley, *The Ethics of Deconstruction. Derrida and Levinas* (Oxford: Blackwell, 1992), 221.

34   H. K. Bhabha, 'The Other Question: Difference, Discrimination and the Discourse of Colonialism', in R. Fergeson, M. Gever, T. T. Minha and C. West, eds, *Out There: Marginalization and Contemporary Cultures* (New York: New Museum of Contemporary Art and the Massachusetts Institute of Technology, 1990), 73.

35   A. Coetzee, 'Reading the Silences. Afrikaner Literature and the Transformation of South African Society', *Southern African Review of Books* 3: 1 (1989).

36   Berman, 'Rights and Writing', 170.

37   E. Laclau, 'Beyond Emancipation', *Development and Change* 23: 3 (1992), 121–37, at 132.

Chapter 14

John Lonsdale

MAU MAUS OF THE MIND

Making Mau Mau and remaking Kenya

WHY WAS MAU MAU BELIEVED to be so evil?[1] The horror story of Britain's empire in the 1950s, it was less of a threat but thought to be more atrocious than either the Communists in Malaya or the Cypriot EOKA. It has lived in British memory as a symbol of African savagery, and modern Kenyans are divided by its images, militant nationalism or tribalist thuggery. This chapter explores some of these Mau Maus of the mind.

War and freedom

The colonial government first knew of the movement in 1948, with the renewal of unrest among Kikuyu labour tenants on white settler farms. 250,000 of these squatters lived on the 'White Highlands', a quarter of the Kikuyu people and half the farm labour force. Mau Mau was banned in 1950. In 1952 violence flared on the farms, where restraints on squatter cultivation and grazing rights were more sternly enforced in the interest of farm capital and resisted in the cause of peasant clientage;[2] in the slums of Nairobi where crime offered more than employment; and in the Kikuyu reserve where Mau Mau's opponents, 'the resistance' as whites first called them, were killed, often by fire and with their kin's assent, a form of execution once reserved for sorcerers.[3] A new governor, Sir Evelyn Baring, declared an emergency in October. Jomo Kenyatta, alleged to be the manager of mayhem, was arrested with 180 others. Mau Mau did not, as expected, collapse in terminal frenzy; after months of phoney war it was transformed into a formidable guerrilla force. The British did not win the initiative until early 1954. Their army was then a full infantry division with six King's African Rifles (KAR) battalions and five British, backed by Royal Air Force bombers. The police had multiplied threefold, and the Kikuyu 'resistance' had become a patchwork private militia, the Kikuyu Guard, over 20,000 strong. The army was withdrawn from operations in late 1956, after a four-year war.

The causal relationship between the containment of Mau Mau and the concession of majority rule has yet to be unravelled, but its intimacy can be suggested by citing three coincidences. Over white protest, the first African was appointed minister in 1954, in a reform of government designed to quicken the war; two months later the army cleared Mau Mau, and thousands of Kikuyu, from Nairobi. Then the first African general election was held in March 1957, barely a month after Mau Mau's forest leader, Field-Marshal Sir Dedan Kimathi as he entitled himself, was hanged. Finally, the emergency ended in January 1960 as delegates went to London for a conference which promised African rule. The right-wing settler leader, Group-Captain Briggs, called this remaking of Kenya 'a victory for Mau Mau'.[4] His supporters felt overcome by the evil out of which they had imaginatively made the rising. In a suitably Biblical gesture one of them threw thirty pieces of silver at the feet of Michael Blundell, whose liberalism they believed had betrayed white supremacy.[5]

Ignorance and imagination

This essay tries to explain neither Mau Mau nor its connexions with decolonisation. It addresses the prior question of how to read the evidence. We must know how Mau Mau was intellectually constructed before we can decide what it was and how it may have changed history. Behind the surface solidarities of war, myths of Mau Mau were more disputed than has been thought, with Africans as divided as whites. This should not surprise us. The future of Kenya was more anxiously contested after the second world war than at any time in its stormy past, behind rival dreams of social order; the social authorisation of murderous violence is an anxious issue in any culture; and all contenders were ignorant of their situation. True of any political conflict, this was true twice over of Mau Mau. It was mainly, but not entirely, a Kikuyu movement, and whites knew little of Kikuyu society. Few spoke Kikuyu. Most were content to know 'what everybody knew', the stereotypes that explained the daily uncertainties of Africa. The ignorance of whites was therefore structured. To them the Kikuyu were a 'tribe', but already an unusual and unsettling one. Mau Mau then fundamentally challenged the imaginative structures of race and tribe which underwrote the colonial order, forcing whites to choose between punishing a tribe and dissolving race as strategies of survival.

Kikuyu were just as ignorant, and as uncertain how to maintain or recreate social order. Always a fragmented set of parochial societies whose ruling principle was 'local government run mad',[6] they were, increasingly, a divided and mutually hostile people. Their oaths of political allegiance reflected both periods of this history. Most remained mundane rituals of initiation which imposed on aspirants the costs which promised seriousness of open, public purpose in a small community. But some now demanded hidden, factional loyalty to persons often unknown, outside the immediate locality, on pain of death. For Mau Mau emerged as the militant wing in a struggle for allegiance in which, as will be shown, authority and energy were ill matched. That is the tragedy which, when carried to extremes, marks all contexts of political terror. Mutually apprehensive ignorance ruled. Competition was secret, not public, since the main issue was not social honour but effective action. In any case, the obvious political vehicle, the Kikuyu Central Association (KCA), was already banned. As subject people, further, Kikuyu were under pressure to cloak real divisions under an invented common front. Political purpose could not be freely debated. Divided loyalties could not be openly recorded. A leader's public authority could with impunity be whisperingly invoked in his followers' private interest. Lies and intrigue flourished. Secrecy exacts that price.

Once battle was joined, ignorance and imagination were poor guides to action. As the enemy had to be better known, allies courted, and decisions faced, so four mutually incompatible meanings of Mau Mau occupied white minds, conservative, liberal, revivalist and military. These divisions were clouded by a common assumption of white superiority and that tacit evasion of dispute which survival demands in horrific times. Whites preserved a united front of counter-insurgency by damning what all saw as Mau Mau's savagery which, all agreed, had to be destroyed. But they divided over its civil remedies, which governed their view of its causes. Their debates sometimes forced their way furiously to the surface. The ostensible issues of dissension were generally military, over rules of engagement and interrogation, how clean or dirty, and surrender talks, whether Mau Mau should be offered them at all. But the conduct of war was disputed, as always, with an eye to the construction of peace. As peace neared and the future had once more to be faced directly, so the coalition fell apart. This was because the war had only doubtfully been won. Briggs was soon to say it had been lost. For the settlers had become dependent upon dubious allies with diverse Kenyas in mind: the British government, the leaders of 'loyal tribes' which had furnished police and troops, and, above all and most ominously, the 'loyalist' Kikuyu guard (KG).

While whites negotiated unity, it seems that the Kikuyu were forced into it by the first fury of repression. An official enquiry secretly admitted as much. Mau Mau members generally had one set of enemies. Their opponents often had two, 'Mau Mau on the one hand and the forces of law and order on the other'. Many Kikuyu, who had welcomed the emergency as a defence against terror, 'became disllusioned' when all Kikuyu were treated as rebels.[7] Kingsley Martin, visiting Kenya, reported the same effect of 'Black-and-Tannery'. This caused bitter hatred of whites among Kikuyu, of whom 'only a very small section' had supported Mau Mau a few weeks earlier.[8] These views were part of the liberal construction of the movement; it was a product of its environment. But many settlers believed that up to 80 per cent of Kikuyu had taken the first oath of initiation by October 1952, in agreement with or out of fear of their fellows, not from fear of whites.[9] This reflected the conservative view, that terror was inherent in Kikuyu society. Estimates of the movement's growth were political claims on the future. The more initiates there were before the emergency, the more the entire tribe was a criminal gang which had forfeited all prospective liberties. The very limited data available from the screening teams, which certified people's loyalties, support the liberal view. They suggest that half the Kikuyu men on white farms or in Nairobi had been oathed before Kenyatta's arrest, and under 20 per cent in the Kiambu district of the reserve. This last figure more than doubled in the first five months of the emergency. If one were treated as Mau Mau by police, it looks as if it seemed prudent to become one.

Even while Kikuyu were being lumped into Mau Mau by casual white violence, the government anxiously split them more sharply between Mau Mau and 'loyalist' resistance, by arming chiefs and tribal policemen. These latter suffered terribly in the first year of war, with a death rate of around 10 per cent,[10] perhaps because they had what Mau Mau needed most, guns. Chiefs then enlisted among waverers and those who had joined Mau Mau under duress, creating the KG by a similar mix of threat and persuasion. Recruits had to prove themselves with public confession and a traditional oath of cleansing.[11] Most KG units had substantial numbers of ex-Mau Mau. The insurgents also used these early months to gather their forces, with larger units and stronger oaths.[12] A Kikuyu civil war was being prepared. But many on both sides tried to evade the barbed invitation to fight the wider battle by local feud. While the KG killed more Mau Mau than any other formation and in some places acquired a grisly reputation, some units conspired with insurgents to keep the local peace. Conversely, Mau Mau leaders claimed to subjugate violence to the social audit of local communities which would have to live with the aftermath of murder.[13] And Mau Mau warriors, like any soldiers in battle, displaced their guilt and fear on to gangs other than their own. Like Kikuyu society it was a parochial war, obsessed with parochial honour. When the war was over, many were obsessed with its shame.

These blurred distinctions on both sides, in which the divided opinions of peace were compromised by the tactical agreements of war, have been insufficiently recognised. The evidence must be read with these tensions in mind. The white conventional wisdoms of the day glossed over them, skimming with care the fragile surface of racial solidarity. They only begin to address the question of evil. But one has to start with them before one can follow the divisions, white and black, which lead one down to the roots of social dread.

Conventional wisdom and private doubt

What then did whites at the time say publicly about the Mau Mau evil? Many thought it uniquely depraved, even in the dirty annals of modern terror and partisan war. There were three parts to the conventional answer, its leader's treachery, the bestiality of its ritual, and its savage method of killing. Kenyatta, who had enjoyed the best that Britain could offer, study at the London School of Economics (LSE) and the love of an English wife, was the probable artificer of the oaths, British propaganda found it easy to present these as utterly debased and degrading. Mau Mau oaths produced Mau Mau murders. Like most conventional answers they say more about the interpreter than the matter 'explained'. It will be convenient to take the murder and magic first, leaving the making of Mau Mau's manager till later.

In a big book twice reprinted, which probably introduced more western readers to modern Africa than any other, the American journalist John Gunther remarked that Mau Mau killings were, 'as everybody knows, peculiarly atrocious'. Victims might be 'chopped to bits', partly for security's sake; all gang members had to join in and share the guilt. They might also remove a corpse's accusing eyes, for Kikuyu, after all, were 'profoundly superstitious'.[14] Perhaps some reporters were too superstitious of what 'everybody knew'; for another, Graham Greene, thought that a Bren gun wounded as savagely as a *panga*, the heavy farm knife used by Mau Mau, as the British pointedly demonstrated by exposing guerrilla corpses.[15] There was also scandal over the army's habit of severing the hands of insurgents killed in action, to save the labour of carrying their bodies away to be identified by finger print.[16] The only systematic survey of Mau Mau victims suggests that chopping up on the other side was in fact rare. Dr Wilkinson examined 210 dead. Yes, many had multiple wounds. But these were generally superficial. The fatal ones were commonly six blows to the head, almost as if insurgents had been trained to make 'a quick and certain death for their victims'.[17]

Total casualty figures also suggest a picture different to Gunther's. The disparity in death is striking. On official data, Mau Mau (or Africans so described) lost 12,590 dead in action or by hanging over the four most active years of war; 164 troops or police died in the same period, most of them Africans. Mau Mau killed 1,880 civilians, nearly a third of them KG and all but 58 of them black.[18] This is a tragic total, but it may be thought to be not large when one considers how vulnerable their targets were at night, dispersed in broken country without light, guns, or wire until the villagisation programme of mid-1954. Settlers believed that all Kikuyu domestic and farm servants had taken at least one oath,[19] yet very few felt impelled to kill their masters. Mau Mau killing looks on the whole to have been rather restrained, at less than one sixth of their own dead, as if it was indeed under some social control. Against this, it should be said that insurgent attacks were largely confined to the first two years of war, and to specific battle zones in the districts of Nyeri and Fort Hall (Murang'a). Again, it was a parochial war and on both sides, in some places, dirty and bloody, with local peasant conflicts driving on the bitterness as much as wider political frustration.

As to the oaths, they made sensational reading which official sources and journalists exploited with a coyness which titillates while it repels. It was reliably reported that recruits committed their lives to the cause in swallowing a stew of mutton or goat, vegetables and cereals, sprinkled with soil, marinated in goat's blood, watched by uprooted sheep's eyes transfixed on thorns. All this was cruel, not bestial. But that was just the beginning of horror. For it was reported, possibly less reliably in some respects, that oaths became more ghastly as the war dragged on and insurgents despaired. Many writers left the details unsaid and readers' imaginations free to range in fascinated self-disgust. Police interrogators, rather less delicately, may have invited their prisoners to invent some more.[20] Other authors adopted a formula which claimed to deny the reader 'the full details' but then gave specifics which one could scarcely bear to think of as less than complete. If it was enough to say, with Blundell, that they included 'masturbation in public, the drinking of menstrual blood, unnatural acts with animals, and even the penis of dead men', then even a dirty mind must shrink from exploring further.[21] A parliamentary delegation thought the rituals too beastly to lay before the British public. They were hidden in an appendix to their report, privately available only in the House of Commons library.[22] Similarly, while fresh British troops were given a booklet, *The Kenya Picture*, to prime them against the enemy, the account of the 'advanced' oaths was inserted on a loose sheet of paper. This had to be returned after being read, a charming protection for wives and girlfriends in the days before the photocopier.[23] Yet, in spite of everything, many whites continued to employ Kikuyu. They badgered officials to waive emergency rules in respect of their employees.[24] Whatever they said in public, whites acted in private as if cross-racial trust and the wage relation were stronger than any oath, however bestial.[25]

Boundaries and infiltrators

After this public horror it is instructive to remember that the principal white authority on Mau Mau, Dr Louis Leakey, said absolutely nothing about their ritual in his initial explication of the oaths. Their malign power lay, rather, in combining a heightened tradition with its deliberate violation. The initiates' deeds did not offend custom; in any culture legal oaths were strong meat. It was the sociology of oathing which, he thought, subverted Kikuyu values. Customary oaths-at-law were voluntary acts of responsible adults, taken in the open, before witnesses and by agreement with relatives who risked magical harm in the event of a litigant's perjury. Mau Mau oaths, by contrast, were often taken under duress, at night, in unlit huts, in the presence of persons unknown, without consent of kin. Worse still, in order to tie their proverbially loose tongues, Mau Mau officers oathed legal minors, women and children, on whom such heavy moral demands ought not to be made.[26] While Leakey did briefly mention the Mau Mau cocktail in his second book, nearly two years later, he again stressed something different, the morally liminal status of initiates. These had to undergo for a second, customarily unthinkable, time the passage between careless youth and tested adulthood, by crawling through the circumcision arch of sugar cane and banana leaves before taking the oath. Leakey believed that enforced and unexpected re-entry into this fluid state must cause intense shock.[27] Blundell thought that oathing sowed a 'mind-destroying disease'.[28]

Leakey was no disinterested expert; he was committed to the fight against Mau Mau, as Kikuyu elder first and settler second. From his accounts one can infer an explanation of the evil imputed to Mau Mau not only deeper than any mere drinking of a devil's brew, but one to which many Kikuyu also subscribed. What disturbed Leakey was the mixing of moral and social categories which Kikuyu culture had previously separated in creating order. This was to take the liberal view, that Mau Mau was a product of cultural decay; the more common preoccupation with the paraphernalia of the oaths reflected the conservative position, that Kikuyu were savages. But Leakey may also have come close to portraying the horror with which Kikuyu faced the problem of violence far more intense and internal than could be controlled by conventional ritual means.[29] Mau Mau's offence lay in its confusion between persons of hitherto distinct legal status, gender and generation; its subversion of morally responsible legal tests, which resolved disputes, into coerced submission to unknown wills; and its inversion of actions proper to the day, social time, into the deeds of anti-social time, of darkness visible and spiritual.

Disease enters society, body and mind by subverting order or infiltrating boundaries, natural or socially constructed. This was the internal Kikuyu evil of which Leakey warned, with the elders. But Mau Mau presented whites with a violent concentration of all the dangers to which their own Kenya was also exposed, seemingly suddenly since the second world war. The essence of treason was social dissolution, twice over. If tribes were tottering, could white supremacy survive?

Before the war the colonial world had rested on a mental construction of social separations. Rulers and ruled were distinguished, and differentially valued, by race. Different subjects, otherwise anonymous, were recognised by tribe. Tribal authority and the extended family underpinned control. It was believed, even by sympathetic observers, that tribal character was inherited in a mystic union protected from neighbours by cultural isolation, 'like a fragile orchid, native of some windless forest'.[30] Africans had never enjoyed that secret of British progress, a vigorous commerce of ideas and social conflict. Nor did tribes produce workers. Colonial rule, cash and Christianity, in creating 'useful citizens' and 'industrious assets',[31] must come as a whirlwind of change which uprooted communal fences, especially around the fields of labour and learning. Here Africans invaded the white world[32] and injured their own. 'Detribalised' and 'semi-educated', they were failures in themselves and a reproach to whites, as well as a threat. To profit by Africans it seemed that whites must subvert them. On entering Kenya, therefore, settlers also entered a nineteenth-century South African debate on how to construct political security and morality on shifting sands. It was never resolved, whether in white opinion or in the priorities of the colonial state. Conservatives thought Africans inherently primitive, liberals that they were retarded children who promised well as modern men. The former thought order lay in 'adaptation', propping up reformed tribal authorities against the gale in segregated local governments; the latter trusted in 'assimilation' to replace external controls with the self-disciplines of educated Africans, westernised men. Similarly, some reckoned the answer to African unrest was repression, others that cooptation was cheaper and even safer in the end. Africans were similarly divided. More tried to link the imperial and household civilising missions within invented ethnic nationalisms than in a still more imaginary 'Kenya'.

After 1945 these border issues became ever more complex. The segmentary domains of political control were subject to trespass by competing economic interests seeking access to the centre, Nairobi. Conflict wracked all political levels. At the centre, the watchword of cooptation was 'multiracialism'. The first African was nominated to the legislature in 1944: Eliud Mathu, witchdoctor's son and Balliol man. But settler obduracy denied Mathu's moderate supporters, the Kenya African Union (KAU), the political resources which might have secured their effective cooperation. The governor, Sir Philip Mitchell, combined belief in education as a cultural bridge between the races with contempt for the idea that African nationalism might creatively purge the confusions of communal identity.[33] In the segregated reserves the local politics of control rested on the growing powers of African councils. Officials promoted progress but distrusted its twin foundations, peasants who exhausted the soil and 'progressives' not in chiefs' uniform, the egotists and agitators. In the deeper politics of work, the labour department struggled to open gateways of industrial relations through the emerging fences of class, against the opposition of both capitalists and workers, neither of whom saw themselves in such exclusive terms. Farmers refused, and urban employers were reluctant, to recognise trades unions; most workers preferred general to craft organisations. Yet white paternalists and anonymous black townsmen personified conflict, not control.[34] The deepest politics of all opposed labour and land on the White Highlands. The Maasai had formerly grazed most of this area. Little more than one per cent – but the richest part – had been Kikuyu land. Settlers claimed sole right to the land by virtue of treaty and achievement; it was their one sure footing in uncertain times. Their squatters claimed a share. They had given two generations of labour to taming the land and had made it ritually home by initiating their young and burying their dead on white farms. White farmers no longer wanted a tenantry, and squatters had no wish to become free labour. Settlers called in the police, squatters called on what they now saw as a tribe. Here was a thicket of cross-cutting boundaries indeed. The conflict between settler and squatter, capital and labour, class and tribe, was the most bitterly complex border dispute in all the unfinished business of Kenya.[35]

Mau Mau blew indecision apart. It outraged tribal elders and household authority at the foundations of control. Kikuyu militance also subverted, fractured and then seemed to dominate the pan-ethnic urban elite in the KAU, the only possible basis of African cooptation. Mau Mau thus destroyed past and blasted future images of social control, communal segregation and a multi-racial state. Policy could no longer wait on events. It had to be made. But a scapegoat must also be found for the catastrophe of confusion, an infiltrator-in-chief. It could only be the culture-rustler, Kenyatta.

Most whites feared and loathed Kenyatta, probably more for his English marriage than his trips to Moscow. District officers resented the way in which his oratory had broken the politics of progress in Kikuyuland, when women downed hoes and refused to terrace hills against erosion.[36] Missionaries, who may once have nursed him back to life, feared him.[37] After his return home in 1946, Kenyatta presided over the Teachers' Training College at Githunguri, the apex of the Kikuyu independent school system which competed with the missions; he was also said to attack the Christianity which had saved him.[38] Settlers blamed him for stirring up squatters.[39] Governor Mitchell must have included him in his scorn for the manufacturers of premature nationalisms. The rise of Mau Mau then proved Kenyatta, the enemy of tribal progress, to be a tribalist traitor to the African elite. Only he was thought clever enough to invent the oaths, perhaps from his reading in the LSE where, it was guessed, his anthropology had covered European witchcraft.[40] He also had charisma. His campaign tours in early 1952 had everywhere been followed by, and must therefore have instigated, spates of Mau Mau oaths and murder. He had got Kikuyu to boycott bottled beer. Yet his denunciations of Mau Mau, at government request, were ineffective; his heart therefore cannot have been in them. This was the chief supporting evidence in Baring's request to call an emergency.[41] The presumed backwardness and conformity of tribes did not admit of any other than a sorcerous origin for the cunning and internecine ferocity of Mau Mau.

To deconstruct the evil of Mau Mau is to reconstruct past boundaries of morally valid knowledge and power. To summarise the rest of the argument, it is to find not that Mau Mau was an official invention, as the British left thought, an alibi for suppressing legitimate African politics, but dreadful reality, a pathological image of the right social group relations which ought to order colonial life. These relations were in any case in disarray, between the myth of what once had been and the mirage of what they might become. In the several Mau Maus of their minds whites negotiated fresh African stereotypes, to bring new order out of confusion. In simpler times the white model of African cultural transition had been a linear, compensating, process of loss and gain in which small, tribal identities were diluted into a larger, civilised one; educated natives might agitate the untouched, but each could be calmed by a combination of adaptation and assimilation. Mau Mau smashed that innocent picture. Transition now looked like trauma. Loss of identity seemed to stir somnolent savagery. Education did not lead modern men out of the past; it made amoral men who manipulated its darkest fears. With a linear, if always subversive, model of progress now challenged by a movement which suggested that modernity could recreate savagery, whites had to rethink their ideas of social explanation. Mau Mau was bound to be made in divergent ways.

Two ideas competed to control the conduct of war, with different border trespass in mind. Conservatives stressed the unchanging danger of the primitive. Race was the most obvious boundary under threat and was simplest defended by hardening the polemical frontier between white civilisation and black savagery. They demanded an end to the liberal imperial promises which had aroused primitive envy. But if that had been Mau Mau's only border outrage, it could never have been punished with such cost and brutality in a just war by the decolonising Empire of the 1950s. After all, Kwame

Nkrumah was already the Queen's chief minister in the Gold Coast. The compelling construction of Mau Mau, which won the whites the right to fight the war, was more subtle and of wider application. Liberals saw border unrest within the African soul, on its psychic frontier between tradition and modernity, community and society, past tribe and future nation. Racial repression might have sharpened the conflict, but was not its cause. This lay in the trauma of transition. Mau Mau had to be destroyed, of course. But while diehards fought to keep the Kikuyu on the far bank of the river of transition – *The river between* as Ngugi the Kikuyu novelist had it[42] – white liberals knew it had to be crossed. Peace would come only when Kikuyu society was on the modern side. The need for wartime allies, local Africans and the home government, nerved the liberal imagination as never before to convert this conventional wisdom into government action. Whites thus failed to agree on a fresh African stereotype; Mau Mau split their previous indecisions into opposite camps. They fought the war on different premises. Privately, many thought any means tolerable for punishing ancient savagery; publicly, government strove to force the modern transition.

This public, liberal construction of the issue did not, however, win the peace. Nor did its Christian subtext of spiritual conversion. Measures of modernity, education and loyalty were, it is true, used to ration out the franchise for the first African general elections in 1957. This was seen as a precondition for a colour-blind common electoral roll in due time, in which white 'standards' would be safe. But this liberal control over the future had no future. It was blocked by African parliamentary boycotts and then killed by the deaths of eleven Mau Mau detainees at Hola camp in early 1959. At the Lancaster House conference in 1960, the modernizing liberal mission gave way to hard political bargaining. The ideas which cleared the way for, and then controlled, this longer future were held by those who fought the war and who were, under any circumstances, bound to outlast it, the British army and members of Kikuyu agrarian society. Generals asked not how one modernised Africans but who would hold power. They were part of the British establishment; Tory ministers, their civil partners, finally accepted the army's view of the war. Mau Mau fighters, on the other hand, were not privy to Kikuyu authority; they called themselves its *itungati*, its warrior servants. Their seniors, most of them 'loyalists', begrudged their service but enjoyed its rewards.

Settlers and supremacy

The iconography of the war was horrible, with pictures of hamstrung cattle grotesquely knelt upon the grass and burned black babies lying decapitated in the ashes of their homes. It looked very like a war between savagery and civilisation. On the side of order blond youths in slouch hats, backed by honest spearmen in blankets, represented the finest examples of their race, each in their proper place. African troops were also shown with guns, starched into civilisation by the creases in their khaki. On the side of chaos crouched wild-eyed men in rags and ringlets, just out of the trees.[43] A local publisher toasted the 'emergency alliance of men and women of all races and tribes' which gave hope for the future.[44] That was too simple. The ambiguities of adaptation and assimilation were now armed. Spearmen in blankets were politically sound but militarily doubtful. Trousered gunmen were essential in war but rivals in peace.

Mau Mau's horror united whites in demanding its forcible suppression. But the ambiguities of security, based on adapting African authorities or assimilating black individuals, divided them over the sort of power to which force must answer. Conservatives demanded a return to white supremacy and tribal discipline. Liberals thought that white control would be more surely preserved if Mau Mau were isolated in African opinion. This must mean some sharing of power between the races, as represented by their educated individuals. Divided contemplation of the future invited new appropriations of the past. White Kenyans wrote history now as never before, their own and that of the African peoples. One cannot reduce their mutual differences to class interest, between, say, liberal businessmen and hardline farmers. Theirs was too small a community for that, too closely tied by marriage, church and club. Nonetheless, the insecurity of farming on a mortgage was probably the closest that Europeans came to living out a personal analogy of their community as a whole, an experience which put 'firmness' foremost in race relations.

The highland farm mocked white supremacy in its daily confusion of categories. A tribute to middle class English effort, it was also the site of black peasant expansion. In hock to the banks, whites had made the 'untouched land of Africa' into farms, 'with all that a farm implies'.[45] Farms meant civilisation; farms pleased. They were fenced against the bush; water glinted in their dams; windbreaks marched straight over the horizon; lawns were greener than any 'at home'. Farms also satisfied. They supported not only a white family but dozens of black ones too. Only the ignorant or malevolent could talk of 'stolen lands'. Most of the Highlands had been wastefully grazed by a few Maasai in the past; even a Fabian critic said so.[46] African farm families were immigrant strangers too, other than on the coffee estates of Kiambu. To employ resident labourers was an act of generosity. Colonial rule had brought peace, health and rising population; some settlers added to these general benefits the paternal care of black communities who owed them the reciprocal duty of loyal service. But that was the problem; farms also unsettled. Squatters were not a dependent class, tied by a moral community of protection and service. They were not a conquered people who had lost the right to liberty. They were a fifth column, a menace. They created their own communities in hidden corners of white estates. They reintroduced the African bush within the fences of the farm. Nobody knew how many there were. Part of white domestic life and yet unknowable, the sullenness of race undid the duty of class. Worse still, after the war farms began to accuse. The tensions of the squatter relationship broke into conflict. White district councils enacted orders to restrict squatter rights to cultivation and pasture, and to require of them more labour. Settlers squeezed their dependants' livelihood partly because wartime profits enabled them to farm intensively, using more capital than labour. But the political consolidation of civilisation was still more urgent. The highland achievement must become unequivocally white, and farmworkers' claims be met with a wage alone, not land. Squatters resisted the new contracts, muttering among themselves of settler 'sin' and 'hypocrisy'. Even white officials used the language of 'moral entitlement' on behalf of labour.[47] Many settlers refused or failed to repudiate their squatters' rights. Nonetheless, squatter resistance had to be deprived of legitimacy. Some settlers regained the moral ground by infantilising their workers. One district council urged that 'the African', 'still a savage and a child', would respond to 'firmness' with a new 'respect' for whites who removed his freedoms.[48] It is difficult not to conclude that white guilt was assuaged by racial contempt. Africans ought not to make their masters behave so badly.

Most whites knew Mau Mau as the squatter armed. The frontline was at home, between supper and bedtime. Tools became weapons. The man with one's cast-off trilby fingered his panga.[49] Mau Mau was an ungrateful stab in the back, 'a revolt of the domestic staff . . . It was as though Jeeves had taken to the jungle'.[50] Two of the first settlers murdered were doctors, known for giving free treatment to squatter families;[51] the six year-old son of one of them was also killed; the press pictured his bloodstained bed, with chamber pot and clockwork train set on the floor. And what must, alas, be the best known account of Mau Mau, Ruark's oft-reprinted novel *Something of Value*, centres on the friendship between the settler's son Peter and the squatter's son Kimani. Kimani grew up in Nairobi's slums to become Mau Mau. Friend was now beast. In a blood-curdling book, the most chilling sentence for its settler readers must have been Ruark's statement of Kimani's purpose when he left the forest, gun in hand and murder in mind: 'This time Kimani was going home.'[52]

The conservative response was the settler alarmed. It had six strands, entwined in a circular argument. The first related grievance and terror. Kikuyu had no grievance; white settlement had allowed them to colonise Maasailand. Since Mau Mau could not appeal against wrong, it had to impose by fear.[53] Then why had it emerged? Since 1945, in Kenya as elsewhere, 'the spineless policies of the rulers seemed to encourage the revolt of their subjects'.[54] Savages respected firmness. Talk of democracy showed weakness, which invited questions. Once privilege was questioned, envy stirred; if not, then agitators were free to stir it. Thirdly, democracy was a 'fantastic idea'[55] for people whose recent history showed them unfitted to exercise it. Settlers were prepared to accept that Africans were potentially equal; but they were observedly different, improvident, incurious, ungrateful, superstitious and slothful. Search their history and one found alternating autocracy and anarchy. Mau Mau warned how thin was the modern veneer; it foreshadowed an African self-rule as bloody as the court of Kabaka Mutesa, not a century before. Fourth, western education had not improved Africans; Kenyatta's career suggested the reverse. Islam might be better than Christianity; it neither demanded nor promised so much. Fifthly, as for the squatters, so for Africans generally, firmness, even force, was the language they understood. This was especially true of the Kikuyu, once terrorised by a secret council of wizards, from which Mau Mau was perhaps descended. Finally, the answer was plain. European dominance must be restored. In centuries to come, white discipline might have shaped African potential. For the moment, they must respect whites more than they feared Mau Mau. The chief instrument of correction ought to be, not blundering British battalions, but an expanded KAR 'drawn largely from tribes inimical to the Kikuyu', officered by settlers 'experi-enced in dealing with black men.'[56] If all this was too much for Whitehall, lately ruled by woolly minded socialists, then the settlers knew where to find friends, further south in Africa.[57]

For many whites the emergency offered, more simply, the prospect of revenge. That was why Baring had to reinforce its declaration with airlifted British troops. He feared that settlers would otherwise supply, privately and without restraint, any violence the state appeared to lack.[58] From the start, the governor was deter-mined not to fight a racial war. In the empire of 1952 that would in any case have been impossible.

Liberals and transitionals

Conservatives said what they meant. Liberals dissembled. This was partly because ignorance and panic made them share conservative views. It also preserved a united front. On his first visit to Nairobi, Lyttelton, colonial secretary, maintained that Mau Mau was not the child of economic pressure.[59] That was to calm the settlers; he himself knew better. Two months earlier his officials had considered reforms which might meet 'any legitimate grievance of law-abiding Africans' and raised them with Baring before he flew to Kenya. They had discussed housing schemes, civil service promotion, crop prices, even the question of African farming on the White Highlands. Baring called reform his 'second prong', to make his first, repression, look presentable. It was also an essential tactic of war. The government must stop driving moderate Africans into the arms of the extremists and, instead, split the KAU, Baring might well have to decide 'either to "bust" or "buy" Kenyatta'.[60] Events precluded that. But London had to buy the settlers or they might bust the government. Some cried 'appeasement' when Baring revealed the second prong. If he was to keep the settlers at heel he would have to mind his tongue.[61] Official statements followed the conservative line.

Official action was different, and action remade Mau Mau in many official minds. Policy steered between two rocks of disaster. First, the settlers must be allowed no increase in influence; the precedents of two world wars were ominous in that respect. Nor must they be stampeded into a ferment which could be calmed only by concession. Yet the state had to answer African grievances, despite white fears of betrayal. For the second need was to prevent Mau Mau 'infecting' other African peoples; there was anxious evidence that it might. Brutal repression of their fellows was stirring angry passions.[62] The deputy head of the colonial office, Sir Charles Jeffries, squared the circle with some dog-eared official wisdom. 'The only sound line', he believed, was to 'build up a substantial "middle class" of *all* races to be the backbone of the country.'[63] He did not know how it should be done; nobody did, but it was by now the standard magical spell for conjuring new order out of colonial confusion. Racial barriers must melt into class coalitions. Meanwhile a war had to be fought, and its methods were hardly middle class. Yet most of Kenya was at peace and must so remain. African rural ambitions must be satisfied, urban discontents relieved and, more urgently, tens of thousands of Kikuyu in detention weaned from Mau Mau. An awful war needed a beastly enemy. A solid peace needed radical reform. An ideology which joined the two in causal sequence emerged from the daily discourse of harassed men.

This liberal doctrine adopted as its subject a new stereotype, 'the African in transition'. It diagnosed Mau Mau as a disease which demanded as cure none other than the government's best intentions of the postwar years. It was offered by Dr Colin Carothers, who had been a local medical officer for twenty years and now practised psychiatry in England. He had been asked back to reassure the commissioner for community development, Askwith, that his approach to rehabilitating Mau Mau detainees was on the right lines.[64] He assumed that they were possessed by evil and must be cleansed by public confession as performed in Kikuyu law, paid manual labour, literacy classes, instruction in the beneficent colonial history of Kenya and, if they chose, by Christian witness.[65] It was a working theory of a guided transition. Carothers was asked to comment on the ideas of practical men; his doctrine was dug from experience, theirs and his. He himself was a self-taught psychiatrist.[66] But he did much more.

Carothers' contribution to constructing Mau Mau was to theorise the detention camps' commonsense concept of a crisis in modernisation, a war for the soul of transitional man. He had just published a general treatment of the liberal approach to African psychiatry, which stressed the influence of environment rather than heredity on mental capacity. The preliterate tribal personality, he had argued, was moulded from outside by the conformity of the community. Literate western man was inner-directed, disciplined by the competition of society. This general work neither mentioned Mau Mau nor forecast any unusual psychiatric problems for 'the African in transition'.[67] But when he came to investigate, he found that Mau Mau was, in part, a reaction to psychic insecurity. Transitional men would have lost many cultural supports while still dreading the power of external, magical 'wills'. Their grievances would tell them that whites controlled a richer store of these than they did themselves. Here lay the cunning of Mau Mau; its oaths promised redress of the magical balance.[68]

Carothers has often been misinterpreted, perhaps because he allowed his understanding to change as he wrote, without then revising earlier passages, 'an approach which held the writer in as much suspense as any of his readers'.[69] It is remembered that he thought that the Kikuyu, as secretive forest-dwellers with little of the music of social cohesion in their souls (he was badly advised on both counts), unusually ill-fitted for the transition. It is forgotten that his report concluded with a call for deliberate modernisation. If Mau Mau abused the inner bewilderment of transitional man, Africans must be given the self-assurance of modernity. Confusion of category must cease, especially in the family. Disorder reigned where the river of transition separated traditional woman from modern man.[70] New boundaries of order must be drawn around modern genders. Again, this was the view of practical men. Askwith believed that recovery from Mau Mau was confirmed only by regular employment and the companionship of family life. Other senior officials had long called for a similar remedy for wider ills.

Post-war British colonial policy assumed that neither peasant economy nor unskilled urban labour could sustain social order much longer, let alone provide for development and improved welfare. Neither side of African life was self-sufficient; each was debilitated by what connected them, the oscillation of male wage labour. As Carothers fitted Mau Mau into his concept of transition, officials did likewise. Their transitional man was flesh and blood in the migrant worker. Mau Mau had travelled home with him. The slum had infected the countryside with the incessant movement between them. Two government plans and unprecedented sums of public finance were now devoted to separating them. The labour department pressed for improved wages and conditions, to create a new basis for society, the urban African family, where before Nairobi had accommodated loose atoms, labour units, bachelor workers.[71] The department of agriculture embraced a freehold revolution in land tenure to produce the rural mirror image, the peasant family able to earn a rapidly increasing income on its own land by its own labour, neither subsidising bachelor sons in town nor yet needing their monthly remittances. The conflicting bundles of rights which confused customary land tenure, fragmented holdings, the constant drain of litigation, must be swept aside with registration, consolidation, fencing, contour-ploughing and tree-crops.[72] Disorder would give way to cadastral survey and straight lines. Both departments seized on the emergency to argue, with a conviction which more than a decade of frustrated persuasion had sharpened, that the risks of pushing African communities through the transition to market society were as nothing to leaving them hanging betwixt and between. If Mau Mau was a disorder of the beginnings of progress the cure must be to bring progress to a successful end. Moreover, and this was vital, they could not be accused of appeasing Mau Mau; to the contrary, they were disciplining with individual obligation the collective disorders of transitional society. Each talked openly of class as the basis of order and power.

Liberal beliefs, reinforced by pragmatic action, helped officials to fight the war of transition with a clear conscience and to bring to justice some at least of their subordinates who fought a different, dirty, racial war. But this construction of Mau Mau failed to provide a foundation for peace. Two men at the centre of the bid for liberal authority warned explicitly that it would not. The forgotten part of Carothers' report on Mau Mau psychology argued that it was futile to try to remake the Kikuyu in the individualist English image unless they were given the chance to exercise the responsibility of power. Rehabilitation would be complete only with some kind of democracy, however that was defined.[73] Askwith conducted rehabilitation on the same assumption. The first was only an adviser, the second was sacked for not forcing the pace, when in 1957 the African elections demanded altogether more urgency, and the administration decided that persuasion must be stiffened with 'compelling force'.[74] The views of the army were quite a different matter. It trusted neither in controlled reform nor in compelling force.

Soldiers and politics

The army fought against Mau Mau's military confusions. These were very different from those which haunted the liberal myth of modernisation. General Erskine, commander during the critical first part of the war, took a simple soldierly view of the oaths which so disturbed the understanding of most observers. He recognised that Mau Mau had grievances and an aim, to eject Europeans. The connexion between strategic end and nauseating means was crisply rational.

> Secrecy was necessary, hence oaths were administered. Money was necessary, hence the oath had to be paid for. The whole tribe had to act as one, hence oaths were administered forcibly. Discipline was necessary, hence judges and stranglers became part of the organisation. It was perfectly clear from the nature of the oaths that violence was intended. Oaths became more and more binding and bestial.[75]

Cooling the mind the better to know the enemy was carried still further by the soldier who had the best Mau Mau war and later became a theorist of similar 'low intensity operations', the then Captain Kitson. He found the conservative obsession with savagery bad for tactical intelligence. 'Looked at over one's shoulder the oath was a frightful business, suffused in evil.' If one looked at it straight, what was left?

> A cat hung on a stick; poor pussy. An arch of thorns with goat's eyes impaled on them: a silly scarecrow to frighten the feeble . . . what next? The initiates are abusing themselves into a bowl of blood – prep school stuff

. . . The whole business when looked at carefully is no more than the antics of naughty schoolboys.[76]

Kitson made his sense of Mau Mau by assimilating it to his own experience, more lurid than that of many of his compatriots one might think, even of those who had endured boarding school. At a more workaday level, he recognised the guerrillas as army types, skivers and time-servers whose kindred spirits once swarmed over base areas in the second world war.[77]

The colonial secretary, Oliver Lyttelton, was struck by a nobler likeness between forest fighter and British soldier. A veteran of the Great War, he respected men who, contrary to their 'tribal reputation', had 'more than once pressed home attacks against wire, and in the face of hot fire, and heavy casualties.' He had asked no more of his Grenadiers. If Mau Mau gallantry was explained by 'dutch courage . . . doped with hemp', had he not too, like others in his war, braced himself with rum before battle?[78] Such recognition of equivalence, so contrary both to the racialism which denied a common humanity and the liberalism which pitied dupes, was politically important. On a visit to London, Blundell (whose own respect for Africans came from commanding them in war), was shocked to find that Churchill thought the 'fibre, ability and steel' of the Kikuyu deserved to be acknowledged by an offer of terms.[79]

Erskine thought like Churchill. The settlers never trusted him after his statement that Mau Mau required a political rather than military solution.[80] But that was a soldier's reaction to guerrilla war, the most difficult of all wars to fight. It poses the keenest moral problems for its participants, on both sides of the hill. It blurs the distinction between military and civil and so too, more than other wars, between victory and massacre, gallantry and crime.[81] Insurgents can win political battles by an underhand refusal to fight open, soldierly, ones; they muddy the aims and reputation of security forces by denying them the clean tactical objective of a 'fair target' or 'fair fight'.[82] After clearing the army of the political confusions created by others, Erskine then strove to restore proper distinctions to the battlefield itself. Forest and mountain became pro-hibited areas, where troops could operate on a 'straight forward [sic] war basis knowing that anybody they met must be an enemy.' He reserved these zones of simplicity to the army, leaving to the police the inhabited areas where 'pressure and persuasion' had their murkier role. White settlers were as messy as Mau Mau. Erskine's compulsory evacuation of elderly and isolated white farmers from the front line, to avoid dissipating his forces as scattered farm guards, was almost his most unpopular act.[83]

Erskine angered whites most with his successive surrender offers to the forest fighters. These thwarted the lust for revenge. Negotiation also denied two fundamental beliefs of the conservative myth, that the obscenities of the oath turned men into beasts and that Mau Mau lacked rational aims. Even Kenyan-born white police found that Mau Mau commanded their respect. After sixty-eight hours of interrogating the captured 'General China', superintendent Ian Henderson, the boys' own hero of the settlers' war, concluded that his prisoner was 'a complete fanatic'. Was he then mentally ill? Not at all. China had 'a good brain and a remarkable memory'. He knew why he was fighting; 'his sole wish was to expound his political testament before Legislative Council and then walk to the gallows without trial.'[84] When he too was captured, China's successor in Mount Kenya's forests, General Kaleba, outlined his objective as the achievement of more land and power of self-determination. They do not consider this will be achieved by violence alone, but they firmly believe that those who are sympathetic to their cause can only succeed if Mau Mau continue to fight.[85]

The opposing generals understood each other. Each acknowledged their limitations in a political war. They could only exert the military pressure needed to force a political peace.

It took the tragedy of Hola camp, when eleven 'hard core' detainees were beaten to death in the name of modernisation, to bring the British government round to the military view. As Margery Perham put it, the hard core were determined to prove that they 'were not in the grip of some remedial obsession but pursuing logical and irrevocable political aims'.[86] The detainees might have put it differently. The immediate issue was work and its refusal. Their case was simple. They were political prisoners, not criminals. To work to order would be to admit to wrong. Work was a proper demonstration of responsibility for free men; under any other condition it was slavery. The colonial government did not agree, but that was no longer relevant. The liberal campaign for westernisation, as both the bridge of transition and condition of political rights on a qualified franchise, could no longer govern policy. Political change could not wait on repentance and the development of a politically responsible (that is, guilt-conscious) middle class. Britain could not continue to remake Kenya by force when other European powers were abandoning attempts to remodel colonial rule for the moral high ground of informal empire.[87] A political war must be ended by political means. Civilisation had to be gambled on concession and agreement, not enforced by the tyranny of good intentions and warders' truncheons. Within months of Hola came Lancaster House and the prospect of majority rule.

Freedom and crime

The remaking of civilisation in Kenya, then, had to be a political creation, not a confessional crusade. But whose? The man who won the peace was the man found guilty of causing the war, Kenyatta. The government had charged him with imposing evil on the Kikuyu. But Mau Mau could never have been a simple imposition. There were too many Mau Maus for that. They were the product of deep political conflict within Kikuyu society. Their militants were inspired by Kenyatta, of that there is no doubt. But his exhortations were overtaken by their compulsions.[88]

On the surface, Mau Mau was an anti-colonial revolt to recover Kikuyu land and to press the claim to much of the remainder of the White Highlands which had been lodged by two generations of squatter labour.[89] But what gave the revolt its shape and inner meaning was its junior status in a long struggle for patriotic virtue within Kikuyuland. Kikuyu virtue lay in the labour of agrarian civilisation, directed by household heads. Honour lay in wealth, the proud fruit of burning back the forest and taming the wild, clearing a cultivated space in which industrious dependants too might establish themselves in self-respecting independence; the possibility of working one's own salvation was the subject of more Kikuyu proverbs than any other.[90] But by the 1940s this myth of civic virtue began to mock the majority rather than inspire. Big men no longer welcomed dependants, they expropriated them. Wages fell behind prices, whether of food, housing, land, or marriage transfers. Young men asked if they would ever earn enough to marry and mature. Those who had most cause to fight colonial rule had the least chance to merit responsibility. Those whose deeds might deliver power would have no right to enjoy it. That was the Kikuyu tragedy, a struggle over the moralities of class formation, not mental derangement.

Kikuyu were engaged in a struggle about class, not in class struggle. They were not yet morally divided, however much their material chances diverged. They argued within one myth of virtue. A Mau Mau leader recalled how the trade unionist Makhan Singh taught him that the Kikuyu were once communist; but he meant a communalist society, in which 'the community took care of everyone and his family.'[91] Nobody had a socialist Mau Mau in mind. The right to force political change was contested between the men of authority like Kenyatta, who was the son-in-law of not one but two official chiefs, and the dispossessed, legal minors. The reputable, it began to appear, could not win power except at the appalling price of owing its achievement to men they despised. These latter, the hard men of Nairobi, took over the oath of respectable unity which Kenyatta knew and pressed it, by force, deception, and persuasion on those who hoped that desperate deeds, *ngero*, would earn them what they needed, the adulthood which would entitle them to share the fruits of victory. These were the men and women whom Kikuyu knew as Mau Mau, not all those who had taken the oath of unity but the few who had taken the second, fighting oath.[92] But, however much Kikuyu may have denounced Mau Mau within, few were so careless of communal solidarity or their own lives that they betrayed it without. Europeans mistook this fear and solidarity for tribal unity, a mystic force. This myth of tribal unity found Kenyatta guilty. If he was the tribal leader he was responsible for everything done in his name.

Throughout his career, with sustained consistency over fifty years, Kenyatta taught that authority was earned by the self-discipline of labour, as he had learned from his grandparents. In 1928 he had warned of the fate of native Australians, whom the British 'found were decreasing by reason of their sloth . . . and so they got pushed to the bad parts of the land'. Kikuyu ought to follow the Maori example. The British had found them 'to be a very diligent people. And now they are permitted to select four men to represent them in the Big Council . . .'[93] This simple contrast summed up all his later political thought. On numerous occasions, between his return from England in 1946 and his arrest in 1952, Kenyatta publicly denounced those who no longer worked their land as the enemies of political advance: 'if we use our hands we shall be men; if we don't we shall be worthless.' Among the vast crowds who listened, those who no longer had land did not thank him for this sermon.[94]

So Kenyatta also made a meaning for Mau Mau. In front of a huge crowd at Nyeri in July 1952 he compared it with theft and drunkenness. Henderson, the police observer, thought he equivocated; and the provincial commissioner believed this meeting marked a turning point in the swing of opinion towards Mau Mau.[95] But Henderson also reported Kenyatta as asking the crowd to 'join hands for freedom and freedom means abolishing criminality'.[96] That may not be an obvious point for a nationalist orator to make, but precisely what one would expect of a Kikuyu elder. Freedom and criminality were at opposite poles in Kikuyu thought. Freedom was *wiathi*; this enjoined not only independence from others but also self-mastery. It came from disciplined effort, whether as herdboy, warrior, dependent worker, or household head. Criminality was *umaramari* or *ngero*. The former term derived adult delinquency from childhood disobedience; the latter carried connotations of failing a test. Kenyatta was not alone in making a delinquent Mau Mau in the mind. A former Mau Mau fighter has called it a council of *ngero*.[97] Even the chairman of its central committee or *kiama kia wiathi*, Eliud Mutonyi, would have not demurred. A self-made businessman himself, he regretted that in the Nairobi slums, from which Mau Mau recruited so many fighters, 'poverty knows no patriotism',[98] a modern rendering of the old, dismissive proverb, 'poverty has no responsibilities'. The path of crime, *umaramari*, could never lead to its opposite, self-rule, *wiathi*.

In the forests the struggle for respectability was as fierce as the fight for freedom. Guerrillas remembered in song what Kenyatta had said at Nyeri: 'Vagrancy and laziness do not produce benefits for our country.'[99] Perhaps also revealing their own anxieties about socially unauthorised killing, they anathematised ill-disciplined gangs, always the ones over the next hill, as *komerera*, an appellation which pairs the concepts of idleness and concealment, mere thugs who perpetrated anti-social violence and refused to cook for their leaders. They personified the nightmares not only of military discipline but also of civic virtue.[100] Forest fighters also argued out the question of gender and the social order. They divided between literates, who assumed the adult status required to form a household, and illiterates, the 'Kenya *riigi*', who saw themselves as a warrior age-set below the age of marriage, for whom sexual relations were more free.[101] Even in the forest, to outsiders the very fount of evil, literacy was becoming associated with respectable class formation, threatened by the illiteracy of a junior generation, in which one can dimly discern the emerging contradiction of a lower class. Mau Mau faced within itself the confusions of the rest of Kenya.

But while Nairobi's hooligans crawled under the arch of Mau Mau circumcision in search of the responsible 'spirit of manhood' and then persevered in the forests to earn their right to land,[102] they did not win. The remaking of Kenya and their place in it were decided by others. The agrarian revolution of the war of modernisation had gone on without them. On emerging from forest or detention they were landless still, indeed more so than before in a rural world now realigned by land consolidation and freehold title. They remained debarred from the creation of order, outside its boundary fence. And on his release back to political life in 1961 Kenyatta took up his old refrain. His government would not be hooligan rule; Mau Mau had no moral claim on power. He no doubt intended to calm white farmers and foreign investors. But he had a still more anxious audience to reassure, with nowhere else to go. Most Kenyans, certainly all household heads, were relieved to discover that Kenyatta was on the side of domestic order, after all. Their traditional civilising mission had now become a modern ruling ideology. By criminalising Mau Mau once more in the public mind, as he had tried a decade earlier, Kenyatta reasserted his authority to remake Kenya.[103]

There are therefore many answers to the question I was asked two years ago by a landless taxi-driver. As a schoolboy he had taken General Matenjagwo – General matted hair – his last bowl of beans before he met his death in action. His mother had lost their land rights to the senior wife during land-consolidation. 'Why', he asked in some indignation, 'why did they call us *imaramari?*' They still do. White conservatives and liberals may have gone, and the regiments departed. Household heads, many of them now reinforced with fundamentalist Christianity, remain.

Notes

1   Much of the impact of 'Mau Mau' on the mind lay in its name; many different origins have been proposed for it. The most plausible comes from Thomas Colchester, lately of the Kenya administration: in Swahili *ka* is a diminutive prefix, *ma* an amplifying one, enhanced by repetition. *Mau* would thus connote something larger than *Kau* (the colloquial form of the Kenya African Union).

2   Tabitha Kanogo, *Squatters and the Roots of Mau Mau* (London, 1987), 129–37; Frank Furedi, *The Mau Mau War in Perspective* (London, 1989), chapters 3 and 4.

3   Willoughby ('Tommy') Thompson, Kandara division (Fort Hall) handing over report, 1 March 1955: Rhodes House, Oxford, [RH] Mss. Afr. s. 839 (1); Jomo Kenyatta, *Facing Mount Kenya* (London, 1938), 304.

4   George Bennett and Carl Rosberg, *The Kenyatta Election: Kenya 1960–1961* (London, 1961), 22.

5   Sir Michael Blundell, *So Rough a Wind* (London, 1964), 283.

6   W. S. and K. Routledge, *With a Prehistoric People* (London, 1910), 195.

7   'Report on the sociological causes underlying Mau Mau with some proposals on the means of ending it' (mimeograph, 21 April 1954, seen by courtesy of Greet Kershaw), paras. 2 and 34.

8   Kingsley Martin, 'Kenya report', *New Statesman and Nation* (London), 15 November 1952.

9   Rob Buijtenhuijs, *Essays on Mau Mau* (Leiden, 1982), 35–6, discusses Mau Mau recruitment rates.

10   S. H. Fazan, *History of the Loyalists* (Nairobi, 1961), 78.

11   *Ibid.* 12–16.

12   Donald L. Barnett and Karari Njama, *Mau Mau from Within* (London, 1966), 153–97.

13   Barnett and Njama, *Mau Mau from Within*, 138–9, 142, 155, 193–5; 'Interrogation of Waruhiu s/o Itote, alias "General China" ' (Kenya Police Special Branch, Nairobi, 26 January 1954), para. 219: privately held.

14   John Gunther, *Inside Africa* (New York, 1953, 1954, 1955), 361.

15   Graham Greene to editor, *The Times* (London) 1 December 1953, under the heading 'A nation's conscience'.

16   Anthony Clayton, *Counter-insurgency in Kenya 1952–60* (Nairobi, 1976), 42, n. 84.

17   J. Wilkinson, 'The Mau Mau movement: some general and medical aspects', *East Africa Medical J.*, xxxi (July, 1954), 309–10.

18   Statistics from Colonial Office, *Historical Survey of the Origins and Growth of Mau Mau* (Cmnd. 1930, May 1960), 316 (hereafter cited as *Corfield report*), and Clayton, *Counter-insurgency*, 53.

19   As in Nellie Grant to Elspeth Huxley, 20 Oct. 1952, in Elspeth Huxley (ed.), *Nellie: Letters from Africa* (London, 1980), 179.

20   As suggested by Josiah M. Kariuki, *'Mau Mau' Detainee* (London, 1963), 33.

21   Blundell, *Wind*, 168.

22   *Report to the Secretary of State for the Colonies by the Parliamentary Delegation to Kenya January 1954* (Colonial Office: Cmd. 9081, 1954), 1.

23   Clayton, *Counter-insurgency*, 7, n. 12.

24   R. D. F. Ryland (Officer-in-charge, Nairobi extra-provincial district) to R. G. Turnbull (Minister for African Affairs), 23 December 1954: Kenya National Archives, Nairobi [KNA], MAA. 9/930.

25   KNA, Rift Valley Province annual report (1953), 2, 16.

26   L. S. B. Leakey, *Mau Mau and the Kikuyu* (London, 1952), 98ff.

27   L. S. B. Leakey, *Defeating Mau Mau* (London, 1954), 77–81.

28   Blundell, *Wind*, 171.

29   Leakey, *Southern Kikuyu*, vol. 3, 1037–48, 1056–67, 1234, 1238, 1269–70, 1276, for the customary controls on violence.

30   Norman Leys, *Kenya* (London, 1924), 303.

31   *Ibid.* 305–6, quoting an *East African Standard* editorial of February 1924.

32   The metaphor is John Gunther's: *Inside Africa*, 9.

33   Governor Mitchell to Secretary of State Creech Jones, confidential despatch 16, 30 May 1947; KNA, African Affairs file ii (reference noted in 1965 but not checked since the revision of the archives classification).

34   Anthony Clayton and Donald C. Savage, *Government and Labour in Kenya 1895–1963* (London, 1974), 265–346; Sharon B. Stichter, 'Workers, trade unions and the Mau Mau rebellion', *Canadian J. Afr. Studies*, IX (1975), 259–75; Frederick Cooper, *On the African Waterfront* (New Haven and London, 1987), 78–203.

35   Kanogo, *Squatters*; Furedi, *Mau Mau War*; Throup, *Origins*, chapter 5.

36   D. W. Throup, *Economic and Social Origins of Mau Mau* (London, 1987), 152–64, shows that the administration little understood Kenyatta's position in this heavily politicised 'terrace war'.

37   Jeremy Murray-Brown, *Kenyatta* (London, 1972), 45.

38   M. G. Capon, 'Kikuyu 1948, a working answer', September 1948: KNA, DC/MUR. 3/4/21.

39   Throup, *Origins*, 129–30.

40   J. C. Carothers, *The Psychology of Mau Mau* (Nairobi, 1954), 16, is cautious on this point; Bishop L. J. Beecher, 'Christian counter-revolution to Mau Mau', in F. S. Joelson (ed.) *Rhodesia and East Africa* (London, 1958), 82, much less so.

41   Baring, top secret telegram to Lyttelton, 10 Oct. 1952: PRO, CO 822/443, and reproduced in Charles Douglas-Home, *Evelyn Baring, the Last Proconsul* (London, 1978), 227–8.

42   (James) Ngugi (wa Thiong'o), London, 1965.

43   Two illustrated accounts of Mau Mau are Granville Roberts, *The Mau Mau in Kenya* (London, 1954), and anon, *Mau Mau, a Pictorial Record* (Nairobi, nd., ?1954).

44   *Ibid.* Foreword.

45   J. F. Lipscomb, *White Africans* (London, 1955), 82; C. J. Wilson, *Kenya's Warning* (Nairobi, 1954), 13.

46   Kingsley Martin, 'The settler case', *New Statesman*, 29 November, 1952.

47   Kanogo, *Squatters*, 45, 65, 72.

48   Uasin Gishu district council resolution, April 1947, quoted in Furedi, *Mau Mau War*, 35–6.

49   Pictured on the blood-red dustcover of Wilson, *Kenya's Warning*.

50   Graham Greene, *Ways of Escape* (London, 1980), 188.

51   Wilson, *Kenya's Warning*, 56.

52   Robert Ruark, *Something of Value* (London, 1955), 368.

53   Most succinctly put by Wilson, *Kenya's Warning*, 59.

54   C. T. Stoneham, *Out of Barbarism* (London, 1955), 105.

55   'The voice of the settler', anonymous correspondent to *New Statesman*, 4 October 1952, 378.

56   Stoneham, *Barbarism*, 122.

57   This composite picture is drawn from *ibid.*; and C. J. Wilson, *Before the Dawn in Kenya* (Nairobi, October and December 1952, January 1953) and *Kenya's Warning*.

58   Baring to Lyttelton, 9 October 1952: PRO, CO 822/443.

59   Lyttelton, radio broadcast from Nairobi, 4 November 1952 (transcript in KNA, CD, 5/173); and repeated in his statement to parliament: *House of Commons Debates*, 5th series, vol. 507 (7 November 1952), col. 459.

60   W. Gorell Barnes to Baring, 10 September 1952; note of a meeting with Baring, 23 September 1952: PRO, CO 822/544.

61   I have adopted Kingsley Martin's reading of the situation: *New Statesman*, 8 November 1952.

62   Rogers, minute to Gorell Barnes, 24 October 1952; Rogers, minute to Sir Charles Jeffries, 16 February 1953; Lyttelton to Baring, 5 March 1953: PRO, CO.822/440.

63   Jeffries, minute to Lloyd, 17 February 1953 (original emphasis): CO.822/440.

64   T. G. Askwith, typescript memoirs, chapter on 'Mau Mau', p. 8, seen by courtesy of the author.

65   Colony and Protectorate of Kenya [CPK], *Community Development Organization Annual Report 1953* (Nairobi, 1954), 2–3; CPK, *Annual Report of the Department of Community Development and Rehabilitation 1954* (Nairobi, 1955), 21–33.

66   Dr J. C. Carothers, in conversation, 26 July 1989.

67   J. C. Carothers, *The African Mind in Health and Disease* (World Health Organization, Geneva, 1953), 54–5, 130–3.

68   CPK: Carothers, *Psychology*, 6–18.

69   J. C. Carothers, 'The nature-nurture controversy', *Psychiatry: J. for the Study of Interpersonal Processes*, xviii (1953), 303.

70   Carothers, *Psychology*, 22–4.

71   CPK, *Report of the Committee on African Wages* (Nairobi, 1954).

72   CPK, *A Plan to Intensify the Development of African Agriculture in Kenya* (Nairobi, 1954).

73   Carothers, *Psychology*, 19–20, 28–9.

74   T. G. Askwith, in conversation, 27 July 1989; Terence Gavaghan, in conversation over the years.

75   General Sir George Erskine, despatch, 'The Kenya emergency June 1953–May 1955', 2 May 1955: PRO, WO 236/18 (seen by courtesy of Mr Heather).

76   Frank Kitson, *Gangs and Counter-gangs* (London, 1960), 131.

77   *Ibid.* 158.

78   Lyttelton, secret and personal telegram to prime minister Churchill, 18 May 1953: PRO, CO 822/440; Oliver Lyttelton, *The Memoirs of Lord Chandos* (London, 1962), 41, 59.

79   Blundell, *Wind*, chapter 4 and p. 184.

80   James Cameron, 'Bombers? Kenya needs ideas', *News Chronicle* (London), 15 Nov. 1953.

81   Michael Walzer, *Just and Unjust Wars* (Harmondsworth, 1980), chapter 11.

82   The quoted phrases come from Erskine's despatch of 2 May 1955, para. 17: PRO, WO 236/18; and Kitson, *Gangs*, 46.

83   Erskine's despatch, 2 May 1955, paras. 15, 17, 40, 74.

84   'Interrogation of "General China" ', para. 14.

85   'Flash Report No. 1 – Interrogation of Kaleba', Special Branch headquarters, 28 Oct. 1954, para. 37: KNA, DC/NYK. 3/12/24 (by courtesy of Mr Heather).

86   Foreword to Kariuki, *'Mau Mau' Detainee*, xv.

87   As argued by John Darwin, *Britain and Decolonisation: the Retreat from Empire in the Post-war World* (London, 1988), 244–69.

88   As African leaders complained to Kingsley Martin: 'The case against Jomo Kenyatta', *New Statesman*, 22 November 1952.

89   As Governor Mitchell almost said in retirement: *Afterthoughts*, 268.

90   G. Barra, *1000 Kikuyu Proverbs* (Nairobi, 1974, first edition 1939); Ngumbu Njururi, *Gikuyu Proverbs* (Nairobi, 1983).

91   'Classification report no. 3468: John Michael Mungai', (17 May 1956), 9–10: RH, Mss.Afr.s.1534.

92   Carl G. Rosberg and John Nottingham, *The Myth of Freedom 1921–63* (Nairobi, 1975), 234–76; Kaggia, *Roots of 'Mau Mau' Nationalism in Kenya* (New York and London, 1966), 78–115, 193–5; M. Tamarkin, 'Mau Mau in Nakuru', *J. Afr. Hist.*, xvii (1976), 119–34; John Spencer, *KAU, the Kenya African Union* (London, 1985), 202–49.

93   Editor (Kenyatta), 'Conditions in other countries', *Muiguithania*, i, 3 (July 1928), translation by A. R. Barlow of the CSM. KNA, DC/MKS.10B/13.1.

94   Profile of Jomo Kenyatta in *The Observer* (London), 2 November 1952, doubtless by Colin Legum. The *Corfield report*, 301–8: Appendix F (Assistant Superintendent Henderson's report on KAU mass meeting at Nyeri on 26 July 1952, with 25,000 estimated present) shows the difficulty Kenyatta could have in controlling a crowd.

95   KNA: Edward Windley, Central Province annual report (1952).

96   *Corfield report*, 305.

97   Joram Wamweya, *Freedom Fighter* (Nairobi, 1971), 52.

98   Eliud Mutonyi, 'Mau Mau chairman', undated typescript, copy in author's possession.

99   Barnett and Njama, *Mau Mau from Within*, 180.

100   *Ibid.* 213, 221, 293–5, 376, 390, 397, 479, 498; Waruhiu Itote (General China), *Mau Mau General* (Nairobi, 1967), 139–41.

101   Barnett and Njama, *Mau Mau from Within*, 471–8; Itote, *Mau Mau General*, 78, 127–38. White, 'Separating the men from the boys', has much more on all this.

102   The full title of Gakaara wa Wanjau's 1952 pamphlet was 'The spirit of manhood and perseverance for Africans', as translated in an appendix in Gakaara wa Wanjau, *Mau Mau Author in Detention* (Nairobi, 1988), 227–43.

103   Jomo Kenyatta, *Suffering without Bitterness* (Nairobi, 1968), 124, 146, 147, 154, 159, 161, 163–8, 183, 189, 204.

PART SIX

Gender and Sexuality

GENDER AND SEXUALITY

ONE OF THE MORE INTERESTING and well-developed areas in the literature of decolonization is that which focuses on gender and sexuality. Like other social changes triggered by the shifting balance of power, changes in the representations of gender and sexuality occurred in the midst of anticolonial and nationalist movements. At the very least, these changes mirrored larger social contests and also spoke to the issue of the political and social roles that women and men played during decolonization. The essays selected here illustrate several ways in which gender and sexuality permeated political discussions, and in many instances, fueled anticolonial activity. I have chosen an article on the Mau Mau along with a provocative article on Mahatma Gandhi's celibacy because together they afford extremely dynamic insights into the relationship between gender, sexuality, and decolonization.

Cora Ann Presley's essay "The Mau Mau Rebellion, Kikuyu Women, and Social Change" also addresses the issue of gender construction and historiography vis-à-vis decolonization in Kenya. However, rather than discussing the representation of male gender, Presley focuses on women's contributions to the nationalist movement. As Presley argues, women nationalists have not received due attention because many earlier historians too often relied on stereotypical colonial representations of African women either as victims or prostitutes during the rebellion. Kikuyu women did in fact play active roles in the struggle and were, for example, instrumental in maintaining supply routes for the rebels. This is best illustrated by the fact that only the eventual arrest and detention of women supporting the rebellion allowed the British forces to subdue the Mau Mau. As a corrective to the literature on women during decolonization, Presley's article opened important ground in colonial history, especially in the historiography of gender studies during decolonization.

Joseph S. Alter turns the question of gender in another direction. In "Celibacy, Sexuality, and the Transformation of Gender into Nationalism in North India," Alter highlights how Gandhi's celibacy related to Indian nationalism. According to

Alter, celibacy, as a concept, was used to stand against the inherent threat of Westernization. Analysing Gandhi's writings on celibacy and nationalism, Alter buttresses claims that Gandhi's philosophy of non-violence was very much informed by Hindu practices and teachings, which, for Gandhi, translated into asexual notions of political emancipation for all Indians. These teachings, according to Alter, rendered the physiology of sex and gender irrelevant in the quest for a higher truth. Ultimately, Alter argues, sexual abstinence would be translated into independence from European domination.

Chapter 15

Cora Ann Presley

THE MAU MAU REBELLION, KIKUYU WOMEN, AND SOCIAL CHANGE

Introduction

IN HIS 1982 WORK, *Essays on Mau Mau: Contributions to Mau Mau Historiography*, Robert Buijenthuis surveys the state of scholarship on the Mau Mau rebellion in Kenya from the 1950s to the 1980s. Buijenthuis, an early scholar of the Mau Mau rebellion and Kenyan nationalism, ably assesses the questions that researchers and participants in Mau Mau have addressed. Some of the fundamental questions explored are: What were the origins of Mau Mau? What were its patterns of recruitment and definition of membership? A second level of questions attempts to delineate the political, ideological, and personal connections of Mau Mau to nationalist associations in the pre-1948 period. Third, the historiography has focused on the different phases of the Mau Mau rebellion. A fourth concern has been how the colonial state and the British government marshalled their forces to counter and defeat Mau Mau. These questions were widely explored from the 1950s to the 1970s. Beginning in the 1970s, questions of class and local level analysis came into vogue. Typical questions were: Which of the Kikuyu districts in the Central Province contributed members to the rank and file as opposed to the Mau Mau leadership? Was Mau Mau a conflict or civil war between rural/urban populations and elite mass/sectors of society? Or was it best understood as labor conflict which evolved between the lumpenproletariat and the skilled workers in the trade unions?

All of these questions have deepened our understanding of the multifaceted nature of Mau Mau and have revealed cleavages in Kikuyu society. Some cleavages began in the pre-colonial period. Others were introduced under the colonial regime. While debate rages over some of these issues, in particular over local level and class differences in Mau Mau participation, scholars still exclude from consideration women's contribution to the rebellion and to Kenyan nationalism in general. The earlier Mau Mau studies did not examine women's participation.[1]

With the exception of a few works, such as Tabitha Kanogo's recent book on Mau Mau and squatters in the Rift Valley, 1980s scholarship accords women only token acknowledgement as participants in the "passive wing" of Mau Mau (Kanogo 1987). By not questioning women's contribution to Kenyan nationalism and Mau Mau, analyses continue to project a view that Mau Mau was a conflict among males. The following dyads were created:

Africans *versus* Europeans
nationalists *versus* loyalists
mass *versus* élites
rural *versus* urban
lumpenproletariat *versus* trade union members

Research has ignored an important aspect of Kenyan nationalism: the development of nationalist sentiment and activity among women since the 1920s; and the colonial state's response to women's nationalism.

The Government's response was to alter social policy. The center-piece of this was the development of a department whose policies and programs were directed specifically to wean women away from Mau Mau. These policies were developed in response to two needs. The first was to isolate the military force of Mau Mau and to defeat it by attacking and cutting off its popular support, which the British called the "passive wing," composed largely of women. Their function was to supply information, to smuggle arms, food, clothing, and medicine to the guerilla army, and to maintain the lines of transit for recruits travelling from the urban and rural sectors of the Central Province to join the military forces in the forest. The phrase "passive wing" hides the importance of this type of activity. The women and men who were the support troops of Mau Mau should more aptly be termed the non-combatant forces. They were treated as a serious force by the British.

The second part of the Government's policy was a program aimed at capturing the loyalty of the Kikuyu. This involved villagization and a full-blown propaganda program whose major purpose was to detach women from Mau Mau. The Government paid special attention to women's activism since key officials believed that women were "far more rabid and fanatical than the males" and more violent in their support of Mau Mau.[2] In response to women's "fanaticism" institutions designed to address such unmet needs as education, health care, access to a clean and reliable water supply, and child-care were created. The policy acknowledged, perhaps for the first time, that the colonial government had a primary responsibility for the welfare of rural populations. The Community Development Department, which was created in 1954, addressed these problems. It was given a large annual budget of £250 000 and a staff which included Africans as well as Europeans (Great Britain 1954, 80).

This Department was part of the British struggle to control women. Before the 1920s, the contest over who would control women, African or European males, revolved around jural issues: chiefly the marriage laws. The colonial state, of course, won the contest (Presley 1986, 149–200).[3] Other conflicts of this nature revolved around female circumcision and women's wage labor. Women's massive participation in Mau Mau contributed to the rebellion's initial psychological, if not military successes. A total of 34 147 women were sentenced to prison for violation of the Emergency Regulations from 1952 to 1958 (see Table 1). Thousands of these women were repeat violators of the regulations, which included taking oaths and aiding the forest fighters through

Table 1 Women admitted to prisons, 1952–1958

Year	Number	Number Sentenced	Recidivists	First Offenders
1952	347	n/a	n/a	n/a
1953	4 415	3 132	55	3 077
1954	9 609	8 494	290	3 204
1955	13 265	11 467	1 506	9 961
1956	8 900	7 906	1 627	6 279
1957	8 854	7 472	2 068	5 404
1958	7 295	5 976	1 873	4 103

Source: Kenya Colony and Protectorate, Kenya Prisons. *Annual Report*, 1953, 8; Kenya Prisons, *Annual Report*, 1956, 8–9; Kenya Prisons, *Annual Report*, 1958, 10.

supplying food, guns and information. Thus, from the standpoint of both the British and the nationalists, wooing women's loyalty was an essential ingredient in winning the war.

The image of women nationalists

When women's activities are described in the pro-colonial histories, two pictures of women emerge. Women are seen either as victims of Mau Mau or as prostitutes who, through personal contact with male nationalists, were drawn to Mau Mau while resident in Nairobi. The view of women as victims of Mau Mau originates from the colonial record. Women are presented by officials as the physical and psychological victims of atavism. The first type of victimization characterizes women as being forcibly compelled to take the oath of allegiance to Mau Mau. A 1952 Special Branch report on intimidation in oathing recounted the forced oathing of a Catholic Kikuyu woman. She was stripped naked, severely beaten to the point of unconsciousness, and upon her revival compelled to "drink blood from a bottle, and perform the other disgusting rites constituting the Mau Mau ceremony" (Corfield 1960, 155–156.) Another 1952 incident contributed to the view of women as victims. In Nyeri, the District Commissioner reported that forcible oathings of women and children were widespread (Corfield 1960, 134). Further fuel was added to this image of women by writers who were openly antagonistic to Mau Mau. In *State of Emergency*, F. Majadalany portrayed women's attraction to Mau Mau as being caused by a misdirected hero-worship of nationalists, described as "young thugs and criminals." According to Majdalany, however: "When the fighting gangs were formed each included its quota of women, and though their first function was to act as pack transport (with some concubinage on the side) many of them became ferocious and implacable fighters too" (Majdalany 1963, 60).

Both F. D. Cornfield and Majdalany ascribe irrationality and bestiality to Mau Mau. One measure of its supposed fanaticism was the repeated attacks on Loyalist women (Corfield 1960, 101). In the Lari Massacre (26 March 1953) eighty-four Loyalists were killed, two-thirds of the victims women. During 1952 Mau Mau military actions killed twenty-three loyalists of whom two were women and three were children (Corfield 1960, 157; Majadalany 1963, 137–147). While the rebellion was in progress, a popular British tactic was to portray women as Mau Mau's principal victims. However, only ninety eight of the 1024 Kikuyu killed by Mau Mau were women (Buijenthuis 1982, 184). This figure represents actual deaths and does not include threats, beatings, and other intimidation.

The image of women nationalists as prostitutes originates from district and provincial reports. Women nationalists began to be described as prostitutes when the Kenya African Union (KAU) successfully staged mass rallies. For example, a rally in Nyeri on 26 July 1952 was described by the District Commissioner: "Over 20 000 men, women and children attended. KAU insinuated over 40 bus loads of Nairobi thugs and prostitutes, who were clearly under instructions to excite the crowd" (Corfield 1960, 136–137). In describing the participation of the Meru in Mau Mau, J. T. Kamunchulah repeats the theme of a connection between prostitution and women's activism. He attributes the success of the Mau Mau in acquiring arms from government soldiers from 1950 to 1952 to "a network of communication with prostitutes, who lay 'tender traps' for African askaris, of ambushing the African askaris in dark streets and abducting and later suffocating them to death" (Kamunchulah 1975, 193).

Women in the Mau Mau rebellion

Colonial assertions that "respectable" women were not involved in politics were created to minimize women's participation in public politics. Women's participation in public arena politics was indeed alien to Kikuyu custom. Colonialism changed women's political roles. This change did not originate in the decade before the State of Emergency was declared but predated Mau Mau by twenty years. Small groups of women became nationalists in the 1930s. Over the next twenty years, they recruited thousands of other women to the nationalists' cause.[4] Women gained recognition from the major nationalist associations, the Kikuyu Central Association (KCA) and the Kenya African Union (KAU) before these organizations were proscribed by the government. Their roles in the Mau Mau rebellion were as multifaceted as the revolt itself. Women had primary responsibility for the organization and maintenance of the supply lines which directed food, supplies, medicine, guns, and information to the forest forces. They also recruited for Mau Mau. They officiated at and participated in oathing ceremonies (Corfield 1960, 84). In 1950 the Kiambu District Commissioner reported to his superiors that men were no longer administering oaths of loyalty to Mau Mau:

> Women, however, were proceeding with the work of oath-giving . . . For a woman to administer a Muma oath would be utterly contrary to Kikuyu custom, although it must be admitted that until the Dedan oaths were started it was also unknown for a woman to have a Muma oath.
>
> (Corfield 1960, 90)

A break with custom in giving and taking oaths was one of the many changes in gender roles nationalism introduced for women. They also joined the forest forces and served as combat troops. They were so important to the movement that the British rounded them up in the military sweeps, aimed at arresting the leaders and the more active Mau Mau adherents who were not in the forests. Their high visibility in the movement is indicated by their mention in colonial records. In 1953 women's activism caused the District Commissioner of Kiambu to pass on this observation to his superiors:

> In September, the Chura location appeared to become a centre of the Mau Mau central committee, and every Itura had its own sub-committee, nor did they lack a women's section. The latter throughout may well be described as the "eyes and ears of Mau Mau."[5]

The 1953 *African Affairs Report* notes:

> The part played by women to aid the terrorists was considerable. They not only fed them but carried food to gangs in the forest, and some were caught dressed as Mau Mau "askari" [soldiers]. The attitude of the women of the tribe towards the Emergency was, in general, particularly distressing . . . the primitive and indigenous cult of Mau Mau has had for many a powerful appeal. There have been instances of female relatives being privy to the murder of their loyal menfolk.[6]

Kikuyu women joined the nationalist associations to improve their economic status, to gain access to the political process, to further their education, and to abet the return of alienated land. Muthoni wa Gachie was a member of KCA and KAU in the 1940s. She recounted women's motives as being political in origin:

Q: When did you join?
A: I joined in April of 1945.
Q: Why did you become a member?
A: So that I could be a politician of the country.
Q: Were there other women who were members?
A: Yes, there was a group of us.
Q: How many?
A: The whole of Central Province.
Q: Were women already members when you joined?
A: Yes, very many were already members.
Q: What did KCA want?
A: We wanted only to make the Europeans to go from the country.
Q: What were your responsibilities as a member?
A: I was cooking for visitors and I contributed for Mzee [Kenyatta] to go to Europe. We were fighting so we would know how to become independent . . .
Q: Were you a leader?
A: Yes, even I was taken to prison. When the war started we thought of some people going to the forest. We were cooking food and taking it to the forest. We were carrying guns, if we would give it to her and she would take it to the forest. We went during the night. During the day the Homeguards came to collect us. We were brought here to dig the ground with our hands. Some were killed. Others were jailed for some years. Then from there the war slowly came to an end.

Q: How long did you spend in jail?

A: In one year I was jailed three times. This was in 1958. Then I was detained in 1959 for one year. I was detained at Athii River, then I was taken to Embu.[7]

Wagara Wainana also described herself as a leader of Mau Mau. Unlike Muthoni wa Gachie, she was able to avoid being placed in detention.

Q: When did you take your first oath?

A: About 1948.

Q: How many did you take?

A: Only two.

Q: Were you a member of the Mau Mau committee?

A: I was a committee member of KAU and of Mau Mau.

Q: Which area did you represent?

A: I represented Karura (Muthurura) Kiambaa.

Q: Was your husband involved in politics?

A: Yes.

Q: How was it that you were not put in prison?

A: I was not detained because my husband was beaten. My co-wife's son was also detained. The co-wife was sick so that there was no one left so that the Europeans left me to care for the sick.

Q: Did they know that you were an active Mau Mau?

A: They knew [there were Mau Mau in the area] but not who the actual person was unless the other Kikuyu told them.

Q: Did you get put into the villagization program?

A: Yes, we built the villages.

Q: Did you carry on the work of Mau Mau from the villages?

A: Yes, we continued after that. We women were taken to a place and forced to do work for nothing. This place was called Kianjogu . . . We did digging and we didn't know the reason we were doing this digging. We dug all around the camp, sweeping and clearing the camp. Then we were taken to another camp. We stayed in Kianjogu for seven months. Then we were taken to a village for four years and then I went to my farm. This was in 1955. We were only fighting and in the end we were helped by God. In the 1930s the women started the Mumbi Central Association and when Kenyatta came back from England he called us all together and organized us. I took food to the Mau Mau. We also took guns. When I was taking food, I was hiding from the Europeans when another one of us saw the police, she started screaming and ran down to the river. I grabbed her by the throat so that we could not be heard. When the soldiers came near, I ran away and the other one was screaming again. Then the other one was caught and put into detention.[8]

Wangui wa Gikuhiu joined KCA when it was first organized. Though an active supporter of Mau Mau, she described herself as "only a member." Women leaders "did the work of talking about how to get the land."[9] Priscilla Wambaki, a leader before Mau Mau and a KANU (Kenya Africa National Union, the ruling party) leader in her division in the independence period, recalled the beginning of women in politics:

Q: Were you a member of a political party?

A: Yes, I was a member of KAU.

Q: Did you belong to KCA?

A: KCA was the one before KAU, but I was only a member of KAU.

Q: Did you ever hear of an organization called Mumbi Central Association?

A: I was a member of Mumbi Central Association. I was also a member of KAU.

Q: When did you join Mumbi Central Association?

A: I can't remember the year but I joined it with Wambu Wangaram and I worked with Rebecca Njeri . . .

Q: What did Mumbi Central Association want to accomplish?

A: Kiama kia Mumbi had the aim to preserve the customs, to not allow them to dissolve. But before we went further the war started . . . First women were not invited to join Kikuyu Central Association. We met together and decided we didn't like this so we asked the pastor of the church to help us. He did and we raised money and started Mumbi Central Association. We would have dances to raise money and the men could not matter. It was only Mbiyu Koinange who was allowed. After a while we joined the men again.

Q: How much money did you raise for Kiriri?[10]

A: I don't know since the books were destroyed, but it was much more than 100 000 shillings.

Q: How many oaths did you take?

A: . . . Only children did not take the oath. I won't talk about that. I want to tell how Mbiyu helped to build the dormitories so that you can understand the role women played when Mzee [Kenyatta] came from Europe. We met with him. We had not completed the dormitories. We had no windows. He helped us, he was on our side. From that time on he was on our side. If there were no women, then the war would not have been carried on. And the women were mostly girls, because if the men were beaten, they would tell the secrets and the girls would not. Even Mzee knew that the girls played a great part and that is why he gave us Madaraka . . .[11]

Women's activism sparked a response from the Government. They were arrested, detained, and interrogated in large numbers. When the Emergency officially ended in 1956, of the 27 841 Kikuyu who were still in the detention camps, 3103 were women (*Daily Chronicle* 7 September 1956). Tables 1 and 2 reveal the number of women imprisoned during the Mau Mau period compared to the total number of Africans detained in the camps. Of the 13 265 females admitted to prison in 1955, 1714 were discharged from prison custody, 11 467 were sentenced to imprisonment (9 961 of these were first offenders, the balance were repeat offenders.[12] Virtually all women imprisoned were suspected of Mau Mau involvement.

Table 2 All Africans admitted to detention camps,
1948–1957

Year	Number
1948	16 369
1949	16 637
1950	18 037
1951	18 257
1952	23 201
1953	32 862
1954	25 979
1955	30 247
1956	41 441
1957	53 080

Source: Kenya Colony and Protectorate, *Annual Report on the Treatment of Offenders*, 1957, 2.

Before the Emergency, there was so little female crime that no particular prison facilities had been built. To the surprise of the colonial government, when Mau Mau activities became pronounced, women's participation was on such a large scale that a facility had to be built to house them. The Kamiti prison was extended to accommodate the upsurge in women prisoners and detainees; the camp included 1335 women prisoners and 1010 women detainees by the end of 1954.[13] Women were also detained in other facilities. The Athii River detention camp which was built in 1953 to contain violaters of the Emergency Regulations had ten compounds containing 1429 detainees. One of the compounds was reserved for twenty-seven female detainees.[14] Most women prisoners were sentenced for violations of the Emergency regulations.[15] A large proportion of the women sentenced were first time offenders. Sentences ranged from short terms of one or two months to the full duration of the Emergency, with a majority sentenced to terms of six months or less – twenty percent (1952) and twenty-seven percent (1953) were sentenced to six months to two years. As Mau Mau became more threatening, the length of sentences increased.

The camps were not merely holding facilities. Prisoners were required to work and also to go through a re-socialization process whose goal was to get them to renounce Mau Mau and be "cleansed."[16] The Community Development organization was involved in rehabilitating prisoners.[17] At Kamiti, the Department was given some control over the detainees' "leisure time."[18] Nearly three hundred female detainees attended classes. They received instruction in animal husbandry, hygiene, health, agriculture, and local government.[19] However, these classes were not the most important aspect of the organization's work in the struggle to defeat Mau Mau. The Department also ran child-care facilities.[20]

Most of the apparent success the Government achieved in converting Mau Mau detainees in 1955 and 1956 was among female prisoners in Kamiti prison. Several facilities for women were maintained around the colony, but Kamiti was for the "hard-core" Mau Mau women.[21] The number of women released from the Kamiti facility in

1956 was 1194 leaving 1384 women in the camp. In 1957 4 220 women were released and 174 remained in detention. Many "hardcore" women were not released until 1960. The rehabilitation efforts among women were so "successful" that by 1957 Mau Mau women detainees were:

> . . . processed straight to their homes on release and have not passed through the pipe line camps in their own areas as is the case with men. This is a tribute to the thorough and successful rehabilitation work undertaken at the camps.[22]

Community Development officers were aided in their work of detaching women from Mau Mau by the missionaries. The Christian Council of Kenya sent representatives to the camps to hold Christian services and "cleanse" women prisoners of their radical beliefs.[23] The Department categorized prisoners according to the strength of their attachment to Mau Mau and response to rehabilitation. The "Y" category were those who were responding to re-socialization.[24] Kamiti women prisoners were considered to be in the "Y" category of rebels. Confession was stressed. When word circulated that those who confessed could gain an early release, the number of penitents rapidly soared (Wipper 1977, 255).

Conditions in the prisons

Former women prisoners at Kamiti described conditions of terror, physical punishment, and forced labor. They received inadequate food and clothing. Conditions for women Mau Mau and/or Mau Mau suspects were similar to those for males who were arrested and detained. Interviews with former Mau Mau female prisoners reveal a prison system which meted out harsh treatment.[25] Women in Kamiti were required to work for the prison system.[26] Light work of raising vegetables and fruit was given as a reward for co-operating with the rehabilitation program, another impetus to confess. This co-operation usually took the form of taking a pledge renouncing Mau Mau and giving information about Mau Mau activity in the prisons and elsewhere. The more intransigent were required to work on road-building and quarrying stone. The prison commandant reported in 1955 that 199 000 running feet of stone was quarried by Kamiti prisoners.[27] Once the stones were quarried and dressed, women prisoners transported them on their heads. In 1954 women helped to terrace the thirty-five acre prison farm. The value of the labor extracted from these women through the cultivation of the 197 305 pounds of vegetables they raised in 1956 was £1973.[28] Other forms of punishment included solitary confinement, the withholding of food, and corporal punishment.[29] Harsh and inhuman treatment was the rule in the prisons and detention camps according to former Mau Mau prisoners. The following is from an interview with one of them, Priscilla Wambaki:

Q: Were you detained?
A: Yes.
Q: Where were you taken?
A: I was taken to Kajado in Maasailand.

Q: When was this?

A: It was in 1952. That was the time when Mzee [Kenyatta] was detained with Rebecca Njeri . . . [Njeri was the most prominent woman nationalist, detained at the same time as Kenyatta]. I was in detention for one year then I was taken to the Athii River [camp] . . . At Kajado only the women leaders were detained. Men were there also but the women were kept separate. We were not forced to work but kept locked in our rooms. There we were beaten but not too much. But when we were taken to the Athii River, we were beaten very much. All of the members of KAU, men and women were detained. Women were not many at Athii River, we were about two hundred, but the men were uncountable. Those who were involved in politics or any other movement but not the church were taken to Kamiti. This was in 1954, and only women were there. We were beaten and very many died. During that time people were hanged in great numbers and we buried many there. We were not afraid of the corpses, even if we were doing this job we were still beaten. We could see some corpses with the blood from the beating still on them. During the time of getting food in the prison the young girls would pull the carts, they were tied three by three to the carts in order to pull them to where they were to get the food and then they had to pull the carts back to Kamiti. Even now, I remember what was done when I see a young girl like you . . . We would leave the prison to dig the terraces. We took breakfast at 5:00 a.m. We had *uji* [boiled ground maize meal]; the girls would bring it from two miles away; then we took the *jembes* [hoes] and basins to dig the terraces; we were only women . . . We got *ugali* [boiled ground maize meal] with boiled beans or boiled cabbage. We worked up to three then we took supper at four. After that we were locked in the house and one could go to wash. We were fed *ugali*, and it was not well cooked. If there were no beans or cabbage, we got only one boiled potato with the *ugali*.

Q: Was there any meat, eggs, milk or tea?

A: No! Even the children couldn't get these things. I am disappointed to hear that many people believe that women did nothing in the war; we buried the bodies. The children of Kamiti were tied with ropes together to be guarded while we women worked. They gradually died off. It was due to hunger. We suffered a lot from hunger . . . Kamiti was a hell prison. Some were dying, some were beaten to death, sometimes they died after work. We were happy when someone died because we said "Now she is free!" I was still in Kamiti in 1956.[30]

Muthoni wa Gachie was detained in 1959. Her experiences were consistent with those recounted by other respondents. She talked of torture inflicted by the Homeguards

Q: Were you a leader?

A: Yes, even I was taken to prison . . . When we were in detention the work was only to be beaten, given hard work and not enough food. We spent one week digging trees with other women.

Q: Why were you detained?

A: Because I was speaking about the Government.

Q: What did you say?

A: I was saying that Europeans should be taken to their homes and our children should be given education.

Q: How did the European know about you?

A: Other people reported me.

Q: Were you married then?

A: Yes.

Q: Did your children go to detention with you?

A: No, they were not in detention with me but they suffered because they lacked food, clothing and education.

Q: Was your husband involved?

A: He was also jailed but not put into detention.

Q: Who took care of the children while you were in jail and detention?

A: Only God. Our homes were burnt, cattle were taken, we were left with no clothing and wore banana leaves. Even that women gave birth on the way. We had nothing to help the child. We removed the headscarf to carry the child. Bottles were put in our private parts as a punishment.

Q: Where were you detained that they did these things?

A: Just here at Githunguri. The Homeguards were doing this.

Q: Were they doing this to make you admit Mau Mau?

A: They were doing this so that the Europeans could give them something.[31]

The fact that women were a significant portion of the prison population and that they were not accorded any special treatment because of gender is little known and rarely mentioned in the historiography of Mau Mau, although these facts were not hidden from public view during the Emergency. Indeed, the treatment of women prisoners caused a minor scandal in 1956 in Kenya and England. Eileen Fletcher, a former member of the Kamiti Prison staff, revealed the poor conditions and abuse by officials at Kamiti in her testimony before members of the House of Commons in London and in statements and interviews with the British press. She recounted that under-age girls were wrongfully detained. In the course of several House of Commons debates on the subject, an official inquiry into the prison system was initiated [Presley 1986, 256–264; *Tribune* [London] 16 November 1956; *Daily Chronicle* [Nairobi] 31 May and 7 September 1956]. After the inquiry, annual reports on the conditions in the prisons included detailed information on the treatment of prisoners and the punishment or dismissal of wardens and staff for their mistreatment of prisoners.

Greater administrative attention to reporting on prison conditions was not enough, however, to ensure the end of abuse. The scandal involving the murder of eleven male detainees at the Hola Camp in 1959 finally brought an end to the detention system and the "pipeline" process of gradually releasing detainees from high to ever lower security facilities until finally they were released to their home villages.[32]

The impact of social policy on women's nationalism

When the remaining women detainees were released and returned to their villages in 1960, they discovered that the Government had radically altered village life as a part of its war against Mau Mau. The campaign against women was a major part of this. This change was achieved through the villagization program. Initially begun as a punitive measure, the project became a centerpiece of social policy.[33] The turning point in defeating Mau Mau on the home front was achieved when activists or those suspected of being activists were rounded up. The entire Kikuyu population was semi-imprisoned in guarded villages. The importance of the villagization program in the defeat of Mau Mau was recognized in official circles. Addressing the Legislative Assembly in 1955, the Governor, Sir Evelyn Baring stated:

> . . . it has been possible in many areas to arrange a system of movement control by which villagers going to work on their *shambas* [farms], or herding their cattle, do so under escort from either the Tribal Police or the Watch and Ward Units. It is the establishment of this system which in many areas has broken the physical contact with the gangs. The individual gangsters must often have hidden in a hole in a sisal hedge and have slipped out for a few minutes to tell a woman working in her field that food must be left at a certain place at a certain time or else there would be trouble. In this way the fear of the terrorist was maintained. Now, there can be no absolute certainty, but it appears probable that the new system has in most areas broken that physical contact and dissipated that fear . . . As a result too, the flow of information from the villagers has greatly improved.[34]

The breaking of contact between villagers and Mau Mau fighters meant that women who were not imprisoned during the Emergency had their own intensive encounters with the regime. The object of these encounters was, of course, to defuse nationalism and curtail their Mau Mau activities. Just as in the prisons and detention camps, the main plank of the policy was the withholding and granting of benefits to sway the non-combatant wing away from radical nationalism. One of the consequences of being identified as Mau Mau was loss of land. The Government confiscated the land of Mau Mau members and reallocated it to "deserving Loyalists." The instrument for this policy was the Community Development Department. It was thought to have the potential for creating a true social revolution in the villages, its major goal being:

> . . . to teach the women in the new villages a new way of life and to show them that the possibilities of community life in a smaller area offer better opportunities for improved homes than the old scattered villages – as indeed they do.[35]

The relocation scheme was begun in 1954 and began to be phased out in 1958.[36] It involved the forced relocation of the entire Kikuyu population of the three Kikuyu districts in Central Province. More than eighty thousand Kikuyu households were uprooted in Kiambu District in 1954 and 1955. Also, more than seventeen thousand squatters who were ejected from the Rift Valley by settler farmers joined the Kikuyu who were required to live in the new villages.[37] For Kiambu District, the focus of my research, this involved over 300 000 men, women, and children. They were compelled to build new villages and tear down or abandon their homesteads. They lived under guard behind barbed-wire fences. To farm, women were escorted to their fields by the Homeguard. Everyone had to be back behind the barbed-wire fences by the 4:00 p.m. curfew.[38] In 1955 threats of the confiscation of land and the imposition of a twenty-four hour curfew were used in Kiambu District to break the "passive wing."

Abuse of villagers under the authority of the Homeguard was reported. Milka Ngina who spent the Emergency in the guarded villages recalled:

> A: We were beaten and forced to dig the terraces. They beat us very much and it was the Homeguard who did the beating.
> Q: Did you take the oath?
> A: Yes, I took very many, and we were beaten when we took the oath.
> Q: Were you put into detention?
> A: Some women were detained but not all of them.
> Q: Did Kenya become independent because of Mau Mau?
> A: Yes, because they bought the freedom with blood.
> Q: Did others in your family take the oath?
> A: All the Kikuyu took the oath at that time.
> Q: Was there any fighting around your home?
> A: Yes.
> Q: What happened?
> A: We were beaten by the Homeguard because the Mau Mau passed through our homes. I myself was almost beaten to death.
> Q: Why did the Homeguard help the British?
> A: We were beaten by the Homeguard because the Mau Mau were not on good terms with the Homeguard and those who were giving food were on good terms with the Mau Mau.[39]

Catherine Wajiru, who lived in Embu during the Emergency, was also exposed to the civil war between Mau Mau supporters and the Loyalists [Kikuyu seen as loyal to the colonial regime].

> Q: Did you help the freedom fighters?
> A: Yes.
> Q: How did you help?
> A: I gave them cooked food.
> Q: Does that mean that there were freedom fighters in Embu?
> A: Yes, they were there because they were living in the forest near us.
> Q: Were you happy to give them food?
> A: We gave them food because we had no security and if we refused to give them food, they could beat us.
> Q: Were you living near Embu people?
> A: Yes, we were mixed. We built the homes in the same place and we worked on the *shambas* with other groups.

Q: Did the Embu give food?

A: Yes, they did. They stopped giving them food when the villages were built but before that the Mau Mau would take goats and even cows by force. Also we were beaten by the colonials if they found that we were giving food. There were spies called Homeguard who would tell when you helped.

Q: Were you beaten?

A: Yes, I was beaten very much and my husband died during that time because of the beating.[40]

Villagization was successful in demoralizing the non-combatant wing. The African Affairs Department recorded:

> The withdrawal of the surrender terms on 10 July was combined with local propaganda, so that at the end of June and the beginning of July the volume of confession swelled to such a degree that the teams were unable to cope. A very great deal of Mau Mau funds was handed in as well as guns and ammunition. The threat of confiscation of land, together with the imposition of 24-hour curfews also had a considerable effect in breaking the last efforts of the *Mau Mau* to conceal information. The confession teams in the settled areas . . . had an extremely difficult job to begin with . . . they subsequently achieved remarkable and effective results in breaking the passive wings on the farms and discovering the main gang bases or food depots.[41]

The major point of contact under these semi-concentration camp conditions was through the Community Development Department. Initially, most of the Department's annual budget of 250 000 pounds was spent on the work of rehabilitation.[42] The Department focused on women:

> In view of the large numbers of women and children to be found in these villages whose husbands are either serving sentences, detained, working in the home guard, operating in the forests or living in the towns, the accent of rehabilitation must be on women.[43]

The Department's major vehicle for influencing women was through the Maendeleo ya Wanawake (Progress among Women) clubs. The clubs had begun in the late 1940s but did not have a significant membership until the Emergency. Membership in the organization expanded tremendously during the Emergency years since it could be the crucial difference between survival and starvation under the villagization program. The work of the clubs included running day nurseries, making and supervising the distribution of soup, distributing milk to hungry children, and "caring for children whose parents were missing or dead."[44]

These humanitarian efforts were affected by the Emergency since the "Work of Maendeleo clubs [was] hampered by subversive propaganda and additional communal work necessary in the rehabilitation of and fortifying villages." The clubs were only able to meet after the four o'clock curfew.[45] The Department measured its success through

Table 3 Maendeleo ya Wanawake clubs

District	Clubs	Members
Army Camps	8	400
Kiambu	45	5 050
Fort Hall	35	3 250
Nyeri	100	7 500
Embu	25	1 250
Meru	1	20
Settled Areas	10	300
Naivasha	1	45
Thompson's Falls	1	85
Nairobi	5	400
Machakos	94	10 000
Other Districts	183	8 510
Total	508	36 810

Source: Kenya Colony and Protectorate, Community Development Department, AR/1954, 13.

the increase in membership. In 1954 the membership totalled 36 810 in 508 clubs (see Table 3). Kiambu women joined forty-five of the clubs with a membership of 5050.[46] Forty-five percent of the members came from the three Kikuyu districts of Kiambi, Fort Hall and Nyeri, and Nairobi where Mau Mau activities were greatest.

In addition to administering to the needy, the Community Development programs were "responsible for internal broadcasting, libraries, the distribution of papers, classes, *barazas* [public gatherings], recreation and instruction in various forms."[47] The purpose of the education component of the program was to counteract Mau Mau by providing a course of "general knowledge."[48] Typically, this included bringing books, pamphlets, and a film truck to villages. This information stressed the positive benefits of colonialism and the evils of Mau Mau.[49] The Government viewed the clubs as "an effective instrument against subversive elements."[50]

In the guarded villages, the clubs were used to aid the security forces. Club members gathered information about Mau Mau activities and tried to persuade Mau Mau adherents to abandon the movement.[51] Women were told that they had to become allied with the Government rather than with Mau Mau. If they chose to remain publicly sympathetic to Mau Mau, they lost access to the services which the clubs offered.[52]

> In most areas where the backbone of Maendeleo clubs had been in existence since 1951–53, the club members have in many cases been of value to the Security forces giving information freely and persuading others to give up *Mau Mau*. In at least one case they played an important part in the capture of a *Mau Mau* general. The women realized that the ideals of *Maendeleo* and *Mau Mau* were incompatible and they would have to choose between them. It is very encouraging to note that the numbers of clubs and members in these areas are on the increase as more and more realize that *Mau Mau* has brought nothing but distress and sorrow.[53]

This persuasive message resulted in a tremendous growth in membership. By 1955 the number of clubs increased to 596 with a membership of 43 000.[54] The benefits of belonging or simply being associated with the clubs were particularly crucial in 1955 and 1956 when famine struck Kiambu District.[55] A scarcity of food was induced by the curfew, for women had fewer hours available to them in which to fetch water and fuel and to cultivate their fields. During the famine, the 107 clubs in Kiambu District operated soup kitchens and increased their milk allotments.[56] In 1956 there were 34 500 fully paid members, in addition to 11 500 women who benefited from the club services but were unable to pay the membership fees.[57] By the end of 1957, the number of clubs had grown to 986, but fully paid membership had declined to 33613.[58]

One of the goals of the Community Development Department was to train Africans to be good citizens according to British standards. A byproduct of this was women's representation on the village and district councils. By 1955 "Maendeleo members [were] coming forward to take their place on locational and District Councils in greater numbers, so that in future there is hope that the voice of the women will be heard more and more."[59]

Conclusion

Viewing Mau Mau from the female perspective adds several important aspects to the understanding of the rebellion. It illuminates an often repeated statement that landless and less affluent Kikuyu were more likely to take part in Mau Mau whereas the better off Kikuyu publicly took sides with the British and joined the loyalist forces as Homeguards. In some families, women were deeply involved in Mau Mau while males publicly disassociated themselves from it. There are two possible explanations for this phenomenon. First, women's involvement with Mau Mau cut across "class" lines. Wives of prominent Kikuyu were jailed. At least one woman organizer was the wife of a chief. Second, women's involvement in radical nationalism expresses the ambiguity of prominent families' identification with Mau Mau. Males of such families might have silently supported Mau Mau while maintaining a public face as Loyalists. If men openly supported the rebellion, the consequence was loss of more land and privileges. This may have led to a perception that it was marginally safer for women to carry out the family's commitment to Mau Mau. The entire family need not then be impoverished by supporting it. A nationalist female, if arrested and detained, could be easily discredited and disowned. Whether this was deliberate family policy among a number of families is of course unknown. It may, however, explain some of the curious features of Mau Mau reported by the Government and uncovered in oral interviews. Specifically, it may explain the Government's contention that women were more rabid and fanatical, that men had stopped giving oaths, and that women were assuming these responsibilities. It may also explain the Government assertion that women of loyalist families were involved with Mau Mau. Mau Mau women reported to the author that their husbands, though considered loyal to the Government, knew of the aid they gave to the Mau Mau rebels and did not report them.

Women's participation in the violent Mau Mau revolt focused Government attention on the need to use some of its resources to develop programs to serve women and their needs. In order to defeat Mau Mau militarily, it was crucial for the British to isolate the guerilla fighters from their supplies. Mere isolation, however, was not sufficient. The non-combatant force, led and organized to a large degree by women, had to be engaged with force and persuasion. Thus, women were jailed in increasing numbers from 1954 to 1957. The increase occurred at the same time that the British victory over Mau Mau was assured. It is my contention that this was not mere coincidence, but that success in the war against women was a necessary ingredient in the war against Mau Mau. The campaign of propaganda and education was designed to convince women not already Mau Mau activists that disassociation from Mau Mau held positive rewards. First, the entire Kikuyu population was relocated to villages which were closely supervised by the Security Forces, the Homeguard, and the new Community Development Department. Within three years of this policy, a drop in Mau Mau activities occurred. The British government started a social revolution by providing an extensive social services program. Women were the first to be experimented upon since the Government recognized that they had to be detached from Mau Mau for final victory to occur. This had consequences for post-Mau Mau Kenya. The creation of the Community Development Department was the precursor of the Community Development Program in independent Kenya and, much later, the Women's Bureau. The contemporary Maendeleo ya Wanawake clubs also owe their origin to women's vigorous nationalism during Mau Mau. In the 1980s the Maendeleo clubs number over six thousand. Maendeleo is Kenya's largest women's organization (Ndumbu 1985, 86; Wipper 1975; Wipper 1975–76).

One reason for the lack of research on women's nationalism is that scholars followed the line taken by the colonial government. Until thousands of women were imprisoned for Mau Mau offenses, colonial administrators dismissed incidents which indicated that women were actively involved in resisting colonialism. In the case of labor stoppages and protests against terracing, district officers maintained that women's activism was caused by male agitators. Therefore, psychologically, the administrators were unprepared for women's protest. It seemed to them to be sudden, fanatical and unexpected.

Historians of Mau Mau have also treated women's nationalism as incidental to the main currents of nationalism. Their sources of data for the study of Mau Mau have been almost exclusively male, whether they were Europeans or Africans. The use of this data source and perspective has created the false paradigm that politics was mainly a male concern. Consequently, the questions posed to male respondents and the official records focus on the actions of men. When men did comment on women's involvement, it did not seem to be a major thread of the rebellion. In searching for answers to a political dilemma, scholars have naturally looked to those departments which had responsibility for political and economic issues. The full story of the colonial battle against women's nationalism is not revealed by political records, though important indicators occur there. In the social services area, even more revealing data surface. Since the colonial officials were trapped in their 1950s perceptions of women, they relegated policies dealing with women to community development. As the Community Development report noted, the voice of women began to be heard during the Mau Mau rebellion, although women had spoken out through their protest, be it on economic, political, or social issues, for over twenty years in colonial Kenya. When they took up arms and supported violent rebellion, their voices began to be heard. The legacy for contemporary Kenyans is to acknowledge women as equal partners in politics.

Notes

1   See Rosberg and Nottingham 1966; Tignor 1976; Kilson 1955; Buijenhuis 1973, 1982; Kanogo 1987; Barnett and Njama 1966; Clayton and Savage 1974; Furedi 1974, 1975; Tamarkin 1976, 1978; Coray 1978; Newsinger 1981; Stichter 1975; Leakey 1952, 1954; Majdalany 1963; Ogot 1972; Sorrenson 1967.

2   Kenya National Archives [KNA], Native Affairs Department (NAD), *Annual Report (AR) 1953*, 25; Kenya Colony and Protectorate (KCP), Community Development Department (CDD), *AR 1956*, 4.

3   KNA. *Political Record Book, Kiambu District 1912*, KBU/109/Part II(K), 10; KNA. *Political Record Book, Kiambu District 1908–1912*, KBU/76, 85–87.

4   Interviews with former women nationalists conducted in 1978. The main women who described the organization of the women's network are: Wambui Wagarama, Nduta wa Kore, Phillis Wanjiko (Margo) wa Mimi, Priscilla Wambaki and Mary Wanjiko. See Presley 1986, 222–227.

5   KNA. *Political Record Book, Kiambu District 1953*, KBU/44, 1.

6   KNA. AAD. CP. *AR 1953*, 27.

7   Interview on 10 January 1979 in Githunguiri, Kiambu District.

8   Interview on 29 April 1978 in Kiambu.

9   Interview on 13 May 1979 in Ruiru, Kiambu.

10 Kiriri was the women's dormitory at the Githunguri Independent School which was established by nationalists after the break with church and government controlled education which resulted from the circumcision controversy.

11 Interview on 23 May 1979 in Juja, Kiambu. Madaraka Day marks the granting of internal self-government in 1963, about half a year before independence.

12 KCP. *Treatment of Offenders Annual Report 1957*, 10.

13 KCP. "Report on the General Administration of Prisons and Detention Camps in Kenya," by G. H. Heaton 1953, 3; KCP. *Report on the Treatment of Offenders for the year 1953*, 4; KCP. *Report on the Treatment of Offenders for the year 1954*, 4.

14 KCP. *Report on the Treatment of Offenders for the year 1953*, 16–17.

15 KCP. *Treatment of Offenders Annual Report 1956*, 8–9.

16 KCP. CDD. *AR 1954*, 21–24; KCP. CDD. *AR 1955*, 22–26.

17 KCP. *Treatment of Offenders Annual Report 1955*, 2.

18 Ibid.

19 KCP. *Treatment of Offenders Annual Report 1956*, 2.

20 KCP. CDD. *AR 1956*, 6.

21 KCP. CDD. *AR 1954*, 30.

22 KCP. CDD. *AR 1956*, 4.

23 KCP. CDD. *AR 1955*, 22–23.

24 There were four categories: (1) Z1 – Mau Mau leaders who refused to respond to the rehabilitation program; (2) Z2 – rank and file who refused to renounce Mau Mau; (3) Y – those who responded to rehabilitation; and (4) X – those who were rehabilitated and placed on parole. See KCP. CDD. *AR 1956*, 3–6.

25 Oral interviews: Tabitha Mumbi, Thika, 24 May 1979; Elizabeth Gachika, Kianibu Town, 7 January 1979; Nduta wa Kore, Tingang'a, 13 January 1979; Wambui Wangarama, Kabete, 29 April 1979. See Presley 1986c for extensive oral interviews with Mau Mau women.

26 KCP. *Report on the Treatment of Offenders for the year 1953*, 4–5; KCP. *Treatment of Offenders Annual Report 1955*, 16, 18.

27   KCP. *Treatment of Offenders Annual Report 1955*, 15.

28   KCP. *Treatment of Offenders Annual Report 1956*, 14.

29   KCP. *Report on the Treatment of Offenders, Kenya Prisons for the year 1954*, 11.

30   Interview 23 May 1979 at Juja, Kiambu.

31   Interview 10 January, 1979, Githunguri, Kiambu.

32   KNA. *Records of Proceedings and Evidence into the Deaths of Eleven Mau Mau Detainees at Hola Camp in Kenya*, 1959; Rosberg and Nottingham 1966, 335–344.

33   KCP. AAD. CP. *AR 1954*, 33.

34   KCP. *Legislative Council Debates* 18 October 1955, 4.

35   KCP. CDD. *AR 1954*, 31.

36   KCP. CDD. *AR 1958*, 7.

37   KCP. AAD. CP. *AR 1955*, 35, 51.

38   KNA. CDD. *AR 1957*, 33; KNA. AAD. *AR 1954*, 33.

39   Interview 11 May, 1979, Kiambu town.

40   Interview with Catherine Wajiru, Kitambaya, Kiambu, 11 May 1979.

41   KCP. AAD. *AR 1955*, 37.

42   KCP. CDD. *AR 1955*, 1.

43   KCP. CDD. *AR 1954*, 31.

44   KCP. CDD. *AR 1955*, 7.

45   Ibid.

46   KCP. CDD. *AR 1954*, 13.

47   KCP. CDD. *AR 1955*, 25.

48   Ibid.

49   KCP. CDD. *AR 1952*, 9; KCP. CDD. *AR 1956*, 1–10.

50   KCP. CDD. *AR 1954*, 12–13.

51   KCP. CDD. *AR 1955*, 7. These activities caused the Maendeleo movement to be severely stigmatized among the Kikuyu in the early period of independence. (See Wipper 1975–76, 199–204.)

52   KCP. CDD. *AR 1955*, 7.

53   Ibid.

54   KCP. CDD. *AR 1955*, 12.

55   KCP. AAD. CP. *AR 1955*, 48.

56   KCP. CDD. *AR 1956*, 13–14.

57   KCP. CDD. *AR 1956*, 10.

58   KCP. CDD. *AR 1957*, 8.

59   KCP. CDD. *AR 1955*, 6.

Bibliography

Barnett, Donald and K. Njama. 1966. *Mau Mau From Within: Autobiography and Analysis of Kenya's Peasant Revolt*. New York and London: Monthly Review Press.

Buijenthuis, Robert. 1973. *Mau Mau Twenty Years After: The Myth of the Survivors*. The Hague/Paris: Mouton.

—— 1982. *Essays on Mau Mau: Contributions to Mau Mau Historiography*. Leiden: African Studies Centre No. 17.

Clayton, Anthony. 1976. *Counter-Insurgency in Kenya, 1952–60*. Nairobi: TransAfrica Publishers.

Clayton, Anthony and Donald Savage. 1974. *Government and Labour in Kenya, 1895–1963*. London: Frank Cass.

Coray, Michael. 1978. "The Kenya Land Commission and the Kikuyu of Kiambu." *Agricultural History* 52, no. 1: 179–193.

Corfield, F. D. 1960. *Historical Survey of the Origins and Growth of Mau Mau*. London: HMSO (Cmnd 1030).

Furedi, Frank. 1974. "The Social Composition of the Mau Mau Movement in the White Highlands." *Journal of Peasant Studies* I, no. 4: 486–505.

—— 1975. "The Kikuyu Squatters in the Rift Valley, 1918–1929." *Hadith* 5: 177–194.

Furley, Q. W. 1972. "The Historiography of Mau Mau." *Hadith* 4: 105–133.

Great Britain. 1954. *Colonial Office Report on the Colony and Protectorate of Kenya*. London: HMSO.

Kamunchulah, J. T. 1975. "The Meru Participation in Mau Mau." *Kenya Historical Review* 3, no. 2: 193–216.

Kanogo, Tabitha. 1987. *Squatters and the Roots of Mau-Mau 1905–1963*. Columbus: Ohio University Press.

Kilson, Martin. 1955. "Land and the Kikuyu: A Study of the Relationship Between Land and Kikuyu Political Movements." *Journal of Negro History* 40: 103–153.

Leakey, L. S. B. 1952. *Mau Mau and the Kikuyu*. London: Methuen & Company.

—— 1954. *Defeating Mau Mau*. London: Methuen and Company.

Majdalany, F. 1963. *State of Emergency: The Full Story of Mau Mau*. Boston: Houghton Mifflin Company.

Mungai, Evelyn and Joy Awori. 1983. *Kenya Women Reflections*. Nairobi: Lear Publishing Co.

Murray, Jocelyn. 1974. "The Kikuyu Female Circumcision Controversy with Special Reference to the Church Missionary Society's 'Sphere of Influence.' " Ph.D thesis, University of California, Los Angeles.

Ndumbu, Abel. 1985. *Out of My Rib: A View of Women in Development*. Nairobi: Development Horizons.

Newsinger, John. 1981. "Revolt and Repression in Kenya: The 'Mau Mau' Rebellion, 1952–1960." *Science and Society* 45, no. 2: 159–185.

Ogot, B. A. 1972. *Politics and Nationalism in Colonial Kenya*. Nairobi: East African Publishing House.

Presley, Cora. 1986a. "The Transformation of Kikuyu Women and their Nationalism." Ph.D. thesis, Stanford University, Stanford, California.

—— 1986b. "Labor Protest Among Kikuyu Women, 1912–1947." In *Women, Race and Class in Africa*, edited by Claire Robertson and Iris Berger. New York: Holmes and Meier Press.

—— 1986c. "Women in the Mau Mau Rebellion." In *In Resistance: Studies in African, Afro-American and Caribbean Resistance*, edited by Gary Okihiro. Amherst: University of Massachusetts Press.

Rosberg, Carl and John Nottingham. 1966. *The Myth of Mau Mau: Nationalism in Kenya*. New York Washington: Frederick A. Praeger.

Sorrenson, M. P. K. 1967. *Land Reform in the Kikuyu Country*. London: Oxford University Press.

Spencer, John. 1974. "The Kikuyu Central Association and the Genesis of Kenya African Union." *Kenya Historical Review* 2, no. 1: 67–79.

—— 1985. *The Kenya African Union*. London: KPI Limited.

Stichter, Sharon. 1975. "Workers, Trade Unions and the Mau Mau Rebellion." *Canadian Journal of African Studies* 9, no. 2: 259–275.

Tamarkin, M. 1976. "Mau Mau in Nakuru." *Journal of African History* 17, no. 1: 119–134.

—— 1978. "Loyalists in Nakuru During the Mau Mau Revolt and its Aftermath." *Asian and African Studies* 12, no. 2: 247–261.

Temu, A. J. 1972. *British Protestant Missions*. London: Longman Group.

Tignor, Robert. 1976. *The Colonial Transformation of Kenya: The Kamba, Kikuyu and Maasai from 1900 to 1939*. Princeton: Princeton University Press.

Wipper, Audrey. 1975. "The Maendeleo ya Wanawake Organization – The Co-optation of Leadership." *African Studies Review* 18, no. 3: 329–355.

—— 1975–76. "The Maendeleo ya Wanawake Movement in the Colonial Period: The Canadian Connection, Mau Mau, Embroidery and Agriculture." *Rural Africana*: 195–214.

—— 1989. "Kikuyu Women and the Harry Thuku Disturbances: Some Uniformities of Female Militancy." *Africa 59*, no. 3: 300–337.

Chapter 16

Joseph S. Alter

CELIBACY, SEXUALITY, AND THE TRANSFORMATION OF GENDER INTO NATIONALISM IN NORTH INDIA

IT IS WELL KNOWN THAT Mahatma Gandhi felt that sexuality and desire were intimately connected to social life and politics, and that self-control translated directly into power of various kinds, both public and private. Gandhi's enigmatic genius and his popular appeal among India's masses may be attributed, at least in part, to the degree he was able to embody a powerful ideal of sexual self-control that linked his sociopolitical projects to pervasive Hindu notions of renunciation (S. Rudolph 1967). Affecting the persona of a world-renouncer, Gandhi was able to mix political, religious, and moral power, thus translating personal self-control into radical social criticism and nationalist goals. Gandhi's mass appeal was partly effected on a visceral level at which many Hindu men were able to fully appreciate the logic of celibacy as a means to psychological security, self-improvement, and national reform. Although my concern in this paper is not directly with Gandhi's notion of self-control, it is against the larger backdrop of his political legacy that I situate this discussion of sexuality, gender, and nationalism in contemporary India.

My specific purpose is to analyse the Hindu concept of *brahmacharya* (celibacy) as it relates to questions of gender and politics. I will show that a male concern with celibacy is couched in terms of a discourse about truth, and that truth translates directly into the moral politics of nationalism. At the outset, I must point out that the nationalism that emerges out of this discourse is of an oblique and somewhat utopian sort. In other words, it is not formalized or institutionalized in any sense, but takes shape culturally, I would argue, on two primary levels, that of rhetoric on the one hand, and the body on the other. Rhetoric and the body come together in terms of health, for the celibate body is regarded as supremely fit, and as such evokes a divine and heroic mystique of epic proportions. What emerges is a kind of medical poetics in which the male body is sexually analysed, systematically diagnosed and, finally, as rhetoric and theory are put into practice, disciplined according to a rigorous regimen. This regimen is thought to produce a citizen who embodies the essence of national integrity and strength.

There is not a great deal in the standard literature on nationalism to help make sense of this process. For the most part, contemporary writers such as Dumont (1986), Hobsbawm (1990), Smith (1983) and Gellner (1983) focus on the overtly political, institutionalized forms of nationalism wherein the primary issues are ethnic, religious, or linguistic ideologies. Benedict Anderson, whose analysis of nationalistic "imagined communities" is less formal and more open to the dynamics of power/ knowledge and cultural transformation, is still primarily concerned with questions of language and the history of ideas, even when those ideas concern the political implications of such somatic signs as the color of a person's skin (Anderson 1983: 129–47).

A small but significant literature is being developed on the relationship between explicitly somatic problems and nationalist sentiments (cf. Martin 1990; Mosse 1985). Much of this work emerges from the intersection of feminist scholarship and critical studies of colonialism (cf. Alloula 1987; Ballhatchet 1980; Callaway 1987; Etienne and Leacock 1980; Hyam 1990; Stoler 1989; Cooper and Stoler 1989; Strobel 1987). British imperialism in India seems to have provided particularly fertile ground for the study of sexual politics, and some innovative recent work has been done on the place of female bodies in the nationalist projects of the late nineteenth and early twentieth centuries (cf. Chakravarti 1990; Chatterjee 1986, 1989, 1990; Sangari and Vaid 1990; Tharu 1990; Mani 1987). Discussions of male bodies in this context are, unfortunately, more difficult to find (cf. Alter 1992, 1994; Rosselli 1980). However, my own research in North India clearly shows that physical fitness and nationalism are dramatically embodied in the heroically masculine physique of the Indian wrestler (pahalwan), and that this masculine physique took shape as a form of colonial and postcolonial critique (Alter 1993).

Along these lines, Partha Chatterjee's general formulations about gendered nationalism are of particular relevance. He argues that Indian nationalists in the mid- to late nineteenth century made a distinction between a material sphere of power, regarded as exterior to the individual, where the British were superior, and a spiritual sphere of moral value where "traditional" Hindu beliefs, located within the individual, were regarded as superior to, and somewhat immune from, the Western culture of imperialism (Chatterjee 1989: 624). He concludes that the notion of an inner purity of tradition—imputed by colonized men onto the bodies of colonized women—was the product of an alien discourse of power that classified certain aspects of Hindu culture as inherently private and apolitical (p. 631), thus producing what he calls "the new patriarchy" of modern liberalism (p. 627).

While I agree in general with the distinctions Chatterjee makes, I think his use of the term "spiritual" is somewhat misleading since it evokes notions of mystical devotion and secret knowledge about mysterious truths. Clearly, Hindu notions of somaticity— both in terms of ritual, health, and social hierarchy—fall within the domain of what Chatterjee refers to as the spiritual discourse of nationalism, and yet bodies are concrete material objects. While certain aspects of Hindu physicality may, indeed, be construed as "inner" and therefore outside the purview of imperial power, in other ways the material body is a naked object upon which the forces of imperial power directly impinge. As distinct from ideologies about the body, physiological issues of gender, health, and hygiene tend to blur the important distinctions that Chatterjee argues the early nationalists were trying to make. The literature on brahmacharya clearly illustrates the extent to which, in the late twentieth century at least, the "spiritual" male body became a focal site for a discourse of nationalism.

Celibacy, semen, and the science of sex

Many scholars have noted that *brahmacharya* is a concept with social, psychological, medical and religious significance in Hindu society (Carstairs 1958; Kakar 1981, 1982, 1990; Obeyesekere 1981; O'Flaherty 1973; Spratt 1966), and there can be no doubt that semen retention is a theme with powerful resonance in the psyche of many Hindu men who feel that sex is enervating. While the basic theory of celibacy has been analysed and explained in various ways by many authors, my concern is primarily with the technical aspect of the *brahmachari*'s regimen, and with what the logic of those techniques implies. Aside from Gandhi's own writings, there is very little on the mechanics—the science—of being and becoming celibate.

The modern concept of *brahmacharya* clearly derives from the classical life-cycle prescriptions of *dharma* articulated by Manu (1886 [1964]), among others. The four-fold *ashrama* cycle of life stages, of which *brahmacharya* (initiated studentship) is the first, when understood in conjunction with the "four ends of man"—*dharma, artha, kama*, and *moksha*—clearly articulates an encompassing code of moral, civic, ritual, political, and economic conduct. The status of the initiated student defines one specific phase in the larger structure of society, and the "structured" integration of the individual into that society. Specifically, it marks the second birth of Brahman, Kshatriya, and Vaishya boys and sets them on a path of disciplined Vedic learning. In this regard, *brahmacharya* may be seen as a crucial phase in the articulation of difference within society insofar as the ritual of initiation defines the particular trajectory of the various *Varna* categories and who has what rights and duties within those categories.

Most of the rules of conduct for the *brahmachari* concern his religious status *vis-à-vis* his *guru* and the ritual protocol of his community. It is clearly within the ritualized contexts defined by *The Sacred Laws of the Aryas* (Muller 1879 [1965], *Bhagavad Gita* (1945), and the *Ashvalayana Grihya-Sutra* (1923) that the *brahmachari*'s vow of chastity must be understood. For the initiated twice-born student, chastity in particular and self-control in general were requisite for learning the *Vedas*, since sex was regarded as both defiling and distracting. In this regard, chastity was a practical pedagogical principle and not a general rule of moral conduct prescribed for all Hindus. Nor was the ritual vow of chastity—as distinct from the modern concept of nationalistic celibacy— medicalized in any sense; the initiated student did not, it seems, practice celibacy as a form of personalized public health. It was simply part of his religious training.

Despite the very narrow, ritualized meaning of celibacy within the classical life-cycle scheme of the twice-born (cf. Stevenson (1920 [1971]), one is able to discern a nascent political agenda in Vedic and post-Vedic discourse on sexuality. Within the life-cycle of the twice-born male, there was most certainly a time and place for sex. However, the *Vedas* and other classic texts sought to regulate the nature of who, what, where, and how one might engage in sex (cf. *Kama Sutra*), but not sex itself as a monolithic construct that defined the moral conduct of some equally monolithic Hindu citizen. Social, political, aesthetic, and economic distinctions were all important when reckoning the moral propriety or appropriateness of sex, whereas universal standards were virtually meaningless: what was good for one was by no means good for all, particularly when it came to abstinence. In this regard, the classical authors seemed to see sex as one behavioral facet among many others to be regulated in the interest of maintaining the social hierarchy. As Romila Thapar has noted, however, the world-renouncer who abstained from sex completely was able to act as a social critic precisely by virtue of his position outside of this hierarchy. Similarly, for the Naga sect of the Ramanandi order, the discipline of *brahmacharya* was central to the practice of various martial arts put to use in sixteenth- and seventeenth-century political campaigns. Thus, asexuality functioned as a form of socio-political power while deriving its authority from the renouncer's mystical, "other-worldly" spirituality. It was this connection between sex, spirituality, and social criticism that Gandhi was able to translate so effectively into his program of militant nonviolence. Although I think the Vedic and post-Vedic perspective on sex is radically different from the modern discourse on sex and nationalism that emerged in the twentieth century—since the classical renouncer, unlike Gandhi and his modern heirs, did not advocate that everyone become like him in order to reform society—it is important to keep in mind that the "laws of *dharma*" were incipiently political. It is easy, therefore, for modern Hindu advocates of reform to recast the narrow rules of "ancient sex" in terms of social criticism and a more encompassing, nationalistic vision of moral propriety.

Like his classical forebear, the modern *brahmachari* is, first and foremost, celibate, but to maintain absolute control over his sexual desire his discipline mandates that he must control all of his senses by means of a rigid and carefully regimented program of diet, exercise, and rest. Moreover, control of the senses entails careful management of a wide array of daily activities, including what and how to read, where and how to sleep, and what to wear, among many other things. In other words, *brahmacharya* is a way of life that is focused on sexuality but includes a much broader spectrum of activities and concerns.

In contemporary North India, a genre of popular/technical literature on *brahmacharya* is published by large, mainstream establishments as well as by smaller, regional presses. Booklets, pamphlets, and "medical" manuals advocate celibacy, explain its merits, and provide precise instructions on how to control desire and stay healthy. These publications also, and perhaps primarily, offer home-remedy treatments to cure specific ailments that threaten to undermine self-control. In virtually all of this literature, the concept of *brahmacharya* is systematically opposed to Indian modernity. Although it is only logical that this literature should have proliferated in the decades of rapid change and increasing literacy after independence, my argument is that *brahmacharya* developed as a strategic concept opposed to Westernization. More specifically, it was developed as the moral/physical alternative to various forms of postcolonial desire—both gross and subtle—which were thought to directly afflict the body and undermine its strength and integrity. The forces of postcolonial desire are manifold, and mostly defined by way of contrast to the pristine, natural, and non-erotic environment of "traditional" India. As one critic writes:

> Because the youth of today are destroying their semen they are courting the worst disaster and are daily being condemned to hell . . . Mother nature stands, stick in hand, watching their abominable behavior, and for every drop of semen spilled she lashes out and strikes their vital organs . . .

These days it is common to see the deep wounds of her stick on young people's backs. How many of these unfortunate people lie shaking on their cots like the grievously ill? Some are suffering from the heat. And others, carrying the same deep wounds, pretentiously puff out their chests and walk about piously exchanging garlands while nervously checking their pulse for any sign of illness. There is no trust of God in their hearts, only lust. Now tell me, what future do such people have? . . . They only glow with the light of fireflies, and neither humility nor glory are found in their flickering hypocrisy.

(Shivananda 1984: 41)

Many authors are very specific about what forms of erotic and sensual stimulation cause young people to destroy their semen. Popular cinema, which is saturated with romantic themes and suggestively lurid images, is unanimously regarded as the most debauched aspect of modern life.

As a form of entertainment, cinema is a great enemy of modern society. It is full of obscene, erotic, and indecent images which enter the sub-conscious, lie dormant, and then result in night-emission.

(Shastri n.d.: 29)

Similarly, so-called "pornographic" novels and magazines are said to stimulate desire through fantasy. However, it is the whole ethos and institutional structure of modernity that is considered sensually decadent, including everything from effete toiletries and coeducation to hair-styles and family-planning policies. While sex is certainly not said to be categorically bad, its public manifestation and subtle permeation of the culture is thought to be fundamentally disruptive.

The literature on *brahmacharya* is directed specifically, but not exclusively, at teen-age boys and young men in college who would be the primary consumers of films, "pornography," and the other effete products of modernity. Books on celibacy are often sold at school bookstores along with classroom texts and other educational literature. Although their precise circulation is unknown, the extent to which young men are familiar with the principles and practice of celibacy indicates that the literature is widely read. Among wrestlers, who comprise a broad class and caste spectrum of society, the practice of *brahmacharya* is highly developed and provides a clear example of how the discourse on celibacy finds popular, public expression. In many North Indian villages and cities, wrestling is a popular sport that attracts tens of thousands of spectators who are exposed to a dramatic display of how semen retention can enhance the character, strength, and skill of otherwise ordinary men. The wrestling *akhara* (public gymnasium) provides a social environment in which the ideas expressed in the popular literature on celibacy are both confirmed by practice and disseminated among village and neighborhood communities of men. The public gymnasium thus provides a context within which the critique of postcolonial desire finds popular expression. Thereby a "moral" form of popular culture is pitted against the popular hedonism of modernity.

What is most striking about the literature on *brahmacharya* is the degree of detail provided about all facets of male sex, "sexuality," and health. Rather than focusing on the moral psychology of erotic desire—as might similar books published by, say, church groups in America, or the Boy Scouts—books on *brahmacharya* strive to analyse the mechanics, hydraulics, and chemistry of sex with particular emphasis on the various properties of semen, since semen is regarded as the most essential fluid of life. The whole purpose of *brahmacharya* is to build up a resilient store of semen so that the body—in a holistic, psychosomatic sense—radiates an aura of vitality and strength.

The production and protection of semen is based on what might best be described, somewhat awkwardly, given the incompatibility of English with the language of Hindu sexuality, as a regimen of the plain and simple truth. One writer explains that the term *brahmacharya* is a conjunction of two words which mean truth and conduct (Saraswati 1982: 89). More specifically, conduct is of three types—diet, exercise, and work. To be a *brahmachari* is to eat simple food, live simply, and engage in the simple exercise of walking. The term simple, as Saraswati uses it, is synonymous with truth, and may be contrasted to the imbalanced chaos of modern life—the deceit of modernity.

The process by which the body makes semen is fundamental to the *brahmachari*'s regimen. Diet is perhaps the single most important variable. According to a clearly defined and predictable ratio, food is transformed into blood, blood into flesh, flesh into fat, fat into bone, bone into marrow, and marrow into semen. Thus, semen is a highly condensed distillate of pure and wholesome food. As Shastri notes, the *brahmachari*'s food should be of the purest quality, since "pure food produces pure truth, and pure truth produces pure wisdom. With great and absolute wisdom one will always be successful" (Shastri n.d.: 50). He then provides a long list of specific items which, on account of being either *tamasi* or *rajasi*, ought to be avoided.*

As the most primary of fluid substances, semen is thought to permeate and flow within the body much the way blood does. However, as a vital fluid, its properties are not only life-giving, but energizing in a heroic, epiphanal, and almost supernatural way:

> The more a person conserves his semen, the greater will be his stature and vitality. His energy, ardor, intellect, competence, capacity for work, wisdom, success and godliness will begin to manifest themselves, and he will be able to profit from a long life. . . . To tell the truth, semen is elixir.
>
> (Shivananda 1984: 10–11)

Although semen has phenomenal properties, it is regarded as a tangible, natural substance. This point must be emphasized because the reader is likely to forget that semen is an elemental fluid with basic physical properties when its power to transform is taken into consideration. No distinction should be made here between the gross nature of seminal fluid and the subtle properties of *ojas*, which animate the body with vital energy. The regimen of *brahmacharya*, and the analysis and rationalization of that regimen in the popular medical literature, fundamentally conflates concrete substance—the stuff of wet dreams, masturbation, and intercourse—with abstract social, political, and spiritual power. Celibacy is not a theory based on analogy and metaphor, but a practical scheme based on the metonymical correspondence of somatic health, psychological and intellectual maturity, and the sociopolitical power to change the nature of society. It is, therefore, not the action of self-control that builds character and resolve

---

* *Tamas* and *rajas*, along with *sattva*, comprise a triadic scheme of food classification. *Tamasi* foods make one dull and lethargic, while *rajasi* foods make one feel hot, agitated, and restless.

through a discipline of the disembodied self in a game of mind over matter. It is the matter itself from which the essentials of character and virtue emanate.

Gender and postcolonial desire

A discourse on the power of semen produces an unambiguously male ideology. In spite of the fact that some authors, in keeping with Ayurvedic theory, say that women's bodies also contain semen, albeit of a different kind and nature than that of men, there can be little doubt that the entire construct of *brahmacharya* is conceived of in male terms. Although it is intriguing to consider the implications of genderless semen for a discourse on sexuality and nationalism, typical discussions of the subject consist of one or two disappointingly vague and insignificant lines.

One might argue that the distinctly male features of celibacy render the whole question of gender moot and uninteresting by virtue of the relatively two-dimensional relationship between social, political, and physical power that is implied. However, in most instances of male dominance, power is largely an ideological construct that is only nominally, and therefore tenuously—although often forcefully and vigorously—based on images of strength (cf. Brown 1988; Elshtain 1981). It is relatively rare, and therefore of some theoretical interest, to find a case in which a logic of male dominance is inverted, so to speak, where what becomes problematic is not the politics of status and authority, or the production of a heroic identity, but that which might seem most essentially and ineluctably male: the nature of semen.

In *The Woman in the Body: A Cultural Analysis of Reproduction* (1987), Emily Martin clearly shows how women's bodies have been fragmented by science, technology, and labor (cf. also Martin 1989, 1991). Most significantly, she shows how an opposition to fragmentation and alienation is often effected through the medium of the body in general, and specific parts of the body or body processes in particular, menopause and birthing, for example. Martin's argument is that disempowered women are not only able to see the process of fragmentation for what it is, but are able to imagine "alternative visions" to that process. Significantly, these reconfigurations of the self are not only imagined, they are embodied, and the logic of embodiment is worked out in exact detail.

Distinct from the medical discourse by men about women's bodies, which Martin critically deconstructs, the discourse on semen within the literature on *brahmacharya* is both by and about men. However, it is "unreflexively" male, which is to say that the men writing about semen write, for the most part, as though the world were exclusively, if unremarkably, male. Clearly this discourse emerges from a comfortable position of unself-conscious power; a world in which women simply do not figure except in their sharply circumscribed roles as mother, sister, and wife, on the one hand, and seductive whore, on the other. The whole discourse on *brahmacharya* is so fantastically skewed that gender—what it means to be a man in modern India—becomes a purely self-referential question rather than a problem of distinguishing between masculine and feminine attributes, between male and female roles, or, indeed, between male and female aspects of sexual intercourse. A preoccupation with the nature of semen—rather than, say, machismo or masculine values—tends to structure the discourse on male identity in a way that unintentionally deconstructs a mythology of dominance by penetrating deep into the body and soul of everyman. However, the deconstruction is only nominal, for the male discourse on semen ends up constructing an alternative and perhaps more covert mythology of gendered truth.

Although the men who write about celibacy do so—in terms of gender, at least— from a position of almost total power, their motivation to write comes from a feeling of impending powerlessness in the face of radical sociomoral change. In other words, they feel compelled to reconfigure the nature of identity in order to prevent nothing less than the debauchery of everyman and the total disintegration of society. It is this feeling of impending powerlessness and disintegration that puts those who write about celibacy in a frame of mind to reflect critically—if not always self-consciously—on the nature of the "man in the body." The impending fragmentation of the male body in terms of modernity and the various forces of postcolonial desire entail a radical reconfiguration of "self and body image," to again adapt Martin's phrase. These reconfigurations are, needless to say, quite different from those of "the woman in the body" where powerlessness is real and encompassing rather than putative and contextual, and where there is a gendered world of difference between those who structure the discourse about bodies and those who "live" those bodies. Under certain circumstances, Emily Martin argues, women are able to see through the thick walls of patriarchal ideology and see it for what it is. My argument is that men in a position of power, confronted by what they perceive to be an almost apocalyptic transformation of society, are forced to see the extreme contingency of their gendered position—the fictional basis of their ideology, if you will. As a result, what they do is to critically deconstruct the elements of that ideology in search of a more primary, natural truth about themselves—which is, in essence, what some of the women Emily Martin writes about are trying to do. Although there are phenomenal differences between these women and the Indian men who advocate celibacy, lessons may be drawn from the former about how the latter seek to embody their gender.

To understand the problematic nature of male identity in contemporary India, it is necessary to consider briefly a few historical points. Edward Said, among others, has argued that there is a close connection between the culture of imperialism and the power and imagery of male-oriented aggressive sex (Said 1978; cf. also Ballhatchet 1980; Stoler 1989; Alloula 1987). While the connection is perhaps most apparent in the common metaphor and experience of rape, there were more subtle, if no less insidious, ways in which the Orient, as female, was eroticized and then passionately consumed by those in positions of power. This power depended not only on the construction of an erotic feminine mystique, but also on the deconstruction of an indigenous male identity.

From a British perspective—and I use "a" rather than the more general and totalizing "the" advisedly (cf. Cooper and Stoler 1989)—it was relatively easy to conclude that Indian men, in general, and upper-caste Hindu men, in particular, were effete. They had, after all, been defeated and turned into subject citizens by a dominant power. Accusations of political, military, and sexual impotence were powerful metaphors in the context of this kind of argument. Although there were loud and sustained protests by Indian politicians, reformers, and educators alike, John Rosselli has indicated, through historical research in Bengal, that for a significant period of time this image of effeteness was accepted and perhaps even affectedly popularized by a certain class of Indian men, primarily, although not exclusively, the educated *babus* and clerks who worked in the vast imperial bureaucracies (Rosselli 1980). The trend was certainly strong enough to elicit a powerful nationalist response by those who felt compelled to "remasculate" their impotent brethren through the medium of physical education (Nandy 1980: 60). A striking example is provided by Abdus Salam's short treatise, *Physical Education in India* (1895). After applauding the vitality and vigor of India's early Muslim heritage, Salam makes the following observation, which, although directed at the Bengali Muslim intelligentsia, may be taken as a more general statement on the condition of all "Westernized" Indians.

> In contrast with this brilliant past as regards physical vigour and manliness, the lack of physical energy which now more or less characterises the Mahomedans [*sic*] in India stands out in bold relief. Our one-sided Western education, so far . . . has acted with us like a bad liver: it is making us assimilate what has to be rejected of the Western import, and reject what has to be assimilated. We are rapidly parting with our own national ways and manners. . . . In the case of a few here and there, there might be visible some surface Western polish, but it is no more than skin deep; the result being that whilst the sweet guilelessness and gentle suavity of the East is absent, the genuine sturdiness and masculine straightforwardness of the West is also wanting
>
> (Salam 1895: 17–18).

At issue amidst all this acrimony, from a British perspective at least, was the largely metaphoric connection between heroism, strength, and courage, on the one hand, and virility, on the other. Their disparagement of Indian men was, in effect, based on an analogic theory of how personal strength translated into public virtue. Virility was a metaphor for political power and sociomoral strength; a metaphor that mixed together elements of masculine psychology and colonial ideology. Virility, in British terms was, of course, associated with a particular form of sexuality wherein strength and power was a function of potency, stamina, size, and appetite. In other words, power was measured in terms of one's ability to spend semen—either literally or figuratively—which was, in turn, dependent on one's ability to control the conditions under which it was spent. An echo of this reverberates in Salam's anglicized, English prose.

> [I]n these piping-days of peace and high intellectual pressure and especially in this enervating Indian climate, when more than ever a race is apt to get emasculated, it is absolutely necessary that we should have recourse to physical exercise . . .
>
> (Salam 1895: 22)

It is important to point out that the effete, Westernized *babu* was only one of a number of sexually based stereotypes of Indian men. As many scholars have pointed out, the British in India were intent on various schemes of racial/caste classification. One of the categories developed in these schemes was that of the so-called martial castes, who, in direct contrast to the effete Bengali *babu* and merchantile *vaishya*, were aggressive, virile, and courageous. These martial castes, which included Maratthas, Pathans, and Rajputs, were constructed in terms of a classical masculine image that probably had as much to do with imputed British ideals as with indigenous values (Nandy 1980: 72). One can, for example, clearly locate the moral empathy in the opening sentence of Sir George MacMunn's *The Martial Races of India*.

> Who and what are the martial races of India, how do they come, and in what crucible, on what anvil's [*sic*] hot with pain spring the soldiers of India, whom surely Baba Ghandi [*sic*] never fathered?
>
> (MacMunn 1977[192?]: 1)

Although bombastic almost to the point of parody, MacMunn's rhetoric serves to illustrate the extent to which a scheme of sexual classification functioned to make sense of Indian masculinity. Whereas Salam blamed Western education for sapping the strength of India's young and noble, MacMunn places the blame on religion and "early marriage, premature brides, and juvenile eroticism" (MacMunn 1977[192?]: 2). Applauding the chivalry of Rajput soldiers and other "virile races" who would rather immolate their wives than have them captured in war, MacMunn again castigates Gandhi and "the mass of [Indian] people [who] have neither martial aptitude nor physical courage . . ." (ibid.).

> The gentle yet merciless race of hereditary moneylenders, from which Lala Ghandi [*sic*] springs, only kept within bounds by an occasional flaying and roasting, have never been able or even tried to protect their own hoards.
>
> (ibid.: 3)

Despite their radical differences, the effete *babu*, the gentle yet merciless *vaishya*, and the heroic Rajput were conceived of in terms of a single theory of sexual power: aggressive virility or a lack thereof.

The logic of this analogy between semen and power is, I believe, crucial to understanding the nature of what I am calling postcolonial desire and the logic of various indigenous responses to it. In most general terms, the colonial conception of sexuality in particular, but sensuality in general, with its emphasis on male potency and personal gratification, helped change what might be referred to as the structure of erotic passion in late nineteenth- and twentieth-century India. Needless to say, eroticism was not a British invention, and it could be argued that Victorian prudishness militated against the public—as distinct from private and elite—proliferation of erotica in colonial India. However, it was, in part, this same prudishness that contributed to the "pornographication" of erotica in India culture, on the one hand, and on the other, the construction of a moralistic, Christian discourse on sex in general. As Ballhatchet (1980) and Hyam (1990) show, there was a great deal of disagreement about, and ambivalence toward, alien sexuality, prostitution, concubinage, and interracial marriage among the British in India. Attitudes and practices did not always conform to policy. Regardless, what is most significant about colonial sexuality was the tremendous politicomoral discourse it generated by linking sex and identity with questions of power and authority. The modern advocates of celibacy who criticize the youth of modern India for being "sex addicts" often trace the history of their addiction back to the virtual invention of "sexuality"—in the modern Foucaultian sense of the term—during the colonial period.

Prior to that time there was sex, passion, and sensuality, to be sure, and there was an elaborate discourse on the art of sex—replete with categories and modes of classification (cf. Cakravarti 1963; Meyer 1930)—but there was no sense in which an apparatus of sexuality provided a definitive moral yardstick against which to measure the appropriateness of various acts or the status of the actors. Sex was a thing unto itself, but certainly not an encompassing, sociomoral force whose seductive influence permeated the entire cultural fabric.

Those who advocate *brahmacharya*, however, argue that sex began to permeate society at about the turn of the century and since that time men have become progressively more enslaved to the idea that sex is the most important aspect of life. One might say that a more encompassing, libertine self-concept emerged out of the self-image of effeteness, and the ascribed identity of race-specific martial virility—at least in the critical, conservative judgment of those who favored celibacy. The colonial discourse on sex seduced those who were colonized and distorted their self-concept by structuring the very nature of sexuality.

Rather than celebrate Independence and the achievements of modern India, those who write about celibacy often point out that postcolonial India is enslaved by its "freedom" to develop and Westernize; enslaved not so much to sex itself—although certainly that—as to the idea that power is a function of potency, and virility the coefficient of modernization. In other words, these authors are adamantly opposed to the institutionalized sex of prostitution and concupiscence, but they are more strongly opposed to a Victorian theory of sexuality that underwrote the vast industry of prostitution and attitude of covert concupiscence in colonial India; a theory whose legacy they regard as a form of neocolonial domination. They would most likely agree with Lawrence Birken's general analysis of modern Western sexuality as a "consuming desire," and with the notion that sexualization and the idiosyncratic nature of desire is a function of radical "neoclassical" individualism (1988: 35; cf. Dumont 1986 for the basis of this kind of individualism).

Those who champion the cause of *brahmacharya* target for particular criticism the gross manifestations of sex. However, the larger issue they address is the nature of modern sexuality in India and the impact of colonial domination on male identity. As they see it, the basic problem is hydraulic. Modern life, in general, and a discourse preoccupied with intercourse and erotic stimulation, both figuratively and literally cause semen to flow and then structure identity in terms of that flow. In the context of postcolonialism, where sex is measured in terms of the gratification it gives, power is defined in relation to the flow and expenditure of semen. You are who you are in terms of the sex you have. For example, one might look, to adapt the rhetoric of the *brahmachari*, at the way popular film heroes and villains are portrayed; at the accusations leveled against corrupt, licentious policemen; at the proliferation of sex manuals; and, perhaps most alarmingly, at the rate of population growth and all it signifies in the ways men are trying to define themselves and assert their position in society. In other words, everywhere one looks there are more or less horrific signs of men trying to build themselves up by the very means that will ultimately bring them down, quite literally, by drying up their liquid assets.

The celibate, on the other hand, is defined by the sex he does not have, and by the semen that he does not allow to flow. However, there is a more fundamental distinction between the *brahmachari*'s conception of sex and that of the postcolonial "libertines" whom he criticizes. For the *brahmachari*, it is not sex as an act that defines identity nor is power conceived of in terms of one's sexual prowess—quite the opposite: identity and power are inherent in semen and not in those situations in which semen is made to flow. What this means is that gender gets defined in two radically different ways by the *brahmachari* and his "libertine" counterpart: for the postcolonial "libertine," masculinity is an ideology of domination, self-gratification, and the control of others, an ideology almost pathologically individualistic in the priority it places on the egocentric self in relation to others. For the *brahmachari*, on the other hand, gender identity derives from a regimen of self-control, balance, and integration of the self with natural truth. It is, in part, the sheer abomination of contemporary masculinity, the utter waste of vital fluids, which has made celibacy a persuasive form of embodied opposition to the legacy of colonial sexuality.

Nationalism and truth

In his treatise on night emission and celibacy, Kaviraj Jagannath Shastri writes:

> Today the disease of night emission is widespread. It not only afflicts the young and unmarried, but also those who are married and old. Wherever you look you will see that about 85 percent of the population suffers from this disease.
>
> But the greatest sorrow is in the fact that it is these same people who man the rudder of this dear country of ours; who must shoulder the heavy burden of protecting India; who must steer the nation into the future; who provide the standard upon which all else rests; and who are the heart and soul of our society. These students, children, and youth are worn down and left virtually defeated by the battle this evil power wages against them.
>
> (Shastri n.d.: 17)

Shastri and many others feel that India's vital potential is being wasted on a scale that only those who believe in the phenomenal power of a single drop of semen can truly appreciate. As Shastri concludes, the loss of semen means the total demise of "the nation, the present era, prevailing circumstances, the environment, the natural order of things, and the social order of caste and religion" (ibid.). Although the magnitude of the problem here imagined is noteworthy, it is the nature of the problem that has particular relevance. Shastri and others believe fundamentally that the body is the site of national reform; that nationalism must be embodied to have any real effect. On the other hand, the nationalism of "pure ideology," is "like the roar of a paper tiger, and the loud rhetoric of false prophets." As Shivananda writes:

> Without reforming the body one will never achieve a state of freedom and satisfaction; nor will one ever be successful. There is nothing—no substance or person—who can give satisfaction and peace to one whose body is unhealthy. You alone can make yourself free and blissfully happy. In other words, physical reform must be our primary goal, for it is the

basis for all of man's other four aims, and essential for our salvation and independence.

(Shivananda 1984: 29)

As a tangible, corporeal whole, the body is regarded as more fundamental and natural than are ideas and concepts; it is incontrovertible, and therefore moral in a biological rather than an ideological way. As the body is made the site of nationalism, and *brahmacharya* its agency of reform, the individual is held responsible for embodying such things as freedom, glory, peace, and happiness, as well as more typically physical attributes such as strength and good health. The regimen of celibacy is clearly meant to turn sick men into progressive citizens who could, single-handedly, reform the nation. Shivananda writes:

> Open your eyes and set your resolve in order to regain the glory of the past through the regimen of celibacy. One who is able to control a single drop is able to control the seven seas. There is nothing in the world—no object or condition—which a celibate man cannot overcome.
>
> (Shivananda 1984: 34–35)

As we have noted, celibacy is an inwardly focused regimen. The logic of self-control is also purely reflexive in a microscopic mode, insofar as the ultimate goal of celibacy is to magnify the power of that which is most elemental, essential, and basic—the smallest common denominator of everyman. But as the regimen of *brahmacharya* turns inward and becomes concerned with the minute intricacies of how to breath, bathe, defecate, and eat, it becomes less and less individuated and progressively more integrated into the "natural environment" of Mother India.

The place of nature in the regimen of *brahmacharya* is important, for there is a logical correspondence between each drop of semen on a microscopic level and the natural order of things on a universal level. Harmony and balance—which translate easily into the freedom, happiness, and peace of national revival—are achieved when the body and its reservoir of semen are enveloped by, or in tune with, the natural world. "Brothers!", writes Shivananda, and the reader should not forget the implications of his gender-specific appeal:

> [r]eturn to the arms of Mother Nature. She is truly compassionate! She will help you reform. Have faith. You cannot live for even one hour without the kindness of Mother Nature. Through the nose, ears, mouth, anus, skin, and hair she takes the poison out of our bodies and keeps us fit. We should daily avail ourselves of the "five natural substances"—light, water, earth, air, and space. Abandon those things which aggravate in favor of things which impart happiness and bring redemption. Salvation is in our own hands.
>
> (Shivananda 1984: 43)

Although the nationalism invoked through this kind of rhetoric is embodied on an individual level where citizenship is constructed as a kind of psychosomatic attribute, there are some important ways the body has an impact on social institutions. As noted above, those who advocate celibacy are critical of postcolonial sexuality in general, but they are adamantly opposed to "legitimate" sexuality as it is practiced within the family. In their view, the family is not a place where one may freely indulge in sex. In fact, it is precisely the notion that one may freely have sex with one's wife as often as one likes—"every hour of every night," as Shivananda sarcastically quips (Shivananda 1984: 51–52)—which makes the family a dangerous and potentially destructive institution, a kind of sanctioned den of iniquity where the veneer of public morality—to say nothing of social status and prestige—hides the truth of a more insidious demise. One's legal rights as a spouse in no way change the biomorality of semen flow. On the other hand, one can certainly be married and remain "celibate" as long as one engages in sex only for procreation. The argument presented for this case is drawn from animals and the natural environment, where relationships are balanced, rather than from the world of modern society, which is corrupt. Men are admonished to draw their genitals up like horses and bulls, thus limiting sex to the act of intercourse while remaining otherwise passively unsexed. Unlike the late nineteenth-century discourse on "spiritual" nationalism (cf. Chatterjee 1989) wherein the family was constructed as pure, impervious, and outside the purview of politics, the discourse on *brahmacharya* not only makes the family a focal site of national reform, but directly criticizes the basic sexual premise upon which the family itself is founded.

Although institutionalized sex within the family is generally regarded as dangerous precisely because it appears to be "legitimate," *brahmacharis* reserve their harshest criticism for the practice of child marriage. The logic of this position is not hard to grasp. Youth in general are thought to be easily seduced by the pleasure of sex and particularly apt to take advantage of the sexual license that early marriage provides. To put children in a situation where they can easily satisfy their erotic appetites clearly undermines every principle of self-control and all potential for self-development. Shivananda writes:

> In this country we even undermine the potential of our children. Before teaching them how to swim, parents tie the lead weight of a young wife around their sons' necks and then push them out mercilessly into the ocean of life. How can a country in which this kind of thing goes on advance!?
> (Shivananda 1984: 56)

The nation of which the reformist celibate speaks is both a figment of his utopian imagination—a world where every man is strong, hard working, happy, and free—as well as a world where the natural order of things—clean air, pure food, cool water, and fresh air—prefigures, and to some extent supersedes, the social order. In general, modern social life, which from most perspectives would be the central constituent category of a reformist ideology, is in this case both preempted and subverted. In part, this is because postcolonial modernity is regarded as irredeemably debauched but, in an important sense, Hindu epistemology also makes it difficult to separate out social facts from biological or natural ones (cf. Marriott 1991). This point brings us back to the question of truth and its relationship to the nation and to the body.

Mahatma Gandhi's autobiography appears in translation as *The Story of My Experiments With Truth* (1927). Although it is an account of his early political and social life, the autobiography is intensely personal and, as Sudhir Kakar has noted, characterized by extreme "candor and honesty" (Kakar 1990: 85). Gandhi was preoccupied with issues of social and political justice and felt that truth was the only means by which justice could be achieved. For Gandhi, however, truth was far from self-evident; one had to experiment in various ways to both realize its nature and subscribe to its tenets. Although he was concerned to some extent with abstract metaphysics, what is most striking about Gandhi's experiments is their utterly banal character, and Gandhi's own virtual obsession with seemingly mundane, utilitarian issues of diet, health, and, above all else, the control of sexual passion. Although Gandhi's own theory of celibacy was derived in more or less equal parts from Christian and Hindu doctrines, the regimens he developed were extreme and highly idiosyncratic. However, it is clear that Gandhi, in keeping with classical Hindu teaching, believed in the power of semen, that there was an intimate connection between the elusive nature of truth and the seductive power of sexuality: to conquer the latter was to realize the former.

Although Gandhi believed in the power of celibacy and was keenly aware of what Kakar refers to as the "metaphysical physiology" of semen (Kakar 1990: 119), it would seem that for him truth was a somewhat mystical function of the regimen he devised rather than the actual, biomoral substance itself: a problem of overcoming the body in order to realize truth through enlightenment rather than embodying truth as semen itself. At times Gandhi seems to write as though it is the semen itself that matters, but more often it is what the spillage or waste of semen represents in terms of his personal failure to put mind over matter. For Gandhi, celibacy was a physical and personal means to a sociopolitical, and ultimately spiritual, end.

Unlike Gandhi, whose enigmatic genius was in part the function of his vital suspension between the world of Christian and Hindu ethics, contemporary advocates of *brahmacharya* provide a much more tangible and one-dimensional version of what constitutes truth, and the connection between that truth and national reform. For them celibacy is not the means to an end; it is an end in and of itself, a way to engender nationalism by cultivating the seeds of truth.

Conclusion: gender into nationalism

The ideology of nationalism is arguably one of the most masculine expressions of patriarchal politics. Certainly, the rhetoric of *brahmacharya* is aggressively male. And yet, male sexuality—the metaphors of conquest, penetration, and violent domination—are strikingly absent from the whole scenario of celibate power. In a similar vein, Gandhi's nationalist politics of nonviolence seems to cut against the grain of overt masculinity (cf. Nandy 1980: 73, 74). Despite his preoccupation with sex and semen—and perhaps on account of it—Gandhi felt that women could be celibate, and through their celibacy work toward a realization of the truth. As Kakar has argued and others have noted, Gandhi's personal treatment of women was not particularly enlightened, but at least on the level of theory he did not discriminate and may, in fact, be regarded as a champion of gender equality, remembering, of course, with a caveat drawn from Chatterjee (1989), that Gandhi's discourse on women was part of the larger "new patriarchy" of liberal nationalism. A number of scholars have pointed out the ways Gandhi's ambivalence toward women and femininity and men and masculinity led to the construction of what might be called an androgynous politics (cf. Erikson 1969; Kakar 1990; Nandy 1983; Rudolph and Rudolph 1967). The notion that one could become powerful by dominating others—sexually or physically—was anathema to Gandhi, whose most cherished ideal was that of selfless service. Gandhi's regimen of *satyagraha*, with its emphasis on celibacy and dietetics, was designed to translate selfless service into national reform. To this end, Gandhi made it clear that both men and women were equally qualified to experiment with truth, equally qualified to turn themselves into citizens who would work to reform India, equally qualified to turn willpower into social service—but only if they stopped being sexual objects to one another. In the Gandhian utopia—to paraphrase an often-quoted model—male and female citizens would be as brother and sister, mother and son, father and daughter, with all that these relationships imply in the context of the new patriarchy of modern India.

I do not want to get into the particulars of either Gandhi's ideology or his program of reform. However, Gandhi's concern with celibacy and his policy toward women provide an important point of contrast to the engendered nationalism of contemporary *brahmacharis*. One might say, to somewhat oversimplify, that Gandhi undermined the old ideology of patriarchal politics by turning the aggression of virility into the energy of androgynous nonviolence. Although Gandhi's nonviolence, in particular, and theory of political action, in general, were based on a regimen of self-control, the ultimate goal was to overcome the body's physical limitations, a fact that ultimately rendered the physiology of sex and gender irrelevant to the realization of truth, while allowing for the reconstruction of such purportedly asexual and apolitical roles as brother/sister, mother/son, father/daughter. If Gandhi's larger agenda was patriarchal in any sense, and I am sure the argument could be made that it was, it was patriarchal despite itself on the level of institutionalized ideological structures, but not on the level of biomoral substance.

By contrast, I am arguing, that the contemporary nationalist regimen of *brahmacharya* seems to go beyond the metaphysical limitations of Gandhi's experiments by postulating a substantial, incarnate, seminal truth. Although semen is inherently male, the *brahmacharya* postulate is that it is protosexual; its power derives not from the kinetic agency of masculine sexuality, but from the potential energy manifest in the essence of male substance. By locating truth in the male body, the contemporary *brahmachari* translates an ideology of domination into a particularly insidious form of biological determinism while, ironically, appearing to deconstruct the whole edifice of sex as such. Thus, truth becomes not just a male virtue, but something that only men can embody by virtue of who they are. Such a proposition has often been the substance of patriarchal myths of power and glory but, in the case of *brahmacharya*, one finds a version of that myth in which embodiment is virtual rather than putative, a myth in which gender emerges more powerful on account of being essentialized as a biomoral substance. In these terms, nationalism is not synonymous with the ideals of "humanism," as Gandhi might have it, but with an exclusive form of truth that heroically animates the "man in the body."

> Brothers! Liberate our dear Mother India from poverty and resurrect her true power and glory! India's freedom is dependent on each and everyone's freedom, and everyone's freedom is achieved once the yoke of poisonous slavery has been caste off. We, like our forefathers, must achieve this end by controlling our semen.
>
> (Shivananda 1984: 156)

The tragic contradiction—or perhaps ominous indictment—of such a heroic vision is, of course, that "everyone's freedom" cannot be based on the seminal truth of biological determinism, no matter how fluid.

The question remains, however, what brings gender and nationalism together? What factors are involved in bringing about the transformation of one conception of the body into another? I have argued that postcolonial desire, and the history of sexuality in colonial India played an important part in this process. As a secret vice that permeated society, sex came to be regarded as a key to power and truth. What emerged was a discourse on sexuality that radically essentialized the practice of sex. To construct an opposing discourse to this essentialism required a degree of what I suppose must be called counter-essentialism, that is, the production of a theory of power and truth that could deconstruct the hegemony of sexuality at its most basic level. What the *brahma-charya* argument does is to effect this deconstruction on two planes: the protosexual level of semen, thereby relocating power to a more primary position within the body, and the utopian level of national harmony, where debauchery is preempted by the balanced integration of body and nature. The whole discourse of postcolonial desire that afflicts contemporary society is thus crushed, it is hoped, by the logic of an argument that both undermines and preempts the structure of modern sexuality in India.

List of references

Alloula, Malek. 1987. *The Colonial Harem*. Manchester and Minnesota: Manchester University Press.

Alter, Joseph S. 1992. *The Wrestler's Body: Identity and Ideology in North India*. Berkeley and Los Angeles: University of California Press.

—— 1993. "The Body of One Color: Indian Wrestling, the Indian State and Utopian Somatics." *Cultural Anthropology* 8.1: 49–72.

—— 1994. "Somatic Nationalism: Indian Wrestling and Militant Hinduism." *Modern Asian Studies* 28.3: 557–588.

Andersen, Walter K., and Sharidhar D. Damle. 1987. *The Brotherhood in Saffron: The Rashtriya Swayamsevak Sangh and Hindu Revivalism*. Boulder, Colo.: Westview Press.

Anderson, Benedict. 1983. *Imagined Communities: Reflections on the Origin and Spread of Nationalism*. London and New York: Verso.

Ashby, Philip H. 1974. *Modern Trends in Hinduism*. New York: Columbia University Press.

Ashvalayana. 1923. *Grihya-Sutra*. Edited by Ganpati Shastri. Trivandrum: Government Press.

Ballhatchet, K. A. 1980. *Race, Sex and Class Under the Raj: Imperial Attitudes and Policies and Their Critics, 1793–1905*. New York: St. Martin's Press.

Bhagavad Gita. 1945. Edited by Shripad Krishna Belvalkar. Poona Bhandarkar Oriental Research Institute.

Birken, Lawrence. 1988. *Consuming Desire: Sexual Science and the Emergence of a Culture of Abundance. 1871–1914*. Ithaca and London: Cornell University Press.

Brown, Wendy. 1988. *Manhood and Politics: A Feminist Reading in Political Theory*. Totawa, N.J.: Rowman and Littlefield.

Cakravarti, Candra. 1963. *Sex Life in Ancient India: An Explanatory and Comparative Study*. Calcutta: Firmal K. L. Mukhopadhyay.

Callaway, Helen. 1987. *Gender, Culture and Empire: European Women in Colonial Nigeria*. London: Macmillan Press.

Carstairs, G. Morris. 1958. *The Twice-Born*. London: Hogarth Press.

Chakravarti, Uma. 1990. "Whatever Happened to the Vedic *Dasi?* Orientalism, Nationalism and a Script for the Past." In Kumkum Sangari and Sudesh Vaid, eds., *Recasting Women: Essays in Indian Colonial History*, pp. 27–87. New Brunswick: Rutgers University Press.

Chandra, Bipin. 1984. *Communalism in Modern India*. New Delhi: Vikas.

Chatterjee, Partha. 1986. *Nationalist Thought and the Colonial World*. London: Zed Books.

—— 1989. "Colonialism, Nationalism, and Colonized Women: The Contest in India." *American Ethnologist* 16.4: 622–33.

—— 1990. "The Nationalist Resolution of the Women's Question." In Kumkum Sangari and Sudesh Vaid, eds., *Recasting Women: Essays in Indian Colonial History*, pp. 233–53. New Brunswick: Rutgers University Press.

Cooper, Frederick, and Ann L. Stoler. 1989. "Introduction—Tensions of Empire: Colonial Control and Visions of Rule." *American Ethnologist* 16.4: 609–21.

Daniel, E. Valentine. 1984. *Fluid Signs: Being a Person the Tamil Way*. Berkeley: University of California Press.

Dumont, Louis. 1986. *Essays on Individualism: Modern Ideology in Anthropological Perspective*. Chicago: University of Chicago Press.

Edwards, James. 1983. "Semen Anxiety in South Asian Cultures: Cultural and Transcultural Significance." *Medical Anthropology*, Summer: 51–67.

Elshtain, Jean Bethke. 1981. *Public Man, Private Woman*. Princeton: Princeton University Press.

Embree, Ainslie T. 1990. *Utopias in Conflict: Religion and Nationalism in Modern India*. Berkeley: University of California Press.

Erikson, Erik H. 1969. *Gandhi's Truth*. New York: Norton.

Etienne, Mona, and Elenor Leacock. 1980. *Women and Colonization*. New York: Praeger Press.

Fox, Richard. 1989. *Gandhian Utopia: Experiments with Culture*. Boston: Beacon Press.

Gandhi, M. K. 1927. *The Story of My Experiments with Truth*, Mahadev Desai, trans. Ahmedabad: Navjivan Prakashan Mandir.

Gellner, Ernest. 1983. *Nations and Nationalism*. Oxford: Basil Blackwell.

Hobsbawm, Eric J. 1990. *Nations and Nationalism Since 1780: Programme, Myth, Reality*. Cambridge: Cambridge University Press.

Hyam, Ronald. 1990. *Empire and Sexuality: The British Experience*. Manchester: Manchester University Press.

Kakar, Sudhir. 1981. *The Inner World: A Psycho-analytic Study of Childhood and Society in India*. Delhi: Oxford University Press.

—— 1982. *Shamans, Mystics and Doctors: A Psychological Inquiry into India and its Healing Traditions*. Delhi: Oxford University Press.

—— 1987. *Tales of Love, Sex and Danger*. London: Unwin Hyman.

—— 1990. *Intimate Relations: Exploring Indian Sexuality*. Chicago: University of Chicago Press.

Laqueur, Thomas. 1986. "Orgasm, Generation and the Politics of Reproductive Biology." *Representations* 14: 1–41.

MacMunn, Sir George. 192? [1977]. *The Martial Races of India*. Quetta (Pakistan): Gosha-e-Adab.

Mani, Lata. 1987. "Contentious Traditions: The Debate on *Sati* in Colonial India." *Cultural Critique* 7: 119–56.

Manu. 1886 [1964]. *Dharma Shastra*. F. Max Muller, ed. Delhi: Motilal Banarsidass.

Marglin, Frederique Apffel. 1985. *Wives of the God-King: The Rituals of the Devadasis of Puri*. Delhi: Oxford University Press.

Marriott, McKim. 1990. *India Through Hindu Categories*. New Delhi: Sage Publications.

—— 1991. "On 'Constructing an Indian Ethnosociology.' " *Contributions to Indian Sociology* (n.s.) 25.2: 295–308.

Martin, Emily. 1987. *The Women in the Body: A Cultural Analysis of Reproduction*. Boston: Beacon Press.

—— 1989. "The Cultural Construction of Gendered Bodies: Biology and Metaphors of Production and Destruction." *Ethnos* 54.3–4: 143–60.

—— 1990. "Toward an Anthropology of Immunology: The Body as Nation State." *Medical Anthropology Quarterly* 4.4: 410–26.

—— 1991. "The Egg and the Sperm: How Science Has Constructed a Romance Based on Stereotypical Male-Female Roles." *Signs* 16.3: 485–501.

Meyer, Johann Jakob. 1930. *Sexual Life in Ancient India*, 2 vols. New York.

Mosse, George. 1985. *Nationalism and Sexuality*. Madison: University of Wisconsin Press.

Muller, F. Max. 1879 [1965]. *The Sacred Laws of the Arayas*. Delhi: Motilal Banarsidass.

Nandy, Ashis. 1980. *At the Edge of Psychology: Essays in Politics and Culture*. Delhi: Oxford University Press.

—— 1983. *The Intimate Enemy: Loss and Recovery of Self Under Colonialism*. Delhi: Oxford University Press.

Obeyesekere, Gananath. 1976. "The Impact of Ayurvedic Ideas on the Culture and the Individual in Sri Lanka." In Charles Leslie, ed., *Asian Medical Systems*. Berkeley and Los Angeles: University of California Press.

—— 1981. *Medusa's Hair: An Essay on Personal Symbols and Religious Experience*. Chicago and London: University of Chicago Press.

O'Flaherty, Wendy Doniger. 1973. *Asceticism and Eroticism in the Mythology of Siva*. London: Oxford University Press.

—— 1980. *Women, Androgynes and Other Mythical Beasts*. Chicago: University of Chicago Press.

O'Hanlon, Rosalind. 1991. "Issues of Widowhood: Gender and Resistance in Colonial Western India." In Douglas Haynes and Gyan Prakash, eds., *Contesting Power: Resistance and Everyday Social Relations in South Asia*, pp. 62–108. Berkeley and Los Angeles: University of California Press.

Oldenberg, Veena Talwar. 1991. "Lifestyle as Resistance: The Case of the Courtesans of Lucknow." In Douglas Haynes and Gyan Prakash, eds., *Contesting Power: Resistance and Everyday Social Relations in South Asia*, pp. 23–61. Berkeley and Los Angeles: University of California Press.

Rosselli, John. 1980. "The Self-Image of Effeteness: Physical Education and Nationalism in Nineteenth-Century Bengal." *Past and Present* 86: 121–48.

Rudolph, Susanne. 1967. "Self-Control and Political Potency." *American Sociological Review*.

Rudolph, Susanne, and Lloyd Rudolph. 1967. *The Modernity of Tradition*. Chicago: University of Chicago Press.

Said, Edward. 1978. *Orientalism*. New York: Vintage.

Salam, Abdus. 1895. *Physical Education in India*. Calcutta: W. Newman and Co.

Sangari, Kumkum, and Sudesh Vaid. 1990. *Recasting Women: Essays in Indian Colonial History*. New Brunswick: Rutgers University Press.

Saraswati, Swami Yogananda. 1982. *Brahmacharya Raksha Hi Jiwan Hai* (Celibacy is Life Itself). Alwar: Pandit Ramji Lal Sharma.

Shastri, Kaviraj Jagannath. N.d. *Brahmacharya Sadhana: Virya Raksha Hi Swasthya ka Sar Hai* (The Means by Which to Maintain Celibacy: Semen Protection is the Way to Health). Delhi: Dehati Pustak Bhandar.

Shivananda, Swami. 1984. *Brahmacharya Hi Jiwan Hai* (Celibacy Itself is Life). Allahabad: Adhunik Prakashan Graha.

Smith, A. D. 1983. *Theories of Nationalism*. London.

Spratt, P. 1966. *Hindu Culture and Personality*. Bombay: Manaktalas.

Stevenson, Sinclair. 1920 [1971]. *The Rites of the Twice-Born*. Delhi: Munshiram Manoharlal.

Stoler, Ann L. 1989. "Making Empire Respectable: The Politics of Race and Sexual Morality in 20th-century Colonial Cultures." *American Ethnologist* 16.4: 634–60.

Strobel, Margaret. 1987. "Gender and Race in the 19th and 20th Century British Empire." In R. Bridenthal et al., eds., *Becoming Visible: Women in European History*, pp. 375–96. Boston: Houghton and Mifflin.

Tharu, Susie. 1990. "Tracing Savitri's Pedigree: Victorian Racism and the Image of Women in Indo-Anglian Literature." In Kumkum Sangari and Sudesh Vaid, eds., *Recasting Women: Essays in Indian Colonial History*, pp. 254–68. New Brunswick: Rutgers University Press.

PART SEVEN

Culture and Contests

CULTURE AND CONTESTS

I T HAS OFTEN BEEN SAID that cultural conflicts were at the heart of decolonization. Europeans, it is true, evidenced little patience for indigenous cultural demands and certainly tended to use their overseas empires as an instrument to instill their own values and attitudes on other cultures. This section attempts to bring together three provocative essays on popular culture that demonstrate the degree to which "culture" factored into decolonization. The three territories under consideration are Northern Rhodesia, Africa broadly considered, and Shanghai. The issues discussed are alcohol and popular politics, sport and soccer, and the leisure and sex industries.

In "Alcohol, Racial Segregation and Popular Politics in Northern Rhodesia" Charles Ambler presents readers with an extremely convincing case of how European regulations on alcohol consumption for Africans in Rhodesia fueled African resentment for European colonial rule and led to popular resentment of the colonial system. As Ambler points out, the British controllers of Northern Rhodesia allowed racial and cultural stereotypes of Africans (as sexually aggressive, etc.) to inform colonial policies on alcohol. As a result, Europeans concocted elaborate oversight schemes and confined drinking to a limited number of beerhalls that were overseen by whites. The refusal to let Africans consume alcohol unharassed provoked beerhall protests sponsored by nationalists who challenged the colonial status quo on drinking through boycotts. Similarly, Ambler underscores the divergent cultural and political concerns within African nationalist movements on the eve of independence, which Northern Rhodesia achieved under the name of Zambia in 1964.

Coming at the question of culture from a different angle, Paul Darby demonstrates in "Football, Colonial Doctrine and Indigenous Resistance: Mapping the Political Persona of FIFA's African Constituency" that the history of sport affords fascinating insights into the study of nationalism and decolonization. Darby argues that football in Africa was an outgrowth of European cultural influences, yet as Africans developed the game it increasingly became a marker of resistance against imperial rule. Darby makes his case about football becoming a cultural site of anti-colonial resistance through a unique comparative approach to colonial sport that examines British, French, and Belgian colonial doctrines in Africa. This comparison allows readers to situate sport within the larger colonial project of European cultural imperialism and to test the traditional assumptions about Europe's hegemonic relationship with its colonies. Darby is thus able to demonstrate how football – as a cultural phenomenon in Africa – became increasingly central to both indigenous resistance to colonialism as well as subsequent efforts of the international community to redefine the game in the aftermath of decolonization. In this sense, Darby presents football as something that eventually inverted the traditional metropolitan–colonial relationship.

While the football in Africa helped unbalance Europe's hegemonic cultural forces and prohibitions on alcohol consumption in Northern Rhodesia fueled nationalist resentment, Frederick Wakeman, Jr. argues in "Licensing Leisure: The Chinese Nationalists' Attempt to Regulate Shanghai, 1927–47" that Asian nationalists were confronted with a host of very different obstacles as they wrestled Shanghai – culturally and politically – from Western influences. In an effort to reestablish a notion of civic culture, Chinese nationalists fought hard to control the definitions of proper social behavior and encouraged their police force to discipline those who veered into the French and British nightclubs and bordellos. Narcotics and racing also proved difficult for nationalists to regulate, as Europeans in Shanghai continually fought against the nationalists' objections to Western cultural vices. While Chinese nationalists attempted to regulate vice and keep communism at bay, they failed to provide the Chinese in Shanghai with a notion of civic culture that could compete with Western cultural influences such as drugs, prostitution, gambling, and political corruption. However, as Wakeman argues, this was not the case for the communists, who in 1949 began to eliminate (rather than regulate) urban Western vices from Shanghai in the pursuit of an authentic social revolution.

Chapter 17

Charles Ambler

ALCOHOL, RACIAL SEGREGATION AND POPULAR POLITICS IN NORTHERN RHODESIA

I N   J U N E   O F   1 9 6 2 , during a debate in the Northern Rhodesia Legislative Assembly, one of the few African members made a prediction: 'I think as soon as we have an African government in this country, [beerhalls] will be the first thing it will hit at.'[1] It may seem unusual that, in the midst of a bitter and violent racial and inter-party contest for the political destiny of this territory, a prominent African politician could suggest that changing liquor laws would be the first order of business of a future African government. In fact, his prediction proved accurate; when elections brought an African-dominated government to power in 1964 one of the first acts of the new administration was to eliminate the beerhalls. There was nothing frivolous, however, in the decision of this new government to dismantle the colonial structure of legislation governing the consumption of alcohol by Africans. During the two decades of political struggle that preceded Zambian independence, popular actions had repeatedly challenged restrictive and racially discriminatory alcohol regulations. Examination of these often acrimonious conflicts illuminates some of the varied and sometimes contradictory social forces shaping a nationalist movement that to date has been studied largely in terms of the development of party politics.

Alcohol regulation

International agreements dating from the late nineteenth century obligated the European powers to ban the production and importation of distilled spirits for African consumption in most of tropical Africa. In Northern Rhodesia, as in their other east and central African dependencies, the British went even further and prohibited African consumption of all European-type bottled beers and wines as well. Before the 1920s, however, colonial authorities paid little attention to the production and consumption of traditional alcoholic drinks. In rural households across Northern Rhodesia women brewed various fermented grain beers for domestic use, for tribute, to compensate labourers, and to mark ceremonial and social occasions. Because brewing was hard work and required substantial amounts of grain, drinking was for most people an occasional activity – but an activity that was to be enjoyed to the fullest when the opportunity arose. During the times of year when grain was plentiful and women had less work to do in the fields, communal beer parties lasting long into the evening were the main source of entertainment in village communities. Since grain beers are highly perishable, there was little point in going home until the beer pots were empty. In these circumstances, men saw beer parties as opportunities to relax, to let down their guard – to get a bit drunk. They generally succeeded, even if in fact the amount of beer consumed was actually relatively small and the alcohol content low.

With the development of the copper-mining industry in Northern Rhodesia in the late 1920s and the concomitant growth of the Copperbelt towns and mining compounds, colonial authorities sought much stricter regulation of brewing and drinking by Africans. In rural areas officials might regard customary drinking patterns as harmless or even quaint; in urban areas these same patterns looked disruptive and dangerous. The rapid commercialization of grain beer production and sales in the town setting during the 1920s only increased the determination of white authorities to bring alcohol use in urban areas under state control.

Beginning in the early 1930s, the administration aggressively pressed a policy of municipal control over the production and sale of grain beer in towns. While continuing to permit private, non-commercial, brewing in the countryside, the British effectively banned all African brewing in towns and strongly encouraged the white-settler controlled municipalities to brew and sell grain beer at beerhalls modelled on those established in Durban, South Africa, in the early part of the century. As in Durban, profits from sales of beer were to be dedicated to the provision of basic amenities in African residential areas; in other words beerhall proceeds would foot the bill for maintaining a strict system of residential segregation. Not surprisingly, the local white settler community – notable for its virulent racism – gave strong support to this policy.

The alcohol regulations imposed in Northern Rhodesia clearly reflected British conceptions of the role of alcohol in society and its effects on human behaviour. As the international restrictions on trade in liquor suggest, the British, like most Europeans, generally believed that where possible Africans should not be permitted to drink spirits. The introduction of hard liquor, it was argued, would make Africans unruly and difficult to govern and would inexorably demoralize and impoverish African societies. The regulations on African beer adopted in Northern Rhodesia make it clear that similar racial assumptions shaped the attitudes of many whites toward the consumption by Africans of traditional, fermented drinks as well. Whites, and particularly employers, favoured limited hours of sale because they felt that Africans could not restrain their drinking and therefore could not be trusted to come to work sober.[2] Yet those who represented mining companies or the colonial administration ordinarily took a more relaxed view of African drinking than did white farmers and mine-workers, many of whom were of South African extraction.[3]

The requirement that drinking be confined to a few beerhalls under the strict control of a white supervisor in itself implied a fear, notably among the white settlers who controlled municipal governments, that widespread drinking would threaten the security of white residential areas. That the beerhalls had to be fenced and were permitted to open only during daylight hours underscored those worries.[4] Embedded within concerns about unregulated drinking were fears that alcohol made Africans sexually aggressive and violent, and that white women might become the targets of those impulses.[5] Northern Rhodesian whites, like their counterparts in other settler colonies, displayed a preoccupation that bordered on paranoia about the 'indecent curiosity' that African men were claimed to display toward white women.[6] During World War II, when many white settlers left their families alone on their farms, this phobia surfaced repeatedly in complaints to authorities about raucous and aggressive drunkenness.[7]

Although colonial authorities intended liquor laws to suppress the supposedly dangerous repercussions of alcohol consumption by Africans, officials certainly did not intend these regulations to prohibit drinking. Whatever their fears of the effects of alcohol on Africans, most Europeans also believed that Africans needed to drink to be content. Mine company officials especially saw beerhalls as places where Africans would maintain some semblance of their home lives, while releasing, in carefully monitored surroundings, the frustrations that accumulated in industrial employment. Whatever attempts whites later made to assign a traditional pedigree to beerhalls, they clearly began as alien institutions constructed according to the European specification that in urban areas African drinking would be purely a leisure activity.[8]

Alcohol and opposition to racial discrimination

The conscious African assault on racially inspired liquor laws began in the years immediately following World War II with a challenge to the prohibition on African consumption of European-type bottled beer and wine. A few of the relatively well-off and well-educated men who protested this ban had acquired a taste for bottled beer while in the armed services or by buying from bootleggers, but for most the issue was mainly symbolic. The consumption of bottled lager beer was an emblem of the European life-styles and values that they had been encouraged to aspire to and which separated them from the masses of Africans; the law forbidding that consumption continually reminded these members of the African élite that in a racist society like Northern Rhodesia those aspirations were chimerical.

In 1946, immediately after the government had confidently asserted that Africans in Northern Rhodesia had no interest in consuming bottled beer and wine, members of the newly formed African Representative Council (A.R.C.) vigorously disputed that contention.[9] Much to the surprise of government officials, the members devoted a good portion of their opening debate to an attack on racially discriminatory liquor laws and in particular the ban on bottled beer and wine. Nelson Nalumango claimed that 'wherever I have travelled in my area in the Southern Province, I have been asked why we, the leaders who have been chosen to represent the views of the people, should not approach the Government about Africans being granted permission to buy European beer'.[10] Another member hit directly at the racial assumptions of the prohibition: 'It is a very surprising thing that Africans are allowed to drink their own beer in the beer hall and that they are prevented from drinking European beer. I cannot see any difference between a person who drinks European beer and a person who drinks African beer — the intoxication is just the same.'[11] The member for the Copperbelt region put it most starkly: 'I beg the Government to remove this discriminatory law.'[12] In the course of debate, various speakers argued for an end to the prohibition on the grounds that similar bans were being eliminated in neighbouring colonies, that returning soldiers had become accustomed to such drinks, and that legalization of beer and wine would undermine any market for illicit spirits, 'the coming concoctions and Barbertons which are now growing rapidly in the south and some parts of this country'.[13]

No mass action supported these protests, but they nevertheless had an immediate and telling impact; within two years the government had pushed through the Legislative Council a law that allowed Africans to purchase bottled beer and wine. The arguments advanced by members of the A.R.C. were persuasive on several crucial points. The recent decision of the East African colonies of Uganda, Kenya and Tanganyika, encouraged by the Colonial Office, to permit bottled beer consumption by Africans had in fact created a precedent that would have been difficult to ignore.[14] But the mention of demands of ex-servicemen hit a particularly sensitive nerve. The Northern Rhodesia administration, like many others, was concerned about the possibilities of heightened aspirations and loss of habits of deference of returning African soldiers. Letting them drink bottled beer might side-track more fundamental challenges.[15]

The emotion that members of the A.R.C. brought to their denunciations of the beer and wine prohibition made it clear that they cared deeply about this issue. These were men whose support the Northern Rhodesia administration had determined to win. Prodded by London, the government was installing a network of representative institutions in both urban and rural areas which were designed to provide popular legitimacy for the colonial regime and draw support away from the African welfare society movement that was then gathering strength.[16] It was, of course, precisely those men who were involved in both the new councils and the welfare societies who had the desire to drink bottled beer and the resources to buy it. Moreover, these men were conscious, as were the British, of the line that such drinking would draw between them and most of their fellow Africans. Indeed, at least one member of the A.R.C. suggested that drinking bottled beer ought to be the privilege of Africans of 'good character'.[17] Several years later another prominent A.R.C. member, Dauti Yamba, would argue for similar discriminatory provisions in the liquor laws on the grounds that 'class distinction would give encouragement to the advancement of all Africans wishing to get to that class so that he gets better treatment'.[18]

Although the pleas for modification of the liquor laws won government support, the proposed changes met considerable opposition from segments of the white population for whom the prohibition on beer and wine consumption by Africans had as much symbolic importance as it had for blacks. Whites viewed the ban on bottled beer as an important barrier to inter-racial contact. A former African policeman recalled that Europeans thought. 'If we allow the people to drink European beer that would be mixing.'[19] Even a decade later, the stalwart if highly paternalistic defender of gradual African advancement, Sir Stewart Gore-Browne, insisted that 'the dangers inherent in allowing coloured persons [i.e. Africans] to mix with Europeans in bars are too obvious to need discussion'.[20] Racist assumptions surfaced also in concerns that Africans – supposedly unable to resist the lure of bottled beer – would spend beyond their means.[21] Even after the consumption of bottled beer and wine was legalized, Europeans continued to warn against permitting Africans to drink wine, pointing time and again to the havoc that wine was believed to have caused among the black population of the Cape Province of South Africa.[22] For their part, most African drinkers avoided wine anyway, perhaps thanks to the popular belief that the cheap South African wines imported into Northern Rhodesia were fed to horses elsewhere.[23]

What finally overcame any reluctance of the white authorities to liberalize the liquor laws was their hope that permitting Africans to consume bottled beer and wine would keep them away from spirits. Even African promoters of reform pushed the dubious line that the availability of beer and wine would steer consumers away from illegal rotgut. European fears of the effects of African consumption of spirits were so extreme and widespread that they came to see the provision of beer and wine as a crucial defense against the introduction of hard liquor – legal or illegal – in African society.[24] Beginning with the very first debates in which Africans put forth their demands for the relaxation of alcohol regulations, Europeans stated and restated their vehement opposition to Africans drinking spirits. In 1946 Gore-Browne told A.R.C. members, 'I would resist with all my effort any idea of allowing Africans to buy spirits'.[25]

All this concern among whites regarding the effects of wine and spirits upon Africans ensured that liquor laws would remain a point of contention and a symbol of discrimination.[26] In 1948, in a Copperbelt urban council meeting, one questioner challenged the racist foundations of this concern when he asked 'if it was written on the books of the Government that all Africans were drunkards'.[27] Two years later, an African member of the Legislative Council noted that 'the impression is that an African is a weak victim of any drink. I do not believe in this, because the poison that kills an African also kills a European.'[28] Even though Africans could now buy beer and wine, they had for many years to purchase and consume them at beerhalls, a restriction that particularly irritated the more prosperous and better educated segment of the population.[29] Throughout the 1950s strict racial segregation continued to prevail in public facilities including especially hotels and bars. Even the tentative suggestion that bottle stores be opened to Africans was summarily rejected on the grounds that spirits were also sold on those premises, a rationale that prompted a sarcastic promise in the A.R.C. from Dauti Yamba that 'when we enter a store we will only enter to buy beer and not ask for a poison'.[30] Increased African involvement in politics brought a few colonial officials to speak of the 'soothing effect' that they imagined might come with the legalization of spirits; but most whites remained adamantly opposed to African consumption of hard liquor.[31] It was not until the very eve of independence that this last vestige of racially discriminatory liquor legislation was discarded.

For many whites, African demands for legal spirits, coupled with the spread of illicit liquor and the rapid rise in the consumption of bottled beer, both reflected and encouraged a dangerous breakdown in traditional values as well as a blurring of essential racial boundaries. Some advocated a campaign to draw Africans back to traditional drinks (which in urban areas were now mass-produced), as if filling men with grain beer would cause them to forget their demands for higher pay and political rights.[32] But the main emphasis in the policies of both the government and the mining companies lay in the improvement of beerhalls and beergardens and in the construction of alternative drinking facilities that would attract the urban élite. Whatever the appeal of new clubs and 'cocktail bars' (that did not serve cocktails), prosperous African town dwellers preferred to celebrate important events and meet and entertain their friends in private homes where the refreshments were often blackmarket imported gins and whiskeys.[33] In this contemptuous rejection of alcohol regulation they allied themselves with a broader movement of opposition to state-controlled leisure.

The anti-beerhall movement

Popular opposition to liquor control arose over the issue of state regulation of the production and consumption of traditional-type grain beers, rather than over access to bottled beer and wine or spirits. From the 1930s the expansion of the monopolistic beerhall system had generated growing anger among town residents; in the 1950s this anger surfaced in a dramatic series of mass protests and boycotts. The boycott, and especially the beerhall boycott, became one of the most potent protest weapons in the arsenal of the Northern Rhodesian African National Congress (A.N.C. or Congress), the nationalist organization formed in 1948 in response to the settler movement that led in 1953 to the Central African Federation. But popular action against the beerhalls had its own roots and momentum; and if African politicians were sometimes able to use beerhall boycotts and protests to good effect, they were never able to define or control the popular feeling against the beerhall monopoly.

People first opposed the beerhall system because it disrupted traditional patterns of social drinking and prevented the ritual use of alcohol for occasions such as funerals.[34] Although whites often saw beerhalls as well suited to the supposed natural gregarious-ness of Africans, Africans themselves originally regarded the beerhalls as impersonal mass institutions that undermined the established patterns of social interaction that traditional drinking reinforced. When drinking in beerhalls it was impossible to pre-serve the private character or ambience of the communal beer party.[35] Town residents complained repeatedly that they were forbidden to drink at night, that in beerhalls they were thrown together with all kinds of people, and above all that the beer served in the halls was bad-tasting and weak.[36] Many Africans as well as whites came to feel that the beerhalls bred crime and immorality. Critics blamed beerhalls for encouraging drunkenness, profligacy and increased juvenile delinquency, and especially for unseemly behaviour on the part of women. Members of the 'respectable' class of Africans increasingly dismissed beerhalls as tawdry and unpleasant – hence the push for the legalization of other kinds of alcoholic beverages and for the opening of small bars and bottle stores to Africans.[37]

Denunciations of the supposedly degrading environment of beerhalls also gave moral flavour to objections that were essentially commercial.[38] As early as 1928, in their protest against plans to open a beerhall in the Copperbelt town of Ndola, a group of African church members made it clear that they objected not only to the problems that would come with the encouragement of drinking but also to the establishment of a European monopoly over what until that time had been – although illicit – an African-dominated commerce. In their words, 'the beerhall is a means of keeping us [in] an inferior position because our money will be snatched from us daily'.[39] No matter how often the colonial authorities pointed out that beer profits were spent on 'native welfare', the beerhall would remain for many Africans a symbol of colonial political and economic domination.[40] When in 1957 the A.R.C. debated a motion to permit African businessmen to operate private bars, members argued that beerhalls were overcrowded, sordid and dangerous; but their main objective was to open a new area of legitimate trade to Africans.[41] In a statement greeted with huzzas, one supporter noted that 'this motion is advocating the distribution of income amongst the Africans . . . I must emphasize . . . what an economic question it is and how important it is equally as owning shops, farms and anything at all that will lead to the development and progress economically of the African people. It has nothing to do with Christianity, this question of economy.'[42]

The people who went to live in Northern Rhodesia's growing towns first resisted state alcohol regulations by ignoring them; instead of patronizing beerhalls, migrants attempted to recreate as much as possible traditional patterns of drinking. The realities of urban and industrial life rapidly transformed cottage brewing into a commercial activity; nevertheless, the beer prepared by private female brewers was relatively authentic and the circumstances in which it was sold and served far more closely resembled a village setting than did the new beerhalls. During the 1930s and 1940s, as municipalities across the territory established beerhalls, illegal private brewing expanded even more rapidly.[43] Despite its illegality, brewing became an established occupation for women in Northern Rhodesian towns – and increasingly in the country-side as well. The preparation and sale of beer was simply one of the very few means that they had at their disposal to support themselves and their families.[44] One woman recalled that brewing was the only way she could raise school fees for her children; in the words of another, 'that is how we clothed our children'.[45] At a 1943 meeting a group of chiefs asked the government 'to allow the people to brew and sell beer so that they will be enabled to get money to buy clothes'.[46] Thus, when the authorities used police to suppress beer production, the brewers fought back. Some women organized them-selves into mutual support circles so that if arrested they could raise fines and quickly get back into business; others abandoned the towns and established themselves in the surrounding countryside where detection was much more difficult.[47] On more than one occasion, brewers and their customers attacked or stoned the police and forced them to retreat.[48]

What most shocked the government about this lawlessness was the failure of African opinion to condemn it.[49] Because most Africans believed that beer regulations were designed primarily to generate revenue for the state, they tended to view police campaigns against illegal brewing and beer-selling as the suppression of competition.[50] They despised the frequent midnight police raids on suspected brewers as disruptive invasions of privacy.[51] Even members of the African Representative Council, normally sympathetic to official policies, denounced the arrests of female brewers as an unwarranted criminalization of women.[52] Recognizing the impossibility of stamping out brewing and the animosity that attempts to do so engendered, a 1948 government report on the subject advocated the gradual introduction of private, licensed brewing. But opposition from mining companies, which feared loss of control over their work-force, and from municipalities, which had come to depend upon alcohol revenues, doomed that proposal.[53] The stage was thus set for a confrontation over beerhalls.

The first direct popular challenge to the monopoly system came in 1954 in Lusaka.[54] There, competition from illicit producers had sharply reduced beerhall revenues and caused municipal officials to step up police raids on brewers.[55] But the local African community refused to acquiesce in this intensified enforcement of liquor law. According to a contemporary report by an African researcher, 'forbidding illegal brewing in Lusaka is now a political matter since women feed their own families, pay rent, and supplement their husbands' income on the African beer they brew'.[56] In April the women brewers, working with the women's wing of the Lusaka branch of the African National Congress, began holding meetings to protest against the actions of the police.[57] These women were moved above all by their desperate need to earn money. In the words of one participant, 'our husbands get low wages and we have large families'.[58]

The women's protests culminated at the end of May in a mass demonstration of thousands of women at government headquarters in the centre of Lusaka.[59] Leaders of the protesters appealed to colonial officials at least for a modification of the beer monopoly that would permit women to brew beer for sale at the municipal beerhalls, arguing that since Africans were forbidden to consume *white* liquors such as whiskey and gin they ought to be free to produce and consume their own *African* drinks.[60] But the District Commissioner informed the crowd that there was no way he could accommodate their demands as the law forbade private brewing. According to the press account, after he withdrew 'the women rushed forward and adopted a hysterical attitude, and attempted to force an entry into the office'.[61] Police then used tear gas to disperse the demonstrators. In the aftermath there were reports that men who had been watching the protest engaged in rock-throwing, and police made a number of arrests. During the days that followed there were sporadic recurrences of unrest, and in the compounds residents intimidated government supporters and tried to enforce boycotts of the beerhalls.[62]

The British authorities found it difficult to respond to or even to comprehend the anger and militancy of the women. Officials ultimately concluded, or preferred to believe, that the demonstration had not been a spontaneous action, but rather a well-orchestrated manipulation of the beer issue by Congress leaders bent on furthering their campaign to discredit the Federation. In the end all those charged with major offences in relation to the demonstrations were male officials of the Congress whom the presiding judge held had 'deliberately engineered a violent assault on constituted authority'. Against overwhelming contrary evidence, he went on to claim that the women had been forced against their will to participate.[63] Ironically, male African nationalist politicians were probably as much disconcerted by this display of female determination as were white officials. In fact, in the next major challenge to the beerhall system the preservation of male control over women emerged as a major issue.

During the next several years, municipalities substantially expanded their beerhall operations. As profits increased, towns became ever more dependent on beer sale revenues, and thus more vulnerable to boycotts.[64] Recognizing these circumstances, the Congress organized a national campaign against beerhalls in 1957 that caused considerable disorder in both Lusaka and in the Copperbelt and effectively shut down beerhalls in many towns for extended periods. The campaign began in Lusaka in early July. Organized by the local Congress branch, women and men armed with sticks and stones began to picket the beerhalls. They permitted purchases of bottled beer but not grain beer, 'as it was being sold to fill the pockets of Europeans with money'.[65] Africans who supported the government or violated the boycott found themselves the subject of intimidation, their houses stoned and in some cases smeared with excrement. Several confrontations with police followed, and protestors burned to the ground part of one of the municipal beerhalls.[66]

The anti-beerhall movement spread quickly from Lusaka to the Copperbelt towns where with varying degrees of success and persistence local Congress branches organized boycotts.[67] Frightened by the substantial crowds that gathered at public meetings, the authorities confronted beerhall pickets and protesters with a provocative police presence. At Chingola demonstrations developed into a riot that left several whites and numerous Africans injured and forced municipal employees and police into humiliating retreat over the beerhall wall. While the protests continued in Chingola and the police arrested hundreds of the women and men involved, the boycott gained virtually total effectiveness in the Copperbelt municipalities if not in the mineworker compounds.[68] The protests clearly frightened local whites and cut deeply into revenues; nevertheless, within weeks the campaign began to disintegrate and at the end of the month the local newspaper smugly reported that 'beer flowed normally down thousands of African throats on the Copperbelt as the African Congress beerhall boycott died – of thirst – today'.[69] But this obituary was somewhat premature. Congress youth and women's organizations revived the effort in several towns during September. In Mufulira, for example, more than five hundred demonstrators blocked beer deliveries, while in Luanshya the government called in the special paramilitary anti-riot force to quell protests.[70] Later in the month, however, the Congress head, Harry Nkumbula, rejected a call for an expansion of the anti-beerhall campaign and instead declared it over.[71] Even then a number of local branches ignored the directive.[72]

Northern Rhodesian whites saw the boycotts essentially in political terms. According to the major local newspaper, 'The whole basis of the boycotts seems to be changed . . . They have a look of nationalism, naked and unashamed'.[73] It was certainly true that A.N.C. leaders and militants viewed the anti-beerhall campaign both as a test of political strength and as a weapon of political action against the government – especially the settler-dominated municipalities. But if the demonstrators who blocked the Chingola beerhall in August chanted, 'We are fighting for our country', the masses of men and women who supported the boycotts acted out of motivations that were as much social and economic as they were directly political.[74]

Although the grievances of women brewers did not dominate the 1957 boycotts as they had the 1954 demonstrations, anger at the state monopoly over a potentially lucrative area of commerce still shaped the objectives of protesters. As the 1957 boycott was launched in Lusaka, for example, the local A.N.C. leader stated, 'We shall continue to struggle peacefully until the Government considers our demand to allow Africans to brew beer without licence', and protest leaders elsewhere made similar demands.[75] Although many continued to object to the criminalization of women brewers, it was quite plain that men also had hopes of profiting from a business whose illegality froze them out. An African critic of the boycott charged the Congress with 'encouraging the economic exploitation of Africans by Africans', but the commercially-minded men and women who dominated the A.N.C. would certainly not have seen it that way.[76]

Many of the leaders of Congress recognized moral as well as economic advantages in sweeping away the beerhalls. Whereas in 1954 protesters had objected to the system of state monopoly that the beerhalls represented, in 1957 they attacked the evils of the beerhall as an institution. In speeches and letters activists and sympathizers called the beerhalls 'places where people have gone and decayed', blaming them for poverty, juvenile delinquency, and especially idleness and improper behaviour among women.[77] An African member of a local management board claimed that 'most women were absent from their homes drinking and did not prepare lunch or supper for their husbands and children'.[78] Another African man noted, 'I give my wife money to buy meat and she comes home drunk and without the money or the meat.'[79] According to another, 'I never go to the Beer Hall with my wife . . . that way can easily lead to fighting between you and even divorce'.[80] Hence the boycotters called for a reduction of beerhall hours, Sunday closings and a total ban on women customers.[81] This ban won strong support not only from men concerned over the growing independence of urban women, but from female Congress supporters as well. For the 'respectable' married women who populated the nationalist ranks, such support made perfect sense. To them the 'loose' women who frequented the beerhalls lured their husbands into dalliances and drank away their paychecks, in the process upsetting aspirations for stable homes and companionate marriages.[82]

The politics of beerhalls

Although the 1957 boycott campaign mobilized mass support for the nationalist cause on an unprecedented scale, the protests over the beerhalls also illuminated the sharp fissures that would divide opposition forces during the years before independence. The repeated refusal of relatively radical Congress branches to accept direction from the more conservative national leadership indicated the existence of divisions within the party that in the following year resulted in the departure from the A.N.C. of the group led by Kenneth Kaunda and the eventual formation of the United National Independence Party (U.N.I.P.).[83] Equally important, the boycott campaign displayed the substantial differences in perspective that separated the nationalist politicians from leaders of an African Mineworkers Union bent on preserving the relatively privileged position of the mineworkers.

Proposals for the privatization of beer production and sales, demands for reduced beerhall hours and condemnations of the moral evils of the beerhalls won little support from the working men who regularly patronized the halls.[84] In July, when Nkumbula, president of the A.N.C., made his first unsuccessful attempt to cancel the campaign, the union president sent him a congratulatory telegram assuring him that 'all sensible Africans are behind you in your wise moves'.[85] If in this case Nkumbula opposed the boycott tactic, he nevertheless shared the distaste that most political leaders and other members of the African élite felt toward beerhalls, and perhaps their patrons. Differences in drinking preferences had long been markers of status distinction. In the beerhalls, more prosperous and better-educated men had often ceremoniously segregated themselves, earning the resentment of their poorer fellow drinkers. This resentment persisted through the 1950s and early 1960s when the élite turned to the consumption of bottled beer and migrated to clubs and smaller bars that were never the subject of boycotts.[86] When African politicians and intellectuals denounced the beerhalls as degrading and untraditional, they failed to comprehend that the beerhalls had gradually evolved into genuine and vibrant community institutions – managed but not entirely controlled by the state.

Despite the apparent failure of the 1957 campaign, local political activists continued to organize beerhall boycotts to confront the white authorities. In April 1958 when Ndola imposed rent increases on African residents the local people fought back by boycotting and attacking the main beerhall.[87] Later in 1958 and again in 1959, A.N.C. activists attempted to organize boycotts at Chingola.[88] In 1960 militants attacked the only beerhall in Kitwe that was not affected by a boycott. These actions culminated in 1961 in a U.N.I.P.-organized 'Keep Sober' campaign that attempted a nation-wide beerhall boycott.[89] As the 'keep sober' theme suggests, the nationalists maintained their moral objections to beerhall drinking. In the politicians' view, beerhall boycotts prevented workers from squandering their wages and, not incidentally, made money available for political donations.[90]

The British decision to support an eventual transition to majority rule in Northern Rhodesia and the concomitant disintegration of the Federation shifted the focus of political action from racial confrontation to a bitter struggle for preeminence between the two main African political parties, the A.N.C. and U.N.I.P. This period of political conflict climaxed in early 1963 in a series of often violent confrontations that rocked the Copperbelt.[91] The report of the commission that investigated the disorders concluded that 'many of the major disturbances had their origin in or around beerhalls'.[92] More to the point, when one member of the commission asked a police official the question, 'Does the battle for [the Copperbelt town of] Mufulira centre around the beerhalls?', the answer came back, 'Mainly, yes, Sir.'[93]

In the commission's view the unrest at the beerhalls was the natural product of large crowds of drinkers gathering in a confined area; in fact the cause was the determination of competing political activists to win control over these institutions.[94] In the aftermath of the entry of A.N.C. and U.N.I.P. representatives into the national government and in anticipation of elections that would be based on universal suffrage, the two parties struggled to gain the upper hand, especially in the mining towns. In this conflict, the masses of working class and unemployed urban residents became critical players and the beerhalls, as strongholds of working class culture, became the focus of political organization and action. Not surprisingly, this development finally convinced the mining companies and municipalities that beerhalls, however profitable, had to be replaced with smaller drinking establishments.[95]

During this period local chapters of the A.N.C. and U.N.I.P. in effect appropriated many of the beerhalls in Lusaka and in the Copperbelt towns.[96] Party loyalists gave the halls nicknames that signified their political identities. In Mufulira, for example, one of the beerhalls was known as 'Kapwepwe's Bar' after the U.N.I.P. official and future Zambian Vice-President, Simon Kapwepwe. Signs posted by the entrance displayed that nickname and the message, 'A.N.C. stay away'. Outside the Mufulira hall associated with the A.N.C., party supporters had written, 'Mukuba Bar-A.N.C. If any U.N.I.P. is killed it is his fault'.[97] At some of the party-controlled beerhalls, party workers stationed themselves at the entrances demanding that those who entered show their membership cards and in some cases pay a fee.[98] According to the District Commissioner in the mining town of Bancroft, beerhall patrons had 'a rather elaborate procedure to go through. You arrive at the beerhall and you run the gamut of a band of the U.N.I.P. Youth Brigade who inspect your credentials and if you have the necessary credentials you are allowed to go in, if you don't you are either sent to get them or you are beaten up.'[99] Militants used these party-controlled halls as bases of organization and various operations, including attacks on political opponents.[100] Beerhalls that were less thoroughly under party control were periodically invaded by activists who would intimidate patrons by demanding that membership cards be shown or that the appropriate hand sign be given.[101] If a political rally was scheduled, party workers might swoop down on a beerhall and force the patrons out of the hall to the meeting.[102] Needless to say, such tests of strength often led to confrontations and violence.[103]

Despite this pragmatic recognition of the importance of the beerhalls in the organization of urban communities, leaders of the two parties held on to more than a little of their antipathy to these institutions. In towns where U.N.I.P. had succeeded in establishing its dominance, the local party resorted once again to the beerhall boycott to cut off revenues to hostile municipal officials and to stop residents from spending too much of their money on beer.[104] When the youth wing members swept through beerhalls, overturning tables and dumping beer, they aimed a clear message at their elders, the patrons of the halls: at a time of political crisis drinking was a waste of time and money.[105] Numerous leaders in both parties made strong statements against beerhalls, or against any kind of excessive drinking.[106] On more than one occasion Kenneth Kaunda asserted, 'I hate beer . . . more than Federation'.[107]

This concern about the destructive social impact of the beerhalls persisted most prominently and effectively, however, in the continuing campaign to exclude women. In many beerhalls across the territory, the pressure of public opinion, in some cases reinforced by picketing, kept women away from the halls.[108] According to a U.N.I.P. women's brigade leader, the party's actions to prevent women from drinking in public were designed to strengthen the family. Too many husbands and children had gone hungry and too many marriages had broken down, she argued, because wives and mothers were wasting time and money in the beerhalls: 'If we are going to build a respectable society and a proud nation, a start aimed at reforming women must be made.' She continued: 'All we want is that women can buy their beer and have it at their homes in a dignified manner. If this is done the woman has a chance to see to domestic chores.'[109]

Given the persistence of such attitudes, it is hardly surprising that, once U.N.I.P. had gained power, the traditional distaste for beerhalls among leaders such as Kaunda, now Prime Minister, would re-emerge as strong as ever. Indeed, within months of taking office in early 1964 this new government ordered that the beerhalls be closed.[110] In taking this action, the new leadership revealed some of its fundamental concerns. Rather than legalize the existing illicit trade in traditional beer dominated by women brewers, the Kaunda government permitted municipalities to maintain their beer monopolies through the creation of networks of small-scale beerhalls that would purvey industrially-produced grain beer. In contrast, with all restrictions on the African consumption of other alcohol swept away, private individuals – presumably men with some capital – were free to enter the profitable trade in lager beer and spirits.[111] The moralistic opposition to alcohol use expressed by Kaunda and others in the leadership apparently made little if any impact on Zambian drinking habits. During the colonial years alcohol regulation had been inextricably linked to issues of racial discrimination and perhaps as a consequence efforts to control alcohol after independence won little support. Indeed, in the years immediately following independence consumption of both grain beer and lager beer increased dramatically.[112]

Notes

1   Job Michello, *Proceeding of the Northern Rhodesia Legislative Council (NRLC)*, 18 June 1962, para. 804.
2   Provincial Commissioner, Broken Hill, to Member for Health and Local Government, 13 Nov. 1951, Sec 5/444 no. 287, National Archives of Zambia (NAZ); and G. Quick,

Missionary in Charge, Mbereshi Boys' Training School, Kawambwa, to Chief Secretary, 13 July 1941, Sec 2/421 vol. 1, no. 116, NAZ.

3   Minutes, Executive Committee Meeting, Northern Rhodesia Chamber of Mines, 21 Nov. 1946, RST 202.7, Roan Consolidated Mines (formerly Rhodesia Selection Trust Corporation) Deposit (RCM), Archives of Zambia Consolidated Copper Mines, Ltd, Ndola, Zambia.

4   Secretary for Native Affairs to Chief Secretary, 6 Dec. 1929, ZA 1/9/83/1, no. 2, NAZ; Provincial Commissioner, Northern to Chief Secretary, 28 Nov. 1939, Sec 2/421, Lusaka, 29 Sept. 1943, Sec. 2/424, no. 109/5, NAZ.

5   Rex vs. Mambwe, Sub-Court of Resident Magistrate, Ndola, Criminal no. 289/1937, Sec 421, vol. 1, no. 9/1, NAZ.

6   Elena Berger, *Labour, Race and Colonial Rule: The Copperbelt from 1924 to Independence* (Oxford, 1974), 42.

7   File on 'Control of beer drinking on farms', Sec. 2/424, NAZ.

8   See F. Spearpoint, 'The African native and the Rhodesia copper mines', *J. Royal Afr. Soc.*, xxxvi, supplement (July 1937), 28–39.

9   Statement attributed to the Northern Rhodesia Government, quoted by Chief Secretary, East Africa Governors' Conference: memo to governments, 8 Jan. 1946, Sec 1/1573 no. 129, NAZ.

10 Nelson Nalumango, *Proceedings of the Northern Rhodesia African Representative Council (ARC)*, 16 Nov. 1946, cols. 123–4.

11 Chief Ikelenga, *ARC*, 16 Nov. 1946, col. 126.

12 Moses Mubitana, *ARC*, 16 Nov. 1946, col. 125.

13 Nelson Nalumango, *ARC*, 16 Nov. 1946, cols. 12, 123–4, 125–8.

14 Proceedings of the Conference of the Governors of Kenya, Uganda and Tanganyika, August 1945, CO 822/113/1, PRO.

15 File of the Post-War Problems Committee, Labour Department, NR 3/245, NAZ; and Labour Officer, Lusaka to Labour Commissioner, 24 Sept. 1945, Sec 2/424 no. 137B/1, NAZ.

16 See L. H. Gann, *History of Northern Rhodesia: Early Days to 1953* (London, 1964), 379–88.

17 Nelson Nalumango, *ARC*, 14 Nov. 1946, col. 12.

18 Dauti Yamba, *ARC*, 26 Jan. 1951, col. 245.

19 Mr Jubani, interview by author, 5 July 1988, Lusaka. Transcripts of all the interviews cited in the notes are in the author's possession.

20 Stewart Gore-Browne, Summary Response of Committee [on liquor law] Question-naire, 1955, Sec 5/443, NAZ.

21 E. G. Nightingale, *NRLC*, 15 March 1948, para. 160.

22 'Alcohol and the African', *Central African Post*, 6 May 1948, extracted in Sec 1/1573, NAZ.

23 Mr Kacheche, interview by J. Mwondiwa, Lusaka, June 1988.

24 Minute, 28 Oct. 1948, re Sec 1/1573, no. 192, NAZ.

25 *ARC*, 16 Nov. 1946, col. 130. See also extract of letter, Gore-Browne to Sec. for Native Affairs, 29 Oct. 1947, Sec 1/1573 no. 190; and Secretary for Native Affairs, *NRLC*, 15 March 1948, para. 167 (extract in Sec 1/1578, NAZ).

26 Sykes Ndilia, editor, *The African Mineworker*, Summary Response of Committee [on liquor law] Questionnaire, 1955, Sec 5/443, NAZ.

27 Minutes, Mufulira African Urban Advisory Committee Meeting, 12 May 1948, Sec 2/421 vol. 11, no. 438, NAZ.

28 *NRLC*, 6 Dec. 1950, para. 442.

29   Mr Mukupo, *ARC*, 20 Dec. 1952, cols. 146–8. People in rural areas were also effectively denied access to bottled beer. Stewart Gore-Browne, Summary Response of Committee [on liquor law] Questionnaire, 1955, Sec 5/443, NAZ.

30   Dauti Yamba, *ARC*, 20 Dec. 1952, col. 149.

31   'African liquor experiment', by J. Miller, *Northern News*, 3 June 1955 (extracted in Sec 5/443, NAZ); and G. S. Jones to Member for Commerce and Industry, 19 Oct. 1955, Sec 5/443, NAZ.

32   Minutes of the Northern Province District Commissioners Conference, No. 1954, Sec 5/443. Also, *Nchanga Drum* (a mining company newspaper), 13 June 1958.

33   Reuben Musonda, interview by J. Mlondiwa, Lusaka, 27 June 1988; 1954 report by D. Chansa summarized in Vernon X. Smith, 'Excessive drinking and alcoholism in the Republic of Zambia' (M.A. thesis, Howard University, 1973), 82.

34   Minutes of the African Provincial Council, Western Province, Kitwe, 24–26 June 1946, Sec 2/421 vol. 11, no. 362, NAZ; Mr Chilambwe, interview by author, Lusaka, 22 June 1988; Mr Million, interview by J. Mlondiwa, Lusaka, June 1988.

35   R. T. Chicken, *A Report on an Inquiry into the Prevalence of Illegal Brewing and Its Causes and Effects on Urban Areas near the Railway Line in Northern Rhodesia* (Lusaka, 1948), 7. Mr Kacheche, interview by J. Mlondiwa, Lusaka, June 1988.

36   Mr Jubani, interview with author, Lusaka, 5 July 1988; Mr Chilambwe, interview with author, Lusaka, 22 June 1988; and Chief Ikelenga, *ARC*, 16 Nov. 1946, col. 126.

37   'African views on beerhalls', selections of comments by African readers of the *Bantu Mirror* (Bulawayo, S. Rhodesia), 4 Jan. 1941 in Sec 2/421 vol. 1, NAZ. Of the ninety who wrote only seven commented favourably on the beerhalls. Chief Kopa, *ARC*, 16 Nov. 1946, col. 127.

38   See Provincial Commissioner, Eastern to Chief Secretary, 29 Nov. 1939, Sec 2/421, vol. 1, no. 35, NAZ; and Rev. Kasokolo, *NRLC*, 6 Dec. 1950, para. 439 (extracted in Sec 5/444, no. 283, NAZ).

39   Members, Ndola District Native Christian Church to Ndola Village Management Board, 4 Sept. 1928, forwarded to Secretary for Native Affairs, ZA 1/9/83/9/1, no. 1, NAZ.

40   As early as 1935 Copperbelt strikers attacked a mine compound beerhall. *Report of the Commission Appointed to Enquire into the Disturbances in the Copperbelt* (Lusaka, 1935), 29–30.

41   *ARC*, 7 June 1957, cols. 245–56.

42   L. Katilungu, *ARC*, 7 June 1957, col. 247.

43   Minute, 13 Oct. 1939, Sec 2/421 vol. 1, no. 29, NAZ; Chicken, *Report on Illegal Brewing*; and A. Lynn Saffery, *Report on Some Aspects of African Living Conditions on the Copperbelt of Northern Rhodesia* (Lusaka, 1943), 15, 20, 63.

44   George Chauncey, 'The locus of reproduction: women's labour in the Zambian Copperbelt, 1927–1953', *J. Southern Afr. Studies*, 7 (1981), 135–64.

45   Mrs White, interview by author, Lusaka, 5 July 1988.

46   Extract of minutes of a meeting between the Chief Secretary and Chiefs, Lundazi, 31 Aug. 1943, Sec 2/421 vol. 1, no. 185A, NAZ.

47   Mr Jubani, interview by author, Lusaka, 5 July 1988. Minute by Governor Maybin, 25 Oct. 1939, Sec 2/421, vol. 1, no. 32, NAZ; and Officer in Charge, N.R. Police, Broken Hill, to Commissioner of Police, Lusaka, 26 Nov. 1947, Sec 2/421, vol. 1, no. 406/1, NAZ.

48   Acting Provincial Commissioner, Southern, to Secretary for Native Affairs, 7 June 1947, Sec 2/421, vol. 11, no. 390, NAZ; Commissioner of Police to Secretary for

Native Affairs, 22 July 1947, Sec 2/421, vol. 11, no. 404, NAZ; T. R. Pickard, General Manager, Rhodesia Broken Hill Development Co., Ltd, to Labour Commissioner, Lusaka, 20 Sept. 1943, Sec 2/424, no. 109/2, NAZ; and Chicken, *Report on Illegal Brewing*, 6.

49   Proposed changes in draft report by R. T. Chicken on illegal brewing (1948), Sec 2/421, vol. 11, no. 465, NAZ. *ARC*, 14 and 16 Nov. 1946.

50   Mr Chandipo, interview by J. Mlondiwa, Lusaka, June 1988.

51   Chicken, *Report on Illegal Brewing*, 6; and Labour Officer, Nkana, 'Report on a visit to Broken Hill Mine, Sept. 21–24 1942', Sec 2/421, vol. 1, no. 181, NAZ.

52   *ARC*, 10 July 1948. Also, Minutes, African Provincial Council, Southern Province, Livingstone, 11–12 June 1946 (extract, Sec 2/421, vol. 11, no. 357, NAZ); and Minutes of a meeting between the Governor and the Livingstone African Urban Advisory Council, African Welfare Association and Livingstone Urban Native Court, 21 Sept. 1946 (extract, Sec. 2/421, vol. 11, no. 364, NAZ).

53   Chicken, *Report on Illegal Brewing*, 9. Also, Northern Rhodesia, *Report of the Committee to Consider the Liquor Licensing Ordinance* (Lusaka, 1955), 12.

54   There had been earlier boycotts over price rises. Provincial Commissioner, Western to Secretary for Native Affairs, 31 Oct. 1952, Sec 5/444, NAZ.

55   *Central African Post*, 28 May 1954.

56   D. Chansa quoted in Smith, 'Excessive drinking in Zambia', 84.

57   *Ibid.* 72; *Central African Post*, 21 May 1954; and W. Sikalumbi, *Before UNIP* (Lusaka, 1977) [written before 1965, some before 1960], 49.

58   Quoted in Smith, 'Excessive drinking in Zambia', 72.

59   *Central African Post*, 16 June 1954; and Sikalumbi, *Before UNIP*, 49.

60   Norman C. Rothman, 'The liquor authority and welfare administration in Lusaka', *Afr. Urban Studies*, 1 (Spring 1978), 34.

61   *Central African Post*, 21 May 1954.

62   *Ibid.*

63   *Ibid.* 16 June 1954.

64   Rothman, 'The liquor authority'.

65   *Northern News*, 3 July 1957.

66   *Ibid.* 3, 4, 5, 27 July 1957.

67   *Ibid.* 24 Sept. 1957; and David Mulford, *Zambia: The Politics of Independence, 1957–1964* (London, 1967), 64.

68   *Northern News*, 5 Aug. 1957.

69   *Ibid.* 29 Aug. 1957.

70   *Ibid.* 2, 18, 19 Sept. 1957.

71   *Ibid.* 24 Sept. 1957. Mulford, *Zambia: The Politics of Independence*, 64.

72   Sikalumbi, *Before UNIP*, 113; and *Northern News*, 1 Nov. 1957.

73   *Northern News*, quoted in Mulford, *Zambia: The Politics of Independence*, 64.

74   *Northern News*, 15 Aug. 1957.

75   *Ibid.* 4 July 1957, and 27 July 1957.

76   *Ibid.* 27 July 1957.

77   H. D. Banda, letter to the editor, *Ibid.* 5 Aug. 1957; and *Ibid.* 24 July 1957.

78   *Northern News*, 24 July 1957.

79   *Ibid.* 5 Aug. 1957.

80   A. L. Epstein, *Politics in an Urban African Community* (Manchester, 1958), 107.

81   Sikalumbi, *Before UNIP*, 113; *Northern News*, 31 July, 10 Aug. 1957. Restrictions on beerhalls would, of course, have benefited the illegal competition.

82   *Nchanga Drum*, April 1957, report on a meeting of the 'Young Wives Club'.

83   *Northern News*, 10 Aug., 5 Sept. 1957; and Mulford, *Zambia: The Politics of Independence*, 64.

84   *Northern News*, 10 Aug. 1957.

85   *Ibid.* 29 July 1957.

86   Commission of Inquiry into Unrest on the Copperbelt, July–August 1963, Evidence, mimeo, Lusaka, 1963, M. Adams (District Commissioner, Kitwe), 270; Nelson Kumwanda, interview with author, Lusaka, 22 June 1988; *Nchanga Drum*, Dec. 1957; and *Northern News*, 15 May and 23 July 1957.

87   Northern Rhodesia, 'Report of the Commissioner for the Ndola Riot Damage Area', mimeo, Lusaka, 23 May 1968, Box 57G, NAZ; and *Northern News*, 10 April 1958.

88   *Nchanga Drum*, 17 Oct. 1958, 21 Aug. 1959.

89   1963 Copperbelt Commission, Exhibits, 'Incidents of violence', Kitwe Municipal Council, July 1963; Northern Rhodesia, 'An account of the disturbances in Northern Rhodesia, July to October, 1961', Lusaka, 1961, 2; Nephas Tembo, *The Lilian Burton Killing* (Lusaka, 1986), 13; and Mulford, *Zambia: The Politics of Independence*, 199.

90   1963 Copperbelt Commission, Evidence, M. Chona (U.N.I.P. leader), 1328, 1336, 1346; and Harry Nkumbula (A.N.C. leader), 1252.

91   See 1963 Copperbelt Commission, Report, Evidence, and Memoranda.

92   1963 Copperbelt Commission, Report, 6.

93   1963 Copperbelt Commission, Evidence, L. Clark (Police Official), 529.

94   1963 Copperbelt Commission, Report, 6, 11–12.

95   African Personnel Manager, Roan Antelope Copper Mine, Memorandum on 'African beer', 11 May 1961, RCM/RST 203.8.1.

96   1963 Copperbelt Commission, Report, 5; 1963 Copperbelt Commission, Evidence, L. Clark, 528; Abel Mulenga, interview by J. Mlondiwa, Lusaka, June 1988; and Wellington Yakobe Nkosi, interview by J. Mlondiwa, Lusaka, 10 July 1988.

97   1963 Copperbelt Commission, L. Clark, Evidence, 512. Also, Festus Chileshe (shopkeeper), 1890; and Dominic Mwenya (mineworker), 2005.

98   *Ibid.* S. P. Bourne (deputy Provincial Commissioner), 49; L. Clark, 512; and 1963 Copperbelt Commission, Memoranda, L. K. Lombe, letter dated 21 July 1963.

99   1963 Copperbelt Commission, Evidence, R. Cunningham (District Commissioner), 858.

100 *Ibid.* G. Walsh (District Commissioner), 375; G. Lane (police official), 449–50; K. Pickles (District Commissioner), 489; L. Clark, 512; and H. Philpot (police official), 607.

101 *Ibid.* F. Roberts (police official), 104.

102 *Ibid.* M. Adams (District Commissioner), 225.

103 *Ibid.* L. Clark, 520; H. Philpot, 607; and Francis Mukuka (township secretary), 1905.

104 *Ibid.* A. Black (municipal official), 2079; and *Northern News*, 1 Aug. 1963.

105 Statement from Combined Kitwe Youth Clubs, 1963 Copperbelt Commission, Memoranda.

106 1963 Copperbelt Commission, Evidence, M. Adams, 270; and Harry Nkumbula, 1252.

107 *Zambia Times* (U.N.I.P. paper), 14 May 1963, in 1963 Copperbelt Commission, Memoranda.

108 1963 Copperbelt Commission, Evidence, M. Chona, 1506; and Rhodesia Broken

Hill Development Company, Ltd, Compound Report for Nov. 1963, Nchanga
Consolidated Copper Mines (formerly Anglo-American Corporation) deposit,
Zambia Consolidated Copper Mines Archives, NCCM/CSD/MO/220.

109   Ester Banda quoted in *Northern News*, 31 Aug. 1963.

110   Northern Rhodesia, Ministry of Local Government, 'Local authority liquor
undertakings', Circular 5/64, 11 April 1964.

111   A. Haworth, M. Mwanalushi and D. M. Todd, *Community Response to Alcohol-Related
Problems in Zambia*, vol. 1, *Historical and Background Information* (Institute for African
Studies, University of Zambia, 1981), 35–45.

112   *Ibid.* 49–50.

Chapter 18

Paul Darby

FOOTBALL, COLONIAL DOCTRINE AND INDIGENOUS RESISTANCE

Mapping the political persona of FIFA's African constituency

T HE INITIAL ANALYSIS CONTAINED WITHIN this article provides a broadly representative account of the diffusion and early development of football on the African continent by examining the spread of the game to a selection of former colonies that were controlled by three of Europe's primary imperial powers (Britain, Belgium and France). Attention is accorded to illuminating the nature of the linkages between football's diffusion to Africa and the various forms of colonial doctrine and imperialist policy that were prevalent throughout that continent during the first half of the twentieth century and this reveals that the game has featured in colonial exploitation and cultural imperialism. However, as the study goes on to illustrate, towards the latter stages of colonialism in Africa, football increasingly came to represent a forum for protest and resistance against European rule and the economic and cultural imperialisms that it engendered. The functioning of football in Africa as a form of resistance is also highlighted by examining the ways in which the game and its national, regional and international administrative structures were appropriated by newly independent African states, for the purposes of constructing a national identity and communicating that identity on an international basis. FIFA's limited role in mediating football's early growth in Africa and its subsequent reluctance to countenance Africa's lobby for a democratization of the game's global institutional and competition structures is also critically analysed. It is argued that the approach of the world governing body during the first 60 years of its existence was in many ways resonant of the missionary philosophy and, at times, élitist and exploitative attitudes that characterized the administration of the colonies by their European 'masters'. The article concludes by asserting that any understanding of the politicized nature of African football's contemporary aspirations within FIFA and the world game must be informed by an appreciation of the ways in which football in Africa became intertwined with independence, nationalism and the broader struggle for global recognition.

Colonial doctrine, sports diffusion and football in Africa

Although an analysis of French, British and Belgian colonial activity in Africa reveals common economic and political motives, it is possible to detect variation and distinctiveness in the way that each of these colonial powers went about governing their territories. One of the most striking divergences in European colonial doctrine in Africa can be found in the use of direct and indirect systems of governance. Whilst the boundaries between the two forms of administration were relatively fluid and all colonial powers used each system according to historically specific circumstances and objectives,[1] the adoption of direct or indirect forms of control not only had a significant impact in the political and economic sense but also had a strong bearing on social and cultural life within the colonies. Regardless of which system of colonial doctrine was used to facilitate the maintenance of European empires in Africa, the advent and development of colonialism, in its various guises, has undeniably been the most significant factor in the socio-cultural transformation of African society. At the time, the missionaries and colonial administrators heralded their presence and the societal change which the infiltration of their customs and culture initiated as a morally improving and 'civilizing' force for the benefit of all Africans. However, others have argued convincingly that the diffusion of Western cultural products, including modern sport, impacted negatively on existing indigenous culture and was motivated more by a desire to uphold the prevailing colonial political and economic order through the Europeanization and de-Africanization of Africa rather than by any sense of utilitarianism.[2] It would be naïve to overlook the adaptive powers of indigenous Africans as well as their ability and desire either to assimilate into or resist imperial culture or deny that the consequences of cultural exchange between the colonizer and colonized could be unintentional, accidental or informal.[3] However, traditional African customs and belief systems were clearly transformed and eroded with the influx of Western cultural forms. The extent to which this occurred was not only influenced by the interpretation of hegemonic culture by local peoples, but was also dependent upon the particular variant of colonial policy through which it was diffused. Indeed, differentiating between the various modes of colonialism reveals certain nuances in the process of Western driven sports diffusion and nowhere is this more apparent than in the advent and development of football in those territories that were governed by Europe's three main colonial powers.

Whilst it is difficult to generalize about the spread of popular cultural forms to an area which is as geographically vast and ethnically diverse as Africa, it is possible to identify a number of central features of the game's development throughout the continent. That football in Africa is a legacy of European colonialism is undeniable. It is somewhat paradoxical to observe that the vehicle for the creation and maintenance of the material conditions which facilitated the mass popularization of football in Africa also brought with it a system of economic exploitation and impoverishment that wrought so much havoc on African society. Population transfers and urban environments created by the migratory movements of both indigenous and foreign peoples had already proved conducive to the diffusion of the game throughout many of the other European empires during the late nineteenth and early twentieth centuries. In Africa, the destruction of traditional agricultural communities and the resultant massive migration into wage labour in the new cities and mining regions that developed during the first four decades of the twentieth century, also proved to be fertile ground for the games growth.

The European education system which was invariably transported to the formal colonies throughout the world was also a feature of late nineteenth and early twentieth century African society and it too was instrumental in introducing the game to Africans. Schools were specifically established for the African élite which in its eagerness for the higher status afforded for cultural imitation of their colonial masters, began to take up the game of soccer. Thus, participation in football in the early part of the twentieth century was largely dependent upon privileged contacts with Europeans and hence, the game developed as a somewhat élitist enterprise.[4] Later, the local populations also had the opportunity to participate as a result of contact with the new settlers and traders in the cities and urban sprawls, as had Africans recruited into European armies to lend their weight in colonial wars.

The work of the missions was also vital in terms of the dissemination of football not just to Africa but also to the furthest flung corners of the European Empire. The self-stated aim of the missionaries in Africa during the colonial period was to civilize the local population by imbuing them with Christian values and beliefs. However, other writers, particularly those indigenous to the African continent, argue that the role of the Christian Church in colonial Africa was not just confined to spreading the Gospel, but also to upholding the colonial political, social and economic order.[5] A debate of the benefits or otherwise of the missionary impulse in Africa is beyond the scope of this article, but what should be emphasized here is that the ethnocentric certainty of many missionaries in relation to the moral virtues and qualities that would be bestowed upon indigenous populations by a combination of Christianity and Western, predominantly British, games resulted in the 'overestimation of Western tradition', and the 'under-estimation of indigenous tradition'.[6] This was critical for the continued diffusion of football to Africa because, for as long as the game was viewed by educators and churchmen as possessing a civilizing and educative function as well as acting as a potential recruitment mechanism for the mission schools[7] then football would remain central to missionary endeavour. As will be illustrated later, this missionary approach to the spread of soccer to Africa was so deep rooted that it persisted within the higher echelons of FIFA until well into the 1970s.

Football, independence and nationalism in Africa: 1945–60

The years immediately following the Second World War marked the beginning of a defining period in the development of modern Africa. Much of the continent became caught up in the massive waves of global transformation that were heralding the collapse of empires and the emergence of a new world order. Despite the pace and apparent inevitability of global change which had already precipitated the independence of European colonies elsewhere in the world, the continent's imperial powers remained steadfast in their determination to maintain control of their African colonies, not least because the war effort had drained off much of their wealth and resources. However, in the face of continued colonial exploitation, the aspirations of Africans in the post-war world began to reflect a growing desire for independence. The experiences of those who had been educated in Europe or who had fought in wars to defend the Empire were particularly significant in that that they helped many Africans to develop an awareness of the world which had hitherto not been available to them. During the 1950s, this awareness was mobilized by various nationalist leaders who combined a growing sense of national consciousness with the principles of pan-Africanism and national unity to form the cornerstone of a politically focused campaign for independence.[8]

In the decade and a half leading up to the shedding of colonial authority, football assumed a more central place in African society and increasingly came to represent a vehicle for expressing aspirations for African emancipation and harnessing resentment towards the exploitative and oppressive conditions which typified much of colonial life in Africa between 1945 and 1960. Building on its growth before the War, football achieved immense popularity amongst the local population, leading to the gradual emergence of an indigenous infrastructure for African football. Indeed, with a broad range of socio-political organizations either proscribed or coming under colonial control, football represented one of the few meaningful institutions over which the local population could realistically secure ownership. The formation of an independent football association in colonial Zimbabwe in 1949 (Bulawayo Football Association), following disputes with the municipal authorities, represented a watershed in terms of African ownership of the game, and was soon followed by the inauguration of a range of independent football associations during the early 1950s which took over responsibility for the organization of the game in many colonial towns and cities. Whilst these associations may not have been as successful as their heavily subsidized colonial counterparts, the fact that they were being run independently of European influence not only had huge symbolic significance, but also contributed in a very practical sense to the politics of football was not lost upon indigenous nationalist political leaders and they proceeded to utilize the opportunities afforded to them within the relative sanctuary of local football matches to express their ambitions for a new Africa openly and recruit members of the labouring classes and the African élite to their cause. The significance of the local game in terms of acting as a symbol of African identity and resistance against colonial rule is articulated by Stuart:

> . . . in the decades that followed its introduction, soccer became an African possession. It was part of the experience of living in Bulawayo, Johannesburg, Lagos or anywhere else that it was played across the continent. The game was wrested from European control and used by the African population to assert their new urban identity. The game became an expression of defiance towards the state and of independence from their colonial oppressors.[9]

In north Africa, for example, many soccer clubs acted as centres of anti-colonial sentiment and the promotion of a nationalist tradition. In Morocco, clubs like Wydad of Casablanca and the US Meknes club became closely associated with criticism of French and Spanish colonial activities, whilst Tangier and Larrache were notable for their particularly fervent opposition to Spanish rule.[10] In the Belgian Congo during the 1950s, football also developed as an agent for the articulation of an emerging sense of national spirit and, indeed, the formation and subsequent performances of the first

Congolese national team in 1957 served to heighten the awareness of nationhood which culminated in 1960 with the granting of independence. Furthermore, in the early years of independence in the newly named Zaire, football and the consolidation of a national consciousness went hand in hand as was evidenced when the Congress of the Popular Movement of the Revolution, the nation's only political party, passed a motion which led to the changing of team names of foreign origin. For example, the St. Eloi of Elisabethville became the Lupopo of Lubumbashi whilst Daring of Léopoldville were renamed the Imana of Kinshasa.[11] The strong correlation between football and resistance was also apparent in Tanganyika (later Tanzania) where football clubs were centrally involved in the liberation movement. Research undertaken by Hamad NDee reveals that, during the 1950s, when the struggle for emancipation from British rule was at its height, sports clubs in Dar es Salaam are known to have acted as a front for otherwise prohibited political gatherings. For example, sports meetings at the Young Africans Sports Club were used by the nationalist political party Tanganyika African National Union (TANU) to discuss strategies aimed at delivering independence. In recognition of the Young Africans Sports Club's contribution to the fruition of TANU's political objectives in 1961, the club enjoyed a special relationship with Tanzania's ruling party which manifested itself not only in financial aid for new clubhouses, but also in the fact that the majority of the sports club's members, particularly its leaders, were also members of TANU.[12]

The connection between football and the quest for independence in Africa was perhaps most explicit in Algeria. The organization of the insurrection against the French, which came to prominence in the mid-1950s and eventually led to Algerian independence, was co-ordinated by the Front de Libération National (FLN) which was founded in 1951. Building upon a tradition of using sport for nationalist expression which stretched back to 1926 and the formation of the Étoile Nord-Africaine (a centre for sports and politics) by Arab nationalists,[13] the FLN drew on the mobilizing power of football to further the cause of Algerian independence and, in 1958, they introduced a 'Revolutionary Eleven' team. The FLN XI, based in Tunisia, was made up predominantly of Algerians who had been playing in France, but unhappy with the colonial system back home, had returned to play their part in the drive for independence. From 1958 until 1962, the FLN team, acting as a focus for anti-French feeling, toured 12 countries in north Africa, Eastern Europe, the Middle East and China, playing 53 matches, winning 39, drawing 10 and losing only four.[14] The successes of the FLN XI were perceived to be symbolic of the strength and unity of the Algerian people, and the team members were portrayed as patriotic heroes, further helping to imbue the Algerian youth with national pride and a desire for freedom from colonial rule. Such was the extent of the connection between football and the politics of protest in Algeria that many of the players in the team were rewarded with prominent government positions when the nation gained its independent status in 1962. Furthermore, the success of the FLN in galvanizing support for the revolutionary regime in the late 1950s and early 1960s has ensured that, to this very day, football in Algeria continues to represent a vehicle for political protest and propaganda.[15]

FIFA and African football in the colonial period: imperialism vs. resistance

The dichotomy of football's role as a reservoir of cultural imperialism in Africa and a source of resistance is also apparent in FIFA's relationship *vis-à-vis* African football during the colonial era. The International Federation was founded in 1904 following an initiative by seven European nations and in its formative years FIFA's constituency list was entirely northern European. Despite the fact that the global spread of the game was a stated aim of the fledgling organization, the task of disseminating football around the world was left to the colonial administrators, industrialists and European settlers, thus ensuring that FIFA played little part in the early diffusion and mediation of the game in Africa. Although the performances of South American footballers and administrators had elevated the status of that continent within FIFA, for the first 50 years of its existence, the International Federation remained an insular body whose primary aim was to oversee the development of the European game.

FIFA's Eurocentric disregard for the *international* nature of football's appeal was particularly apparent in the world body's relationship with Africa. The development of football in Africa was clearly rooted in the colonial experience and, as a reflection of this experience, FIFA's attitude towards African football laid the foundations for the inequality and power imbalances which have underpinned relations between FIFA and the Confédération Africaine de Football (CAF) in the second half of the twentieth century. For example, as President of FIFA from 1921 until 1954, the Frenchman Jules Rimet had a conception of the world body which followed a paternal and neo-colonial view of global development in which economic and cultural hegemony radiated from a 'modern', European centre to a 'pre-modern' third world periphery. Indeed, this continued to be the basis upon which FIFA expanded under the stewardship of the Englishmen Arthur Drewry and Stanley Rous. Under Rous, in particular, FIFA adopted a missionary approach to the development of football and hence FIFA's relationship with its African constituency was marked by a patronizing, Eurocentric and neo-imperialistic style. Evidence of Rous' attitudes towards FIFA's less-established constituencies can be found in an interview which he conducted shortly before his death in July 1986 when he described the initiation of a programme of coaching and refereeing courses in a number of African and South American countries as the beginning of the 'general missionary work'.[16] Sugden and A. Tomlinson elaborate further on the imperialistic nature of the approach adopted by FIFA's leaders with respect to the spread and administration of football in Africa: 'For figures like Jules Rimet, Arthur Drewry and Stanley Rous, football, like Christianity was viewed as something which was good for the savages and as such it was FIFA's mission to develop the game in the farthest flung corners of the globe.'[17] Despite this self professed 'mission', any inclination to mount a concerted effort to encourage and support the development of the game in Africa was precluded by FIFA's European insularity and the narrow-mindedness that its founding members exhibited. The outbreak of the Second World War and the International Federation's preoccupation with securing the re-entry of the isolationist British football associations further diminished any desire on the part of FIFA to nurture an African constituency for the world game. With Africa's presence within FIFA in the immediate post-war period limited to four members, attempts to foster the growth of African football and raise its profile were routinely frustrated. However, the dramatic expansion which had increasingly marked the world body's development as a result of the collapse of empires elsewhere in the world, and a recognition of the imminence of African independence within Europe, gradually made prominent figures within the world body alive to the fact that a restructuring of the world body was necessary in order to adapt to and reflect the changing environment in which it was operating. Thus, the first FIFA Congress of 1950 opened with Jules Rimet speaking of the 'extraordinary development' and 'unparalleled success' of football and of the need for the organization to respond to 'the new conditions under which it is evolving'.[18] However, rather than grasping the opportunity to mould FIFA into a body that acted in the interests of the *international* football community, Rimet sought to maintain the status quo and protect Europe's privileged position at the helm of world football. Despite Rimet's conservatism, other leading figures within FIFA began to acknowledge that football was developing into a global passion and that an international body which espoused as its primary goal '*world* football unity'[19] whilst operating in the interests of one or two continents, was becoming increasingly impractical. Stanley Rous, for example, expressed his concerns for the development of FIFA in a rapidly globalizing world in the following terms: 'It was essential in my view that FIFA decentralise rather than become a vast bureaucracy based on Europe and out of touch – or thought to be out of touch and unsympathetic to the needs of other continents.'[20]

That the initial push for decentralization in the game's administrative structures should come from Rous is an ironic feature of FIFA's development because the establishment of confederations, at various stages during the 1950s and early 1960s, in the continents of Africa and Asia not only served to unify and co-ordinate the efforts of the emergent footballing nations in their quest for equity on the world stage, but also gave them the confidence upon which to base their challenge to Europe's hegemony and ultimately end Rous' reign as FIFA President.

It was during the 1950 Congress that the idea of confederations first appeared on FIFA's agenda. Prior to the Congress, England and Argentina had circulated a number of proposals suggesting changes in FIFA's statutes that would pave the way for the grouping of national associations according to the continents in which they were situated. In keeping with his opening address, Jules Rimet introduced the discussion of the proposals in a manner which not only emphasized his conservative nature, but also with sentiments that were broadly reflective of the views of those who were committed to maintaining Europe's grip on the world game. His assertion that 'it is only with great prudence that its [FIFA's] statutory rules . . . should be touched', combined with the warning that 'improvization is the expedient of the irresponsible' can clearly be interpreted as evidence of his desire to maintain the distribution of power in world football at that time and of his reluctance to introduce statutory change which might threaten Europe's privileged position.[21] Whilst administrative reorganization would have benefited those countries where the development of the game was in its early stages, thus helping FIFA fulfil its self-proclaimed global mission, Rimet and Europe remained diffident.[22] However, the discussions surrounding the formation of confederations not only heightened awareness of the need for the International Federation to accommodate its newer constituents, but also placed statutory reform, and Africa's place within it, firmly on the political agenda.

Increasing pressure on the FIFA leadership resulted in an Extraordinary Congress in 1953 at which the statutory reform necessary for any reorganization of FIFA could be openly discussed. The crux of the meeting was a debate surrounding a proposed amendment to Article 17 of the statutes which was intended to provide Africa and Asia with one place apiece on the Executive Committee, thus making the world body a more representative forum. The heated exchanges which ensued revealed that FIFA's small third world constituency was rapidly developing the confidence to promote its sporting interests on the world stage whilst the core European members remained resolute in their opposition to democratization within the International Federation.[23] Ernst Thommen, a Swiss member of the Executive Committee, expressed views that were broadly representative of the European contingent at the meeting, asserting his belief that Africa and Asia had not yet sufficiently organized themselves to merit a say within world football's decision-making body. The patronizing, Eurocentric response of the northern European administrators evoked considerable outrage amongst many of the delegates. For example, Ratklo Pleic, representing the Yugoslav Association, argued that, 'the basis of any organization should be the equality of rights and obligations for all members', and cited an article containing a legal analysis of FIFA's statutes, by a Professor of Law at Limoges University in France, which concluded that the associations of FIFA did not enjoy the same rights.[24] By way of a compromise, the northern European associations eventually agreed that, when Africa and Asia formed an organization or grouping that would ensure direct nomination of their representative, they would be provided with the right to a seat on the Executive Committee. This compromise served to preserve the status quo and temporarily placate the representatives of Asia and Africa, but not before the Egyptian delegate had criticized what he perceived to be a lack of global equity in relation to the composition and activities of the Executive Committee, 'the statues of FIFA should be adapted to the *world* situation and safeguard the interests of *all* its members'.[25]

The events of the 1953 Extraordinary Congress marked something of a watershed in terms of the politics of FIFA. For the first time the football associations of Africa and Asia had registered dissatisfaction with their exclusion from world football's corridors of power. Perhaps more significantly, those delegates representing the emerging nations must have left the Congress with a clear understanding of the need to organize themselves into unified, co-ordinated confederations. Not only was this imperative in terms of the development of the game on their own continents, but it was also critical if their voice was to be heard within the governance of world football. Any remaining doubts as to the need for a formal continental organization to protect the interests of African football were soon dissipated at FIFA's Congress in the following year. The African delegates met in Berne prior to the Congress, and in a move which they believed satisfied the requirements of the 1953 Extraordinary Congress in respect of nominating an Executive Committee member, Abdelaziz Abdallah Salem from the Egyptian Federation was put forward as Africa's representative. The ensuing discussions exhibited a condescending and patronizing attitude towards the African associations with the view being expressed on a number of occasions, particularly by Rudolfe Seeldrayers, the Belgian vice-president and later President of the world body, that Africa's loosely defined forum, convened prior to the meeting, did not constitute the necessary basis from which to elect a member onto FIFA's Executive Committee. Dr Halim, the Sudanese representative retorted that FIFA's attitude in this matter was 'very unfortunate', pointing out that the long distances involved in convening a meeting between the African associations had made it difficult to organize a formal confederation. The Egyptian nominee for Africa's Executive Committee berth, Salem, was also critical of FIFA's attitude and suggested that FIFA was being controlled by a European and South American duopoly.[26] In perhaps the most scathing attack on FIFA's refusal to recognize the organization of the African game, Victor Antipenok, the Russian delegate, pleaded for the right of the African and Asian associations to nominate their members of the Executive Committee and suggested that FIFA had neglected the interests of both continents:

> If it were said that the standard of play was not yet high enough, the Executive Committee might be held responsible for it as they were apparently not interested enough in what went on in these two continents. They must receive help and in this connection they must be entitled to nominate their member of the Executive Committee.[27]

Inspired by those who had displayed such resilience in organizing indigenous teams and leagues, despite continued colonial oppression, FIFA's African delegates strengthened their resolve against the Eurocentrism clearly apparent at the Congress, and when the motion was put to the vote they eventually secured their seat on the world body's Executive Committee. The events of this meeting clearly illustrate that, in much the same way that African solidarity and a growing sense of national identity found expression through the medium of football within many of the colonies, the world games' institutional infrastructure also increasingly figured as a site for articulating the growing confidence of African nations. Perhaps of more significance was the fact that the politicking surrounding the Congress provided the impetus for the formation of a continental structure for African football, thus providing those countries that were on the verge of independence and otherwise politically invisible with a potent stage in which to root their struggle against FIFA's first world bias.

African football unites

The formation of the Confédération Africaine de Football in Khartoum in February 1957 by the only independent African nations at that time (Egypt, Ethiopia, Sudan and South Africa) was a critical juncture in the development of the game on that continent. Indeed, Mahjoub has observed that 'with the founding of the African Football Confederations, the year 1957 was to prove the launching pad for what is indisputably the continent's most popular sport'.[28] The rationale behind the formation of CAF can be found in the desire to develop football throughout Africa, introduce continent-wide competition and promote the African game on the global stage.[29] The need for the co-ordination of the game throughout the continent was great, but the promotion of a pan-African sporting body, which limited its membership to independent states, was also indicative of the general political mood at that time. The inception of CAF was crucial in a political sense in that it lent considerable weight to the use of the game as a tool for asserting African and pan-African identity and represented a highly visible podium for mediating that identity both throughout Africa and on a global basis. The organization of the first African Cup of Nations, which was hosted by Sudan and won by Egypt, further awakened national consciousness throughout the continent. As Quansah has observed, 'when Egypt were crowned champions of Africa at the first championship, the rest of Africa looked on in envy, unable to participate because of colonial rule'.[30] However, when the shackles of colonialism were removed from the majority of African states by the mid-1960s, membership of CAF and a general desire to join the wider international sporting community became available to young African nations eager to draw on the African confederation and the Cup of Nations to exert their independence and identity.

The capacity of sport to help imbue the local population of newly independent states with a sense of nationhood which could potentially transcend the parochialism of tribal loyalties and bind Africans to common social, economic and political objectives was recognized at an early stage in their development. Anver Versi, for example, recalls how Kwame Nkrumah, the leading Ghanaian nationalist and champion of the pan-African cause, saw sport as going hand in hand with the birth of a new Africa.[31] For Nkrumah, football in particular had a vital role to play in moulding the youth of the nation and he recognized the value of sporting victories for creating pride and dignity in the people of Africa. The response of the Ghanaian people to their national team's success in the 1963 African Cup of Nations provides evidence of the role of football in this respect: 'their [the Ghanaian national team] picture, with the late Dr Kwame Nkrumah, first President of Ghana sitting in the middle, adorned almost every Ghanaian home'.[32] Almost 20 years later, Nigeria's Minister of Sport, Sylvannus Williams, reaffirmed Nkrumah's beliefs by suggesting that sporting achievements not only help to integrate people but are also a measure of a nation's greatness.[33] The erection or refurbishment of football stadiums in celebration of hard-won emancipation provides another tangible manifestation of the way that football figured in the construction of national identity in independent Africa. Indeed, the names of these stadiums signify the strength of the relationship between the game and nationalist sentiments. For example, Accra's main venue is named the Independence Stadium as is the national stadium in Lusaka. Both Benin and Senegal have a Stade de l'Amitié (stadium of friendship) whilst other nationally evocative names are Liberty in Ibadan, Reunification in Douala and Revolution in Brazzaville.

CAF's desire to be viewed as an organization which was a symbol of African unity was made explicit not only in CAF's statues,[34] but also in its early policy direction. This was particularly evident in relation to South Africa, whose refusal to enter a multi-racial squad for the first Cup of Nations resulted in its removal from the competition before a ball had been kicked. When the competition moved to Cairo in 1959, South Africa was again banned following its decision not to accede to CAF's request that it submit a national team which was drawn from all racial groups. In 1961, at the pre-championship Congress in Ethiopa. CAF decided to expel South Africa formally and exclude it from all continental football championships whilst its apartheid system was replicated in the sporting domain. The way in which South Africa was dealt with by CAF sent out a clear political message to aspiring members that any actions which contravened or jeopardized the spirit of all-African unity which was sweeping the continent at that time would result in sporting prohibition. CAF's role in the promotion of a sense of African community was recognized by Kwame Nkrumah in 1964 when he donated a trophy for another CAF organized competition:

> It is encouraging to note that with progress towards the attainment of African unity at the political and economical levels, the interchange of

sports and cultural activities is making its influence felt in the creation of a healthy atmosphere for African unity and total independence. It is for this reason that I, as a citizen of Africa, have donated the Osagyefo trophy for the annual African clubs' championship to help consolidate the foundation of a continental movement to bring all Africa together in the field of sports.[35]

The emphasis which leading nationalist politicians and newly formed governments placed on football as a medium for national expression and a way of registering their presence in the international arena was grounded in a sense of realism about their limited ability to project themselves in a military or economic sense. However, it was also rooted in a recognition of the massive symbolism that the game and its associated institutional and competition structures had acquired for emerging African nations. As Mahjoub has observed:

> Football can also be seen as symbolising the liberation of the African continent. No sooner had some of the new states become members of the United Nations or the Organisation of African Unity, than they joined the International Federation of Association Football or the CAF and competed for the Africa Cup, enjoying one of the first opportunities of expressing their new-found and ambitious national identity. Football can also provide a symbolic parallel for the difficult and tentative steps Africa has made forging ahead in the modern world.[36]

So important was football and membership of CAF for the new states that, 'to this day, CAF is among the first international organizations that any nation achieving independence in Africa applies to join. Application for membership of the United Nations, the Organization of African Unity and CAF go hand in hand'.[37] Joining CAF was clearly central to the ambitions of newly independent African states; however, a realization that any struggle for global recognition would be best achieved by seeking affiliation to international organizations led to a rapid expansion of FIFA's African constituency. Having acquired membership of the world body, African nations were eager to ensure that the international games' institutional and competition structures developed in ways that were sympathetic to their needs and aspirations. Given that FIFA's electoral franchise at Congress operated on the principle of one nation one vote, it might have been expected that CAF would be in a position to project itself politically. However, European administrators, anxious to maintain hegemony within FIFA, had organized themselves into a politically unified confederation in 1954[38] and almost immediately they set out to consolidate their position within FIFA whilst at the same time marginalizing Africa and Asia. Stanley Rous, then a FIFA vice-president, summed up the prevailing mood within UEFA:

> Many people are convinced that it is unrealistic, for example, that a country like England, where the game started and was first organized, or that experienced countries like Italy and France, who have been pillars of FIFA and influential in its problems and in world football affairs for so many years, should have no more than equal voting rights with any of the newly created countries of Africa and Asia.[39]

Concerned about being pushed further into the electoral minority at FIFA Congress. UEFA made several attempts during the late 1950s and early 1960s to introduce a pluralist voting system that would more adequately reflect their self-perceived standing in world football[40] but their failure to effect electoral reform persuaded them to attempt to maintain their hegemony in other ways. Chief amongst these was a strategy aimed at ensuring that the format of the World Cup Finals continued to reflect élite European and South American dominance at the expense of FIFA's rapidly expanding third world constituency. Although membership of CAF had increased to more than thirty by the mid-1960s, most of whom had joined FIFA, African representation at the World Cup Finals could only be achieved via a play-off between the winner of the African Cup of Nations and the Asian equivalent. This was in marked contrast to Europe and South America whose football-playing nations enjoyed the lion's share of World Cup berths. Whilst Europe's dogged refusal to redress such imbalances frustrated African aspirations for fulfilment on the international stage, failure to participate in FIFA competitions also had crippling political consequences. The world body's statutes decreed that 'National Associations which do not take part in two successive World Cups or Olympic tournaments will be stripped of their right to vote at the Congress until they fulfil their obligations in this respect.'[41] Thus, because many African nations did not feel that they could afford or justify the financial outlay necessary for qualification matches given the restricted opportunity for reaching the Finals, CAF remained impotent and peripheral as a political force within FIFA.

In view of the role which football played in terms of African independence and solidarity and the significance apportioned to it as a barometer of international standing, it is not surprising that adequate representation in the game's most visible international arena became a central plank in Africa's struggle for global equity. Africa's response to such obvious discrimination in respect of the allocation of places for the World Cup Finals manifested itself in the form of a campaign, initiated by Kwame NKrumah to boycott the 1966 Finals in England. The idea of a boycott quickly secured approval from CAF and, at its Executive Committee meeting in Cairo in July 1964, a resolution was passed in opposition to Africa's 'outrageously unfair' allocation of places for the World Cup Finals. Charged with the objective of contributing to 'the cause of making the World Championship a real world manifestation far from any exclusivism', the Executive Committee proceeded to inform FIFA of the intention of all African national associations to withdraw from the qualifying competition for the 1966 Finals.[42] The Asian nations soon followed suit, arguing that 'as a *World* Cup, the competition should represent the world and not just Europe and South America'.[43] FIFA's response to the boycotting nations was a fine of 5,000 Swiss Francs, which not only placed a considerable financial burden on African football, but also increased the antipathy of CAF's constituents towards the world body. A reduction of the fine by 1,000 Swiss Francs, following the intervention of CAF, did little to abate the African nations' enmity and, in a letter to his counterpart in FIFA, Ydnekatchew Tessema, CAF's Secretary General, registered the anger of his constituents by arguing that the allocation of one World Cup Final berth to three continents comprising more than 65 Associations was 'absurd' and did not adequately reflect the prevailing situation in world football.[44] Furthermore, Tessema challenged FIFA's assertion that the boycott was totally without justification as the basis for the fines:

> FIFA has adopted a relentless attitude against the African Associations and its decisions resemble methods of intimidation and repression designed to discourage any further impulses of a similar nature. In our opinion, the African National Associations which, in spite of the flagrant injustice that drove them to abandon the World Cup series, submitted sportingly to the regulations in force, so as to consolidate the moral authority of the FIFA, really deserved a gesture of respect rather than a fine.[45]

The boycott marked the beginning of Africa's campaign for a more equitable World Cup and, despite FIFA's initial hard-line response, it soon had the desired effect. Indeed, as Quansah observed, the withdrawal of all African and Asian competitors from the World Cup qualifying tournament 'shook the very foundations of FIFA which voted at its pre-tournament Congress in London to allow African representation on their own merit'.[46]

The proactive, politicized approach to tackling inequalities within FIFA had clearly proved successful in this instance. However, it is important to stress that a complex equation involving the socio-economic and political legacy of European colonialism,[47] and a set of statute provisions which clearly favoured the established soccer-playing nations of Europe, not only served to restrict CAF's capacity to effect sustained and meaningful reform within FIFA, but also precluded any genuine development of the international game in Africa. Although many of the newly independent states had recognized the utility of sport for creating social cohesion and pan-African unity, in the context of the massive foreign debts, indigenous impoverishment and ethnic conflict which characterized the aftermath of the colonial era, governments found it increasingly difficult to justify theinvestment of scarce resources into sport.[48] Quite simply, for many African nations the finances necessary for developing the grass roots of the game and for participating in international competition were simply not available. Thus, unable to afford the costs incurred in World Cup qualifying rounds, or dissuaded from competing given the limited scope for proceeding to the Finals, a significant proportion of the International Federation's African constituency forfeited their voting rights at Congress and hence their ability to redress imbalances within FIFA. Despite the fact that Africa has since considerably improved its political profile within the world body, it is these same problems, combined with a number of flaws inherent within African football, which have continued to frustrate CAF's desire to rectify the global inequalities which it believes still lie at the heart of FIFA.

Conclusion

It may appear incongruous that attempts to withstand colonial dominance, promote nationalism throughout the African colonies and project a positive international image in the aftermath of independence were not combined with sustained efforts to reconstruct or re-invent sports forms or structures which more clearly reflected indigenous culture, as occurred in the United States or Ireland, for example. Within the current debate on the globalization of sport, some writers have highlighted a considerable tension or paradox in the use of Western sports forms for the articulation of non-Western nationalist expression and, whilst not going as far as to claim that this is indicative of the strength of global cultural homogeneity, they argue that it at least sensitizes us to the limited capacity of the local to resist hegemonic cultural diffusion effectively. Indeed, Sugden and Tomlinson have felt it necessary to qualify the ability of football and its world governing body to serve as vehicles for resistance to imperialism and neo-imperialism:

> . . . for the post-colonial Third World, affiliation to FIFA and participation in international football represented a tacit acceptance of the deep structure left behind by the colonists. Football was a European game and, while some of the names might have changed, the shape and ethnic contents of the new nation states which affiliated to FIFA were the same as those imposed by the old colonial powers a century earlier. By playing inter-national football, countries like Sudan, Nigeria, Malaysia, Singapore and South Africa are confirming a social and political map imposed by the First World.[49]

The fact that a European sports form has featured so strongly in African national self-definition can certainly be interpreted as evidence of the pervasiveness and strength of the cultural imperialisms which permeated the colonial period and beyond. Football, intentionally or otherwise, has clearly served as a mechanism for creating the con-ditions of conformity to hegemonic culture. However, this is not to say that cultural imperialism represents an entirely satisfactory explanation of what occurred at the interface of cultural exchange in Africa during the colonial period because that would be to significantly underplay the capabilities of indigenous populations to absorb, modify and adapt cultural imports such as sport, to fit their own needs and values. It would clearly be frivolous to suggest that Africans have been duped into accepting incoming Western sports forms or have played a negligible role in their interpretation. Indeed, one of the striking features of football's diffusion to Africa has been its eager acceptance and popularization by indigenous groups. Furthermore, in much the same way that Western sports forms have served as a forum for resistance against external cultural and economic exploitation in Latin America and the Caribbean,[50] African peoples, football administrators and nationalist leaders have displayed a skilful capacity to adapt football and redefine its institutional infrastructures in ways that are supportive of local values and political aspirations. This has been achieved by utilizing the game as a mechanism for radical political expression and resistance to hegemonic pressures from Europe in the first instance and subsequently by harnessing it as a mobilizing force in the construction and promotion of nationhood both within domestic confines and on the international stage. Notions of African resistance to first world hegemony have clearly played a major role in forging both CAF's and FIFA's organizational and political visage. Whether or not CAF has actually been successful in acquiring parity of esteem within world football is a matter of great conjecture, but it can be said without any doubt that the political persona of the African game, developed in the latter years of colonialism and its immediate aftermath, has continued to constitute a central theme around which the governance of the world game is conducted.

Notes

1   R. V. Albertini, *European Colonial Rule, 1880–1940: The Impact of the West on Southeast Asia and Africa* (hereafter *European Colonial Rule*) (Oxford: Clio Press, 1982), p. 490.

2   A. Mazrui and M. Tidy, *Nationalism and New States in Africa* (hereafter *Nationalism*) (Nairobi, London, Abadan: Heinemann, 1984), p. 40.

3   J. A. Mangan (ed.), *The Cultural Bond: Sport, Empire, Society* (London and Portland, OR: Frank Cass, 1992), pp. 1–9.

4   O. Stuart, 'The Lions Stir: Football in African Society' (hereafter 'The Lions Stir'), in S. Wagg (ed.), *Giving the Game Away: Football, Politics and Culture on Five Continents* (London and New York: Leicester University Press, 1995), pp. 27–8.

5   Mazrui and Tidy, *Nationalism*.

6   J. A. Mangan, *The Games Ethic and Imperialism: Aspects of the Diffusion of an Ideal* (hereafter *The Games Ethic and Imperialism*) (London and Portland, OR: Frank Cass, 1998), p. 191.

7   Stuart, 'The Lions Stir', p. 27.

8   B. Davidson, *Modern Africa: A Social and Political History*, 2nd edition (London and New York: Longman, 1989), pp. 31–43.

9   Stuart, 'The Lions Stir', p. 34

10 A. Versi, *African Football* (London: Collins, 1986) p. 41.

11 B. Lema, 'Sport in Zaire' in E. A. Wagner (ed.), *Sport in Asia and Africa: A Comparative Handbook* (New York/London: Greenwood Press, 1989), pp. 234–6.

12 Faxed correspondence with Hamad Ndee, International Research Centre for Sport, Socialization and Society. University of Strathclyde (2 Feb. 1998).

13 A. Guttmann, *Games and Empires: Modern Sports and Cultural Imperialism* (New York: Columbia University Press, 1994), p. 69.

14 Versi, *African Football*, p. 24.

15 B. Murray, *Football: A History of the World Game* (Aldershot, Scolar Press, 1994), pp. 242–3.

16 K. Goldman, 'My Life and Times in World Football – Sir Stanley Rous', *World Soccer* (Sept. 1986), 12.

17 J. Sugden and A. Tomlinson, 'Football and Global Politics: FIFA, UEFA and the Scramble for Africa' (unpublished paper presented at the British Sociological Association annual conference, 1996), 31.

18 FIFA, *Minutes of the XXVIIIth Ordinary Congress*, Rio de Janeiro, 22/23 June 1950.

19 Ibid.

20 S. Rous, *Football Worlds: A Lifetime in Sport* (London and Boston: Faber and Faber, 1978), p. 130.

21 FIFA, *Minutes of the XXVIIIth Ordinary Congress*.

22 S. Rous, 'The Role of Confederations', in *Handbook of UEFA* (Zurich: Berichthaus, 1963/64), pp. 87–9.

23 FIFA, *Minutes of IInd Extraordinary Congress*, Paris, 14/15 Nov. 1953.

24 Ibid.

25 Ibid.

26 FIFA, *Minutes of XXIXth Ordinary Congress*, Berne, 21 June 1954.

27 Ibid.

28 F. Majhoub, 'The Cup of Nations 1957–1990: From Khartoum to Algiers', *West Africa – Special Edition*, March 1990, 7.

29 Versi, *African Football*, pp. 9–10.

30 E. Quansah, 'The Cup to Surpass All Cups', *Africa Today* (Jan./Feb. 1996), 26.

31 Versi, *African Football*, pp. 33–4.

32 E. Quansah, 'The Fall of a Soccer Empire', *West Africa – Special Edition* (March 1990), 37.

33 G. Jarvie, 'Sport, Nationalism and Cultural Identity', in L. Allison (ed.), *The Changing Politics of Sport*, pp. 69–70.

34 *Statutes of the Confédération Africaine de Football* (Cairo: Nubar Printing House), p. 7.

35 Versi, *African Football*, p. 33.

36 F. Majhoub, 'African Cup of Nations', *Balafon: Air Afrique Onflight Magazine* (Dec./Jan. 1995). No. 125, 46.

37 Quansah, 'The Cup to Surpass All Cups', 26.

38 J. Crahay, 'The Foundation of UEFA', in *Handbook of UEFA*, pp. 92–7.

39 *UEFA Official Bulletin*, No. 16, April 1961.

40 H. Bangerter, 'UEFA. Past and Present', in U. R. Rothenbuhler (ed.), *25 Years of UEFA* (Berne: UEFA Publications, 1979), pp. 42–4.

41 FIFA, *Statutes of the Fédération Internationale de Football Association* (Zurich: FIFA Publications), article 42: 5.

42 SCAIR (Sports Cultures Archive for Investigative Research), *CAF Circular Letter to FIFA Executive Committee*, 21 Aug. 1964.

43 G. Oliver, *World Soccer: The History of the Game in over 150 Countries* (London: Guinness Publishing, 1992), p. 24.

44 SCAIR, *Personal Communication to Dr Helmut Kaeser from Ydnekatchew Tessema*, 16 Aug. 1965.

45 Ibid.

46 Quansah 'The Cup to Surpass All Cups', 27.

47 T. Monnington, 'The Politics of Black African Sport', in L. Allison (ed.), *The Changing Politics of Sport* (Manchester: Manchester University Press), pp. 149–51.

48 Ibid., pp. 154–5.

49 J. Sugden and A. Tomlinson, *FIFA and the Contest for World Football: Who Rules the People's Game?* (Cambridge: Polity Press, 1998), pp. 228–9.

50 A. Klein, 'Baseball as Underdevelopment: The Political Economy of Sport in the Dominican Republic', *Sociology of Sport Journal*, 6 (1989), 95–112; A. Klein, 'Sport and Culture as Contested Terrain', *Sociology of Sport Journal*, 8 (1981), 79–85; J. L. Arbena, 'International Aspects of Sport in Latin America', in E. Dunning *et al.* (eds.), *The Sports Process: A Comparative and Developmental Approach* (Champaign, IL: Human Kinetics Publishers, 1993).

Chapter 19

Frederic Wakeman, Jr.

LICENSING LEISURE

The Chinese Nationalists' attempt to regulate Shanghai, 1927–47

Shanghai has often been called the Paris of the Orient. This is only half true. Shanghai has all the vices of Paris and more but boasts of none of its cultural influences. The municipal orchestra is uncertain of its future, and the removal of the city library to its new premises has only shattered our hopes for better reading facilities. The Royal Asiatic Society has been denied all support from the Council for the maintenance of its library, which is the only center for research in this metropolis. It is therefore no wonder that men and women, old or young, poor or rich, turn their minds to mischief and lowly pursuits of pleasure, and the laxity of police regulations has aggravated the situation.

(*China Weekly Review*, 14 June 1930)

IN THE THREE DECADES BEFORE the nationalist regime seized power in Shanghai in 1927, China's greatest city experienced the rise of modern industrial entertainment. As Shanghai changed from a pre-electric city of pleasure, centered on teashops and courtesans' quarters, to a garishly illuminated metropolis of night-life vice in cabarets, dance halls, and bordellos, its inhabitants' leisure-time activities shifted correspondingly

from the elite parlor to the mass movie theater;
from games (majiang, huahui) to gambling (casinos, canidromes, horse racing);
from fixed regional pastimes (local opera in native dialect) to a more eclectic department-store culture, where customers shopped for entertainment by moving from one floor to another in multi-storied amusement centers that offered a wide variety of merchandised performances;
from courtesans to prostitutes;
from Sino-foreign segregation to intermixed social intercourse;
from "soft" pre-modern intoxication with opium and wine to "hard" industrial addiction to acetylated heroin and distilled alcohol.

As the domestic rituals of the household gave way to the social mores of the race track or nightclub, private punctiliousness deferred to public policing. The new Nationalist leaders welcomed this opportunity to regulate Chinese Shanghai's entertainment industries, both to raise revenue and to prove to the imperialists who controlled the French, international, and Japanese sectors of the city—each patrolled by separate semi-colonial police forces—that the Chinese were perfectly capable of maintaining "order" (*zhixu*) themselves. Indeed, from the very beginning of the establishment of a Nationalist municipality in Shanghai in 1927, the Guomindang insisted that if it could bring law and order to the city, then it deserved to recover sovereignty and abolish extraterritoriality in the foreign concessions (Wakeman 1988).

Even after the April 1927 purge of the left wing, the leaders of the Nationalist regime considered themselves revolutionaries. As such they were committed to modernization without undue Westernization, which they regarded as potentially corrupting and corrosive. They correctly identified Shanghai's "vice industry" as an extractive mechanism that could be used by the imperialists to fleece Chinese citizens. It was therefore a sacred duty of patriots to police urban society by overseeing proper dress rules, guiding public demeanor, licensing places of entertainment, and regulating communications and traffic. Punishments for the "infringement of police [rules]" (*weijing*) had a direct impact on Shanghai's Chinese citizens. During the twelve months between July 1929 and June 1930, for instance, the Nationalists' Public Security Bureau detained, fined, or reprimanded more than 29,000 Shanghainese for disorderly conduct, disturbing communications, harming public customs, injuring others' persons and property, destroying evidence, and disturbing the peace (*Shanghai shi gong'anju yewu baogao 1931*, table after p. 108).

The Chinese police force's interference in urbanites' personal lives represented the new state's effort to create a civic culture. This determined quest to create a modern municipal culture was thus part of a national effort to make "citizens" (*gongmin*) out of "people" (*renmin*). Although some historians now claim to see the emergence of a "public sphere" in late nineteenth-century cities like Wuhan (Rowe 1990), the evidence from Shanghai of a strong endogenous "civic culture" in the 1920s and 1930s is not so compelling.

There were collective movements, to be sure, but the appearance of a civic culture —a strong municipal identity—was a creation from the top down: part of a larger plan, drawn from Sun Yat-sen's testament for national reconstruction, to build a new Shanghai (Shen Yi 1970). The Guomindang authorities, striving to combat Communist and National Salvationist mass movements, contrived their own municipal demonstrations and political rituals. These symbolic events, however, were ultimately corporatist occasions, arranged and led by party and police agents, whose musical bands headed the parades through Chinese Shanghai's streets.

The Nationalists' effort to police society culminated in the New Life Movement in 1934. In a cultural potpourri such as Shanghai, the justification for a conformist moral rearmament campaign seemed obvious. After all, how could the authorities hope effectively to license acceptable forms of leisure when "good" cultural events were only one floor down from "bad" cultural activities in the Great World amusement center on Tibet Road? The distinction between "good" and "bad" leisure, between entertainment such as modern films and storytelling and vices such as gambling and prostitution, was never clearly drawn in Republican Shanghai. This was partly because of conservative nativists' identification of "bad" leisure with Westernizing influences, partly because a metropolis such as Shanghai condenses and amplifies urban subcultures, and partly because the city itself was divided into four different sectors, each with its own definition of political and social morality (see Fischer 1975). The necessity of whipping together an altogether New Life by combining traditional Neo-Confucian fussiness with the barracks discipline of Chiang Kai-shek's Whampoa cadets seemed an attractive alternative to décolletage, expectoration, permanent waves, and unbuttoned trousers.

Needless to say, when it came to disciplining Shanghai's rowdy and restless urbanites, this intrusive dressing-down of casual habits, provocative clothing, and slovenly comforts sufficed only to arouse resentment. Even if good bourgeois citizens believed that by not spitting on the sidewalk they would be helping gird the nation for war with Japan, the police regulation of private mores—however well meaning—was compromised by other forms of maintaining the regime's version of probity: the overwhelming censorship, especially after 1932, of books, newspapers, magazines, and movies.

As authorities increasingly linked moral licentiousness with political subversion, the formal preservation of law and order turned out to be mainly the maintenance of order. Since law enforcement only requires the assessment of guilt, whereas order maintenance also entails "a dispute in which the law must be interpreted, standards of right conduct determined, and blame assigned," actions between the Shanghai police and its citizenry mainly invoked the former (Wilson 1976: 85).

This police interference not only provoked mass resentment; it also, in the context of the National Salvation movement of the 1930s, ran counter to the collective nationalism of Shanghai's urbanites. And because there was a fateful confusion by the Guomindang authorities between anti-Japanese patriotism and anti-Chiang radicalism— a confusion abetted by the Communists' claims of leadership within the National Salvation movement—the Nationalists' attempts to regulate public life were identified by many patriotic Chinese as a reactionary defense of the privileges of Shanghai's "playboys" against the city's immiserated "black insects."

The Shanghai police authorities themselves were sullied as well by charges of collusion with the Japanese. The Chinese police's readiness to control National Salvation demonstrations in order to avoid handing the Imperial Japanese Army and Navy a *casus belli* already linked the Nationalists, in some people's eyes, with appeasement well before the Marco Polo Bridge incident. Even more damaging, once the Chinese armies lost the battle of Shanghai in the fall of 1937, was the readiness with which many former Public Security Bureau agents joined the puppet police at 76 Jessfield Road, called the "Hotel Lucrèce" of Shanghai, after the Gestapo headquarters in occupied Paris.

Political collaboration was invariably accompanied by social corruption, which coincided with the displacement of foreign control of modern vice industries by Chinese management. The illicit traffic in narcotics was the most prominent example of this form of import substitution: first, the imperialists' opium smuggled in by foreign syndicates; then, the Chinese substitute grown in their own poppy fields; and finally, acetylated drugs like heroin and morphine processed by government—gangster combines that brought the Chiang regime close to racketeers like Du Yuesheng. When the Wang Jingwei regime was granted control of occupied Shanghai by the Japanese occupation forces, the Nationalists' henchmen in the Green Gang were ousted by rival Chinese gangsters and *yakuza* supported by the puppet police and the Japanese Special

Services. Revenues from the narcotics trade, in turn, helped finance the puppet government.

An analogous process took place in the gambling industry. In 1928–1929 the new Nationalist regime at first tried to get the concessions' authorities to close down the casinos and racetracks operating under extraterritoriality. They were partially successful in the International Settlement, but not in the French Concession. After 1932, however, this campaign waned. Once connections between the Shanghai Chinese police and the Nanjing regime were severed by the Japanese in 1937, local law enforcement authorities actually licensed gambling: first, in the "Badlands" of western Shanghai, then throughout the entire city under puppet rule. The same was true for prostitution, which continued to flourish under informal license even after the Pacific War was over, partly because of the presence of American military men whose sexual demands correspondingly increased the supply of prostitutes from the civil war-torn hinterland. Indeed, after the Nationalists recovered Shanghai, a special red-light zone was established by the Chinese police. As we shall see, the sum effect of this political and social corruption within China's metropolis was to help bring about the delegitimation of the Guomindang, whose rule was compromised in 1949 by the very social setting it had so firmly resolved to reform in 1927.

The new civic culture

The possibility of a new civic culture for the Chinese-administered portions of Shanghai seemed about to be realized on 7 July 1927, when General Huang Fu was formally installed as mayor of the Special Municipal Government established by the Nationalist regime (*Shenbao*, 7 July 1927). After the opening ceremonies, with martial music played by the Shanghai and Wusong police bands, Chiang Kai-shek invoked Sun Yat-sen's program of national construction.

> All eyes, Chinese and foreign, are focused on the Shanghai Special Municipality. There simply has to be a successful completion of its construction. If all is managed according to the way described by the *zongli*, then it will be even more perfect than in the foreign concessions. If all of the public health, economic, and local educational affairs are handled in a completely perfect way, then at that time the foreigners will not have any way to obstruct the recovery of the concessions.
>
> (*Shenbao*, 7 July 1927)

Huang Fu also emphasized the importance of creating a modern municipal government in Shanghai "so as to pave the way for the eventual restoration of the foreign settlements." With the help of the party and the city's people (*shimin*), the newly appointed municipal administration would demonstrate the way in which "our Chinese people are spiritually capable of reconstruction" (*Shenbao*, 8 July 1927).

Civic culture was to begin with the maintenance of *zhixu*. This repeated emphasis upon bringing order to the unruly and chaotic life of the city was a primary theme in the governing of the Greater Municipality of Shanghai from that very moment of its inception. This is why the establishment of a modern police force to enforce that order, a

Public Security Bureau (*Gonganju*), was envisaged even before the new mayor took his oath of office (*Shenbao*, 4 July 1927). From the very beginning, one of the major responsibilities of the PSB was the imposition of this new social order by concrete means: the control of traffic and the licensing of vehicles (in the 1920s, half of China's automobiles were on Shanghai's streets), and the supervision of leisure-time activities and the regulation of vice (Clifford 1988: 6; *Shenbao*, 12 July 1927).

Narcotics and gambling

Shanghai's worst vice, in the eyes of most onlookers, was narcotics abuse, which was a national problem as well. Drug use was virtually ineradicable during those years, when the illicit revenue from the narcotics trade became such an important source of warlords' income. According to one estimate, in the 1920s and 1930s, at least 90 percent of the world's supply of narcotic drugs was consumed in China. Although heroin and morphine addiction was on the increase, the most visible manifestation of this vice in Shanghai was opium smoking. Consequently, one of the first acts of the new municipal government was to set up an Opium Suppression Bureau (*Jinyanju*), which cooperated closely with the new Public Security Bureau (Parssinen and Meyer n.d.: 2). Control (and even licensing) of opium-smoking divans did take place, but in general narcotics abuse was a much less manageable vice than gambling, which soon became one of the primary concerns of the police throughout Shanghai.

During the late 1920s and early 1930s, commercialized gambling in Shanghai existed on a larger scale than in any other city in the world. In 1935 the Shanghai Municipal Police estimated that slot machines alone in the International Settlement took in approximately $1,000,000 per annum (letter from the Director-General of the Shanghai Municipal Council to the Commissioner of Police, cited in *The China Critic*, 30 October 1930). The turnover from professionally conducted gambling, including roulette and horse and dog racing, exceeded one million dollars a week; and some claimed that Shanghai deserved to usurp Monte Carlo's title as the gambling center of the world (*China Weekly Review*, 13 July 1929).

Horse racing was initially an amusement of the foreign community (Coates 1983: 21–44, 113–30, 231–35). Trackmeets at the Shanghai Race Club, which, with its adjoining recreation grounds, covered sixty-six acres of the choicest property in the city, were originally held twice a year, during the first week in May and the first week in November (Gamewell 1916: 46). Ordinarily, Chinese were kept out of the racetrack grounds by guards—except on race days. On those occasions, Chinese could line up at the racetrack window and buy a one dollar ticket to get in to bet (*The China Critic*, 27 June 1935). The bets placed by these Chinese gamblers constituted about 95 percent of the club's revenue, and as a result the Shanghai Race Club was said to be the wealthiest foreign corporation in China except for one or two banks and shipping companies (*China Weekly Review*, 13 July 1929).

An even more profitable form of track betting was greyhound racing, which was introduced in 1927–28. The dog tracks featured parimutuel betting, which was outlawed in England. The owners published daily advertisements in the Chinese newspapers and distributed free admission tickets. If you did not have a free ticket, you could buy one for ten cents from one of the urchins lining the streets leading to the greyhound racecourses (Meng 1929a: 420). It was estimated that greyhound racing took about US$250,000 a month out of mainly Chinese pockets (*China Weekly Review*, 1 June 1929, 13 July 1929).

But an even greater cause of gambling losses than dog racing was the popular "huahui" numbers game, which appealed to upper and lower classes alike, "ranging from rich people to the poorest ricksha coolies" (Meng 1929b: 334; Wu Yü, Liang, and Wang 1988: 123). Each winner took home twenty-nine times his bet; the organizers, who were powerful "local magnates" (*tuhao*), then pocketed the remaining 7/36ths of the money wagered, or about $48,000 per day (Meng 1929b: 334).

Not only did gambling encourage crime (armed robberies increased appreciably just before the autumn horse races each year); it also was associated with the ruin of ordinary urban residents who all too often lost their money at the dog track, in a casino, or playing popular lotteries like "huahui," and who ended up—in the slang of the time—by "taking a jump in the Huangpu" (*tiao Huangpu*) or by leaping off the roof of the Great World amusement center (*The China Critic*, 30 October 1930; Xu Zhucheng 1982: 29; Browning 1987: 25a).

Although the SMP periodically did try to close down gambling establishments and arrest their operators during the first two years of the new Chinese municipal government's rule, the latter's Public Safety Bureau officers continued to believe that the International Settlement and French Concession police forces were not to be trusted to carry out a thoroughgoing crusade against gambling. In their view they would be able to close down the "huahui" lottery and other gambling rackets only by getting their own government to require that the Settlement authorities help them enforce anti-gambling bans (*Shanghai tebie shi gonganju yewu jiyao*, 1928, *jishi*: 53).

In May 1929, consequently, the Chinese government officially protested against public gambling in the International Settlement to the British Minister, Sir Miles Lampson, noting that greyhound parimutuel racing was actually contrary to British law and should therefore be outlawed in Shanghai (*China Weekly Review*, 13 July 1929). In response to this pressure, British members of the Shanghai Municipal Council wrote the British directors of the dog tracks on 25 May, asking them to restrict their races to one night a week and threatening to close the municipal roads leading to the race club entrance if the proprietors refused to comply (*China Weekly Review*, 1 June 1929). The greyhound stadium proprietors asked, in turn, what the Council intended to do about other forms of gambling in Shanghai. Less than twenty-four hours later, before dawn on Sunday 26 May, the Shanghai Municipal Police staged a spectacular siege in front of the building at 151C Bubbling Well Road, popularly known as "The Wheel."

The "Wheel Case," which had its first hearing on 12 June 1929, was described in the press as a "gang war" between the British-owned greyhound gambling resorts (whose board members and investors included SMC members and British police officers) and the Latin American and Chinese-owned roulette casinos. Meanwhile, despite the orders to restrict their races to one night a week, the British dog track owners were able to maintain their profits simply by increasing the number of events they ran on a particular race night (*China Weekly Review*, 13 July 1929).

The Nationalist government refused to relent. As agitation for the abrogation of the unequal treaties mounted, the Chinese authorities demanded that the Luna Park and Stadium be closed (*China Weekly Review*, 22 February 1930). The SMC tried to stand firm, but the consular body found it difficult not to respond to this pressure. On

8 July 1930, the Nanjing government finally announced that it would stop greyhound racing in Shanghai by issuing arrest warrants for Chinese employees and habitués of the dog tracks. Shares prices of the two enterprises slumped toward zero, and shortly afterwards the two tracks shut their gates and went out of business (Pal 1963: 16; *China Weekly Review*, 19 July 1930).

But the French Concession proper's refusal to clean up its vice establishments (including closing down its dog track, the "Canidrome") was at the time blamed almost invariably upon extraterritoriality (*China Weekly Review*, 26 September 1931). French tolerance of vice was also attributed to a kind of colossal colonial indifference to the sufferings of the native population and a willingness to tolerate the most blatant forms of criminality in exchange for bribes and favors (Han 1932: 239). Except for a few desultory raids, nothing much was done about gambling by the French police until a short-lived reformist administration tried to get the racketeers out of "Frenchtown" (Martin 1992: 296). Throughout this period, and on up to 1935–36, gambling continued to be an annoyance to the police forces of Greater Shanghai, and to the Public Security Bureau in particular. Efforts to control the vice were sporadic and ineffective, especially since gambling was part of a larger world of entertainment that included amusement centers and dance halls (*China Weekly Review*, 26 January 1935).

Amusement centers

During the boom years of World War I, a Chinese medicine millionaire named Huang Chujiu decided to build a modern amusement center for the common folk of the city. It was opened on 4 July 1917, as The Great World [*Da shijie*] (Scott 1982: 75–76). The central attraction of the original amusement center was a set of several dozen funhouse mirrors imported from Holland. Later, cinemas were added, along with food stands and galleries. The layout of the building resembled one of the modern department stores on Nanking Road, so that customers moved from floor to floor, shopping from one layer of entertainment to the next: from theaters to puppet shows, wrestlers, singsong girls, restaurants, and games of chance (Carney 1980: 19). Yet there was also an air of the Chinese country fair about the building, with a rich offering of regional drama and traditional storytelling (Scott 1982: 76).

> There were all kinds of opera here: Beijing, Shaoxing, Shanghai, Ningbo, Huaiyin, and Yangzhou; there were conjurers, acrobats, film-shows and puppets; and besides all these things there were also places to eat and drink . . . A ceaseless medley of sounds clamoured for every visitor's attention: the clashing gongs and drums of the Beijing Opera, the stirring drum-beats and bugle-notes that accompanied the acrobats, the plaintive melodies of the Shaoxing opera . . . Yes . . . this really was a Great World, with everything that the heart could desire. It was quite true that one had never been to Shanghai until one had been here.
>
> (Zhou Erfu 1981, vol. 1: 215)

Huang Chujiu went broke in 1931 and had to sell the amusement center to former Green Gang head Huang Jinrong (Ke Zhaojin 1985: 5; Browning 1987: 25a). The amusement center thrived through becoming more licentious; it quickly acquired a notorious reputation as a gathering center for gamblers, prostitutes, and thieves (Ke Zhaojin 1985: 5).

Prostitutes

As streetwalkers became common in Shanghai, the business of prostitution became increasingly impersonal (Hershatter 1989: 494). In 1920 the Shanghai Municipal Council calculated that more than 70,000 prostitutes were in the foreign concessions: 12,000 high-class *changsan*; 490 second-class *yao'er*; 37,140 unregistered streetwalkers or "pheasants" (*yeji*), of which 24,825 were to be found in the International Settlement and 12,315 in the French Concession; and 21,315 women working in "flower-smoke rooms" (*huayan jian*, where men smoked opium and visited prostitutes afterward), and "nailsheds" (*dingpeng* or crib joints that catered to laborers) (Sun Guoqun 1988: 3–4; Hershatter 1989: 466). If these figures are approximately correct, then in the French Concession in 1920, where there were 39,210 female adults on the population registers, one in every three women was a whore (Sun Guoqun 1988: 4). Altogether, it was estimated at the time that Shanghai's ratio of one prostitute to every 137 inhabitants was the highest among major world cities; Tokyo's ratio being 1:277; Chicago's, 1:437; Paris's, 1:481; Berlin's, 1:582; and London's, 1:906 (Yang Jiezeng and He Wannan 1988: 1).

It was the presence of prostitutes on the streets that Western commentators found offensive. High-class cabarets and brothels along The Line (the International Settlement's red-light district), such as Gracie Gale's glamorous American bordello at Number 52 Kiangsi Road, were another matter. The era of American madams and prostitutes came to an end with the Russian revolution. By 1930 there were about 8,000 White Russian prostitutes in Shanghai, either working openly in "Russian Houses" (*Luosong tangzi*) in Hongkou and the French Concession or as taxi dancers selling their sexual services on the side (Hershatter 1989: 473).

American and White Russian prostitutes had mainly Western clients, but the vast majority of Shanghai prostitutes catered to a Chinese clientele. Many of the girls and young women who worked in Shanghai brothels had originally been sold into prostitution by family members. Many came from Hangzhou and Suzhou, where they were bought cheaply at a tender age. In districts beset by flood or famine, they could be had for a couple of dollars apiece (Hauser 1940: 268). Others had been seized by kidnappers either in the countryside or just after getting off the boat when arriving in this strange and confusing metropolis (Xu Huifang and Liu Qingyu 1932: 79–84). The magnitude of the traffic in children and women was extraordinary. During the period 1913–17 the Anti-Kidnapping Society in Shanghai rescued 10,233 women and children, an average of 2,533 cases per year (*The China Critic*, 1 April 1937).

Brothels were regulated by the police in the International Settlement under By-law 34, which gave the Shanghai Municipal Council the right to license all commercial establishments. By-law 34 was attacked by the Settlement's Moral Welfare League, which opposed the medical examination of prostitutes on the grounds that clients were given a false sense of security, which encouraged vice. In 1919 the ratepayers voted to establish a Special Vice Committee, which submitted a report in March 1920 advocating the ultimate suppression of brothels by a gradualist method: first, By-law 34 would be enforced strictly so that every brothel had a municipal license with an assigned number; second, every year one-fifth of the numbers would be drawn at random and those licenses would then be withdrawn. In this way, the Special Vice Committee hoped to eliminate prostitution from the International Settlement altogether within five years (Hershatter 1988: 35–37).

The SMC tried to ignore the report of the Special Vice Committee, favoring regulation over elimination of the brothels on the grounds that if the houses of prostitution had no licenses, they would simply move outside the Settlement. Also, if brothels were not licensed, they would proliferate, and more police would be needed to suppress them. However, in April 1920 the Special Vice Committee brought its report before the ratepayers, who approved the proposal. Protesting, the SMC nonetheless began to take steps in May 1920 to license and then close down all brothels per the SVC's instructions (Hershatter 1988: 35–37).

Within a year, 210 bordellos had closed their doors. But all this did was to put prostitutes on the street with—in the words of the police commissioner—"a consequent impossibility of any effective police control" (Finch 1953: 226; Yen Ching-yueh 1934: 103). The brothels soon reopened, especially on streets along the Settlement borders; and when the new Nationalist government inaugurated the Chinese Municipality, protests were sent to the consular authorities asking them to take steps to close these houses of prostitution (*China Weekly Review*, 20 August 1929). Yet at the same time, the 1928 banning by Chiang Kai-shek's government of prostitution in all the cities of Jiangsu, Zhejiang, and Anhui led to an even greater influx of prostitutes into Shanghai (Sun Guoqun 1988: 4). The result was a schizophrenic social policy on the part of the British and Chinese police authorities of Shanghai. While they ostensibly opposed prostitution (*The China Critic*, 1 April 1937; Hershatter 1988: 42–43), they continued to license brothels. In 1936 the International Settlement issued brothel licenses to 697 people; 558 people received licenses in 1937, 585 in 1938, 1,155 in 1939, and 1,325 in 1940 (Sun Guoqun 1988: 4).

National culture

These were also years, of course, during which the Nationalist government was devoting a large portion of its control efforts to extirpating Communists. As the New Life movement was later to demonstrate, in the eyes of the Nationalist right wing, political radicalism and cultural permissiveness were cut from the same cloth. The Chinese Communist movement was deliberately tainted by its association with foreign Bolshevism, and both were, in turn, linked in Nationalist propaganda with attacks upon the Confucian family and with the advocacy and practice of free love. During the Nanjing decade of 1927–37, the Nationalist policy of outlawing prostitution and gambling was thus one aspect of growing censorious control of public life, including the expression of political opinions. While it became a crime in 1931 to criticize the Nationalist Party in the press, it was also seditious to publish and disseminate "reactionary printed materials." Together with the British police of the International Settlement, the Chinese police subsequently raided and closed down some twenty bookshops publishing or circulating books bearing such "ominous" titles as *Materialistic Philosophy*,

Materialism and Religion, Oulinoff, the Materialist, Soviet Farmers, and *Women* (Shanghai Municipal Police Files, D-7873, 14 April 1927).

This right-wing ideological repression was accompanied by a conscious endeavor to provide positive alternatives to the "negative" culture of left-wing radicalism. The government proposed to open in Shanghai a Nationalist bookshop where "the tastes of youth shall be ignored and youth be given what is good for them," and at least one international lecturer was brought to the city to guide the young away from Communism and into better ways (Isaacs 1932: 76).

The authorities also began to organize counter-holidays to enforce their own vision of the new municipal civic order. For example, the Shanghai branch of the Guomindang notified various public bodies on 3 May 1936, that: "May 5 being the anniversary of the inauguration of our revolutionary government, the local party branch will convene a meeting of representatives of various circles at its auditorium at 10:00 a.m. to celebrate the occasion . . . The national flag should be hoisted, and separate meetings should also take place to celebrate the anniversary" (*Central China Daily News* (trans.) 1936).

National salvation

The Manchurian Railway Incident of 18 September 1931, expanded the boundaries of civic dissent in Shanghai dramatically. On 22 September 1931, thirty local university representatives gathered at the Shanghai Baptist College to form an alliance of all the college Resist-Japan-to-Save-the-Nation societies (Wasserstrom 1988, ch. 5: 20).

The local Guomindang branch instantly tried to gain control of this newly formed youth league by founding a Resist-Japan Society (*Kang-Ri hui*) run by Party leaders and members of the Chinese Chamber of Commerce. It also tried to steal the thunder of the colleges' Resist-Japan league by lowering flags on all government buildings to half mast on 24 September 1931, a day that was already declared "national humiliation day" (Wasserstrom 1988, ch. 5: 19).

The 9 December 1931 incident—in which students occupied the Chinese municipal administration building, sacked and wrecked the Guomindang headquarters, held a kangaroo court that interrogated and beat a PSB detective, and issued a warrant for the arrest of the commissioner of police—led to the resignation of General Zhang Qun as mayor of Shanghai on 10 December and provoked a spate of other demonstrations that were treated by the Japanese as provocations likely to lead to war (*North China Herald*, 13 January, 16 December 1931; Wang Min, et al. 1981: 140).

After the Japanese invaded Zhabei on 28 January 1932, "the dancing girls disappeared from our cinema"—Communist filmmaker Xia Yan claimed hyperbolically— "and we started on the new road of courage" (Kaufman 1982: 2). Once the "peace truce" was signed with the Japanese on 5 May 1932, the various police forces of Shanghai were more than ever concerned to keep such strong anti-Japanese feeling from providing another *casus belli* to justify intervention. As members of the left and of the Communist Party sought to take advantage of nationalistic outrage against the aggressors by mobilizing protests against the Chiang government's policy of appeasement, the Chinese municipality's Public Security Bureau linked its assault against the CCP with continuing control of urban demonstrations.

Authorities throughout Shanghai feared "possible communistic uprisings" on

18 September 1932, the first anniversary of the Manchurian Railway Incident (Shanghai Municipal Police Files, D-4003, 17 September 1932). Requests for help from the PSB, however, mobilized all of Shanghai's police forces, including the Japanese consular police, on emergency standby on that particular day. Their presence was so overwhelming that only one minor incident occurred. The Japanese were much relieved, and a spokesman for the Naval Landing Party told the press, "At no time in recent local history has there ever been seen such effective cooperation taken by the authorities of different nations for the preservation of peace and order in the city" (Shanghai Municipal Police Files, D-7333, 19 September 1932).

Shanghai's future: utopia or apocalypse?

The "peace and order" lauded by the Japanese was built upon the ruins of major portions of the Chinese Municipality, and especially of bombed and burned Zhabei. The civic order that Mayor Huang Fu had hoped to achieve still remained out of reach—even though Wu Tiecheng, the dynamic and powerful new mayor who sought to rebuild Chinese-administered Shanghai after the January 1932 fracas, had similar visions of his own. "If you will permit me to guide your thoughts into a state of idealism," he told his fellow citizens, "you will form a picture in your mind of a city, a sort of Utopia, which embodies the world's latest and most approved form of municipal government . . . Such is the Greater Shanghai that we would like to see" (Wu Tiecheng 1933: frontispiece).

It was not difficult to parody such a utopian fantasy. Ming San wrote that the Shanghai of the future would be "modernized" (*jinhua*) into a "heaven on top of a heaven" where there would no beggars, no criminals, no vagabonds, no homeless.[1] "The streets will be filled only with the most illustrious, with celebrities, with the most successful, with the gentry, with philanthropists, and with the geniuses of the International Settlement, including great foreign men and their wives." Youth will be "modernized" (*modenghua*) into the "modern boy" (*mopu*) with a foreign suit and moustache, and the "modern girl" (*moge*) with a permanent wave and high-heeled shoes; and when these members of the opposite sex meet each other, they will speak together in a foreign language (Xin Zhonghua zazhi she, 1934: 2).

Yang Yibo, on the other hand, was too deeply depressed by the devastation Shanghai suffered from the Japanese to be so sanguine—even in sarcasm.

> Shanghai is a seething cauldron. Did you not see the phenomenon several months ago when the Huangpu River in raging tide overflowed its banks and completely washed away the major roads? This appears to be exactly like the first act of the great masses of China taking back Shanghai by force. A Chinese poet's prophetic words went something like this (I remember just the general meaning): "Along these smooth and well oiled streets / There is going to explode a mountain of fire." Is that true? I hope utterly to destroy this old Shanghai, to smash asunder this oriental bastion of imperialist domination, to inter forever those golden dreams of bloodsucking vampires! Rage on, Shanghai!
>
> (Xin Zhonghua zazhi she, 1934: 10–11)

Slightly less apocalyptic, though strikingly Kafkaesque, was Liu Mengfei's prognostication of Shanghai's future, when there would no longer be a distinction between "masters" and "slaves," between "high-level Chinamen" and the shriveled beggars of the sidewalk, between the oppressors and the "black insects." The poor people will move from their rat holes to the "high-rise mansions" (*gaolou dasha*) of the "playboys" (*anlegong*), who will flee by airplane to some distant place where they can continue to be pampered. The British and French barracks will be blown up and the foreign banks, factories, and printing presses will be taken over by the masses, the "black insects," who will enjoy an ultimate and total victory over the imperialists (Xin Zhonghua zazhi she, 1934: 5).

New life

It was precisely to hold back the tide of "black insects" that the Shanghai party branch of the Guomindang initiated the New Life Movement on 8 April 1934. By 11 April, more than 5,000 people had registered with the Shanghai New Life Movement Acceleration Association; and, during the next three days, public propaganda meetings were held at the recreation ground in Wusong, followed by lantern processions through the streets (Shanghai Municipal Police Files, D5729/1, 17 April 1934). At the end of the first week of the New Life Movement, another lantern procession involved more than six thousand people, including 500 members of the Peace Preservation Corps, 300 PSB policemen, and 100 military policemen. The parade began at 6:00 p.m., wound its way through South Market, and broke up at 10:10 p.m. at West Gate (Shanghai Municipal Police Files, D-5729/1, 17 April 1934).

The new civic center at Jiangwan was supposed to be the symbolic center of this movement. But only the town hall had been finished in time for the demonstrations; the library, museum, and municipal stadium were still under construction (Henriot 1983: 250–51). Consequently, the New Life Movement lacked a ceremonial forum—a concentrated arena to celebrate mass spontaneity and elevate it to a form of ritualized political consciousness. It remained a top-down affair, organized with the help of the police and the local party organization, which worked mainly through professional groups, educational institutions, and other organs open to GMD manipulation. By the end of May 1934, it was beginning to decline into routine, although the Chinese police continued to try to enforce their own regulations of public conduct along New Life lines (Shanghai Municipal Police Files, D-5729, 3 April, 9 May 1934; *Shanghai shi gonganju*, File 21).

Of course, radical right-wing core groups continued to wage cultural war on the left. The Blue Shirts raided the Yihua Film Company, which was dominated by underground CCP members, and warned that their Society for the Eradication of Communists in the Film Industry was going to "cleanse the cultural world" of makers of leftist films. These bully-boy tactics went hand-in-hand with the work of the GMD censors, who rejected eighty-three film scripts and closed fourteen film studios between 1934 and 1934 (Kaufman 1982: 2–3; Hunter 1973: 263).

The left fought back as best it could. Censors were bribed, pseudonyms were used, and "pigeon films" were made to draw the censors' fire on purpose so that one's crucial line of protest in a serious film would get through. The greatest leftist coup in the cinema world was conducted by Xia Yan, who got the support of Chiang Kai-shek and Madame Chiang for a film, "Morals of Women," released at the beginning of the New Life Movement (Kaufman 1982: 2–3). In the meantime, filmmakers also had to cope with the censors of the International Settlement and French Concession with seventeen and eight cinemas, respectively. In 1937 the SMP and French police censored 451 feature films, 932 shorts, and 269 newsreels (Shanghai Municipal Council, 1938: 95).

Attacks on movies were part of the larger effort at censorship that deeply affected the cultural life of Shanghai. In February 1934 the Guomindang banned 149 books in Shanghai and forbade the circulation of seventy-six magazines, including *The Dipper* and *Literature Monthly*. More than twenty-five bookstores were threatened with closing because they sold the works of Lu Xun, Guo Moruo, Mao Dun, and Ba Jin. The following June, just after the New Life Movement began to wind down, a law made it compulsory for publishers to submit all manuscripts for books and magazines to a special committee for inspection before they could be printed (Hunter 1973: 265–66, 273).

National salvation

The main targets of Chinese Nationalist censorship were Communist and "National Salvation" publications. The Public Security Bureau frequently requested International Settlement police aid in seizing such materials, but, although the SMP needed no special urging to ferret out Communist propagandists, it hesitated to confiscate "National Salvation" materials (Shanghai Municipal Police Files, D-7855, 6 April 1937).

The International Settlement authorities were reluctant to persecute "National Salvation" patriots because the line between patriotism and radicalism was becoming blurred as the imperial Japanese armies expanded into North China and as the Nanjing regime stolidly stuck to its determination first to *annei* (subjugate the internal enemy, the Communists) before *rangwai* (expelling the external enemy, the Japanese). Gradually the New Life Movement paled beside this much more striking national issue, especially after the December Ninth Movement erupted in 1935 and was captured by the left.

The Xi'an Incident changed this alignment virtually overnight. After Chiang Kai-shek was released on Christmas Day 1936, there was a spontaneous surge of public support for the Generalissimo. The Shanghai Guomindang branch leader, Wu Kaixian, decided to harness this support by holding a mass meeting on 28 December (Shanghai Municipal Police Files, D7674A, 29 December 1936).

The mammoth civic rally of 150,000 people that subsequently assembled at the public recreation grounds opened by singing the Guomindang anthem and bowing in respect to the national and party flags and to the portrait of Dr. Sun Yat-sen. (The crowd estimate was that of the *Shanghai Times*. The police estimated 30,000 persons, mainly students.) After three minutes of silence in honor of the comrades killed in the Xi'an Incident, Dr. Sun's will was read aloud, members of the presidium made a report to the audience, Wu Kaixian gave an oration, and short speeches were delivered by representatives of local public bodies. The crowd passed a resolution to send a telegram to General Chiang, welcoming him back to Nanjing and hailing him "as the sole national leader of

China in view of his great personality and the meritorious service he had rendered to the country." Then the enormous crowd conducted "one of the biggest and most colorful parades staged in recent years in Shanghai." Led by the musical bands of the PSB and Shanghai-Wusong Garrison force, the procession marched for nearly four hours through Nandao, while two airplanes chartered by the China Aviation Club scattered colored paper slips with pro-Chiang slogans along the way. Similar meetings, followed by processions, were held in Pudong, Jiangwan, and Wusong, with a total of 12,000 people participating (*Shanghai Times*, 29 December 1936).

The December 1936 rally was the regime's most successful counter-procession. Like the radical political assemblies it was intended to displace, the rally was supposed to mobilize public support to help create a common sense of civic culture. When we compare it to such urban activities of late-imperial Chinese cities as ritualized competitions between various labor groups, it is easy to see how much of this new civic culture had to be fabricated *ab novo* by political authorities both licit and clandestine.

Wartime Shanghai

After the battle of Shanghai in August 1937, when the Japanese occupied the Chinese sectors of the city, an illusory air of prosperity, even frivolity, settled over the foreign concessions (Honig 1982: 28; but see also Fu 1989: 9–13). The various authorities of the city were initially too preoccupied by refugee settlement problems to pay much attention to the western suburbs outside the International Settlement—an area that quickly became known as the "Badlands" after the regular PSB fell under Japanese domination and lawless elements were allowed to roam unchecked there (Ma Jun 1988: 206–8). Gambling flourished, and kidnapping, extortion, highway robbery, and murder became rampant (Shanghai "Shanghai Mayor . . ." 1941: 3–4). "A large criminal community has gradually established itself around the gambling operations organized in that area, and this has in recent months been further increased by the formation of large political and plainclothes armed groups. Any man bringing a pistol can enlist in such groups" (Bourne 1939).

Although the puppet city government of Shanghai under Mayor Chen Gongbo ordered all of the gambling dens in the Badlands to close down in the spring of 1941, at least four major casinos—luxurious gaming resorts operating in several of the large country houses with imposing gates and long driveways located west of the city—continued to keep their doors open (Shanghai Municipal Police Files, D-8039A, 15 May 1941; *Shanghai*, "Shanghai Mayor . . ." 1941: 2–4). The owners of these four gambling dens had an "understanding" with Wu Subao and the Japanese military police whereby a daily protection fee of $15,000 was paid to the "East Asia Charity Association," headed by one of the senior Japanese police officers (*China Weekly Review*, 2 August 1941).

Meanwhile, other rackets were also thriving in occupied Shanghai. The drug trade surged, both nationally and in Shanghai, after the Japanese special services organs began to carry out a "narcotization" policy that was expected to raise $300,000,000 per year when fully implemented (reports from U.S. Treasury Agent Nicholson, in Parssinen and Meyer, n.d.: 49). In Shanghai's Badlands, forty-two opium hongs reportedly had been granted licenses by the Japanese and municipal authorities in exchange for certain fees (Shanghai Municipal Police Files, D-8039, 15 March 1941).

By June 1941 these gambling houses and opium dispensing dives constituted a chief source of income for the puppet Nanjing government. Monthly receipts from these rackets came to about $3,750,000, of which $750,000 was contributed in the form of "special taxes" to the Treasury in Nanjing. Smaller sums were given to local municipal officials. Journalists estimated that these payments amounted to 50 percent of the gross income of the gambling houses (*China Weekly Review*, "Wang's Moral Crusade . . ." 1941: 108; "Wave of Local Terror . . ." 1941: 361).

At this same time, however, the Japanese home government was becoming concerned about the stupendous extent of crime in occupied Shanghai (Wakeman 1994: 29–30). Ambassador Honda Kumataro was recalled to Tokyo both to prepare for a state visit from Wang Jingwei in June 1941 and to put pressure on the puppet ruler to clean up some of Shanghai's more egregious vices (*China Weekly Review*, "Wang's Moral Crusade . . ." 1941: 108).

Even before setting sail for Japan, Wang Jingwei had ordered his police commissioner in the Badlands, C. C. Pan (Pan Da), to close all the gambling houses between 31 May and 2 June. Mayor Chen Gongbo firmly supported this plan. Special Services chief Wu Subao managed temporarily to thwart Wang's plans (Cai Dejin 1987: 108–9; *China Weekly Review*, 12 July 1941). When Commissioner Pan learned that the gambling ban was being ignored, he personally led a raid on two of the biggest casinos. But he could not singlehandedly prevail. The other Badlands "joints" were never forced to close, and a major new casino was opened in one of Shanghai's best residential districts (Cai Dejin 1987: 109; *China Weekly Review*, 26 July, 2 August 1941).

The Nationalist government tried to make the best propaganda use it could of the Wang Jingwei regime's toleration of massive vice activities in Shanghai (Wakeman 1994: 30). Chiang Kai-shek personally sent a note in July 1941 to the Shanghai press excoriating the puppets and calling for a fight against gambling and opium. In self-defense, puppet Mayor Chen Gongbo subsequently insisted upon having the regular Chinese police take over the Badlands operations (*China Weekly Review*, 12 July 1941).

In late July 1941 General Lu Ying, director of the Shanghai Special Municipality police headquartered in Nandao, sent his assistants to seize control of Commissioner C. C. Pan's Western District Special Police headquarters. The coup was a momentary success. On 16 August, Captain Wu Subao was removed from his post at 76 Jessfield Road. The "king of racketeers" refused to depart from Shanghai, but at least his criminal activities had to be conducted under other guises (*China Weekly Review*, 12 July, 2 August 1941; Argus 1941).

By then the harm had been done, at least as far as Wang Jingwei's fate was concerned. Wang's association with these gangsters badly tarnished his "reform" government, and his decision in November 1941 to lift the ban on prostitution (which further inundated Shanghai with unlicensed streetwalkers) simply confirmed earlier impressions of corrupt and tawdry misrule (Sun Guoqun 1988: 4). By the end of 1942, in fact, Japanese occupation authorities reported a total of 3,900 licensed brothels throughout the city (Yang Jiezeng and He Wannan 1988: 3). Wang Jingwei hoped to win patriotic loyalty and international esteem when the Japanese transferred sovereignty over the foreign concessions to Chinese hands on 1 August 1943. But as vice continued to flourish during the remaining years of the Pacific War with the help of Japanese *yakuza* working hand-in-glove with military and civilian police, Shanghai's own internal civic order seemed irreparably eroded; it was riddled with corruption and corroded by collaboration (Tang Zhenchang, et al. 1989: 829, 846–48).

Postwar Shanghai

Licensed night-life continued after the Pacific War was over. Shanghai's demimonde seemed irrepressible, dancing to Li Jinhui's catchy "yellow music" in the cabarets and dance halls of the now unified Chinese city. One banal favorite, "Ye Shanghai" (Shanghai Night), had these lyrics:

> Shanghai is not a dark city at night.
> Only seeing her smiling face, who can be gloomy at heart?
> I would not exchange the new heaven on earth for any other place.
>
> (Scott 1982: 70–72)

The American GIs who arrived in 1945 brought with them an extraordinary demand for prostitutes, and unlicensed brothels appeared all over the city, causing the Nationalist chief of police in March 1946 to turn Hongkou's Lanqiao precinct into a controlled red light zone (*fenghua qu*) (Yang Jiezeng and He Wannan 1988: 4). Taxi dancers flourished, and the waltz, fox trot, and tango recovered all the popularity these dances had enjoyed before Pearl Harbor. At the Wing On Company's Seventh Heaven ballroom:

> The orchestra on the stage was playing a waltz and couples whirled round the floor to the left. The lights were low and changed from red to blue and from blue to purple as the tempo of the music changed. . . . Some [of the women dancing beneath the colored lights] wore dresses of patterned velvet georgette, some of plain purple velvet and some of black satin, and on their feet they had silver-coloured high-heeled shoes that flashed and glinted as they danced.
>
> (Zhou Erfu 1981, vol. 1: 217)

In 1947 the Nationalist government banned dance halls, and 200,000 Shanghai taxi dancers threatened to march on Nanjing (Zhou Erfu 1981, vol. 1: 217). Less than a year later, on 30 January 1948, 6,000 dance hostesses marched to the Shanghai Bureau of Social Affairs and demanded that the government lift its ban on commercial dance halls. When the Guomindang cadres demurred, the dance hall hostesses rioted. In the end, the officials gave in and the dance halls remained open.[2]

A very different outcome resulted when prostitution riots broke out again after 1949. Even though many prostitutes fled to Hong Kong during the civil war, over 800 bordellos were doing business openly with 40,000 licensed and unlicensed prostitutes when the Communists took over the city in May of that year (sun Guoqun 1988: 5).[3] During the following three years, the municipal authorities conducted a major reform of prostitution, closing most of the brothels in 1951, shutting down additional bordellos in February 1952, rounding up clandestine streetwalkers in September 1952, and outlawing bar girls and taxi dancers in July 1953 (Hershatter 1992: 170–79).

Under the Communists' domination of an undivided city as well as a reunited hinterland, most of the prostitutes were put in labor reform camps where they often had to go "cold turkey" in giving up drug habits. These women were not an easy population to control, especially since their pimps and panderers wanted them released so that they could go back in business again. Several hundred gangsters surrounded a labor reform school that housed prostitutes in October 1952, and they rioted tumultuously until the Public Security Bureau's men arrived and broke up the demonstration (Zhang Xinxin and Sang Ye 1986: 151–52). This was the last gasp of Shanghai's underworld sex merchants. Finally, under a government truly capable of re-educating social deviants, the vices of modernity were being brought under control (Beijing shi gonganju: 32–33). This was certainly not the "Paris of the Orient," but neither was it the civic order that Wu Tiecheng had once envisaged.

The Nationalists' earlier attempts to regulate popular culture, to stifle left-wing criticism, and to repress patriotic dissent had been an authoritarian reaction against Shanghai's moral unruliness, social turmoil, and political restiveness. The city itself was thought to be "a vast dye-vat that would change the colour of any political party that came along" (statement attributed to the *North-China Daily News*, Zhou Erfu 1981, vol. 1: 572). Shanghai's modernity, foreignness, and heterogeneity seemingly defied the Guomindang regime's longing for military orderliness and traditional simplicity.

The Nanjing government's constant preoccupation with *zhixu*, however, was more of an effort to police social forces than to mobilize them. In that sense, the Guomindang government's civic order was only one step above traffic control and municipal licensing; it failed to articulate a Republican political identity vital and vigorous enough to displace all the attractive amusements that constituted the new urban culture of the 1920s and 1930s. Moreover, the other side of political policing was social corruption—corruption so massive that it compromised the national government itself. It might even be argued that the effect of the new state's initial decision in 1927 to intervene so readily in regulating society, in publicly "licensing" its private pursuits, yielded more than proof of the government's inability to mobilize popular support. That decision also aroused expectations that only a better organized, mass-based movement could ultimately fulfill.

When the Communists captured Shanghai in 1949 they, too, feared the taint of the "dye-vat," but their austere and ascetic political ways ultimately prevailed over the indulgences of Shanghai's sophisticated consumers. For these new cadres, leisure no longer had to be licensed because it was essentially eliminated—expunged, not just disregarded. After all, Liu Mengfei's "black insects" were finally in charge, and leisure was the last thing on their minds as genuine social revolution was imposed upon Shanghai at last. Spontaneous civic culture, needless to say, was yet to come.

Notes

1   The description "heaven on top of a heaven" was playing off of Xia Yan's famous description of Shanghai as "a city of forty-eight-storey skyscrapers built upon twenty-four layers of hell" (Xia Yan 1978: 26).
2   Communication from Emily Honig, based on her own interviews.
3   After Liberation, 30,000 prostitutes were sent off for re-education and several hundred thousand opium addicts were detoxified (Wren 1982: 4).

References

Argus. *China Weekly Review*. 1941. "Motives Behind the Reorganization of the Puppet Government," 6 September.

Beijing shi gonganju, *Da shiji* [Major chronicle]. 1986. Beijing: Gonganbu.

Bourne, K. M. 1939. Memorandum to C. Akagi, enclosure in Shanghai depatch to Embassy, Shanghai, 635, 22/11/1939, dated 16 November 1939, in British Foreign Office Records. London: Her Majesty's Public Record Office, F1006, 2 September 1940, FO371–24682.

Browning, Michael. 1987. "Mirrors Reflect Racy Past of Chinese Den of Iniquity." *The Miami Herald*, 22 March: 25a.

Cai Dejin. 1987. *Wang Jingwei ping zhuan* [Critical biography of Wang Jingwei]. Chengdu: Sichuan renmin chubanshe.

Carney, Sanders. 1980. *Foreign Devils Had Light Eyes: A Memoir of Shanghai, 1933–1939*. Ontario: Dorset Publishing.

Carte, Gene E., and Carte, Elaine H. 1975. *Police Reform in the United States: The Era of August Vollmer, 1905–1932*. Berkeley: University of California Press.

Central China Daily News. 1936. "The Anniversary of the Assumption of Office by the Late Dr. Sun Yat-sen and the Canton Government," 5 May. Translated in Shanghai Municipal Police (International Settlement) Files. Microfilms from the U.S. National Archives, D-7333.

The China Critic. 1937. "Shanghai's Housing Report." Shanghai: 17.2: 34. Also issues of 30 October 1930; 27 June 1935; 1 April 1937.

China Weekly Review. 1941. "Wang's Moral Crusade Short-Lived; Police Permit Gamblers to Resume Operations," 28 June: 108. "Wave of Local Terror Rises as Gunmen Kill Chinese Banker Here," 23 August: 361. Also issues of 1 June, 13 July, 20 August 1929; 22 February, 19 July 1930; 26 September 1931; 26 January 1935; 12 July, 26 July, 2 August 1941.

Clifford, Nicholas R. 1988. "The Western Powers and the 'Shanghai Question' in the National Revolution of the 1920s." Paper given at the International Symposium on Modern Shanghai, Shanghai Academy of Social Sciences, 7–14 September.

Coates, Austin. 1983. *China Races*. Hong Kong: Oxford University Press.

Cressey, Paul G. 1932. *The Taxi-Dance Hall: A Sociological Study in Commercialized Recreation and City Life*. Chicago: The University of Chicago Press.

Finch, Percy. 1953. *Shanghai and Beyond*. New York: Charles Scribner's Sons.

Fischer, Claude S. 1975. "Toward a Subcultural Theory of Urbanism." *American Journal of Sociology* 80.6: 1319–41.

Fu, Po-shek. 1989. "Passivity, Resistance, and Collaboration: Intellectual Choices in Occupied Shanghai, 1937–1945." Ph.D. diss., Stanford University.

Gamewell, Mary Ninde. 1916. *The Gateway to China: Pictures of Shanghai*. New York: Fleming H. Revell Co.

Green, O. M., ed. 1927. *Shanghai of Today: A Souvenir Album of Thirty-Eight Vandyke Prints of the "Model Settlement."* Shanghai: Kelly and Walsh, Ltd.

Han, M. K. 1932. "French Colonial Policy in China as Reflected in the Shanghai French Concession." *The China Weekly Review*, 23 January: 239.

Hauser, Ernest O. 1940. *Shanghai: City for Sale*. New York: Harcourt, Brace and Co.

Henriot, Christian. 1983. "Le gouvernement municipal de Shanghai, 1927–1937." Thèse pour le doctorat de 3ème cycle présenté à l'Université de la Sorbonne Nouvelle (Paris III), Juin.

Hershatter, Gail. 1988. "Prostitution in Shanghai, 1919–1949." Paper given at the International Symposium on Modern Shanghai, Shanghai Academy of Social Sciences, 7–14 September.

—— 1989. "The Hierarchy of Shanghai Prostitution, 1870–1949." *Modern China* 15.4: 463–98.

—— 1992. "Regulating Sex in Shanghai: The Reform of Prostitution in 1920 and 1951." In Frederic Wakeman, Jr., and Wen-hsin Yeh, eds. *Shanghai Sojourners*, pp. 145–185. Berkeley: Institute of East Asian Studies.

Honig, Emily. 1982. "Women Cotton Mill Workers in Shanghai, 1919–1949." Ph.D. diss., Stanford University.

Hunter, Neale. 1973. "The Chinese League of Left-Wing Writers, Shanghai, 1930–1936." Ph.D. thesis, Australian National University.

Isaacs, Harold R., ed. 1932. *Five Years of Kuomintang Reaction*. Shanghai: China Forum Publishing Company.

Kaufman, Peter. 1982. "The Film *Street Angel*: A Study in Camouflaged Dissent." History seminar paper, University of California, Berkeley.

Ke Zhaojin. 1985. " 'Great World' a Must for Amusement Seekers." *China Daily*, 27 April: 5.

Lethbridge, H. J., intro. 1983 (1934–35). *All About Shanghai: A Standard Guidebook*. Hong Kong: Oxford University Press.

Liu Guangqing. 1988. "Kangzhan hou de Shanghai jinyan" [The suppression of opium in Shanghai after the War of Resistance]. In Shen Feide, et al., eds., *Jiu Shanghai de yan du chang* [Old Shanghai's drugs, gambling, prostitution]. Shanghai: Baijia chubanshe.

Ma Jun. 1988. "Gudao shiqi de Hu xi daitu" [Island Shanghai's western badlands]. In Shen Feide, et al., eds., *Jiu Shanghai de yan du chang* [Old Shanghai's drugs, gambling, prostitution]. Shanghai: Baijia chubanshe.

Mao Xiaocen. 1963. "Jiu Shanghai de da duku—huili qiuchang" [A big gambling den of old Shanghai—the Jailai fronton]. In Chinese People's Political Consultative Conference, Shanghai weiyuanhui, Wenshi ziliao gongzuo weiyuanhui, comps. *Wenshi ziliao xuanji (Shanghai)* [Selections of historical materials (Shanghai)], fascicle 15. Shanghai: Zhonghua shuju.

Martin, Brian G. 1992. " 'The Pact with the Devil': The Relationship between the Green Gang and the French Concession Authorities, 1925–1935." In Frederic Wakeman, Jr., and Wen-hsin Yeh, eds., *Shanghai Sojourners*, pp. 266–304. Berkeley: Institute for East Asian Studies.

McCormick, Elsie. 1923. *Audacious Angles on China*. New York: D. Appleton and Company.

Meng, C. Y. W. 1929a. "A Tale of Two Cities." *The China Weekly Review*, 27 July: 420.

—— 1929b. "The 'Hwa Hui' Gambling Evil." *The China Weekly Review*, 19 January: 334.

North China Daily News, cited in Zhou 1981.

North China Herald. Shanghai: 13 January, 16 December 1931.

Pal, John. 1963. *Shanghai Saga*. London: Jarrolds.

Pan Ling. 1982. *In Search of Old Shanghai*. Hong Kong: Joint Publishing Company.

Parssinen, Terry M., and Meyer, Kathryn B. N.d. "International Narcotics Trafficking in the Early Twentieth Century: Development of an Illicit Industry." Unpublished paper.

Rowe, William T. 1989. *Hankow: Conflict and Community in a Chinese City, 1796–1895*. Stanford: Stanford University Press.

—— 1990. "The Public Sphere in Modern China." *Modern China* 16.3: 309–29.

Scott, A. C. 1982. *Actors Are Madmen. Notebook of a Theatregoer in China*. Madison: The University of Wisconsin Press.

Shanghai. 1941. "Shanghai Mayor Keeps His Promise to the Public." Shanghai: Metropolitan Publishing Company, July 1.3: 3–4.

Shanghai Municipal Council. 1938. Report for the Year 1937 and Budget for the Year 1938. Shanghai: *North China Daily News* and *North China Herald*.

Shanghai Municipal Police (International Settlement) Files. Microfilms from the U.S. National Archives.

Shanghai shi gonganju, *Jingcha changshi huibian* [Compilation of general knowledge about the police]. 1937. Shanghai Municipal Archives, Microfilm No. 1–2660–895.24.

Shanghai shi gonganju yewu baogao, 1930 [Shanghai Municipality Public Security Bureau report of affairs, 1930]. 1930. Shanghai: Shanghai Municipal Public Security Bureau.

Shanghai shi gonganju yewu baogao, 1931 [Shanghai Municipality Public Security Bureau report of affairs, 1931]. 1931. Shanghai: Shanghai Municipal Public Security Bureau.

Shanghai tebie shi gonganju yewu jiyao, Minguo shiliu nian ba yue zhi shiqi nian qi yue [Summary of the affairs of the Shanghai Special Municipality Public Security Bureau from August 1927 to July 1928]. 1928. Shanghai: Shanghai Municipal Public Security Bureau.

Shanghai Times. 1931. Cited in Harold R. Isaacs, ed., *Five Years of Kuomintang Reaction*: 11.

—— 1936. In Shanghai Municipal Police (International Settlement) Files, D7675A, 29 December 1936.

Shenbao. Shanghai: 4, 7, 8, 12 July 1927.

Shen Yi. 1970. "Shanghai shi gongwuju shi nian" [Ten years in the Shanghai Municipal Bureau of Works]. *Zhuanji wenxue* 70.2: 11–18.

Spence, Jonathan D. 1981. *The Gate of Heavenly Peace: The Chinese and Their Revolution, 1895–1980*. New York: Viking Press.

Sun Guoqun. 1988. "Lun jiu Shanghai changji zhidu de fazhan he tedian" [On the development and characteristics of the prostitute system in old Shanghai]. Paper given at the International Symposium on Modern Shanghai, Shanghai Academy of Social Sciences, 7–14 September.

Tang Zhenchang, et al., eds. 1989. *Shanghai shi* [History of Shanghai]. Shanghai: Shanghai renmin chubanshe.

Tu Shipin, ed. 1948. *Shanghai shi daguan* [Overview of Shanghai city]. Shanghai: Zhongguo tushu zazhi gongsi.

Wakeman, Frederic, Jr. 1988. "Policing Modern Shanghai." *China Quarterly* 115: 408–40.

—— 1994. "The Shanghai Badlands: Wartime Terrorism and Urban Crime." Paper given at the Conference on National Identity and State Formation, Institute of Modern History, Academia Sinica, Nan-kang, 12–14 January.

Wang Min, et al., eds. 1981. *Shanghai xuesheng yundong da shi ji* [Record of major events of the Shanghai student movement]. Shanghai: Xuelin.

Wasserstein, Bernard. 1994. "Collaboration in Wartime Shanghai." Paper given at the annual meeting of the American Historical Association, San Francisco, 9 January.

Wasserstrom, Jeffrey. 1988. "Student Protest in Shanghai." Ph.D. thesis, University of California, Berkeley.

Westley, William A. 1970. *Violence and the Police: A Sociological Study of Law, Custom and Morality*. Cambridge, Mass., and London, England: The MIT Press.

Wilson, James O. 1976. *Varieties of Police Behavior: The Management of Law and Order in Eight Communities*. New York: Atheneum.

Wren, Christopher S. 1982. "Once-Wicked Shanghai Is a Puritan Port of Call." *New York Times*, 5 November: 4.

Wu Tiecheng. 1933. "Greater Shanghai: Its Present and Future." *People's Tribune*, 3.11: 403, 1 January. Cited in Henriot 1983.

Wu Yü, Liang Licheng, and Wang Daozhi. 1988. *Minguo hei shehui* [Black society of the Republic]. Jiangsu: Jiangsu guji chubanshe.

Wu Zude. 1988. "Jiu Shanghai de da huahui" [Playing huahui in old Shanghai]. In Shen Feide, et al., eds., *Jiu Shanghai de yan du chang* [Old Shanghai's drugs, gambling, prostitution]. Shanghai: Baijia chubanshe.

Xia Yan. 1978. *Baoshen gong* [Collected works].

Xin Zhonghua zazhi she, eds., 1934. *Shanghai de jianglai* [The Future of Shanghai]. Shanghai: Zhonghua shuju.

Xu Huifang and Liu Qingyu. 1932. "Shanghai nüxing fan de shehui fenxi" [A social analysis of female crime in Shanghai]. *Dalu zazhi* 1.4: 79–84.

Xu Zhucheng. 1982. *Du Yuesheng zhengzhuan* [A straightforward biography of Du Yuesheng]. Hangzhou: Xinhua shudian.

Yang Jiezeng and He Wannan. 1988. *Shanghai changqi gaizao shihua* [A history of the reform of Shanghai prostitutes]. Shanghai: Shanghai sanlian shudian.

Yeh Wen-hsin. 1987. "The Liu Geqing Affair: Heroism in the Chinese Secret Service during the War of Resistance." Paper presented to the Regional Seminar, Center for Chinese Studies, University of California, Berkeley, 21 March.

Yen Ching-yueh. 1934. "Crime in Relation to Social Change in China." Ph.D. diss., University of Chicago.

Zhang Kaimin, ed. 1989. *Shanghai renkou qianyi yanjiu* [Research on Shanghai population migration]. Shanghai: Shanghai shehui kexue yuan chubanshe.

Zhang Xinxin and Sang Ye. 1986. *Chinese Profiles*. Beijing: Panda Books. *Zhongyang ribao*. Translated in Shanghai Municipal Police (International Settlement) Files, D-7333, 4 May 1936.

Zhou Erfu. 1981. *Morning in Shanghai*, A. C. Barnes, trans. Beijing: Foreign Languages Press.

PART EIGHT

Postcolonialism:
After Decolonization

POSTCOLONIALISM

After decolonization

EUROPEAN DECOLONIZATION in Africa and Asia initiated many questions, not the least of which is how to write about events and changes in the aftermath of the collapse of empire. Debates over the interpretations of the past have led to provocative and eloquent theoretical analyses of the postcolonial condition; and researchers have tracked with care many historical and political transitions in the former colonies. The articles presented here focus on several aspects of postcolonial society and are intended to highlight both historical and theoretical contributions to our understanding of the postcolonial condition.

Since the legacy of decolonization and nationalism also lingers in all postcolonial societies, it seems natural to ask what sort of legacy did decolonization leave in European metropolitan societies. Perhaps one of the best examples in Christopher Flood and Hugo Frey's article "Questions of Decolonization and Postcolonialism in the Ideology of the French Extreme Right." Flood and Frey describe how decolonization resonates in the anti-immigration discourse of the contemporary French right wing. The French anti-immigration and xenophobic discourse is marked by the fear of die-hard French nationalists that French culture is threatened by the practice of Islam in contemporary France. French politicians such as Jean Marie Le Pen attempt to restore the so-called grandeur of the French empire by transforming the legacy of decolonization into a battle cry against North Africans and immigrants.

Crawford Young's 1994 article "Zaire: The Shattered Illusion of the Integral State" investigates postcolonial politics in the former Belgian Congo. As Young states, the colonial legacy hung heavy in the wake of decolonization. Under African leaders such as Patrice Lumumba, the Congo witnessed an attempt to create an integral state in which nationalism would be both ideological and radical. This nationalist discourse unfortunately spun the Congo into the vortex of the Cold War, which had dramatic repercussions for the Congolese. Following Lumumba's assassination, Young traces the effects of Mobutu Sese Seko's vision of the state and the Congolese economy.

Ultimately, according to Young, the legacy of colonialism and decolonization in the former Belgian Congo remains yet to be settled.

Moving to an analysis of current debates about the postcolonial condition and the role of historians, Dipesh Chakrabarty seeks to displace Eurocentrism in the historiography of colonial India. In an effort to push Europe out of its privileged epistemological status, Chakrabarty calls for a "provincialization" of Europe by which is meant that colonial historians must self-consciously keep from reproducing western stereotypes and teleologies *vis-à-vis* India. Historians considering the process of decolonization, for example, would, according to Chakrabarty, need to marginalize considerations of Europe because most historians practicing colonial history start with Europe at the center and then work toward the colonies as a peripheral concern. A major indictment of colonial historiography, Chakrabarty's essay is eloquent and provocative.

Chapter 20

Christopher Flood and Hugo Frey

QUESTIONS OF DECOLONIZATION AND POST-COLONIALISM IN THE IDEOLOGY OF THE FRENCH EXTREME RIGHT

Introduction

THE PROCESS OF DECOLONIZATION and its long-term consequences are central issues for extreme right-wing intellectuals grouped in, or ideologically close to, the Front National (FN). The meanings which these writers ascribe to the age of empire and to the post-imperial period feed into the controversy over non-European immigration into France. They also bear on extreme right-wing approaches to French foreign and defence policy, including relations with France's remaining overseas territories and with former colonies. Furthermore, these questions are framed in the wider context of the extreme right's assessments of the overall development of inter-national relations, and especially the issue of American power since the end of the Cold War.

The extreme right was not always committed to French empire-building. In the 1880s many of its members had objected to Jules Ferry's expansionist colonial policy on the ground that it was a costly distraction from the necessary tasks of restoring France's status in Europe and preparing for war against Germany to recover the provinces lost in 1871. Opposition in this area also provided a vehicle for the extreme right's perennial hostility to the Republic itself. It could even feed on anti-Semitism, as some extreme right-wingers saw the commercial forces which supported colonial expansion as knowingly or unwittingly serving the objectives of Jewish capitalism at the expense of the French national interest.

However, several factors encouraged a gradual, though not entirely unanimous, conversion to support for colonialism from the 1890s onwards. This support could draw on the cherished belief in France's pre-eminent, God-given role as Eldest Daughter of the Church. Colonial expansion thus became acceptable to many Catholic traditionalists who believed that missionary activity would not only redeem subject peoples and help to civilize them, but would function as a spiritual counterbalance to secularism in metropolitan France. At the same time, in the light of attacks on the reputation of the French military establishment during the Dreyfus Affair, support for the actions of French armed forces around the globe offered a defence against left-wing accusations of military corruption or incompetence at home. Equally, the extreme right began to see the colonial arena as an extension of intra-European conflicts. Instead of dissipating national energies, it could be viewed as a projection of France's rivalry with both Britain and Germany. In the discourse of the extreme right colonial epic, military ethic, religion and nationalism could go hand in hand as expressions of the values of heroism, authority, obedience, faith and patriotic sacrifice which they revered. Even if they did not hold the same conceptions of civilization and progress as republicans, and even if they did not believe that non-white races could be raised eventually to the same level as white Europeans, many extreme right-wingers came to endorse the belief that France was engaged in a civilizing mission.

Support for the empire was maintained during the first half of the twentieth century. During the inter-war years it was reinforced by the development of an anti-colonial stance on the communist left. The Vichy regime and its adherents attached enormous importance to the empire as a bastion of French sovereignty. By the 1950s, the wars of decolonization led the extreme right to the high point of its commitment. During the conflicts in Indochina and Algeria, defence of colonialism was closely entangled with fear of the worldwide spread of communism as well as with despair at the decline of France's international power. Having only recently begun to return from the political margin to which it had been driven after the Liberation, the extreme right ultimately suffered a further catastrophic defeat through its virulent, and sometimes physically violent, opposition to decolonization.

From the time of the Evian accords of 1962 until the FN began to make electoral headway some twenty years later, the extreme right remained impotent and embittered on the edge of political life, alienated from the Gaullists who had accepted the General's cession of Algeria, disdained by ambitious conservatives seeking careers in mainstream politics, and unable to retaliate effectively against the claims of leftists, third-worldists, multiculturalists and liberal humanitarians who demanded moral and material recognition of the exploitative and oppressive aspects of the colonial era. Yet, amid the economic anxieties, stubbornly high levels of unemployment, and political polarization in the mid-1980s, with the left in power for the first time under the Fifth Republic, the issue of immigration from the former colonies was to serve the FN well as an ideological battering-ram in its attempt to thrust itself into contention for public support.

The demand for halting and radically reversing non-European immigration could not simply be a matter of domestic policy. It inevitably raised larger questions concerning France's past and present relationship with Algeria and other ex-colonial states which had supplied so many immigrants and asylum seekers. More recently the issue has been sharpened further by the rise of Islamic fundamentalism in some of the states within France's traditional sphere of influence, and radiating out from those states to sections of the immigrant population within France itself. In any case, besides its various agreements with former dependent territories, France still has the remains of its empire. In a post-colonial – and now post-Cold War – world France is one of the powers which still has colonies, albeit small ones, scattered across the southern Atlantic, Pacific and Indian Oceans. Questions relating to France's responsibility, obligations and national interest in these regions are perceived by the extreme right as vitally important.

Why did France lose the empire?

FN intellectuals and their ideological allies have to deal with a paradox. On the one hand, they wish to defend many aspects of France's past record as an imperial power, and hence the nationalist right's own record of diehard support for colonialism. On the other hand, they have to explain the fact that subject peoples of the empire were in some cases willing to die in bloody wars to rid themselves of their colonial overlords. If France had indeed been engaged in a civilizing mission, as so many of its politicians had claimed at the time, why had the empire disintegrated? The questions must be answered in terms which exempt the extreme right from serious blame by ascribing the faults to their political enemies. The need is all the stronger and more heartfelt, because some of the older generation of activists and intellectuals on the extreme right were involved in the wars of decolonization as soldiers (Jean-Marie Le Pen, Roger Holeindre, Jean Mabire, for example), and/or as activists in the OAS or other kindred organizations during the death throes of French Algeria (Jean-Claude Bardet, Pierre Montagnon Pierre Sergent, Jean-Jacques Susini, Dominique Venner, for example).

These issues have been addressed in the context of a major effort of ideological renewal. The essence of the New Right intellectual-drive from the late 1960s onwards was to modernize and revitalize the ideology of the extreme right. The FN, which has absorbed many of the intellectuals formerly associated with the New Right, also wishes to present itself as a modernizing party which has a new ideological synthesis to offer in opposition to the tired ideas of the left and the mainstream right. Furthermore, within this synthesis, retrospective assessment of the empire has to be reconciled with the extreme right's self-proclaimed, neo-nationalist role as defender of the right of all nations to their own identity and ethnic culture. Therefore, it is not a case of maintaining a wholesale, revisionist defence of the empire against those who have claimed that it was an exploitative, corrupt and unjust system. The stakes are much higher than that, and the arguments are, in any case, more sophisticated.

In fact, the discourse of the extreme right on the colonial period is deeply ambivalent. It includes a strong critique of the principles which shaped the governance of the empire, but it does not attack the activity of building and holding the empire in itself. Traditional nationalists are heirs to an ideological tradition of social Darwinism, mixed with borrowings from Nietzsche and other sources. In the past, exponents of this viewpoint took it for granted that nations, like individuals, are driven by a will to power and possession. They also assumed that nations, and even races, like individuals, are unequal in their capacities, so that one will dominate another, but may be dominated in its turn by a third, and so on. A second related strand was the nationalist right's emphasis on particularism in opposition to left-republican universalism. That is to say, nations, like individuals, are unique products of an infinitely complex combination of heredity and environment interacting over time (the Catholic traditionalist version attributes God-given collective vocations to nations). Implicitly, when fused together, these beliefs formed the basis for a type of nationalism which was undemocratic, as well as anti-egalitarian. It also lent itself to imperialism by virtue of a further assumption that the French people were an élite nation which was destined to play a leading role in the world.

Today, in keeping with the claim to have moved on from the racist, élitist and authoritarian ideas of the past, the discourse tends to be more nuanced. Race is rarely mentioned. The stress is on recognizing and preserving ethnic and national differences, rather than on superiority and inferiority. This requires a degree of intellectual acrobatics in discussion of the French empire. Of course, not everyone bothers with such subtleties. In accounting for the imperialism of France and other European powers, the FN's president, Jean-Marie Le Pen, is an unabashedly deterministic élitist and political realist of the old school. For him, colonialism was merely an expression of fundamental laws of predatory human behaviour throughout history:

> Mus par la volonté de puissance inhérente à leur nature, les hommes ont toujours cherché à dévorer l'espace de leurs voisins. N'en déplaise aux beaux esprits des salons parisiens, l'histoire des relations internationales s'écrit en premier lieu en termes de puissance et de domination et se measure à l'aune des rapports de force. L'habiller sous les atours clinquants des idéologies ou du 'politically correct' ne change rien à l'affaire. Cette constante est aussi vieile que la politique elle-même.[1]

However, many writers are inclined simply to take the empire as historical fact, while emphasizing that the great drive to expansion in the late nineteenth century was carried out under the auspices of the republican centre and left. This enables them to concentrate on the defects of French colonial policy or other factors contributing to the eventual loss of the greater part of the empire. In so doing, they seek to settle old political scores by casting historical blame on the political enemies of their own ideological precursors. At the same time, they attempt to undermine the more recent charge that the extreme right had stood unsuccessfully against the tide of history in the two decades after the Second World War and had blindly defended exploitative imperialist practices which were no longer acceptable to their subjects or to enlightened opinion in the West. Their contention is that the administration of the empire from the late nineteenth century onwards was persistently distorted by republican ideology translated into colonial theory. This observation also forms a vital element of the explanation of what brought the empire down and of the negative consequences of decolonization. Much of the argument in this area by FN intellectuals such as Pierre de Meuse and Didier Lefranc echoes the thinking of the New Right theorist, Alain de Benoist, in his critique of the notion of the *mission civilisatrice* and of the assimilationist underpinning of French colonial administration – both of these errors being predicated on the false, universalistic assumption inherited from the Enlightenment and the Revolution, to the effect that all human beings are fundamentally equal and identical the world over, so that imperialism was a force of emancipation for raising the level of those human groups which had not yet achieved the advanced stage of development epitomized by France.[2] Instead of governing the colonies on the basis of flexible procedures appropriate to their specific conditions, traditions and historical patterns, it is argued, France had tried to fit its colonial subjects into a preconceived, uniform mould dictated by Parisian centralists and had set out to eradicate their ethnic particularities. This prepared the way for eventual reaction by native peoples of the empire against the enforced loss of identity.

Thus, while acknowledging that many right-wingers also rallied to some of these assumptions in due course, FN writers place the primary historical responsibility firmly to the left of their own ideological predecessors. Le Pen equally emphasizes that the ideological error was compounded in the course of the twentieth century when the communist left found it expedient to propagate a different, anti-colonial version of the universalist ideology by preaching the universal right of self determination, coupled with the claim that imperialism was a stage in the process of capitalist exploitation which would eventually be surpassed through revolutionary wars of liberation.[3] During the post-war years, weakened by the recent conflict, undermined from within by the Marxist anti-colonial discourse in the service of the USSR, and overshadowed from the West by the US, which had its own ambitions for world hegemony, French political leaders had faltered in the face of rising militancy within the empire. The tragedy of the Algerian war had, of course, been the real culmination of the process. France's inability to hold the line there can easily be interpreted as the result of a failure of political will which was itself symptomatic of the nation's loss of direction. As one writer puts it, 'pour la France, ces épreuves, fruits de l'incapacité et de la duplicité de ses gouvernants successifs, de la lâcheté de sa population, sont la preuve tangible de sa décadence.'[4]

Post-colonial angst, retro-colonialism and American neo-colonialism

According to intellectuals of the extreme right, the disaster did not end with decolonization. On the contrary, decolonization can be depicted as the preface to a period of ill-judged post-colonial policy which coincided with France's continuing national decline. With the focus on Africa in particular, post-colonial errors can be explained in terms of similar ideological factors as those used to account for the previous mis-management of the empire itself. The left is again set up as the force driving French policy towards disaster in pursuit of its own ideological and party-political ends. The interpretation is as follows. Preaching the gospel of loathing for France's imperial past, the communists, followed later by the socialists, alongside a host of third-worldist pressure groups, have continued to use France's alleged guilt as an exploitative colonial power to push successive French governments into pursuing ill-conceived, ineptly executed policies of *coopération*. These policies have had disastrous effects through the channelling of huge quantities of money to corrupt élites in the former colonies, while the mass of ordinary people have been reduced to pitiful levels of subsistence. The damage has been exacerbated by the economic dislocation of these countries through varying mixtures of ideological contamination, adoption of inappropriate socialist or liberal models of development, mis-government, cultural disorientation, external interference, the creation of an aid-dependent mentality and the consequent inability to compete in world markets. Thus, Bernard Lugan, the FN's leading Africanist, remarks:

> Dans le meilleur des cas, l'Afrique a stagné depuis les indépendances. Mais, plus généralement, elle a reculé. Pourtant, dans l'euphorie de la décolonisation, les tiers-mondistes et les libéraux lui prédisaient un avenir radieux. Les premiers privilégiaient alors les luttes de libération et la voie socialiste vers les lendemains qui chantent, les seconds misaient sur le marché des matières premières qui devait provoquer l'entrée du continent

dans l'économie mondiale. L'échec de ces deux idéologies est total: marxistes ou capitalistes, tous les pays africains sont en effet ruinés. Et l'Afrique paraît imperméable aux modèles importés.[5]

Lugan is also at pains to point out that more recently, under Mitterrand's presidency, French interference in the government of these territories became a hallmark of the Socialist Party's policy as it coerced them in the name of universal rights and equality to adopt Western-style democratic regimes which ran directly contrary to traditional customs and social divisions, thereby promoting murderous inter-ethnic conflicts.[6]

Immigration into France from the former colonies, especially the African territories, and above all the Maghreb, can be presented as a further aspect of the same problem. The primacy given to the immigration issue in recent extreme right-wing discourse is now so well known that it hardly needs further discussion. But for present purposes the instrumental value of the link to decolonization needs to be underlined. The echoes are captured in expressions such as *colonisation à rebours* or *colonisation inversée*. While extreme right-wing writers can acknowledge that temporary immigration by individual workers was of value up to the end of the colonial period, the continuation of immigration to France since that time, establishing patterns of permanent settlement, family regrouping, illegal entries and applications for asylum can be understood as a form of retro-colonization which brings with it a wide range of economic, social and cultural ills. When adherents of the extreme right wish to attack its political enemies within France, retro-colonization can be explained in terms of combinations of factors such as the pervasive acceptance of moral guilt, the influence of the Communist Party in its effort to recruit among immigrant workers to compensate for the loss of support among the native French working class, the preference of many French employers for cheap labour rather than technological modernization, and the willingness of the mainstream conservative parties to bow to the pro-immigration lobbies. Governments of both right and left are accused of having colluded in a double lie to the effect that immigration has virtually been halted since the early 1970s and that the immigrants already resident in France would be successfully integrated into French society.

Combined with the effects of demographic explosion, the economic and political chaos in the African ex-colonies can be cited as a major factor in propelling the flow of would-be immigrants in search a better life in France. But beyond that, the extreme right's habitual tendency to explain unwelcome developments in terms of conspiracies presents immigration as a concerted effort to harm France. Indeed, the very notion of *colonisation à rebours* conjures up the impression of settlement as an instrument of domination. When FN publicists are arguing in melodramatic mode, the flow of immigrants can be presented as an unarmed invasion which is the preface to even greater inundations in the future. It is not surprising that the latest edition of Jean Raspail's *Le Camp des saints*, an apocalyptic novel of the arrival of a massive armada of immigrant ships on the south coast of France, has been marketed through *National hebdo*, and its author given a forum in the FN's theoretical magazine, *Identité*. The impression that parts of the country have been ex-territorialized and entirely taken over by third-world immigrants is captured, for example, in an unsigned *National hebdo* article on the concentrations of immigrants in the Nord department, under the title 'La Minorité française en voie d'assimilation' on the subject of what its author called 'l'intégration à rebours' (5–11 Dec. 1996). In acidly humorous vein, much the same idea was conveyed in a series of articles for *National hebdo* by Françoise Monestier in the summer of 1996 on the theme of travels in Paris to visit districts swamped by immigrants. Thus, for example, in the article entitled 'Pour Alger et Konakry, descendez à Barbès-Rochechouart' Monestier remarks that 'on pourrait se croire en plein Maghreb si le Sacré-Cœur de Montmartre n'était pas là, planté en plein cœur de Paris noir et arabe, pour rappeler au promeneur qu'il n'est pas victime d'une hallucination' (18–24 July 1996). The issue of swamping is, of course, very frequently linked to claims concerning the levels of violence and juvenile delinquency in the ghettos which allegedly make them into no-go areas for the police. This factor, in its own right, offers grounds for the FN to argue that the internal security of immigrant-saturated areas of France should be treated as part of France's military defence.[7]

But violence can also be presented in an even more sinister way as intrinsic to the decolonization/retro-colonization process itself. The connection here is religion, and the argument needs to be viewed in the wider context of deterministic arguments concerning cultural identity and difference, which have been propagated by the New Right and the FN in place of the older, less publicly acceptable discourse of racial inequality.[8] The claim is not explicitly that some cultures are superior to others, but that each represents a unique combination of features which shape the thinking and behaviour of those who are part of it, and which binds them together as a community. To adulterate a culture by introducing large numbers of persons from fundamentally dissimilar cultures inevitably leads to the disintegration of society. From the cultural standpoint, given their numbers, immigrants can be presented as a significant threat to French identity, and this is all the more true because of the very many Moslems among the Maghrebi and other African communities. In common with intellectuals of the New Right outside the party, FN publicists do not argue that the immigrants should shed their own cultures or their original national identities. On the contrary, FN theorists claim to defend the right of all peoples to protect their own identities, so long as they do so in their own countries, not in France.

FN intellectuals can explain the rise of Islamic fundamentalism in parts of the former empire as a natural reaction against the ideas and the practices of France and more generally of the West, as an expression of the renewal of native identities. However, while this is entirely understandable to extreme right-wing intellectuals, ever eager to denounce the practical consequences of philosophical errors passed down from the Enlightenment and the Revolution, it is also a weapon to be used against immigrants and an additional warrant for criticism of French policy towards former colonies. Against multiculturalists and integrationists who claim that Islam can be tolerated in France like any other religion, FN writers such as Pierre Vial, Max Cabantous, Jean-Yves Le Gallou and Pierre Milloz argue from historical and current examples that it is not a case of there being an aggressive version of Islam held by an extremist minority, while the true, tolerant version is held by the majority. Islam has been in perpetual conflict with Europe since the time of its emergence in the seventh century, despite periods of calm. It has a prodigious capacity to absorb conquered peoples, or even conquerors, such as the Seljuk Turks. Now it is engaged in a return to its religious and cultural sources accompanied by a violent antagonism to European culture. Thus, Vial presents a panorama of history in terms of the conflict between the two in the mode of the holy war and challenges Europe to reawaken the spirit of the *Reconquista*.[9] Cabantous points out that Christian European culture is necessarily incompatible with Islamic because Islam does not separate human law from divine law, and has no conception of the proper functions of the state, the dignity of labour, civil rights, or respect for women. In France, he alleges, wherever the balance of power favours Moslems, the Sharia is asserted over French civil law. In short, Moslems potentially form an extremely dangerous state within the state.[10]

In terms of foreign and security policy the Islamic threat can be understood as replacing the old East–West conflict between capitalism and communism, democracy and totalitarianism. Changing the axis of socio-economic and geopolitical division, it is presented as a dimension of the fundamental North–South divide which places rich nations with ageing populations opposite poor nations undergoing demographic explosion. It is perceived as a political threat because the Islamic revival extends from parts of the ex-USSR to Morocco. It is also seen to pose a military threat because the Arab states are extremely heavily armed. For France and the rest of Europe, then, radical Islam is a powerful enemy to be faced abroad.[11] But the enemy is within the gates as well. Not all Moslem immigrants are portrayed as radicals but they are considered to form a reservoir of potential recruits as they see the gains made by the fundamentalists in Islamic countries. France is particularly threatened, not merely because of the size of its Moslem population, or because of the savage conflicts between different factions within the North African immigrant community, but, some extreme right-wingers argue, because the decolonization of Algeria by the FLN was already a disguised extension of the eternal holy war against the infidel. Parasitic swamping of France through retro-colonization pursues the same goal by non-violent means, but in the future the option of armed struggle on French soil may well be increasingly exercised – thousands of weapons supplied by the FLN to its supporters in France before 1962 have never been confiscated and new arms are smuggled in. Guy Chambarlac raises the prospect in these terms:

> Tout en changeant d'appellation, l'emprise de l'organisation politico-administrative du FLN n'a pas cessé et s'est même renforcée. Elle bénéficie depuis 1962 du soutien d'un État indépendant auquel les gouvernements français successifs ne refusent rien. La vague de terrorisme qui a frappé la France durant la seconde moitié de 1995 a révélé que les banlieues à forte concentration immigrée constituent des enclaves de non-droit propices au développment d'une véritable guérilla urbaine pouvant dégénérer en une véritable guerre civile. Elle est alimentée à terme par le sentiment fanatique d'une guerre religieuse (djihad) et par une xénophobie antifrançaise qui se propage comme une épidémie chez les plus jeunes des binationaux.[12]

The spectre of militant Islam caters to the extreme right's tendency to link external and internal enemies as participants in organized action against the nation. But while Islamic fundamentalism is viewed as the re-emergence of an essentially primitive force, a more sophisticated and in some ways more dangerous threat allegedly arises from the neo-colonialist machinations of the United States. Political, economic and cultural anti-Americanism – sometimes coloured by anti-Semitism – has been part of French extreme right-wing thinking since the inter-war years, but until the end of the Cold War it was massively outweighed by hostility towards the USSR, with its link to the Communist Party inside France. Anti-communism has not entirely disappeared during the 1990s, but anti-Americanism has expanded to become a central focus for explanation of the factors which are dragging France and the rest of Europe down. In this respect it is underpinned by the FN's need to define a distinctive foreign policy stance which sets it apart from the mainstream parties, enabling it to accuse them of selling out French national interests to the US (and to the EU, depicted as a pawn of the US).

The linking of anti-Americanism with colonialism can be twofold here. History can be taken to show that decolonization after the Second World War was forced on France and other weakened European powers partly by American pressure. This is not interpreted as having been motivated by a real belief that imperial rule was contrary to the democratic right of national self-determination. Instead, it is seen as a manipulation to weaken the former great powers in the hegemonic interest of the US. Thus, General Jordis von Lohausen argues: 'La Seconde Guerre mondiale a produit le résultat escompté: la destruction de la puissance européenne et par voie de conséquence l'accès du capital américain à tous les marchés jusqu' alors réservés prioritairement aux puissances coloniales européennes.[13]

But denunciations of the US focus most often on the damage caused by American neo-colonialism since the period of decolonization, and particularly since the end of the Cold War. The claim is that the US has pursued ruthless policies of economic expansionism and political coercion behind the cover of a humanitarian discourse. However, American neo-colonialism in the Third World is presented by the extreme right as only one dimension of the all-encompassing strategy aimed at what Yvan Blot calls 'la vassalisation du monde'.[14] This objective is both concealed and promoted by the ideologies of cosmopolitanism (the encouragement of rootlessness and detachment from national loyalties), multiculturalism (advocating shapeless mixtures of peoples deprived of the sense of identity essential to the preservation of autonomy), globalism (the creed of free trade, free movement of capital, transnational ownership and mobility of production, without reference to social consequences at national level), universalism (the gospel of human rights, self-determination and democracy, on condition that they follow Western models and do not threaten American interests), and one-worldism (legitimizing political and military intervention in the guise of protecting human rights).

According to this view, Europe has effectively bowed out of the historical arena, exhausted by the two world wars, then subjected to the tutelage of the US and USSR, blamed for the destruction, condemned for being the home of nationalism and colonialism, and governed by politicians who willingly tied themselves to the superpowers. The slavish subservience of the European powers collectively, through the European Union, and individually, has allowed the US a virtual free hand in the Third World – in competition with the USSR until the end of the Cold War, and alone since then – including the areas traditionally within the French sphere of influence. France has even submitted itself to covert American neo-colonial domination. That is why the FN, while declaring somewhat hollowly that France should remain on terms of friendship with the US, rejects the idea of the New World Order, denounces the EU's endorsement of American pressure for generalized free trade, execrates the insidious penetration of debased American culture via the media, and calls for resistance to 'l'Amérique, ennemi des peuples'.[15]

National grandeur once again

It follows from what has been said so far that FN intellectuals and those of like mind wish to present their own current of thought as the only one capable of producing action to reverse France's disarray on post-colonial issues. Part of the solution depends on throwing off the burden of post-colonial guilt. This can function as part of the wider claim to restore France's national pride, in contrast to other political groups which have allegedly promoted its humiliation. It likewise serves to reassert the honourable motives of the extreme right in having resisted decolonization in the first place. There is a substantial historical literature devoted to memorializing the epic, adventurous aspects of colonialism, and especially to what Benjamin Stora would call 'nostalgeria'.[16] While the errors of the imperial era can be acknowledged up to a point, particularly when they are attributable to the left, it is also a case of pointing to the worthy and sometimes heroic qualities of soldiers, explorers, doctors, engineers, missionaries, pioneers and others who made and defended the empire. While condemning the weaknesses and duplicity of the politicians who sold out the empire – although de Gaulle attracts a more nuanced appraisal than was once the case – it involves rehabilitating the military struggle against the nationalist movements opposed to French rule. This extends especially to those who fought to the end to hold Algeria. It includes the OAS. In the words of Dominique Venner, former member of the OAS and a progenitor of the New Right, 'malgré bien des torts, ce fut l'honneur des partisans de l'OAS d'avoir tenté de défendre jusqu'au bout les Français d'Algérie et les musulmans fidèles, livrés par le gouvernement de la République à l'exode ou au massacre.'[17]

Moreover, despite the damage done to ethnic identities in the name of assimilation, it is an inescapable fact, in the eyes of the extreme right, that for the most part their country had provided far better administration of its colonies than those same states had given to themselves since decolonization. Under the Fourth Republic particularly, as French rule came increasingly under challenge, vast resources had been poured into many of the territories to develop their economic infrastructure, building roads, air-fields, ports and railways, as well as hospitals, dispensaries and schools. On balance, whatever the original hopes in some circles, France had not derived commercial profit from colonial exploitation, it is argued. On the contrary, the empire had been extremely costly to sustain, and France has misguidedly continued to pour in money since decolonization. Besides reinforcing the case for rejecting the cult of post-colonial guilt, this line of argument allows the FN to claim that there is no longer any obligation to judge post-colonial issues on the basis of considerations beyond France's own national interest. Lugan declares: 'Notre seule responsabilité est d'avoir decolonisé sous la pression des États-Unis et sans vouloir admettre que l'Afrique noire n'était pas en mesure de surmonter ce traumatisme.'[18] That being the case, there are four main issues to be addressed: (i) what to do about the remaining overseas territories; (ii) what do about the territories with which France has co-operation arrangements; (iii) what to do about the alleged retro-colonization of France by immigrants from the former empire; (iv) what to do about the insidious processes of American neo-colonialism at home in Europe.

As to the first issue, the FN has not resolved the contradiction between colonialism and defence of identities, although it has attempted to blunt it. As we have already seen in the case of Le Pen's deterministic remarks on the quest for power and domination in international relations, there are those in the FN who undoubtedly hold to the old mixture of social Darwinism and nationalistic élitism, if not racism. At the time of the agitation for independence of New Caledonia in the mid-1980s, Jean-Claude Martinez stated categorically: 'Quelle que soit la légitimité des aspirations que pourraient avoir certains des 61.870 Mélanésiens, la France millénaire ne peut pas compromettre son destin de grande puissance pour les satisfaire'.[19] Having compared the glory of France's history with the insignificance of New Caledonia's, Martinez pointed out that there could be no question of placing the interests of New Caledonia's native people on an equal footing with those of the French, and that *le droit des peuples à disposer d'eux-mêmes s'arrête là où commence le droit d'un peuple à se survivre à lui-même.*[20] In short, the overriding imperative was that France needed New Caledonia in order to remain a great power. Beyond that, it could merely be a question of discussing the terms on which French control operated. Furthermore, Martinez was even willing to revive the traditional religious justification for France's imperial role as Eldest Daughter of the Catholic Church:

> La fille aînée de l'Église ne peut renoncer ni à son rang, ni à son destin. Si elle rencontre dans le Pacifique les oppositions des Églises presbytériennes et anglicanes, les stratégies des impérialismes anglophones, les rancœurs de l'affaire Pritchard et les idéologies tiers mondistes manipulées, la conduite à suivre est très simple. Elle est dictée par mille ans d'histoire. Relever le défi. Et repartir au combat.[21]

The official discourse of the FN in the mid-1990s tends to be more subtle. Nevertheless, the need for an assertive foreign and colonial policy is still based on the assumption of a privileged historical destiny reflecting French national qualities which need to be revitalized. That is why Bruno Mégret, co-ordinator of the party's ideological and policy production, often echoes de Gaulle's rhetoric in this area – for example, when he says of France that 'aujourd'hui, pour rester fidèle à elle-même, il lui faut de nouveau prétendre au premier rang des nations: la grandeur est pour elle un impératif d'existence.'[22] Yet, the FN still has to square this with its claim to defend the identities of all peoples, not merely that of the French nation. Indeed, the party's programme proclaims its emancipatory mission in unambiguous terms which also display its apparent endorsement of the principle of democratic self-determination as a universal right:

Défendre l'idée nationale dans le monde

La France se fera dans le monde l'avocat de la cause des nations. Elle œuvrera au plan diplomatique dans les enceintes internationales et par des actions spécifiques pour que le fait national soit reconnu comme fondateur de l'ordre international. Elle prendra systématiquement position en faveur des nations, de la souveraineté des peuples, de leur droit à l'autodétermination et de la nécessité pour eux de disposer d'un territoire qui soit le leur.[23]

Nevertheless, without acknowledging the inconsistency, Mégret and other FN ideologues present their party as the bearer of a dynamic programme for the remaining overseas territories as part of the overall strategy for promoting France's national revival. They argue that, far from allowing the remains of the empire to wither, as they say successive governments have done in the recent past, the overseas territories should be massively developed to make full use of their material resources and those of the seas around them. The location of the DOM-TOMs across the southern oceans makes them vital attributes of French trade and strategic power in a region of the world which is predicted to become a hub of commercial activity. On this basis, it is claimed, France can maintain a place as one of the world's major powers, with a strong voice inside and outside Europe. However, in deference to the defence of identities (and implicitly in keeping with the associationist colonial tradition favoured by many on the extreme right in the past), it is accepted that the territories should be grouped into three autonomous regions under decentralized government which would be sensitive to the cultures of the regions concerned. Just as France should always give priority to the interests of its own native people on its own metro-politan territory, the interests of native peoples in the overseas territories should be given priority in matters of employment, accommodation, welfare, etc. What this would mean for French colonists in New Caledonia, for example, is not clear. All the same, the FN is careful to indicate that France would retain control of all security matters.[24]

The second and third issues – aid and immigration – are bound together by the FN in an ingenious, if mean-spirited fashion. As regards the former colonies with which France has co-operation agreements, one way of combining the self-interested appeal to French national interest with respect for the sanctity of identities would be for France to withdraw from such arrangements, stop pouring good money after bad, stop interfering in their internal politics and leave them to sort out their own affairs as best they may. This approach appeals to Bernard Lugan, for example, on the further grounds that, in Africa at least, it would allow the re-emergence of traditional patterns of government within new states organized on ethnic lines – each around a single group or on the basis of several groups in which a clear hierarchy was sustained.[25] However, while Lugan and others argue that France has no further responsibility towards the ex-colonies, they allow for the fact that France may neverthe-less have an interest in dealing with them on a new basis. The FN does not envisage complete disengagement, because this would further diminish France's international influence and allow the Americans to fill the vacuum in francophone Africa left by French withdrawal. Instead, it argues for an approach based on the principles of bilateralism and reciprocity – and, implicitly, the ruthless use of leverage for France's advantage. Agreements would be negotiated with individual states on a case-by-case basis, subject to the level and security of French interests there, the ideological orientation of their governments, and the strategic value of the countries to France. Aid would be channelled through private banks in the recipient countries to prevent it falling into the clutches of corrupt state élites. It would be tied to the promotion of French business interests in the countries concerned. Above all, aid would be conditional on recipient states accepting the return of their nationals and former nationals who had previously emigrated to France.[26] This, then, would be an element in the FN's scheme for repatriating 3 million immigrants in the space of seven years, allegedly solving many of France's economic, social and cultural problems almost at a stroke.

As for the huge issue of American domination of France and other European countries, the policies already mentioned are conceived in part as counterweights aimed at increasing France's independence. Others, which cannot be discussed in detail here, involve pressing for changes of policy within the EU to move away from the GATT regime and towards some degree of protectionism. Failing that, there have been hints that France ought to pursue its own bilateralist trade policies in ways which would imply withdrawal from the EU as constituted at present. Similarly, the FN is committed to persuading France's European partners to abandon NATO in favour of a purely European defence alliance, buttressed by institutions to promote collective security. It would entail non-participation in international, American-driven global policing activities, except where French interests were at stake. In the cultural sphere, which is viewed as crucial to the preservation of French identity, the defence of Frenchness at home and its promotion throughout the world are taken to depend on a range of measures, such as the inculcation of a proper understanding of French history and of national values in school curricula, and reserving financial support to the arts for work which was identifiably rooted in French traditions. Proposed measures relating to art teaching, the restoration of the purity of the French language, the promotion of French folk culture, the renaming of streets, or the institution of new public holidays on major historical anniversaries all tend in the direction of cultural nationalism. Beyond these specific proposals, FN publicists would undoubtedly argue that the totality of their policies set out the path towards national self-awareness, including rejection of what their party programme calls 'l'invasion de notre pays par la sous-culture américaine qui dévore nos écrans, nos ondes, nos modes vestimentaires, nos habitudes alimentaires et nos loisirs'.[27]

Conclusion

The discourse of the extreme right on colonial and post-colonial issues has multiple, mutually reinforcing functions. It defends the ideological record of the nationalist right in the past and attacks that of its enemies. While acknowledging lesser errors on its own side, it places the primary responsibility for imperial failures on misguided, assimilationist policies promoted by the mainstream parties of the Third, Fourth and Fifth Republics. By denouncing the politicians and bureaucrats in Paris, but praising the qualities of many of those who served in the colonies, it uses the empire as a source of negative and positive justifications of the extreme right's own positions. It seeks to rescue those who refused to accept Algerian independence, and by this means it strives to transform the memory of the past from an encumbrance into an asset. By defending the practical benefits which France brought to its colonies, the extreme right attempts to profile itself as the defender of a balanced view of imperial history against those who have represented that history as purely exploitative and oppressive in order to promote their own anti-patriotic creeds. It also distances the extreme right from costly post-colonial aid policies which it deems to have failed. These failures can be taken as a logical outcome of the perverse mixture of post-imperial guilt and neo-assimilationist interventionism which drives the parties of the left and the moderate right. The spectre of parasites (immigrants and aid-dependent ex-colonies) or predators (Islamic fundamentalism and the US) is used to explain the long-term results of decolonization in terms which allow the extreme right to present its own policies as the key to revival of France's strength in the domestic and international spheres. Whatever the inconsistencies of this discourse, it serves the FN's efforts to present itself as the only political force able to restore national pride at a time when other parties have no stirring vision to impart.

Notes

1   J. M. Le Pen, 'Le Sinistre Mea Culpa de l'homme blanc', *Identité*, 22 (1994), 3.

2   Pierre de Meuse, 'Le Colonialisme, enfant de la gauche', *Identité*, 22 (1994), 5–8, 34; Didier Lefranc, 'Le Tiers Monde à libérer', *ibid.*, 13–17; Alain de Benoist, *Europe, Tiers monde, même combat* (Paris: Robert Laffont, 1986).

3   Le Pen, 'Le Sinistre Mea Culpa', 3.

4   Raymond Muelle, 'Une guerre contre les Français', *Enquête sur l'histoire*, 25 (1996), 47.

5   B. Lugan, 'Décolonisation: un cadeau empoisonné', *Identité*, 22 (1994), 9; and see Lefranc, 'Le Tiers Monde à libérer'; Pierre Bonnefont, 'Les Pièges de la coopération', *Enquête sur l'histoire*, 8 (1993), 74–5.

6   See Lugan, 'Les Nouvelles Africafolies', interview with Philippe de Baleine, *Paris-Match*, 24 Aug. 1995; and *Afrique: de la colonisation philanthropique à la recolonisation humanitaire* (Paris: Christian de Bartillat, 1995).

7   Jean du Verdier, *Éléments de réflexion sur la défense de la France* (Paris: Editions Nationales, 1991); Hervé Morvan, 'La Défense intérieure', *Identité*, 14 (1991), 14–17.

8   Pierre-André Taguieff, *La Force du préjugé: essai sur le racisme et ses doubles* (Paris: La Découverte, 1987), esp. Chapter 8; *Sur la nouvelle droite* (Paris: Descartes, 1994), 64–106.

9   See P. Vial, 'L'Islam contre l'Europe', *Identité*, 6 (1990), 5–8.

10   See M. Cabantous, 'Deux cultures incompatibles', *Identité*, 6 (1990), 9–15; and 'Dreux en voie d'islamisation', *National hebdo*, 18–24 April 1996.

11   Pierre Milloz, 'Face à l'Islam, l'Afrique francophone', *Identité*, 9 (1990), 23–5; Jean-Yves Le Gallou, 'La Menace est au sud', *Identité*, 6 (1990), 20–3.

12   G. Chambarlac, 'Tueurs et porteurs de valises', *Enquête sur l'histoire*, 15 (1996), 54; and see Jean Grondin, 'Le Djihad algérien', *ibid.*, 39–41.

13   J. Von Lohausen, 'Main basse sur l'Europe', *Eléments*, lxxxiv (1996), 41; and see his *Les Empires et la puissance: la géopolitique aujourd'hui* (Paris: Labyrinthe, 1996).

14   Y. Blot, 'La Vassalisation du monde', *Identité*, 23 (1996), 9–12; and see Pascal Gannat, 'Le Nouveau Visage du colonialisme', *Identité*, 22 (1994), 18–21.

15   Title of the dossier of articles in *Identité*, 23 (1996), 3–21.

16   B. Stora, *La Gangrène et l'oubli: la mémoire de la guerre d'Algérie* (Paris: La Decouverte, 1992), 239.

17   D. Venner, 'Trente ans après', *Enquête sur l'histoire*, ii (1992), 5.

18   Lugan, 'Décolonisation: un cadeau empoisonné', 12.

19   'Conclusion', in Association pour le Respect des Lois de la République/Jean-Claude Martinez (ed.), *La Nouvelle-Calédonie: la stratégie, le droit et la République* (Paris: Pédone, 1985), 209.

20   *Ibid.*, 210.

21   *Ibid.*, 211.

22   B. Mégret, *L'Alternative nationale: les priorités du Front National* (Saint-Cloud: Éditions Nationales, 1997), 213.

23   Front National, *300 Mesures*, 343.

24   *Ibid.*, 338–40, 378–84.

25   Lugan, *Afrique: de la colonisation philanthropique à la recolonisation humanitaire.*

26   See FN, *300 Mesures*, 342–4, 348–51.

27   *Ibid.*, 341.

Chapter 21

Crawford Young

ZAÏRE: THE SHATTERED ILLUSION OF THE INTEGRAL STATE

Va, c'est trop te celer le destin du Zaïre . . .
Le ciel, pour terminer les malheurs de nos jours,
D'une main plus puissante a choisi le secours . . .
(Voltaire, *Zaïre*, edited by Eva Jacobs (London, 1975), pp. 86–7)

ZAÏRE, BY THE EARLY 1990s, by some accounts had all but vanished. One senior American diplomat described it as nothing more than the presidential vessel 'Kamanyola' anchored safely offshore in the Zaïre River, an élite praetorian guard compensated in hard currency, the remote marble city of Gbadolite, a shrivelled state superstructure nourished by diamond smuggling. Its perennial President, Mobutu Sese Seko, was characterised contemptuously by a French official as 'a walking bank account in a leopard-skin cap'. More than a decade ago, a former publicist for the central régime had relegated the once-powerful state to a zone of non-existence: 'The state does not exist or no longer exists in Zaïre. It is no more than a skeleton that entertains the illusion'.[1] The 1992 National Conference resolved to expunge Zaïre from history by restoring its earlier colonial and post-colonial nomenclature of 'Congo'.

Whatever the present derelictions and future uncertainties surrounding the Zaïrian state, through a thousand survival strategies Zaïrian societies persist. Beneath the hollow shell of a state in full decomposition there is evidence that they are seeking to recover their birthrights. Zaïre, as first introduced to the world in a once-popular eighteenth century Voltaire play, was the fair captive damsel whose noble birth awaited redemption. Zaïre, reincarnated in the late twentieth century as the crippled, ill-starred giant of central Africa, again awaits payment of her ransom. When deliverance finally comes, the new political dispensation for Zaïrian society will surely need to set aside the baneful state legacy of the past.

The heritage of the past century, I wish to argue, is the persistent effort to construct a leviathan state invested with the mission of transforming society according to an image of its rulers. This project, ultimately undermined and defeated by what Achille Mbembe aptly terms 'the historical capacity for indiscipline' of the society,[2] none the less reappears in various incarnations since the creation of the Léopoldian colonial state. President Mobutu, driven – as officially inspired commentary would have it – by 'the inflexible will to transform the equatorial forest into terrestrial paradise',[3] is the most recent architect of autocracy.

The vision of an omnipotent state reached its apotheosis in the hegemonical pretensions of the 1974 constitution that were of extraordinary scope. The 'nation politically organized' through the agency of its political instrument, the *Mouvement populaire de la révolution* (M.P.R.), had a stupendous destiny. Its will was absolute, and expressed by Mobutu, who presided over all branches of government, and in effect named all members of party ruling organs, ministers, legislators, and judges. In design and doctrine, the state was monolithic; 'deviationism' was declared a constitutional crime.

In this imagined polity, we find a notion of rule characterised by Christian Coulon as the 'integral state'. Speaking of Senegal at the beginning of the 1980s, he discerned an emergent project to supplant the 'soft state' with one acting more directly upon civil society through its 'hegemonical apparatuses'. The integral state, he argued, sought a dominant presence in those sectors of society previously touched only through political intermediaries (clientelistic networks) or through ideological mediation (for example, by marabouts).[4] Jean Copans offered a parallel judgement of state ambitions in Senegal:

> The objective of the dominant groups in the state apparatus is the control, the maintenance, the augmentation of surplus extraction . . . The lesson of recent years is the following: the interests of the Senegalese state have triumphed over local private interests . . . this growing role of the state, rendered concrete through the remodelling and multiplication of institutions for control of the peasantry, leads to a new policy. The Senegalese state aims more and more at direct administrative, ideological and political control over the dominated masses, be they urban or rural.[5]

The concept of the 'integral state' is a reasonable characterisation of the hegemonical project of the Mobutist state at its apogee in the early 1970s. By 'integral state', I have in mind a design of perfected hegemony, whereby the state seeks to achieve unrestricted domination over civil society. Thus unfettered, the state is free to engage in rational pursuit of its design for the future, and to amply reward the ruling class for its governance services. The integral state requires not only the autonomy from civil society achieved through comprehensive instruments of political control, but a suzerainty, if not monopoly, extending over social and economic vectors of accumulation. As, in Weberian terms, 'a compulsory association which organizes domination', the integral state, with rationality suffusing its operative logic, supplies purposive rule guided by an inspirational charter for the future.[6]

The integral state, in the comprehensive apparatus of domination it proposes, erects a sharp distinction between state and society. Even though, in its post-colonial forms, it may seek a guided politicisation through the single party, the powerful legacy of the colonial state directs these impulses towards exclusion rather than incorporation. Rather than transforming civil society into a willing agent of its own domination, as in the 'totalitarian' model, the integral state envisages passive subjects, even if mobilised into ritual expressions of their deference. Civil society is to be kept, in Gramscian terms, 'gelatinous', so that the massive superstructure of terror and coercion characteristic of a true totalitarian state is less necessary. Confronting civil societies far less structured by collective solidarities and corporate social bodies than polities which gave rise to the idea of totalitarianism, notably Nazi Germany and the former Soviet Union, the integral state could pursue its vocation of domination and autonomy on less all-embracing terms. Nor was its amorphous vision of the future cast in the mould of a 'totalist ideology'.

One may note that notions akin to the integral state emerged in a number of monographs based upon observation of patterns of power and enunciation of ruling class ambitions of the 1970s. Jean-François Bayart conceptualised the Ahmadou Ahidjo era in Cameroon as grounded upon a 'hegemonical project':

> from the moment of his accession to office, [Ahidjo] held a vision at once precise and vast of the hegemonical quest which it was his task to direct, and understood at once that he needed to transcend the clientelistic state which he inherited . . . the nomination of Ahidjo as Prime Minister inaugurated in reality a process of autonomisation of the state which constituted a global and coherent response, a Bonapartist stripe, to a structural crisis almost a century old . . .
>
> . . . the struggle against 'under-administration' . . . had always been conceived in terms of *encadrement* of the population . . . By means of the development of its structures, the territorial administration pretended, in barely concealed form to guarantee the essence of social control and political direction of the country.[7]

A few years later Comi Toulabor presented a similar portrait in his penetrating analysis of the Eyadéma régime in Togo.[8] The deleterious schemes of 'cultural revolution' in the final phases of the N'Garta Tombalbaye régime in Chad perhaps illustrate the idea of the integral state, borrowed in this instance to a large degree from Mobutu's Zaïre, in its ultimate absurdity.

The integral state in Zaïre

I wish to examine three versions of the integral state which have punctuated the history of Zaïre, leading up to its recent decline. The first was erected under Belgian auspices, and reached a pinnacle of apparently unchallenged hegemony from the 1920s until the mid-1950s. The second was a merely latent (and hence problematic) version, implicit in the nationalist vision of the forces of Lumumbism, which external intervention and historical conjuncture aborted. The third was constructed by the 'new régime' headed by Mobutu after the military high command had seized power in November 1965. The fact that two of these projects decomposed in spectacular fashion, and that the other was stillborn, suggests that the integral state was a flawed notion from the outset. Such an appraisal finds strong reinforcement in the astonishing collapse of régimes in the former Soviet bloc whose design, although in some respects more far-reaching, none the less bore a family resemblance to the integral state.

1. First version: the Belgian model

The colonial state in Zaïre, whose informal creation dates from 1876, and whose formal anointment by the European powers followed in 1885, acquired from its earliest days the profoundly revealing metaphorical representation as *Bula Matari*, or 'crusher of rocks'. This monicker first attached to Léopoldian agent Henry Morton Stanley, inspired by his feat of driving a caravan of porters bearing dismantled steamers over the tortuous terrain between the Zaïre River estuary and the vast navigable watercourses extending inward from Kinshasa. By semiotic transformation, it soon came to apply to the alien colonial state and the European agents who exercised its hegemony, reflecting the images of overwhelming, crushing force by which its subjects knew them. As explained by N'Kanza Lusibu Zala, a Zaïrian scholar, 'For all Bakongo the name of Bula Mata(r)i signified terror'.[9]

In its early Léopoldian form, the state sought a skeletal framework of hegemony, mainly to ensure international confirmation of the huge territorial claims staked out by the Congo Free State, a largely successful undertaking. By 1900, 183 outposts were created, with some 1,500 European military and civil agents assuring an embryonic infrastructure of domination. Its resource base was assured by primitive extraction, whose mechanisms were suggestive of the future scope of the integral colonial state.

Application of the European doctrine of sovereignty gave juridical cover to the state claim to propriety over all 'vacant lands', a concept applying to the entire territory save the small surface physically occupied by Congolese communities. The decree asserting land nationalisation appeared on the official birth date of the Congo Free State, 1 July 1885. The wild products of this land – initially, rubber and ivory – could only be expropriated by the state through parallel assertion of regalian rights over African labour by taxation (forced rubber deliveries) and conscription (especially porterage), combined with direct or indirect state-assigned mercantile monopolies. The revenue requirements of the Léopoldian state, needed to assure its survival and reproduction, could only be imposed upon subject society by huge doses of brutality and intimidation. The hegemonical superstructure remained very thin; thus violence was decentralised and mediated by an array of African sentinels, chiefs and other auxiliaries backed in their coercive mission by regular punitive expeditions by the armed bands under (more or less) direct state control.

The Léopoldian state was propelled by its determination to consolidate proprietary claim on its vast dominions. As well, it was intended to operate as a capitalist enterprise, returning an eventual profit to its sole proprietor, King Léopold himself. The monarch, beyond his colonial dreams, nurtured a compelling private project: to endow the royal family with a fortune to be used for the national good as they saw fit. In the words of his biographer, 'Leopold had discovered a way to reverse the historical victory of the middle classes over their kings: a new path to absolutism'.[10] The Léopoldian state, however, lacked a theory of hegemony; this was to emerge only with the formalisation of Belgian rule from 1908 onwards.

Building on a process already begun before the *reprise*, the Belgian colonial state moved beyond primitive extraction to develop a permanent base of accumulation. Export agriculture and mining were to provide a secure revenue source for the state, and reward its partners in exploitation. The central infrastructure of domination was systematised and rationalised by the imposition of a prefectoral grid of European administration, extending downwards from provinces to districts and territories, staffed by agents screened by formal recruitment criteria and schooled for their services. At the bottom tier, African intermediaries were incorporated according to the new dictates of 'colonial science'. This corpus of thought, strongly marked by the formal juridical reason which permeated state discourse, was given exhaustive codification in the Decree of 5 December 1933, whose guiding precepts were summarised by the accompanying legal note:

> While respecting traditional administration, the legislator wanted to establish a single administrative system; he made chieftaincy the lowest echelon of the administrative organisation, and the chief a functionary integrated into the system without prejudice to his traditional rôle.[11]

By way of being a general vehicle for *Bula Matari* hegemony, the Decree of 24 July 1918 vested territorial agents with plenary power to impose seven days prison and/or a 200 franc fine for 'Any disrespectful act or word committed or uttered towards a European agent of public authority in his presence'. In similar vein, immediate arrest and imprisonment awaited any African who 'was guilty of threatening state security, provoking disobedience of the laws, or in other ways compromising public tranquillity or the stability of institutions'.[12] Collective insubordination by a village could bring, at the discretion of the administrator, a military occupation, 'with the obligation, for the inhabitants, to provide the occupying personnel, if need be without remuneration, lodging, food and service'.[13]

The direction and control of African labour was crucial to state purposes. This occurred through several devices. The coercive arsenal of the state was stocked with legal weapons; in the agricultural sphere, this was especially the Ordinance of 20 February 1917, which imposed upon the peasantry 60 days annually of obligatory cultivation according to norms established by the state agricultural services. As Mulambu Muvulya observes, local administrators immediately learned by circular that the penal sanctions accompanying this legislation equipped them with 'the means necessary to induce cultivators to expand their crops', and that these 'were nothing other than military or police occupation'.[14]

Large amounts of labour needed to be removed from village communities and directed towards European mines, plantations, transportation, and military service. During the 1920s, and the two world wars, direct state intervention was required to meet manpower needs. From 1920 to 1926, the number of wage earners reportedly rose from 125, 120 to 421, 963;[15] to meet these requirements, the territorial administration in many regions became a man-catching machine. At the level of state doctrine, the obligation of all African subjects to render labour service was axiomatic, as was the duty of the regional administration to ensure that this requirement was fulfilled. As the Governor-General, Maurice Lippens, put the matter in 1922, every official had to be 'penetrated with the idea that his reason for existence is to favor and develop our occupation and that this duty consists in supporting every enterprise'. Under no circumstances could an official express the view that 'once taxes are paid and other legal obligations met the native may remain inactive'.[16] The male subject, as conceived by the integral state, was a functional unit of labour, symbolised by the evocative census designation as '*homme adulte valide*'.

A comprehensive legal web of regulations was spun around African behaviour. Here we encounter in the integral state project the *gouvernmentalité* dimension that Bayart borrows from Michel Foucault: a bundle of actions by political power which operate upon the field of action open to subject actors.[17] Voluntary migration was subject to the pleasure of the territorial administrator, whose issue of an internal passport was indispensable. Urban Africans were denied the right of land ownership, unauthorised presence in European quarters in the evening, and viewing of any films not approved by a rigorous censor. Print media were subject to careful control.

The comprehensive paternalism of colonial state ideology is well reflected in a 1946 memorandum by the copper mining corporation, *Union minière du Haut-Katanga*:

> The coloniser must never lose sight of the fact that the Negroes have the souls of children, souls which mould themselves to the methods of the educator; they watch, listen, feel, and imitate. The European must, in all circumstances, show himself a chief without weakness, good-willed without familiarity, active in method and especially just in the punishment of misbehaviour, as in the reward of good deed.[18]

Bruce Fetter makes a compelling case for the extraordinary scope of the domination achieved by the colonial state and its partners in locations of maximal impact; writing of the urban copperbelt, he concludes that a veritable 'totalitarian society' had been created. The *Union minière*, in alliance with the state and the Benedictine mission, was able to exert 'full control over its human milieu', extending to 'virtually all aspects of the life of its African workers'.[19]

The colonial state lacked the resources or capacity to directly organise the economic realm, an option in any case precluded by the distant overlayer of liberal ideology central to metropolitan state doctrine, not to mention the dominant social and economic interests to which it was accountable. However, the terms of entry into the colonial domain were subject to negotiation, and key sectors found the state taking substantial equity participation in return for the 'patrimony' contributed from its sovereign domains: mineral rights, often extensive land concessions. In the case of the economically strategic gold mines of the far northeast, the state initially tried to exploit these directly, but discovered that it lacked the technical competence to do so.[20]

In the cultural domain, the Catholic missions were indispensable auxiliaries. Their task was to displace customary African religion with Christianity, an alteration which, according to a leading Catholic prelate, was commanded by the conviction that 'only the Christian-Catholic religion, based on authority, is capable of changing native mentality, of giving to our Africans a clear and intimate consciousness of their duties, of inspiring in them respect for authority and a spirit of loyalty towards Belgium'.[21] In those zones in east-central Zaïre where Islam gained a fragile foothold in the years immediately before colonial conquest, state and missions were to join forces to isolate and contain this potential cultural threat. Muslims according to Louis Franck, the Colonial Minister, had the 'hope, founded on divine decree, to become masters of the country; one recently told a Greek trader that "we shall see how much longer Bula Matari remains master in the country".'[22]

The ultimate object of Christian conversion was not full assimilation; indeed, especially in the early years, many missionaries strongly opposed the 'Westernisation' of their African disciples, whom they wished to mould into purified rural communities protected from what they perceived as the corruption of Western commercial and industrial life. The integral state had not the least desire to transform its 'empire of silence' into a true civil society. Its *telos* was well summarised by Franck:

> In other words, we do not have an obstinate wish to create an imitation European, a Black Belgian, but rather a better Congolese, that is, a robust, vigorous and hard-working Negro, proud of a conscientiously accomplished task, respectful of the collectivity to which he belongs.[23]

The colonial version of the integral state, closely examined, fell far short of its claims in terms of its actual exercise of control over subject society. In manifold ways, African society displayed a capacity for evasion and inner autonomy. None the less, at its peak – from the early 1920s until the mid-1950s – it was a formidable aggregation of power. At the same time, it created the conditions for its own accelerating decomposition.

The increasing sophistication and complexity of the Belgian Congo's economic infrastructure made impossible by the 1950s any further delay in introducing secondary and higher education. The dramatically altered international environment exposed it to pressures which it was ill equipped to withstand, and corroded its communications monopoly and capacity to insulate its subjects from external influences. Its mission partner began to distance itself from the integral colonial state, in keeping with a global Vatican design of adaptation to prospective decolonisation. The swift growth of the European population in the post-war years inevitably introduced fissures related to the complex fracture lines of Belgian society. The loosening of the shackles of hegemony designed to win African consent for the Eur-African future proposed by Belgium created the political space needed to reject such schemes. The solidity of the apparatus of surveillance and control eroded before the sheer scale of population shifts towards wage labour and urban residence.

What finally shattered the colonial apparatus and undermined its will was its incapacity to master spontaneity, in a scenario which bears intriguing resemblance to Eastern Europe in 1989. The pivotal event which triggered the unravelling process was the wave of rioting in Kinshasa in January 1959. This leaderless and unplanned social explosion shook the colonial edifice to its foundation and, as one immediate consequence, provoked King Baudouin to upstage the anticipated cautious political reforms of a Belgian working group by the explicit promise of independence 'without undue delay or precipitate haste'. In turn, the territorial administration in some key areas – lower Congo, Kwilu, Maniema – all but lost control in the face of a wave of civil disobedience, now open rather than concealed. The rapidly proliferating political parties, Herbert Weiss argues, were themselves under intense pressure from the exploding social anger and soaring aspirations of their peasant constituents, especially the youth.[24] By the end of 1959, the now discredited colonial régime suffered a spiralling deflation of its authority. Both the metropolitan state and the nationalist parties were sharply divided; no accord could be reached except on the basis of the maximum demands then being aggressively advocated: immediate independence.

2. Second model: the Lumumbist vision

The most consequential of the nationalist parties, the *Mouvement national congolais-Lumumba*, developed a project which married retention of the centralised, bureaucratic force of the colonial state with a political overlayer inspired by radical populist national-ist thought. Although ephemeral and submerged by the nearly-instant post-colonial crisis, embedded within the political doctrine of Lumumbism – subsequently appro-priated in part by the Mobutu régime, transformed for its own purposes – was a vision of the post-colonial polity bearing the seeds of a new version of the integral state. Even though unfulfilled, its merits brief examination.

To grasp the ideological project of the radical wing of anti-colonial nationalism in Zaïre, one must recollect its point of departure and temporal context. As articulated by the embryonic intelligentsia it can be traced back to the grievances of the *évolués*, whose first expressions were formulated as demands for equal treatment with European residents. Initially, these accepted the conceptual distinction fundamental to colonial state doctrine that its human estate was divided into zones of 'civilisation' and a negative 'other' (the *basenji*, or 'savage'). A celebrated 1944 memorandum from an anonymous group of *évolués* in Kananga (then Luluabourg) stated this clearly:

> We ask that the government recognise that, alongside the native mass, backward or little developed, a new social class emerges, which is becoming a kind of native bourgeoïsie . . .

> The members of this native intellectual élite are doing everything possible to instruct themselves, and to live decently, as do respectable Europeans . . . These *évolués* believe that they deserve . . . a particular protection from the government, sheltering them from certain measures or treatments which may apply to an ignorant or backward mass.[25]

Until 1955, the 'reform' discourse of the terminal colonial state was dominated by the theme of recuperating the influential *évolués* by defining legal conditions of respectability.

This conceptualisation remains prominent in the posthumously published 1956 text by Patrice Lumumba:

> Many criticise the régime of tutelage and see only the negative side. This . . . is the protection of the native against the abuses of certain unscrupulous persons; its object is the direct amelioration of the moral and material conditions of native existence . . .
>
> If this régime is outdated for a certain class of the population . . . it is still necessary for the broad mass, which has not yet evolved to the point of defending or guiding itself alone.[26]

Lumumba quotes with apparent approval a definition of colonisation as 'the action exercised by a civilised people upon a people of an inferior civilisation with the object of progressively transforming it by the development of its natural resources and amelioration of the moral and material conditions of native existence'. He cites the

1908 Colonial Charter as an authoritative source of colonial state doctrine, calling for 'a more and more complete organisation of the country to reinforce order and peace and assure the protection and expansion of the diverse branches of economic activity'. The colonial state, he concludes, despite its errors, 'has realised many great and beautiful things'.[27] The nature of *Bula Matari* as integral state is not at issue, but rather the need to associate the leading strata of its subject population to its direction.

From 1956 onwards, nationalism incorporated the goal of independence, and began to assimilate themes from radical anti-imperial discourse more broadly, from which the colonial *évolués* had long been effectively insulated. Pivotal events were the attendance of a sizeable number of African élites in the 1958 Brussels World Exposition, as living exhibits of the achievements of the colonial state, and the participation of a Congolese delegation, including in particular Lumumba, at the 1958 All-African People's Conference in Accra. A swift infusion of radical African nationalist themes into the anti-colonial corpus of thought followed at once. Lumumba was especially drawn to the political vision of Kwame Nkrumah, both its pan-African dimension, and the concept of the comprehensive nationalist party as a weapon of liberation.

The formidable acceleration of events from January 1959 gave a strong conjunctural imprint to the political discourse of the final colonial months. A crucial theme was the preservation of the centralised state as the indispensable instrument of national unity; the appearance of 'federalist' claims by parties in western and south-eastern Zaïre (lower Congo and Katanga) lent urgency to this commitment. The Lumumbist party – or at least a bloc of radical nationalists – viewed itself as the necessary spinal column of the future independent state.

The political overlayer was to guide and direct the more enduring ossature of the state, the colonial bureaucracy, and the army. As Lumumba stated in his investiture speech as Prime Minister on 23 June 1960, 'The members of the former colonial administration, having ceded their powers of command to the Congolese, will remain by their advice and their experience the surest guarantees of a healthy management of public affairs'.[28] Other themes from the Lumumbist text echoed integral state notions of the past:

> this government will maintain intact, against all challengers, the integrity of the territory and the unity of the Nation . . . This government will act to maintain order, without weakness, throughout the country . . . This government will assume as its first duty to lead the popular masses along the path of social justice, welfare, and progress . . .[29]

The very essence of the gamble known as the *pari congolais*, on the basis of which Belgium agreed in January 1960 to risk immediate independence, was the erection of a political superstructure – African ministers and legislators – atop the robust apparatus of the colonial state, whose leading bureaucratic and security cadres would remain for some time overwhelmingly European. Radical Lumumbist leaders believed that by controlling the steering mechanism of *Bula Matari*, its nature could be transformed into a genuine instrument of mass well-being. The core values of national unity and accelerated development could only be accomplished by the preservation of a powerful, centralised state.

The Lumumbist project of an integral state under radical nationalist direction was torn apart before its implementation had begun by a congeries of hostile forces. The rank-and-file of the army, discontented at the prospect of remaining mere unrewarded foot soldiers in the new order, mutinied against their Belgian officers five days after independence. Almost immediately, the European armature of the *Bula Matari* base of the post-colonial state vanished, which resulted in an instant deflation of its power and authority. European interests, especially in Katanga, perfectly content with the integral state under Belgian management, were fearful of this juggernaut with nationalist direction, and thus encouraged its fragmentation. The United States, driven by a cold war geo-political reason then at its pavlovian peak, conflated the increasingly intense anti-imperial discourse of a Lumumba beset by enemies with servitude to Soviet designs, and by August 1960 was scheming his overthrow, and thereafter plotting his assassination.

Any evaluation of this second version of the integral state must remain in the realm of speculation. A clear distinction must be drawn between Lumumba as martyred symbol of African liberation and victim of imperialist machinations – so eloquently portrayed in the captivating *cinéma-vérité* of Raoul Peck, the Haitian producer, in his film 'Lumumba: Death of a Prophet' – and the actual political project of the 1960 leadership. One can suggest that the profound contradiction between the *Bula Matari* base and the proposed superstructure in itself made failure likely. Just possibly, the populist discourse of Lumumbism might have transformed attitudes towards the state. But the retrospective evidence concerning the fate of first generation post-colonial African régimes, based upon comprehensive mass nationalist single parties, permit doubt as to whether the radical populism could overcome the premise of the integral state, within the limits set by the discourse of decolonisation.

3. Third version: The Mobutist state

The severity of the 'Congo crisis' – both in the disorders engulfing the country during 1960–1, and the renewed dislocations ensuing from the 1963–5 wave of rebellions affecting a large portion of the territory – supplied the initial legitimating text for the 'new régime' of Mobutu Sese Seko which seized power in November 1965. The 'oasis of peace' and orderly progress bequeathed by *Bula Matari* had degenerated into 'chaos', which only a restoration of the powerful unitary state could remedy. The 'very existence of the Nation was threatened', proclaimed Mobutu. 'The social, economic, and financial situation of the country is catastrophic'.[30] 'Congolisation', he lamented, had entered French dictionaries as a synonym for a shameful *pagaille* (shambles).

The idea of the state persisting from the Léopoldian policy provided a doctrinal vessel for the Mobutist project. The provinces were restored to a close approximation of their colonial physiognomy. Administration, from its presidential centre, was reunified into a single hierarchical apparatus, grounded in 'unity of command'. In a speech intended as an authoritative formulation of state ideology, Engulu Baanga Mpongo well expressed the continuities in hegemonical concept:

> The administrative organisation of the Colony, the hierarchical military type, was a heritage of the structure established by Léopold II for the occupation of Zaïre. It was founded on the principle of unity of command,

which means that, for whatever action, an official receives his orders only from one chief. Wishing to create and maintain in the administration, as among the people, a unity of views and action, Belgium entrusted complete responsibility for the colonial enterprise to a single cadre: the territorial service.

The real motivation for the concentration of function in the territorial cadre was political. It was necessary to indicate to the population that authority was one and indivisible.[31]

Old parties were swept away, and first republic politicians were gradually transformed into courtiers; the incipient state bourgeoisie was converted into a service class, dependent on prebends from the prince. As the supreme instrument for the management of patrimonial politics, the M.P.R. was founded in 1967, and endowed with a political monopoly.

The scope of the hegemonical claims of the new régime was extraordinary. The 1973 'Zaïrianisation' measures transferred a vast swathe of the economy in the agricultural and mercantile realm to Zaïrian *acquéreurs*, as presidential patrimony. The 1974 'radicalisation of the revolution' completed the seizure of most colonial enterprises, vesting them for a brief period in the state (until the utter fiasco of these measures compelled 'retrocession' in 1976). The entirety of the agricultural sector was covered by a network of state marketing monopolies. Customary chiefs were by 1973 legislation declared to be 'politico-administrative' cadres that were subject to transfer, just simple local bureaucratic agents at the bottom of the hierarchical ladder (another measure made short-lived by its impracticality).

At the ideological level, the new régime initially appropriated Lumumbist symbols and unitarian nationalism. Over time 'authentic Zaïrian nationalism' was transformed and personalised, first as '*authenticité*', subsequently as 'Mobutism'. Emblematic of the extravagant pretensions of the Mobutist state at its peak was a brief period in 1974 when the press was forbidden to use the names of any state official other than the President. The integral state was served, in this imagery, by depersonalised human agents who were anonymous instruments of its hegemonical will.

From 1975 onwards, a new epoch of state deflation opened. The once-imposing hegemony of the Mobutist state corroded, as the now 'lame leviathan', to borrow Thomas Callaghy's apt imagery,[32] lost its hold on civil society and international standing. Copper prices broke; a large debt acquired almost overnight in the early 1970s affixed the stigma of bankruptcy. The grandiose projects which were to make 1980 a rendezvous with abundance – the Maluku steel mill, the Inga-Shaba power line, and the Tenke-Fungurume copper mines, among others – were spectacular disasters, matched by the dislocation of the 'Zaïrianisation' and 'radicalisation' measures. Diplomatic standing was sullied by the unsuccessful intervention in the Angolan civil war in partnership with the United States and South Africa. A former security agent, Emmanuel Dungia, suggests that 'by 1979, the *Maréchal* [Mobutu] no longer had any illusions about his capacity to build a modern country and to restore a badly compromised situation. His ambition thereafter became limited to accumulation of personal wealth to prepare his retirement'.[33] Jan Vansina adds an eloquent portrait of decay:

Legitimacy is gone, citizens are alienated, the intelligentsia dream of revolution or reform, some others expect liberation or a millennium, most have sunk into a gloomy resignation. Naked power and bribes erode the law. In turn, the strongly centralized state has lost much of its effective grip, because its legal directives are ignored, except under duress or when they seem to be opportune. Lack of security does not allow anyone to plan for the long term.[34]

Demise of the integral state

The scope of state decline in contemporary Zaïre is a familiar tale, and need not be described in further detail. Those segments of the state realm crucial to its survival and minimal reproduction – the security agencies, the presidential staff, the central bank, the diplomatic cadre – continue to operate. The regional administration persists in a pre-emptive presence, but certainly cannot fulfill the governance designs of the integral state. Most affected by state decline are basic public services. Overall, the state has suffered a loss of its probity, competence, and credibility.

State deflation in this third round, although less sudden and spectacular than the collapse of *Bula Matari*, or the 1960 'Congo crisis', is none the less of broader scope, and more permanent impact. Civil society has now experienced nearly two decades of decline, and has increasingly developed institutionalised responses. New economic and social space is created, in the parallel economy,[35] religious sphere, and informal association realm. Erected in the shadow of the state in decline, these shelters offer protection for what Ilunga Kabongo has labelled 'the zone of non-existence'.[36] Much more doubtful is whether a new relationship between state and civil society can be reconstructed from these nucleii.

Surely a reinvented Zaïre, whatever name it will bear, will be grounded in a relationship between state and civil society profoundly different from that imposed by the integral state. The cultural heritage must serve as anchorage; in the absence of such rooting, Peter Ekeh's portrait of the moral realm associated with the state devoid of normative ties with society remains a true visage.[37] To transcend what Basil Davidson has called the 'curse of the nation-state',[38] to bridge what Jan Vansina terms the 'baneful dichotomy' between Western influence and the majority tradition,[39] a new concept of state is indispensable.

The illusion of the integral state lies shattered, but we still await the requiem. The nature of its successor has yet to be revealed. The ransom of ill-starred Zaïre has yet to be paid.

Notes

1   Bwaria Kabwe, *Citoyen Président, Lettre ouverte au Président Mobutu Sese Seko . . . et les autres* (Paris, 1978), p. 23.
2   Achille Mbembe, *Afriques indociles: Christianisme, pouvoir et État en société postcoloniale* (Paris, 1988), p. 148.

3 Manwana Mungonga, *Le Général Mobutu Sese Seko parle du nationalisme zaïrois authentique* (Kinshasa, n.d. 1972?), p. 116.

4 Christian Coulon, *Le Marabout et le prince (Islam et pouvoir au Sénégal)* (Paris, 1981), pp. 289–90.

5 Jean Copans, *Les Marabouts et l'arachide: la confrérie mouride et les paysans du Sénégal* (Paris, 1980), p. 248.

6 Max Weber, 'Politics as a Vocation', reprinted in H. H. Gerth and C. Wright Mills, *From Max Weber: essays in sociology* (New York, 1958), pp. 82–3.

7 Jean-François Bayart, *L'État au Cameroun* (Paris, 1979), pp. 52 and 222.

8 Comi M. Toulabor, *Le Togo sous Eyadéma* (Paris, 1986).

9 N'Kanza Lusibu Zala, 'The Social Origins of Political Underdevelopment in the Belgian Congo (Zaïre)', Ph.D. dissertation, Harvard University, Cambridge, MA, 1976, pp. 232–4.

10 Neal Ascherson, *The King Incorporated: Leopold II in the age of trusts* (London, 1963), p. 11.

11 Pierre Piron and Jacques Devos, *Codes et lois du Congo belge* (Brussels, 8th edn 1960), Vol, 11, p. 211.

12 Royaume de Belgique, Ministère des colonies, *Recueil à l'usage des fonctionnaires et des agents du service territorial* (Brussels, 5th edn 1930), pp. 119–20 and 134–5.

13 Ibid. p. 141.

14 Mulambu Muvulya, 'Le Régime des cultures obligatoires et le radicalisme rural au Zaïre (1917–1960)', Ph.D. dissertation, Université libre de Bruxelles, 1974, p. 96.

15 Rapports Annuels sur l'Administration du Congo Belge, présentés au Chambres legislatifs, cited in Crawford Young, *Politics in the Congo* (Princeton, 1968), p. 206.

16 Cited in Raymond Leslie Buell, *The Native Problem in Africa* (New York, 1928), Vol, 11, p. 506.

17 Michel Foucault, 'Le Pouvoir, comment s'exerce-t-il?', in H. L. Dreyfus and P. Rabinow (eds.), *Michel Foucault, un parcours philosophique* (Paris, 1984), pp. 313–14, cited in Jean-François Bayart, 'L'Hybridation du politique en Afrique noire: les églises chrétiennes et la gouvernmentalité du ventre', Conference on Relationships between the State and Civil Society in Africa and Eastern Europe, Bellagio, Italy, February 1990, p. 8.

18 L. Moutoulle, *Politique sociale de l'Union minière du Haut Katanga* (Brussels, 1946), pp. 5–6.

19 Bruce Fetter, 'L'Union minière du Haut-Katanga, 1920–1940: la naissance d'une sous-culture totalitaire', in *Cahiers du CEDAF* (Brussels), 6, 1973, p. 38.

20 Bakonzi Agayo, 'The Gold Mines of Kilo-Moto in Northeastern Zaïre, 1905–1960', Ph.D. dissertation, University of Wisconsin-Madison, 1982.

21 Mgr. Roelens, cited in Louis Franck, *Le Congo belge* (Brussels, 1930), Vol. 11, pp. 208–9.

22 Ibid. p. 208.

23 Franck, op. cit. Vol. 1, p. 282.

24 Herbert F. Weiss, *Political Protest in the Congo: the Parti Solidaire Africain during the independence struggle* (Princeton, 1967).

25 Reprinted in *Dettes de guerre* (Elisabethville, 1945), pp. 128–9.

26 Patrice Lumumba, *Le Congo, terre d'avenir, est-il menacé?* (Brussels, 1961), p. 22.

27 Ibid. pp. 19–20.

28 Jean van Lierde, *La Pensée politique du Patrice Lumumba* (Brussels, 1963), p. 192.

29 Ibid. p. 191.

30   Mobutu Sese Seko, *Mobutu: discours, allocutions, et messages, 1965–1975* (Paris, 1975), Vol. 1, pp. 20–1.

31   Engulu Baanga Mpongo, speech to the Makanda Kabobi Institute for party ideological instruction, N'sele, 1974.

32   Thomas M. Callaghy, *The State-Society Struggle: Zaïre in comparative perspective* (New York, 1984), passim.

33   Emmanuel Dungia, *Mobutu et l'argent du Zaïre* (Paris, 1992), p. 15.

34   Jan Vansina, 'Mwasi's Trials', in *Daedalus* (Cambridge, MA), 111, Spring 1982, p. 69.

35   Janet MacGaffey et al., *The Real Economy of Zaïre: the contribution of smuggling and other unofficial activities to national wealth* (London and Philadelphia, 1991).

36   Ilunga Kabongo, 'Baffling Africa or the Dying Gasps of a Discourse', Conference on African Crisis Areas and United States Foreign Policy, Los Angeles, march 1993.

37   Peter Ekeh, 'Colonialism and the Two Publics in Africa: a theoretical statement', in *Comparative Studies in Society and History* (Cambridge), 17, 1, 1975, pp. 91–112.

38   Basil Davidson, *The Black Man's Burden: Africa and the curse of the nation-state* (London and New York, 1992).

39   Jan Vansina, 'A Past for the Future?', in *Dalhousie Review* (Halifax), 68, 102, 1989, pp. 21–3.

Chapter 22

Dipesh Chakrabarty

POSTCOLONIALITY AND THE ARTIFICE OF HISTORY

Who speaks for "Indian" pasts?

> *Push thought to extremes.*
> (Louis Althusser)

I

IT HAS RECENTLY BEEN SAID in praise of the postcolonial project of *Subaltern Studies* that it demonstrates, "perhaps for the first time since colonization," that "Indians are showing sustained signs of reappropriating the capacity to represent themselves [within the discipline of history]."[1] As a historian who is a member of the *Subaltern Studies* collective, I find the congratulation contained in this remark gratifying but premature. The purpose of this article is to problematize the idea of "Indians" "representing themselves in history." Let us put aside for the moment the messy problems of identity inherent in a translational enterprise such as *Subaltern Studies*, where passports and commitments blur the distinctions of ethnicity in a manner that some would regard as characteristically postmodern. I have a more perverse proposition to argue. It is that insofar as the academic discourse of history—that is, "history" as a discourse produced at the institutional site of the university—is concerned, "Europe" remains the sovereign, theoretical subject of all histories, including the ones we call "Indian," "Chinese," "Kenyan," and so on. There is a peculiar way in which all these other histories tend to become variations on a master narrative that could be called "the history of Europe." In this sense, "Indian" history itself is in a position of subalternity; one can only articulate subaltern subject positions in the name of this history.

While the rest of this article will elaborate on this proposition, let me enter a few qualifications. "Europe" and "India" are treated here as hyperreal terms in that they refer to certain figures of imagination whose geographical referents remain somewhat indeterminate.[2] As figures of the imaginary they are, of course, subject to contestation, but for the moment I shall treat them as though they were given, reified categories, opposites paired in a structure of domination and sub-ordination. I realize that in treating them thus I leave myself open to the charge of nativism, nationalism, or worse, the sin of sins, nostalgia. Liberal-minded scholars would immediately protest that any idea of a homogeneous, uncontested "Europe" dissolves under analysis. True, but just as the phenomenon of orientalism does not disappear simply because some of us have now attained a critical awareness of it, similarly a certain version of "Europe," reified and celebrated in the phenomenal world of everyday relationships of power as the scene of the birth of the modern, continues to dominate the discourse of history. Analysis does not make it go away.

That Europe works as a silent referent in historical knowledge itself becomes obvious in a highly ordinary way. There are at least two everyday symptoms of the subalternity of non-Western, third-world histories. Third-world historians feel a need to refer to works in European history; historians of Europe do not feel any need to reciprocate. Whether it is an Edward Thompson, a Le Roy Ladurie, a George Duby, a Carlo Ginzburg, a Lawrence Stone, a Robert Darnton, or a Natalie Davis—to take but a few names at random from our contemporary world—the "greats" and the models of the historian's enterprise are always at least culturally "European." "They" produce their work in relative ignorance of non-Western histories, and this does not seem to affect the quality of their work. This is a gesture, however, that "we" cannot return. We cannot even afford an equality or symmetry of ignorance at this level without taking the risk of appearing "old-fashioned" or "outdated."

The problem, I may add in parenthesis, is not particular to historians. An unself-conscious but nevertheless blatant example of this "inequality of ignorance" in literary studies, for example, is the following sentence on Salman Rushdie from a recent text on postmodernism: "Though Saleem Sinai [of *Midnight's Children*] narrates in English . . . his intertexts for both writing history and writing fiction are doubled: they are, on the one hand, from Indian legends, films, and literature and, on the other, from the West—*The Tin Drum, Tristram Shandy, One Hundred Years of Solitude*, and so on."[3] It is interesting to note how this sentence teases out only those references that are from "the West." The author is under no obligation here to be able to name with any authority and specificity the "Indian" allusions that make Rushdie's intertexuality "doubled." This ignorance, shared and unstated, is part of the assumed compact that makes it "easy" to include Rushdie in English department offerings on postcolonialism.

This problem of asymmetric ignorance is not simply a matter of "cultural cringe" (to let my Australian self speak) on our part or of cultural arrogance on the part of the European historian. These problems exist but can be relatively easily addressed. Nor do I mean to take anything away from the achievements of the historians I mentioned. Our footnotes bear rich testimony to the insights we have derived from their knowledge and creativity. The dominance of "Europe" as the subject of all histories is a part of a much more profound theoretical condition under which historical knowledge is produced in the third world. This condition ordinarily expresses itself in a paradoxical manner. It is this paradox that I shall describe as the second everyday symptom of our subalternity, and it refers to the very nature of social science pronouncements themselves.

For generations now, philosophers and thinkers shaping the nature of social science have produced theories embracing the entirety of humanity. As we well know, these statements have been produced in relative, and sometimes absolute, ignorance of the majority of humankind—i.e., those living in non-Western cultures. This in itself is not paradoxical, for the more self-conscious of European philosophers have always sought theoretically to justify this stance. The everyday paradox of third-world social science is that *we* find these theories, in spite of their inherent ignorance of "us," eminently useful in understanding our societies. What allowed the modern European sages to develop such clairvoyance with regard to societies of which they were empirically ignorant? Why cannot we, once again, return the gaze?

There is an answer to this question in the writings of philosophers who have read into European history an entelechy of universal reason, if we regard such philosophy as the self-consciousness of social science. Only "Europe," the argument would appear to be, is *theoretically* (i.e., at the level of the fundamental categories that shape historical thinking) knowable; all other histories are matters of empirical research that fleshes out a theoretical skeleton which is substantially "Europe." There is one version of this argument in Edmund Husserl's Vienna lecture of 1935, where he proposed that the fundamental difference between "oriental philosophies" (more specifically, Indian and Chinese) and "Greek-European science" (or as he added, "universally speaking: philosophy") was the capacity of the latter to produce "absolute theoretical insights," that is *"theoria"* (universal science), while the former retained a "practical-universal," and hence "mythical-religious," character. This "practical-universal" philosophy was directed to the world in a "naive" and "straightforward" manner, while the world presented itself as a "thematic" to *theoria*, making possible a praxis "whose aim is to elevate mankind through universal scientific reason."[4]

A rather similar epistemological proposition underlies Marx's use of categories like "bourgeois" and "prebourgeois" or "capital" and "precapital." The prefix *pre* here signifies a relationship that is both chronological and theoretical. The coming of the bourgeois or capitalist society, Marx argues in the *Grundrisse* and elsewhere, gives rise for the first time to a history that can be apprehended through a philosophical and universal category, "capital." History becomes, for the first time, *theoretically* knowable. All past histories are now to be known (the-oretically, that is) from the vantage point of this category, that is in terms of their differences from it. Things reveal their categorical essence only when they reach their fullest development, or as Marx put it in that famous aphorism of the *Grundrisse*. "Human anatomy contains the key to the anatomy of the ape."[5] The category "capital," as I have discussed elsewhere, contains within itself the legal subject of Enlightenment thought.[6] Not surprisingly, Marx said in that very Hegelian first chapter of *Capital*, vol. 1, that the secret of "capital," the category, "cannot be deciphered until the notion of human equality has acquired the fixity of a popular prejudice."[7] To continue with Marx's words:

> Even the most abstract categories, despite their validity—precisely because of their abstractness—for all epochs, are nevertheless . . . themselves . . . a product of historical relations. Bourgeois society is the most developed and the most complex historic organization of production. The categories which express its relations, the comprehension of its structure, thereby also allow insights into the structure and the relations of production of all the vanished social formations out of whose ruins and elements it built itself up, whose partly still unconquered remnants are carried along within it, whose mere nuances have developed explicit significance within it, etc. . . . . The intimations of higher development among the subordinate animal

species . . . can be understood only after the higher development is already known. The bourgeois economy thus supplies the key to the ancient.[8]

For "capital" or "bourgeois," I submit, read "Europe."

II

Neither Marx nor Husserl spoke—not at least in the words quoted above—in a historicist spirit. In parenthesis, we should also recall here that Marx's vision of emancipation entailed a journey beyond the rule of capital, in fact beyond the notion of juridical equality that liberalism holds so sacred. The maxim "From each according to his ability, to each according to his need" runs quite contrary to the principle of "Equal pay for equal work," and this is why Marx remains—the Berlin Wall notwithstanding (or not standing!)—a relevant and fundamental critic of both capitalism and liberalism and thus central to any post-colonial, postmodern project of writing history. Yet Marx's methodological/epistemological statements have not always successfully resisted historicist readings. There has always remained enough ambiguity in these statements to make possible the emergence of "Marxist" historical narratives. These narratives turn around the theme of "historical transition." Most modern third-world histories are written within problematics posed by this transition narrative, of which the overriding (if often implicit) themes are those of development, modernization, capitalism.

This tendency can be located in our own work in the *Subaltern Studies* project. My book on working-class history struggles with the problem.[9] Sumit Sarkar's (another colleague in the *Subaltern Studies* project) *Modern India*, justifiably regarded as one of the best textbooks on Indian history written primarily for Indian universities, opens with the following sentences:

> The sixty years or so that lie between the foundation of the Indian National Congress in 1885 and the achievement of independence in August 1947 witnessed perhaps the greatest tradition in our country's long history. A transition, however, which in many ways remains grievously incomplete, and it is with this central ambiguity that it seems most convenient to begin our survey.[10]

What kind of a transition was it that remained "grievously incomplete"? Sarkar hints at the possibility of there having been several by naming three:

> So many of the aspirations aroused in the course of the national struggle remained unfulfilled—the Gandhian dream of the peasant coming into his own in *Ram-rajya* [the rule of the legendary and the ideal god-king Ram], as much as the left ideals of social revolution. And as the history of independent India and Pakistan (and Bangladesh) was repeatedly to reveal, even the problems of a complete bourgeois transformation and successful capitalist development were not fully solved by the transfer of power of 1947. (p. 4)

Neither the peasant's dream of a mythical and just kingdom, nor the Left's ideal of a social[ist] revolution, nor a "complete bourgeois transformation"—it is within these three absences, these "grievously incomplete" scenarios that Sarkar locates the story of modern India.

It is also with a similar reference to "absences"—the "failure" of a history to keep an appointment with its destiny (once again an instance of the "lazy native," shall we say?)—that we announced our project of *Subaltern Studies*:

> It is the study of this *historic failure of the nation to come to its own*, a failure due to the *inadequacy* [emphasis added] of the bourgeoisie as well as of the working class to lead it into a decisive victory over colonialism and a bourgeois-democratic revolution of the classic nineteenth-century type . . . or [of the] "new democracy" [type]—*it is the study of this failure which constitutes the central problematic of the historiography of colonial India.*[11]

The tendency to read Indian history in terms of a lack, an absence, or an incompleteness that translates into "inadequacy" is obvious in these excerpts. As a trope, however, it is an ancient one, going back to the hoary beginnings of colonial rule in India. The British conquered and represented the diversity of "Indian" pasts through a homogenizing narrative of transition from a "medieval" period to "modernity." The terms have changed with time. The "medieval" was once called "despotic" and the "modern," "the rule of law." "Feudal/capitalist" has been a later variant.

When it was first formulated in colonial histories of India, this transition narrative was an unashamed celebration of the imperialist's capacity for violence and conquest. To give only one example among the many available, Alexander Dow's *History of Hindostan*, first published in three volumes between 1770 and 1772, was dedicated to the king with a candor characteristic of the eighteenth century when one did not need a Michel Foucault to uncover the connection between violence and knowledge: "The success of Your Majesty's arms," said Dow, "has laid open the East to the researches of the curious."[12] Underscoring this connection between violence and modernity, Dow added:

> The British nation have become the conquerors of Bengal and they ought to extend some part of their fundamental jurisprudence to secure their conquest. . . . The sword is our tenure. It is an absolute conquest, and it is so considered by the world. (1: p. cxxxviii)

This "fundamental jurisprudence" was the "rule of law" that contrasted, in Dow's narrative, with a past rule that was "arbitrary" and "despotic." In a further gloss Dow explained that "despotism" did not refer to a "government of mere caprice and whim," for he knew enough history to know that that was not true of India. Despotism was the opposite of English constitutional government; it was a system where "the legislative, the judicial and the executive power [were] vested in the prince." This was the past of unfreedom. With the establishment of British power, the Indian was to be made a legal subject, ruled by a government open to the pressures of private property ("the foundation of public prosperity," said Dow) and public opinion, and supervised by a judiciary where "the distributers of justice ought to be independent of everything but law [as] otherwise the officer [the judge] becomes a tool of oppression in the hands of despotism" (1: pp. xcv, cl, cxl-cxli).

In the nineteenth and twentieth centuries, generations of elite Indian nationalists found their subject positions, as nationalists, within this transition narrative that, at various times and depending on one's ideology, hung the tapestry of "Indian history" between the two poles of the homologous sets of oppositions, despotic/constitutional, medieval/modern, feudal/capitalist. Within this narrative shared between imperialist and nationalist imaginations, the "Indian" was always a figure of lack. There was always, in other words, room in this story for characters who embodied, on behalf of the native, the theme of "inadequacy" or "failure." Dow's recommendation of a "rule of law" for Bengal/India came with the paradoxical assurance (to the British) that there was no danger of such a rule "infusing" in the natives "a spirit of freedom":

> To make the natives of the fertile soil of Bengal free, is beyond the power of political arrangement. . . . Their religion, their institutions, their manners, the very disposition of their minds, form them for passive obedience. To give them property would only bind them with stronger ties to our interests, and make them our subjects; or if the British nation prefers the name— more our slaves. (1: pp. cxl–cxli)

We do not need to be reminded that this would remain the cornerstone of imperial ideology for many years to come—subjecthood but not citizenship, as the native was never adequate to the latter—and would eventually become a strand of liberal theory itself. This was of course where nationalists differed. For Rammohun Roy as for Bankimchandra Chattopadhyay, two of India's most prominent nationalist intellectuals of the nineteenth century, British rule was a necessary period of tutelage that Indians had to undergo in order to prepare precisely for what the British denied but extolled as the end of all history: citizenship and the nation state. Years later, in 1951, an "unknown" Indian who successfully sold his "obscurity" dedicated the story of his life thus:

> To the memory of the
> British Empire in India
> Which conferred subjecthood on us
> But withheld citizenship;
> To which yet
> Everyone of us threw out the challenge
> "Civis Britanicus Sum"
> Because
> All that was good and living
> Within us
> Was made, shaped, and quickened
> By the same British Rule.[13]

In nationalist versions of this narrative, as Partha Chatterjee has shown, it was the peasants and the workers, the subaltern classes, who were given to bear the cross of "inadequacy," for, according to this version, it was they who needed to be educated out of their ignorance, parochialism, or, depending on your preference, false consciousness.[14] Even today the Anglo-Indian word *communalism* refers to those who allegedly fail to measure up to the "secular" ideals of citizenship.

That British rule put in place the practices, institutions, and discourse of bourgeois individualism in the Indian soil is undeniable. Early expressions—that is, before the beginnings of nationalism—of this desire to be a "legal subject" make it clear that to Indians in the 1830s and 1840s to be a "modern individual" was to become a "European." *The Literary Gleaner*, a magazine in colonial Calcutta, ran the following poem in 1842, written in English by a Bengali schoolboy eighteen years of age. The poem apparently was inspired by the sight of ships leaving the coast of Bengal "for the glorious shores of England":

> Oft like a sad bird I sigh
> To leave this land, though mine own land it be;
> Its green robed meads,—gay flowers and cloudless sky
> Though passing fair, have but few charms for me.
> For I have dreamed of climes more bright and free
> Where virtue dwells and heaven-born liberty
> Makes even the lowest happy;—where the eye
> Doth sicken not to see man bend the knee
> To sordid interest:—climes where science thrives,
> And genius doth receive her guerdon meet;
> Where man in his all his truest glory lives,
> And nature's face is exquisitely sweet:
> For those fair climes I have the impatient sigh,
> There let me live and there let me die.[15]

In its echoes of Milton and seventeenth-century English radicalism; this is obviously a piece of colonial pastiche. Michael Madhusudan Dutt, the young Bengali author of this poem, eventually realized the impossibility of being "European" and returned to Bengali literature to become one of our finest poets. Later Indian nationalists, however, abandoned such abject desire to be "Europeans" themselves. Nationalist thought was premised precisely on the assumed universality of the project of becoming individuals, on the assumption that "individual rights" and abstract "equality" were universals that could find home anywhere in the world, that one could be both an "Indian" and a "citizen" at the same time. We shall soon explore some of the contradictions of this project.

Many of the public and private rituals of modern individualism became visible in India in the nineteenth century. One sees this, for instance, in the sudden flourishing in this period of the four basic genres that help express the modern self: the novel, the biography, the autobiography, and history. Along with these came modern industry, technology, medicine, a quasibourgeois (though colonial) legal system supported by a state that nationalism was to take over and make its own. The transition narrative that I have been discussing underwrote, and was in turn underpinned by, these institutions. To think this narrative was to think these institutions at the apex of which sat the modern state,[16] and to think the modern or the nation state was to think a history whose theoretical subject was Europe. Gandhi realized this as early as 1909. Referring to the Indian nationalists' demands for more railways, modern medicine, and bourgeois law, he cannily remarked in his book *Hind Swaraj* that this was to "make India English" or, as he put it, to have "English rule without the Englishman."[17] This "Europe," as Michael Madhusudan Dutt's youthful and naive poetry shows, was of course nothing but a piece of fiction told to the colonized by the colonizer in the very process of fabricating colonial domination.[18] Gandhi's critique of this "Europe" is compromised on many points by his nationalism, and I do not intend to fetishize his text. But I find his gesture useful in developing the problematic of nonmetropolitan histories.

III

I shall now return to the themes of "failure," "lack," and "inadequacy" that so ubiquitously characterize the speaking subject of "Indian" history. As in the practice of the insurgent peasants of colonial India, the first step in a critical effort must arise from a gesture of inversion.[19] Let us begin from where the transition narrative ends and read "plenitude" and "creativity" where this narrative has made us read "lack" and "inadequacy."

According to the fable of their constitution, Indians today are all "citizens." The constitution embraces almost a classically liberal definition of citizenship. If the modern state and the modern individual, the citizen, are but the two inseparable sides of the same phenomenon, as William Connolly argues in *Political Theory and Modernity*, it would appear that the end of history is in sight for us in India.[20] This modern individual, however, whose political/public life is lived in citizenship, is also supposed to have an interiorized "private" self that pours out incessantly in diaries, letters, autobiographies, novels, and, of course, in what we say to our analysts. The bourgeois individual is not born until one discovers the pleasures of privacy. But this is a very special kind of "private"—it is, in fact, a deferred "public," for this bourgeois private, as Jürgen Habermas has reminded us, is "always already oriented to an audience [*Publikum*]."[21]

Indian public life may mimic on paper the bourgeois legal fiction of citizenship—the fiction is usually performed as a farce in India—but what about the bourgeois private and its history? Anyone who has tried to write "French" social history with Indian material would know how impossibly difficult the task is. It is not that the form of the bourgeois private did not come with European rule. There have been, since the middle of the nineteenth century, Indian novels, diaries, letters, and autobiographies, but they seldom yield pictures of an endlessly interiorized subject. Our autobiographies are remarkably "public" (with constructions of public life that are not necessarily modern) when written by men, and they tell the story of the extended family when written by women.[22] In any case, autobiographies in the confessional mode are notable for their absence. The single paragraph (out of 963 pages) that Nirad Chaudhuri spends on describing the experience of his wedding night in the second volume of his celebrated and prize-winning autobiography is as good an example as any other and is worth quoting at some length. I should explain that this was an arranged marriage (Bengal, 1932), and Chaudhuri was anxious lest his wife should not appreciate his newly acquired but unaffordably expensive hobby of buying records of Western classical music. Our reading of Chaudhuri is handicapped in part by our lack of knowledge of the intertextuality of his prose—there may have been at work, for instance, an imbibed puritanical revulsion against revealing "too much." Yet the passage remains a telling exercise in the construction of memory, for it is about what Chaudhuri "remembers" and "forgets" of his "first night's experience." He screens off intimacy with expressions like "I do not remember" or "I do not know how" (not to mention the very Freudian "making a clean breast of"), and this self-constructed veil is no doubt a part of the self that speaks:

> I was terribly uneasy at the prospect of meeting as wife a girl who was a complete stranger to me, and when she was brought in . . . and left standing before me I had nothing to say. I saw only a very shy smile on her face, and timidly she came and sat by my side on the edge of the bed. I do not know how after that both of us drifted to the pillows, to lie down side by side. [Chaudhuri adds in a footnote: "Of course, fully dressed. We Hindus . . . consider both extremes—fully clad and fully nude—to be modest, and everything in-between as grossly immodest. No decent man wants his wife to be an *allumeuse*."] Then the first words were exchanged. She took up one of my arms, felt it and said: "You are so thin. I shall take good care of you." I did not thank her, and I do not remember that beyond noting the words I even felt touched. The horrible suspense about European music had reawakened in my mind, and I decided to make a clean breast of it at once and look the sacrifice, if it was called for, straight in the face and begin romance on such terms as were offered to me. I asked her timidly after a while: "Have you listened to any European music?" She shook her head to say "No." Nonetheless, I took another chance and this time asked: "Have you heard the name of a man called Beethoven?" She nodded and signified "Yes." I was reassured, but not wholly satisfied. So I asked yet again: "Can you spell the name?" She said slowly: "B, E, E, T, H, O, V, E, N." I felt very encouraged . . . and [we] dozed off.[23]

The desire to be "modern" screams out of every sentence in the two volumes of Chaudhuri's autobiography. His legendary name now stands for the cultural history of Indo-British encounter. Yet in the 1500-odd pages that he has written in English about his life, this is the only passage where the narrative of Chaudhuri's participation in public life and literary circles is interrupted to make room for something approaching the intimate. How do we read this text, this self-making of an Indian male who was second to no one in his ardor for the public life of the citizen, yet who seldom, if ever, reproduced in writing the other side of the modern citizen, the interiorized private self unceasingly reaching out for an audience? Public without private? Yet another instance of the "incompleteness" of bourgeois transformation in India?

These questions are themselves prompted by the transition narrative that in turn situates the modern individual at the very end of history. I do not wish to confer on Chaudhuri's autobiography a representativeness it may not have. Women's writings, as I have already said, are different, and scholars have just begun to explore the world of autobiographies in Indian history. But if one result of European imperialism in India was to introduce the modern state and the idea of the nation with their attendant discourse of "citizenship," which, by the very idea of "the citizen's rights" (i.e., "the rule of law"), splits the figure of the modern individual into "public" and "private" parts of the self (as the young Marx once pointed out in his *On the Jewish Question*), these themes have existed—in contestation, alliance, and miscegenation—with other narratives of the self and community that do not look to the state/citizen bind as the ultimate construction of sociality.[24] This as such will not be disputed, but my point goes further. It is that these other constructions of self and community, while documentable in themselves, will never enjoy the privilege of providing the metanarratives or teleologies (assuming that there cannot be a narrative without at least an implicit teleology) of our histories. This is so partly because these narratives often themselves bespeak an antihistorical consciousness; that is, they entail subject positions and configurations of memory that challenge and undermine the subject that speaks in the name of history. "History" is precisely the site where the struggle goes on to appropriate, on behalf of the modern (my hyperreal Europe), these other collocations of memory.

To illustrate these propositions, I will now discuss a fragment of this contested history in which the modern private and the modern individual were embroiled in colonial India.

IV

What I present here are the outlines, so to speak, of a chapter in the history of bourgeois domesticity in colonial Bengal. The material—in the main texts produced in Bengali between 1850 and 1920 for teaching women that very Victorian subject, "domestic science"—relates to the Bengali Hindu middle class, the *bhadralok* or "respectable people." British rule instituted into Indian life the trichotomous ideational division on which modern political structures rest, e.g., the state, civil society, and the (bourgeois) family. It was therefore not surprising that ideas relating to bourgeois domesticity, privacy, and individuality should come to India via British rule. What I want to highlight here, however, through the example of the *bhadralok*, are certain cultural operations by which the "Indians" challenged and modified these received ideas in such a way as to put in question two fundamental tenets underlying the idea of "modernity"—the nuclear family based on companionate marriage and the secular, historical construction of time.

As Meredith Borthwick, Ghulam Murshid, and other scholars have shown, the eighteenth-century European idea of "civilization" culminated, in early nineteenth-century India, in a full-blown imperialist critique of Indian/Hindu domestic life, which was now held to be inferior to what became mid-Victorian ideals of bourgeois domesticity.[25] The "condition of women" question in nineteenth-century India was part of that critique, as were the ideas of the "modern" individual, "freedom," "equality," and "rights." In passages remarkable for their combination of egalitarianism and orientalism, James Mill's *The History of British India* (1817) joined together the thematic of the family/nation and a teleology of "freedom":

> The condition of women is one of the most remarkable circumstances in the manners of nations. . . . The history of uncultivated nations uniformly represents the women as in a state of abject slavery, from which they slowly emerge as civilisation advances. . . . As society refines upon its enjoyments . . . the condition of the weaker sex is gradually improved, till they associate on equal terms with the men, and occupy the place of voluntary and useful

coadjutors. A state of dependence more strict and humiliating than that which is ordained for the weaker sex among the Hindus cannot be easily conceived.[26]

As is well known, the Indian middle classes generally felt answerable to this charge. From the early nineteenth century onward a movement developed in Bengal (and other regions) to reform "women's conditions" and to give them formal education. Much of this discourse on women's education was emancipationist in that it spoke the language of "freedom," "equality," and "awakening," and was strongly influenced by Ruskinian ideals and idealization of bourgeois domesticity.[27] If one looks on this history as part of the history of the modern individual in India, an interesting feature emerges. It is that in this literature on women's education certain terms, after all, were much more vigorously debated than others. There was, for example, a degree of consensus over the desirability of domestic "discipline" and "hygiene" as practices reflective of a state of modernity, but the word *freedom*, yet another important term in the rhetoric of the modern, hardly ever acted as the register of such a social consensus. It was a passionately disputed word, and we would be wrong to assume that the passions reflected a simple and straightforward battle of the sexes. The word was assimilated to the nationalist need to construct cultural boundaries that supposedly separated the "European" from the "Indian." The dispute over this word was thus central to the discursive strategies through which a subject position was created enabling the "Indian" to speak. It is this subject position that I want to discuss here in some detail.

What the Bengali literature on women's education played out was a battle between a nationalist construction of a cultural norm of the patriarchal, patrilocal, patrilineal, extended family and the ideal of the patriarchal, bourgeois nuclear family that was implicit in the European/imperialist/universalist discourse on the "freedoms" of individualism, citizenship, and civil society. The themes of "discipline" and "order" were critical in shaping nationalist imaginings of aesthetics and power. "Discipline" was seen as the key to the power of the colonial (i.e., modern) state, but it required certain procedures for redefining the self. The British were powerful, it was argued, because they were disciplined, orderly, and punctual in every detail of their lives, and this was made possible by the education of "their" women who brought the virtues of discipline into the home. The "Indian" home, a colonial construct, now fared badly in nationalist writings on modern domesticity. To quote a Bengali text on women's education from 1877:

> The house of any civilised European is like the abode of gods. Every household object is clean, set in its proper place and decorated; nothing seems unclean or smells foul. . . . It is as if [the goddess of] order [*srinkhala*, "order, discipline"; *srinkhal*, "chains"] had become manifest to please the [human] eye. In the middle of the room would be a covered table with a bouquet of flowers on it, while around it would be [a few] chairs nicely arranged [with] everything sparkling clean. But enter a house in our country and you would feel as if you had been transported there by your destiny to make you atone for all the sins of your life. [A mass of] cowdung torturing the senses . . . dust in the air, a growing heap of ashes, flies buzzing around . . . a little boy urinating into the ground and putting the mess back into his

mouth. . . . The whole place is dominated by a stench that seems to be running free. . . . There is no order anywhere, the household objects are so unclean that they only evoke disgust.[28]

This self-division of the colonial subject, the double movement of recognition by which it both knows its "present" as the site of disorder and yet moves away from this space in desiring a discipline that can only exist in an imagined but "historical" future, is a rehearsal, in the context of the discussion of the bourgeois domestic in colonial India, of the transition narrative we have encountered before. A historical construction of temporality (medieval/modern, separated by historical time), in other words, is precisely the axis along which the colonial subject splits itself. Or to put it differently, this split *is* what is history; writing history is performing this split over and over again.

The desire for order and discipline in the domestic sphere thus may be seen as having been a correlate of the nationalist, modernizing desire for a similar discipline in the public sphere, that is for a rule of law enforced by the state. It is beyond the scope of this paper to pursue this point further, but the connection between personal discipline and discipline in public life was to reveal itself in what the nationalists wrote about domestic hygiene and public health. The connection is recognizably modernist, and it is what the Indian modern shared with the European modern. What I want to attend to, however, are the differences between the two. And this is where I turn to the other important aspect of the European modern, the rhetoric of "freedom" and "equality."

A similar connection between the modern, "free" individual and selfishness was made in the literature on women's education. The construction was undisguisedly nationalist (and patriarchal). *Freedom* was used to mark a difference between what was "Indian" and what was "European/English." The ultra-free woman acted like a *memsahib* (European woman), selfish and shameless. As Kundamala Devi, a woman writing for a women's magazine *Bamabodhini patrika*, said in 1870: "Oh dear ones! If you have acquired real knowledge, then give no place in your heart to *memsahib*-like behaviour. This is not becoming in a Bengali housewife."[29] The idea of "true modesty" was mobilized to build up this picture of the "really" Bengali woman. Writing in 1920, Indira Devi dedicated her *Narir ukti* [A Woman Speaks]—interestingly enough, a defense of modern Bengali womanhood against criticisms by (predominantly) male writers—to generations of ideal Bengali women whom she thus described: "Unaffected by nature, of pleasant speech, untiring in their service [to others], oblivious of their own pleasures, [while] moved easily by the suffering of others, and capable of being content with very little."[30]

This model of the "modern" Bengali/Indian woman—educated enough to appreciate the modern regulations of the body and the state but yet "modest" enough to be unselfassertive and unselfish—was tied to the debates on "freedom." "Freedom" in the West, several authors argued, meant *jathechhachar*, to do as one pleased, the right to self-indulgence. In India, it was said, *freedom* meant freedom from the ego, the capacity to serve and obey voluntarily. Notice how the terms *freedom* and *slavery* have changed positions in the following quote:

To be able to subordinate oneself to others and to *dharma* [duty/moral order/proper action] . . . to free the soul from the slavery of the senses, are the first tasks of human freedom. . . . That is why in Indian families boys and girls are subordinate to the parents, wife to the husband and to the parents-in-law, the disciple to the guru, the student to the teacher . . . the king to *dharma* . . . the people to the king, [and one's] dignity and prestige to [that of] the community [*samaj*].[31]

There was an ironical twist to this theorizing that needs to be noted. Quite clearly, this theory of "freedom-in-obedience" did not apply to the domestic servants who were sometimes mentioned in this literature as examples of the "truly" unfree, the nationalist point being that (European) observers commenting on the unfree status of Indian women often missed (so some nationalists argued) this crucial distinction between the housewife and the domestic. Obviously, the servants were not yet included in the India of the nationalist imagination.

Thus went the Bengali discourse on modern domesticity in a colonial period when the rise of a civil society and a quasimodern state had already inserted the modern questions of "public" and "private" into middle-class Bengali lives. The received bourgeois ideas about domesticity and connections between the domestic and the national were modified here in two significant ways. One strategy, as I have sought to demonstrate, was to contrapose the cultural norm of the patriarchal extended family to the bourgeois patriarchal ideals of the companionate marriage, to oppose the new patriarchy with a redefined version of the old one(s). Thus was fought the idea of the modern private. The other strategy, equally significant, was to mobilize, on behalf of the extended family, forms and figurations of collective memory that challenged, albeit ambiguously, the seemingly absolute separation of "sacred" and "secular" time on which the very modern ("European") idea of history was/is based.[32] The figure of the "truly educated," "truly modest," and "truly Indian" woman is invested, in this discussion of women's education, with a sacred authority by subordinating the question of domestic life to religious ideas of female auspiciousness that joined the heavenly with the mundane in a conceptualization of time that could be only antihistorical. The truly modern housewife, it was said, would be so auspicious as to mark the eternal return of the cosmic principle embodied in the goddess Lakshmi, the goddess of domestic well-being by whose grace the extended family (and clan, and hence, by extending the sentiment, the nation, *Bharatlakshmi*) lived and prospered. Thus we read in a contemporary pamphlet: "Women are the Lakshmis of the community. If they undertake to improve themselves in the sphere of *dharma* and knowledge . . . there will be an automatic improvement in [the quality of] social life."[33] Lakshmi, regarded as the Hindu god Vishnu's wife by about A.D. 400, has for long been held up in popular Hinduism, and in the everyday pantheism of Hindu families, as the model of the Hindu wife, united in complete harmony with her husband (and his family) through willful submission, loyalty, devotion, and chastity.[34] When women did not follow her ideals, it was said, the (extended) family and the family line were destroyed by the spirit of Alakshmi (not-Lakshmi), the dark and malevolent reverse of the Lakshmi principle. While women's education and the idea of discipline as such were seldom opposed in this discourse regarding the modern individual in colonial Bengal, the line was drawn at the point where modernity and the demand for bourgeois privacy threatened the power and the pleasures of the extended family.

There is no question that the speaking subject here is nationalist and patriarchal, employing the clichéd orientalist categories, "the East" and "the West." However, of importance to us are the two denials on which this particular moment of subjectivity rests: the denial, or at least contestation, of the bourgeois private and, equally important, the denial of historical time by making the family a site where the sacred and the secular blended in a perpetual reenactment of a principle that was heavenly and divine.

The cultural space the antihistorical invoked was by no means harmonious or nonconflictual, though nationalist thought of necessity tried to portray it to be so. The antihistorical norms of the patriarchal extended family, for example, could only have had a contested existence, contested both by women's struggles and by those of the subaltern classes. But these struggles did not necessarily follow any lines that would allow us to construct emancipatory narratives by putting the "patriarchals" clearly on one side and the "liberals" on the other. The history of modern "Indian" individuality is caught up in too many contradictions to lend itself to such a treatment.

Those voices, combining the contradictory themes of nationalism, of patriarchal clan-based ideology, of women's struggles against men, and opposed at the same time to friendship between husbands and wives, remind us of the deep ambivalences that marked the trajectory of the modern private and bourgeois individuality in colonial India. Yet historians manage, by maneuvers reminiscent of the old "dialectical" card trick called "negation of negation," to deny a subject position to this voice of ambivalence. The evidence of what I have called "the denial of the bourgeois private and of the historical subject" is acknowledged but subordinated in their accounts to the supposedly higher purpose of making Indian history look like yet another episode in the universal and (in their view, the ultimately victorious) march of citizenship, of the nation state, of themes of human emancipation spelled out in the course of the European Enlightenment and after. It is the figure of the citizen that speaks through these histories. And so long as that happens, my hyperreal Europe will continually return to dominate the stories we tell. "The modern" will then continue to be understood, as Meaghan Morris has so aptly put it in discussing her own Australian context, "as *a known history*, something which has *already happened elsewhere*, and which is to be reproduced, mechanically or otherwise, with a local content." This can only leave us with a task of reproducing what Morris calls "the project of positive unoriginality."[35]

V

Yet the "originality"—I concede that this is a bad term—of the idioms through which struggles have been conducted in the Indian subcontinent has often been in the sphere of the nonmodern. One does not have to subscribe to the ideology of clannish patriarchy, for instance, to acknowledge that the metaphor of the sanctified and patriarchal extended family was one of the most important elements in the cultural politics of Indian nationalism. In the struggle against British rule, it was frequently the use of this idiom—in songs, poetry, and other forms of nationalist mobilization—that allowed "Indians" to fabricate a sense of community and to retrieve for themselves a subject position from which to address the British. I will illustrate this with an example from the life of Gandhi, "the father of the nation," to highlight the political importance of this cultural move on the part of the "Indian."

My example refers to the year 1946. There had been ghastly riots between the Hindus and the Muslims in Calcutta over the impending partition of the country into India and Pakistan. Gandhi was in the city, fasting in protest over the behavior of his own people. And here is how an Indian intellectual recalls the experience:

> Men would come back from their offices in the evening and find food prepared by the family [meaning the womenfolk] ready for them; but soon it would be revealed that the women of the home had not eaten the whole day. They [apparently] had not felt hungry. Pressed further, the wife or the mother would admit that they could not understand how they could go on [eating] when Gandhiji was dying for their own crimes. Restaurants and amusement centres did little business; some of them were voluntarily closed by the proprietors. . . . The nerve of feeling had been restored; the pain began to be felt. . . . Gandhiji knew when to start the redemptive process.[36]

We do not have to take this description literally, but the nature of the community imagined in these lines is clear. It blends, in Gayatri Spivak's words, "the feeling of community that belongs to national links and political organizations" with "that other feeling of community whose structural model is the [clan or the extended] family."[37] Colonial Indian history is replete with instances where Indians arrogated subjecthood to themselves precisely by mobilizing, within the context of "modern" institutions and sometimes on behalf of the modernizing project of nationalism, devices of collective memory that were both antihistorical and antimodern. This is not to deny the capacity of "Indians" to act as subjects endowed with what we in the universities would recognize as "a sense of history" (what Peter Burke calls "the renaissance of the past") but to insist at the same time that there were also contrary trends, that in the multifarious struggles that took place in colonial India, antihistorical constructions of the past often provided very powerful forms of collective memory.[38]

There is then this double bind through which the subject of "Indian" history articulates itself. On the one hand, it is both the subject and the object of modernity, because it stands for an assumed unity called the "Indian people" that is always split into two—a modernizing elite and a yet-to-be-modernized peasantry. As such a split subject, however, it speaks from within a metanarrative that celebrates the nation state; and of this metanarrative the theoretical subject can only be a hyperreal "Europe," a "Europe" constructed by the tales that both imperialism and nationalism have told the colonized. The mode of self-representation that the "Indian" can adopt here is what Homi Bhabha has justly called "mimetic."[39] Indian history, even in the most dedicated socialist or nationalist hands, remains a mimicry of a certain "modern" subject of "European" history and is bound to represent a sad figure of lack and failure. The transition narrative will always remain "grievously incomplete."

On the other hand, maneuvers are made within the space of the mimetic—and therefore within the project called "Indian" history—to represent the "difference" and the "originality" of the "Indian," and it is in this cause that the anti-historical devices of memory and the antihistorical "histories" of the subaltern classes are appropriated. Thus peasant/worker constructions of "mythical" kingdoms and "mythical" pasts/ futures find a place in texts designated "Indian" history precisely through a procedure that subordinates these narratives to the rules of evidence and to the secular, linear calendar that the writing of "history" must follow. The antihistorical, antimodern subject, therefore, cannot speak itself as "theory" within the knowledge procedures of the university even when these knowledge procedures acknowledge and "document" its existence. Much like Spivak's "subaltern" (or the anthropologist's peasant who can only have a quoted existence in a larger statement that belongs to the anthropologist alone), this subject can only be spoken for and spoken of by the transition narrative that will always ultimately privilege the modern (i.e., "Europe").[40]

So long as one operates within the discourse of "history" produced at the institutional site of the university, it is not possible simply to walk out of the deep collusion between "history" and the modernizing narrative(s) of citizenship, bourgeois public and private, and the nation state. "History" as a knowledge system is firmly embedded in institutional practices that invoke the nation state at every step—witness the organization and politics of teaching, recruitment, promotions, and publication in history departments, politics that survive the occasional brave and heroic attempts by individual historians to liberate "history" from the metanarrative of the nation state. One only has to ask, for instance: Why is history a compulsory part of education of the modern person in all countries today including those that did quite comfortably without it until as late as the eighteenth century? Why should children all over the world today have to come to terms with a subject called "history" when we know that this compulsion is neither natural nor ancient. It does not take much imagination to see that the reason for this lies in what European imperialism and third-world nationalism have achieved together: the universalization of the nation state as the most desirable form of political community. Nation states have the capacity to enforce their truth games, and universities, their critical distance notwithstanding, are part of the battery of institutions complicit in this process. "Economics" and "history" are the knowledge forms that correspond to the two major institutions that the rise (and later universalization) of the bourgeois order has given to the world—the capitalist mode of production and the nation state ("history" speaking to the figure of the citizen). A critical historian has no choice but to negotiate this knowledge. She or he therefore needs to understand the state on its own terms, i.e., in terms of its self-justificatory narratives of citizenship and modernity. Since these themes will always take us back to the universalist propositions of "modern" (European) political philosophy—even the "practical" science of economics that now seems "natural" to our constructions of world systems is (theoretically) rooted in the ideas of ethics in eighteenth-century Europe—a third-world historian is condemned to knowing "Europe" as the original home of the "modern," whereas the "European" historian does not share a comparable predicament with regard to the pasts of the majority of humankind. Thus follows the everyday subalternity of non-Western histories with which I began this paper.

Yet the understanding that "we" all do "European" history with our different and often non-European archives opens up the possibility of a politics and project of alliance between the dominant metropolitan histories and the subaltern peripheral pasts. Let us call this the project of provincializing "Europe," the "Europe" that modern imperialism and (third-world) nationalism have, by their collaborative venture and violence, made universal. Philosophically, this project must ground itself in a radical critique and transcendence of liberalism (i.e., of the bureaucratic constructions of citizenship, modern state, and bourgeois privacy that classical political philosophy has produced), a ground that late Marx shares with certain moments in both poststructuralist thought and feminist philosophy. In particular, I am emboldened by Carole Pateman's courageous declaration—in her remarkable book *The Sexual Contract*—that the very conception of the modern individual belongs to patriarchal categories of thought.[41]

VI

The project of provincializing "Europe" refers to a history that does not yet exist; I can therefore only speak of it in a programmatic manner. To forestall misunderstanding, however, I must spell out what it is *not* while outlining what it could be.

To begin with, it does not call for a simplistic, out-of-hand rejection of modernity, liberal values, universals, science, reason, grand narratives, totalizing explanations, and so on. Fredric Jameson has recently reminded us that the easy equation often made between "a philosophical conception of totality" and "a political practice of totalitarianism" is "baleful."[42] What intervenes between the two is history—contradictory, plural, and heterogeneous struggles whose outcomes are never predictable, even retrospectively, in accordance with schemas that seek to naturalize and domesticate this heterogeneity. These struggles include coercion (both on behalf of and against modernity)—physical, institutional, and symbolic violence, often dispensed with dreamy-eyed idealism—and it is this violence that plays a decisive role in the establishment of meaning, in the creation of truth regimes, in deciding, as it were, whose and which "universal" wins. As intellectuals operating in academia, we are not neutral to these struggles and cannot pretend to situate ourselves outside of the knowledge procedures of our institutions.

The project of provincializing "Europe" therefore cannot be a project of "cultural relativism." It cannot originate from the stance that the reason/science/universals which help define Europe as the modern are simply "culture-specific" and therefore only belong to the European cultures. For the point is not that Enlightenment rationalism is always unreasonable in itself but rather a matter of documenting how—through what historical process—its "reason," which was not always self-evident to everyone, has been made to look "obvious" far beyond the ground where it originated. If a language, as has been said, is but a dialect backed up by an army, the same could be said of the narratives of "modernity" that, almost universally today, point to a certain "Europe" as the primary habitus of the modern.

This Europe, like "the West," is demonstrably an imaginary entity, but the demonstration as such does not lessen its appeal or power. The project of provincializing "Europe" has to include certain other additional moves: (1) the recognition that Europe's acquisition of the adjective *modern* for itself is a piece of global history of which an integral part is the story of European imperialism; and (2) the understanding that this equating of a certain version of Europe with "modernity" is not the work of Europeans alone; third-world nationalisms, as modernizing ideologies *par excellence*, have been equal partners in the process. I do not mean to overlook the anti-imperial moments in the careers of these nationalisms; I only underscore the point that the project of provincializing "Europe" cannot be a nationalist, nativist, or atavistic project. In unraveling the necessary entanglement of history—a disciplined and institutionally regulated form of collective memory—with the grand narratives of "rights," "citizenship," the nation state, "public" and "private" spheres, one cannot but problematize "India" at the same time as one dismantles "Europe."

The idea is to write into the history of modernity the ambivalences, contradictions, the use of force, and the tragedies and the ironies that attend it. That the rhetoric and the claims of (bourgeois) equality, of citizens' rights, of self-determination through a sovereign nation state have in many circumstances empowered marginal social groups in their struggles is undeniable—this recognition is indispensable to the project of *Subaltern Studies*. What effectively is played down, however, in histories that either implicitly or explicitly celebrate the advent of the modern state and the idea of citizenship is the repression and violence that are as instrumental in the victory of the modern as is the persuasive power of its rhetorical strategies. Nowhere is this irony—the undemocratic foundations of "democracy"—more visible than in the history of modern medicine, public health, and personal hygiene, the discourses of which have been central in locating the body of the modern at the intersection of the public and the private (as defined by, and subject to negotiations with, the state). The triumph of this discourse, however, has always been dependent on the mobilization, on its behalf, of effective means of physical coercion. I say "always" because this coercion is both originary/ foundational (i.e., historic) as well as pandemic and quotidian. Of foundational violence, David Arnold gives a good example in a recent essay on the history of the prison in India. The coercion of the colonial prison, Arnold shows, was integral to some of the earliest and pioneering research on the medical, dietary, and demographic statistics of India, for the prison was where Indian bodies were accessible to modernizing investigators.[43] Of the coercion that continues in the names of the nation and modernity, a recent example comes from the Indian campaign to eradicate smallpox in the 1970s. Two American doctors (one of them presumably of "Indian" origin) who participated in the process thus describe their operations in a village of the Ho tribe in the Indian state of Bihar:

> In the middle of gentle Indian night, an intruder burst through the bamboo door of the simple adobe hut. He was a government vaccinator, under orders to break resistance against smallpox vaccination. Lakshmi Singh awoke screaming and scrambled to hide herself. Her husband leaped out of bed, grabbed an axe, and chased the intruder into the courtyard. Outside a squad of doctors and policemen quickly overpowered Mohan Singh. The instant he was pinned to the ground, a second vaccinator jabbed smallpox vaccine into his arm. Mohan Singh, a wiry 40-year-old leader of the Ho tribe, squirmed away from the needle, causing the vaccination site to bleed. The government team held him until they had injected enough vaccine. . . . While the two policemen rebuffed him, the rest of the team overpowered the entire family and vaccinated each in turn. Lakshmi Singh bit deep into one doctor's hand, but to no avail.[44]

There is no escaping the idealism that accompanies this violence. The subtitle of the article in question unselfconsciously reproduces both the military and the do-gooding instincts of the enterprise. It reads: "How an army of samaritans drove smallpox from the earth."

Histories that aim to displace a hyperreal Europe from the center toward which all historical imagination currently gravitates will have to seek out relentlessly this connection between violence and idealism that lies at the heart of the process by which the narratives of citizenship and modernity come to find a natural home in "history." I register a fundamental disagreement here with a position taken by Richard Rorty in an exchange with Jürgen Habermas. Rorty criticizes Habermas for the latter's conviction "that the story of modern philosophy is an important part of the story of the democratic societies' attempts at self-reassurance."[45] Rorty's statement follows the practice of many Europeanists who speak of the histories of these "democratic societies" as if these were self-contained histories complete in themselves, as if the self-fashioning of the West were something that occurred only within its self-assigned geographical boundaries. At the very least Rorty ignores the role that the "colonial theater" (both external and internal)—where the theme of "freedom" as defined by modern political philosophy was constantly invoked in aid of the ideas of "civilization," "progress," and latterly "development"—played in the process of engendering this "reassurance." The task, as I see it, will be to wrestle ideas that legitimize the modern state and its attendant institutions, in order to return to political philosophy—in the same way as suspect coins returned to their owners in an Indian bazaar—its categories whose global currency can no longer be taken for granted.

And, finally—since "Europe" cannot after all be provincialized within the institutional site of the university whose knowledge protocols will always take us back to the terrain where all contours follow that of my hyperreal Europe—the project of provincializing Europe must realize within itself its own impossibility. It therefore looks to a history that embodies this politics of despair. It will have been clear by now that this is not a call for cultural relativism or for atavistic, nativist histories. Nor is this a program for a simple rejection of modernity, which would be, in many situations, politically suicidal. I ask for a history that deliberately makes visible, within the very structure of its narrative forms, its own repressive strategies and practices, the part it plays in collusion with the narratives of citizenships in assimilating to the projects of the modern state all other possibilities of human solidarity. The politics of despair will require of such history that it lays bare to its readers the reasons why such a predicament is necessarily inescapable. This is a history that will attempt the impossible: to look toward its own death by tracing that which resists and escapes the best human effort at translation across cultural and other semiotic systems, so that the world may once again be imagined as radically heterogeneous. This, as I have said, is impossible within the knowledge protocols of academic history, for the globality of academia is not independent of the globality that the European modern has created. To attempt to provincialize this "Europe" is to see the modern as inevitably contested, to write over the given and privileged narratives of citizenship other narratives of human connections that draw sustenance from dreamed-up pasts and futures where collectivities are defined neither by the rituals of citizenship nor by the nightmare of "tradition" that "modernity" creates. There are of course no (infra)structural sites where such dreams could lodge themselves. Yet they will recur so long as the themes of citizenship and the nation state dominate our narratives of historical transition, for these dreams are what the modern represses in order to be.

Notes

1   Ranjit Guha and Gayatri Chakravorty Spivak, eds., *Selected Subaltern Studies* (New York, 1988); Ronald Inden, "Orientalis: Constructions of India," *Modern Asian Studies* 20, no. 3 (1986): 445.

2   I am indebted to Jean Baudrillard for the term *hyperreal* (see his *Simulations* [New York, 1988]), but my use differs from his.

3   Linda Hutcheon, *The Politics of Postmodernism* (London, 1989), 65.

4   Edmund Husserl, *The Crisis of European Sciences and Transcendental Philosophy*, trans. David Carr (Evanston, Ill., 1970), 281–85.

5   Karl Marx, *Grundrisse: Foundations of the Critique of Political Economy*, trans. Martin Nicholas (Harmondsworth, England, 1973), 469–512; and in Marx, *Capital: A Critique of Political Economy*, 3 vols. (Moscow, 1971), 3: 593–613.

6   See Dipesh Chakrabarty, *Rethinking Working-Class History: Bengal, 1890–1940* (Princeton, N.J., 1989), chap. 7.

7   Marx, *Capital*, 1: 60.

8   Marx, *Grundrisse*, 105.

9   See Chakrabarty, *Rethinking Working-Class History*, chap. 7, in particular.

10   Sumit Sarkar, *Modern India, 1885–1947* (Delhi, 1985), 1.

11   Guha and Spivak, *Selected Subaltern Studies*, 43.

12   Alexander Dow, *History of Hindostan*, 3 vols. (London, 1812–16), dedication, vol. 1.

13   Nirad C. Chaudhuri, *The Autobiography of an Unknown Indian* (New York, 1989), dedication page.

14   Partha Chatterjee, *Nationalist Thought and the Colonial World: A Derivative Discourse?* (London, 1986).

15   *Mudhusudan rachanabali* [Bengali] (Calcutta, 1965), 449. See also Jogindranath Basu, *Michael Madhusudan Datter jibancharit* [Bengali] (Calcutta, 1978), 86.

16   See the chapter on Nehru in Chatterjee, *Nationalist Thought*.

17   M. K. Gandhi, *Hind swaraj* (1909), in *Collected Works of Mahatma Gandhi*, vol. 10 (Ahmedabad, 1963), 15.

18   See the discussion in Gauri Visvanathan, *Masks of Conquest: Literary Studies and British Rule in India* (London, 1989), 128–41, passim.

19   Ranajit Guha, *Elementary Aspects of Peasant Insurgency in Colonial India* (New Delhi, 1983), chap. 2.

20   William E. Connolly, *Political Theory and Modernity* (Oxford, 1989). See also David Bennett, "Postmodernism and Vision: Ways of Seeing (at) the End of History," in *History and Post-war Writing*, ed. Theo D'haen and Hans Bertens, Postmodern Studies 3 (Amsterdam/Antwerp, 1991), 259–79.

21   Jürgen Habermas, *The Structural Transformation of the Public Sphere: An Inquiry into a Category of Bourgeois Society* (Cambridge, Mass., 1989), 49.

22   Sumit Sarkar, "Social History: Predicament and Possibilities," in Iqbal Khan, ed., *Fresh Perspective on India and Pakistan: Essays on Economics, Politics, and Culture* (Oxford, 1985), 256–74.

23   Nirad C. Chaudhuri, *Thy Hand, Great Anarch!: India, 1921–1952* (London, 1987), 350–51.

24   See Karl Marx, *On the Jewish Question*, in *Early Writings* (Harmondsworth, England, 1975), 215–22.

25   Meredith Borthwick, *The Changing Role of Women in Bengal, 1849–1905* (Princeton,

N.J., 1984); Ghulam Murshid, *Reluctant Debutante: Response of Bengali Women to Modernisation, 1849–1905* (Rajshahi, 1983).

26   James Mill, *The History of British India*, vol. 1, ed. H. H. Wilson (London, 1840), 309–10.

27   Borthwick, *Changing Role*.

28   Anon., *Streesiksha*, vol. 1 (Calcutta, 1877), 28–29.

29   Borthwick, *Changing Role*, 105.

30   Indira Devi, *Narir ukti* (Calcutta, 1920), dedication page.

31   Deenanath Bandyopadhyaya, *Nanabishayak prābandha* (Calcutta, 1887), 30–31.

32   Peter Burke, *The Renaissance Sense of the Past* (London, 1970).

33   Bikshuk [Chandrasekhar Sen], *Ki holo!* (Calcutta, 1876), 77.

34   David Kinsley, *Hindu Goddess: Visions of the Divine Feminine in the Hindu Religious Tradition* (Berkeley, 1988), 19–31; Manomohan Basu, *Hindu acar byabahar* (Calcutta, 1873), 60; H. D. Bhattacharya, "Minor Religious Sects," in R. C. Majumdar, ed., *The History and Culture of the Indian People: The Age of Imperial Unity*, vol. 2 (Bombay, 1951), 469–71; Upendranath Dhal, *Goddesses Lakshmi: Origin and Development* (Delhi, 1978).

35   Meaghan Morris, "Metamorphoses at Sydney Tower," *New Formations* 11 (Summer 1990): 10.

36   Amiya Chakravarty, quoted in Bhikhu Parekh, *Gandhi's Political Discourse* (London, 1989), 163.

37   Gayatri Chakravorty Spivak, "Can the Subaltern Speak?," in Cary Nelson and Lawrence Grossberg, eds., *Marxism and the Interpretation of Culture* (Urbana, Ill., 1988), 277.

38   *Subaltern Studies*, vols. 1–7, and Guha, *Elementary Aspects*.

39   Homi Bhabha, "Of Mimicry and Man: The Ambivalence of Colonial Discourse," in Annette Michelson et al., eds., *October: The First Decade, 1976–1986* (Cambridge, Mass., 1987), 317–26; also Bhabha, ed., *Nation and Narration* (London, 1990).

40   Spivak, "Can the Subaltern Speak?" Also see Spivak's interview published in *Socialist Review* 20, no. 3 (July–September 1990): 81–98.

41   Carole Pateman, *The Sexual Contract* (Stanford, Calif., 1988), 184.

42   Fredric Jameson, "Cognitive Mapping," in Nelson and Grossberg, *Marxism and the Interpretation of Culture*, 354.

43   David Arnold, "The Colonial Prison: Power, Knowledge, and Penology in Nineteenth-Century India," in D. Arnold and D. Hardiman, *Subaltern Studies*, vol. 8.

44   Lawrence Brilliant with Girija Brilliant, "Death for a Killer Disease," *Quest*, May/June 1978, 3.

45   Richard Rorty, "Habermas and Lyotard on Postmodernity," in Richard J. Bernstein, ed., *Habermas and Modernity* (Cambridge, Mass., 1986), 169.

Index